JOURNAL FOR THE STUDY OF THE NEW TESTAMENT
SUPPLEMENT SERIES
24

Executive Editor, Supplement Series
David Hill

Publishing Editor
David E Orton

JSOT Press
Sheffield

APOCALYPTIC
AND THE
NEW TESTAMENT

Essays in Honor of
J. Louis Martyn

edited by
Joel Marcus and
Marion L. Soards

Journal for the Study of the New Testament
Supplement Series 24

Copyright © 1989 Sheffield Academic Press

Published by JSOT Press
JSOT Press is an imprint of
Sheffield Academic Press Ltd
The University of Sheffield
343 Fulwood Road
Sheffield S10 3BP
England

Printed in Great Britain
by Billing & Sons Ltd
Worcester

British Library Cataloguing in Publication Data

Apocalyptic and the new testament.
1. Bible. N.T. Eschatology
I. Marcus, Joel   II. Soards, Marion L.   III. Martyn,
J. Louis   IV. Series
236

ISSN 0143-5108
ISBN 1-85075-175-7

CONTENTS

FOREWORD

In his nearly thirty years at Union Theological Seminary, New York, J. Louis Martyn has had a subtle but profound effect upon a variety of areas of New Testament study. To the present time he is best known for his seminal labors on the Gospel of John,[1] but even before *History and Theology in the Fourth Gospel* appeared in 1968, he had done ground-breaking exegetical work on the relation between Paul and apocalyptic theology.[2] In a set of recent articles[3] he has returned to this theme, and his forthcoming Anchor Bible commentary on Galatians will bring this work to fruition. As is evidenced in this volume, some of his students and friends have, in dialogue with him, taken Martyn's awareness of the importance of apocalyptic and explored its relevance for study of other areas of the New Testament.

The interpenetration between apocalyptic and the New Testament will be further explored in this volume. As any reader of contemporary New Testament scholarship knows, the precise definition of the word 'apocalyptic', and even the legitimacy of using it as a noun, are matters of intense debate, and readers of this volume will note that the authors have assumed a variety of explicit or implicit working definitions of the term. At times the word describes a genre of literature (apocalypse), at times it describes a type of eschatology, at times it describes a social movement (apocalypticism), and at times it describes a way of looking at the world.

This volume deals primarily with 'apocalyptic' as a way of looking at the world. After a tribute to Prof. Martyn from his colleague Raymond E. Brown, the first essay, by Richard E. Sturm, explicitly addresses the problem of defining 'apocalyptic'. Then a series of essays relates apocalyptic to the Synoptic Gospels and the Pauline corpus (here including Hebrews). Next two essays by theologians, Nancy J. Duff and Martyn's friend and former colleague Paul Lehmann, explore the ramifications of apocalyptic for contemporary theology and ethics. Finally, the essay by Dorothy W. Martyn (Mrs. J. Louis Martyn) illustrates that the significance of New Testament apocalyptic reaches beyond what are normally thought of as 'theological' topics into fields such as psychology and psychotherapy.

J. Louis Martyn has steadily reminded his students and friends that one does exegesis in much the same manner that one engages in conversation. All of us who have contributed to this volume present these studies to him in the hope and confidence that the conversation will continue.

The editors wish to thank the Presidents of Princeton Theological Seminary and United Theological Seminary, Dayton, Dr Thomas W. Gillespie and Dr Leonard I. Sweet, for their generous support of this project.

NOTES

1. *History and Theology in the Fourth Gospel* (2nd rev. edn; Nashville: Abingdon, 1979; orig. 1968); *The Gospel of John in Christian History: Essays for Interpreters* (Theological Inquiries; New York: Paulist, 1978). *Gospel* consists of a collection of essays published in the mid-1970s.

2. 'Epistemology at the Turn of the Ages: 2 Corinthians 5.16' in *Christian History and Interpretation: Studies Presented to John Knox* (ed. W.R. Farmer et al.; Cambridge: Cambridge University Press, 1967), pp. 269-87.

3. 'From Paul to Flannery O'Connor with the Power of Grace', *Katallagete* 6 (1981), pp. 10-17; 'Apocalyptic Antinomies in Paul's Letter to the Galatians', *NTS* 31 (1985), pp. 410-24.

A PERSONAL WORD

In a *Festschrift* the intellectual quality of the contributions pays tribute to the scholarship of the one being honored. I wish to go beyond such formal acknowledgment by expressing what many of us owe to Lou Martyn as a person and a scholar, for in that combination lies what I do not hesitate to call his greatness.

The first contact with Martyn that I remember came in the spring of 1968 when, largely through the persuasion of Jim Sanders, I came as a visiting professor to Union Theological Seminary in New York. By that time I had published my first Anchor Bible volume on John; and it was a pleasure to discover that Lou (who had been almost a decade at Union) was also working on John—his highly influential *History and Theology in the Fourth Gospel* would appear that year. During that semester I can recall speaking before a group of scholars on John and someone asking me if I thought that my approach meant that the Bultmannian consensus on John might now be breaking up. My response was that I had never understood that there was a consensus since the English and most Roman Catholics had never accepted Bultmann's unprovable thesis that the roots of John were not in Judaism but in gnosticism. At that time I did not yet understand the way in which some Americans, influenced by German scholarship, created the appearance of unanimity by quoting each other and their masters; and the reaction to my remark by the audience was as if I had eaten peas off my knife. Lou said to me afterwards that he was delighted to hear someone from a different background who was open to a new approach. I understood the full implications of his remarks only later when I read his book and saw that he had carried the synagogue matrix of John farther than I and thus had truly breached the Bultmannian 'consensus'. On another occasion, when a group of us were theorizing about John, Lou graciously noted that I was the only one present who had written a commentary and worked with every verse to put my theories to the test. Those two incidents—the only significant ones in relation to Martyn that I recall from my first stay at Union—were already a key to two facets of his scholarship that I would see over and over again. He has never been a 'school man'; he appreciated his masters, but he has continually thought in his own way. His basic test is always the text, verse by verse, so that the theory has to fit the text and not vice versa.

When I came back to Union seminary in 1971 as a permanent faculty member, I would have guessed that Jim Sanders would be the colleague most influential in my life there, especially when he shaped a Department of Biblical Studies to bridge the Testaments and to support an emphasis on the relationship between Christianity and Early Judaism. Alas, Jim departed for Claremont in 1976. But even before his departure, other factors were influential in drawing me close to Lou Martyn. In 1971 there were ten professors in the Biblical Field; but by 1972, with Reginald Fuller's departure and James Smart's retirement, the Field was down to eight. By 1973, as part of Union's financial retrenchment, the Field was at seven; and by 1977, at six. For a decade and a half, then, with the aid of a junior colleague rotated on a regular basis, Martyn and I have had to work together on all the Field exams and dissertations of a very active New Testament doctoral program. In twelve years of previous biblical teaching at St Mary's Seminary in Baltimore, I had never worked with doctoral students. Thus Martyn had to teach me as well as the students the method of doctoral training. (My own doctor-father, W.F. Albright, inspired us to scholarship but would scarcely have been a model to be emulated in methodical guidance.) With sensitive tact Lou never did this heavy-handedly, but by imitation I learned how and when to be demanding for the sake of the students. I knew that my labors had not been in vain when one day in the early 1980s Lou said to me that the doctoral dissertations we were directing and the students in attendance were the best he had experienced in his two decades at Union. The thought that a small department by working together in friendship and respect, had achieved the level of the larger departments of the past meant something to the doctoral students as well, for consistently they treated both of us as their friends. Never, to my awareness, have they found us undermining each other or using them against each other—a blessing true in our relation to our Old Testament colleagues as well. If at times because of my background I have felt myself even briefly a stranger at Union, I have never felt myself a stranger in the Biblical Field.

I have concentrated on our doctoral work together because that enterprise has brought me so often and so profitably in contact with Lou Martyn, and because some of the contributors to this volume are recent Union PhDs who will know the truth whereof I speak. Martyn's contribution to the MDiv program was just as important and cooperative. I enjoy lecturing to large groups; he enjoys working with smaller groups, so that our courses dovetailed and were not competitive. We even worked out a system where I would initiate seminary students en masse to John, and he would follow up the next semester with the detailed treatment of a particular section of the Gospel. Neither of us was worried that we might be open to students' comparison. When we had both written on the same aspect of John, e.g. the Johannine Community, and there were points of disagreement, we were able to call attention to the other's work with the confidence that each of us had something to say. The seminars that we taught together (alas, not frequently enough) gave me an insight into why the students so appreciated Lou Martyn: he always asked questions that made all of us think. Invitations to move to other institutions came my way, but part of my resistance to the siren's attraction was a doubt that I could ever find such a colleague elsewhere.

Of course our styles differ. Lou thinks parabolically and often expresses himself thus; my logic is more pedestrian, shaped perhaps by the struggle to make things 'absolutely clear' to students. My appeals to Lou over the years to tell me very clearly what he means have sometimes brought a bemused smile to his face as if he wondered that communication needed to be so prosaic. Again, while I hope that both of us are ethical, my approach to the ethics of the complex situations that we have faced in academic and institutional unrest has been shaped by the carefully articulated system found in Roman Catholicism. Lou's answers have been directly biblical. Over and over again I have seen him indignant about some procedure because it was against the principles he was commenting upon in the New Testament. No one who has dealt with Lou Martyn long can doubt that he is a man who lives by what he teaches.

By what I have written it should be clear that as Lou retires in his 62nd year on June 30th, 1987, I shall miss his wise guidance and so will his students. Our consolation is that this youthful retirement is for the purpose of his finishing writing-projects on which he has set his heart. He wants to complete his Commentary on Galatians and produce a book on the Parables. Students at Union have profited from his superb teaching on these subjects; now when his writing appears a wider world will be in his debt.

Friend, scholarly tributes (including one from me) will appear here and elsewhere, but no volume would do justice to your career unless someone had said a personal word from the heart.

Raymond E. Brown

ABBREVIATIONS

AB	Anchor Bible
AnBib	Analecta Biblica
BAG	W. Bauer, W.F. Arndt, and F.W. Gingrich, *Greek-English Lexicon of the New Testament*
BCE	Before the Common Era
BDB	F. Brown, S.R. Driver, and C.A. Briggs, *Hebrew and English Lexicon of the Old Testament*
BETL	Bibliotheca ephemeridum theologicarum
Bib	*Biblica*
BT	*The Bible Translator*
CBQ	*Catholic Biblical Quarterly*
CBQMS	Catholic Biblical Quarterly, Monograph Series
CE	Common Era
EBib	Etudes Bibliques
EKKNT	Evangelisch-katholischer Kommentar zum Neuen Testament
ET	English Translation
ExpTim	*Expository Times*
FRLANT	Forschungen zur Religion und Literatur des Alten und Neuen Testaments
HNT	Handbuch zum Neuen Testament
HTKNT	Herders theologischer Kommentar zum Neuen Testament
HTR	*Harvard Theological Review*
HUCA	*Hebrew Union College Annual*
Int	*Interpretation*
JAAR	*Journal of the American Academy of Religion*
JB	The Jerusalem Bible
JBC	Jerome Biblical Commentary
JBL	*Journal of Biblical Literature*
JSJ	*Journal for the Study of Judaism in the Persian, Hellenistic and Roman Period*

JSNT	*Journal for the Study of the New Testament*
JSNTS	Journal for the Study of the New Testament, Supplement Series
JSOT	*Journal for the Study of the Old Testament*
JTS	*Journal of Theological Studies*
LCL	Loeb Classical Library
LSJ	Liddell–Scott–Jones, *Greek-English Lexicon*
LXX	Septuagint
MeyerK	H.A.W. Meyer, *Kritisch-exegetischer Kommentar über das Neue Testament*
MT	Masoretic Text
NEB	The New English Bible
NICNT	New International Commentary on the New Testament
NIV	The New International Version
NovTSup	Supplement to *Novum Testamentum*
NTS	*New Testament Studies*
RB	*Revue Biblique*
RSV	The Revised Standard Version
SBLDS	Society of Biblical Literature Dissertation Series
SBLMS	Society of Biblical Literature Monograph Series
SBLSP	Society of Biblical Literature Seminar Papers
SBT	Studies in Biblical Theology
SE	Studia Evangelica
TDNT	*Theological Dictionary of the New Testament*
TS	*Theological Studies*
TSK	*Theologische Studien und Kritiken*
ZAW	*Zeitschrift für die alttestamentliche Wissenschaft*
ZNW	*Zeitschrift für die neutestamentliche Wissenschaft*

LIST OF CONTRIBUTORS

Raymond E. Brown, S.S., is Auburn Distinguished Professor of Biblical Studies, Union Theological Seminary, 3041 Broadway, New York City.

Richard E. Sturm is Director of the Evening Theological Education Program, New York Area, and Associate Professor of Biblical Studies, New Brunswick Theological Seminary, New Brunswick, New Jersey.

Joel Marcus is Assistant Professor of New Testament, Princeton Theological Seminary, Princeton, New Jersey.

Jane Schaberg is Professor of Religious Studies, University of Detroit, Detroit, Michigan.

Stephenson Humphries-Brooks is Assistant Professor of Religion, Hamilton College, Clinton, New York.

Lamar Cope is Professor of Religion, Carroll College, Waukesha, Wisconsin.

Robin Scroggs is Professor of New Testament, Union Theological Seminary, 3041 Broadway, New York.

Thomas E. Boomershine is Professor of New Testament Studies, United Theological Seminary, Dayton, Ohio.

Martinus C. de Boer is Assistant Professor of New Testament, Princeton Theological Seminary, Princeton, New Jersey.

Richard B. Hays is Associate Professor of New Testament, Yale Divinity School, New Haven, Connecticut.

Judith L. Kovacs is Lecturer in Religious Studies and Classics at the University of Virginia.

Marion L. Soards is Professor of New Testament and Early Christianity, United Theological Seminary, Dayton, Ohio.

Charles P. Anderson is Associate Professor of Religious Studies, University of British Columbia, Vancouver, British Columbia, Canada.

Nancy J. Duff is Assistant Professor of Christian Theological Ethics at Brite Divinity School of Texas Christian University, Fort Worth, Texas.

Paul Lehmann is Charles A. Briggs Professor Emeritus of Systematic Theology, Union Theological Seminary, 3041 Broadway, New York.

Dorothy W. Martyn, PhD, is a psychotherapist in private practice in New York City, and is married to Professor J. Louis Martyn.

DEFINING THE WORD 'APOCALYPTIC':
A PROBLEM IN BIBLICAL CRITICISM*

Richard E. Sturm

It is common knowledge that the word 'apocalyptic' is derived from the Greek verb and noun *apokalyptō/apokalypsis*, 'to unveil/unveiling', and that the English words 'to reveal/revelation' are based on the Latin equivalents *revelare/revelatio*. Nevertheless, definition of the term 'apocalyptic' has been a matter of controversy in biblical criticism throughout the one hundred fifty years it has been used. For some, 'apocalyptic' has positive connotations as a key to understanding Jesus and Paul and as relevant to faith today. For others, 'apocalyptic' connotes something strange, important for Jesus and Paul, but inappropriate for contemporary religious belief. For others, 'apocalyptic' has such negative connotations it is considered to be alien to the thought of Jesus and Paul in the first century AD, and to be descriptive in the present day only of biblical literalism and religious fanaticism. One might conclude that 'apocalyptic' is a word too confusing and ambiguous to be of constructive use,[1] but such a desperate conclusion is unnecessary. True, the word 'apocalyptic' is used variously and even contradictorily. But the very fact that the word continues to be used shows that there must be a need for it. Rather than abandon the word, then, let us explore the problem of definition.

This investigation reviews the history of research on apocalyptic in order to see the ways in which others have approached the topic, and thereby to determine their working definitions and discern the aspects of ambiguity or issues of controversy associated with the word. This review is something like a detective story, a search for a missing person on the basis of reports from acquaintances over the past one hundred fifty years. But the search is complicated by the fact that these acquaintances differ widely regarding both the character and the identity of apocalyptic. One particular question we shall have in mind is whether or not we can identify the apostle Paul's thought as 'apocalyptic'.

The Earliest Research on Apocalyptic

In the first book of historical-critical research published on apocalyptic, Friedrich Lücke states two goals: first, to determine 'the concept and character of apocalyptic literature', and second, to describe the history behind the literature.[2] These goals dominate all research on apocalyptic from Lücke's time to the present. Although Lücke lays the foundations for this research clearly and comprehensively, he also includes in his definition of apocalyptic an ambiguity that survives to this day. This ambiguity arises from Lücke's handling of his first goal: theoretically the concept and character of apocalyptic are presented as a unity, but they are approached as though they were independent of one another. As a result, Lücke's analysis of the conceptual basis of apocalyptic has virtually no impact on his subsequent study of its characteristics.

Lücke's interest lies mainly with the two 'biblical apocalypses', Daniel and the book of Revelation. Clustered around these two apocalyptic masterworks are the lesser Jewish and Christian apocryphal apocalypses: the *Sibylline Oracles*, the *Book of Enoch*, *4 Ezra*, the *Ascension* and *Vision of Isaiah*, the apocryphal *Apocalypse of John*, and 'apocalyptic ideas' in the apocryphal *Testaments of the Twelve Patriarchs* and the *Shepherd of Hermas*. But Daniel and Revelation are presented, respectively, as the first and the last true apocalypses, the former both 'a development and a variant [degeneration?]' of OT prophecy, and the latter, the Christian fulfillment of OT 'prophecy of hope'.[3] Lücke approaches these works critically, attempting to resolve such questions as pseudonymous authorship, dating, and historical context. From this research on the book of Daniel, Lücke gleans the following list of apocalyptic characteristics: a universal perspective as the scope of revelation, a particular reckoning of time, pseudonymity, an artistic presentation, a combination of visions and images, and the interpretive mediation of angels. Lücke sees apocalyptic literature as both related to, and in tension with, prophetic literature, but he indicates that apocalyptic is somehow inferior to prophecy. Such positive qualities as the 'clarity of thought, simplicity and beauty of pure prophetic literature' are contrasted with the 'human capriciousness and phantasizing' of apocalyptic.[4]

Lücke is not concerned with apocalyptic only as a literary phenomenon, however. He also intends to explore apocalyptic as a theological concept. At the outset of his chapter on the 'establishment of the concept or theory of apocalyptic', he notes that as far back as 'the Greek church', the 'title' *apokalypsis*, the heading traditionally given to the NT book of Revelation, has denoted the 'essential content' of various works of Jewish and Christian literature.[5] He believes, therefore, that the word *apokalypsis* is the place to begin his theological exploration. On the basis of specific uses of the word *gālāh/gĕlā'* in the OT and its Greek equivalent *apokalyptō* in the NT, Lücke finds the word intimately related to *mystēria*, *optasiai*, *horasis*, and *prophēteia* and defines the essence of *apokalypsis* most simply as 'the revelation of God'. He sees the book of Daniel asserting that God alone has, knows, and reveals the secrets of God. These secrets, 'the OT mysteries', Lücke names as 'the essence and will of God, the ordinances and laws of His kingdom, which no human being from his own capacity and by way of natural knowledge can perceive'.[6] He describes Christ as 'the objective fulfillment of OT revelation, and hence the objective ground and beginning of all NT revelation'. Likewise, from his study of the use of *apokalyptō* by Paul, Lücke describes *apokalypsis* as essentially an act of God, by the mediation of the spirit of God. Lücke sums up such discoveries to define *apokalypsis* as '*the eschatological dogma, the Jewish and Christian faith in the future consummation of the kingdom of God*'.[7] But this theological link between 'apocalyptic' and 'revelation' is never really argued in his subsequent study of either the characteristics of, or the history behind, apocalyptic literature. Lücke's methodology treats apocalyptic as if it were fundamentally a literary genre.

Lücke foreshadows the course of subsequent research on apocalyptic in more ways than he intends. One approach of later research studies the characteristics and the history of the literary genre, offering critical interpretation of the corpus of apocalyptic literature. Another surveys the theological contours of a thought-complex called 'apocalyptic', exploring its relationship to the thought of the OT, Jesus' teaching, and the church's faith. But Lücke's methodological failure to pursue more fully the theological focus of apocalyptic may also initiate a troublesome ambiguity that can still be seen in the way the word is defined and used. Let us consider the two main approaches in turn.

Apocalyptic as a Literary Genre[8]

Adolf Hilgenfeld, in the full title of his book, *Die jüdische Apokalyptik in ihrer geschichtlichen Entwicklung: Ein Beitrag zur Vorgeschichte des Christentums* (Jena, 1854), indicates his major goal: to explore the historical development of Jewish apocalyptic, which is a study as well of the pre-history of Christianity. In pursuing this interest, Hilgenfeld defines apocalyptic primarily in terms of literary genre. This can be seen by the fact that he includes Daniel with other 'related Jewish scriptures' under the name 'Jewish Apocalyptic', to distinguish them from 'genuine prophetic scriptures'.[9] Hilgenfeld shows that, although the earlier *Codex Pseudepigraphus Vet. Test.* (1713) of J.A. Fabricius included a collection of 'apocryphal apocalypses', it was not until the nineteenth century that knowledge of the genre was widened and made accessible.[10] Hilgenfeld explores apocalyptic literature as an expression of the historical experience of Judaism under Seleucid and Roman domination, arising out of the contradiction between contemporary circumstances and hope in a future kingdom of God. He criticizes Lücke for allowing the book of Revelation to dominate his research, and he attempts to approach Jewish apocalyptic literature without reading back from the NT or the church. He thus wants to consider 'Jewish apocalyptic' as an historical entity in and of itself, including canonical and non-canonical works, both to be valued equally. But he sees apocalyptic as significant because it links OT and NT, prophecy and Christianity.

Hilgenfeld's positive approach to apocalyptic is not frequently followed. Emil Schürer, a forerunner of the *religionsgeschichtliche Schule*, in his monumental *Geschichte des jüdischen Vokes im Zeitalter Jesu Christi* (Leipzig, 1873), does include 'Apokalyptik' as one section in his first edition, but he discards the section in his second edition (1886), incorporating its ideas under the heading 'messianic hope', and dealing with the literature only under a section entitled '*prophetische Pseudepigraphen*'. Such low estimation of apocalyptic is also seen in Schürer's distinction between later apocalyptic and older genuine prophecy: he sees apocalyptic expressing revelation not in prophecy's distinct speech, but rather in a secretive form of riddles.[11] Here Schürer defines apocalyptic as a literary form related to, but distinct from, messianic dogma. Similarly, researchers of the *literargeschichtliche Schule*, including most notably Wellhausen and Duhm, envision such a radical break between Israel and Judaism that they discern Jewish literature after the Exile and beginning with Ezra as showing signs of 'degeneration'. A vast gulf is posited for the centuries between the great prophets and Jesus, and apocalyptic is consequently defined as a body of literature that carries prophetic form and thought off onto an unfortunate tangent. Julius Wellhausen, in *Geschichte Israels* (Berlin, 1878), barely mentions the 'gap' in which apocalyptic literature arose, and in *Israelitische und Jüdische Geschichte* (Gütersloh, 1884), he describes the book of Daniel as a step back to what 'the Israelites had in common with the heathen', a retreat from the monotheism of the prophets.[12] Bernhard Duhm, in *Israels Propheten* (Tübingen, 1922), argues that the apocalyptic literature of these supposedly vacuous centuries excessively emphasized the Law and eschatological hope: a reduction of prophetic ethical demands, on the one hand, and of prophetic 'threats and promises', on the other.[13]

Despite such assessments generally demeaning of apocalyptic, two major contributions to research on apocalyptic are made at the beginning of this century: in Germany, by Emil Kautzsch, *Die Apokryphen und Pseudepigraphen des Alten Testaments* (Tübingen, 1900), and in England, by R.H. Charles, *Apocrypha and Pseudepigrapha of the Old Testament* (Oxford, 1913).[14] By translating, editing, annotating, and publishing the collected literature, these scholars make the history, identity, and characteristics of the apocalyptic genre more accessible and the significance of apocalyptic more apparent than ever before. Kautzsch's edition is less annotated than Charles's, and he does at times speak pejoratively of apocalyptic.[15] Charles's work shows a higher value for apocalyptic literature, explicitly countering the assumption (by Wellhausen and others) of an historical gap from Malachi to the Christian era that was without inspiration and prophets. Charles sees the relationship of apocalyptic and prophecy to be extremely close, but differing in four ways: Apocalyptic expands the 'scope' of prophecy (1) to encompass all of time and the universe, adding to prophecy (2) the belief in a blessed future life, (3) the expectation of a new heaven and new earth, and (4) the catastrophic end of the present world.[16] On the basis of these four elements of apocalyptic, Charles concludes that pseudonymity is not a universal or essential characteristic of apocalyptic, and he even speaks of a 'Pauline apocalypse'.[17] Historically, Charles sees apocalyptic arising out of prophecy in the fourth century, when the claims of the Law began to diminish the significance that prophecy had enjoyed since the eighth century. Charles also affirms that under the rubric of prophecy, apocalyptic and revelation are intimately related; but his observation is only noted in passing.[18]

In England, appreciation of apocalyptic based largely on the work of R.H. Charles is voiced first by H.H. Rowley and later by D.S. Russell. In *The Relevance of Apocalyptic* (London, 1944), Rowley reviews the history and literature of apocalyptic. He asserts that one must distinguish between apocalyptic and eschatology; and since 'ideas of apocalyptic eschatology may be found in works that could not be described as apocalypses', he purposely omits any reference to the writings of Paul.[19] Rowley holds that when late prophecy saw history as moving swiftly toward a great climax and birth of a new age for a remnant of Israel, it was only a short step to apocalyptic, from which messianism developed, incorporating Son of Man traditions and giving increased prominence and definiteness to the concept of a great world judgment. Most importantly, Rowley sees the following distinction between apocalyptic and prophecy with regard to their respective views of time:

> Speaking generally, the prophets foretold the future that should arise out of the present, while the apocalyptists foretold the future that should break into the present.[20]

D.S. Russell, in *The Method and Message of Jewish Apocalyptic* (Philadelphia, 1964), distinguishes 'pseudepigrapha' (as form) from 'apocalyptic' (as content). He would derive apocalyptic from *apokalypsis*, 'revelation', which he interprets as first being identical with *vision* but then becoming identified with *books* on visions. Once again, Russell holds that the book of Revelation title was a technical term that came to signify a body of literature which was diverse yet also similar to the book of Revelation, and 'with certain well-defined characteristics which mark it off from other literary productions of the same period'.[21] These idiosyncrasies of apocalyptic literature include '*an impression or mood* of thought and belief, more than essential concepts, features which characterize the *literature* of the apocalyptists as distinct from their teaching'.[22] As the 'message' of Jewish apocalyptic, Russell includes such characteristics as time and history, angels and demons, messianic kingdom, Son of Man, and life after death. Russell's stated purpose in his book is 'to work out the theological implications of these characteristics for New Testament study'[23] by referring directly to apocalyptic texts and recently published literature from Qumran and by studying the history behind them. His work is helpful, but it provides information on the literature of apocalyptic more than on its theology.

Philipp Vielhauer, in his 'Introduction to Apocalypses and Related Subjects',[24] asserts that apocalyptic literature is characterized by a doctrine of the two ages, pessimism and hope of the beyond, universalism and individualism, determinism and imminent expectation, and lack of uniformity of characteristics within the genre. For Vielhauer 'apocalyptic' designates primarily 'the literary genre of the Apocalypses, i.e. revelatory writings which disclose the secrets of the beyond and especially of the end of time, and then secondly, the realm of ideas from which this literature originates'.[25] According to Vielhauer, the 'character, formal peculiarities and fixed features' of apocalyptic are *literary*, so that the following are 'elements in the style of this literary genre': pseudonymity, account of the vision, rapture and ecstasy experiences, surveys of history in future-form, and literary forms and their combinations, e.g. symbolic utterances, visions, blessings, wisdom sayings, sacred sayings, farewell discourses, and paraenesis.[26]

Vielhauer considers unresolved the question of the origin of apocalyptic, but he gives an excellent summary of previous theories: (1) that apocalyptic arose out of foreign ideas, especially Persian cosmological dualism, stimulating eschatological thinking in post-exilic circles around 400–200 BC, as those communities became sectarian under pressure from the anti-foreign Jewish theocratic establishment; (2) that apocalyptic is a continuation of prophecy; (3) that apocalyptic is an expression of 'folkbooks' or esoteric literature of rabbis; and (4) that apocalyptic is a product of Wisdom tradition. Vielhauer basically accepts the first view: Apocalyptists combine eschatological expectation, dualistic ideas, and esoteric thought in a manner like that of the community at Qumran; they use the organization, materials, and forms similar to those of Wisdom circles; and they write their literature to strengthen and comfort their own particular community. In research to date on apocalyptic, Vielhauer's summaries on the origin and characteristics of apocalyptic are often considered to be definitive.

John J. Collins, in *The Apocalyptic Vision of the Book of Daniel* (Missoula, 1977), 'Apocalypse: The Morphology of a Genre' (*Semeia* 14, 1979), and *The Apocalyptic Imagination: An Introduction to the Jewish Matrix of Christianity* (New York, 1984), is convinced of some prophetic origin of apocalyptic, but he argues for closer connection between prophecy and 'mantic wisdom', as well as later apocalyptic influence on Wisdom writers. Thus Collins sees the relationships between prophecy, Wisdom, and apocalyptic as complex, and he finds it impossible to trace apocalyptic back to a single origin.[27] In his article, Collins clearly describes his main purpose as that of identifying and defining a literary genre, 'apocalypse'.[28] Although Collins acknowledges that 'the term "apocalypse" is simply the Greek (*sic*) word for revelation', he sees the term commonly used as follows:

> in a more restricted sense, derived from the opening verse of the book of Revelation (The Apocalypse of John) in the NT, to refer to 'literary compositions which resemble the book of Revelation, i.e., secret divine disclosures about the end of the world and the heavenly state'.[29]

Briefly summarizing apocalyptic works of 'late Antiquity',[30] Collins adds some precision to Vielhauer's list of elements by discerning that the content of the 'temporal axis' of apocalyptic literature includes protology (theogony and/or cosmogony), historical recollections of prophecy, and evidence of eschatological crisis, judgment, and salvation. He even provides a chart to show which of these elements are evident in each of the major apocalypses. His concluding definition of the genre is quite comprehensive:

> 'Apocalypse' is a genre of revelatory literature with a narrative framework, in which a revelation is mediated by an otherworldly being to a human recipient, disclosing a transcendent reality which is both temporal, insofar as it envisages eschatological salvation, and spatial, insofar as it involves another, supernatural world.[31]

More particularly, Collins believes that 'the inner coherence of the genre' is *transcendence*, 'as seen in the otherworldly being mediating revelation'.[32] In this statement Collins attempts to evaluate or give priority to the various literary characteristics he discerns. But his definition of 'apocalypse' is so sweeping, transcendence may sound less like the heart of apocalyptic and more like a lowest common denominator of the genre.

Let us now evaluate the strengths and weaknesses of the research that has approached apocalyptic primarily as a literary genre. Although the estimation and origin of apocalyptic have been radically disputed by researchers, now the scholarly consensus values this body of literature as our major source of information on the development of various religious ideas and traditions in the centuries between OT prophecy and the NT. Genre study has also made it possible to characterize the general boundaries of apocalyptic literature: (1) the literary form of visionary narrative, (2) pseudonymous authorship, and (3) temporal dualism. Moreover, this research has helped to determine the relationship of newly discovered documents (e.g. from Qumran and Nag Hammadi) to the larger body of literary works. On the other hand, the literary genre approach is limited both by the fact that general characteristics may not apply to every work and by the need to weigh the significance of elements for each text to show how priorities may differ form work to work. If one takes literary genre as a starting point for research, the ideas of apocalyptic are important but *secondary*, as general features characteristic of the literature. Even if a link between apocalyptic and revelation is posited, what 'revelation' really means remains unclear. Major questions must therefore be considered: If one approaches apocalyptic primarily as a literary genre, must persons who did not write apocalypses, like Jesus or Paul, be neglected or ignored? Would their omission mean that it is improper to refer to their ideas and images as 'apocalyptic?'

Apocalyptic as a Theological Concept[33]

In the research of the *religionsgeschichtliche Schule* at the end of the last century, we begin to find apocalyptic defined as a phenomenon that is literary in form but, more significantly, theological in content, so that it must be interpreted in light of precedents in religious thought. Here apocalyptic is generally considered to be an example of the way in which Judaism and Christianity incorporated foreign religion and mythology. To be sure, not all researchers of the *religionsgeschichtliche Schule* portray apocalyptic thought as something positive. For example, Hermann Gunkel, in *Schöpfung und Chaos in Urzeit und Endzeit* (Göttingen, 1895), describes the apocalyptic tradition behind the book of Revelation as symptomatic of 'a passionately aroused fantasy' with analogies in mythology'.[34]

More than anyone else, Johannes Weiss, in his *Die Predigt Jesu vom Reich Gottes* (Göttingen, 1892), is the first to compel NT scholarship to begin focusing on apocalyptic *eschatology*. His book is a turning point in biblical criticism, for he demonstrates how the kingdom of God, which his liberal contemporaries all held to be a central theme of Jesus' ministry, is utterly 'eschatological-apocalyptic'.[35] Weiss's point of departure is the kingdom of God in the proclamation of Jesus, a concept which he sees as an 'objective messianic Kingdom' that is 'inextricably tied to "eschatological-apocalyptical" views'.[36] To be sure, Weiss's terminology only rarely includes the word 'apocalyptic', used positively, as above, when linked with the term 'eschatological'.[37] But by focusing on the centrality of 'eschatological apocalyptical' thoughts in the mind of Jesus, clearly Weiss is defining apocalyptic primarily as a concept, an eschatological perspective in which God's sovereignty over human affairs is known. From now on in research on apocalyptic as a theological concept, apocalyptic is generally considered to be a subdivision of eschatology, the doctrine of 'last things'.

In *Jesu Predigt in ihrem Gegensatz zum Judentum* (Göttingen, 1892), Wilhelm Bousset affirms 'the demand for a consistent—not merely occasional—use of the world of religious ideas and moods of late Judaism[38] for the understanding of the historical phenomenon of Jesus'.[39] Appreciation for such a 'consistent eschatology' as central to the thought of Jesus and Paul becomes one of the hallmarks of twentieth-century NT interpretation, and Bousset is to be credited in large part with helping to begin this emphasis.[40] In his later works,[41] Bousset continues to argue that Jewish apocalyptic is an undeniable influence on the gospel, especially as it was proclaimed by the apostle Paul.[42]

The first full discussion of Paul's apocalyptic eschatology appears in *Die Eschatologie des Paulus* (Göttingen, 1893) of Richard Kabisch, who sees 'the last things' as not merely part of Paul's theology but as the rubric under which the whole of his thought is to be subsumed. Kabisch's description of Paul's eschatology is similar to Weiss' use of the term 'eschatological-apocalyptic', i.e. that the coming of the Messiah is a matter not of ethical subjectivity or abstraction, but of the world and its end.[43]

Albert Schweitzer, in his *Skizze des Lebens Jesu* (Tübingen, 1901), forcefully articulates that eschatology must be 'consistent' and thoroughgoing, or it is not eschatology at all: 'Jesus ... must have thought either eschatologically or uneschatologically, but not both together'.[44] Likewise, in *Von Reimarus zu Wrede: Eine Geschichte der Leben-Jesu-Forschung* (Tübingen, 1910), Schweitzer credits the early eighteenth-century scholar Reimarus as the first in modern biblical research to understand 'Jesus' conceptual world historically, that is, as an eschatological world-view'. And he praises Weiss' *Predigt* as a genuine contribution to our knowledge of Jesus, because Weiss also shows that 'Jesus' message is solely eschatological'.[45] Schweitzer goes on to define the eschatology of John the Baptist, Jesus, and Paul as 'the culminating manifestations of Jewish apocalyptic thought'.[46] Similarly, in his *Geschichte der paulinischen Forschung* (Tübingen, 1911), Schweitzer argues that the theology of Paul is to be understood on the basis of apocalyptic Judaism. Paul's thought here is like the teaching of Jesus, which also 'represents a deeply ethical and perfected version of the contemporary Apocalyptic. . . . The Gospel is at its starting-point exclusively Jewish-eschatological'.[47] To substantiate this thesis, in *Die Mystik des Apostels Paulus* (Tübingen, 1931), Schweitzer gives a critical interpretation of the *ideas* of apocalyptic literature, especially the forms of messianic expectation. Surprisingly, however, Schweitzer was reluctant to question the theology of his own day on the basis of the ancient and extreme form of eschatological thought he was exploring. Thus, Schweitzer could advocate a Jesus 'spiritually arisen within' us, considering Jesus' own apocalyptic expectations 'crushed' by the fact that his death did not immediately bring about the end of time.[48]

Rudolf Bultmann is the one who goes furthest in attempting to interpret the gospel anew for the present generation. In numerous books and essays,[49] Bultmann undertakes the task of distinguishing the substance of the gospel from its particular historical expressions, the well-known process he called 'de-mythologization'. Even Jesus' own 'mythological' framework of thought, which Bultmann acknowledges to be thoroughly apocalyptic, must be discarded or translated for contemporary faith. For example, at the beginning of *New*

Testament Theology, Bultmann agrees that the dominant concept of
Jesus' message is the Reign of God coming as 'a miraculous event,
which will be brought about by God alone without the help of
men'.[50] Bultmann's contemporary translation of Jesus' apocalyptic
proclamation of the Kingdom of God would uncover 'the conception
of man' which underlies the eschatological message and thus would
affirm the relevance of individual human will and decision.[51] In spite
of Bultmann's claim to the contrary, we see here a deliberate attempt
to define apocalyptic in the light of an existentialism that emphasizes
the individual and the will. Apocalyptic is thus translated into a sense
of urgency in one's *decision* to live as though the kingdom of God is
at hand. Bultmann's consistent existentializing of the gospel inhibits
for decades (especially in Germany) further historical research into
apocalyptic on its own terms.

Meanwhile, in the United States, we find that the influential work
of George Foot Moore, *Judaism in the First Centuries of the Christian
Era* (Cambridge, 1927), dismisses apocalyptic as 'extraneous books'
embodying an eschatology which is tangential to the thought of
'normal Judaism'. Since these writings were not canonized by
Judaism and were ignored in the Tannaitic literature, he reasons, 'it
is fallacy of method for the historian to make them a primary source
for the eschatology of Judaism, much more to contaminate its
theology with them'(!).[52] As comprehensive and helpful as Moore's
work is in introducing Americans to the rich tradition of rabbinic
Judaism, his assessment of apocalyptic seems based on an uncritical
value for canon and an assumption that Wisdom and rabbinic
traditions are utterly separate from apocalyptic, a thesis which others
have demonstrated to be unfounded.[53]

In Germany, Gerhard von Rad, in his impressive *Theologie des
Alten Testaments* (München, 1960), contends that since 'knowledge is
the nerve-center of apocalyptic literature', then its real matrix must
be Wisdom. He substantiates this thesis by noting, for example, how
important Daniel's wisdom is to the book of Daniel, and how the
importance of *secret* or esoteric knowledge utterly differentiates
apocalyptic from prophecy's open proclamation.[54] Stressing definite
links between apocalyptic and Wisdom is von Rad's most valuable
contribution to research on apocalyptic. Nevertheless, von Rad also
drives a wedge between apocalyptic and prophecy by asserting that
'their views of history are incompatible' and that the view of

apocalyptic is 'really devoid of theology'.[55] Reviving previous criticism, von Rad sees the apocalyptists' sense of being the last generation as myopic, their view of a unified world-history as grandiose, and their sense of evil ever increasing as being 'pessimistic in the extreme'.[56] What is 'wrong' with apocalyptic, according to von Rad, is (1) its characteristic 'eschatological *dualism*, the clear-cut differentiation of two aeons', and (2) its *deterministic* view of history. In apocalyptic 'the real salvation event has moved out to the fringes of history, to the primeval election and determination and to the dawning of salvation at the end... [resulting in a] theological or, to be more precise, soteriological depletion of history'.[57]

Finally, although von Rad defines apocalyptic as a literary genre of pseudepigraphical works beginning with Daniel and ending with *4 Ezra*, he points out that 'this definition of apocalyptic (as a literary phenomenon of a particular kind) is inadequate'; an adequate definition must 'also try to describe a theological phenomenon with its own view of the world'.[58] Here von Rad is noting the central ambiguity of character *versus* concept in the definition of apocalyptic, which we first saw in Lücke, and on the basis of concept von Rad denigrates apocalyptic as theologically inferior to wisdom and prophecy. Such a denigration, which remains popular today, rests on the assumption that apocalyptic has an inadequate appreciation for history. Von Rad's assessment of apocalyptic in this regard has been challenged.[59]

Ernst Käsemann is primary in expressing a contrary view that affirms a positive and crucial significance for apocalyptic. A student of Bultmann, Käsemann seeks directly to counter his teacher's views, in the publication of 'Sätze heiligen Rechtes im Neuen Testament' (*NTS*, 1954), and even more in 'Die Anfänge christlicher Theologie' (*ZTK*, 1960) and 'Zum Thema der christlichen Apokalyptik' (*ZTK*, 1962). Recognizing the thrust of eschatological judgment behind examples of holy Law in Paul and the synoptics, Käsemann goes on to proclaim apocalyptic as 'the mother of all Christian theology'.[60] First of all, then, Käsemann underscores the significance of apocalyptic as essential to all Christian thought:

> We bar our own access to the primitive Easter kerygma if we ignore its apocalyptic content.... Paul's apostolic self-consciousness is only comprehensible on the basis of his apocalyptic.[61]

But Käsemann also narrows the focus on eschatology by defining more precisely what is meant by apocalyptic. In 'Die Anfänge', for example, he describes apocalyptic both in terms of the lordship of Christ, in which the Son of Man effects God's eschatological judgment over Creation, and also in terms of 'the Pauline doctrine of God's righteousness and our justification'.[62] In 'Zum Thema', Käsemann describes *the* apocalyptic question as 'To whom does the sovereignty of the world belong?'[63] Thus, Christ's role as Lord of the universe, subjugating the rebellious world, is apocalyptic *par excellence*.[64] Käsemann had stated earlier, in 'Die Anfänge', that 'it was apocalyptic which first made historical thinking possible within Christendom'.[65] Most important for our understanding of apocalyptic as a theological concept, then, Käsemann describes how 'apocalyptic' refers to 'the particular kind of eschatology which attempts to talk about ultimate history'.[66] Here Käsemann is challenging the opposition of apocalyptic and history, as argued, for example, by von Rad.

Käsemann's contribution to research on apocalyptic is remarkable. In a sense, he single-handedly 'rediscovers' apocalyptic in the tradition of Weiss and Schweitzer; and unlike Weiss and Schweitzer, Käsemann allows the apocalyptic of the primitive church to challenge and redefine our contemporary understanding of time and history. He counters Bultmann by refusing simply to translate apocalyptic into more modern dress. Thus, Käsemann restores for today the significance of apocalyptic as a thought-complex that must include a cosmology. Apocalyptic is by no means restricted to an individual and the power of one's will. Instead, Käsemann finds apocalyptic focusing on the sovereignty of God and its implications for all Creation, *including* humanity's understanding of time and history. Käsemann may be criticized for sometimes equating 'primitive Christian apocalyptic' with 'the expectation of an imminent Parousia' without adequately explaining why this particular expression of apocalyptic (rather than, for instance, the cross/resurrection) is to be interpreted as central. Moreover, Käsemann believes that Jesus' 'own preaching . . . did not bear a fundamentally apocalyptic stamp but proclaimed the immediacy of the God who was near at hand'.[67] In this regard, Käsemann implicitly accepts the widely held opinion that Jesus' Son of Man sayings are not authentic, but he uniquely and problematically defines 'theology' as something Jesus does not do.[68]

Since Käsemann, researchers begin more and more to explore the relationship of apocalyptic to history. For example, in the essay, 'Das Geschichtsverständnis der alttestamentlichen Apokalyptik' (1957),[69] Martin Noth explores the understanding of history evident especially in Daniel 2 and 7. Noth grounds his interpretation both in the biblical text and in the text's historical *Siz im Leben*, and he draws conclusions concerning the apocalyptic conception of history. For example, Noth finds in Daniel's apocalyptic the Jewish perception of 'once-and-for-all happenings of history as the true sphere of human life'.[70] Apocalyptic for Noth presents history as a whole, focusing on the sovereignty of God. Noth binds together apocalyptic and history and again counters the argument, for example, of von Rad.

Ulrich Wilckens, in 'Die Bekehrung des Paulus als religionsge-schichtliches Problem' (1959) and 'Das Offenbarungsverständnis in der Geschichte des Urchristentums' (1961),[71] focuses on the relation of apocalyptic to the theological doctrines of God, salvation, and revelation. Wilckens begins with the riddle of Paul's conversion and the apostle's antinomy between the Law and Christ, a problem that is comprehensible, he argues, only if we recognize Paul the Pharisee as an apocalyptic thinker. For Wilckens the soteriological function of the Law in apocalyptic Judaism is excluded by Paul's apocalyptic understanding of Christ crucified.[72] In his later essay, Wilckens describes Jesus' antithesis between himself and the Law in the Sermon on the Mount as an issue of authority which again is comprehensible only as an expression of apocalyptic thought. From this connection between christology and apocalyptic, Wilckens concludes that faith in Jesus 'is based on the actuality of Jesus' resurrection as the decisive inauguration of the eschatological self-revelation of God'. He goes on to describe the cosmic repercussions of the resurrection and the link between resurrection and revelation:

> The event that has already been inaugurated will catch up the whole cosmos in a universal way. To this extent, the fate of Jesus is understood in connection with the Jewish apocalyptic thought as the self-revelation of God. Revelation is the one definitive event as the 'sum' of universal history.[73]

For the first time since the work of Lücke, Wilckens explores in some depth the connection between apocalyptic and revelation. He brings together the resurrection and God's self-revelation to express the totality of history.

In *Offenbarung als Geschichte* (Göttingen, 1961) and *Grundfragen systematischer Theologie* (Göttingen, 1967), Wolfhart Pannenberg, the systematic theologian who shared years of collaborative thought with Wilckens (and Rössler) at Heidelberg, carries further this interrelationship of history, revelation, and apocalyptic. In an attempt to overcome the distance between biblical-critical research and dogmatic theology, Pannenberg defines history as 'the most comprehensive horizon of Christian theology'. Moreover, 'Jewish apocalypticism completed the extension of history so that it covered the whole course of the world from Creation to the End'. For Pannenberg, history itself is 'comprehensible only in light of the End, its resolution, the ultimate future goal of universal history'. That ultimate perspective on history is a present reality 'made possible because the final condition of man is proleptically anticipated in the destiny of Jesus Christ, and in his resurrection in particular'.[74] In this regard, revelation is defined in terms of God's own self-disclosure in God's historical acts, but it is comprehended completely only at the *end* of history. Such a perspective comes from the tradition of prophetic and apocalyptic expectation, and from this perspective Pannenberg would 'understand the resurrection of Jesus and his pre-Easter life as a reflection of the eschatological self-vindication of Jahweh'.[75] Pannenberg thus presents as incomprehensible, apart from an inextricable connection with apocalyptic, Christ's resurrection, God's self-revelation, and the ultimate judgment of God which makes history a whole.[76]

Dietrich Rössler, in *Gesetz und Geschichte* (Neukirchen, 1962), contributes to the exploration of the theological conception of apocalyptic by tracing its link with history. Although his book is more criticized than praised,[77] Rössler recognizes, as did Wilckens, that the Law has a significant function in apocalyptic soteriological and cosmological thought. Rössler argues that apocalyptic presents the first view of history in which history is viewed as a whole unit and linked to a pre-destined plan in which every event, from Creation to the End, has its place.[78]

In *Verhängnis und Verheißung der Geschichte* (Göttingen, 1966), Wolfgang Harnisch uses 'Apokalyptik' and 'apokalyptisch' to describe a theological conception of specific authors. He focuses on the theological understanding of time and history in *4 Ezra* and *2 Baruch*, exploring how these two major apocalypses handle two motifs central to apocalyptic thought: dualism and determinism. For him, *4 Ezra* and *2 Baruch* present a single theological perspective, apparently arising out of the same tradition and self-understanding of a specific group in Pharisaic Judaism shortly after AD 70. Crucial to both texts is a dualistic conception of history (the doctrine of two aeons). On the one hand, history develops not gradually but as one aeon of fallenness (*Unheilzeit*) marked by death, affliction, distress, and pain. On the other hand, there is the Last Judgment, a terminating moment of decision, wherein salvation in the future aeon is assured for those who have been obedient to Torah. The Law is thereby a means of encounter between the transcendent God and the realm of history. It is taken no longer as the document of Israel's election, but rather as the norm of God's ultimate *ius talionis*. In such apocalyptic thought, this aeon is depreciated as a mere state of passage (*Durchgangsstadium*) in which salvation is concealed and inaccessible; and yet, through the Law, this aeon is the only time in which those addressed by God find eschatological salvation named and mediated.[79]

Harnisch's contribution to our understanding of apocalyptic is considerable. First of all, he illustrates the soteriological function of the Law in the first century as apocalyptic. Secondly, with regard to *4 Ezra* and *2 Baruch*, two long-standing and pejorative generalizations of apocalyptic are disproved: apocalyptic as primarily the calculating of the coming of the Endtime, and apocalyptic as a pessimistic product of skepticism. Harnisch demonstrates that the two apocalypses incorporate a teaching of determinism in world history which does *not* emphasize the calculation of the amount of time to the End. Instead, their teaching underscores the certainty of hope in God as the Lord of time who guarantees the imminent coming of salvation. In the apocalyptic theology of *4 Ezra* and *2 Baruch*, the Two-Aeon doctrine polemically *responds to* the questions of doubt and the absence of promise, experienced historically in Rome's destruction of the Temple, by presenting a positive theocentric view of time, a theological apology of promise, and a theodicy.[80] By showing how two apocalypses embody ideas that contradict a general picture of apocalyptic, Harnisch demonstrates the need either to continue searching for the theological focus of apocalyptic or to limit characterizations of apocalyptic to specific works.

Jürgen Baumgarten, in *Paulus und die Apokalyptik* (Neukirchen,

1975), focuses on the undisputed letters of Paul in the larger context of research on apocalyptic and explores particularly 'urchristliche Eschatologie'.[81] Baumgarten challenges the assumption that Paul was single-handedly taking ideas directly from *4 Ezra*, *1 Enoch*, or any other apocalyptic text or the Dead Sea scrolls. Baumgarten also raises the question whether certain concepts or motifs that appear in 'apocalypses' can be identified as 'apocalyptic' if they are also met in prophecy, wisdom, Sibylline writings, rabbinic writings, Qumran, or gnosticism. Baumgarten believes that the definition of apocalyptic as a literary genre is 'greatly complicated' by the discoveries of Qumran and Nag Hammadi texts; and he argues that the origins of apocalyptic in the traditions of the Hasidim, Essenes, Pharisees, splinter groups, and proto-christian prophecy are too intricate to unravel. Moreover, Baumgarten rejects the attempt to discover a conceptual center of apocalyptic thought, asserting that such attempts are too exclusivistic.[82] Baumgarten's own interpretation of Paul's apocalyptic posits Paul's 'Entapokalyptisierung' ('de-apocalyptic-ization') and 'Entkosmolosierung' ('de-cosmologization') of received traditions, so that traditional apocalyptic elements are translated into anthropology and ecclesiology. Here Bultmann's influence is unmistakable.[83]

Paul D. Hanson, in his book *The Dawn of Apocalyptic* (Philadelphia, 1975), makes eschatology the rubric for his study of apocalyptic. His insistence that we look for the origin of apocalyptic in pre exilic and exilic prophecy is, on the whole, persuasive. Critical of von Rad for attempting to sever apocalyptic from Israel's other traditions, especially prophecy, Hanson argues that apocalyptic is a natural outgrowth of Israel's own prophetic tradition and not primarily the offspring of foreign influence. Looking within the prophetic tradition of Israel in the Second Temple period of the sixth to fifth centuries BC, Hanson sees the birth of apocalyptic in the inner-community struggle between visionary prophets and hierocratic (Zadokite) priests. The latter disenfranchise the former, who are then forced to abandon the traditional task of prophecy (i.e., translating visions of the divine council into historical terms) and begin to produce apocalyptic literature instead. Hanson's exploration of the origin of apocalyptic significantly adds to the contribution of Vielhauer by concentrating on the sociological and literary evidence for the development of eschatological thought within Judaism. Hanson examines the earliest examples of such apocalyptic creativity: 2 and 3 Isaiah and Zechariah 9-14.

At the beginning of his book and in three later essays,[84] Hanson attempts to clarify the ambiguous definition of apocalyptic by distinguishing: (1) 'apocalypse', a particular literary genre incorporating 'the revelation of future events by God through the mediation of an angel to a human servant'; (2) '"apocalyptic eschatology", a religious perspective, a way of viewing reality in relation to divine providence'; and (3) 'apocalypticism', the religious movement in which an apocalyptic community codifies its identity and interpretation of reality. This three-fold distinction is helpful, as is Hanson's description of the limitations that one encounters in approaching apocalyptic only as a literary genre. He also shows care in exploring the historical and sociological matrix of apocalyptic in ancient Israel.

Following Hanson, some of the most recent research has continued this attempt to understand apocalyptic, especially its origins, through sociology and anthropology.[85] Nevertheless, in studying the origins of apocalyptic eschatology 'within the conceptual framework of the tension . . . between vision and reality',[86] Hanson claims that the prophets were committed to 'plain history' whereas the apocalypticists 'increasingly abdicated responsibility to the politico-historical order of translating the cosmic vision into terms of the mundane'.[87] Here, Hanson's focus seems to be primarily on the 'politico-historical order'. Thus, his conception of apocalyptic is somewhat negative, and he almost reduces the term to a sociological construct.

J.C. Beker, in *Paul the Apostle: The Triumph of God in Life and Thought* (Philadelphia, 1981), finds the coherent center of Paul's gospel in the apocalyptic theme of God's triumph. He explores the way Paul translates that apocalyptic theme into contingent particularities of the human situations addressed in each of his letters. Beker declares the significance of apocalyptic as 'the indispensable means of [Paul's] interpretation of the Christ-event'.[88] Against Bultmann, Beker argues that the inextricable ties of the gospel to apocalyptic include cosmology more than anthropology.[89] Beker generally succeeds exegetically, and he demonstrates why the apostle necessarily expresses apocalyptic thought in various ways, depending upon the time and place addressed in his specific letters. Nevertheless, the book is disappointing with regard to a major point, for Beker's very definition of 'apocalyptic' is ambiguous. When he seems ready to define exactly what he means by 'apocalyptic', he turns not to Paul but to Koch and Vielhauer for their lists of apocalyptic characteristics.[90] To be sure, Beker claims that 'dualism, the cosmic rule of God, and the hope of its imminent coming form the crux of apocalyptic thought'.[91] Yet Beker's less than thorough examination of his most important term results in occasional problems of interpretation. He does not see, for example, that Galatians may be as profoundly apocalyptic a letter as 1 Corinthians.[92]

In *The Open Heaven: A Study of Apocalyptic in Judaism and Early Christianity* (New York, 1982), Christopher Rowland seeks to explore apocalyptic without allowing it to be 'dominated by its eschatological elements'. Distinguishing apocalyptic from eschatology by reserving 'eschatology' to refer to 'the future hope of Judaism and Christianity', he claims 'apocalyptic is as much involved in the attempt to understand things as they are now as to predict future events'.[93] What is new about *The Open Heaven* is the importance Rowland gives to his definition of 'the essential character of apocalyptic, [namely] the disclosure of the divine secrets through revelation'.[94] The apocalyptic movement from c. 300 BC to AD 300 is grounded in 'the belief that God reveals his mysteries directly to man and thereby gives them knowledge of the true nature of reality so that they may organize their lives accordingly'.[95] But in claiming that what is central to apocalyptic is not eschatology, but rather such disclosure of God, Rowland excludes many works generally conceived as apocalyptic, most notably the War Scroll of Qumran. Moreover, when he discusses apocalyptic in Paul, Rowland places greatest emphasis on 2 Cor. 12.1-10, and he equates 'revelation' with 'vision'. Several questions emerge that severely undermine, by their omission, Rowland's contribution. How is apocalyptic related to eschatology? Is revelation-as-vision the 'essence' of apocalyptic? If so, how is apocalyptic distinguished from gnosticism? What, finally, is the theological content of apocalyptic 'revelation'?

Having completed our survey of this second approach of research on apocalyptic, we can again evaluate our findings. There is strength in the way this research generally attempts to weigh theologically the significance of apocalyptic concepts. These concepts include (1) the idea of two Aeons, (2) the embattled sovereignty of God over time and cosmos, (3) the revelation of an imminent eschaton. Indeed, clarity about the content of apocalyptic seems to be achieved in the way some researchers describe apocalyptic as an eschatological frame of mind in which history and God's rule are perceived and finally understood. We also see that socio-historical concern in this research has done much toward establishing the *Sitz in Leben* and origin of apocalyptic. Finally, the theological concept research not only includes the thought of Jesus and Paul, in it their theological expressions of apocalyptic become central. Thus, this second approach to apocalyptic is invaluable. Nevertheless, it is disputed whether any single concept or cluster of ideas is central or 'essential' to apocalyptic, and it remains uncertain how one can most adequately approach the problem of defining 'apocalyptic'.

Conclusion Noting the Particular Contribution of J. Louis Martyn

In our survey of research on apocalyptic, we have observed that the word 'apocalyptic' derived from the transliteration of the Greek noun *apokalypsis* has often connoted something negative, abstruse, or fantastic, whereas the translation 'revelation' has been one of the most positive words in our theological vocabulary.[96] One reason for this discrepancy may be that the general use of the term 'apocalyptic' is derived primarily from the literary genre characterized by the book which concludes the NT, the Apocalypse. Defining the term by taking genre as one's point of departure has tended to emphasize characteristics of the larger body of intertestamental and apocryphal literature, much of which is indeed abstruse and fantastic. A few scholars who have explored the relationship between apocalyptic and Jesus or the apostle Paul, like Schweitzer and Käsemann, have avoided basing their research on assumptions drawn from a study of literary genre and have instead focused on apocalyptic as a theological concept. But since there is wide disagreement here, too, there is still need for analysis of definition and point of departure, as well as for more thorough grounding of the argument in exegesis. Exegesis is crucial, since each ancient text and author needs to be interpreted separately to discern individual emphases of apocalyptic thought.

One of the most promising points for doing such exegesis is the *intersection of apocalyptic and revelation*. Friedrich Lücke began to explore the etymological root of both words beyond the function of

Apokalypsis as a title for the book of Revelation. A century later, Wilckens and Pannenberg pursued at some length the theological implications of inter-relating apocalyptic and revelation. Although this link was not an explicit part of his argument, Harnisch also studied apocalyptic as a theological perspective on time and history in a way that seemed closely related to the concept of revelation. And even though Rowland's narrow definition of 'revelation' raised other questions for investigation, his claim that revelation constitutes the form and content of apocalyptic literature suggested an important focus. Do we have, in this almost unnoticed line of research, a clue for resolving some of the confusion in the way the word 'apocalyptic' functions? A positive answer may first be found in a provocative essay, 'Epistemology at the Turn of the Ages: 2 Corinthians 5.16',[97] where J. Louis Martyn makes a major contribution to the study of Paul's understanding of the gospel. Although again no such claims are made in the essay, Martyn's description of the eschatological *epistemology* in Paul's gospel expresses much of what we have been considering as the conceptual essence of apocalyptic. Let us conclude, then, with a closer look at the way in which Martyn approaches our problem.

In 'Epistemology', Martyn exegetes the broad context of 2 Cor. 2.14 to 6.10, in order to interpret 5.16. Here he discovers two basic facts:

> (1) Paul defends his apostleship by various arguments, all of which refer to the turn of the ages; (2) he mounts these arguments in a way which makes clear that only at that juncture is man granted the new means of perception which enable him to distinguish true from false apostles. To put it in the prosaic language of scholarly investigation, Paul's statements establish *an inextricable connexion between eschatology and epistemology.*[98]

The 'new means of perception' that is part of Paul's eschatology helps explain his use, in 2.16, of the phrase *kata sarka*, knowing Christ 'according to the flesh':

> He is saying that there are two ways of knowing and that what separates the two is the turn of the ages, the eschatological event of Christ's death/resurrection. There is a way of knowing which is characteristic of the old age (*ginōskein* or *eidenai kata sarka*), and by clear implication there is a way of knowing which is proper either to the new age or to that point at which the ages meet.[99]

Martyn's conclusion is simply astonishing: 'it is clear that the implied opposite of knowing *kata sarka* is not knowing *kata pneuma* but rather knowing *kata stauron*'.[100] But is such knowing, 'according to the cross', what we can properly call 'apocalyptic'? The apodosis, 2.17, confirms that Paul is using apocalyptic imagery to describe 'an event of cosmic proportions': *kainē ktisis, ta archaia parēlthen, idou gegonen kaina*.[101] And as the context again makes clear, that event which has made all things new is the cross/resurrection of Jesus Christ. In 2 Corinthians, then, the 'super' apostles have proven themselves 'false' apostles by failing to discern what Paul knows has brought an apocalyptic turn of the ages: the cross/resurrection of Christ, to which the daily death/life of the true apostle corresponds.[102]

Here Martyn demonstrates the way the apostle Paul finds in the cross of Christ a lens through which all things are viewed and interpreted apocalyptically. Indeed, Paul's focus on the cross expresses an apocalyptic encounter between God and humanity that brings God's judgment and grace whenever the gospel is proclaimed and lived. Martyn's contribution is significant in presenting not merely the horizon of Paul's thought as apocalyptic, but even Paul's *focus* on Christ's cross/resurrection, the heart of his gospel. This insight surpasses Käsemann's definition of apocalyptic by concentrating, *as Paul does*, on the cross/resurrection more than the parousia. Indeed, Martyn helps correct the imbalance in Beker's understanding of apocalyptic that neglects Galatians by missing the fact that for Paul the cross/resurrection seems as thoroughly apocalyptic as the parousia. Martyn perceives that nothing could be more apocalyptic than Paul's theology in Galatians.

Martyn provides exegetical confirmation for this interpretation in his essay, 'Apocalyptic Antinomies in Paul's Letter to the Galatians'.[103] Here Martyn describes four reasons for an inextricable link between epistemology and apocalyptic in Paul's thought:

> Epistemology is a central concern in all apocalyptic, because the genesis of apocalyptic involves a) developments that have rendered the human story hopelessly enigmatic, when perceived in human terms, b) the conviction that God has now given to the elect true perception both of present developments (the real world) and of a wondrous transformation in the near future, c) the birth of a new way of knowing both present and future, and d) the certainty that

neither the future transformation, nor the new way of seeing both
it and present developments, can be thought to grow out of the
conditions in the human scene.[104]

This apocalyptic hermeneutic is one that sees through the enigma of
past, present, and future in a perspective that comes solely from God.
And it is expressed not only in the promise of Christ's triumphant
parousia, but also in the gospel of Christ crucified:

> For Paul the developments that have rendered the human scene
> inscrutable are the enigma of a Messiah who was crucified as a
> criminal and the incomprehensible emergence of the community of
> the Spirit, born in the faith of this crucified Messiah. The new way
> of knowing, granted by God, is focused first of all on the cross, and
> also on the parousia, these two being, then, the parent of that new
> manner of perception. Galatians is a strong witness to the
> epistemological dimension of apocalyptic, as that dimension bears
> on the cross.[105]

Granted, in Galatians we do not encounter the traditionally
perceived motifs of apocalyptic as in 1 Thessalonians 4, 1 Corinthians
15, or Romans 8. Nevertheless, Galatians presents us with cosmic
pairs of opposites, or antinomies, that are connected with God's *New
Creation*, clearly 'an expression at home in apocalyptic texts'.[106] For
example, the Spirit and the Flesh function in Galatians 'not as an
archaic pair of opposites inhering in the cosmos from creation [as we
seem to find in the Doctrine of the Two Ways at Qumran, for
example], but rather as an *apocalyptic antinomy* characteristic of the
dawn of God's New Creation'.[107] Paul does not believe that the
messianic 'Age to Come' has replaced or made irrelevant the
historical 'present evil age', but in Christ crucified/resurrected he
knows what time it really is:

> It is the time after the apocalypse of the faith of Christ, the time
> therefore of rectification by that faith, the time of the presence of
> the Spirit, and thus the time of the war of liberation commenced by
> the Spirit.[108]

Here Martyn is using the word 'apocalypse' not in its common
literary sense, but as a literal translation of Paul's theological use of
the noun and verb *apokalyptō/apokalypsis*. The word in Galatians is
used most significantly, to *reveal* the coming of Christ, the Spirit,
and faith, as well as the true course of cosmic history, the ground of

his own apostleship, and the battle commands for obeying the gospel:

> The advent of the son and of his Spirit is also the coming of faith, an event that Paul explicitly calls an *apocalypse* (note the parallel expressions 'to come' and 'to be apocalypsed' in 3.23). Indeed it is precisely *the Paul of Galatians* who says with emphasis that the cosmos in which he previously lived met its end in God's apocalypse of Jesus Christ (1.12,16; 6.14). It is this same Paul who identifies that apocalypse as the birth of his gospel-mission (1.16), and who speaks of the battles he has to wage for the truth of the gospel as events to be understood under the banner of apocalypse (2.2,5,14).[109]

Paul's letter to the Galatians is fully as apocalyptic as his other epistles, but with an extraordinary emphasis on crucifixion:

> The motif of the triple crucifixion—that of Christ, that of the cosmos, that of Paul—reflects the fact that through the whole of Galatians the focus of Paul's apocalyptic lies not on Christ's parousia, but rather on his death. There are references to the future triumph of God (5.5,24; 6.8), but the accent lies on the advent of Christ and his Spirit, and especially on the central facet of that advent: the crucifixion of Christ, the event that has caused the time to be what it is by snatching us out of the grasp of the present evil age (1.4). Paul's perception of Jesus' death is, then, fully as apocalyptic as is his hope for Jesus' parousia (cf. 1 Cor 2.8). Thus the subject of his letter to the Galatians is precisely an apocalypse, the apocalypse of Jesus Christ, and specifically the apocalypse of his cross.[110]

For Paul, Martyn perceptively concludes, the gospel itself is an 'apocalypse'. That is, not in some ahistorical ecstatic vision, but in 'the word of the cross' (1 Cor. 1.18), apocalyptic and revelation intersect. In Paul's gospel the power and purpose of God are ultimately disclosed.

To be sure, one must acknowledge that words are defined functionally more than etymologically. Whatever the ancient root of a word may be, it may legitimately come to be used in ways that are quite different from its origin. Moreover, the way one person (even the apostle Paul) uses a word can hardly be normative or authoritative for others. Nevertheless, it is unfortunate when a word is used haphazardly in contradictory ways, and Martyn's discoveries regarding

Paul's epistemological understanding of the gospel link apocalyptic and revelation in a way that may provide the theological focus that would allow us at least to define *Paul's* apocalyptic comprehensively and in depth.

NOTES

*An expanded version of much of this research appeared in my thesis, 'An Exegetical Study of the Apostle Paul's Use of the Words *apokalyptō/ apokalypsis*: The Gospel as God's Apocalypse' (Dissertation, Union Theological Seminary, 1984).

1. T.F. Glasson, for example, believe. that apocalyptic 'is a useless word which no one can define and which produces nothing but confusion and acres of verbiage'. See his essay, 'What is Apocalyptic?', *NTS* 27 (1980), pp. 98-105.

2. *Versuch einer vollständigen Einleitung in die Offenbarung des Johannes, oder allgemeine Untersuchungen über die apokalyptische Litteratur überhaupt und die Apokalypse des Johannes insbesondere* (Bonn: Weber, 1832, 1st edn), p. 22. Unless otherwise indicated, all references are to the second edition (1852); quotations from the 1st edition were available to me through J.M. Schmidt's *Die jüdische Apokalyptik* (see n. 8 below).

3. *Versuch*, pp. 40, 30. In the first phrase, Lücke's words are 'eine Fortsetzung und zugleich eine Abart'. Elsewhere Lücke comes even closer to saying that apocalyptic is a 'degeneration' of prophecy: 'Die Apokalyptik ist an und für sich noch keine Entartung des prophetischen Geistes, aber sie ist nahe daran, es zu werden, und ist es oftmals gewesen' (*Versuch* [1st edn], p. 26). He seems to believe that apocalyptic becomes 'degenerate prophecy' in apocryphal (i.e. non-canonical) works.

4. *Versuch* (1st edn), pp. 25-26.

5. *Versuch*, p. 17. 'Die Griechische Kirche' is a recurring term apparently referring to the Greek-speaking early church of Paul and the Greek Fathers (cf. Lücke's use of the term 'Roman church': 'Das sehr alte Fragm. anonymi bey Muratori über den Kanon der Rom. Kirche kennt keine andere Ueberschrift' [*Versuch*, p. 509 n. 1]). By saying that 'the authentic heading' of the book of Revelation became 'a technical literary expression in the Greek church', Lücke means that the most ancient codices of the NT (as well as Origen, Clement of Alexandria, and the Muratori Canon) give *Apokalypsis Iōannou* as 'probably the original library title' for this work.

6. *Versuch*, p. 20.

7. *Versuch*, p. 15.

8. This section, although extensive, can be brief, thanks to the reviews of J.M. Schmidt, *Die jüdische Apokalyptik* (Neukirchen: Neukirchener Verlag,

1969), and K. Koch, *Ratlos vor der Apokalyptik* (Gütersloh: Mohn, 1970; ET = *The Rediscovery of Apocalyptic* [Naperville: Allenson, no date]).

9. *Jüdische Apokalyptik*, p. 2. His other texts include Daniel, *Sibylline Oracles 3*, *Enoch*, *Apocalypse of Ezra* (*4 Ezra*), (*Syriac*) *Baruch*, and 'Essene' writings. For him, the major characteristics of apocalyptic literature are pseudonymity and a universal perspective of history.

10. R. Lawrence published an edition of *4 Ezra* in 1820, *Enoch* in 1821; and J.H. Friedlieb published his edition of the Sibylline writings in 1852.

11. Schürer, *Geschichte*, p. 260.

12. Wellhausen, *Israelitische und Jüdische Geschichte*, pp. 288-89 (1958 edn).

13. Duhm, *Israels Propheten*, p. 460.

14. Charles's two volumes were preceded by *Jubilees* (1895), *Assumption of Moses* (1897), *1 Enoch* (1906), *Testaments of the Twelve Patriarchs* (1908), and were followed by *Religious Development between the Old and the New Testaments* (1914), and Commentaries on Revelation (1920) and Daniel (1929). Charles's work has only recently been significantly expanded, by *The OT Pseudepigrapha*, 2 vols., ed. James H. Charlesworth (Garden City: Doubleday, 1983).

15. For example, Kautzsch speaks of how nearly all the 'elements of apocalyptic' are to be found in Enoch, but he specifically names such things as 'die mythologisierenden Berichte über den Fall und die Bestrafung der Engel [und] Phantasien über die Geheimnisse des Weltalls' (*Apokryphen*, pp. xx-xxi).

16. Charles, *Religious Development*, pp. 18-23 (1948 edn).

17. Charles cites 1 Corinthians and 2 Thessalonians 2 (*ibid.*, p. 46).

18. *Ibid.*, p. 14 n. 1.

19. Rowley, *Relevance*, p. 51.

20. *Ibid.*, p. 35.

21. Russell describes the apocalyptic mood as (1) esoteric in character, (2) literary in form, (3) symbolic in language, and (4) pseudonymous in authorship (*Method and Message*, p. 36).

22. *Ibid.*, pp. 104-105; see also pp. 106-39.

23. *Ibid.*, p. 9.

24. His essay appears in E. Hennecke & W. Schneemelcher's *Neutestamentliche Apokryphen in deutscher Übersetzung*, Vol. II (Tübingen: Mohr, 1964). My citations are taken from the ET edition by R.McL. Wilson, *New Testament Apocrypha*, II (Philadelphia: Westminster, 1965), pp. 581-607.

25. Vielhauer holds that by analogy to the Christian use of *Apokalypsis Iōannou* as the title of the book of Revelation, attested since the Muratori Canon 1.71-72 (AD 200?), 'the name was applied to similar Jewish works, e.g. *Syriac Baruch*, and to a genre' (ibid., p. 582).

26. *Ibid.*, pp. 582-87.

27. Collins, *The Apocalyptic Vision*, pp. 54-59.

28. Collins defines 'literary genre' as 'a group of written texts marked by distinctive recurring characteristics which constitute a recognizable and coherent type of writing' (see 'Apocalypse', p. 1). Collins considers his task to be literary and therefore primary, since, for example, even the 'sociological study of apocalyptic depends almost entirely on evidence of a literary nature' (*ibid.*, p. 4).

29. *Ibid.*, p. 2 (Collins's quotation is from K. Koch, *Rediscovery*, p. 18).

30. Collins dates 'late Antiquity' from 'c. 250 BCE to 250 CE' (*ibid.*, p. 5).

31. *Ibid.*, p. 9.

32. *Ibid.*, pp. 10-11.

33. Here again, J.M. Schmidt and K. Koch include helpful discussion of most of the major figures and their discoveries (see n. 8 above). Even more helpful in this theological review is the work of W.G. Kümmel, *Das Neue Testament: Geschichte der Erforschung seiner Probleme* (Marburg: Alber, 1970); ET = *The New Testament: The History of the Investigation of its Problems* (New York: Abingdon, 1972).

34. Gunkel, *Schöpfung*, pp. 272-73 (cited in Kümmel, *The New Testament*, p. 250).

35. For Weiss's substantiation of his view see *Predigt*, in the ET, *Jesus' Proclamation of the Kingdom of God*, ed. R.H. Hiers, D.L. Holland (Philadelphia: Fortress, 1971), pp. 78-79. Weiss's argument seeks to contradict Ritschl and the prevailing assumption that Jesus believed (as did nineteenth-century theologians) in a gradually developing kingdom of God within the world, a kingdom that was the embodiment of presently realized or spiritualized ethics.

36. *Jesus' Proclamation*, pp. 114, 133. Weiss sees the imminence of the kingdom as also motivating Jesus' ethics, the 'new morality' (*ibid.*, p. 106).

37. On the other hand, Weiss twice uses the word 'apocalyptist' negatively, contrasting Jesus first, with those who seek to calculate how long it will be until the Kingdom of God comes (*ibid.*, p. 90), and second, with those who are not sparing in their descriptions of the 'color' of messianic salvation (*ibid.*, p. 104).

38. Kümmel perceptively explains why the term 'late Judaism' does not appear in his own history of research, except in the quotations of others: 'The designation of post-Old Testament Judaism as 'late Judaism' arose at the end of the eighteenth century ... and was generally in use among Christian scholars until the middle of our century, but it is factually in error' (*The New Testament*, p. 439 n. 294).

39. Bousset, *Jesu Predigt*, p. 6 (cited in Kümmel, *The New Testament*, p. 230).

40. Bousset is nevertheless unwilling to see Jesus as 'under the spell of

Judaism', which is to say, thoroughly heir to the traditions of Israel (including apocalyptic).

41. See *Die Offenbarung Johannis* (1896), *Die Religion des Judentums im neutestamentlichen Zeitalter* (1903), and especially *Die jüdische Apokalyptik, ihre religionsgeschichtliche Herkunft und ihre Bedeutung für das Neue Testament* (1903).

42. *Jüdische Apokalyptik*, p. 56 (cited in Kümmel, *The New Testament*, p. 261).

43. Kabisch, *Eschatologie*, p. 317 (cited in Kümmel, *The New Testament*, pp. 234-35); again, the argument is *contra* Ritschl.

44. Schweitzer, *Skizze*, pp. ix-x (cited in Kümmel, *The New Testament*, p. 235).

45. *Von Reimarus zu Wrede*, p. 24 (cited in Kümmel, *The New Testament*, p. 238).

46. *The Quest of the Historical Jesus* (New York: Macmillan, 1961), p. 367. (This is the ET of *Von Reimarus zu Wrede*.)

47. *Forschung*, p. viii (cited in Kümmel, *The New Testament*, p. 242).

48. *Quest*, p. 401. Likewise, after presenting a radical picture of Jesus' message, Weiss could shrink from rejecting his contemporaries' thoughts (see Weiss, *Proclamation*, p. 135).

49. See especially *Jesus* (1926; ET = *Jesus and the Word*, 1934, 1958); 'Das Neue Testament und Mythologie: Das Problem der Entmythologisierung der neutestamentlichen Verkündigung' (1941, reprinted in *Kerygma und Mythos*, 1948; ET = *Kerygma and Myth*, 1953); *Theologie des Neuen Testaments* (1941; ET = *Theology of the New Testament*, 1955), and, in response to E. Käsemann, 'Ist Apokalyptik die Mutter der christlichen Theologie?' in *Apophoreta: Festschrift für E. Haenchen*, BZNW 30 (1964), pp. 64-69, later in *Exegetica* (1967), pp. 476-82.

50. *Theology of the New Testament*, pp. 4-5.

51. *Jesus and the Word*, pp. 55-56.

52. Moore, *Judaism* (1950) edn), pp. 126-27.

53. See e.g. Koch, *Rediscovery*, 86-92.

54. Von Rad notes here that 'Daniel must use a Persian loan word *räz* for "secret"' (*Old Testament Theology*, II [New York: Harper, 1965]), p. 308.

55. Von Rad, ibid., p. 303.

56. *Ibid.*, p. 305.

57. *Ibid.*, p. 273.

58. *Ibid.*, p. 301. Cf. G. Ebeling, 'Der Grund christlicher Theologie', ZTK 58 (1961), pp. 231-32; and H.D. Betz, 'Zum Problem des religionsgeschichtlichen Verständnisses der Apokalyptik', ZTK 63 (1966), p. 392.

59. See e.g. P. von der Osten-Sacken, 'Die Apokalyptik in ihrem Verhältnis zu Prophetie und Weisheit' (*Theologische Existenz Heute* 157; München: Kaiser, 1969).

60. Käsemann, 'Die Anfänge'; ET= 'The Beginnings of Christian Theology', *NT Questions of Today* (Philadelphia: Fortress, 1969), p. 102. 'Holy Law' is *nomos Christou* in e.g. 1 Cor. 3.17; Rom. 10.11, 13; Mk 8.38; Mt. 10.32-33; 16.27.

61. *Ibid.*, p. 96.

62. *Ibid.*, p. 105.

63. *Ibid.*, p. 135.

64. *Ibid.*, pp. 133-34.

65. *Ibid.*, p. 96.

66. *Ibid.*, p. 109 n. 2.

67. *Ibid.*, p. 101.

68. See *ibid.*, p. 102.

69. Noth's essays appears in his *Gesammelte Studien zum Alten Testament* (München, 1957); ET = 'The Understanding of History in OT Apocalyptic', in *The Laws in the Pentateuch and Other Studies* (Philadelphia: Fortress, 1967).

70. *Ibid.*, p. 214.

71. 'Die Bekehrung des Paulus' appeared in *ZTK* 65 (1959), pp. 273-93, and 'Das Offenbarungsverständnis', in *Offenbarung als Geschichte*, ed. W. Pannenberg (Göttingen: Vandenhoeck & Ruprecht, 1961); ET = 'The Understanding of Revelation in the History of Primitive Christianity', in *Revelation as History* (New York: Macmillan, 1968).

72. 'Bekehrung', p. 285 (cited in Koch, *Rediscovery*, p. 73).

73. 'Understanding of Revelation', in *Revelation as History*, p. 70.

74. Pannenberg, 'Heilsgeschehen und Geschichte', in *Grundfragen*; ET = 'Redemptive Event and History' in *Basic Questions in Theology* (London: SCM, 1970), p. 20.

75. 'Dogmatic Theses on the Doctrine of Revelation', in *Revelation as History*, p. 127.

76. *Ibid.*, p. 193.

77. See e.g. Koch, *Rediscovery*, pp. 40-42, 89-90; Vielhauer, 'Introduction', p. 593; W.R. Murdock, 'History and Revelation in Jewish Apocalypticism', *Int* 21 (1967), pp. 167-87; and W. Harnisch, *Verhängnis und Verheißung der Geschichte* (Göttingen: Vandenhoeck & Ruprecht, 1969).

78. Rössler, *Gesetz und Geschichte*, p. 111.

79. Harnisch, *Verhängnis und Verheißung*, p. 247.

80. *Ibid.*, p. 326.

81. Baumgarten, *Paulus*, p. 16.

82. *Ibid.*, pp. 13-14.

83. See especially *ibid.*, pp. 241-43.

84. Hanson, 'Apocalypse (Genre)' and 'Apocalypticism' in the *IDBSup* (New York: Abingdon, 1976), and 'Appendix' in *Dawn* (2nd edn, 1979).

85. See e.g. R.R. Wilson, 'From Prophecy to Apocalyptic: Reflections on

the Shape of Israelite Religion', *Semeia* 21 (1981), pp. 79-95; and W.A. Meeks, *The First Urban Christians: A Social Description of Pauline Christianity* (New Haven: Yale University, 1982), especially ch. 7.

86. *Dawn* (1st edn), p. 29.

87. *Ibid.*, pp. 17, 26.

88. Beker, *Paul the Apostle*, p. 143. Cf. *ibid.*, p. 152: 'Only a consistent apocalyptic interpretation of Paul's thought is able to demonstrate its fundamental coherence'.

89. In this regard, Beker is confirming (but may not really be adding to) the thought of Käsemann; nevertheless, Beker also uses language which sounds very much like Bultmann (see e.g. *ibid.*, p. 179).

90. Beker sees Koch's list as giving 'a more comprehensive picture', differing in many ways from Vielhauer's list; but Beker does not explore what makes Koch's picture better or why either list is helpful (*ibid.*, p. 135).

91. *Ibid.*, p. 138.

92. See J.L. Martyn's review of Beker's book in *Word & World* 2 (1982), pp. 194-98, and Martyn's essay discussed below (see n. 103).

93. Rowland, *The Open Heaven*, pp. 1-2.

94. *Ibid.*, p. 20. Cf. R.E. Brown, *The Semitic Background of the Term 'Mystery' in the NT* (Philadelphia: Fortress, 1968), pp. 1-30.

95. *Ibid.*, p. 11.

96. K. Koch observes this in *Rediscovery* (see n. 8 above), p. 18.

97. J.L. Martyn, 'Epistemology at the Turn of the Ages: 2 Corinthians 5.16', W.R. Farmer, C.F.D. Moule, R.R. Niebuhr (eds.), *Christian History and Interpretation: Studies Presented to John Knox* (Cambridge: Cambridge University Press, 1967), pp. 269-87.

98. *Ibid.*, pp. 271-72 (emphasis mine).

99. *Ibid.*, p. 274.

100. *Ibid.*

101. *Ibid.* Elsewhere Martyn notes that 'in rabbinic Judaism seeing and/or knowing perfectly appears to be consistently reserved for the messianic age or the age to come. "The things that are concealed from you in this world, you will see in the World to Come, like a blind man who regains his sight," *Num. R.* 19.6' (*ibid.*, p. 280).

102. To be sure, Paul finds the Last Judgment imposing significant epistemological limitations for the present: e.g. in 1 Cor. 4.3 'notice that in this passage Paul, far from claiming for himself the capacity to judge (contrast 2.15!), insists that only the returning Lord is capable of judgment. . . . [U]ntil we all stand before the *bēma tou Christou*, there is only one point at which the epistemological question can be legitimately posed: the death/resurrection of Christ and the daily death/life of the disciple' (*ibid.*, p. 287).

103. J.L. Martyn, 'Apocalyptic Antinomies in Paul's Letter to the Galatians', *NTS* 31 (1985), pp. 410-24.

104. *Ibid.*, p. 424.

105. *Ibid.*

106. *Ibid.*, p. 417.

107. *Ibid.*

108. *Ibid.*, p. 418.

109. *Ibid.*, p. 417 (first emphasis mine).

110. *Ibid.*, pp. 420-21.

'THE TIME HAS BEEN FULFILLED!' (MARK 1.15)

Joel Marcus

'Get a dictionary and learn the meaning of words!' Ford Maddox Ford's imperious command to the young Ezra Pound, as recollected years later by Pound,[1] could well have been uttered by J. Louis Martyn to his students. In his teaching, Lou has always insisted on precise definitions, believing that only they can lead to clear thought, the sort of thought he has exemplified to generations of students. Sometimes, in fact, as Lou has shown, a precisely defined word or phrase, heard with the ears of its first hearers, can become the entryway into the apocalyptic truth of the gospel.[2]

An example is provided, I believe, by the first words Jesus speaks in the Gospel of Mark, 'The time has been fulfilled' (*peplērōtai ho kairos*, 1.15). Most interpreters translate *kairos* here, in line with classical Greek usage, as 'decisive moment',[3] and speak confidently of the 'fulfillment' of this moment without appearing to ask themselves how a *moment* can be *fulfilled*.

Although *kairos* certainly *can* mean 'decisive moment' in Mark (12.2; 13.33), it can also mean a longer (10.30) or shorter (11.13) span of time. This study will examine and defend F. Mussner's argument that *kairos* in Mk 1.15 refers to a span of time. It will then offer, I hope in the spirit of Lou Martyn, a more consistently apocalyptic interpretation of the verse than Mussner presents, and finally advance a hypothesis about its *Sitz im Leben*. I begin with a translation of the verse.

1.15a   *peplērōtai ho kairos*
       'The time has been fulfilled,
1.15b   *kai ēngiken hē basileia tou theou*
       and the kingdom of God has drawn near.

1.15c	*metanoeite*
	Repent,
1.15d	*kai pisteuete en tǭ euangeliǭ*
	and believe in the gospel.'

1. *Appointed Time or Span of Time?*

In an oft-overlooked article, Mussner opposes the translation 'decisive moment', arguing that the punctiliarity of this concept contrasts distressingly with the linearity implied in the verb 'to fulfill'.[4] A glance at Liddell–Scott supports this argument; the root image behind *plēroun*, like that behind our English verb, is of a container receiving more and more contents until it is full.[5]

Since *peplērōtai* would have initially evoked for Greek speakers this image of a container, and since *kairos* can indicate, indeed in the LXX and NT usually *does* indicate, a span of time,[6] it seems more logical to begin with the hypothesis that Mk 1.15a speaks of a span of time that has now become full, i.e. is over, and only to deviate from this interpretation if impressive reasons for doing so can be adduced. Mussner strengthens the case for staying with the translation 'span of time' by pointing to evidence from secular Greek,[7] the LXX,[8] and the NT[9] which shows that *plēroun* in conjunction with expressions of time, including *kairos*, denotes a span of time.[10]

G. Delling, however, in his *TDNT* article on *plērēs*, claims that *kairos* in conjunction with *plēroun* can denote a point in time. Taking a careful look at Delling's evidence, one notes first his citation of Aelius Aristedes *Or.* 22.9. *panēgyreis. . . plērountai*, which Delling translates '*festivals. . . fall due* every five and three years'.[11] *Panēgyris*, however, is not an expression of time. Moreover, the translation of *plērountai* as 'fall due' is unlikely; neither LSJ nor Moulton–Milligan shows this meaning or anything like it. The normal meaning of *plēroun*, 'to fulfill', in this case to fulfill the rites of, yields perfectly good sense.[12] In addition, since a *panēgyris* is a festal *assembly*,[13] the usage of *plēroun* in the passive to mean 'assemble, muster'[14] would also be appropriate.

In his consideration of the LXX passages,[15] Delling recognizes that *plēroun* with expressions of time usually denotes extent. He suggests, however, that in Lev. 8.33; Gen. 25.24; 1 Kgdms 18.27 (A) it refers to a point in time. Two of these examples, however, Gen. 25.24 and the variant reading from 1 Kgdms 18.27, speak of the fulfillment (= the end) of *hai hēmerai*, 'the days', in the first case the days of Rebekah's pregnancy, in the second case the days of David's wedding engagement; a span of time is therefore in view. In the third example, Lev. 8.33, Aaron is instructed not to go out from the door of the tabernacle 'for seven days, until the day is fulfilled (*heōs hēmera plērōthē*), the day of your consecration'. Delling paraphrases, 'until the appointed day has come', but Aaron is supposed to leave the tabernacle *after* the day of his consecration, not *on* it.[16] In the LXX, too, then, *plēroun* speaks of the fulfillment or completion of a *span* of time.

Delling also cites Josephus, *Ant.* 6.49:[17] *Samouēlos. . . exedecheto ton kairon genesthai, plērōthentos d'autou katabas* ('Samuel awaited the arrival of the time, and when it was fulfilled he descended'). Here *kairos* means 'point of time' in the first clause, but does that meaning control the second clause as well? It seems more likely that the meaning of *kairos* oscillates here between 'point of time' and 'span of time', as it does in the Alexandrinus reading of Esth. 2.12: 'This was the time (*kairos*) for a maiden to go in to the king, when the time (*kairos*) of the maiden was fulfilled (*plērōthē*)'; the other manuscripts of Esther read 'when twelve months were fulfilled' in the second clause. In Esth. 2.12, then, and probably also in *Ant.* 6.49, the reader would have been alerted to the switch from the punctiliar nuance of *kairos* to the linear one by the introduction of the verb *plēroun*.[18]

Finally, Delling points to two NT passages (besides Mk 1.15) where he believes that *kairos* in conjunction with 'fulfillment' verbs refers to a point in time: Acts 2.1 and Jn 7.8.[19] I grant Delling's point about Acts 2.1, but here the verb is not *plēroun* but the compounded form *symplēroun*, which already in classical Greek can mean 'attain', a meaning not attested for the uncompounded form.[20] Acts 2.1, then, proves nothing about the meaning of the uncompounded form *plēroun* in conjunction with expressions of time.

John 7.8 is worth pondering longer; for *kairos* is used in conjunction with an uncompounded form of *plēroun* (*peplērōtai*), and the alternation with *parestin* in 7.6 convinces most interpreters[21] that the *arrival* of the *kairos* (= the decisive moment) is being discussed. It is possible, however, that the meaning of *kairos* changes from 'decisive moment' to 'span of time' in the transition from Jn 7.6 to Jn 7.8, as we have seen that it does in Esth. 2.12 and probably in Jos.

Ant. 6.49. As in those cases, in Jn 7.6-8 readers would be alerted to the change in nuance by the change in verbs. John certainly likes to play with the different nuances of important words (e.g. *kosmos* in Jn 1.9-10, *anōthen* in Jn 3.3-7), so it is not implausible that he is doing so here.

The probability of such an oscillation is increased by the observation that *kairos* is a synonym for the more frequent Johannine *hōra*;[22] the latter term, however, can have an element of linearity: it includes Jesus' whole ministry, seen from the standpoint of the crucifixion.[23] This linearity is suggested by expressions such as, 'The hour is coming and now is', and 'the hour is coming and has come' (4.23; 5.25; 16.32). Moreover, the notion that Jesus' allotted span of time (= the *kairos* of 7.8) is fulfilled at the crucifixion is consonant with the declaration in 19.28, 30, 'It has been accomplished' (*tetelestai*), which is quite close in meaning to 'it has been fulfilled'.[24] It is more than possible, then, that *kairos* in Jn 7.8 refers to a span of time.

Mussner's interpretation is strengthened by the structure of Mk 1.15 and by its Markan context. Jesus' announcement in 1.15 consists of two main clauses with perfect tense verbs, connected by *kai* (1.15ab); these are followed by two imperatives connected by *kai* (1.15cd). The second main clause (1.15b) looks to the future; the kingdom has come near but has not yet fully arrived.[25] The second imperative (1.15d) also looks to the future; the good news must be *believed* because it announces a dawning reality, one that has not yet arrived in power. By contrast, the first imperative, the exhortation to repent (1.15c), is primarily a call to *turn away* from what lies in the past.[26] Thus, in order to preserve the parallelism, the first main clause, the announcement of the fulfilled time (1.15a), should also refer to what is past, and therefore to the end of a time rather than to the arrival of a time. We might diagram this parallelism thus:

the time has been fulfilled	and	the KOG has drawn near
OLD AGE		NEW AGE
repent	and	believe in the gospel
TURN AWAY		TURN TO

As M.-J. Lagrange describes this correspondence: 'The fulfilled time, a negative condition to which one responds by repentance; the approaching kingdom, a positive condition to which one adheres by faith'.[27] This correspondence, however, is present only if *kairos* has an extensive meaning, referring to the span allotted to the old age.

The probability of such a meaning is further increased by Mussner's citation of 1QpHab 7.1-2, a contemporary Hebrew parallel for the phrase 'to fulfill a span of time': 'God told Habakkuk to write down the things which would come upon the final generation, but the consummation of the time (*gmr hqṣ*) he did not make known to him'.[28] In support of the extensive translation of *qṣ*, which some have questioned,[29] W.H. Brownlee points to its usage at Qumran in the phrase *aḥryt hqṣ*, 'the end of the time' (4QpNah 3.3; 4QpPss^b frag. 1.51.5); this phrase corresponds to the more usual *aḥryt hymym*, 'the end of the days'.[30] Furthermore, in both biblical and Talmudic Hebrew, *gmr* means 'to finish, complete, be completed',[31] and there is no reason to doubt that it retains this meaning in 1QpHab 7.2.[32]

We have seen, then, that parallels from the QL, the LXX and the NT, as well as the very structure of Mk 1.15, support the view that the latter speaks of the fulfillment of a span of time.[33] The previous epoch is pictured as a container that has been filling up and is now full, so that the eschaton is imminent. The Jewish apocalyptic concept of the eschatological measure, therefore, is in view;[34] when the measure of time allotted to the old age is full, the new age will come. As the classic expression of this concept, *4 Ezra* 4.36-37, puts it: '[God] has weighed the age in the balance, and measured the times by measure, and numbered the times by number; and he will not move or arouse [the souls of the just] until that measure is fulfilled'.[35]

Here it is the measure of the *times*, plural, that must be fulfilled, whereas Mark speaks of the fulfillment of the *time*; but D, significantly, reads *kairoi* in Mk 1.15, revealing that at least one early scribe interpreted 1.15 as a reference to the eschatological measure. Apocalyptic texts attest an alternation between 'time' and 'times' in such contexts,[36] so that Mark's use of the singular is not an argument against an apocalyptic interpretation; central to apocalyptic is the doctrine of the *two ages*, not the doctrine of *several* ages leading up to the eschaton.[37] The use of the singular in Mk 1.15 is of a piece with the comment that humanity's hardness of heart is the reason Moses permitted divorce (Mk 10.5-6): the whole age stretching from the Fall to the advent of Jesus is viewed as a unity of disobedience, so that any division into epochs (including the epoch of the Law) would be irrelevant.[38]

2. *Time of Waiting or Time of Satan's Rule?*

These last comments, however, raise a question about Mussner's study. He refers to the *kairos* as 'the time of the promises' and its fulfillment as 'the end of the time of waiting'.[39] But is this exactly Mark's nuance? Does God's kingdom replace a situation in which there is *no* kingdom, or does it overthrow an *opposing* kingdom?

Already we have seen indications that the Markan *kairos* has a more negative meaning than Mussner gives it. One *turns away* from something that is evil, not from something that is as hopeful as a 'time of waiting'. The *kairos*, I have suggested, is the old age that is mired in a spirit of disobedience. Before and outside of the advent of Christ, human beings *are* subject to a *basileia*, namely one that impels them toward sin, death, and destruction. This apocalyptic reading of *kairos* is supported by its use in 10.30, where in true apocalyptic fashion the present evil age (=*kairos*) is contrasted with the coming age.[40]

This interpretation of *kairos* is supported by comparison with a fascinating passage the structure of which is in many ways similar to that of Mk 1.15. In the Freer Logion, which appears in a fifth-century Greek uncial (W) in the longer ending of Mark and is also known from Jerome, Jesus replies to the disciples' request that he reveal his righteousness: *peplērōtai ho horos tōn etōn tēs exousias tou satana, alla engizei alla deina*, 'The term of the years of the dominion of Satan has been fulfilled, but other terrible things draw near'. The continuation lacks a main clause: 'And on account of which (*kai hyper hōn*) sinners I was handed over to death, in order that (*hina*) they might turn to the truth and no longer sin, in order that they might inherit the spiritual and immortal glory of righteousness in heaven'.

The formal similarities to Mk 1.15 of this logion, which seems to be an isolated saying embodying a local tradition,[41] are striking, as the following comparison demonstrates:

Mark 1.15	*Freer Logion*
has been fulfilled (*peplērōtai*)	has been fulfilled (*peplērōtai*)
the time	the term of dominion of Satan
and	but
has drawn near (*ēngiken*)	draw near (*engizei*)
the kingdom of God	other terrors. . .
repent	in order that they might turn. . .
and believe in the gospel	that they might inherit glory

The first sentence, like Mk 1.15, begins with the verb *peplērōtai* and is followed by its subject, which describes an eschatological terminus. As in Mark, there then follows a conjunction and a form of the verb *engizein*, and there is a tension between the 'not yet' expressed by this second clause and the 'already' expressed by the first clause. Although what next follows in the Freer Logion is in the subjunctive rather than the imperative mood, the same basic idea is expressed as in Mk 1.15cd: turning *from* sin and turning *to* God's eschatological gift. Overall, this section of the Freer Logion reads like a bloated and somewhat scrambled version of the saying in Mk 1.15.

The correspondence between the Freer Logion and Mark 1.15 is even closer if K. Haacker[42] is right in his reconstruction of a Semitic original to the Logion,[43] for in this reconstruction the second main clause reads, 'and the end of terrible things is near', and the first *hina* clause becomes an imperative ('let them turn to the truth'). It seems probable in any case that there is some sort of tradition-historical relationship between Mk 1.15 and this section of the Freer Logion.

In the light of these formal parallels, it is significant that what is fulfilled in the Freer Logion is 'the term of the years of *the dominion (exousia) of Satan*'. I would suggest that this is exactly the sense of *peplērōtai ho kairos* in Mk 1.15. The *kairos* that is fulfilled with Jesus' advent is the time of the dominion of Satan; his reign is now over.[44]

That we are not simply imposing this interpretation on Mark from the Freer Logion emerges from a consideration of the Markan context of 1.15. Just before he comes proclaiming the fulfillment of the time, Jesus is opposed by Satan (1.13); the continuation of the narrative suggests that this contest did not end in a draw, but rather in a defeat for Satan: his minions, the demons, shriek in terror as Jesus exorcizes them (1.24, 39).[45]

This line of reasoning is strongly supported by *T. Naph.* 8.3-4:

> Through his *kingly power* (*skēptros*) God will appear
>   to save the race of Israel. . . .
> If you achieve the good, my children,
> men and *angels* will bless you. . . .
> The *devil* will flee from you;
> *wild animals* will be afraid of you,
> and the *angels* will stand by you.

Here we find the same three actors who are associated with Jesus in

Mk 1.13 (Satan, wild animals, and angels) in a passage that deals with the revelation of God's kingly power.[46] If Mark's readers knew this tradition,[47] then even before reading the rest of ch. 1, they would have interpreted 1.13 as a description of the dethronement of Satan. This exorcistic understanding of 1.13 is supported by the parallel between Jesus' being with the wild animals here and the picture of him 'taming' (*damasai*, 5.4) the Gerasene demoniac in 5.1-13. Mark's readers would therefore have been primed to think of the end of Satan's rule when they read in 1.15 of the fulfillment of the time and the advent of the kingdom.[48]

In light of the argument thus far, a paraphrase of 1.15 can now be presented which highlights its implicit alternation between the *basileia* of Satan and the *basileia* of God (cf. 3.23-27):

> The time of the dominion *of Satan* has been fulfilled,
> and the kingly power *of God* has drawn near.
> Turn away, therefore, from the dominion *of Satan*,
> and turn to the coming manifestation of the power *of God*.

The imperatival section of this passage is a call to recognize the new situation that has been created by God's action in Jesus Christ. God has judged the *kairos* of Satan and brought it to an end;[49] therefore the only sane thing for human beings to do is to withdraw their recognition from Satan's regime and to acknowledge the new *basileia* that is about to replace it. Jesus' hearers are urged to make this acknowledgment not only because they can thereby guarantee their survival but also, more basically, because recognizing the new regime is the only way of acting that corresponds to *reality*. One world has died, another is being born; Jesus calls his hearers to recognize the new world in which they live.

3. *Sitz im Leben*

In Mk 1.15, then, Jesus announces the termination of one age and the beginning of another; he then calls his hearers to turn away from the age that is over and to turn to the age that is beginning. This exact pattern recurs in Rom. 13.12:

> The night is far gone,
> and the day has drawn near (*ēngiken*);
> let us therefore take off the works of darkness,
> let us put on the weapons of light.

Since the old age, the night, is about to end, the works associated with that age are to be left behind; since the new age, the day, is about to arrive, the weapons that draw their strength from that age are to be girded on. Similarly, 1 Thess. 5.5-6 implies a cosmic change (night/darkness to day/light) and exhorts human beings to enter into that change; cf. Col. 1.13; Acts 26.18 (see Figure 1).

Figure 1

Mk 1.15	Rom. 13.12	1 Thess. 5.5-6	Col. 1.13	Acts 26.18
time has been fulfilled	night is far gone	you are sons of light and of day	rescued us from dominion of darkness	
kingdom of God has drawn near	day has drawn near	we are not of night or of darkness	transferred us into kingdom of loved son	
repent	let us put off works of darkness	let us not sleep like others		to turn from darkness to light
believe in the gospel	let us put on weapons of light	let us wake up and be sober		from dominion of Satan to God

Rom. 13.11-12, however, is probably from a baptismal liturgy,[50] as is indicated by the rhythmic quality of its language; the imagery of illumination,[51] awakening from sleep, and changing clothes (cf. Gal. 3.27); and the correspondence of Rom. 13.11 to Eph. 5.14, which is usually identified as part of a baptismal hymn.[52] For similar reasons, 1 Thess. 5.5-6 and Col. 1.13 have been identified as parts of pre-Pauline baptismal liturgies,[53] and a case can also be made for the adoption of baptismal language in Acts 26.18.[54] One therefore wonders whether the structurally similar 1.15 might also have been used in a baptismal setting before its incorporation into Mark's Gospel.

Several considerations support such a hypothesis. The developed parallelism and solemn cadences of our verse suggest liturgy. Moreover, the call to repent and believe in the gospel fits naturally into a baptismal setting. Mark himself has already linked repentance and baptism by his description of John's 'baptism of repentance' (1.4); and in Acts we find calls to repentance and to faith in narratives having to do with baptism (2.38; 11.16-18; 13.24; 19.4). These narratives, as O. Cullmann has shown, reflect a stage of

Christian liturgical development in which repentance and confession of faith were the sole conditions for baptism.[55]

Not only repentance and faith, but also *the kingdom of God* has baptismal associations in NT texts.[56] This is only natural, since one of the sources of the Christian rite was Jewish proselyte baptism,[57] and the Jewish proselyte was said to take upon himself kingdom of heaven.[58] In Jn 3.5, being born from water and the Spirit (=being baptized)[59] is the condition for entry into the kingdom; this seems to be John's version of the story in Mk 10.13-16,[60] which also concerns the kingdom of God and is probably itself not devoid of baptismal associations.[61] In 1 Cor. 6.9a, Paul warns the Corinthians that the unrighteous will not inherit the kingdom; he then goes on to reassure them by recalling their baptism (1 Cor. 6.11).[62] Finally, in Col. 1.13, which the previous discussion has shown to be part of a baptismal liturgy, we read that God 'rescued us from the dominion of darkness and transferred us into the *basileia* of his beloved Son'.

Not only are the terms of Mk 1.15 associated with baptism in other NT contexts, but there is internal evidence that 1.15 incorporates a previously existing tradition.[63] The Semitic parallelism of the verse, while not conclusive evidence in itself,[64] at least raises the possibility of pre-Markan provenance, for Mark seems to have been neither a Palestinian, nor an Aramaic speaker, nor even perhaps a Jew;[65] more importantly, the Semitic construction *pisteuein en* is a hapax in Mark and in the NT, and is strong evidence for pre-Markan tradition.[66] The presence of the term 'gospel' is no argument against an underlying Semitic tradition, for this term (*bśwrh, bśwrt'*) can be traced back to early Palestinian Jewish Christianity.[67] It is doubtful, however, that Mk 1.15 goes back to Jesus, because of the similarities we have traced to early Christian baptismal formulas. Its origin, therefore, is probably to be sought in Aramaic-speaking Jewish Christianity.[68]

Mk 1.15, therefore, seems to be traditional; and its similarity in form to passages that have been identified as baptismal (particularly Rom. 13.12), and its usage of vocabulary associated with baptism in the NT (repentance, faith, kingdom of God) suggests that it is specifically a *baptismal* tradition. In their original settings, Mk 1.15 and all the other passages displayed in Figure 1 would have identified baptism as the occasion upon which the turn of the ages was appropriated anthropologically. Mk 1.15ab: 'The time of Satan's dominion is over, and the kingdom of God has drawn near!'—the catechumens, approaching the baptismal waters, would have heard this announcement of cosmic juncture as a promise that they might now enter the kingdom. Mk 1.15cd: 'Bury, in your baptismal death, the world that has died, and rise from the waters, over which the Spirit hovers, to view God's new creation!'

In 1.9-15, therefore, Mark has described Jesus' own baptism, then portrayed his proleptic victory over Satan, and finally described his initial proclamation of the kingdom with words drawn from a baptismal liturgy known to the Markan community. Furthermore, this whole section is prefixed by John the Baptist's prophecy in 1.8 that the Stronger One who comes after him will baptize with the Holy Spirit. In Mark's narrative, however, there follows no explicit description of Jesus baptizing with the Spirit.[69] If my argument so far is valid, however, Mark's readers would have recognized in 1.15 words drawn from their own baptismal liturgy, and they thus may have been led to identify Jesus' proclamation of the gospel in 1.14-15, and the events that it inaugurates, with the baptism in the Holy Spirit.[70] The one who has just been baptized in the Spirit (1.9-10) can now himself baptize in the Spirit. Indeed, to hear the preaching and to see the actions of the earthly Jesus *is* to be baptized in the Spirit, to experience the ultimate charismatic manifestation.

Long ago Albert Schweitzer, reflecting on the tension between John's prophecy of a baptizer to follow him and the fact that Jesus did not baptize, proferred an explanation for the behavior of the historical Jesus:[71]

> He dispensed with [baptism] because he held it to be unnecessary. His own presence has in itself sacramental significance. He who attaches himself to Him, the future Messiah, and thereby enters into fellowship with Him, does not need to be baptized in order to receive the Spirit and to be saved at the Judgment.

Our study has shown that Schweitzer's basic insight is consonant with the Markan editing of 1.2-15, though Mark does not play baptism off against fellowship with Jesus. For Mark (as for Paul in Schweitzer's analysis), Jesus' presence does have an apocalyptic sacramental significance, but the new Christian is ushered into this presence and hence proleptically into the orb of the new aeon *at baptism*. In the Markan view discipleship is a matter of 'being with Jesus' (3.14), of following him on his journey from Galilee to

Jerusalem (10.32-34); the Markan community would have read itself into the references (many of them redactional) to the band of disciples accompanying Jesus on his earthly way.[72] And Mark's readers would have believed that it was through baptism that they had gained entrance into this band, entrance into the story of Jesus that is the demonstration in the earthly sphere of the kingly power of God (*basileia tou theou*).[73] It is thus no accident that the baptismal formula in 1.15 is immediately followed by the calling of the first four disciples (1.16-20).

The announcement of Mk 1.15, then, weds baptism firmly to the person of Jesus, and it points forward to the inseparable events that for Mark reveal God's kingship and are constitutive of the Markan community: the death of Jesus, his resurrection from the dead, and his coming again.[74] Mark sees himself and his community as living in the short interval between Jesus' ministry, which culminated in his crucifixion-and-resurrection, and the parousia; and he reminds his readers that it is to these events, and to the interval between them, that the words spoken over them at baptism point. Thus there is no danger that, for Mark, the kingdom of God will become a timeless realm, entered once and for all at baptism; Mark binds the kingdom and baptism to the Jesus who walked the earth, to time, to the world that had been the devil's empire, but that has just as surely become the arena in which God is manifesting his kingly power and vindicating his holy name.

NOTES

1. E. Pound, *The Cantos of Ezra Pound* (New York: New Directions, 1972), Canto 98, p. 689.

2. I am thinking in particular here of Lou's treatment of the phrase *kata sarka* (2 Cor. 5.16) in 'Epistemology at the Turn of the Ages' (*Christian History and Interpretation: Studies Presented to John Knox* [ed. W.R. Farmer et al.; Cambridge: Cambridge University Press, 1967], pp. 269-87) and his discussion of the word *aposynagōgos* in *History and Theology in the Fourth Gospel* (2nd edn; Nashville: Abingdon, 1979).

3. See e.g. E. Lohmeyer, *Das Evangelium des Markus* (Göttingen: Vandenhoeck & Ruprecht, 1951; orig. 1937), pp. 29-30; G. Delling, '*plērēs*', *TDNT* VI (1968; orig. 1959), pp. 459-62; W.L. Lane, *The Gospel of Mark* (NICNT; Grand Rapids: Eerdmans, 1974), p. 64; J. Gnilka, *Das Evangelium nach Markus* (EKKNT 2; Zürich: Benzinger/Neukirchener Verlag, 1978-79),

vol. I, p. 66; apparently J. Schlosser, *La règne de Dieu dans les dits de Jesus* (EBib; Paris: Gabalda, 1980), vol. I, p. 100. V. Taylor (*The Gospel Accordng to St. Mark* [2nd edn; Grand Rapids: Baker, 1981; orig. 1950], p. 166) and B.D. Chilton (*God in Strength: Jesus' Announcement of the Kingdom* [Studien zum Neuen Testament und Seiner Umwelt, Serie B, Band 1; Freistadt: Plöchl, 1979; repr. in the series The Biblical Seminar; Sheffield: JSOT, 1987], pp. 85-86) argue for a related translation, 'appointed time'. On *kairos* in classical Greek, see G. Delling, *'kairos'*, *TDNT* III (1965), pp. 455-58; LSJ, pp. 859-60.

4. F. Mussner, 'Gottesherrschaft und Sendung Jesu nach Mk 1, 14f. Zugleich ein Beitrag über die innere Struktur des Markusevangelium', in *Praesentia Salutis. Gesammelte Studien zu Fragen und Themen des Neuen Testaments* (Düsseldorf: Patmos, 1967), p. 88.

5. *'plēroō'*, LSJ, pp. 1419-20; see also C.F.D. Moule, 'Fulfillment Words in the New Testament: Use and Abuse', *NTS* 14 (1967), p. 315. *Plēroun* in the LXX usually renders *ml'*, which both in the OT and in the QL denotes the completion of a period or of a process (B. Chilton, *God in Strength*, p. 80).

Moule ('Fulfillment Words', pp. 293-94) lists three nuances of *ml'*/*plēroun* in the OT and NT: (1) verification of a prediction, (2) termination, completion, or confirmation of a beginning, project, or promise, and (3) fulfillment of the covenant-promise. None of these three meanings fits the concept 'appointed time'.

6. J. Schlosser, *Règne*, vol. I, pp. 98-99.

7. Pap. Oxyr. 2.275.24 *mechri tou ton chronon plērōthēnai*.

8. See especially his citation of Tobit 14.5: The Israelites will return to Israel *heōs plērōthōsin kairoi tou aiōnos*, 'until the times of the age are fulfilled'.

9. Here the important passages are Lk. 21.24 (Jerusalem will be trodden by the Gentiles until the times of the Gentiles are fulfilled, *plērōthōsin kairoi ethnōn*); Eph. 1.10 (God's plan for the fulness of the times, *plērōmatos tōn kairōn*; cf. the singular 'fulness of the *time*', *plērōma tou chronou* in Gal. 4.4), and the Freer Logion, on which see below, section 2.

10. 'Gottesherrschaft', pp. 84-86, 88.

11. *'plērēs'*, pp. 287, 309.

12. Cf. the usage in IG 12(5).946.1, *plēroun pasan archēn kai leitourgian*, 'to fulfill every office and liturgy' (*'plēroō'*, LSJ, p. 1420 III 6).

13. *'panēgyrizō',* etc.', LSJ, p. 1297.

14. *'plēroō'*, LSJ, p. 1420 III 7. Cf. esp. the usage of *plēroun* with *ekklēsia*, Ar. *Ec.* 89.

15. *'plērēs'*, p. 288.

16. Both the MT and the LXX describe seven days of consecration; Aaron is not to leave the tabernacle until seven days are over (LXX *ouk exeleusesthe hepta hēmeras*, 'you shall not leave for seven days') i.e. until the *conclusion* of

the seventh and culminating day, which is itself called the 'day of consecration' in the LXX.

17. *'plērēs'*, p. 287. Mussner ('Gottesherrschaft', p. 86) cites the same text for his contrary opinion.

18. See H.St.J. Thackeray's LCL translation of *plērōthentos d'autou* in *Ant.* 6.49 as 'when the hour was ripe'.

19. *'plērēs'*, pp. 294, 308.

20. LSJ cites Polystr. *Herc.* 346 *to tēs physeōs telos* ('to attain the end of nature') and a similar usage in the middle, Epicur. *Ep.* 3 *to tēs psychēs kai tou sōmatos agathou* ('to attain the good of the soul and of the body'). Cf. Lk. 9.51, where *symplērousthai* also seems to have the nuance of arrival.

21. E.g. C.K. Barrett, *The Gospel According to St. John* (London: SPCK, 1962), p. 257; R.E. Brown, *The Gospel According to John* (2 vols.; AB 29; New York: Doubleday, 1966-70), vol. I, p. 306; R. Schnackenburg, *The Gospel according to St John* (3 vols.; New York: Crossroad, 1982; orig. 1965-75), vol. II, p. 142.

22. Cf. 7.6, 8 with 2.4; R.E. Brown, *John*, vol. I, p. 306.

23. I am indebted to M.C. de Boer for this observation.

24. Although *plēroun* and *telein* are not synonymous, they are parallel in use; cf. G. Delling, *'teleō'*, *TDNT* VIII (1972), p. 59 n. 6.

25. See W.G. Kümmel, *Promise and Fulfillment: The Eschatological Message of Jesus* (London: SCM, 1957), pp. 19-25 and J. Schlosser, *Règne*, vol. I, pp. 106-108. 1.15a and 1.15b do not necessarily mean the same thing because they are parallel (*contra* A. Ambrozic, *The Hidden Kingdom: A Redaction-Critical Study of the References to the Kingdom of God in Mark's Gospel* [CBQMS 2; Washington: Catholic Biblical Association, 1972], p. 21). The essence of biblical parallelism is not *identity* of the parallel parts but the *sharpening* of the first by the second (see J.L. Kugel, *The Idea of Biblical Poetry: Parallelism and its History* [New Haven/London: Yale University, 1981], p. 51). Mk 1.15a might thus be paraphrased: 'The time has been fulfilled, and *what is more*, the kingdom of God has drawn near'. For Mark, the kingdom already arrives, but in a hidden way, in Jesus' death-and-resurrection, which anticipates its coming in power at the parousia; see J. Marcus, 'Mark 4.10-12 and Marcan Epistemology', *JBL* 103 (1984), pp. 570-72; *idem*, *The Mystery of the Kingdom of God* (SBLDS 90; Atlanta: Scholars, 1986), pp. 51-57.

26. See W. Bauer et al. (*'metanoeō'*, BAG, 2nd edn, p. 512) on the predominance of the negative aspect in the verb *metanoein*.

27. M.-J. Lagrange, *Evangile selon Saint Marc* (Etudes Bibliques; 2nd edn; Paris: Lecoffre, 1911), p. 17; cf. A. Ambrozic, *Hidden Kingdom*, p. 7.

28. 'Gottesherrschaft', p. 87.

29. J. Schlosser (*Règne*, vol. I, pp. 98-100) takes *qṣ* as the point at which the previous age gives way to the messianic era, and B.D. Chilton (*God in*

Strength, p. 83) thinks that it means 'end', as it usually does in rabbinic Hebrew.

30. *The Midrash Pesher of Habakkuk* (SBLMS 24; Missoula: Scholars, 1979), p. 110.

31. BDB, p. 170; M. Jastrow, *A Dictionary of the Targumim, the Talmud Babli and Yerushalmi, and the Midrashic Literature* (New York: Judaica, 1971), pp. 254-55.

32. W.H. Brownlee (*Midrash Pesher*, p. 110) asserts that the last time's 'fulness' should be interpreted not as its chronological limit but as the exact detail of what will happen then. This is implausible in view of the immediately following 1QpHab 7.7-8, where the chronological element is emphasized: 'The final time will last long and exceed everything spoken by the prophets; for the mysteries of God are marvelous'.

33. B.D. Chilton (*God in Strength*, pp. 85-86), in adopting a punctiliar interpretation of *kairos* in Mk 1.15, suggests a different Jewish background, *Tg. Isa.* 60.20-22, where the Aramaic word for 'fixed time', *zmn*, occurs one verse away from an instance of the verb *šlm* = to fulfill. However, this proximity of a verb for 'to fulfill' to a noun for 'fixed time' is irrelevant, since the noun is not used as the subject or object of the verb; the subject of fulfillment is 'the days of mourning', which implies extension in time.

It might at first seem that another Jewish parallel, *2 Bar.* 30.1, 3 presents a counter-instance of the verb 'to fulfill' in conjunction with a noun indicating a point in time: 'When *the time* of the appearance of the Anointed One *has been fulfilled (ntml' zbn' dm'tyth dmsyḥ')*. . . the time has come of which it is said that it is the end of times'. The appearance of the Messiah, however, is for *2 Baruch* not a punctiliar but a linear event, as is demonstrated a few verses earlier (29.3): 'The Anointed One will *begin to* be revealed' *(nšr' dntgl' msyḥ')*.

34. On this concept in the New Testament, see R. Stuhlmann, *Das eschatologische Mass im Neuen Testament* (FRLANT 132; Göttingen: Vandenhoeck & Ruprecht, 1983). G. Delling rejects the apocalyptic idea of a chronological scheme fixed by God as background for Jesus' announcement of the fulfilled *kairos* because for him such a scheme would imply that the time of an event can be calculated from external signs (*'plērēs'*, p. 294). However, one can be convinced that the eschatological measure is being filled up without exploiting that conviction to calculate the time of the eschaton's arrival. In Mk 13.28-29, for example, Jesus uses the concept of the eschatological measure, and then within a few verses warns that no one, not even he, knows the hour of the end (13.32).

35. The translation basically follows that by B.M. Metzger (in J.H. Charlesworth, ed., *The Old Testament Pseudepigrapha* [2 vols.; Garden City: Doubleday, 1983-85], vol. I, p. 531) except for the words in brackets, which are supplied from W. Harnisch, *Verhängnis und Verheißung der Geschichte*.

Untersuchungen zum Zeit- und Geschichtsverständnis im 4. Buch Esra und in der syr. Baruchapokalypse (FRLANT 97; Göttingen: Vandenhoeck & Ruprecht, 196), pp. 285-86. The object is lacking in the Latin; Harnisch supplies it from v. 35.

36. See for example 1QpHab 7, which alternates between *qṣ* in the singular (7.2, 7) and in the plural (7.13) in a passage having to do with the eschatological terminus; F. Mussner ('Gottesherrschaft', p. 84) notes that such alternation is common in the QL. Cf. *4 Ezra* 14.10: 'For the *age* (*saeculum*) has lost its youth, and the *times* (*tempora*) begin to grow old'.

37. *Contra* B.D. Chilton (*God in Strength*, p. 89), who asserts that 'a distinctively apocalyptic conception would take the plural'. On the centrality of the doctrine of the two ages in apocalyptic, see P. Vielhauer, Introduction to 'Apocalypses and Related Subjects' in *New Testament Apocrypha* (ed. E. Hennecke & W. Schneemelcher; Philadelphia: Westminster, 1964), vol. II, pp. 588-89; Vielhauer goes on to remark that because of this centrality 'the division of history into periods lies in the free choice of the individual writer' (p. 592).

38. On the Markan view that 'hardness of heart' has obtained since shortly after the creation, see D.O. Via, *The Ethics of Mark's Gospel in the Middle of Time* (Philadelphia: Fortress, 1985), p. 45 and passim. Contrast the Apocalypse of Weeks in *1 Enoch* 93, where there are some bright moments, including the giving of the Law, in the 'weeks' before the eschaton (93.6).

39. 'Gottesherrschaft', pp. 88, 91.

40. Because of the already/not yet tension in Mark's eschatology, however, 10.30 implies that the blessings of the new age are already present *in the midst of* the old age.

41. W.L. Lane, *Mark*, p. 607; for general background on the logion, see C.R. Gregory, *Das Freer-Logion* (Leipzig: Hinrichs, 1908).

42. 'Bemerkungen zum Freer-Logion', *ZNW* 63 (1972), pp. 125-29; Haacker's study was then refined by G. Schwarz ('Zum Freer-Logion—ein Nachtrag', *ZNW* 70 [1979], p. 119), who supported Haacker's main conclusions but reconstructed an Aramaic original rather than Haacker's Hebrew original.

43. Haacker's theory has in its favor its resolution of two awkwardnesses in the Greek text: (1) The first clause joyfully announces the end of Satan's reign, but then the second clause abruptly changes tone and warns of coming terrors. (2) The lack of a true main clause in the sentence beginning *kai hyper hōn*.

44. On the parallelism of *exousia* and *basileia* in the NT, see J. Schlosser (*Règne*, vol. I, p. 136 and p. 149 n. 709), who cites Col. 1.13; Rev. 12.10; 17.12.

45. R. Pesch (*Das Markusevangelium* [2 vols.; HTKNT 2; Freiburg/Basel/ Wien: Herder, 1976], vol. I, p. 98) calls attention to the parallel between the

usages of *elthein* in 1.14 (Jesus *comes* preaching the gospel) and in 1.24, 39 (Jesus' *coming* as the destruction of demons); note also that 1.39 reproduces exactly the phrase in 1.14, *ēlthen kēryssōn*. Cf. Lk. 10.18-20, where we observe the order: (1) fall of Satan from heaven, (2) disiples' power over the evil spirits.

46. The ministration of the angels to Jesus in Mk 1.13 may itself suggest the *basileia* of God and its defeat of the *basileia* of Satan. See esp. Daniel 7: angels *serve* the Ancient of Days (7.10); the latter then goes on to enthrone the one like a Son of Man, whose kingdom replaces the demonic earthly kingdoms (7.11-14, 23-27).

The preparation for 1.15 in 1.9-13 is important; in the latter, there are two references to the Spirit, and the passage is introduced by the solemn formula *kai egeneto en ekeinais tais hēmerais*. Without this passage, one might get the impression that the filling up of the eschatological measure was an immanental process; with it, the initiative of God in accomplishing this fulfillment is emphasized.

47. The parallel is so striking, and Mark's statement by itself is so cryptic, that it seems reasonable to conclude that Mark and his readers knew either the *T. Naph.* passage or the tradition that it contains. This conclusion is reinforced by the strong case that can be made for a Syrian provenance for both the *Testaments of the Twelve Patriarchs* and the Gospel of Mark. On the former, see H.C. Kee, 'Testaments of the Twelve Patriarchs', *Old Testament Pseudepigrapha* (ed. J.H. Charlesworth), vol. I, p. 778; on the latter, see H.C. Kee, *Community of the New Age: Studies in Mark's Gospel* (Philadelphia: Westminster, 1977), pp. 100-103; W.G. Kümmel, *Introduction to the New Testament* (revised edn, Nashville: Abingdon, 1973), pp. 97-98; H. Koester, *Introduction to the New Testament*, vol. II, *History and Literature of Early Christianity* (Philadelphia: Fortress, 1982), pp. 166-67.

48. See 3.27, which views Jesus' exorcisms as a defeat for Satan, and cf. *T. Moses* 10.1, which connects the manifestation of the kingdom of God with the defeat of Satan.

The attentive reader may wonder how Jesus' defeat of Satan at 1.13 can be reconciled with the continuing opposition that Jesus encounters throughout the Gospel, which culminates in his death. Furthermore, passages such as 4.15 imply that Satan continues to be active in the Markan community after Jesus' resurrection (see J. Marcus, *Mystery*, pp. 69-71). Continued Satanic activity, however, is compatible with dethronement of Satan, as is shown in Rev. 12.7-12. See further below, n. 74.

49. Cf. *Barn.* 15.5: 'When [God's] son comes he will destroy the *kairos* of the lawless one'.

50. E. Käsemann, *Commentary on Romans* (Grand Rapids: Eerdmans, 1980; orig. 1974), pp. 362-63; H. Schlier, *Der Römerbrief* (HTKNT 6; Freiburg/Basel/Wien: Herder, 1977), pp. 395-96; U. Wilckens, *Der Brief an*

die Römer (3 vols.; EKKNT 6; Neukirchen-Vluyn: Neukirchener Verlag 1978-82), vol. III, p. 75.

51. By the middle of the second century, baptism is being called 'enlightenment' (Justin, *Apol.* 1.61.12; 1.65.1), and see already Heb. 6.4, which may be a baptismal reference (M. Bourke, 'The Epistle to the Hebrews', *JBC*, p. 391).

52. M. Barth, *Ephesians* (AB 34; New York: Doubleday, 1974), vol. II, p. 574 n. 83. Eph. 5.14 is introduced by the quotation formula *dio legei*, has a rhythmic quality, and contains imagery of awakening, resurrection, and illumination.

53. On Col. 1.13-14 as part of a baptismal hymn, see E. Käsemann ('A Primitive Christian Baptismal Liturgy', *Essays on New Testament Themes* [Philadelphia: Fortress, 1982; orig. 1949], pp. 159-62), who calls attention to the aorist tense references to deliverance from darkness and forgiveness of sins (cf. Mk 1.4; Acts 2.38), as well as to the remembrance of Jesus' baptism in the phrase 'beloved Son' (see Mk 1.11). On 1 Thess. 5.5-6, see W. Harnisch (*Eschatologische Existenz* [FRLANT 110; Göttingen: Vandenhoeck & Ruprecht, 1973], pp. 117-25), who points to the imagery of illumination and the similarity to Col. 1.12-24; could the switch in 1 Thess. 5.5 from second person plural to first person plural reflect the alternating responses of baptizer and baptizand in the liturgy? Harnisch thinks that the baptismal tradition extends all the way to 1 Thess. 5.10; see the imagery of clothing in 5.8, and the Pauline hapax 'to obtain salvation' in 5.10. (I am grateful to M.L. Soards for calling my attention to 1 Thess. 5.)

54. Note the motifs of illumination, turning, and forgiveness of sins; also the *exousia* language which parallels Col. 1.13.

55. O. Cullmann, *Baptism in the New Testament* (SBT; London: SCM, 1950), p. 79.

56. G. Haufe even goes so far as to claim that most of the Synoptic and Johannine sayings about the kingdom of God have their *Sitz im Leben* in post-Easter missionary preaching and baptismal paraklesis ('Reich Gottes bei Paulus und in der Jesustradition', *NTS* [1985], pp. 467-72).

57. See H.G. Marsh, *The Origin and Significance of the New Testament Baptism* (Manchester: Manchester University Press, 1941), pp. 1-14; R.E.O. White, *The Biblical Doctrine of Initiation* (London: Hodder & Stoughton, 1960), pp. 56-72.

58. Strack–Billerbeck, vol. I, p. 176, citing *Tanḫuma lech lecha* section 6 (Buber, 32a). Baptism was one of three rites of passage for conversion to Judaism, the other two being circumcision and sacrifice; see W.G. Braude, *Jewish Proselytizing in the First Five Centuries of the Common Era: The Age of the Tannaim and Amoraim* (Providence: Brown University, 1940), pp. 74-78. Cf. also 1QS 4.19-21, where God's destruction of the *dominion* (*mmšlt*) of falsehood is linked to his causing the Spirit to gush forth like purifying *waters*.

59. C.K. Barrett, *John*, pp. 174-75; R.E. Brown, *John*, vol. I, pp. 141-44; R. Schnackenburg, *John*, vol. I, pp. 369-70.

60. R.E. Brown, *John*, vol. I, pp. 143-44.

61. O. Cullmann, *Baptism*, pp. 76-79.

62. J. Giblet, 'Baptism—The Sacrament of Incorporation into the Church According to St Paul', *Baptism in the New Testament: A Symposium* (ed. A. George et al.; Baltimore/Dublin: Helicon, 1964), pp. 171-72.

63. This finding goes against the scholarly consensus, which sees 1.15 as a Markan composition; see the summary of opinions in J.H. Charlesworth, 'The Historical Jesus in Light of Writings Contemporaneous with Him', *Aufstieg und Niedergang der römischen Welt. Geschichte und Kultur Roms im Spiegel der neueren Forschung* II.25.1 (Berlin/New York: De Gruyter, 1982), pp. 459-60.

64. This evidence is not conclusive because of the possibility that Mark may have adopted a biblical style in his composition; cf. the discussion by J. Fitzmyer of Septuagintisms vs Semitisms in Luke's Greek (*Luke*, vol. I, pp. 114-25).

65. See H.C. Kee, *Community*, pp. 102-103; W.G. Kümmel, *Introduction*, p. 97; J. Gnilka, *Evangelium*, vol. II, p. 33; E. Schweizer, *The Good News According to Mark* (Atlanta: John Knox, 1984), p. 24; D. Nineham, *Saint Mark* (Pelican New Testament Commentaries; London: Penguin, 1963), pp. 40-41; J. Marcus, *Mystery*, pp. 80-87. Even if he is not himself a Jew, Mark seems to be in touch with both Jewish apocalyptic and Jewish-Christian traditions; see above, n. 47 and V. Taylor, *Mark*, p. 65.

66. Cf. R. Pesch, *Markusevangelium*, vol. I, p. 103. *Pisteuein en* is rare in the LXX, so Mk 1.15d is not a Septuagintism; see J.H. Moulton, *A Grammar of New Testament Greek*, vol. I: *Prolegomena* (Edinburgh: T. & T. Clark, 1908), pp. 67-68. Moulton himself follows A. Deissman's unconvincing translation of *pisteuein en* as 'to believe in the sphere of'; what would such a locution *mean*?

67. Cf. P. Stuhlmacher (*Das paulinische Evangelium. I. Vorgeschichte* [FRLANT 95; Göttingen: Vandenhoeck & Ruprecht, 1968], pp. 209-44), who cites the usages of *euangelion* and *euangelizesthai* in Rev. 14.6; 10.7; Mt. 11.2-6//Lk. 7.18-23, all of which he claims go back to Palestinian Jewish Christianity. Stuhlmacher is unsure whether or not this vocabulary can be attributed to Jesus.

68. P. Stuhlmacher himself (*ibid.*, p. 237 n. 3) thinks that Mark is responsible for 1.14-15, although he incorporated into it older Jewish Christian traditions, particularly 1.15a; but his assertion that the rest of 1.15 stems from the Hellenistic mission field founders on *pisteuein en*.

69. As pointed out by J. Bishop, '*Parabole* and *Parrhesia* in Mk', *Int* 40 (1986), pp. 51-52.

70. The precise meaning of the saying of Jesus found in Mk 1.8 par. was

apparently a subject of discussion in early Christian circles. Luke, for example, offers his interpretation of the saying in Acts 11.16, while Mark, according to my argument here, suggests his exegesis by his placement of Mk 1.15.

71. A. Schweitzer, *The Mysticism of Paul the Apostle* (New York: Holt, 1951; orig. 1927), pp. 227-37, esp. pp. 236-37.

72. See K. Stock, *Boten aus dem Mit-Ihm-Sein. Das Verhältnis zwischen Jesus und den Zwölf nach Markus* (AnBib 70; Rome: Biblical Institute, 1975), passim.

73. On entering the kingdom of God as entrance into the story of Jesus, see D.O. Via, *Ethics*, p. 131.

74. The kingdom does not come, but is only *near*, until the crucifixion-and-resurrection; see above, pp. 52f. and n. 25. Furthermore, in the overall context of the Gospel, the defeat of Satan announced in 1.15 and pictured in the exorcisms of Jesus' ministry is seen to draw its power from the victory that will not truly be achieved until the crucifixion-and-resurrection. The seeming contradiction here is an integral part of the messianic secret motif: Jesus is already the Messiah during his ministry, and his divine power cannot help constantly breaking through; yet on the other hand it is the crucifixion-and-resurrection that truly establishes his identity (W. Wrede, *The Messianic Secret* [Cambridge: James Clark, 1971; orig. 1901], pp. 124-29). Similarly, the disciples already know the mystery of the kingdom of God (4.11), yet throughout the Gospel they are pictured as uncomprehending. All these tensions have to do with Mark's narration of the story of Jesus' ministry from a post-resurrectional perspective. The resultant 'two-level drama' is, of course, a subject upon which Lou Martyn has shed a good deal of light through his work on the Gospel of John.

MARK 14.62: EARLY CHRISTIAN MERKABAH IMAGERY?

Jane Schaberg

It is a pleasure to dedicate this paper to Lou Martyn. He challenges his students to risk the use of disciplined imagination and intuition in the attempt to enter the worlds of the New Testament, and to appreciate trenchant criticism—of which his own has been for me most helpful, courteous, and encouraging.

In response to the high priest's question, 'Are you the Christ, the Son of the Blessed?' Jesus replies in Mark's Gospel, 'I am, and you will see the Son of man sitting at the right hand of Power and coming with the clouds of heaven' (14.62). This is followed by the high priest's tearing of his mantle, the charge of blasphemy, and Jesus' condemnation by the Sanhedrin as 'deserving death' (vv. 63-64). The major difficulties of interpreting this text are well known.[1] The following will be considered here. Are the combined allusions to Ps. 110.1[2] and Dan. 7.13[3] to be understood as a reference to Jesus' exaltation, or to the parousia, or to both? If to exaltation, then how is the present sequence of the imagery (mention first of the Son of man 'sitting at the right hand of Power', then of his 'coming with the clouds of heaven') to be explained, when the reverse sequence (coming to the heavenly world, then sitting at God's right hand) would seem more likely? Further, on what grounds can the saying in 14.62 be considered blasphemy? The hypothesis I wish to explore is that at some pre-Markan level of the gospel tradition the saying was intended as a prediction that the Son of man will be vindicated when he is seen sitting at the right hand of God, who 'takes' him to the heavens. The imagery is of an ascent on the chariot-throne (Merkabah) of God.

It is well to mention from the outset that I am aware that no reference is made in the NT to the chariot of God. Only the throne is represented,[4] fixed in place in the heavens rather than moving as in Ezekiel's visions in 1.1-3.15; 9.3-11.25; 43.1-5.[5] No claim is made here that Mark, Luke or Matthew recognized and exploited the specific imagery I am proposing. For Mark, the saying in 14.62 is one of the major climaxes of his Gospel. Jesus openly reveals his identity, publicly breaking the closely guarded secret. The reader's attention is focused on the vindication to come, perhaps in ambiguous fashion: on Jesus' enthronement at God's right hand, *and* on his return at the parousia (cf. 13.26).[6] The saying for Luke finds its counterpart and completion in Acts 7.55-56, which, it will be claimed, makes use of a common exegetical tradition. Matthew alone among the evangelists speaks of the throne the Son of man (19.28; 25.31) will occupy at the parousia. In the trial scene Matthew's emphasis is on the process which begins at the trial, initiating the reign of the Son of man who is exalted in death. But these redactional stresses are not evidence that support in any way our reading of the isolated saying in Mark 14.62.

To support this admittedly bizarre reading of Mark 14.62, an examination will be made of (I) elements of the saying itself; (II) the use of Merkabah imagery in Jewish literature, especially in the *Testament of Job*, to depict the death and/or final translation of a righteous one; (III) Christian use of Merkabah imagery in the *Odes of Solomon* and elsewhere in the pseudepigrapha to depict the exaltation of Jesus; and NT texts in which there appear to be traces of a presentation of Jesus in terms of the vision of Ezekiel 1. If the hypothesis presented here has credibility, we may have uncovered an important aspect of early christology, and responded to the challenge of M. Hengel, who remarks that the investigation of the Jewish Hekhalot and Merkabah literature for early Christian christology still has a wide field to explore, and that 'Unfortunately, the great work by G. Scholem is still too little used for New Testament exegesis'.[7]

I

The opinion of the majority of critics, that Mk 14.62 is a clear reference to the parousia, is represented by P.M. Casey, who understands the text in this way:

At the time of the parousia people on earth, including those condemning Jesus, will see him sitting at the right hand of God and coming to earth with the clouds of heaven. His Ascension is assumed, but not mentioned. That he will have been sitting at the right hand of God for a period of time is also presupposed, but what is actually stated is that at a particular moment in the not too distant future they will see him sitting there (it may reasonably be assumed that the heavens will open for this purpose), and then coming with the clouds.[8]

The placement of the allusion to Dan. 7.13 in the text as it stands is considered by several scholars to support this traditional understanding of Mk 14.62.[9] According to Hay, the sequence is meant to make clear that when Jesus comes on the clouds at the parousia, he will have the authority and might of the one sitting at God's right hand.[10] For Lindars, 'coming with the clouds', which follows the heavenly session, denotes Jesus' transport for his apocalyptic function as Judge.[11]

A small number of critics, however, reads the reply of Jesus as an announcement of the reversal of judgment against him, of the intervention of God and the inauguration of Jesus' own reign. Both of the OT allusions are seen to carry the same meaning: coming to God. The coming of the Son of man, it is argued, may have been imagined as a coming to heaven at the moment of his vindication, rather than as a coming from heaven back to earth.[12] To explain the sequence ('sitting' then 'coming'), Robinson argues that session at the right hand and coming with the clouds are alternate, parallel expressions, one static and one dynamic, for the same thing: ascension or exaltation. The sequence is indifferent in the original saying, although subsequently Mark may have interpreted Dan. 7.13 as a statement about the parousia.[13] (M. Gourgues remarks that Ps. 110.1 and Dan. 7.13 are used in the same order in *Midr. Pss.* 2.9 to make the one point that Israel is God's son.[14]) M.D. Hooker also thinks the order is unimportant, since the citations are metaphorical and parallel, 'though not necessarily identical in meaning'.[15] Both Matthew and Luke, in her opinion, grasped this idea of imminent vindication: the addition of ἀπ' ἄρτι (Matthew) and ἀπὸ τοῦ νῦν (Luke), in this view, underlines the idea of imminence. Probably no such phrase stood in Mark's original. But Luke may have understood the 'coming with the clouds' as a coming to earth, and therefore omitted the phrase to solve the problem of an unfulfilled prophecy.[16] Matthew understood the parallelism as ways of speaking about 'a vindication which is to follow immediately, and which take place at the resurrection'.[17] According to Glasson, the sequence may be due to the presentation first of the idea of the personal exaltation of Jesus (using Ps. 110.1), and then of the corporate conception of the emergence of the new community of 'holy ones' (cf. Dan. 7.27) in its representative (Dan. 7.13).[18] Another, somewhat more plausible, explanation of the meaning of the two allusions in an exaltation context has been offered by Linton. Ps. 110.1 has been used, according to his line of reasoning, to make explicit the suggestion in Dan. 7.9 that one like a son of man is enthroned, and the cloud imagery makes explicit that the enthronement is celestial.[19] The assumption is that God must be imagined to be in heaven. Casey is unimpressed by such attempts to explain (or explain away) the sequence, which make a 'straightforward interpretation of the verse' impossible, 'since Jesus cannot come to God either at the same time as, or shortly after, he is already sitting at his side'.[20]

Paul Winter, like several of the critics mentioned above, is willing to forego a straightforward interpretation. He writes that Mk 14.62 brings together the two OT texts so as to bring together two christological factions: one which accepted Jesus' messianic dignity (Ps. 110.1) and one which affirmed the belief in his imminent parousia as Son of man (Dan. 7.13). This view is no more satisfying than the ones already mentioned, however; there is an absence of any evidence for the existence of a group or community which understood Jesus only as the Son of man.[21] But Winter's next remarks in this context are interesting, and raise the possibility explored in the rest of this paper. He argues that the fusion of different symbols here

> betrays a conscious effort. So much is evident if one realizes how unimaginable the figure is which emerges from the combination. We are asked to visualize someone who is 'sitting' (stationary) and 'coming' (mobile) at one and the same time. It is impossible to evoke such an image—unless one supposes that the person concerned was seated in a moving carriage! The difficulty of visualization is a sign that the words in verse 62 do not owe their origin to spontaneous, free narration, but result from devious excogitations.[22]

What Winter rejects as unimaginable is precisely what I wish to suggest: that chariot imagery best accounts for this particular combination of OT allusions and their sequence. While the imagery proposed here would be consistent with either an exaltation or a parousia interpretation of Mk 14.62, the extra-biblical parallels to be treated in sections II and III of this article make the former context more likely to be the one intended at a pre-Markan level.

There is a strikingly similar problem with sequence, involving a combination of allusions to Ps. 110.1 and Daniel 7 (but this time to Dan. 7.27 LXX instead of to 7.13) in 1 Pet. 3.22. The Greek text speaks of the resurrection of Jesus Christ 'who is at the right hand of God, having gone into heaven, with angels, authorities and powers subject to him' (ὅς ἐστιν δεξιᾷ [τοῦ] θεοῦ πορευθεὶς εἰς οὐρανόν ὑποταγέντων αὐτῷ ἀγγέλων καὶ ἐξουσιῶν καὶ δυνάμεων). In Dan. 7.27 LXX we have the statement that the kingdom and authority and the majesty and sovereignty of all kingdoms under heaven was given to the holy people of the Most High, 'and all the powers (ἐξουσίαι) will be subject (ὑποταγήσονται) to it'. The use of an allusion to this verse in 1 Pet. 3.22 seems to indicate that Jesus Christ, like the one like a son of man in Dan. 7.13-14, is in some sense understood as a corporate figure, representing the holy people. The Greek sequence of 1 Pet. 3.22 (Christ is at the right hand of God and has gone into heaven) has been changed in the RSV to a more 'logical' sequence: he has gone into heaven and is at the right hand of God.[23] The verb tenses and sequence lead some commentators like Krodel to claim that the allusion to Ps. 110.1 is not part of the tradition here.[24] Bo Reicke translates in this fashion: '. . . through the resurrection of Jesus Christ who is at the right hand of God; since he ascended into heaven, angels, magistrates and powers have become subject to him'. He sees four main points here: (1) Christ's resurrection; (2) his place at the right hand of God; (3) his ascension; (4) his authority. 'Among these four testimonies, the first and third deal with Christ's exaltation, and the second and fourth with his authority over all things'.[25] M. Gourgues, aware of a connection with Mk 14.62, regards 1 Pet. 3.22 as the doubling of a single affirmation of the exaltation, although the aorist participle πορευθεὶς (cf. Acts 1.10, 11) as well as the εἰς followed by the accusative refer to the ascension, a movement preceeding the stable state of actual presence at the right hand of God.[26] If I understand W.J. Dalton correctly, he thinks that the sequence in 1 Pet. 3.22 is to be explained in this way: an original sequence (going into heaven, then sitting at the right hand of God), from an early Christian hymn, has been inverted by the author of the epistle, because in 3.21 the author's thought moves not in the historical but in the sacramental order: God saves the Christian in baptism through the power of the risen Christ. 'Since Christ is conceived as sending the Spirit[27] and operating in power from the right hand of God, it is understandable that this idea ('who is at the right hand of God') should be introduced before the "going" of Christ in his ascension in the resumption of the hymn sequence.'[28] In other words, the emphasis on Christ's power explains a hypothetical inversion of order. In my opinion, however, concern to represent Christ's power has involved a possible change of verb tense (ἐστίν may replace something like ἐκάθισεν), rather than an inversion of order.

The solution I propose is that the allusion to Ps. 110.1 is a reference both to the mode of ascension (hence its placement in 1 Pet. 3.22)[29] *and* to Christ's permanent heavenly session (hence the tense of ἐστίν). If this suggestion has merit, it gives some support to the theory that Mk 14.62 draws on old tradition, in which Jesus was understood to have been taken at the right hand of God into heaven.

Two elements of Mk 14.61-62 may be clues that the tradition used originated in circles acquainted with mystical Merkabah speculation. These elements are the terms, (1) 'Power' (δύναμις) and (2) 'Blessed One' (ὁ εὐλογητός). Both are used as apparent substitutes for the name of God only here in the NT.

(1) If Psalm 80 was involved in the linking of Ps. 110.1 and Dan. 7.13, as some critics have suggested,[30] the mention in Ps. 80.2 of God 'enthroned on the cherubim', being called to shine forth (Hebrew) or manifest himself (LXX), to come save us (v. 3) subtly strengthens the possibility that chariot imagery was intended. The term 'Power' in Mk 14.62 pars. may evoke Ps. 80.3: 'stir up your might' (גבורך; LXX: τὴν δυναστείαν σου; cf. vv. 4, 7, 15, 19: ὁ θεὸς τῶν δυνάμεων).[31]

Even more significant for our thesis here, G. Scholem remarks that גבורה or δύναμις

> was an appellative or metonym of 'The Divine Glory' among the apocalypticists, and with this very meaning entered the Gospels in the famous passage: 'You shall see the Son of Man seated at the

right hand of the Dynamis'. Although in rabbinic sources of the first and second centuries the name 'Dynamis' was widely used as a synonym for God Himself, the esoteric use continued in the circles of the Merkabah mystics.[32]

Scholem cites examples of this esoteric use from such texts as the following.

Life of Adam and Eve: The phrase *virtus magna* is used by Adam to praise the Lord who is sitting on a wind-like chariot with fiery wheels in the Paradise of righteousness (25.3) or 'Paradise of vision and of God's command' (28.3). This is the vision in which Adam learns he will die.[33]

Ma'aseh Merkabah: 'R. Akiba said: 'When I ascended and beheld the Dynamis (צפיתי בגבורה) I saw all the creatures that are to be found in the pathways of heaven'.

Re'uyot Yeḥezkel: 'The Holy One, blessed be He, opened to him (Ezekiel) the seven heavens, and he beheld the Dynamis (הגבורה)'. In this work, a mystical midrash on Ezekiel 1 probably composed in the fourth or fifth century CE, the terms גבורה (= δύναμις) and כבוד (= δόξα) are interchangeably used.[34]

In addition, in DSH 16.3 there is an adaptation of Isa. 6.3: כה גבורותך may have been substituted for the biblical כבוד. 'This seems to represent an exegesis of the KBWD as the *dynamis* of God, which is well developed in later hekhalot literature'.[35] See also *Apoc.Ab.* 19.5 where 'the power of invisible glory' is said to be above the divine throne.[36]

If we follow out Scholem's suggestions, Mk 14.62 can be interpreted to mean that the Son of man will be seen seated at the right hand of the כבוד described in Ezek. 1.26-28. Does כבוד refer in this case not to the vision as a whole, but to the 'likeness as it were of a human form' (1.26)? Ezek. 1.1 calls the whole experience 'visions of God' (מראות אלהים). Verse 28 seems to imply that this means visions in which God was seen; that is, the genitive is objective and 1.26-27 is a theophany.[37] As we will see, however, some read Ezek. 1.26-27 in a different way.

(2) The second term in Mk 14.62, ὁ εὐλογητός, is used eight times in the NT but this is the only time it appears as a substantive; as a circumlocution for the name of God it is almost completely unattested in Jewish literature.[38] It is probably not (a) an abbreviation of 'the Holy One, blessed be He' (הקדוש ברוך הוא),[39] and not (b) an

unquestioned parallel to the rabbinic expression, 'the Lord is (or: is to be) blessed' (ברכו י"י המבורך; *b. Ber.* 7.3; *y. Ber.* 7.11c; *b. Ber.* 50a), since the participle does not function in those phrases as a substitute for the name of God, but as an adjective defining God.[40] The attestation that most resembles ὁ εὐλογητός is found in *1 Enoch* 77.1, which speaks of God as 'the one who is blessed forever' or 'ever-blessed'. The context in which this term occurs is a discussion of the four corners of the world which Enoch saw at the ends of the earth (76.1); the second is called the south 'because there the Most High descends [contrast 25.3; 18.6], and there especially the one who is blessed forever descends'.[41]

Another idea which is worth mentioning is that ὁ εὐλογητός may bear some relation to the strange and probably not original phrase in Ezek. 3.12b. The MT reads ברוך כבוד־יהוה ממקומו (LXX: εὐλογημένη ἡ δόξα κυρίου ἐκ τοῦ τόπου αὐτοῦ; cf. *b. Ḥag.* 13b)—a cry understood to be the voice of an earthquake, or an utterance of the prophet himself?[42] Could 'the Blessed' have evolved as a title by means of a shortening of this phrase?

Some critics, however, have claimed that in Mk 14.61 we have simply 'an echo of the Jewish concern to paraphrase the name of God',[43] or 'a locution new in the Christian community',[44] or even 'a pseudo-Jewish expression' created by Mark as appropriate in the mouth of the high priest.[45] But none of these suggestions explains the precise title used. I think that the resemblance to *1 Enoch* 77.1 and the possibility of some connection with Ezek. 3.12b indicate that the term 'the Blessed' in Mk 14.61 is drawn from Jewish mystical tradition.

In summary, these aspects of Mk 14.61-62 have led me to suspect that the imagery of ascent on the chariot-throne of God may be evoked in the response to Jesus to the high priest. First, the particular placement of allusions to Ps. 110.1 and Dan. 7.13 in this text, especially the sequence of the verbs 'sitting' then 'coming', can be accounted for by Merkabah imagery. This is particularly true if one understands the saying in v. 62 to be about Jesus' vindication and exaltation, rather than as a statement about the parousia (although a parousia meaning is not thereby excluded). A similar verbal sequence, involving a combination of allusions to Ps. 110.1 and Daniel 7 (v. 27) appears in 1 Pet. 3.22, which can be read as a reference to the ascension of Christ at the right hand of God into heaven. So read, there is no need to invert the sequence or argue that the sequence of an earlier hymn has been inverted by the author of the epistle, or to claim that the thought doubles back on itself. Both Mk 14.62 and 1 Pet. 3.22 may draw on old traditions in which the vindication of Jesus was similarly imagined. Secondly, I have argued that the terms 'Power' (Mk 14.62) and 'Blessed One' (v. 61) are clues that Merkabah traditions referring to the כבוד are used here. 'Power' may evoke the might of God mentioned in Ps. 80.3, a psalm in which God is depicted 'enthroned on the cherubim' (v. 3; cf. Ezekiel 10). G. Scholem claims that 'Power' in Mk 14.62 is a metonym of 'The Divine Glory', an instance of an esoteric usage of the apocalypticists and Merkabah mystics which can be documented for the first century CE. 'Blessed One' resembles the phrase 'One who is blessed forever' in *1 Enoch* 77.1, which speaks of a special descent of God. This term in Mk 14.61 may also be a shortening of the utterance in Ezek. 3.12b, 'Blessed be the Glory of Yahweh from his (its) place'.

In addition, let me mention one further point. It has been shown by several scholars that there is a clear literary and theological influence of Ezekiel 1 on Daniel 7.[46] Over and over again in the midrashic history of these two texts, they appear in combination (e.g. in *1 Enoch* 71; *Testament of Abraham* 17; *b. Ḥag.* 13b-14a; *Gen. R.* 78.1; *Lam. R.* 3.8; *Num. R.* 12.8; *Cant. R.* 3.11; *Exod. R.* 15.26; *b. Pesaḥ.* 119a; *Zohar* 3.15a-b). This may indicate that in some circles Daniel 7 was recognized as associated with Merkabah speculation, probably as a secondary text which supplemented in various ways the symbolism and dynamic theology of Ezekiel 1. This frequency of combination offers some minor support to the theory that although Ezekiel 1 is not alluded to in Mk 14.61-62, something of its chariot imagery is nevertheless present.

II

We turn now to the pseudepigrapha for examples of imagery similar to that which I am suggesting for Mk 14.62. In the *Testament of Job*, *Apocalypse of Moses*, *1 Enoch* 70 and *2 (Syriac) Baruch*, Merkabah imagery is used in the context of discussion of the death and/or final translation of a righteous one. Our focus here will be on the first of these works. The *Testament of Job*, written either in Egypt of Palestine in the first century BCE or CE,[47] and reflecting an early stage of Merkabah mysticism,[48] may allude to Daniel and to Ps. 110.1 to depict the eternal, heavenly royalty of the just one. In ch. 32, the 'comforter' Elious wails eleven times, 'Where is the splendour (δόξα) of your throne?' contrasting the throne Job had, made of precious stones, with his seat in the dunghill (vv. 2-12). To this Job responds,

> Be silent! and now I will show you my throne and the splendor of its majesty which is among the holy ones. My throne is in the supraterrestrial realm, and its splendor and majesty are at the right hand of the Father in the heavens. My throne is eternal—and the whole world shall pass away and its splendor shall fade and those who cling to it shall be (caught) in its demise. But my throne is in the holy land and its splendor and majesty are in the chariots of the Father (33.2-5, 9).

The expression, 'my kingdom is forever and ever' (ἐμοῦ δὲ ἡ βασιλεία εἰς τὸν αἰῶνα αἰῶνος) is reminiscent of Dan. 3.33 MT (= Theodotion 4.3) which refers to the kingdom of the Most High, and of Dan. 7.27 Theodotion (cf. 7.14), which refers to the kingdom given to the holy ones of the Most High (ἡ βασιλεία αὐτοῦ βασιλεία αἰώνιος). While the theme of the throne of the righteous individual may have become simply part of the common stock of apocalyptic-based imagery and expectation of the time (see *4 Macc.* 17.5; *Apoc. Elijah* 37.3-4; *1 Enoch* 108.12; *T. Isaac* 1.5-6; *Asc. Isa.* 7.21-22; 9.9, 13, 18), Job's mention of his supraterrestrial throne whose glory is at the right hand of the Father may be considered an interpretation of Ps. 110.1[49] in terms of the kingdom promised in Dan. 7.27 (7.14). J.J. Collins finds the assertion that the kingdoms of the earth will pass away evocative of Daniel (cf. the four kingdoms schema), and argues that the emphasis on Job's insight on heavenly realities recalls the 'wise' of Daniel. The author of the *Testament of Job*, however, is more interested in individual piety than in the fate of the Jewish nation, and a 'vertical eschatology' in which the individual is assumed into heaven replaces eschatological predictions concerning the fate of the nation. 'Apocalyptic elements are placed in the service of personal mysticism'.[50] The throne of Job, which exists even while he is alive on earth, is like the token of his vindication, the place prepared for him, or a projection of himself which he already sees; his faith in this heavenly reality anticipates and is verified by his assumption at the end of the book. The 'chariots of the Father' may be thought of as the support and foundation of the throne of Job.

The death of Job is narrated in terms of the translation of Elijah[51] and of Ezekiel's Merkabah vision.[52] It might be cautiously implied in Ezek. 3.12 that the prophet, lifted by the Spirit, ascends with the heavenly throne. If the word ברוך is corrected to ברום in this verse, it reads, 'Then the Spirit lifted me up, and as the כבוד of Yahweh arose from its place, I heard behind me the sound of a great earthquake'.[53] S.H. Levey remarks that the instances where the prophet is lifted by the Spirit (3.12-15; 8.3; 11.1, 24; 43.5) 'have overtones of the mystic ascent of the Merkabah devotee'.[54] There is no account in Ezekiel, however, of a final ascent. As Job's daughters play music and praise God (*T. Job* 52.3), a chariot comes for his soul. 'The one who sat in the great chariot came out and greeted Job, while the three daughters looked on and their father looked on, but the others did not see. And taking the soul, he flew up while embracing it, and made it mount the chariot and set off for the east' (52.4-5). It is not stated who the 'one who sat in the great chariot' is (God, or an angel or 'a man'), but there is a plural in 52.2 (Job saw 'those who had come for his soul').[55] If this figure is God (cf. Revelation, where God is identified over ten times as the one who is seated on the throne), he is not described,[56] but is depicted as coming for the righteous one, in contrast to those texts which stress the need of a journey or ascent of the human being before God's presence or throne is reached.

In the *Apocalypse of Moses* 33.34, Eve sees Adam's soul taken 'in a chariot of light' borne by four bright eagles (Ezekiel's חיות?) and with angels going before it. This chariot seems to be the throne of God (cf. 37.3), called here 'the Father of all' (cf. 36.3: 'the Father of light'). He stretches forth his hand and takes Adam, handing him over to the archangel Michael to bring him to paradise (37.5-6). In *2 Baruch*, Baruch speaks of his coming death in this way: 'The throne of the Mighty One I cannot resist' (46.4). Again, these are uses of Merkabah imagery to speak of death, not simply of translation. *1 Enoch* 70.2 describes the final translation of Enoch in this way: 'he was raised aloft on the chariots of the spirit and his name vanished among them'. The ascension of Elijah (2 Kgs 2.11) is the model for the ascension of Enoch in *1 Enoch* 14.8-9, and has left traces also on the descriptions of ascensions in *1 Enoch* 70.2; 39.3; 52.1.[57] If Mk 14.62 presupposes Merkabah imagery in the context of a prediction of ultimate vindication, we may have yet another example of this apocalyptic motif.

III

Explicit Merkabah imagery used to depict the exaltation of Jesus is found in the third century *Apocryphon of James* from Nag Hammadi: Jesus tells James and Peter,

> now I shall ascend to the place from whence I came... But pay heed to the glory that awaits me and, having opened your heart, listen to the hymns that await me up in the heavens; for today I must take (my place at) the right hand of the Father. But I have said (my) last word to you, and I shall depart from you, for a chariot (ἅρμα) of spirit has borne me aloft (I, 2 14.20-34).[58]

The use of this imagery in association with the ascension of Jesus and the possible allusion to Ps. 110.1 are significant. If the speaker in *Odes of Solomon* 38 is the Christ (which seems to me at least possible), his ascent is pictured in Merkabah terminology at an earlier date:[59]

1. I went up into the light of Truth as into a chariot (*markabhta*),[60]
    And the Truth led me and caused me to come.
2. And caused me to pass over chasms and gulfs,
    And saved me from cliffs and valleys.
3. And became for me a haven of salvation,
    And set me on the place of immortal life.
4. And He went with me and caused me to rest and did not allow me to err;
    Because He was and is the Truth.

If the speaker here is not the Christ, then the Christ might be referred to in v. 4 as the one ('the Truth') who went with the ascender.[61] As Charlesworth remarks, in some of the odes the Odist and the risen Christ 'coalesce, making it virtually impossible to separate them'.[62]

Explicit imagery of this type is not present in the NT, but there are found there several hints of a primitive conceptualization of the resurrection or exaltation of Jesus in terms of Merkabah traditions. In Rom. 6.4 the resurrection of Christ is said to have been effected διὰ τῆς δόξης τοῦ πατρός: 'Christ was raised from the dead by the glory of the Father'. Jesus is considered 'taken up in glory' (ἀνελήμφθη ἐν δόξῃ) in 1 Tim. 3.16. The combination in Acts 7.55-56 of 'seeing the glory of God' and 'the heavens opened' strongly evokes the experience of Ezekiel by the River Chebar (Ezek. 1.1, 28).

Here in Acts we have a statement that the vision of the כבוד is in some sense the vision of the exalted Son of Man: he may be seen within the כבוד, standing at the right hand of God. While the term δόξα in these passages could simply mean 'power', 'honor', or 'splendor', it is possible that the idea of the visible divine radiance is also present, and associated with this a reminiscence of the כבוד of Yahweh as described by Ezekiel and mediated on in the Merkabah tradition. Acts 1.9 portrays the ascension of Jesus in cloud imagery ('a cloud took him out of their sight') that may be related to Ezek. 1.4 (the vision appears out of 'the great cloud borne on the sweeping wind'; cf. *y. Ḥag.* 2.1; *b. Ḥag.* 14b) as well as to Dan. 7.13.[63]

John 1.51 ('Truly, truly, I say to you, you will see heaven opened and the angels of God ascending and descending upon [ἐπὶ] the Son of Man') has points of contact with Mk 14.62. The verb ὄψεσθε is found in both, but whereas in Jn 1.51 it is a promise to believers, in Mk 14.62 it is apparently a threat to the accusers of Jesus. Both texts speak of a future visionary experience of the glorified Son of Man.[64] There is no indication that John intends his reader to see 1.51 as a reference only to the final moment of Jesus' vindication and exaltation, rather than as a more general statement of the Son of Man's communion with the heavenly world (cf. 1.14; 2.11; 16.14). However, association with the resurrection or the parousia may have been apparent for the saying at some pre-Johannine stage.[65] Further, the context of Jn 1.51, like that of Mk 14.62, is a discussion of messiahship (1.49; cf. v. 41),[66] and divine sonship (1.49). This is the only passage in the Fourth Gospel which speaks of heavenly vision; paradoxically the author has used it to present the Son of Man as a being located exclusively neither in heaven nor on earth.[67] As Brown notes, 'the vision means that Jesus as the Son of Man has become the locus of the divine glory, the point of contact between heaven and earth'.[68] The image intended to be evoked here is unclear, but it is possible it involves angels (related perhaps to the חיות of Ezekiel, bearers of the moving throne [1.22, 26])[69] accompanying the Son of Man[70] as he ascends and descends. The next time the phrase Son of Man appears in the Fourth Gospel it is again with the verbs ἀναβαίνω and καταβαίνω (now in different order), with reference to the Son of Man's capabilities (3.13). This may indicate that the Evangelist has understood the saying in 1.51 as depicting the movement of the Son of Man. Some allusion in 1.51 to Gen. 28.12 is probable, and on the basis of the use of that OT text (often combined with Daniel 7 and Ezekiel 1 in the Haggadah) in *Gen. R.* 68.12,[71] Dahl argues that the Johannine Son of Man may be connected with the human-like form seated above the throne in Ezek. 1.26 (originally Israel?),[72] a figure which descends and ascends. Other critics have also suggested that the Johannine portrait of the descending/ascending Son of Man draws upon Daniel 7 and Ezekiel 1 and on later reinterpretations of those passages.[73] G. Quispel, for example, states that for John Jesus is the Ezekielian Man (who existed from all eternity and appeared to Isaiah and Abraham and perhaps to Jacob) and the Danielic Son of Man (judge of the last times).[74] Such a bold identification in this Gospel would mean that Jesus is imagined not as sitting *beside* God on the throne, but *as* the figure on the throne.

In Rev. 1.12-16 a different but related development appears to have taken place. To 'one like a sone of man' (ὅμοιον υἱὸν ἀνθρώπου) are attributed elements from many OT angelophanies and theophanies, including the characteristics of the Ancient of Days (v. 14; cf. Dan. 7.9; *1 Enoch* 46.1). Two elements of Ezekiel are present in Rev. 1.12-16. The voice of one like a son of man is described in the terms Ezekiel uses for the sound of the wings of the חיות (Ezek. 1.24) and for the coming of the כבוד (43.2): 'like the sound of many waters'. The lampstands (λυχνίας) in the midst of which stands one like a son of man (Rev. 1.12; cf. 4.5) may be drawn from the appearance of lamps (LXX: λαμπάδων) in the midst of the חיות (Ezek 1.13). But the author of Revelation does *not* use the description of the human-like form on the moving throne (Ezek. 1.27) to portray one like a son of man.[75] Nor does he apply to God the anthropomorphic description of Ezek. 1.26.[76] In Revelation 4, God is the one seated on the throne in the heavens who appears 'like jasper and carnelian' (in Ezek. 1.26 the throne itself is 'in appearance like sapphire'); around the throne is a rainbow (cf. Ezek. 1.28). The one who sits on the throne and the Lamb are clearly distinguished (cf. ch. 5; 6.16; 7.10; 19.4). In 3.21 the one like a son of man sits *with* his Father on his throne, and in 22.1, 3 there is a mention of 'the throne of God and of the Lamb' (cf. 7.17). The Lamb, in other words, is pictured *beside* God on the throne. The imagery here is similar to that which I am proposing is implied in Mk 14.62, except that the throne in Revelation is set in place in the heavens, since Revelation uses Ezekiel to depict the accomplished exaltation of Jesus, not the process of his exaltation.

These NT texts, in my opinion, offer some support to the possibility that, although the text of Ezekiel is not cited, it is presupposed in the description in Mk 14.62 of the Son of Man 'sitting' and 'coming'.

Finally, we turn to Mk 13.24-27:

> But in those days, after that tribulation, the sun will be darkened, and the moon will not give its light, and the stars will be falling from heaven, and the powers in the heavens will be shaken. And then they will see the Son of man coming in clouds with great power and glory. And then he will send out the angels, and gather his elect from the four winds, from the ends of the earth to the ends of heaven.

The normal interpretation of 13.26 is that it is a depiction of the parousia of the Son of man: the 'they' who will see him coming (downward) are those on earth.[77] Certainly this is the way that Matthew understood this saying, since the group mentioned just before the 'they' is 'all the tribes of the earth' (Mt. 24.30; cf. Lk. 21.36 which speaks of 'men fainting with fear and with foreboding of what is coming on the world'). But in the Markan version of this section of the Synoptic Apocalypse, no one on earth is named as witness to the coming. Instead, the preceding verses list only the darkened sun and moon, the falling stars, and the 'powers in the heavens' (αἱ δυνάμεις αἱ ἐν τοῖς οὐρανοῖς) which 'will be shaken' (σαλευθήσονται). In my opinion, it is possible that the 'they' in Mk 13.26 may be these heavenly bodies, or more likely these 'powers'. The exaltation of Christ implies the overcoming of cosmic powers in Eph. 1.20-21; 1 Pet. 3.22; Col. 2.15.[78] The sound of a great shaking (רעש) is associated with the movement of the כבוד in Ezek. 3.12-13. In *Apoc. Ab.* 17 the high place pitches and rolls beneath the feet of the seer, and in *4 Ezra* 6.29 the place where Ezra is standing begins to rock to and fro at the conclusion of a description of the end, delivered by a voice whose 'sound was like the sound of many waters' (v. 17; cf. Ezek. 1.24; 43.2). Ezra has been told in advance, 'If the place where you are standing is greatly shaken while the voice is speaking, do not be terrified; because the word concerns the end, and the foundation so the earth will understand that the speech concerns them. They will tremble and be shaken, for they know that their end must be changed' (6.13-16).[79]

Mk 13.26, read as depicting an upward movement of the Son of man to the heavens, matches the imagery I am proposing for 14.62. But again, I am suggesting this imagery for a pre-Markan stage of the tradition.[80]

IV

At this point, let me summarize the reasons given for suspecting that Merkabah tradition lies behind Mk 14.62.

1. Chariot imagery may account for the particular placement of OT allusions in this text and the sequence of the verbs, especially if the saying is understood to be about the exaltation of Jesus.
2. A similar sequence, involving a combination of allusions to Ps. 110.1 and Daniel 7, appears in 1 Pet. 3.22, with reference to the ascension of Christ into the heavens.
3. The terms 'Power' and 'Blessed One' in Mk 14.61-62 may be clues that Merkabah traditions concerning the כבוד are drawn on in this passage.
4. Clear use of Merkabah imagery appears in post-NT Christian material, and hints of such a representation appear in the NT, to portray the exaltation of Jesus. Related exegetical traditions, perhaps with some base in mystical practices, may be posited.

One further aspect of the Markan text remains to be considered briefly, and this may strengthen the argument developed here. This is the charge of blasphemy (v. 64) which follows the saying about the Son of Man. O. Linton insists, I think rightly, that it is this saying of Jesus which is in the present text the motivation for the charge.[81] Most critics agree that there is no reference here to blasphemy in the technical sense used in *m. Sanh.* 7.5, involving a distinct pronouncing of the divine name; nor is a general messianic claim blasphemous. Rather, blasphemy in Mk 14.62-64, as in the rest of the NT, has a broader definition, concerning some sort of violation of the power and majesty of God, an infringement of God's prerogatives (e.g. Mk 2.7 par; Jn 10.33, 36).[82] The attempts to explain Mk 14.62 in this latter sense are numerous [83] The closest analogies to the charge in the Markan trial scene are (1) the opinion of R. Jose that R. Aqiba 'profanes the Shekinah' by his exegesis of Dan. 7.9 (Aqiba said one

throne was for God and one for David; *b. Sanh.* 38b), and (2) the
apostasy of Elisha ben Abuya (Aḥer), consisting in his claim, uttered
when he came to the vision of the Merkabah and saw Meṭaṭron
'sitting on a throne like a king', that there are two Divine Powers in
heaven (*3 Enoch* 16.2-5; cf. *b. Ḥag.* 15a).[84] See also the charge of
Elious that Job has spoken 'grandiosely and excessively (μεγάλως
καὶ ὑπερβαλλόντως), saying that his own throne is in the heavens' (*T.
Job* 41.5). But the claim in Mk 14.62 may have been heard as an even
worse impropriety: it may have been heard (at some level of the
tradition) as the claim that Jesus as the Danielic Son of Man is a co-
occupant of the divine throne.[85] In other words, as a statement made
by the early Christians about Jesus, Mk 14.62 may be close to the
statements made in Revelation about the Lamb (3.21; 22.1, 3). It may
be *less* blasphemous (if we can speak of degrees of blasphemy), from
the perspective of those making this type of charge against the early
Christians, than the implication we have seen some have found in
the Fourth Gospel: that Jesus is *the* occupant of the divine throne,
the Ezekielian Man.

As we have seen, Ezekiel's 'visions of God' (1.1) may be read to
refer to visions in which God was seen, a theophany. Precisely how
the figure on the moving throne was understood by the early Jewish
Merkabah mystics is unknown to us, since the content of Merkabah
sermons was suppressed in rabbinic literature.[86] But mention of the
mystic expounding 'the glory of our (or: his) Father in heaven' in *t.
Ḥag.* 2.1-2 and *y. Ḥag.* 2.1, and of 'the glory of my Creator' in *b. Ḥag.*
14b leads us to believe that the vision of Ezekiel and the expierience
it gave rise to were regarded in these texts as a vision of the form of
God. An ascent to the third level is spoken of in *y. Ḥag.* 2.1; *b. Ḥag.*
14b, but is not depicted there as an ascent on the Merkabah. Passages
which concern the boast of the wicked king of Babylon (*b. Ḥag.* 13a;
b. Pes. 94a-b; *Gen. R.* 25; *'Erub.* 53a) speak of the Throne of glory at
an immense distance, beyond all creation. Mk 14.62, if interpreted as
suggested in this paper, modifies and challenges that understanding
of Ezekiel, not in the sense that the Markan saying refers to the
ascent of a wicked one, nor to a shocking reinterpretation of the
theophany (contrast the Fourth Gospel), but in that it evokes the
image of the divine Throne coming down to take the righteous one.
In this, we can speculate, might have been seen by some a violation
of the majesty of God, or (to borrow a phrase from Winter, quoted

above) 'devious excogitations' which lead to an infringement of God's prerogatives.

There would have been a particular appropriateness in the use of Merkabah imagery to express faith in Jesus' ultimate vindication. In Ezekiel 10 the sight of the כבוד departing from the temple, and in chs. 43–44 the sight of it returning are a way of showing that Yahweh, unvanquished, survived the destruction of the sanctuary. The heavenly Throne is beyond the reach of Babylonian might.[87] So too is the people to whom the כבוד appears in exile, and to whom is promised a return to the land. As Neusner remarks, Yoḥanan ben Zakkai found the visions of Ezekiel crucial to the survival of his faith; they were the source of his courage to confront and interpret the parallel event of 70 CE. Yoḥanan and his disciples 'drew on a continuing tradition of theosophical speculation, using a fund of contemporary, common images as well as ancient Scriptural forms. In moments of ecstasy they confronted the impending disaster in all its metaphysical, mythic and theological dimensions',[88] foreseeing destruction and reconciliation. The analysis offered here suggests that such imagery may have had relevance also to the disaster Jesus endured and was believed to have survived. An important connection may be seen, moreover, to the charge in Mk 14.58 concerning the destruction of the temple and the building of another, not made with hands.

NOTES

1. Good summaries of the major problems are provided by J.R. Donahue (*Are You the Christ? The Trial Narrative in the Gospel of Mark* [SBLDS 10; Missoula MT: SBL, 1973], pp. 139-50, 172-87) and D. Juel (*Messiah and Temple* [SBLDS 3]; Missoula MT: Scholars, 1977], pp. 77-107).

2. LXX: κάθου ἐκ δεξιῶν μου. Mk 14.62: ἐκ δεξιῶν καθήμενον τῆς δυνάμεως. The parallels in Mt. 26.64 and Lk. 22.69 bring the citation closer to its LXX form, putting the participle (respectively, καθήμενον, καθήμενος) before ἐκ δεξιῶν.

3. LXX: ἐπὶ τῶν νεφελῶν τοῦ οὐρανοῦ ὡς υἱὸς ἀνθρώπου ἤρχετο. Theodotion: μετὰ τῶν νεφελῶν τοῦ οὐρανοῦ ὡς υἱὸς τοῦ ἀνθρώπου ερχόμενος [ἤν]. Mk 14.62 (τὸν υἱὸν τοῦ ἀνθρώπου ... ἐρχόμενον μετὰ τῶν νεφελῶν τοῦ οὐρανοῦ) corresponds more closely with Theodotion, whereas the Matthean parallel reads ἐπὶ τῶν νεφελῶν (cf. the similar correction of

Mk 13.26 at Mt. 24.30). Lk. 22.69 does not contain the phrase 'coming with (or: on) the clouds of heaven'.

4. F.T. Fallon, *The Enthronement of Sabaoth: Jewish Elements in Gnostic Creation Myths* (Leiden: Brill, 1978), p. 57.

5. Ezekiel does not call the fiery-wheeled throne a chariot, but it can be imagined to resemble one because of the wheels and the movement. The word Merkabah came to be applied not only to the throne of this vision, but also to the vision as a whole. See Sir. 49.8 Hebrew; Ezek. 43.3 LXX. In Jewish tradition, מרכבה becomes an accepted term referring to visions of the throne, the heavenly palace or palaces (היכלות), divine hierarchies, and the Glory, all dependent in some way on Ezekiel's vision. See G. Scholem, *Major Trends in Jewish Mysticism* (NY: Schocken, 1973; reprint of 1954 edn), p. 46, for discussion of the variety of terminology used in the course of the centuries for the descriptions of the contemplation of God's Glory and the throne. He posits an essential continuity concerning the Merkabah in the three stages of this tradition: (1) its early beginnings in the period of the second temple, in the 'anonymous conventicles' of the old apocalyptics, groups which produced a large portion of the pseudepigrapha and apocalypses of the first centuries BCE and CE; (2) its second stage, that of the Merkabah speculations of the Mishnaic teachers known to us by name, groups of pupils of R. Yoḥanan ben Zakkai; (3) the third stage, that of the Merkabah mysticism of talmudic and post-talmudic times (pp. 40, 42-43, 47). Contrast more recent analyses such as that of Ira Chernus, *Mysticism in Rabbinic Judaism* (NY/Berlin: de Gruyter, 1982).

6. Juel, *Messiah and Temple*, p. 95.

7. M. Hengel, *The Son of God* (Philadelphia: Fortress, 1976), pp. 89, 90 n. 151.

8. P.M. Casey, *Son of Man. The Interpretation and Influence of Daniel 7* (London: SPCK, 1979), p. 180; cf. W.R.G. Loader, 'Christ at the Right Hand: Ps. CX. 1 in the New Testament', *NTS* 24 (1977/78), pp. 200-201.

9. See. H.K. McArthur, 'Mark XIV.62', *NTS* 4 (1958), pp. 156-58 (an enthronement interpretation is 'controverted by the order of the phrases quoted'); H.E. Tödt, *The Son of Man in the Synoptic Tradition* (London: SCM, 1965), p. 39; R.H. Fuller, *The Foundations of New Testament Christology* (NY: Scribner's, 1965), p. 146.

10. D.M. Hay, *Glory at the Right Hand: Ps 110 in Early Christianity* (NY: Abingdon, 1973), p. 66.

11. B. Lindars, *New Testament Apologetic* (Philadelphia: Westminster, 1961), p. 49; cf. Juel, *Messiah and Temple*, p. 94.

12. T.F. Glasson, *The Second Advent* (3rd edn; London: Epworth, 1963), p. 55-59; M.-J. Lagrange, *Evangile selon Saint Matthieu* (7th edn; Paris: Gabalda, 1948), p. clxv; J.A.T. Robinson, *Jesus and His Coming* (London:

SCM, 1957), pp. 44-47; L. Hartman, 'Scriptural Exegesis in the Gospel of Matthew and the Problem of Communication', *L'Evangile selon Matthieu* (ed. M. Didier; Gembloux: Duculot, 1972), pp. 146, 144.

13. Robinson, *Jesus and His Coming*, p. 49; cf. O.F.J. Seitz, 'The Future Coming of the Son of Man: Three Midrashic Formulations in the Gospel of Mark', *SE* VI (=TU 112 [1973], p. 486); F.H. Borsch, *The Son of Man in Myth and History* (Philadelphia: Westminster, 1967), p. 391. E. Schweizer agrees with Robinson, but says that Mark may have inverted the sequence (*Lordship and Discipleship* [Naperville, Ill.: Allenson, 1960], p. 39 n. 4).

14. M. Gourgues, *A la Droite de Dieu: Résurrection de Jésus et Actualisation du Psaume 110.1 dans le Nouveau Testament* (Paris: Gabalda, 1978), p. 157.

15. M.D. Hooker, *The Son of Man in Mark* (Montreal: McGill University, 1967), pp. 179-71.

16. Other explanations of the absence of this phrase in Luke include the opinions that Luke is following a different source here which did not contain the phrase (some think Luke's version of the saying may be earlier), or that he is 'de-eschatologizing', i.e. toning down the eschatology of Mark here and allowing the parousia to recede into the distant future. Discussion of these points is outside the scope of this paper.

17. Hooker, 'Is the Son of Man problem really insoluble?', *Text and Interpretation* (ed. E. Best and R. McL. Wilson; Cambridge: Cambridge University Press, 1979), p. 163.

18. F.T. Glasson, 'The Reply to Caiaphas (Mark XIV.62)', *NTS* 7 (1960), p. 91.

19. See O. Linton, 'The Trial of Jesus and the Interpretation of Psalm CX.1', *NTS* 7 (1960/1), p. 260; M. Gourgues, *A la Droite*, p. 157.

20. Casey, *Son of Man*, p. 179.

21. D.R. Catchpole, *The Trial of Jesus* (Leiden: Brill, 1971), p. 137. Sloyan (*Jesus on Trial* [Philadelphia: Fortress, 1973], p. 60) remarks that Winter's opinion reflects the view held by Perrin ('Mark 14.62: End Product of a Christian Pesher Tradition?', *NTS* 12 [1965/6], pp. 150-55) that 14.62a and 62b first existed separately and were later joined in a harmonizing attempt. But Perrin does not propose two christological factions; rather, he proposes an ascension and then a parousia use of Dan. 7.13.

22. P. Winter, 'The Marcan Account of Jesus' Trial by the Sanhedrin', *JTS* 14 (1963), p. 100. Catchpole (*Trial*, p. 137) thinks this argument is 'over-literal', and does not consider the alternatives (that each verb is an expression of the Son of Man's vindication, or that 'two consecutive insights are intended').

23. Cf. Mk 16.19. J.N.D. Kelly (*A Commentary on the Epistles of Peter and of Jude* [London: Black, 1969], pp. 146, 164) uses without comment this 'logical' sequence.

24. G. Krodel, 'First Peter', *Hebrews, James, 1 and 2 Peter, Jude, Revelation* (ed. G. Krodel; Philadelphia: Fortress, 1977), p. 67.

25. Bo Reicke, *The Epistles of James, Peter and Jude* (AB 37; Garden City, NY: Doubleday, 1964), pp. 107, 115.

26. Gourgues, *A la Droite*, pp. 77, 79, 86 n. 34.

27. Dalton refers here to Acts 2.33; Mt. 28.18-20; Jn 7.39; 20.22-23, and cites F.W. Beare, *The First Epistle of Peter* (Oxford, 1958), p. 150: 'The significance of the Resurrection, as made effectual in the new life of his followers, through baptism, lies in his elevation to the place of supreme authority over the whole of God's universe'.

28. W.J. Dalton, *Christ's Proclamation to the Spirits* (Rome: Pontifical Biblical Institute, 1965), p. 99.

29. In Acts 2.34 such an allusion appears in the context of a discussion of ascension. Cf. *Asc. Isa.* 10.14: 'in glory you (Christ) will ascend and sit at my right hand'. Is the thought here sequential or in parallelism? Note that the next verse concerns the worship of Christ by the princes and powers.

30. C.H. Dodd, *According to the Scriptures* (London: Nisbet, 1952), pp. 101-102; O.F.J. Seitz, 'The Future Coming', pp. 481-85.

31. Ps. 110.2 mentions a 'rod of power' (δυνάμεως) sent out by the Lord, and v. 3 speaks of dominion (ἡ ἀρχή) in the day of the king's power (δυνάμεως).

32. G. Scholem, *Jewish Gnosticism, Merkabah Mysticism and Talmudic Tradition* (NY: Jewish Theological Seminary of America, 1965), p. 67. On the other hand, Grundman ('δύναμαι/δύναμις', *TDNT* II [1964], p. 297) and Dalman (*The Words of Jesus* [Edinburgh: Clark, 1902], p. 200) present the rabbinic and targumic evidence for גבורה as a paraphrase for the name of God; cf. J.R. Harris, 'Traces of Targumism in the New Testament', *ExpTim* 30 (1920/1), p. 375; Seitz, 'The Future Coming', p. 494.

33. There is wide agreement that the original dates from the first century CE and was composed in a Semitic language (J.H. Charlesworth, *The Pseudepigrapha and Modern Research* [Missoula, MT: Scholars, 1976], p. 74).

34. I. Gruenwald, *Apocalyptic and Merkabah Mysticism* (Leiden: Brill, 1980), pp. 134-36. See also I. Chernus, 'Visions of God in Merkabah Mysticism', *JSJ* 13 (1982), pp. 130-31.

35. A.F. Segal, *Two Powers in Heaven: Early Rabbinic Reports about Christianity and Gnosticism* (Leiden: Brill, 1977), p. 195, following L. Schiffman, 'Merkabah Speculation at Qumran: the 4Q Serekh Shirot 'Olat Ha-shabbat', *Mystics, Philosophers and Politicians* (ed. J. Reinharz and D. Swetschinski with collaboration of K.P. Bland; Durham: Duke University, 1982), pp. 27-28.

36. This work probably dates from 80-100 CE and was written in a Semitic language (Charlesworth, *Pseudepigrapha*, p. 68).

37. See G.A. Cooke, *The Book of Ezekiel* (ICC; Edinburgh: Clark, 1951), p. 21; A. Feuillet, 'Le Fils de l'Homme de Daniel et la tradition biblique', *RB* 60 (1953), pp. 321-46; G. Fohrer, *History of Israelite Religion* (NY: Abingdon, 1972), pp. 78, 169. On some later understandings related to the figure in this vision, see G.G. Stroumsa, 'Form(s) of God: Some Notes on Meṭaṭron and Christ', *HTR* 76 (1983), pp. 269-88.

38. 'Son of the Blessed' (which seems to be synonymous here with 'the Christ') is unique in the NT and in all Jewish literature, as far as we know (Juel, *Messiah and Temple*, p. 78).

39. Dalman (*Words of Jesus*, p. 200) calls the phrase הוא ברוך an appendix in the formula.

40. Juel, *Messiah and Temple*, p. 79.

41. M.A. Knibb translation, *The Ethiopic Book of Enoch* (ed. M.A. Knibb in consultation with E. Ullendorf; Oxford: Clarendon, 1978), vol. II, p. 179.

42. See W. Zimmerli, *Ezekiel* (Philadelphia: Fortress, 1979), vol. I, p. 94. The emended text is discussed below.

43. Beyer, 'εὐλογέω, εὐλογητός', *TDNT* II (1964), p. 764.

44. Sloyan, *Jesus on Trial*, p. 48; cf. Fuller, *Foundations*, p. 110.

45. Juel, *Messiah and Temple*, p. 79; cf. Donahue, *Are You the Christ?* p. 180 ('a Marcan surrogate for God').

46. Cooke, *Ezekiel*, p. 16; J. Bowman, "The Background of the Term 'Son of Man'", *Exp. Tim* (1947/8), p. 285; J.A. Emerton, 'The Origin of the Son of Man Imagery', *JTS* 9 (1958), pp. 225-42; O. Procksch, 'Die Berufungsvision Hesechiels', *ZAW* 34 (1920), p. 141; W. Eichrodt, *Theology of the Old Testament* (2 vols.; Philadelphia: Westminster, 1967), vol. II, pp. 32-34.

47. See the annotated bibliography compiled by R. Spittler in *The Testament of Job* (ed. R.A. Draft, et al.; Missoula, MT: Scholars, 1974), pp. 17-20; Charlesworth, *Pseudepigrapha*, p. 135.

48. H.C. Kee, 'Satan, Magic and Salvation in the Testament of Job', *SBL Seminar Papers 1974* (Missoula, MT: Scholars, 1974), pp. 53-55. D. Flusser ('At the Right Hand of Power', *Immanuel* 14 [1982], p. 43 n.2) sees but does not explore a link between Mk 14.62 and *T. Job* 33.3.

49. Hay (*Glory at the Right Hand*, p. 27) recognizes the allusion here to Psalm 110.

50. J.J. Collins, 'Structure and Meaning in the Testament of Job', *SBL Seminar Papers 1974*, pp. 39, 50.

51. Kee, 'Satan, Magic', p. 66.

52. See K. Kohler, 'The Testament of Job: An Essene Midrash on the Book of Job', *Semitic Studies in Memory of A. Kohut* (ed. G.A. Kohut; Berlin: Calvary, 1897), p. 282. The connection with the Essenes, however, is far from certain.

53. Cooke, *Ezekiel*, p. 41; Zimmerli, *Ezekiel*, p. 139.

54. S.H. Levey, 'The Targum to Ezekiel', *HUCA* 46 (1975), p. 145. Cf. S. Niditch, 'The Visionary', *Ideal Figures in Ancient Judaism* (ed. J.J. Collins and G.W.E. Nickelsburg; Chico: Scholars, 1980), pp. 166-67.

55. M. Philonenko (*Le Testament de Job, Semitica* 18 [1968], p. 18) remarks that the chariots have become 'psychopompes': they carry the soul of the just person to God.

56. The mention of the 'father' in 52.4 complicates this question. The S text has 'their father', but the P text reads ('the father'. The V MS omits 'looked on'. Kee, who prefers the P MS here, thinks this verse means that God 'the Father' watches while another (Meṭaṭron-like) figure accomplishes the assumption ('Satan, Magic', p. 66). It seems to me, however, that S is to be preferred, and the meaning is that *only* Job and his daughters (not the others) saw the one on the throne coming for Job; cf. Acts 22.9; 9.7.

57. Gruenwald, *Apocalyptic*, p. 119. *1 Enoch* 14 is discussed in my dissertation, *The Father, the Son and the Holy Spirit* (SBLDS 61; Chico: Scholars, 1982), pp. 174-76; see pp. 179-80 on the linguistic and thematic affinities among Ezekiel 1, 2 Kings 1 and *1 Enoch* 14.

58. Translation by F.E. Williams, *The Nag Hammadi Library* (ed. J.M. Robinson: San Francisco: Harper and Row, 1977), p. 35. *1 Enoch* 70 seems to stand behind this reference to the 'chariot of the spirit'.

59. Most scholars now think the Odes are Jewish Christian, and date them between 70 and 125 CE. A relationship with the ideas peculiar to the Dead Sea Scrolls is widely acknowledged. See the summaries of critical opinion by W. Bauer, 'The Odes of Solomon', in E. Hennecke, *New Testament Apocrypha* (ed. W. Schneemelcher; Philadelphia: Westminster, 1964), vol. II, pp. 808-810; Charlesworth, *Pseudepigrapha*, pp. 189-90.

60. J.H. Charlesworth translation, *The Odes of Solomon* (Oxford: Clarendon, 1973), p. 131. J. Daniélou, following Bernard, thinks that the word *markabhta*, which denotes any kind of vehicle, does not mean chariot here, but ship, as the Greek ὄχημα could similarly refer to either chariot or ship (*Primitive Christian Symbols* [Baltimore: Helicon, 1964], pp. 82-83). See, however, Charlesworth, *Odes*, p. 133 n. 1.

61. It is impossible to be certain which is the case. 'The Lord' is mentioned in vv. 17, 20, but this title is used in the *Odes* to refer both to God and to the Messiah (see *Ode* 29.6). The author could speak of Christ as 'redeemed' (38.17; cf. 8.21; 35.71 [p. 126 n. 11]) and 'made wise' (38.16; cf. 17.8).

62. Charlesworth, *Odes*, p. 126 n. 7 with reference to *Ode* 35; cf. p. 43 n. 7.

63. Fuller sees in Acts 1.9 an Elijah typology, and, with Perrin and Hahn, the influence of Dan. 7.13 (R.H. Fuller, *The Formation of the Resurrection Narratives* [NY: Macmillan, 1971], p. 213 n. 41; N. Perrin, *Rediscovering the Teaching of Jesus* [NY: Harper and Row, 1967] p. 179; F. Hahn, *The Title of Jesus in Christology* [NY: World, 1969], p. 133 n. 4). Clouds, however, are

quite logically associated with heavenly journeys and need not recall these specific texts.

64. See A.J.B. Higgins, *Jesus and the Son of Man* (Philadelphia: Fortress, 1964), p. 157 n. 3.

65. R.E. Brown, *The Gospel according to John* (Garden City, NY: Doubleday, 1966), vol. I, p. 89; cf. H. Windisch, 'Joh 1,51 und die Auferstehung Jesu', *ZNW* 31 (1932), pp. 199-204; R. Hamerton-Kelly, *Preexistence, Wisdom and the Son of Man* (Cambridge: Cambridge University Press, 1973), p. 299.

66. See F.J. Moloney, *The Johannine Son of Man* (Rome: Libreria Ateneo Salesiano, 1976), p. 25.

67. J.L. Martyn, *History and Theology in the Fourth Gospel* (NY: Harper and Row, 1968), p. 137.

68. Brown, *Gospel according to John*, vol. I, p. 91.

69. In *2 Enoch* 21.1 they 'overshadow' the throne.

70. See P. Borgen, 'Some Jewish Exegetical Traditions as Background for Son of Man Sayings in John's Gospel', *L'Evangile de Jean* (ed. M. de Jonge; Gembloux: Duculot, 1977), p. 245. S. Smalley ('The Johannine Son of Man Sayings', *NTS* 15 (1968/69], p. 228), following a suggestion of M. Black, thinks the preposition ἐπί in Jn 1.51 corresponds to the Aramaic עַל, meaning 'unto' or 'towards'. The picture then would be of angels from above and below converging on the Son of Man. Cf. Higgins, *Jesus and the Son of Man*, p. 159 n. 3, and see BAG, p. 285 for the meaning of 'at' or 'near' for ἐπί.

71. This passage interprets the ascending and descending of the angels as 'exalting' and 'degrading' the one who is Israel. On Jacob's ladder in the *Hekhalot Rabbati*, see Gruenwald, *Apocalyptic and Merkabah Mysticism*, pp. 120, 160-61.

72. N.A. Dahl, 'The Johannine Church and History', *Current Issues in New Testament Interpretation* (ed. W. Klassen & G.F. Snyder; New York: Harper & Brothers, 1962), p. 136, 286-87 n. 21; cf. G. Quispel, 'Nathanael und der Menschensohn (Joh 1, 51)', *ZNW* 47 (1956), pp. 281-83.

73. P. Borgen, *Bread from Heaven* (Leiden: Brill, 1965), pp. 185-86 n. 4, 147.

74. G. Quispel, 'Jean et la Gnose', *L'Evangile de Jean* (Louvain: Desclée de Brouwer, 1958), p. 206.

75. Instead, he draws on the angelophany in Dan. 10.5-6 for the description of eyes like a flame of fire and feet like burnished bronze.

76. See R.H. Charles, *Revelation* (ICC; Edinburgh: Clark, 1920; reprinted 1963), vol. I, pp. 113, 115; cf. C.C. Rowland, 'The Visions of God in Apocalyptic Literature', *JSJ* 10 (1979), p. 154.

77. See Casey (*Son of Man*, p. 171) for this parousia interpretation.

78. H. Schlier, *Principalities and Powers in the New Testament* (New York; Herder and Herder, 1961), p. 40; Grundmann, 'δύναμαι/δύναμις', p. 307.

The elect, dead and alive, are gathered by being caught up 'to meet the Lord in the air' in 1 Thess. 4.17.

79. C.C. Rowland (*The Open Heaven* [New York: Crossroad, 1983], pp. 231-32) understands *4 Ezra* 6.29 as a description of the impact of the vision on the mystic; but this is to ignore vv. 13-16.

80. For an argument that Mk 14.62, an allusion to Dan. 7.13, may be an authentic saying of Jesus, see R. Bauckham, 'The Son of Man: "A Man in My Position" or "Someone"?', *JSNT* 23 (1985), pp. 29-31; contrast B. Lindars, 'The Idiomatic Use of Bar Enasha', *ibid.*, p. 40; G. Vermes, *Jesus the Jew*, pp. 180-86; Casey, *Son of Man*, p. 213. W.O. Walker ('The Son of Man: Some Recent Developments', *CBQ* 45 [1983], p. 599) proposes that those NT sayings which reflect the influence of Dan. 7.13 'most nearly represent the earliest stage in the development of the Son of Man title and concept'. In my opinion, we do not yet have a clear sense of the range of meanings drawn from Daniel 7 in the NT sayings.

81. Linton, 'The Trial of Jesus', p. 259.

82. See Juel, *Messiah and Temple*, pp. 102-103.

83. For a review of the major attempts, see Juel, *Messiah and Temple*, pp. 97-106; Catchpole, *Trial*, pp. 72-148. Texts like *Sepher Ha-Razim* (trans. M.A. Morgan; Chico: Scholars, 1983) in its description of the seventh firmament emphasize that God alone sits in the highest heaven ('He is alone; there is no stranger with Him' [p. 831]).

84. On these texts, see R. Bauckham, 'The Worship of Jesus in Apocalyptic Christianity', *NTS* 27 (1981), pp. 326-27; Rowland, *Open Heaven*, pp. 334-39.

85. H. Odeberg (*3 Enoch* [New York: Ktav, 1973], pp. 137ff.) rejects the conjecture that the name Metatron is equivalent to σύνθρονος, understood to mean co-occupant of the divine throne. Gruenwald (*Apocalyptic and Merkabah Mysticism*, p. 235) accepts the equivalence but not the meaning; Metatron has a chair alongside God's throne.

86. See J. Neusner ('The Development of the Merkavah Tradition', *JSJ* 2 [1971], p. 152) on the sermon of Eleazar ben 'Arakh missing from the four texts treated (Mekhilta of R. Simeon ben Yohai, *Mishpatim* 20.1; *t. Ḥag.* 2.1-2; *y. Ḥag.* 2.1; *b. Ḥag.* 14b). Cf. Rowland, 'Visions', pp. 139, 152-53.

87. S. Spiegel, 'Ezekiel or Pseudo-Ezekiel?', *HTR* 24 (1931), pp. 264-65; Levey, 'The Targum to Ezekiel', p. 142.

88. J. Neusner, *A Life of Yohanan ben Zakkai ca. 1-80 C.E.* (Leiden: Brill, 1970), pp. 140-41. On the revitalization movement as a sociological matrix of visionary activity, see Niditch, 'Visionary', pp. 170-74. Chernus (*Mysticism*, pp. 1-16) discusses 'the use of Sinai as a legitimating paradigm' in second century CE midrashim which use terms strikingly like those found in the literature of Merkabah mysticism. Considering the similarities between Merkabah mysticism and non-Jewish traditions of *gnosis* (but not those

between Merkabah mysticism and NT traditions), Chernus argues that the early Merkabah mystics 'must have had a high risk of being labelled '*minim*'—heretics—and being excluded from the rabbinic community, a fate which they obviously wished to avoid'.

APOCALYPTIC PARAENESIS IN MATTHEW 6.19-34*

Stephenson Humphries-Brooks

The rediscovery of primitive Christian apocalyptic by Johannes Weiss and Albert Schweitzer at the beginning of our century continues to haunt the study of the New Testament generally and the interpretation of the Sermon on the Mount (SM) specifically.[1] Two conclusions reached by both Weiss and Schweitzer demand special attention with regard to the SM and its relevance to the modern world. First, both Weiss and Schweitzer correctly perceive that theological ethics as normally understood in systematics is precluded by an apocalyptic understanding of the teaching of Jesus.[2] We suggest that this is so because of the radical discontinuity between the theological category of God as creator of the physical and moral cosmos in systematics and that of God as redeemer of the cosmos fallen to evil powers in apocalyptic thought. Second, according to Weiss and Schweitzer we cannot adopt the perspective of primitive Christian apocalyptic because we no longer share with our spiritual forbears the expectation of an *imminent* end of the present world order. These conclusions lead Schweitzer to understand the SM as an 'interim ethic' suitable only for a community that expected the imminent return of their Lord and therefore largely irrelevant for the modern world. He correctly affirms that the SM cannot be regarded as normative for the organization of a social order, or for that matter for the Church once it is realized that the future will continue in its chronological progress. If Schweitzer is correct, then, an ethics based upon apocalyptic, understood as the belief in the imminent end of the world, must be abandoned by a Church that finds itself concretized as a continuing social institution with an extended past and a limitless future.

Günther Bornkamm, reviewing 'The History of the Exposition of the Sermon on the Mount', specifies a problem in the position of Weiss and Schweitzer,

> Or in other and less figurative words: this interpretation would appear to make the apocalyptic end of the world the ground of Jesus' demands, whereas the love of our neighbour and of our enemy, purity, faithfulness and truth are demanded simply because they are the will of God. The inner relationship between Jesus' requirement and his message of the coming of the Kingdom of God are [sic] not brought out clearly in the apocalyptic interpretation of the Sermon on the Mount.[3]

Bornkamm clearly states the problem for a modern appropriation of the teaching of Jesus embodied not only in the Sermon on the Mount (SM) but throughout the Jesus traditions in the Synoptic Gospels. One interpretative direction that tends to avoid the problem perceived by Weiss and Schweitzer and clarified by Bornkamm, relates the teaching of Jesus in the SM to Jewish models of Wisdom teaching or Greek philosophical ethics either at the level of Matthew's text itself or in the pre-Matthean tradition.[4] Those who advocate this approach, while they may not recognize it, sidestep the fundamental problem of apocalyptic in the teaching of Jesus. The ethical interpretation allows for the discernment of ethical categories from the reasonable structure of the physical and moral universe created by God.[5] We are told by one advocate of the ethical interpretation for example that the SM functions as an *epitome* of Jesus' teachings whose purpose is to make theologians of his disciples.[6] Jesus may be regarded in the SM as the personified Wisdom of God, who by virtue of his special knowledge of the moral structure of the Kingdom of Heaven brings to his followers ethical and moral insight *and the theological method* for continuing to define the Kingdom. Even if we grant that such a method is constrained by the radical demand of the ethics of the Kingdom, all may not be quite right in this interpretation. First, it tends to overlook the apocalyptic nature of Jesus' paraenesis throughout the Jesus tradition. Second, it circumvents certain apocalyptic assumptions present in the text of both the SM and Matthew. Third, and most disturbing, it gives over to the disciple trained as theologian the authority to determine the Kingdom and its ethical boundaries. This authority the First Gospel reserves exclusively to God and Jesus (see especially Mt. 23.8-10).

If we take the challenge of Bornkamm seriously, perhaps the text of the SM itself can provide some indication of the 'inner relationship' that he calls for. If we are to enter these difficult texts we should do so mindful of two rules. First, in a spirit of openness to instruction we should recite three times slowly as instructed by our teacher J. Louis Martyn, 'I do not know'.[7] Second, we should take as our starting point the dictum attributed to Walter Bauer, and often quoted by Professor Martyn, 'Seek to say nothing of the text that the original audience would not have understood'. One section of the SM that resists incorporation into the overall plan and conceptuality of the SM and the First Gospel is Mt. 6.19-34.[8] Is this because the author of the First Gospel is simply a sloppy editor of his traditions? Or does the history of interpretation show resistance to accepting certain presuppositions of the author that would make this section understandable?

So that the reader might know where we are going, the following is the conclusion of our investigation: Mt. 6.19-34 is best characterized as apocalyptic paraenesis that functions to create in the reader an epistemological position within the Kingdom of God, a position from which the reader may seek that Kingdom and the righteousness that belongs to God.

Normally, in reading a text authored by a single person we can assume that the text is intended to be understood as written by an actual historical author for an actual historical audience. Criticism of the First Gospel has long recognized, however, the difficulties attendant upon the reconstruction of the beliefs of the Gospel writer and the original audience since the First Gospel shows signs of being not simply a free creation of an author but also a composite that includes traditions passed on and interpreted by the author. In order to take account of the possibility that Mt. 6.19-34 contains not only the assumptions of the real author and real audience but also the accumulated assumptions present due to the traditions employed, the following study will employ two complementary methods. First, by means of literary criticism we will look at the thought structure implied by the text as it stands in Mt. 6.19-34. This criticism will yield conclusions about the implied author and the authorial audience.[9] Second, we will briefly engage in a redaction-critical analysis that provides the basis for recovering the specific emphases of the real author functioning as an editor. The use of both of these methods underlines the judgment that hermeneutics must take into account the social and historical situation of both the ancient and the modern audience in order to yield theologically significant results. Only at the intersection of both of these lines of analysis may we reach some theological conclusions about the relevance of the text for modern communities.

These tasks of interpretation are of course interrelated, but for clarity and focus the study will be organized as follows:

    I.   Translation
   II.   Literary Criticism
 III.   Redaction Criticism
 IV.   Theological Criticism

I

As a first step in interpretation the following translation of Mt. 6.19-34 (following Nestle's 26th Edition of the Greek text) is provided. The study will refer to the verse divisions and subdivisions as indicated.

19. a. Do not store up for yourselves treasures upon earth
     b. where moth and rust corrode
     c. and where thieves dig in and steal.
20. a. But store up for yourselves treasures in heaven,
     b. where neither moth nor rust corrodes
     c. and where thieves neither dig in nor steal.
21. For where your treasure is, there also your heart will be.
22. a. The eye is the lamp of the body.
     b. Therefore, if your eye is sound,
     c. then your whole body will be illuminated.
23. a. But if your eye is evil,
     b. then your whole body will be dark.
     c. Therefore, if the light in you is darkness,
     d. how great is the darkness.
24. a. No one can serve two lords;
     b. for either she will hate the one and love the other,
     c. or she will be devoted to one and despise the other.
     d. You cannot serve God and Mammon.
25. a. For the above reason I say to you,
     b. do not have anxiety about your life, what you might eat[10]
     c. nor about your body, what you might wear.
     d. Is not life more than food and the body more than clothes?

26. a. Consider the birds of the heavens
    b. that they do not sow, nor reap, nor gather into barns;
    c. indeed your heavenly Father feeds them.
    d. Do you not surpass them greatly?
27. But who of you by worrying can add a single cubit to his height?
28. a. And why be anxious about clothing?
    b. Learn from the lilies of the field how they grow;
    c. they neither work hard nor do they spin.
29. But I say to you that not even Solomon in all of his glory was clothed like one of these.
30. a. But if God in this manner dresses the grass of the field, which is here today and tomorrow is cast into the oven,
    b. how much more you, you people of little faith?
31. a. Therefore, do not worry saying,
    b. 'What shall we eat? Or, what shall we drink? Or, what shall we wear?'
32. a. For the Gentiles seek all of these things;
    b. for your heavenly Father knows that you need all of these things.
33. a. But seek first the Kingdom of God and his righteousness[11]
    b. and all these things will be added to you.
34. a. Therefore, do not be anxious about tomorrow, for tomorrow will be anxious for itself;
    b. its evil is sufficient for the day.

II

As a general literary observation we note that the section is composed of four paragraphs: (1) vv. 19-21; (2) vv. 22-23; (3) v. 24; (4) vv. 25-34. We will read each in sequence noting particularly the explicit and implicit assumptions that each paragraph makes of the reader. In order to concentrate our attention exclusively on the rhetorical strategy of these verses, we will only minimally refer to what the audience has already learned in the SM and the First Gospel, nor will we refer to narrative that follows this passage. This somewhat artificial exercise in literary criticism attempts to bring into sharp focus this passage on its own terms before, in section III, looking at its place in Matthean thought.

1. *Verses 19-21*

The paragraph bears no immediate syntactical connection to Mt. 6.1-18. Nor does its subject matter directly refer to the issues treated in the preceding verses. The authorial audience presumed in these verses supposes a dualistic structure of the cosmos (note the word pair 'upon earth' [v. 19a]/'in heaven' [v. 20a]). Verse 21 as a conclusion to this illustration directs the authorial audience's attention inward to the 'heart' which is understood contextually as the place within a human where allegiances and motivations reside. Since the dualism of vv. 19-21 refers to the opposition between heaven and earth, the authorial audience perceives that this internal seat of allegiance forces one to align one's destiny with one or the other part of the cosmos. More about this relationship becomes apparent in the following verses.

2. *Verses 22-23*

The second paragraph begins in vv. 22-23a with a description of a physiological theory of perception. The theory, however, implies a level other than the physical by a comparison between light and darkness in v. 23c-d. H.D. Betz argues:

> At any rate, the introduction of ethical terms opens up the completely new possibility that the ethical disposition of a person determines whether or not the eyes function properly.[12]

The saying makes the remarkable claim, according to Betz, that one's inner light can be clouded so as to become dark: i.e. physiology is a matter of ethical propriety. This, of course, leads to the audience's questions: What clouds the sight? If my sight is clouded, how may it be restored? Betz answers the first of these questions by asserting that the saying understands sin to be that which clouds the inner light. Within the ethical interpretation offered by Betz, such a suggestion makes sense. The difficulty with this interpretation is that it introduces into the thought-frame of the saying and its literary context a term and conceptuality not otherwise apparent. While such an interpretation may be possible for the saying taken in isolation, it is not an interpretation immediately apparent within the text as it stands.[13]

Based on these observations, we may state several aspects of the thought structure of these verses that are apparent to the authorial audience at this point. Verses 22-23:

a. introduce an interactive dualism between light and darkness;
b. state that the light can actually be darkness;
c. imply that true sight is not a simple physiological function but involves some, as yet unspecified, epistemological power independent of the physical structure of the eye.

The authorial audience may also remember v. 21 and suspect that the heart whose treasure is in heaven is the one that sees rightly; the heart is an internal locus of perception that points to the place from which true sight originates. The audience still must wonder, how do I acqure a 'sound eye'? And if my eye is ill how may I restore it? Compelled by the author's strategy in the composition of these paragraphs, the audience reads ahead.

3. *Verse 24*
As in the previous two paragraphs the verse moves from the mundane physical level to a new level previously not apparent. Service and lordship are the primary categories that define an individual in the cosmos described in v. 24. The individual who makes autonomous decisions has no place in this cosmos. From the apparently mundane social level v. 24d directs the audience's attention to an entirely different level. The contrast between God and Mammon and the assignment of these entities to specific competing lordships forces the audience to see a sharp distinction between the kingdoms over which they rule. Obviously, the first member of this word pair is well known to the audience as a person with power, and is probably to be identified as the lord who governs the statements about heaven and a sound eye in the preceding paragraphs. The second member of the pair, Mammon, by the same contextual comparison is understood as lord over the earth and the evil eye in the preceding paragraphs. Mammon is to be naturally understood in opposition to God as a lord or master (*kyrios* v. 24a). By parallel with v. 19 Mammon rules over the things of the earth.[14] On this reading, it is further implied in v. 23 that Mammon is associated with evil (*poneros*) and darkness (*skoteia*).

We may now clarify the observations listed in regard to vv. 22-23 above:

1. There are two lordships in competition with each other, that of God and that of Mammon.

2. One's place under the power of one of these lords determines one's allegiance (v. 21) and the truthfulness of one's sight (vv. 22-23).

How do I acquire a sound eye? By power derived from God who is my lord. What clouds the inner light? Power derived from the wrong lord clouds it and makes it darkness.

4. *Verses 25-34*

As the audience read v. 25, they encounter for the first time in this section a direct syntactical tie between a paragraph and the preceding verses. 'For the above reason, I say to you' (*dia touto legō hymin*) serves several functions. First, the *dia touto* construction establishes a strong tie to the preceding argument.[15] *Touto* in its most frequent use refers backwards to an antecedent, in this case either v. 24 and/or the examples adduced in vv. 19-24.[16] The audience is referred to what they have learned so far. By use of the *legō hymin* formula, the implied author reminds the authorial audience of who is speaking. Their attention is centered on Jesus' authority. The author expects the audience to understand the saying of Jesus that follows (a) to have the strongest possible relationship to the discourse of vv. 19-24, and (b) to be valid strictly on the authority of Jesus as the speaker.

Verses 25-34, therefore, are to be read by those who perceive the cosmos as structured according to competing lords (v. 24). Verses 26-32 adopt the same form of argument as vv. 19-21 and vv. 22-23; i.e. they describe first the created order as apparent to usual mundane perception. Verse 33 shifts the audience's perception once again to a different epistemology and refocuses the attention from the created order to a new category, the Kingdom of God. The careful reader of the Greek also notices that the personal pronoun *autou* by virtue of its masculine gender refers to God. Therefore, 'his righteousness' demands attention since it is the righteousness that belongs to the lord who grants true sight. The genitive construction here may be read as a simple possessive, but the authorial audience might also suspect that a genitive of source is intended based both upon what they have learned from v. 24 and upon the use of the verb *zētein* ('to seek'). In order to be able to seek God's righteousness and God's Kingdom both of these possessions of God must be available for possession by others.[17] Therefore, the genitive must be understood in some sense as indicating that one is to seek both the Kingdom and the righteousness which belong to God *and come as a gift from God*. The genitive of source fits best the context of the passage. The employment of these two terms completes the picture revealed to the authorial audience in vv. 19-24. The 'Kingdom of God' draws attention to God's lordship as it was articulated in v. 24. The righteousness of God clearly states to the audience what they have suspected since v. 21, that the narrative concerns in some special way the moral structure of God's rule. Verse 33, therefore, serves to shift the audience's inner sight to the epistemology brought into being by the words of Jesus. It presupposes a healthy inner sight. While vv. 24-32 give examples derived from the created order, no principle derivable from creation allows for the jump to the Kingdom of God and his righteousness in v. 33. The guarantee in verse 34 is not based upon a 'wisdom' idea of *creatio continua*[18] but rather on the radical discontinuity created by the confrontation between the Kingdom of God and the earthly kingdom of evil in the proclamation and person of Jesus Christ. Verse 34 presumes that this confrontation will issue in the final victory of God. We may recognize this structure of thought as an *apocalyptic* eschatological perspective similar to structures of thought identifiable in both Jewish and Christian literature.[19] The teaching that defines this confrontation in 6.19-34, therefore, is not best understood as 'new law' or 'ethical paraenesis' but as *apocalyptic paraenesis*. Jesus' apocalyptic paraenesis makes clear to the authorial audience the circle of righteousness that begins and ends with God who establishes their residence by the exercise of his eschatological power.

III

Confirmation that this perspective characterizes the real author and the real audience of the First Gospel comes from a redaction-critical analysis of Mt. 6.19-34. The following table gives the known parallels to Mt. 6.19-34.

Mt.		parallel to Lk.	
	6.19-20		12.33
	6.21		12.34
	6.22		11.34
	6.23		11.35
	6.24		16.13
	6.25-33		12.22-31
	6.34		—

Each verse in Mt. 6.19-33 has a parallel in Luke; verse 34 has no parallel. The parallels in Luke occur in three different contexts. These logia fit in the Lukan narrative as well as they do in the Matthean: therefore, we cannot with confidence assert that either Matthew or Luke preserves the more original order or context of the verses. Some claim could be made that the Lukan order of 12.22-34 may be more original than the Matthean order and that Matthew separates the last pericope (Lk. 12.33-34 par. Mt. 6.19-21) in order to place it at the beginning of the passage. Since there is no direct literary connection nor necessary ideological connection between these two pericopes, however, critical certainty is not possible. We may cautiously conclude that Matthew and Luke have arranged the pericopes in accord with their own literary designs independently of each other. Given that no literary connection is discernable between the pericopes, the most probable conclusion is that Matthew has assembled these pericopes from at least three different contexts in the tradition which he shares with Luke (Q).[20] Therefore, the arrangement of the pericopes is best regarded as due to the redactional activity of the real author. The effect, then, of this arrangement should be taken as indicative of the conscious assumptions of the real author. His strategy in composition most probably is designed to be understandable and revelatory to his real audience.[21]

Aside from the arrangement of the pericopes, the major substantive changes that Matthew makes in his tradition are the addition of the phrase 'and his righteousness' along with the concluding v. 34. Both of the terms 'Kingdom of God' and 'righteousness' call upon the audience to understand v. 33 and by extension the entire section of vv. 29-34 in respect to what they have already learned of these two terms in the First Gospel.

A complete treatment of the concept 'Kingdom of God' (or Matthew's preferred corresponding term 'Kingdom of Heaven') in the First Gospel is neither desirable nor necessary in this context.[22] Let me point out, however, several salient features that the real audience already knows about the Kingdom before coming to this passage. The Kingdom of God (Heaven) refers to an eschatological event. As early as Mt. 3.2 John the Baptist proclaims its arrival (*ēggiken*), a proclamation taken up by Jesus in Mt. 4.17. Most importantly, the Beatitudes of Mt. 5.3-10 promise the reward that belongs to the Kingdom (v. 3), which is fulfillable only in the eschatological future (vv. 4-10). Further, as the *ēggiken* in Mt. 3.2; 4.17 makes clear the eschatological Kingdom is invading here and now. Therefore, the present *ēggiken* of Mt. 5.3 follows the idea that God's kingdom is entering into the present cosmic order in a new way. The presence of this kingdom, its preacher (Jesus), and its children (the real audience), elicits negative response from certain quarters. It is not without significance that the Devil offers Jesus the 'kingdoms of the world' in 4.8. Jesus responds by identifying the lord that he serves in 4.10 as God. Hence a battle is joined between two *lords* and two *kingdoms*. Such a viewpoint is not only eschatological, but more precisely *apocalyptic* and eschatological. It involves the fundamental conceptuality that God is invading the cosmos to claim territory for God's self in the final days. Jesus, by preaching the arrival of the Kingdom in 4.17 publicly identifies himself as under the lordship of God in this final battle. We see here an interactive dualism characteristic of Jewish and primitive Christian apocalyptic perspectives.

A retrospective look at the idea of 'righteousness' in the passages leading up to 6.33 also confirms the assertion that the real audience is to understand the Kingdom of God as the entrance of God into the earthly realm for the purpose of claiming territory. *Dikaiosynē* (righteousness) occurs five times prior to Mt. 6.33 at 3.15; 5.6; 5.10; 5.20; 6.1. At 3.15 *dikaiosynē* is the will of God eschatologically fulfilled by Jesus and John the Baptist. Similarly, in the context of the SM 5.6, 10 reflect the concept that *dikaiosynē* is a power that belongs to the Kingdom of Heaven (5.3) and to anyone found therein. Further, those who participate in this power are under attack (5.10). The use of the term shifts in Mt. 5.20 from something that belongs to God and God's Lordship to something that can be part of the disciples' acitivity:

> For I say to you that unless *your righteousness* exceeds greatly that of the scribes and Pharisees, you will not enter into the Kingdom of Heaven.

The content of Mt. 5.21-6.18 provides the commandments that give content to this excessive righteousness. In this context Mt. 6.1 warns against a different kind of righteousness that is practiced for human reward. Our passage, 6.19-34, becomes crucial for understanding the righteousness of God, because it provides the connection between the Kingdom of God and the righteousness of God.

This key becomes apparent in the use of *zētein* (to seek) in 6.33. The verb means 'to seek, look for in order to find'. It may also carry the connotation of 'to try to obtain, desire to possess'.[23] The first meaning is confirmed by the use of the term in Mt. 7.7-8. The second emphasis is given in the only other passage in the First Gospel where *zētein* and *basileia* occur in context together, at Mt. 13.45 in the Parable of the Pearl. Both meanings may be involved in 6.33. How is this seeking to be accomplished? The answer to this question emerges from a rereading of Mt. 6.19-34 along the lines suggested earlier in our literary-critical analysis. If you have healthy internal sight (v. 22) that comes from the master whom you serve (v. 24), then you can seek the Kingdom of God and his righteousness with the assurance of finding both (7.7-8). If on the other hand your sight is possessed by a master who is evil (Mammon, v. 24), then your seeking will lead only to your own 'righteousness' (6.1) and darkness.[24] Finally, the power for healthy sight finds its concrete historical expression in the eschatological proclamation of Jesus Christ who is God-with-us (1.21; the audience is reminded of this by the introduction of 6.25) who is in the business of preaching the Kingdom of Heaven (4.17) and revealing its mystery to his disciples. (The last point becomes fully apparent only in chapter 13.) In short, one may seek the Kingdom only from within the Kingdom of God. The structure of the conceptual assumptions in Mt. 6.19-34 and elsewhere in the First Gospel allows for the real audience no independent place of judgment.

These redaction-critical remarks allow for the conclusion that the apocalyptic-eschatological perspective of the implied author recovered by literary analysis in II above is the actual perspective of the real author that he assumes his real audience shares. The apocalyptic-eschatological perspective is not a fortuitous structure of thought dependent solely upon the accumulation and preservation of received tradition. It is rather a perspective shared by Matthew and his community who are real living people.[25] This emphasis must be borne in mind as we proceed to the final section of our discussion.

IV

The convergence of these two lines of investigation allows us to conclude that the apocalyptic-eschatological perspective discernable in Mt. 6.19-34 is a perspective shared by Matthew and his community. This perspective views Jesus as the proclaimer of *apocalyptic paraenesis*. Understanding this apocalyptic paraenesis requires that the individual be incorporated already into the lordship of God. Such paraenesis teaches that the person thus created a disciple or child of God will find both the Kingdom of God and righteousness. Apocalyptic paraenesis may be distinguished from ethical paraenesis in that it does not articulate requirements of entry into the lordship of God, but presupposes the creation of an entirely new way of knowing by the lordship of God. The disciple is in a circle of perception. The creation of the insight to seek the Kingdom of God and to find it along with God's righteousness is an act accomplished within the eschatological lordship of God in God's Kingdom as proclaimed by Jesus. The righteousness of God is thus both the presupposition and *telos* of the disciple.

Matthew's claim upon his readers may be restated, 'As children of the Kingdom you have no choice but to follow the paraenesis of Jesus Christ'. Those who by the power of God are set upon the way of righteousness can do nothing other than seek the Kingdom of God and his righteousness. Why then the paraenesis? Mt. 6.19-34 implies that apocalyptic paraenesis given through Jesus becomes a *powerful* education. It does not provide the terms of admission into God's rule. Rather it draws the disciple more deeply into the mystery of the Kingdom which is a new creation by God and in which the disciple is found. The apocalyptic paraenesis of Jesus describes for the child of the Kingdom the boundary line between God's kingdom and the Kingdom of Evil that rules the world. In the terms of our passage, the paraenesis calls the attention of the children of the Kingdom of God to the difference between them and the world. The world thinks that material possessions and the reduction of the anxieties about material security are one of the prime issues in life. The children of the Kingdom of God know what lord they serve and recognize that the righteousness that comes from God is their only pursuit. They are guaranteed on the power-infused authority of Jesus as the Christ, as God-with-us, that they will find this righteousness. Thus they are free from the anxieties of this world.

If Mt. 6.19-34 assumes such an apocalyptic restructuring of the physical and moral cosmos, and if this perspective reflects the conscious religious perspective of an early Christian community, then what are we as twentieth-century readers to make of such a claim?

We began our study with the problem of an apocalyptic interpretation of the SM posed by Bornkamm. Our conclusions suggest that the inner relationship between Jesus' requirement and his proclamation of the Kingdom of God is found not in apocalyptic seen as the imminent expectation of the end of the world, but rather according to Mt. 6.19-34 in an apocalyptic perspective of the inbreaking of God's kingdom and righteousness that is bringing the world to an end. For Matthew and his community the end time has begun (probably with the preaching of Jesus [4.17], certainly with the crucifixion of Jesus [27.51-53]) and continues with his resurrection into his continued powerful presence with his community as definer and proclaimer of the Kingdom of Heaven (28.16-20). As far as Matthew and his community are concerned, while they believe in the final consummation of the world and its judgment by the Son of Man, that occurrence is not essential to their pursuit of the righteousness that comes from God as defined by their Lord's paraenesis.

The inner connection that Bornkamm calls for is precisely this apocalyptic-eschatological perspective that has no temporal limit. It presupposes the powerful lordship of God present in Jesus Christ, his person and proclamation, as the motive force that impels the disciple into the Kingdom and the pursuit of righteousness that belongs only to the Kingdom. In some small way perhaps this exegetical probe has directed attention to this inner relationship. At least the SM is not understandable unless we recognize that Matthew and his community regard Jesus' paraenesis not as admittance requirements but as defining an expectation for those who have been empowered by their lord to seek his righteousness. According to the First Gospel only God and Jesus Christ may define the expectation and the reality of the Kingdom; Christian communities are called into existence to live that definition by seeking the righteousness of God that belongs to God in the power of God. The SM may well define for the modern Christian community as well as for the ancient Matthean community the boundaries between the Gospel and the world, a world which is, in the words of another first-century apocalyptist, 'wasting away'.

NOTES

*For Lou, with thanksgiving for his spirit of gracefilled inquiry that I continue to meet at the hermeneutical roundtable.

1. Johannes Weiss, *Jesus' Proclamation of the Kingdom of God* (Lives of Jesus Series; Philadelphia: Fortress, 1971); Albert Schweitzer, *The Quest of the Historical Jesus. A Critical Study of its Progress from Reimarus to Wrede* (2nd edn; London: A. & C. Black, 1911); *The Mystery of the Kingdom of God. The Secret of Jesus' Messiahship and Passion* (New York: Macmillan, 1950); *The Mysticism of Paul the Apostle* (New York: Henry Holt, 1931).

2. Weiss, *Proclamation*, pp. 131-35; Schweitzer, *Mystery*, pp. 53-60; *Mysticism*, pp. 293-333. See also Warren S. Kissinger, *The Sermon on the Mount. A History of Interpretation and Bibliography* (ATLA Bibliography Series, 3; Metuchen, NJ: Scarecrow Press and The American Theological Association, 1975), pp. 56-60; Günther Bornkamm, 'The History of the Exposition of the Sermon on the Mount', in *Jesus of Nazareth* (New York: Harper and Row, 1960), pp. 221-25; Richard H. Hiers and David Larrimore Holland, 'Introduction', in *Proclamation*, pp. 4-53.

3. 'History', pp. 223-24.

4. For the redactional approach see M. Jack Suggs, *Wisdom, Christology and Law in Matthew's Gospel* (Cambridge: Harvard University, 1970); for the interpretation of the pre-Matthean tradition see Hans Dieter Betz, *Essays on the Sermon on the Mount* (Philadelphia: Fortress, 1985). W.R. Farmer ('The Sermon on the Mount: A Form-Critical and Redactional Analysis of Matt 5.1-7.29', SBLSP 25 [1986], pp. 56-87) may legitimately be regarded as belonging to both redactional and tradition-critical approaches.

5. The cosmos is both physically and ethically structured by the creator in Jewish Wisdom tradition (Gerhard von Rad, *Wisdom in Israel* [Nashville, TN: Abingdon, 1972], pp. 144-76). Stoic ethics depends upon the view, learned from Aristotle, that the moral structure of the cosmos is discoverable by philosophical inquiry (J.M. Rist, *Stoic Philosophy* [Cambridge: Cambridge University Press, 1969], pp. 1-21).

6. Betz, 'The Sermon on the Mount (Matt. 5.3-7.27): Its Literary Genre and Function', in *Essays*, pp. 1-16; see especially pp. 15-16.

7. J. Louis Martyn, 'Glimpses into the History of the Johannine Community', in M. de Jonge (ed.), *L'Evangile de Jean, Sources, rédaction, théologie* (BETL, 44; Leuven, 1977), pp. 149-75; reissued in *The Gospel of John in Christian History* (New York: Paulist, 1978), pp. 90-121. The quotation occurs on p. 92 of the latter volume.

8. Bornkamm attempts such an incorporation by relating each pericope in Mt. 6.9-7.12 to specific clauses in the Lord's Prayer (Mt. 6.7-13). The resulting pattern, however, is so complex that one may reasonably doubt whether the audience of the First Gospel could perceive or was intended to perceive the distinctions ('Der Aufbau der Bergpredigt', *NTS* 24 [1978] pp. 419-32).

9. I have modified the dictum of Walter Bauer in terms of a literary-critical model adapted from the work of Peter J. Rabinowitz ('Truth in Fiction: A Reexamination of Audiences', *Critical Inquiry* [1977], pp. 121-41). Rabinowitz detects four audiences in the text of the modern novel, two of which are of concern to our inquiry: (1) the *actual audience*—flesh and blood people who read the book; (2) the *authorial audience*—the hypothetical audience for whom the work is designed rhetorically. Seymour Chatman (*Story and Discourse. Narrative Structure in Fiction and Film* [Ithaca, NY: Cornell University Press, 1978]) has also contributed to the literary model used here. See especially his diagram on p. 151. The modifications introduced in this study to these critical theories are demanded by th nature of the text of the First Gospel, which is not a modern novel. My thanks to my colleague, Peter Rabinowitz, for personal conversations which helped to clarify my thinking on these matters.

10. Reading with Sinaiticus et al. and omitting *ē ti piēte*. The text was possibly assimilated later to v. 31. The variation in the witnesses between *kai* and *ē* may indicate the secondary nature. See Bruce M. Metzger (*A Textual Commentary on the Greek New Testament* [United Bible Societies, 1971], p. 17) who, reporting on the decision of the Editorial Committee of the United Bible Societies' Greek New Testament, gives these words (present in Nestle's 26th edition) in brackets and a C reading. Verse 25d indicates little evidence for the inclusion of these words if parallelism is to be retained.

11. Reading with the majority of witnesses and including *tou theou*. Matthew almost never employs *basileia* without a modifier (Metzger, *Commentary*, p. 18). The masculine *autou* lacks an antecedent if these words are omitted, *tēn basileian* being feminine. Finally, if the passage relies on Q then the parallel in Lk. 12.31 would further corroborate the inclusion of *tou theou*. In terms of the interpretation of the verse, 'his righteousness' must refer to the righteousness of God, whether or not *tou theou* actually occurred in Matthew's original text.

12. Betz, 'Matthew 6.22-23 and Ancient Greek Theories of Vision', in *Essays*, p. 85.

13. *Ibid.*, p. 86. Admittedly, Betz here is working at the pre-Matthean level of the text and therefore is not bound by the literary context of Mt. 6.22-23. It appears, however, even more difficult to suggest that sin is the agent that clouds the inner sight when vv. 22-23 are taken as an isolated logion, since the only context for interpretation is then the logion itself, or an interpreter's perception of a tradition that is a hypothetical reconstruction. At the pre-Matthean level it makes a great deal of difference whether one understands vv. 22-23 to represent a community or speaker influenced by wisdom tradition or by apocalyptic tradition, for example.

14. *Mamōnas*, a loan word from Aramaic, refers in rabbinic literature to property, sometimes with a negative connotation (F. Hauck, '*mamōnas*',

TDNT IV, pp. 388-90). In Qumran literature it simply refers to property (1QS 6.2; CD 14.20). The determining evidence of its use here, however, must not be the study of parallels, but the structure of thought in its literary context. See S. Safrai and D. Flusser, 'The Slave of Two Masters', *Immanuel* 6 (1976), pp. 30-33.

15. The construction *dia touto legō* is used only two other times in the First Gospel, at 12.31 and 21.43. In each instance it refers to the immediately preceding statement and is followed by a prophetic/apocalyptic saying.

16. H.W. Smyth, *Greek Grammar* (rev. edn; Cambridge, MA: Harvard University Press, 1956), § 1245.

17. *Ibid.*, § 1410.

18. In strong disagreement with Betz ('Cosmogony and Ethics in the Sermon on the Mount', in *Essays*, pp. 89-123, esp. p. 110 and n. 67).

19. P.D. Hanson, 'Appendix', in *The Dawn of Apocalyptic* (rev. edn; Philadelphia: Fortress, 1979), pp. 427-44. J. Louis Martyn, 'Apocalyptic Antinomies in Paul's Letter to the Galatians', *NTS* 31 (1985), pp. 410-24.

20. An understanding of Q as a tradition, perhaps composed of both oral and written units, seems to best account for the text here. I remain convince of the viability of a modified two-source hypothesis as a critical tool in synoptic studies. See Stephenson H. Brooks, *Matthew's Community. The Evidence of his Special Sayings Material* (JSNTS 16; Sheffield: JSOT Press, 1987), pp. 9-11, 111-15.

21. If Betz is correct that the SM relies on a document composed prior to the First Gospel, then this conclusion would require modification ('The Beatitudes of the Sermon on the Mount [Matt. 5.3-12]: Observations on Their Literary Form and Theological Significance', in *Essays*, p. 18). Betz himself, however, notes that this hypothesis requires further and extensive evaluation of the evidence. Farmer asserts that the SM contains 'substantially unaltered' collections of the words of Jesus ('Sermon', p. 58). While Farmer may be correct that the structure of thought involved in Mt. 6.19-34 was generated by Jesus' own historical proclamation of the Kingdom of God (see below n. 25), he has not shown convincingly that these verses in whole or in part go back to semitic originals ('Sermon', p. 77). His work would still suggest that Matthew's audience understood these verses.

22. See Jack Dean Kingsbury, *Matthew: Structure, Christology, Kingdom* (Philadelphia: Fortress, 1975), pp. 128-60.

23. BAGD, pp. 338-39.

24. On Mt. 6.1 as a logion edited by the author of the First Gospel see Brooks, *Matthew's Community*, pp. 42-46

25. Joel Marcus argues persuasively that a similar structure of thought underlies Jesus' sayings about the Kingdom in the Synoptics and that some of these sayings go back to Jesus himself. If so, then Matthew and his audience are exemplary of an attempt to adopt the perspective of the

historical Jesus under the guidance of the resurrected Lord ('Entering into the Kingly Power of God', *JBL* [forthcoming]).

Perry V. Kea, although he retains the use of the word 'ethics', finds a similar structure to the one we have uncovered in Mt. 6.19-34 to be in evidence in the SM generally ('The Sermon on the Mount: Ethics and Eschatological Time', *SBLSP* 25 [1986], pp. 88-98).

'TO THE CLOSE OF THE AGE':
THE ROLE OF APOCALYPTIC THOUGHT IN THE GOSPEL OF MATTHEW

O. Lamar Cope

In spite of the fact that twentieth-century New Testament studies have been so deeply colored by the rediscovery of eschatology by Schweitzer and Weiss at the turn of the century, we often need to be reminded of its importance. One such reminder came from Ernst Käsemann. His provocative line, 'apocalyptic thought is the mother of Christian theology', has called us to consider anew the pervasive influence of apocalyptic forms of thought upon the development of early Christianity.[1] An area where recent scholarship may have seriously underplayed the role of apocalyptic is in the Gospel of Matthew.

A seminal work for the emerging discipline of redaction criticism was Günther Bornkamm's essay, 'End-Expectation and Church in Matthew'.[2] In that 1956 essay Bornkamm carefully surveyed the connections between Matthean eschatology and the Matthean vision of the church. Nevertheless, very little subsequent work on Matthew has followed upon on the insights of the article. There are strong reasons why we should do so.

The first reason is simply that Bornkamm's argument is, for the most part, persuasive. The point of view of the Gospel of Matthew is powerfully shaped by a doctrine of the coming judgment. Bornkamm shows, for example, how deeply both the content and the structure of the Matthean discourses are dependent upon the doctrine of the coming kingdom. The second reason for following out the direction in which the article has pointed us is that Bornkamm may in fact have understated his case both in terms of the influence of apocalyptic upon Matthew and in terms of its significance for our understanding of the situation which called this Gospel forth. Thus the task of the present essay is easily set. Beginning from Professor

Bornkamm's essay, one asks, 'Just how pervasive was an apocalyptic/ judgment backdrop for the Gospel of Matthew?' 'What function(s) did the apocalyptic viewpoint serve in this Gospel?' And, 'what are the implications that the answers to those questions raise for the situation of the writer and intended readers of the Gospel?'

To begin with, some minor exceptions to Bornkamm's work need to be noted so that the role of the essay as a beginning point, but not as objective bedrock, can be established. There are several points where the article's perspective deserves correction in view of further research. For example, like almost all of us, Bornkamm uncritically accepts Matthew's dependence upon Mark and Q as a point of departure. The critic of today should at least note that several judgments about Matthew's work, made on that premise, may be more understandable if the reverse is true. Two brief examples should suffice since the source question is not central to our subject. First, in his assessment of the structure of the Sermon on the Mount, Bornkamm correctly notes the strong parallel between the Sermon and the Didache. The parallel is explained by Bornkamm as the result of a 'catechism pattern' that both writers are relying upon. Yet Bornkamm's argument itself would be much stronger as an argument for the direct redactional use of Matthew by the Didache.[3] Secondly, at several points Bornkamm's recognition of the Christian Jewish nature of Matthew's argument requires him to argue, as Marcan priorists have to argue, that Matthew is 're-Judaizing' the Hellenistic tradition found in Mk (or Q).[4] That argument, too, is turned upon its head in terms of common sense. It is much more likely that the early tradition was already Judaized and that Mark and Luke have Hellenized it.

There are also two specific areas of exegesis where serious exception needs to be taken to Bornkamm's argument. One is his treatment of the 'rich, young ruler' passage, Mt. 19.16-30. Again, of course, his argument is a traditional one of Matthew's deliberate use of the earlier Marcan tradition.[5] Here, however, Matthew's version is more formally pure and logically coherent than the Mark/Luke version, and it rests on a Jewish exegesis of Prov. 3.35-4.4. The Mark/Luke version probably rests on a mistranslation of Mt. 19.17.[6] So whether Matthew is in fact the original, or whether he simply knew the story in its more original Christian Jewish form, this pericope is a direct reflection of Matthean thinking about righteousness/eternal life/reward, but it is *not* a revision of Mark. Moreover, recognition of the thoroughly Jewish-Christian character of the Matthean pericope actually strengthens Bornkamm's point that the pericope underscores Matthew's connection of eternal life with radical obedience.

The other point of correction is in the exegesis of the parable chapter, Matthew 13. Here Bornkamm underplays the role of Matthew's clever exegesis of Isa. 6.9-10 and of Ps. 78.2 in his brief description of the passage. But he does catch the completely eschatological character of Matthew's interpretation of the parables better than most other recent interpreters.[7]

So, to take up our task from a mildly chastened starting point, even if there are flaws in Bornkamm's essay, it still provides us with a sound starting point from which to explore the role of apocalyptic in Matthew. The article lacked a summary conclusion. That may be one of the reasons for its languishing on the sidelines of recent Matthean criticism. So it is necessary to draw together the central thesis as a base for further exploration.

Bornkamm maintains that (1) the discourses in the Gospel are *all* dominated by the interaction of teaching for the church and teaching about the coming judgment. These two themes are so interwoven that one may say that the writer of the Gospel believes that Christians are precisely those who steer their lives by the coming return of Jesus and its attendant judgment. (2) Matthew's famous theme of 'the greater righteousness' required of Christians is just as tightly linked to expectations about the coming end of the world. (3) For the writer of Matthew, and perhaps for his church, 'a consistent and radical acceptance of the law'[8] is the heart of the message of Jesus and in some sense the key to the Kingdom. And (4) Matthew's view of Christ is also deeply colored by his apocalyptic hope. Jesus *will be* the triumphant returning Son of Man who will judge the world. That vision of Christ's future role colors every vision of Christ in Matthew. Thus, in every important area, Matthew's eschatological expectation has shaped his presentation of the gospel. That, in brief, is Bornkamm's thesis.

It is possible, as I have said, that he has understated the case. For, in addition to the thematic consideration of the apocalyptic influence on ecclesiology, ethics and Christology in Matthew, there is also the sheer weight of the cumulative repetition of the apocalyptic/

judgment language. Even is some of the apocalyptic language and tradition in the Gospel is taken over from tradition, as it surely is, the tone of the Gospel is strongly affected by the overall use of such language. One needs only to compare the Gospel of Luke, where similar tradition is carefully edited to take away the apocalyptic edge, to realize that the Gospel of Matthew breathes apocalyptic. Excluding chs. 24-25, where the numbers would of course be very large, there are more than twenty-five clear references in the Gospel to the coming judgment, or to the age to come. From the opening chapter telling of the birth of the Messiah to the closing scene promising his presence until the close of the age, Matthew keeps the readers' attention fixed upon the apocalyptic consequences of discipleship. From the warning message of John the Baptizer in 3.7-10 to the prefiguring of the day of resurrection in the crucifixion scene, Mt. 27.51-54, the Gospel is filled with references to judgment and the final day.

That heavy repetition may be underlined in a number of ways. Note, for example, the way in which the author closes each of the discourses of the Gospel. The Sermon on the Mount closes with a pair of highly apocalyptic, judgment-oriented scenes. The first, 7.21-23, about unChristian disciples, closes, 'And then I will declare to them, "I never knew you; depart from me, you evildoers"'. And the second, the allegory of the two houses, concludes, 'and it fell, and great was the fall of it'. Both paragraphs bear the mark of Matthean themes and language and are probably the writer/editor's creation. The mission discourse ends with an apocalyptic promise for the one who gives hospitality to a Christian emissary, 'Truly I say to you, he shall not lose his reward (Mt. 10.42)'. The closing scene of the parable discourse is the interpretation of the parable of the Net, 13.47-49, and its apocalyptic message is unmistakable. 'So it will be at the close of the age. The angels will come out and separate the evil from the righteous, and throw them into the furnace of fire; there men will weep and gnash their teeth (13.49-50)'. Here, too, it is nearly certain that this interpretation is the work of the Evangelist. That Matthew closes the discipleship discourse with an equally judgmental scene in the parable of the Unforgiving Servant ('So also my heavenly Father will do to every one of you, if you do not forgive your brother from your heart [18.35]') is well known, as is the fact that at least that line, if not the whole parable, is the work of the

Evangelist. And even if one counts the Woes chapter, 23, as a separate discourse, it, too, closes with a futuristic vision, 'For I tell you, you will not see me again, until you say, "Blessed is he who comes in the name of the Lord"' (23.39). And whatever the source of that line (directly from Ps. 118.26 or from the triumphal entry, 21.9) here it points forward to Jesus' final triumphant return. Of course, the last discourse, chs. 24–25, closes with the great judgment scene, a portrait of the judgment of the nations based on their reception of the disciples, which is almost certainly a Matthean creation.[9] Perhaps nothing else so clearly illustrates how deeply the apocalyptic strain is rooted in the perspective of the author of the Gospel as this consistent construction in the most distinctively Matthean part of the Gospel.

So the answer to our first question is clear. The apocalyptic/ judgment backdrop of the Gospel of Matthew is so pervasive that it indelibly colors the two great themes of the work, Christology and discipleship. For the author of the First Gospel not only adopted the apocalyptic viewpoint of some of his source materials, he also formed and framed the Jesus story solidly in the context of an apocalyptic perspective.

The next question is more difficult. What function does this demonstrable emphasis play in the Gospel? How does a focus on apocalyptic expectation fit into the author's overall view? To answer that we must consider the possible functions of apocalyptic thought. The question has been somewhat lost in recent efforts to grasp the literary forms of the genre of apocalyptic.[10] However, some of the functions of apocalyptic are clear enough to us. An apocalyptic expectation can serve the believer as a means of providing hope in a difficult time. That is fairly consistently the role that apocalyptic plays in Paul's thought; for example, Rom. 8.8-25, 1 Thess. 4.13-18. It is at least *one* of the functions of the Apocalypse itself; compare Rev. 21–22.5. And apocalyptic expectation can also function as a way of assuring the believer that the enemy, or evil ones, will be ultimately punished; for example, Rev. 19–20, Isa. 34.8-12. Or, an apocalyptic expectation can serve as a way to warn the believer to walk the straight and narrow path lest punishment strike the believer in the coming day of judgment. That is probably the thinking behind another Pauline paragraph, 1 Cor. 3.10-15, though in Paul the danger is muted. Insofar as there is evidence of an apocalyptic strain in pre-

AD 70 Pharisaic Judaism, it shared this 'ratification' character. Since, then, Matthew's Gospel is so strongly apocalyptic in tone, can one assess which of these functions the expectation serves?

First, one must say that all of the listed functions do occur in the Gospel. For example, the vision of hope is clearly present in the treatment of the 'sheep' in 25.31-46, in the blessings of the Beatitudes in 5.3-12, and in the promises to the commissioned ones in 10.29-33. There are also glimpses in Matthew of awaited vengeance for enemies and evil ones in such passages as the condemnation of the Pharisaic opponents in 12.30-37 or 23.29-36. But the dominant role which the apocalyptic expectation plays in the Gospel of Matthew is the role of avoiding punishment for misdeeds and receiving reward for good deeds. Within that dominant theme the pre-eminent concern of the author is the valuable role which such an expectation plays in directing the behavior of the disciples, that is, of the church. The author is far more concerned with the coming judgment as a testing point for the followers of Jesus than he is with it as punishment for enemies or as punishment for unbelievers, although these themes are probably taken for granted.

Indeed, in the only passage where he ventures to deal with the fate of 'the nations', 25.31-46, he uses a criterion for their judgment that is oriented to the disciples. That is, he says that the fate of 'the nations' depends on their acceptance or rejection of 'the least of these, my brethren', rather than the cumulative good or evil they have done. So it is clear that even in thinking about a universal judgment of mankind the author does not try to look beyond a very parochial viewpoint to consider the larger question of the ultimate justice of God and its relation to unbelievers.

When one collects, and then surveys, the host of future expectation passages in Matthew, their functional effect is as striking as their cumulative one. Time and again the future judgment, or Lord's return, or the return of the Son of Man, is pointed to not as a time of reward or of vindication but as one of potential punishment if one fails to do what Jesus commands. Consider as examples only the references in the Sermon on the Mount.

5.20 unless your righteousness exceeds that of the scribes and Pharisees, you will never enter the kingdom of heaven.

5.22 Everyone who is angry with his brother is liable to the judgment. . . and whoever says, 'You fool!', shall be liable to the hell of fire.

5.29 It is better that you lose one of your members than that your whole body be thrown into hell. (Cf. also 5.30.)

6.15 But if you do not forgive men their trespasses, neither will your Father forgive your trespasses.

7.14 For the gate is narrow and the way is hard, that leads to life, and those who find it are few.

7.23 And then I will declare to them, 'I never knew you; depart from me you evildoers'.

7.26 Everyone who hears these words of mine and does them will be like a foolish man who built his house upon the sand. . . .

The continued repetition of this punishment/judgment theme as a warning to the disciples throughout the Gospel is so powerful as to represent one of *the* major stresses of the book. If Matthew is, as many have said, a book of discipleship, it is also a book filled with warnings about punishment to come for failure in discipleship. The vision of the future in this Gospel is a two-edged motivator to obedient discipleship.

What accounts for this sharp Matthean view of the eschatological future? As Bornkamm said, only once does Matthew speak of a present reward or present reality of the Kingdom, in 12.28, and there the author is almost certainly employing an earlier tradition to buttress his version of the Beelzebul argument.[11] As a partial explanation of the legalist orientation of Matthew, Bornkamm goes on to say, 'Here the picture of the Jewish-Christian congregation arises which holds fast to the law and has not yet broken away from union with Judaism. . . This Jewish-Christian congregation shares the fate of the Jewish nation. . . '[12] That is, the wrestling point for Matthean Christians is still one of understanding their faith under the umbrella of Judaism. That dialogue is the basis for understanding not just Matthean legalism, but, I believe, the apocalyptic stress.

But such an assertion is controversial today. Several interpreters, most notably Jack Kingsbury and John Meier, have found in Matthew a Gospel much more church-oriented in the sense of a Christian community which is at the beginning of early catholicism, mixed with numerous Gentiles, and turning away from a strict Christian Judaism.[13] For such an interpretation, much of the Torah consciousness of the Gospel stems from the writer's sources, and not from the author himself. But, while one might grant that such a view of Matthew is possible, it seems to fly in the face of the multiple stresses of the Gospel. The apocalyptic/judgment motif is one of them. Better, then, to ask how we can account for a Christian Jewish Gospel that is so conservative on Torah and apocalyptic, almost sectarian, and yet one which is so Christocentric (or, better, as Kingsbury has shown us, centered on the Son of God) and which can close with a commission to go to all the nations.

The answer to that question must lie in the Matthean community's reactions to their recent experience. Some of those experiences we can trace with reasonable accuracy. This community has seen the tragedy of the Jewish War and the fall of Jerusalem (21.41; 22.7; etc.). Its members have known the trauma of persecution by Jewish and Gentile authorities (10.16-23). They have experienced bitter intra-family division over allegiance to Christ (10.34-38). Discipleship for this community has been a rocky path and there remains a sense of being beleaguered. So the Gospel must have been written in Syria/ Palestine in the aftermath of the disruption wrought on Judaism there by the First Revolt, and in the aftermath of some bitter internal Christian struggles about true discipleship (5.21; 7.21-23, etc.). In the decades immediately following the fall of Jerusalem, Matthew and his community have turned even more to an apocalyptic hope which looks steadily forward to the return of the Son of Man. In the meantime, they should devote themselves, says Matthew, to a strict obedience, strict as regards the Torah and stricter still as regards the teaching of Jesus.

A number of the studies of the enigmatic Great Commission have focused upon two parts of the Risen Christ's commands in 28.19-20, the command to go to the nations and the command to baptize them.[14] But such a stress ignores what may be for Matthew the key line of the commission, 'teaching them to observe *all* that I have commanded you'. For although Matthew envisions a mission to the Gentiles, it is one which calls such converts to strict adherence to Jesus' teachings, including Torah obedience. To Matthean Christians, as to their Pharisaic opponents, the practice of the community is what matters. It is precisely in the context of a Christian Judaism holding staunchly to its Jewish roots even while being forced to redefine its faith that Matthew's apocalyptic stress makes most sense.

Thus, in Matthew's vision, Jesus, the Son of God, will return at the judgment as the Messiah/Son of Man in Danielic fashion to judge the world. At that great arraignment two groups will have an edge in entry into the kingdom. One is, of course, the faithful followers of Jesus who have been obedient disciples, even through hardship and persecution. The other is the Gentiles who have given hospitality to the disciples of Jesus on their mission to the world (10.40-42 and 25.34-36). And the greatest edge for the disciples is that they already know the criteria of judgment. They have 'the secrets of the kingdom of Heaven' (13.11). So they can prepare themselves. Yet, woe to the disciple who falters! Simply put (but I do not believe oversimplified), that is the expectation of Matthew for the impending future. Naturally it colors everything else. Bornkamm was solidly correct: end expectation, ecclesiology and Christology are inextricably linked in the Gospel of Matthew's Christian Jewish presentation of the faith.

Normally, a critical essay should end here. But it cannot properly do so in view of the person to whom these essays are dedicated. There are two reasons for this. The first is that Lou Martyn has for twenty years been a somewhat lone voice calling the guild of New Testament scholars to responsibility for the content, the truth issue, the theological impact of what they study so diligently. And the second is that he and I have spent some memorable times debating the substantive, or as he likes to say *sachlich*, issues surrounding a reward and punishment apocalyptic view. So I would like to venture some admittedly risky thoughts about the value for the faith of Matthew's apocalyptic stress.

If apocalyptic is indeed the mother of Christian theology, and I believe Käsemann is largely correct in saying this, then Christian theology has a problem with its lineage. And that problem is not just Matthew's, or John of Patmos's. If the Christian movement was born in the call of John the Baptist and Jesus to 'repent, for the kingdom of heaven is at hand', then the fact that its roots are in an intensely eschatological and apocalyptic framework cannot be denied. Moreover, it has often been argued, and eloquently so by Käsemann and Bultmann, that whenever the Christian faith loses the sense of eschatological urgency, it is in an important sense apostate. A sense of the immediacy, the urgency, of the call of God to life or death is intrinsic to the message of Jesus, of Paul, of the Fourth Evangelist and of much of the rest of early Christian literature. I would agree that such a stress ought to be a vital part of any Christian theology.

However, the call to respond to God's gracious invitation, to turn from a self-centered deception to new life, to know oneself as forgiven and thus to be a forgiver is only one side of the eschatological coin. Matthew turns the coin over. In his hands the call becomes a warning to be obedient lest one's sandbuilt house crumble, to be faithful lest one be cast into the outer darkness, to keep one's lamp lit lest one miss the coming of the groom. That is, in Matthew's hands Christian eschatology becomes principally a warning of doom to come for those who fail.

One can, of course, say that it is a matter of emphasis, and that Jesus and John and Paul stress the invitation and the promise while Matthew stresses the threat, but that they all believe both. Again, I agree that such a view is probably true. But I do not believe that this historical fact makes the second side of Matthew's coin any more valid. For what is at stake is crucial. These types of eschatology inevitably help to define both God and the believer. If one claims that God has so designed the world that it is one great test, and one either earns life and its rewards or the outer darkness and its punishment, then one has portrayed an arbitrary and ultimately tyrannical God. For, all other questions aside, what possible value to God can punishment of the failed disciple or unbeliever be? And if one is to be a true disciple only in order to attain the kingdom's reward or to avoid the wrath of judgment, then a crass self-serving motive has been introduced into the new life. If the love of God, however badly thwarted by human sin, is not still the ultimate affirmation one makes about God, then what is distinctive at all about Christian faith? And if one believes that, except for 'threats of hell or hope of Paradise', one could truly 'live it up', then Christian claims to genuine virtue ring hollow. The Christian life surely ought to have its own intrinsic worth, or it has none at all!

So it seems to me that we need to acknowledge that Christian faith did arise out of the seedbed of late Jewish apocalyptic movements, but we should also recognize that its finest insights about God, human life, and discipleship are anchored in a radical understanding of the grace of God which negates the dark side of apocalyptic. In this age of pseudo-evangelical revival, when a rather blatant and negative apocalyptic fills the air, a recognition of and critique of the roles which apocalyptic/eschatological thought played in earliest Christianity is important. For my part it seems clear that the punishment side of the 'rewards and punishments' theology and ethic of apocalyptic is an obstacle and not an assistance to life and faith. It is no accident that most Christians have simply glossed over Matthew's strict apocalyptic stress in their reading and use of this great book. For that stress will not finally rest at home either with Jesus' call to trusting faith or with Paul's call to live by grace.

NOTES

1. On Käsemann's emphasis see, for example, 'On the Subject of Primitive Christian Apocalyptic', in *New Testament Questions of Today* (Philadelphia: Fortress Press, 1969), p. 137.

2. Günther Bornkamm, Gerhard Barth, and Heinz Joachim Held, *Tradition and Interpretation in Matthew* (London: SCM Press, 1963), pp. 15-51.

3. Bornkamm, 'End-Expectation', p. 17.

4. *Ibid.*, pp. 20-22, 25-26.

5. *Ibid.*, pp. 22-30.

6. See L. Cope, *Matthew: A Scribe Trained for the Kingdom of Heaven* (CBQMS 5; Washington: The Catholic Biblical Association of America, 1976), pp. 111-19.

7. *Ibid.*, pp. 16-20, 22-23.

8. Bornkamm, 'End-Expectation', p. 37.

9. Here, too, I am in disagreement with Bornkamm, who maintains that 25.31-46 is a scene of universal judgment ('End-Expectation', pp. 23-24). Compare L. Cope, 'Matthew 25.31-46, 'The Sheep and the Goats' Reinterpreted', *Novum Testamentum* 11 (1969), pp. 32-44. Most recent interpreters concede that the Matthean judgment scene is about the 'nations', excluding the disciples, although it is harder to say whether or not Israel is included.

10. Two examples of the current focus on the genre issue and apocalyptic are *Apocalypticism in the Mediterranean World and the Near East* (ed. David Hellholm; Tübingen, 1983) and *Semeia* 36 (1986) where the entire issue is devoted to the subject.

11. Bornkamm, 'End-Expectation', p. 34; see also p. 29.

12. *Ibid.*, p. 32. It is true that Bornkamm seemed to back away from this judgment in the later essay on the Matthean Great Commission, 'Der Auferstandene und der Irdische (Matt 28.16-20)', in *Zeit und Geschichte: Dankesgabe an Rudolf Bultmann zum 80. Geburtstag* (ed. E. Dinkler; Tübingen: J.C.B. Mohr, 1964), pp. 171-91. But the essay by Schuyler Brown, 'The Matthean Community and the Gentile Mission', *Novum Testamentum*

22 (1980), pp. 193-221, convincingly shows that Bornkamm's initial impulse was correct. Brown says, 'The general situation is clear, and it surely reflects the development which led up to the final break at Jamnia. The bitter polemic against Pharisaism, which permeates the entire gospel, points to the tragic predicament of a community whose attachment to Judaism was being exposed to the harshest possible test'.

'Under such circumstances the option of strengthening the community by admitting to baptism the gentiles who had associated themselves with it and of actively seeking gentile converts must have seemed overpoweringly attractive to many of Matthew's Christians, although others would have considered it a temptation to apostasy, born out of desperation' (pp. 216-17).

But, 'as long as Matthew's community remained a part of Judaism, circumcision would be required for any gentile seeking admission. The question of circumcision does not arise as a separate issue in the gospel because the question facing the Matthean community was not whether to circumcise gentiles, but whether to actively missionize them' (p. 218).

We only have difficulty with such a view of a post-70 Syrian Jewish Christian community because our view of the development of the church is erroneously filtered through Pauline and Lucan lenses. The evidence is growing that there was a Torah obedient Christian Jewish mission to Gentiles. See J.L. Martyn, 'A Law Observant Mission to Gentiles: the Background to Galatians', *Michigan Quarterly Review* (Summer, 1983), pp. 221-36. In this whole issue of the rediscovery of Christian Judaism, to which Lou Martyn has contributed so much, it is worth noting that the Gospel of Matthew, when not read through Lucan/Harnackian eyes, may well be a product of a Christian Judaism exactly parallel to (or derivative from) the kind of Christian community that produced a law-observant mission to Gentiles in the time of Paul's activity in Asia, Macedonia and Greece.

13. A summary of earlier interpretation on this question is found in Joachim Rohde, *Rediscovering the Teaching of the Evangelists* (Philadelphia: Westminster Press, 1968), pp. 47-112. Jack Kingsbury's work, which recognizes the Jewishness of Matthew but which sees the church as a mixture of Jews and Gentiles (though he does not say whether or not the Gentiles are circumcised), is available in *Matthew: Structure, Christology, Kingdom* (Philadelphia: Fortress, 1975), and *Matthew as Story* (Philadelphia: Fortress, 1986). For John Meier's point of view see 'Law and History in Matthew's Gospel', *Analecta Biblica* 71 (1976), or the commentary, *Matthew* (Wilmington: Michael Glazier, 1980).

14. John Meier, 'Salvation-History in Matthew: in Search of a Starting Point', *CBQ* 37 (1975), pp. 203-15, Georg Strecker, *Der Weg der Gerechtigkeit* (3rd edn; Göttingen: Vandenhoeck & Ruprecht, 1971), pp. 208-14, and others have either downplayed the Matthean line, 'Teaching them to obey *all* that I have commanded you' or have denied that for Matthew Jesus' teaching includes Torah obedience.

ESCHATOLOGICAL EXISTENCE IN MATTHEW AND PAUL
COINCIDENTIA OPPOSITORUM

Robin Scroggs

Strange things happen on the way to *Festschriften*. When I was asked to participate in a volume honoring J. Louis Martyn, I knew him as a valuable contributor to current New Testament scholarship, and I was happy to accept the challenge because of his stature as a creative leader among scholars. Little did I know then that before this volume would be published I would count myself as close colleague, dialogue partner, and, indeed, successor to him at Union Theological Seminary. I offer this paper to him out of the admiration I have had for him over the years. The turn of events, however, has added much fear and trembling to my offering. It did not take many days on the Union campus to learn from both students and faculty that Lou Martyn is loved and appreciated for many qualities in addition to his insightful scholarship. One can succeed him, but he cannot be replaced.

For those open to seeing differences of viewpoint among New Testament authors, Matthew and Paul have traditionally seemed poles apart, perhaps even irreconcilably so. From these opposite poles they appear most obviously different in their descriptions of Christian existence. The Apostle looks to a past event of sheer grace on which to found a life based on freedom. The Evangelist looks ahead to the reward of eternal life based on obedience to the Torah, albeit a Torah interpreted by Jesus. For Paul the present life of the believer is in part a realized existence of the new creation; for Matthew, the kingdom of God appears to be a postponed reality, to be realized only in the final future. Indeed, how close is Matthew to the view Paul attaches to his opponents: justification by grace versus justification by works of the law?

The seasoned scholar will recognize, of course, in this polarization oversimplified schematization; yet it is inaccurate to ignore the significant differences in vantage point. That Matthew and Paul *begin* at opposite poles seems, at least to me, clear. The one asserts the continued validity of Torah; the other, that the Torah is at an end.

With regard to the formation of the Christian self, however, beginnings are not as important as endings. When both the Apostle and the Evangelist have finished their descriptions of the self under Christ, how far apart are they then? In this regard the crucial determination is not where they begin but where they *end*.

Nicholas of Cusa, the great Renaissance philosopher and theologian, may provide for us a provocative perspective. He invented a phrase, *coincidentia oppositorum* (the 'coincidence of opposites') to show how seemingly opposing statements about God in a *via negativa* method could be asserted and the opposition overcome in the ultimate divine reality. The image used is a circle revolving at infinite velocity. At this velocity opposite points on the circle coincide.[1]

Using this notion of the *coincidentia oppositorum* in a wildly metaphorical manner, I want to apply it as a kind of *Leitmotif* to aid our interpretations of Christian selfhood given by the two authors under discussion. I accept the judgment that Paul and Matthew begin at opposite places on the circle. I argue that when the two have 'moved' through their full depiction of what this formation looks like, they occupy the same final point. Their opposite beginning points ultimately coincide. The character formed by Matthew's movement looks very much like the person formed by Paul's. Perhaps they are after all the same character?

The Shared World

Unless two structures coexist in the same world, they cannot even be compared. Or, to use the analogy of the circle, unless two thinkers are on the same circle, even their distance from each other cannot be assessed. Clearly there is a shared cultural world in which Paul and Matthew live. Before the differences in their description of Christian existence can be explored, what they have in common must be briefly enumerated. Some of the similarities may seem so obvious as to be trite; just because of this obviousness they need to be before our consciousness.

Both are *Jews*. That Matthew was Jewish has actually been disputed in some quarters, an untenable position in my judgment.[2] Both are *Hellenistic* Jews. Both are '*Pharisaic*' Jews. Paul is because he says he is (Phil. 3.5). Matthew is although he says he isn't! He has Jesus protest violently against the Pharisees; yet the Gospel shows an agreement in the basic posture towards the Torah with the general Pharisaic movement, however that movement may have evolved or been named by the time of Matthew himself.[3] One could even interpret the Gospel as an intra-Pharisaic dispute, of which there were many throughout the period.

Both the Apostle and the Evangelist think within an *apocalyptic* framework. That is, both believe that the ultimate victory of God is to be revealed in a final conclusion to the present ambiguity of history. Both, as is to be expected, have their own distinctive interpretation of the framework, neither of which destroys the framework itself. Both focus on *Jesus Christ* as the central moment within the apocalyptic structure, from which perspective all else is to be interpreted.

There is basic agreement that commitment to Jesus Christ *changes human life*. Here is the point which is perhaps more to be proven than assumed. Certainly there are wide differences between the two about how such a transformation occurs and how it is described. Finally, both stress the seriousness of *ethical performance*. Matthew, with the teaching of Jesus as the focus, clearly emphasizes the centrality of such performance in the Christian life. And while Paul begins with sheer grace as the basis for salvation, he does, as all know, have high expectation of ethical action from his churches.

Such basic agreements indicate that the Apostle and the Evangelist work from the same basic circle and that their structures can thus be compared. In what follows I will lay out for each thinker the beginning point, show the movement of the thought in the structure of each, and suggest as a conclusion that their resting points on the circle coincide even if their beginning points are at opposing places. There is a true *coincidentia oppositorum*.

Paul

The movement of Paul's thinking from the beginning point of grace to the resting point of a transformed life resulting in ethical performance is basically well-known and much of it can be stated in brief summaries.[4] Each statement, of course, will cover many disputed side-issues which cannot be pursued in this paper.

God's Act of Grace

The beginning point is Paul's conviction that God has acquitted the world of humanity by the sending of the Son. Acquittal is necessary because humans have refused to live in obedience to the gracious, creator God and have substituted for the true God a false image of a God who demands righteous performance as a condition for eternal life.[5] Obedience to the true God would have meant acceptance of life as gift. Disobedience has meant the substitution of the performance principle of justification by works for justification by faith.

In the Christ event, made known in death and resurrection, God has cut through the wall of willful ignorance in which people think they must create their own salvation, re-revealing His true identity as a God who gives life and thus making possible true obedience once more. Salvation is thus possible *now*, in this time and space, because salvation *is* the faithful living out of the perspective of life as gift. The eschatological judgment has already occurred. Eschatological existence and eschatological condemnation are present realities.

Annulment of Torah as the Means to Salvation

This radical understanding of God's grace has no room for law *as the means to salvation*. In fact, as Paul tries to make clear in Romans, while the law has its rightful place because it originates from God's will, Judaism, *as Paul understands it*, has drastically and tragically misread God's will and distorted the law into a system of salvation *because* it has replaced the God of grace by a false god of the performance principle.[6]

> I witness about them [unbelieving Israel] that they have zeal for God, but it is not informed. For being ignorant of the righteousness which comes from God, and seeking to stand on their own, they are not obedient to God's righteousness. For the end of the law is Christ for the righteousness of all who believe (Rom. 10.2-4).

If salvation is by gift, it cannot be by human achievement on the basis of conformity to the law.

The Transformation of the Self

The saving, creative act of the creator God breaks through the false world based on the false god and makes possible a new person and a new community. Not forgiveness, but a radical shift, a change of worlds is the result. 'If anyone is in Christ, he is a new creation. The old has passed away; behold the new has come into existence' (2 Cor. 5.17).

This is indeed a transformation of human reality because the person has entered a world different from the old one he or she had been inhabiting. The self based on acceptance of life is qualitatively different from the one based on the necessity of performance. The person sees himself/herself and his/her community differently *because* he/she now sees God differently. And the new community created by God's act in Christ, the church, helps sustain the confidence of the individual in the reality of the new.

The Transformation of the Nous

The essential dimension of this transformation is the new perception of the mind, the *nous*.

> I exhort you, brethren, through the mercies of God, to offer your selves as a living sacrifice, pleasing to God, your *reasoning* service. And do not be conformed to this age, but be transformed by the making-new of your *mind*, that you may *come to know* what is the will of God, that which is good and pleasing and perfect (Rom. 12.1f.).

This key passage, through its use of words pointing to perception (here italicized), shows that the change of world means a change of basic perception. With bold affirmation, Paul claims that the transformed person is able on her own to learn what is the will of God for her life. Obedience to the true God clarifies perception about one's duties in relation to self and to others.[7]

The transformed mind is thus the basis for ethical performance. Paul refers to this ability also in Philippians. 'And it is my prayer that your love may abound more and more with knowledge and discernment, so that you may approve [the word is the same as that in Romans translated above as 'come to know'] what is excellent, and may be pure and blameless for the day of Christ, filled with the fruits of righteousness which come through Jesus Christ, to the glory and praise of God' (Phil. 1.9-11).

Two implications are crucial to note here. 1. Only after the person has accepted the gift of life and is transformed can one begin to speak, in Paul's theological structure, of ethical insight. Knowing how to act is the result, not the cause, of being. 2. The basis of ethical insight does not lie in any external code such as the Torah, but in the eschatological ability of the transformed person to perceive the will of God. The radical relativizing of the Torah's importance in establishing and maintaining the eschatological relationship with God is obvious here. Equally clear is the great distance from Matthew's stucture.

The basic eschatological-ethical stance of the transformed person is thus established from within, not governed by any set of external rules. Paul *does* occasionally appeal to external authorities, but these sporadic occurrences demonstrate, rather than call into question, Paul's independence from any kind of normative rules ethic. He can appeal to the teaching of Jesus (1 Cor. 7.10f.). He can cite Scripture to support his judgment (e.g. Rom. 12.20). He can just as easily (and more frequently) bring in popular Hellenistic wisdom (e.g. the catalogues of vices). The eclecticism of this approach makes it clear that there is no single set of rules which control character formation. Outside rules support and confirm interior insight.[8]

Ethical Performance

Despite the fact that the eschatological self is grounded in sheer gift, Paul so emphatically stresses good deed that he almost seems in contradiction to himself. This tension in his theological structure has always been noted and variously 'solved' by scholars. Perhaps no completely self-consistent solution is possible. At least it is clear that Paul sees no inconsistency.

Why? Clearly one must begin with *being*, but if the being is true eschatological being, it inevitably leads to the right *doing*. Eschatological character formation involves the right relating to others. The Apostle exudes confidence in this connection. The *self*-confidence of Paul in his own ethical insight and performance is famous, perhaps notorious. To think that Paul jealously limits this confidence to apostolic prerogative is, however, unfair to his thinking. Rom. 12.1f.; Phil. 1.9-11; 3.15 show that he expects all believers to participate in the insight, and passages too numerous to cite indicate his expectation of performance in others equal to his own.

The Final Point: Portrait of Eschatological Existence

We are now at the resting place in the journey through Paul's theological structure: the result of eschatological character formation. What does the person look like? Specifically we need to put the question in relation to Torah. How is such a person like or unlike a person conformed to Torah?

Elsewhere I have shown that the key words Paul uses to characterize the eschatological self are freedom, joy, peace, and love.[9] Love, certainly the most famous but equally the most ambiguous of the terms, is given more specificity by Paul's emphasis upon the 'upbuilding' of neighbor and community. Any act which serves to build up the other is an act of love. Indeed, upbuilding takes precedence over other legitimate options, when there is a possible conflict, as the discussion about eating meat demonstrates (1 Cor. 10.23–11.1). The overruling perspective is to seek the good of the neighbor rather than one's own (10.24).

In none of this is it explicitly said that conformity to Torah is involved. And yet it is almost certain that Paul believes such a person is in fact conformed to Torah. 'The law is holy, and the commandment is holy and just and good' (Rom. 7.12). As *description* of righteousness Paul can say the highest things about Torah. Only when the law is misinterpreted as *prescription* does he speak negatively about it.

Furthermore, life in faith confirms the law (Rom. 3.31). Specifically love fulfills the law. In a sweeping statement Paul writes:

> Owe no one anything, except to love one another; for he who loves his neighbor has fulfilled the law. The commandments, 'You shall not commit adultery, You shall not kill, You shall not steal, You shall not covet', *and any other commandment*, are summed up in this sentence, 'You shall love your neighbor as yourself'. Love does no wrong to a neighbor; therefore love is the fulfilling of the law (Rom. 13.8-10; cf. also Gal. 5.14).

The inclusiveness of Paul's equation of Torah fulfillment with the eschatological self acting in love is indicated by his addition to the list of specific commandments taken from the Ten, 'and any other commandment'.

Thus the final point in the movement takes us precariously back to a dialogical relation with the beginning. Torah used as a means to salvation is contrary to God's intent in giving the Torah; but Torah as a declaration of God's will for humanity is 'holy'. Torah as *prescription* is wrong; Torah as *description* is true. As always in his dialogical theology, Paul walks a tightrope. One must affirm both things about Torah. To say only one of them is to fall off into one or another false position.

Inevitably the question about the so-called 'ritual' requirements of Torah arises at this point. When Paul, in the passage of Romans cited just above, lists items from the ten commandments, he cites only those that are 'ethical'. Does this mean that the Apostle has jettisoned the ritual rules, so that only the ethical retain significance as description of eschatological existence?

This claim is repeatedly made, but it has a decidedly 'Protestant' ring to it, and I for one resist 'reading in' to Paul the anti-ritual bias of some forms of Protestantism. Certainly rabbinic theology does not make such a distinction. Where would Paul have learned such a dichotomy, if indeed he actually makes it? Nevertheless, it has to be admitted that *some* sort of distinction is operative in Paul. The issue is, however, more complicated than some have suggested.

Paul does not doubt that believers in their present life need to turn toward God and perform ritual actions (e.g. 1 Cor. 12–14). He clearly does not wish to compromise the first commandment (e.g. 1 Cor. 8.4-7; 10.14). But about all else he shows a flexibility that is frustrating to scholarly urges to provide neat patterns. What lies behind the flexibility is not indifference to the importance of ritual actions but a conviction that genuine ritual actions stem from the unique faithful individual.

Hence different kinds of actions—whether eating meat or not eating meat, observing a day or not observing it—can be faithful ritual actions *if* the action comes from the individual's conviction that this is what he or she must do to praise God. 'So, whether you eat or drink, or whatever you do, do all to the glory of God' (1 Cor. 10.31). But the converse is also true. Ritual actions performed without internal conviction are *not* faithful acts, no matter how ritually correct they may be, from some community's perspective. The rubric here is found in Rom. 14.23: 'For whatever does not proceed from faith is sin'.

The Apostle himself can live within both the ritual rubrics of Judaism or the Gentile church (1 Cor. 9.19-23). He can become 'as one under the law' precisely because he knows his salvation does not depend upon being under the law. He can also live 'outside the law' as well. Justification by grace frees one *from* the bondage to perform, but it also frees one *for* the use of various ritual actions as a vehicle for the praise of God.

Paul thus does not in any way devalue ritual actions. At the same time he can be seen to relativize any specific set of actions, even those found in Torah. For those who in Torah actions have learned to express their faith in God, the ritual life described in Torah is the appropriate way. For those for whom such actions are strange and uncomfortable, other kinds of actions are legitimate. Does Paul set aside the ritual commands of Torah? The answer has to be yes and no. But it cannot be said that he denies that they *can* be a vehicle for faithful worship of God.

Matthew

To discover Matthew's movement to his point of conclusions, a totally different methodology must be followed than that used to explore Paul. With Paul I attempted to reconstruct this theological logic, using scattered texts to illustrate the various stages. There was no single text I could follow from beginning to end in which his progression could be charted.

The Gospel, to the contrary, is a text that is story. It has a plot and to be true to the author's intent, the plot line must be followed faithfully.[10] That is, I assume that the author tells me what he wants to tell me *when* he wants to. Thus any particular statement in the Gospel *cannot* be lifted from its story-context without distorting its meaning. Proof-texting always has its problems; given the plot-character of the Gospels, such a method can only be unfaithful to the intent of the Gospel author. The advantage of interpreting Matthew over Paul here is obvious. While we had to reconstruct the Apostle's movement, the Evangelist explicitly provides us with his.

The plot of Matthew is a rich and complex tapestry. I can only call attention to those threads and the partial design that I see as illuminating our subject. Doubtless there are other threads that are involved in the design that I have missed seeing. I trust, however, that the ones followed below are the most important. I will, of course, skip from one pericope to another, *but I will always take them in the order established by the Evangelist.*

1. *The Setting of the Sermon on the Mount* (4.12–5.1). Despite the

Jewish tone to the Gospel, something everyone recognizes, Matthew, more than any of the other evangelists, sets the ministry of Jesus firmly within a universal context of Jew *and* Gentile. Jesus moves to Capernaum, which is identified as 'Galilee of the Gentiles' (4.15). Not only does his fame spread abroad, but people come to him from 'all Syria' (meaning the entire Roman province?), and the crowds that follow him include people from the Decapolis.

This setting has important implications for the setting of the following sermon. 'Seeing the crowds, he went up on the mountain, and when he sat down his disciples came to him' (5.1). Who are the disciples here? They cannot be just the twelve, because Matthew does not introduce them until their establishment in ch. 10. Thus the disciples must come from or represent 'the crowds', and that word can, given the context, only refer to the crowds of the preceding verses, that is, a mixed group of followers, both Jews and Gentiles.[11] Matthew wants to affirm that the teaching which follows is addressed to Gentiles as well as to Jews. And this means that what Jesus says in his teaching is incumbent upon the Gentile (as well as Jewish) readers of his Gospel (cf. 28.16-20)!

2. *The Validity of the Torah* (5.17-20). That what the disciples first hear is the comfort of the beatitudes must not be forgotten. We must skip, however, to the affirmation that the Torah is binding upon believers. The ambiguity of vv. 17f., whether the fulfillment and accomplishment of the law and the prophet means the culmination in Jesus Messiah or the continued validity of Torah requirements, will never be solved, and interpreters will doubtless always differ.[12] Probably for Matthew both meanings are in his mind. Verse 19, however, is unambiguous: 'Whoever then relaxes one of the least of these commandments and teaches people so, shall be called least in the kingdom of heaven; but he who does them and teaches them shall be called great in the kingdom of heaven'. Whatever it means to be 'called least in the kingdom', that the sentence as a whole asserts the validity of the entire Torah on the reader, Jew or Gentile, seems to me without doubt.[13] This is the rule for Matthew's church.

Thus we have a first statement about character formation. Obedience to God means submission to the entire realm of Torah. The law must be obeyed. Indeed it is to be obeyed in a righteousness that 'exceeds that of the scribes and Pharisees' if one is to 'enter the kingdom of heaven' (v. 20). What the 'more than' means is stated in the next section, the antitheses.

3. *The Antitheses* (5.21-48). In six sweeping judgments, Jesus shows how the believer must live a life that exceeds the righteousness of the scribes and Pharisees. 'You have heard that it was said, but I say to you'. 'You have heard' must mean the interpretation of the law given in the Jewish community—*as Matthew understood that interpretation*. Whether this was *in fact* how the Torah was being interpreted by Jewish authorities in Matthew's day does not need to be explored for our purposes. 'But I say to you' has to mean the interpretation of the Torah that the Evangelist believes is consonant with the will of Jesus Messiah.

In view of v. 20, the Evangelist has to think that the teaching of Jesus in these antitheses points to the true meaning of Torah requirements. That is, he must believe that the antitheses reveal the true meaning of the law. Scholars continue to debate the question whether some of the antitheses actually abrogate rather than intensify Torah requirements.[14] Whatever the *logic* of the matter is, what Matthew *intends* to say seems to me secured by vv. 17-20, which must be seen as an introduction to the antitheses. Jesus in no way abrogates Torah; he shows how to be truly obedient to it.

Not only does Matthew think the antitheses reveal what true Torah obedience means, he thinks conformity to this obedience possible and necessary, without which no one 'will enter the kingdom of heaven' (v. 20). This insistence has always aroused either fright or incredulity in readers. How can one live without anger, without lust? How can one practice non-resistance and love of enemies? And, as all are painfully aware, the climax of the section is the amazing declaration: 'You, therefore, must be perfect (*teleios*), as your heavenly Father is perfect' (v. 48).

Or is 'perfect' (RSV) the correct translation of *teleios*? Certainly it seems to fit the extreme exhortations of the antitheses. There is, however, an inclination among contemporary scholars to give a broader reading, one consonant with both the Greek word (which has a number of meanings) and Jewish thinking implied by the Hebrew/Aramiac word (*tamim*) which would most likely have been translated into Greek as *teleios*. Without getting into the details of the argument, I can only point out that 'whole', 'complete', 'integrated', are better readings of *teleios* than the traditionally accepted 'perfect'.[15] In any case Matthew expects exacting performance on the part of the believer, actually believes that the believer can live up to the 'counsels of perfection' of the antitheses. One thing is important to add. The *perspective* of the antitheses is almost entirely an interest in relations with people, rather than piety toward God (a topic that is, indeed, addressed in the next section of the sermon).

4. *The Gentle Yoke* (11.25-30). Assuming that Matthew worked with some form of the Markan text before him, his structuring of the Gospel is at one point clear. Through ch. 11 he uses various material from his fund of sources but creates his own structure. Beginning with ch. 12, however, he is content to follow the structure Mark had already created. This suggests that chs. 1–11 are meant as an entity in themselves. The Evangelist's intention is reasonably clear. He wants to set out the major activities of Jesus Messiah as teacher, miracle worker, and as creator of a mission to Israel. Chapter 11 functions at least in part as a statement of the priority of Jesus over John as the Messiah. Mt. 11.25-30 then serves as the conclusion to the first part of the Gospel, and we would expect that in it Matthew gives us a summary of what he takes the meaning of the entire section to be. This expectation is, I believe, met.

On the one hand, Jesus is depicted as the revealer of the will of God. 'all things have been delivered (*paredothē*) to me by my Father'—using a word that is in some contexts a technical term for the passing on of tradition. God is the ultimate 'traditioner'! By this time the reader is clear about one thing: Jesus functions as the correct revealer of the meaning of Torah. Indeed, using a traditional metaphor for the acceptance of tradition, Jesus says to the reader: 'Take my yoke upon you, and learn from me' (v. 29). 'My yoke' means here the acceptance of Torah obedience *as interpreted by* Jesus Messiah.

And yet, despite the fact that the antitheses would seem to frighten, acceptance of Jesus' yoke is in this passage presented as something not only possible but easy to accept. 'For my yoke is easy, and my burden is light' (v. 30). And he has already exhorted: 'Come to me, all who labor and are heavy laden, and I will give you rest' (v. 28). Indeed, those who come to Jesus are not the 'wise and understanding' but 'babes'. The interpretation of Torah by Jesus must be one that makes sense to the uneducated, one which perhaps cuts through what the uninitiated often perceive as tedious legalisms (the view of the 'outsider'). It must be one which, despite its 'perfectionism' seems desirable and attainable. At any rate, Matthew must expect his readers to perceive Jesus' yoke as such, and this must be kept in mind as we proceed.

5. *The True Interpretation of the Torah* (15.1-20). Following Mark, Matthew incorporates the long section on debate with the Pharisees and scribes (Mk 7.1-23). Characteristically he shortens and rearranges the Markan text. But Matthew also makes significant changes and additions to his *Vorlage*, and these reveal the next stage of understanding he wishes the reader to appropriate.

Perhaps most importantly he deletes Mark's statement which communicates precisely the point Mark wants to make—that Jesus annuls the part of the written Torah that deals with food taboos ('Thus he declared all foods clean'—Mk 7.19). Since for Matthew the entire Torah is incumbent upon believers, he cannot allow that interpretation to stand (which is, in fact, forced by Mark upon the material). Instead he has Jesus draw the conclusion in relation to the *oral* tradition: 'To eat with unwashed hands does not defile a person' (v. 20).[16]

That the debate deals with oral rather than written law is made unmistakably clear by Matthew's insertion of vv. 12-14.

> Then the disciples came and said to him, 'Do you know that the Pharisees were offended when they heard this saying?' He answered, 'Every plant which my heavenly Father has not planted will be rooted up. Let them alone; they are blind guides. And if a blind man leads a blind man, both will fall into a pit.

This amplifies the distinction already made between tradition and 'word of God' (vv. 6, 9), and sharpens the rejection of the oral tradition as taught by the 'Pharisees'. Clearly the Evangelist is advising the reader to see the falseness of *that* particular interpretation of the meaning of Torah.

For just as clearly the issue is not between accepting the pure 'word of God' and rejecting oral interpretation. There is no such thing as uninterpreted Torah. *Every* community must interpret for itself the 'true' meaning of Torah; *thus every community has an 'oral' tradition.* The issue now becomes explicit that has been there from the beginning. If Matthew's community accepts the Torah it must provide an interpretation of it. One of the key functions of Matthew's Jesus is to provide this 'correct' interpretation, as we have already seen Jesus do in the sermon.[17]

6. *The Hermeneutic of Active Love* (19.16-22; 22.34-40). Matthew here uses Markan material to intensify his understanding of the meaning of 5.17-20, the necessity of keeping the Torah, but he cleverly alters the *Vorlage* to communicate his meaning: Yes, one must obey the Torah, but to say that is not to say enough or even what is crucial. *What does it mean to obey the Torah?* Increasingly, throughout the last part of the Gospel, the reader is confronted with the Evangelist's wrestling with that issue.

In 19.16-22 he subtly reworks Mark's story about the wealthy seeker for eternal life (Mk 10.17-22)—the artistry of his editing can only be seen with the aid of a parallel. In the Markan story the commandments lifted up are already 'ethical' in character. Matthew repeats Mark's list (omitting one) but adds as a climactic commandment: 'You shall love your neighbor as yourself' (v. 19). We must not let our familiarity with this Leviticus command obscure the fact that here is its *first* appearance in Matthew. It now takes its place among the ethical segment of the ten commandments as a guiding rule for one's Torah obedience. To be obedient to the Torah means to perform the ethical acts listed. This of course does not mean one may ignore any of the other commandments. It means rather that *one must fulfill all the commandments, seeing in them all an expression of love of one's neighbor*.

But even this is not the *ultimate* hermeneutic, because one can still ask the question: '*How* do I love my neighbor as myself?' The answer in Mark and Matthew: Give up all one's possessions so as to become a genuine follower of Jesus. Total almsgiving and total poverty now stand as the hermeneutical principle which explains what it *really* means to fulfill the commandments.

Matthew, however, changes Mark at one important point. He introduces that troublesome word, *teleios*, which he used to form the climax to the antitheses (5.48). 'If you would be *teleios*, go, sell what you possess and give to the poor' (19.21). Just as *teleios* described the kind of action demanded of the hearer of the sermon, so here it points to the state out of which the law is totally fulfilled.

Above I suggested that *teleios* is best taken to mean 'whole' rather than literally 'perfect'. It is just possible that in this pericope another nuance to the word surfaces. This possibility is tied in with another apparently slight alteration Matthew makes in the Markan text. Matthew says the questioner is young, *neaniskos*. Both of his added words *can* have cultic signification. *Neaniskos* may indicate a neophyte, an initiate, while *teleios* is used at times to denote a person who is already initiated. Does this text as reworked by Matthew describe the ideal qualifications for initiation into the Christian community? The young man is, in fact, exhorted to 'follow me', a phrase of invitation to true discipleship. If so, then the criterion of accepting the Torah as obligatory is not in itself enough to be a full disciple. One must also accept Matthew's hermeneutical principle as well.

The second pericope (22.34-40), concerning the chief commandments, is also a Markan text reworked by Matthew to clarify his perspective. In his version the question is hostile, and Mark's conclusion is completely replaced by a different rejoinder. After pointing to love of God and love of neighbor as the great commandments, Jesus concludes: 'On these two commandments hang all the law and the prophets' (22.40).

The wording, 'hang all the law and the prophets', puts the pericope into the rabbinic discussion of the perspective from which Torah is given its meaning.[18] These two commandments here receive the status of the key viewpoint from which the entire Torah is to be interpreted, again without any suggestion that the other Torah requirements are devalued, much less abrogated.

7. *Hermeneutical Conflict* (23.23). Chapter 23 presents serious difficulties to the interpreter, since it is virtually impossible to reconcile the positive judgment on the pharisaic oral tradition in vv. 2f. with the explicitly negative statement in ch. 15. Most scholars today correctly conclude that 23.2f. does not represent the present thought of the Evangelist.[19]

At any rate, the author shows in this chapter great hostility and bitterness; in his attitude to the Pharisees he is consistent with other places in the Gospel. They are still 'hypocrites' and 'blind guides' (v. 24). But in what sense are the Pharisees 'blind guides'?

In 23.23f., Matthew gives his answer. They are blind because they 'strain out a gnat and swallow a camel' (v. 24). With this extreme hyperbole, the Evangelist suggests that their hermeneutic is misplaced. A somewhat more rational reason has just been given in v. 23.

> Woe to you, scribes and Pharisees, hypocrites! for you tithe mint and dill and cummin, and have neglected the weightier matters of the law, justice and mercy and faithfulness; these you ought to have done, without neglecting the others.

This is again argument over the principle of interpretation. Matthew charges his opponents not with too-scrupulous obedience to the law of tithing but with so concentrating on such scrupulousness that at least *de facto* it has become the principle of interpretation of the entire Torah.[20] And this has meant, again according to the judgment of the Evangelist, that the proper principles, justice, mercy, and faithfulness, have been ignored. If one begins, so thinks Matthew, with the 'weightier' principles, the lighter ones will be obeyed and fall in their proper place. To strain out a gnat and swallow a camel means, in contemporary metaphor, to fail to see the forest for the trees. Matthew's hermeneutical principle is consistent, if expressed in other terms, with his emphasis upon love for neighbor as lived out in self-giving.

8. *The Final Statement: Hermeneutic in Action* (25.31-46). With this grand, eschatological vision, Jesus ends his teaching in the Gospel. It thus represents the climactic message the earthly Jesus has to give and functions as the last point on the movement of the circle we have been attempting to describe. On the surface, the message seems simply, if eloquently stated. Underneath, however, there are a number of difficult problems standing in the way of a clear intepretation. The description which follows is based on my conclusion that the text, *as Matthew intends it*, is a vision describing how all people, regardless of national or religious affiliation, will be judged in the eschatological day.

Given all we have said so far, the most startling feature of the parable is what is *not* included. Any reference to Torah is completely absent; whether one acts to care for persons in distress is all that matters. Furthermore, they have acted *unknowingly*. They have not performed in order to be saved; they have not looked over their shoulder to see if their actions are Torah-conformable. They have presumably acted simply because they saw someone in need and responded as they thought best. Their response at the throne of glory is one of incredulity: When did we see . . . ?

What can this mean? Can it mean that, despite all the emphasis upon Torah obedience and the need for the correct perspective on the meaning of Torah, when the chips are down, none of this matters? All the careful and deliberate work of literary construction would then have been to no purpose. As the climactic statement in the Gospel, Matthew cannot intend to say that conformity to Torah is suddenly of no import.

He began with the declaration that obedience to Torah is necessary in order to inherit the kingdom of God. He then showed gradually just what true obedience means. It is an intensification of Torah rules from the perspective of love of neighbor. As the Gospel progresses, the reader is impressed more and more with this hermeneutical principle. The vision as the climactic point of this movement thus must show what happens when one is so conformed to this Torah obedience that caring acts toward the other have become habituated, spontaneous and unselfconscious. Torah is not mentioned here because the persons have become so completely conformed to it that they can forget it. Thus the person worthy of eternal life is one who has in wholeness (*teleios*) conformed himself to Torah obedience. The vision demonstrates the fruits of 5.17-20, the conformity to Torah as interpreted by Jesus which results in a righteousness greater than that of scribes and Pharisees.[21]

It is an *internalization* of God's will in Torah such that the hungry are fed, the strangers given hospitality, the sick and imprisoned cared for. Since all nations are to be taught this Torah and exhorted to keep it (28.20), all people are to be judged by this one, ultimate criterion.

Coincidentia Oppositorum in Paul and Matthew

Paul and Matthew begin at opposite points on the circle. For the Apostle the beginning is the gift of life as sheer grace. For the Evangelist it is acceptance of the gentle yoke of the Torah as taught by Jesus. But when they move to their final point, both end in the same place. The acceptance of life as gift leads to loving behavior, the upbuilding of the neighbor, that conforms to God's will and is the fulfillment of that will found in the commandments. The acceptance of obedience to the Torah as interpreted from the hermeneutical perspective of love of God and neighbor leads to internalization of that love such that caring for the needy is the ultimate description of that obedience.

Thus the final description of the transformed person is the same, even though arrived at by different paths, from perspectives which not only begin at different points but actually seem conflictive (and probably would have been considered conflictive by the authors). Each direction has pitfalls along the way. That of Paul tempts one to relax in complacent confidence of God's gift. That of Matthew threatens serious repression in which feelings are not fully brought into the open and worked through.[22] One does not have to fall into either pit, however, and systemic dangers do not mean the structure is itself faulty.

Can these ultimately similar resting points, however, be fairly called descriptions of eschatological existence? For Paul such a claim presents no difficulty. The life of faith culminating in love for others *is* eschatological life.[23] Such a definition for Matthew, due to his essentially future-oriented eschatology, may seem more difficult. Yet there is a real sense in which, at least in the final scene (28.16-20), the power of the kingdom *is* felt as a present reality. Meier, for example, claims that 'MT sees the death-resurrection as an eschatological event in which the Kingdom breaks into this aeon in a new, fuller way'.[24] The least one can say is that conformity to the interpretation of the Torah given by Jesus in the Gospel creates a person worthy of an ultimate relationship with God. What's in a name? Whether we label such an existence eschatological or not, Matthew believes it is in true fulfillment of God's will for humanity.

To juxtapose Paul and Matthew in this way is one way of demonstrating the creative tensions within the Canon of the New Testament (as well as creative interactions with the theologies in the Hebrew Canon). There is no single 'only right way' to work through to an ultimate relation with God. A friend of mine likes to put the question this way: 'Does one think oneself into a new way of acting, or does one act into a new way of thinking?' People are different, and there are different ways of reaching the same goal. For some, Matthew is the more accessible guide; for others, Paul. Maybe each person on the way uses both approaches at different times of his adventure. Ultimately what is important is not where we have begun, but who we are when we have completed our journey.

NOTES

1. The theological point being made by the philosopher is that 'all the things which are separated as opposites exist conjointly in God'. Cf. Nicholas of Cusa, *Trialogus de possest* 20. I use the translation of Jasper Hopkins, *A Concise Introduction to the Philosophy of Nicholas of Cusa* (Minneapolis: University of Minnesota Press, 1978). For Jasper's discussion of the *coincidentia oppositorum* cf. pp. 21f.

2. The Gentile origins of the author are asserted by G. Strecker, *Der Weg der Gerechtigkeit* (Göttingen: Vandenhoeck & Ruprecht, 1966), p. 34; J. Meier, *The Vision of Matthew* (New York: Paulist, 1979), pp. 17-25. It seems to me the arguments in this direction are misguided. The most recent commentator, Ulrich Luz, maintains the Jewish origin of the Evangelist, cf. *Das Evangelium nach Matthäus* (Zürich: Benziger, 1985), pp. 62-65.

3. That 'Pharisees' in Matthew is a name for the post-70 representatives of the Judaism with whom Matthew is in dialogue is widely accepted among scholars.

4. Any unsuspecting reader should know that my perspective on Paul is informed by the classical Augustinian-Lutheran-Bultmannian interpretation, which centers on justification by grace. Cf. my *Paul for a New Day* (Philadelphia: Fortress, 1976).

5. Cf. Scroggs, *New Day*, pp. 5-20; *idem*, 'New Being: Renewed Mind: New Perception. Paul's View of the Source of Ethical Insight', *The Chicago Theological Seminary Register* 72 (1982), pp. 1-12.

6. Scroggs, *New Day*, pp. 5-14.

7. Scroggs, *New Day*, pp. 58-60; *idem*, CTS *Register* 72, pp. 7-10.

8. Scroggs, *New Day*, pp. 63-71; *idem*, CTS *Register* 72, pp. 4f.

9. Scroggs, *New Day*, pp. 29-33.

10. Cf. the discussion in J. Kingsbury, *Matthew* (2nd edn, Philadelphia: Fortress, 1986), pp. 1-13. Also R. Edwards, *Matthew's Story of Jesus* (Philadelphia: Fortress, 1985).

11. Cf. U. Luz, *Matthäus*, p. 197.

12. Cf. the detailed discussion in J. Meier, *Law and History in Matthew's Gospel* (Rome: Biblical Institute Press, 1976), pp. 41-124; also Luz, *Matthäus*, pp. 227-44.

13. Meier strongly disagrees, cf. J. Meier, *Vision* pp. 222-39. For an equally strong statement with the opposite conclusion, cf. G. Barth, in Bornkamm, Barth, Held, *Tradition and Interpretation in Matthew* (Philadelphia: Westminster, 1963), pp. 62-73. One exception is to be granted. The Gospel nowhere commands circumcision. This rite seems to be replaced by that of baptism, at least as far as the Gentiles are concerned, cf. 28.19f.

14. Bornkamm, *Tradition*, p. 25; Meier, *Law and History*, pp. 125-61.

15. Cf. Barth, *Tradition*, pp. 97-100; *TDNT*, VIII (Grand Rapids: Eerdmans, 1972), pp. 73f. In Luke's version, the demand is to be 'merciful' rather than *teleios*.

16. Meier takes Matthew to mean what Mark intends. I find that approach untenable; cf. J. Meier, *Vision*, pp. 101f.

17. In the midst of this passage is a reworking of a Markan sentence that many scholars take to be an annulment of the written Torah. 'There is nothing outside a person which by going into him can defile him; but the things which come out of a person are what defile him' (Mk 7.15). The

Markan context suggests that this is, in fact, how Mark interprets the rather general statement. But is that also Matthew's meaning? The entirely different context of Matthew must make us search for a different sense to the statement.

Rewording Mark, Matthew has Jesus say: 'Not what enters the mouth makes a person unclean, but what *comes out of the mouth* makes the person unclean' (15.11). With the focus on the mouth, (cf. the same addition in v. 18) Matthew signals that what he is thinking of is the *verbal* production of a person. It can hardly be accidental that he inserts just at this point the statement about the offense of the Pharisees and the debunking of their oral tradition. The evil that comes out of a mouth is the false interpretation of Torah! His thought direction can also be seen in his reworking of the vice list of Mark to emphasize evil acts connected with speaking (e.g. he adds 'false witness' to Mark's list). It is important to reflect on the harsh saying about careless words in 12.36f. with the above in mind.

Thus Matthew cannot be thought to entertain any suggestion that the Torah is not valid. There may be, however, a different kind of logical tension revealed in this statement about the origin of false interpretation of Torah. If moral and religious direction is determined from within, why the need for, or the good of, external guidance such as the Torah, or an explicit interpretation of it?

Some tension, perhaps unresolved in the author's consciousness, seems to exist. On the one hand, a fatalistic, deterministic tendency exists in the various statements about the good and the bad trees (e.g. 3.10; 7.17-19; and the startling 12.33-35 which sets up the judgment on careless words already referred to). Here the implication seems to be that people are by nature either good or bad and their actions are revelations of the inner character. What Jesus says in 15.18-20 is consonant with this perspective. In this case, the inner quality of a person determines the hermeneutic he chooses, and thus the legal principles obeyed are revelatory of inner character. Here *law does not produce character; it simply discloses what the character already is*. It must also be admitted that there is a virtual absence in the Gospel of any hint of transformation, change of heart, conversion.

On the other hand, the motivation behind the entire Gospel seems to move in the opposite direction. If one is to repeat to the Gentiles what Jesus has taught (28.20), the only point of mission is to change people by getting them to conform to the righteousness demanded by Jesus. Or is it rather to reveal what is in the heart by whether or not the person accepts the teaching? The same tension is perhaps found in someone like a Calvin who believed in predestination, even if the Evangelist seems more deterministic than predestinarian. Cf. the reflections of R. Mohrland on this tension, *Matthew and Paul* (Cambridge: Cambridge University Press, 1984), pp. 111-14.

18. Cf. Barth, *Tradition*, pp. 77f.

19. Cf. Meier, *Vision*, p. 160; E. Schweizer, *The Good News according to Matthew* (Atlanta: John Knox, 1975), p. 430; Strecker, *Weg*, p. 138. Kingsbury is not so sure, cf. *Matthew*, p. 89.

20. Rabbinic discussion about perspectives which guide one's interpretation of Torah never suggest any Torah is annulled by the principle. The perspective rather shows how obedience to *all* the laws are to be truly offered. The famous, apocryphal story of Hillel, Shammai, and the proselyte is a case in point, cf. *Shab.* 31a.

21. There are problems which the view I suggest here must meet. They fall into two categories.

1. The view I propose cannot have been the original meaning of the story. It is not about individuals at all, but about national groups. The separated sheep and goats do not stand for individuals but for nations (v. 32). Furthermore, there is a third collective entity, namely 'one of the least of these my brethren'. This third group is the elect and it does not enter into the judgment at all. It is *outsiders*, who have nothing to do with Torah obedience at all, who are judged by the criterion of how they have treated the elect. If the vision has originally a Jewish *Sitz-im-Leben*, the elect group is the people of Israel. The story certainly has now a Christian location, and this must mean that the elect is taken by the Gospel to be the church. The same conclusion holds in either case: the sheep and the goats are those outside judged on the basis of how they have treated this elect. Conformity to Torah has nothing to do with their actions.

I think there can be little doubt that this collective interpretation is correct as far as any presumed pre-Matthean meaning of the story is concerned. The issue is then whether Matthew accepts this presumed original meaning, or whether he has a different interpretation.

2. Matthew himself accepted the collective meaning described above, *at least as far as 'the brethren' are concerned*. The brethren are believers in Jesus; hence the sheep and the goats are non-believers (whether taken collectively or as individual people). And this means that non-believers are judged not by fidelity to Torah but on the basis of how they have treated members of the church.

One can argue, more specifically, that the 'brethren' means not simply all believers in Jesus but the wandering and persecuted Christian missionaries. As Gundry suggests, the brethen are 'those who carried the gospel from place to place as they fled from persecution. . . To show the hospitality of faith to such a disciple is to demonstrate the genuineness of one's own discipleship' (R. Gundry, *Matthew: A Commentary on His Literary and Theological Art* [Grand Rapids: Eerdmans, 1982], p. 514).

The implication of these objections is that Matthew accepts a double criterion for admission into eternal life. For the believer in Jesus, the standard is faithful adherence to the Torah as interpreted by the Messiah (the clear message of the Gospel as a whole). For all others it is actions taken towards believers or, more narrowly, the wandering Christian missionaries. This conclusion, in my judgment, is ultimately impossible. With all of the emphasis throughout the Gospel on the necessity of obedience to Torah as interpreted by Jesus, it is hard to imagine that suddenly the Evangelist opens the door to all those who have not performed such obedience.

The final command of the resurrected Jesus as enthroned *kyrios* of the world renders such a double standard unlikely. The disciples are to 'make disciples of all nations, . . . *teaching them to keep all that I have commanded you*' (28.19f.). That can only mean the content of the Gospel, namely the necessity of obedience to the Torah. *All* people enter the kingdom of God on the basis of *one* criterion, conformity to the Torah of the Messiah. Bornkamm expressed this clearly in his early redaction-criticism of Matthew: 'No distinction is made between Jews and Gentiles, nor even between believers and unbelievers. All are gathered before the tribunal of the judge of the world and are judged by the 'one' standard, namely that of the love they have shown towards, or withheld from, the humblest' (*Tradition*, pp. 23f.).

But Bornkamm's statement does not mean (nor does he think it means) that at this point fidelity to Torah has been forgotten. It is, indeed, precisely conformity to the Torah as interpreted by Jesus Messiah that enables one to express care to those in need (cf. *Tradition*, p. 24).

22. The antitheses clearly show this possibility of repression and have doubtlessly encouraged it in many people throughout the centuries. The danger, however, can be avoided if, as suggested above, *teleios* is taken to mean wholeness and integration. The life described by the antitheses is not repressive if undertaken by an integrated, whole self. A person whose constituent functions—mind, body, feelings—are integrated can listen to the antitheses in a creative way not possible for a repressed person.

23. Scroggs, *New Day*, pp. 21-38.

24. J. Meier, *Law and History*, p. 38, a view also held by C.H. Dodd, *New Testament Studies* (New York: Scribner's, n.d.), p. 56, who is appealing to R.H. Lightfoot.

EPISTEMOLOGY AT THE TURN OF THE AGES IN PAUL, JESUS, AND MARK: RHETORIC AND DIALECTIC IN APOCALYPTIC AND THE NEW TESTAMENT

Thomas E. Boomershine

The tendency in the study of the relationship of apocalyptic and the New Testament since Schweitzer has been to concentrate on the content or subject matter of that relationship, particularly in relation to the understanding of the Kingdom of God. The development of literary and structural methods of analysis opens the possibility of comparative listening to the forms or structures of the relationship. How did the seminal figures of the community that formed the New Testament use the forms and structures of apocalyptic? The possibility that will be outlined here is that a common dialectical relationship to the tradition of apocalyptic can be identified in sections of the teachings of Paul, Jesus, and Mark dealing with the turn of the ages.

I

In his seminal essay on Paul's eschatology, J. Louis Martyn pursued the agenda set by his *Doctorvater* and clarified Paul's understanding of the structures of apocalyptic in relation to the assumptions of his Corinthian auditors.[1] A brief survey of Martyn's argument will set the issue. As both Georgi's original proposal and Martyn's application to this text presuppose, Paul's opponents were confident that they were already in the new age as evidenced by their shining faces. That is, they interpreted the basic structure of apocalyptic as meaning that they were already on the other side of the turn of the ages and both knew the world and themselves as being in the new age. In 2 Cor. 5.16-17, Paul did not contrast knowing Christ in an old age way of knowing (*kata sarka*) with a new age way of knowing Christ (*kata pneuma*) because his opponents, the super-apostles, were those who claimed to know *kata pneuma*. Paul's letter is then an undermining of this eschatological self-knowledge of the super-apostles and Gnostics in the community.

Paul deals with the epistemological dualism of apocalyptic by refusing to accept either way of knowing in an unqualified, simplistic manner. At the heart of Paul's appropriation of the epistemological dualism of apocalyptic is a refusal to contrast 'old age' knowing (*kata sarka*) with the 'new age' knowing of those who been given the gift of the spirit (*kata pneuma*). Paul steadfastly confesses to the way of knowing and being known at the juncture of the ages formed by the cross of Christ. To know truly is to know *kata stauron*. As Professor Martyn says, 'the marks of the new age are at present hidden *in* the old age. At the juncture of the ages the marks of the resurrection are hidden and revealed in the cross of the disciple's daily death, and *only* there'.[2] Paul's treatment of the turn of the ages resists the temptation inherent in the structures of apocalyptic to substitute despair about the inevitable domination of the powers of the old age with the confidence and arrogance that the new age and its powers are unambiguously present.

Stated as a description of the effect of Paul's letter when it was read to the Corinthian congregation, Martyn shows how Paul used the structures of epistemological dualism in a way that undermined the confidence and assurance of both the Gnostics and the super-apostles in Corinth. Paul relates to the traditions of apocalyptic and particularly the possibility of a new age epistemology in what can be called a dialectical manner. 'Yes', in the resurrection we know Christ and, therefore, ourselves *kata pneuma*; 'no', until the parousia we do not know either Christ or ourselves *kata pneuma* but only *kata stauron*. Thus, understanding Paul's letter and his epistemology of the turn of the ages is dependent upon hearing it in relation to the equally apocalyptic presuppositions of his listeners.

The character of Paul's use of apocalyptic in relation to the presupposition of his Corinthian audience is clarified by a categorical distinction about different types of literary experience which was generated by Stanley E. Fish and introduced into the biblical discussion by John Dominic Crossan.[3] At the beginning of his book, Fish distinguishes between 'rhetoric' and 'dialectic' as 'two kinds of literary presentation':

A presentation is rhetorical if it satisfies the needs of its readers. The word 'satisfies' is meant literally here; for it is characteristic of a rhetorical form to mirror and present for approval the opinions its readers already hold. It follows then that the experience of such a form will be flattering, for it tells the reader that what he has always thought about the world is true and that the *ways* of his thinking are sufficient. This is not to say that in the course of a rhetorical experience one is never told anything unpleasant, but that whatever one is told can be placed and contained within the categories and assumptions of received systems of knowledge.

A dialectical presentation, on the other hand, is disturbing, for it requires of its readers a searching and rigorous scrutiny of everything they believe in and live by. It is didactic in a special sense; it does not preach the truth, but asks that its readers discover the truth for themselves, and this discovery is often made at the expense not only of a reader's opinions and values, but of his self-esteem. If the experience of a rhetorical form is flattering, the experience of a dialectical form is humiliating.[4]

In relation to the turn of the ages in Paul's letter, what Fish describes as dialectic is a primary dimension of the impact of Paul's way of knowing. Rather than meeting the needs of his readers for confirmation of the rightness of their way, Paul's letters are intended to be profoundly unsettling and precisely humbling for those who fully hear them.

This relationship between 'rhetoric' and 'dialectic' is further developed by Fish in relation to epistemologies, to ways of knowing that are characteristic of two kinds of reading experience. In Fish's sense, 'rhetoric' and 'dialectic' represent:

an opposition of epistemologies, one that finds its expression in two kinds of reading experiences: on one side the experience of a prose that leads the auditor or reader step-by-step, in a logical and orderly manner, to a point of certainty and clarity; and on the other, the experience of a prose that undermines certainty and moves away from clarity, complicating what had at first seemed perfectly simple, raising more problems than it solves. Within this large opposition there are, of course, distinctions to be made. . . but in general the contrast holds, between a language that builds its readers' confidence by building an argument they can follow, and a language that, by calling attention to the insufficiency of its own procedures, calls into question the sufficiency of the minds it unsettles.[5]

Fish's distinction clarifies the character of Paul's response to the Corinthians and their understanding of themselves in relation to the new age. Paul uses the structures of apocalyptic in a dialectical manner, in a way that appeals to the world view based on the turn of the ages while at the same time undermining the confident assumptions about the ways of knowing Christ and themselves that the Corinthians inferred from that world view. To paraphrase Käsemann and Martyn, God in Christ is seen clearly as dealing always with the godless, before whom no human being can know himself or herself as either pious, just, or unambiguously redeemed in the new age but only as one who is known and redeemed by God in the cross of Christ formed by the juncture of the ages. Not only is this a description of the epistemology underlying Paul's thought, I would suggest that it is also a description of the meaning or impact of Paul's letter for its auditors when it was read to the Corinthian congregation.

II

One facet of the riddle of the eschatological center of the NT has been the relationship between Jesus and Paul. Was Jesus' proclamation of the Kingdom of God continued or essentially transformed in the Pauline proclamation of the cross of Christ as the center of the Gospel? The recognition of the apocalyptic womb from which Paul's theology was born only raises the question in a new way. While the four Evangelists were fascinated with the relationship between Jesus and John the Baptist, historical critics who have deconstructed the texts of the New Testament and reconstructed them in the new forms of history and theology in the last two and a half centuries have been fascinated with the relationship between Jesus and Paul. In what sense was apocalyptic the mother of Jesus' proclamation as well as that of Paul? Käsemann, for example, argues that while Jesus' preaching began with the apocalyptically determined message of John, his own preaching 'did not bear a fundamentally apocalyptic stamp but proclaimed the immediacy of the God who was near at hand'.[6] Thus, Käsemann makes a fundamental distinction between the preaching of Jesus and the theology of Paul in its relationship to apocalyptic. This conclusion in turn poses the next question: how did Jesus relate to the structures of apocalyptic in his portrayal of the turn of the ages?

An important element in Jesus' use of the apocalyptic tradition is made clear by an analysis of some of the underlying actantial and rhetorical patterns of apocalyptic and its portrayal of the turn of the ages.[7] A short but characteristic version of the apocalyptic vision is the end of a discourse in the *Assumption of Moses* (10.7-10):

> For the Most High will arise, the Eternal God alone. He will appear to punish the Gentiles, and he will destroy all their idols. And you, O Israel, will be happy. You will mount on the neck and wings of the eagle. They will be abolished, and God will exalt you. He will bring you up to the starry heaven. You will look from on high and see your enemies in Gehenna. You will recognize them and rejoice. You will give thanks and bless your creator.

Implicit in this apocalyptic vision is a long-recognized narrative structure of reversal based on an understanding of the structures of power in this age and the age to come. Translated into the categories of actantial analysis, the structure of this vision is as follows: in this age, the powers of evil are in control (sender) and their agent (subject), the evil one, who is variously characterized in the tradition, is their designated hero. The powers of evil send persecution, sickness, war and death to the world. The Gentiles are the primary helpers for the evil one and Israel is the enemy. This enmity is seen and known in the persecution experienced by Israel in this age:

THIS AGE

Powers of evil	Sickness/Possession/Death	World
Gentiles	The Evil One	Israel

But in the new age this will be reversed. God will intervene and defeat the powers of evil. In the *Assumption of Moses*, the primary agent of this deliverance is 'the Eternal One' along with the eagle who may symbolically represent the Messiah. In the new age, Israel's status will change from being the enemy of the primary subject of the cosmic plot. Israel will become the helper of the Most High. The status of the Gentiles will also shift from that of helper to enemy. And they will be punished.

THE MESSIANIC AGE

God	Salvation	Israel
Israel	The Messiah	Gentiles

Thus, in this age, the powers of evil are in control and the Gentiles are in power as the primary helpers of the evil one. But in the new age, God will intervene and will reverse the roles and Israel will be rewarded as God's faithful helper and the Gentiles will be punished as God's enemy.

Furthermore, the rhetorical dynamics of the vision support this actantial structure. It is assumed that the listeners identify themselves with Israel. This identification is made explicit in the narrative address: 'And you, O Israel, will be happy. . . ' Likewise, those who are the audience's enemies are clearly identified as 'they', that is, the Gentiles. The experience of the turn of the ages in this apocalyptic passage is based, therefore, on an identification of the audience with those who are persecuted as enemies in this age but who will become the primary helpers of the dominant power of the new age. The turn of the ages is experienced by the listeners in this vision as a reversal of roles from being the enemy to being the helper of the dominant power of the age and, therefore, as a confirmation of present patterns of belief and behavior.

Perhaps the most characteristic narratives of the turn of the ages in the apocalyptic tradition are the stories of Shadrach, Meshach, and Abednego in the furnace and of Daniel in the lions' den. A brief analysis of the rhetorical structure of the story of the three men shed further light on some structures of meaning in the apocalyptic tradition. In these narratives, which might be considered parables, in a broad sense of the term, the turn of the ages is experienced as the crisis of persecution. In both narratives, the primary heroes are Israelites who have gained power but who are suddenly and unexpectedly treated as enemies by the powers of this age. The actantial structure is relatively simple: Nebuchadnezzar and Darius are the primary subject in each narrative, the three men and Daniel are cast as enemies, and the helpers are the primary advisors of the king.

A major dimension of the meaning of the narrative is the discontinuity between the actantial structure of this age and the assumed structure of the audience. In this age, righteous Israelites are the enemy of the powers of this age and the helpers are evil men.

THIS PRESENT EVIL AGE

Sender	Object	Receiver
The advisors to the king	Nebuchadnezzar Darius	Shad/Mesh/Abednego Daniel

But the narrator and the audience both share the conviction that the Jews are the helpers and that those who seek to persecute the Jews are the enemies.

THE STRUCTURE OF THE AUDITORS' WORLD

God	Salvation	Israel/World
Shad/Mesh/Abednego	Nebuch/Darius	The Advisors

A high degree of identification with the Israelites who are treated as enemies is both assumed and invited in the narratives. In the story of Daniel, this appeal for identification is heightened by his immediate decision in light of the decree to go to his house and pray three times a day. The turn of the ages in the narrative takes place when God intervenes in the midst of their persecution and reverses the actantial roles. In both stories, the heroes are delivered from death and their persecutors are destroyed.

In narrative terms, the audience is invited to identify with a character who is treated as the enemy and becomes the primary helper. Likewise the audience's enemies, who have the role of helpers to the powers of this age, become the enemy in the new age. The new age is experienced as a vicarious identification with the victory of the righteous and the destruction of those who plotted against them. And the turn of the ages confirms the audience's structural assumptions toward both themselves and their enemies. Thus, the structure of the new age is identical with the structure of the auditors' world in the midst of the old age.

God	Power/Deliverance	Israel/World
The Three Men	Nebuchadnezzar	The advisors

The rhetorical/actantial structure of these stories is that those with whom the listeners are invited to identify are rewarded in the new age and those from whom they are alienated are condemned. The effect of this apocalyptic structure is to provide comfort for those who experience fear and persecution from their enemies in the present age and to confirm them in their knowledge of themselves and their world.

In Fish's terms, the literary experience of this paradigmatic apocalyptic narrative is, therefore, 'rhetorical', in that it satisfies the needs of its audience for approval and comfort and confirms their present ways of thinking both about themselves and their enemies. The experience of the turn of the ages provides certainty about the rightness of present patterns of belief and behavior. The point of view of these stories looks forward from the present evil age to the new age from the perspective of righteous sufferers, enemies of the powers of this age, with whom the auditors are invited to identify. The experience of the turn of the ages is then a 'rhetorical' experience of confirmation and comfort. The degree to which this structure is characteristic of the apocalyptic tradition as a whole remains to be determined. But the suggestion here is that the way of knowing at the turn of the ages that is characteristic of apocalyptic is to provide assurance of true knowledge in the context of the experienced contradiction between the structures of this age and the age to come. In this sense, Paul's opponents stood in the mainstream of the apocalyptic tradition.

III

The actantial/rhetorical structure of the turning of the ages in many of Jesus' parables is radically divergent from these structures of apocalyptic. The parable of the rich fool (Lk. 12.16-21) is a typical instance of a rhetorical/actantial structure that occurs in a number of Jesus' parables[8] which stands in marked contrast to the 'rhetorical' structure of at least these parts of the apocalyptic tradition.

The parable of the rich fool is based on an appeal for a close identification of the listener with the rich man. The inside view of the rich man is longer and more probing than in any of the parables in the Jesus tradition:[9]

> What will I do, since I have nowhere to store my crops? I will do this: I will pull down my barns, and build larger ones; and there I will store all my grain and my goods. And I will say to my soul, 'Soul, you have ample goods laid up for many years; take your ease, eat, drink, and be merry!'

Jesus' auditor is first drawn into the delightful dilemma of the rich man and then invited to join in his rejoicing at being free from any anxiety about the necessities of life. It is the kind of appeal that contemporary lotteries regularly use to induce persons to buy tickets. The structure of the inside view—question, answer, and address to his soul—leads the listener deeper and deeper into the rich man's mind. And everything the rich man says is highly sympathetic.

In Jesus' parable, the underlying structure of the parable is in continuity with the assumed beliefs of the auditors. As in the life of most religious communities then and now, the rich man is assumed to be a helper, a good man who has been blessed in this present age.

THE STRUCTURE OF THE AUDITORS' WORLD

God	Blessing	Israel
Rich man	Messiah	The poor

It is from the perspective of this close identification with the rich man that the listener hears God's judgment: 'Fool!' The shock of this reversal of expectations is psychologically violent and is thoroughly appropriate to a war of myths. The judgment of the rich man and the reversal of his fortunes is not experienced by the auditor from a perspective of detachment or alienation but of identification and sympathetic attachment. Furthermore, the implication of the parable is that the rich man has become an enemy of God. He is addressed as one who is mocked and perhaps even condemned rather than praised.

The turning of the ages in the parable of the rich fool can be identified with precision. The turning of the ages happened for Jesus' listeners in the moment of the statement of God: 'Fool!' The new age enters the world of the rich man/listener as an eschatological negative evaluation.

In this parable, Jesus gave his listeners the opportunity to identify with attitudes and patterns of behavior in the present and to experience their disastrous result in the new age. Having experienced that future, Jesus' listeners could change their ways in the present and have, therefore, a different future. Specifically, the impact of the rich fool parable is to alienate the listeners from both the envy of the rich and from the rich man's attitude towards money. The parable and its meaning are, therefore, inextricably tied to time: the time of the speaking and hearing of the parable and the time of the old and new age as they are experienced in the speaking and hearing of the parable.

Jesus' parable presupposes a different way of knowing in relation to the turn of the ages. Rather than thinking forward in time to the promise of the new age as is characteristic of apocalyptic, the parable requires the audience to think back from the future into the present. As J. Louis Martyn suggested in his lecture on this parable in 1966, the direction of time is experienced in Jesus' parables as flowing not from the past into the future but from the future into the present. The future breaks into the present in the parable as a new age that is experienced as crisis rather than reward. And, for the one with whom the listeners are invited to identify in the parable, the new age is bad news rather than good news. Rather than confirming the rightness of present patterns of behavior and belief, the parable mocks them. This way of knowing is, therefore, a reversal in the understanding of the direction of time and of the expectations of the new age. The epistemology of the turn of the ages in Jesus' parables is to know oneself and the world in the present from the perspective of the future. In turn, the expectations generated by the apocalyptic tradition in the minds of Jesus' listeners provide the background which makes the shock of the reversal of that tradition possible.

Thus, the turn of the ages in Jesus' parable is a radical reversal of expectations. Rather than confirming the auditors' world, the structure of the new age in the parable contradicts it:

THE AGE TO COME

God	blessing and praise	Israel
The poor	Messiah	The rich man

In the actantial structure of the parable, the character with whom the auditors are invited to identify becomes the enemy in the new age. The experience of the turn of the ages is then both a shock of self-recognition and a threat rather than a blessing. It is shocking rather than comforting news.

The meaning of Jesus' parable is dependent, therefore, on the listeners' assumptions about the turn of the ages. In apocalyptic visions such as the *Assumption of Moses* and the stories in Daniel, the turning of the ages confirms the listeners' faith and behavior in the midst of the present evil age. In Jesus' parable, the character with whom the listeners are invited to identify becomes a loser rather than a winner in the new age. Unlike the Daniel stories, the one who is *mocked* in the new age is the one with whcm the auditors are invited to identify. The dawning of the new age is not, therefore, the good news of condemnation for those from whom the listeners are alienated and reward for those with whom they identify. The new age contradicts and reverses the auditors' assumptions about the structures of the new age. The new age is experienced as a reversal rather than a fulfillment of their expectations about themselves and their ways of thought and behavior.

How widely is this turn of the ages shock treatment present in Jesus' parables? I would identify the following parables as having this same basic rhetorical/actantial structure:

1. The parable of the vineyard (Mk 12.1-11/Mt. 21.33-44/Lk. 20.9-18/Thomas 65)—For those who recognize and identify themselves as the tenants of the vineyard of Israel and who stand in the tradition of Isaiah, this parable has precisely the shock of recognition of the justice implicit in their loss of the land.

2. The budding fig-tree (Mk 13.28f./Mt. 24.32f./Lk. 21.29-31; 12.58f.)—The fig tree is one of the most sympathetic characters in the Gospels. By the end of the parable of this poor, innocent tree, the need to bear fruit is evident but the enigma remains and, with the exception of Lk. 12.58f., the appeal for repentance is connected with the Temple.

3. The unmerciful servant (Mt. 18.23-35)—As the closing comment on the parable of the great feast, this is a primary instance of identification with one for whom the turning of the ages is bad news.

4. The good employer (Mt. 20.1-16)—The ending of this parable is similar to the ending of Jonah and the prodigal son. The identification with those who have worked all day and are, therefore, highly sympathetic in their anger is the foundation for the owner's angry critique of those who have been his helpers.

5. The great supper and the guest without a wedding garment (Mt. 22.1-10/Lk. 14.16-24/Thomas 64)—This parable is a classic instance of an appeal for identification with helpers who end up being enemies of the lord of the banquet.

6. The servant entrusted with supervision (Mt. 24.45-51/Lk. 12.42-46)—The parable invites identification with a sympathetic character who is then condemned because of patterns of behavior that are presumably identifiable for the listeners.

7. The ten virgins (Mt. 25.1-13)—This parable appeals for identification with the five foolish virgins who come back to find the door closed in their faces with hostile indifference.

8. The talents (Mt. 25.14-30/Lk. 19.12-27)—The one talent servant is a highly sympathetic character who begins as a 'helper' and ends as an 'enemy'.

9. The last judgment (Mt. 25.31-46)—The identification with the sheep is the set-up for the inevitable identification with the goats. Who in Jesus' audience had not known someone hungry or thirsty or naked or a stranger or sick or in prison and did not minister to them?

10. The prodigal son (Lk. 15.11-32)—This parable has a unique double reversal of actantial roles in which the prodigal enemy from whom the audience is alienated becomes a helper while the sympathetic elder son/helper makes himself an enemy.

11. The rich man and Lazarus (Lk. 16.19-31)—This parable depends on Jesus' extensive appeals for identification with the rich man and ends with an appeal to think back from the future into the present.

In each of these instances the parable invites or requires the listeners to identify with a character or object (the tree) who is initially sympathetic but who is condemned in the parable's turn of the ages. The listeners thereby are invited to make a judgment about themselves and their assumptions about patterns of behavior and belief in relation to the coming new age.

Thus, when seen against the background of parables in apocalyptic, the tradition of Jesus' parables both depends on the presuppositions of apocalyptic and turns them around. Specifically, instead of envisioning from the present to a new age in the future which will reverse the present order in a manner that provides comfort and certainty in the present, these parables present the turn of the ages by reflecting back from the future into the present in a manner that creates discomfort and confusion about the present. Further, whereas in apocalyptic the listener's identification with the major protagonist frequently leads to an experience of the turn of the ages as victory, the identification with the major characters in these parables of Jesus leads to an experience of the new age as rebuke, condemnation, and enmity.

Jesus' parables have clearly been fed by the tradition of apocalyptic. But the epistemological structure of apocalyptic has been radically reformed in a way that changes its impact and meaning. I find Fish's description of 'dialectic' and its epistemology to be appropriate as a distinction between the tradition of apocalyptic and what is found in these parables of Jesus. These parables are shocking and require a rigorous scrutiny of beliefs and patterns of behavior. In each instance, what is known in these parables moves away from certainty and comfort to humiliation and fright. Epistemology at the turn of the ages in these parables is to know oneself in relation to the new age in ways that are profoundly disturbing.

Thus, both Jesus and Paul in their own way relate to the tradition of apocalyptic in a 'dialectical' manner. In the divergent forms of diatribe and parable, each turns the presupposition of the apocalyptic tradition as understood by their auditors on end. The apocalyptic rhetoric of the turn of the ages as comfort and spiritual self-assurance is transformed into a dialectic of confrontation and self-examination. A primary element of continuity between the teaching of Paul and Jesus is, therefore, a dialectical proclamation of the turn of the ages.

IV

The possibility that Jesus and Paul have transformed apocalyptic in a similar manner raises the question whether this pattern may be evident more widely in the New Testament. An initial test case of interest is the parables of Mark 4 as explored in an excellent recent dissertation by Joel Marcus.[10] Building on J. Louis Martyn's suggestions about the relationship of apocalyptic and Jesus' parables, Marcus has done a systematic study of Mark's use of parables in ch. 4 in the context of the apocalyptic tradition.

Marcus's interpretation of the parables in Mark 4 is based on an understanding of the role of parables in apocalyptic. Marcus concludes that the function of parables in apocalyptic is to present enigmatic images which in themselves contain the mystery of the new age. But the clarification of the mystery is communicated in the sage's interpretation which follows the parable. These clarifications of the mysteries of the future are intended for a privileged audience who are the recipients of this revelation.

In Mark 4, this structure is seen in the combination of the parable and its allegorical interpretation. The parable of the sower contains the secret of the Kingdom of God implicitly. But the disciples and the listeners remain confused about its meaning. The allegorical interpretation which follows the parable then makes clear the meaning of the parable for the Markan community. Jesus' first enigmatic explanation (4.10, 11) raises the question of the 'insiders' who understand the mystery of the kingdom of God and the 'outsiders' who do not. The allegorical interpretation of the parable creates a two-level narrative in which the Markan congregation are confirmed as 'insiders' who are being persecuted for the sake of the gospel. As Marcus states, 'Jesus is "doubled" with evangelists who are members of the Markan community',[11] those seeds that do not bear fruit represent the opponents of the Markan community, and the seeds that produce a glorious harvest represent the Markan community. The impact of the ending of the allegory is described as a memory of Marcus's *Doctorvater's* ebullient teaching:

> as J.L. Martyn has suggested, after his description of the 'bad soil' in 4.15-19, Mark turns to his own congregation in 4.20, perhaps even expecting that, when the passage is read in the Markan community, the reader will indicate his audience with a gesture: 'But *these* are those sown on good soil, who hear the word and accept it and bear fruit!'[12]

Thus, those seeds along the path represent the Markan community's enemies, the scribes and the Pharisees, and those who receive the word and fail to persevere are unfaithful disciples who choose not to be martyred. The function of the parable and its allegorical interpretation is to clarify the mystery of the community's present situation: 'The word speaks *in* the present *of* the future, and thus brings the reality of the future into the present for those with ears to hear in the Markan community'.[13] The role of the parable and its interpretation is then to provide comfort for the community in the present.

In light of the possibility of Jesus' dialectical relationship to the apocalyptic tradition, the question is whether Mark may have continued a similar style. Only the outline of an alternative exegesis of Mark 4 is possible in the scope of this essay. Marcus argues rightly in Chapter 2 that 4.11-12 contains statements about the effect of the parables upon 'outsiders'. For the outsiders, the parables are a source of confusion and incomprehension; they are apocalyptic weapons that blind rather than reveal. By implication, therefore, for those who are 'inside' they are the means of revelation of the mystery of the Kingdom of God.

The rhetoric of 4.10-11 raises a question about the identity of the listeners. The criterion for the listeners' identification of themselves as either outsiders or insiders is the effect of the parables upon them. From the listeners' perspective, the logic is as follows: if I understand the parables, I am an insider; if I do not understand the parables, I am an outsider. That is, the effect of the parable and its interpretation determines the self identification of the listener in relation to the actantial roles of the narrative.

God	Revelation of the Kingdom	World
Those who hear/see	Jesus	Those who do not hear/see

If, therefore, the listener remains confused, the logic of the narrative is that the listener is an outsider, an enemy of the kingdom of God. Such a listener is one of those blinded and deafened by the parables 'lest they should turn again and be forgiven'.

The implication of Jesus' statement following the pivotal Isaiah quotation is that the listeners do not understand: 'Don't you understand this parable? How then are you going to understand all the parables?' By implication, at this point in the parable discourse, the identity of the disciples/audience in relation to the kingdom is wholly ambiguous.

Marcus's argument is that for the insiders, the meaning of the parable is *present* in the parable itself, but in the tradition of parables in apocalyptic, is not *understood* until the interpretation is given by the sage. Thus, in the tradition of apocalyptic, the understanding of the revelation in the parable will take place in the interpretation. The impact of the parable on the self-identification of the listeners is then dependent on how they understand themselves in the allegory. Marcus and Martyn conclude that the allegory was understood as a two-level allegory that made clear that their enemies are the 'outsiders' and they are the 'insiders', the good soil that bears much fruit.

The rhetorical structure of the allegory does not support this conclusion. The allegory is about ways of hearing and the first three elements of the allegory are about seeds that bear no fruit. The listeners to Mark's allegory were clearly able to dissociate themselves from the seeds sown by the wayside, but the seeds that are sown in rocky ground and among the thorns are increasingly inclusive. Thus, the descriptions of the responses of the listeners begin with those who are troubled by the possibility of persecution or trouble and progress to those who allow other concerns such as money or pleasure to affect their hearing of the parables and the Gospel. I would argue, for example, that no listener in the entire history of the readings of Mark's Gospel from then until now can honestly say that their hearing of the parables or the gospel has not been affected by the possibility of persecution or tribulation, the anxieties of this world, the delight in riches, and desires for other things.

This last phrase in the description of the thorns is particularly revealing in relation to Mark's purpose. The noun phrase is inclusive in its structure. The phrase *peri ta loipa* is inserted between the article and its noun *epithymiai*. The resulting phrase, literally 'the for other things desires', is as inclusive as possible and covers the waterfront of possible distractions to fruitful hearing. Just what does 'other things' mean? While it is intentionally ambiguous, I do not think it a twentieth-century anachronism to read this phrase as having some sexual connotations. In fact, if there was ever a circumlocution for sex in the Gospels, this is it. The phrase is a typical parabolic trap, a catch-all into which every listener can read whatever fantasies or desires might come to mind.

Thus, while the final element of the allegory is also addressed to the audience, the dynamics of the allegory make an unambiguous judgment about the listener's status impossible. No listener can piously conclude: 'I am the good soil'. The allegory is structurally designed to prevent it. At the end of the allegory, therefore, the logic of the parable and its interpretation leaves the listener in an ambiguous actantial role in relation to the mystery of the Kingdom of God. And for all those who would identify as insiders who understand the mystery and who are therefore going to be saved, the anxiety of the ambiguity is that the possibility remains that they do not understand and are outsiders/enemies of the kingdom.

The intentional character of this rhetorical structure in ch. 4 is confirmed by its frequent repetition throughout the Gospel. The two feeding narrative sections which follow the parable chapter (4.35–6.52 and 6.53–8.21) both end with the implication that the disciples, with whom the listeners are invited to identify,[14] do not understand and have become enemies of the Kingdom. The passion narrative itself is structured as a series of sympathetic characters who either become or ally themselves with the enemies of Jesus: Judas, the disciples, Peter, the people, those crucified with him. The ending of the Gospel is the final shock in which the women who are entrusted with the message of resurrection flee and say nothing.[15] In each instance, there is a consistent rhetorical/actantial pattern. A sympathetic character with whom the audience is invited to identify faces a crisis and shifts her/his allegiance from being a helper of the Messiah to being an enemy. The dynamics of the narrative lead the listeners to a painful and humbling self-recognition.

Therefore, the suggestion that emerges from this comparison is that Mark's use of parables was 'dialectical' rather than 'rhetorical'. Rather than confirming his listeners in their piety, I suspect that the intended impact of the parables was to shake them up and to invite them to reexamine their own commitments and ways of hearing the gospel. There is evidence throughout the Gospel that Mark stood in the same basic dialectical relationship to the apocalyptic tradition that is evident in the parables of Jesus in their pre-Markan context and in the letters of Paul.

V

A common pattern of relationship to the apocalyptic tradition emerges from this comparative analysis of representative sections of the traditions of Paul, Jesus, and Mark. When seen in relation to Fish's distinction between 'rhetoric' and 'dialectic', in different ways, all three have used the basic materials of the apocalyptic description of the new age in a dialectical rather than a rhetorical manner. In the biblical tradition, the tradition with which to associate this common style is prophecy. From Nathan to Jeremiah, the primary intent of the prophetic tradition was to shock Israel and its leaders into reflection about its assumptions that God would protect and comfort them. The prophets' words frequently called upon Israel to experience itself in a word event as the enemy of God in the hope that the nation might change.

The suggestion that emerges from this study is that Paul Hanson's emphasis on the prophetic sources of apocalyptic is reflected in the use of the apocalyptic tradition by these central figures in the emergence of the Christian sect.[16] Jesus, Paul, and Mark use the apocalyptic tradition in a prophetic manner. To be sure, there are strands of comfort and reinforcement in the prophetic tradition. And the apocalyptic tradition appears to have been associated with those currents in the prophetic tradition in the post-Maccabean period. But if Hanson is right that the sources of apocalyptic must be traced back to the prophets of the seventh century BC, the use of the apocalyptic tradition by Jesus, Paul, and Mark may be a reappropriation of the basic spirit of the sources of apocalyptic.

The unique character of the epistemology implied in this comparison is clearest when seen in relation to the epistemological options of apocalyptic. The first option is to look forward to the new age from the perspective of the old age as a time when the structures of this age will be reversed. This appears to be the primary relationship to the apocalyptic tradition that characterized Jesus' audience in the parables. Paul, on the other hand, was dealing with a group who had chosen the other option, namely, to conclude that the new age has already come and is now fully and unambiguously present. All patterns and attitudes from the old age can, therefore, be systematically ignored in light of the abundant gifts of the spirit including the need to suffer. In Mark's context, the perspective of the audience in relation to these epistemological options is more ambiguous and both perspectives may be in the background. That is, the majority of Mark's audience would appear to be persons who are looking forward to the new age as a time of comfort and new life for whom the notion of the suffering Son of Man and the call to taking up the cross are a shock and a scandal. On the other hand, the parable chapter may also be shaped in response to a group that assumes they are already 'insiders' in the Kingdom and need to be shocked into realization of the possibility that they are still 'outsiders' in need of repentance.

But the common element is that Jesus, Paul, and Mark all maintain the dialectic between the old age and the new age. God is known in the 'turn of the ages' and in the steady experiencing anew of that turn of the ages in the word events of the parables, the epistles, and the narratives of the Gospels. Thus, while the cross of Christ became a primary center for understanding the turn of the ages for both Paul and Mark, many of the same elements of meaning are present in Jesus' parables. There is, therefore, a straight line of tradition from Jesus to Paul to Mark in their steady refusal to collapse the apocalyptic dialectic into either of its more simplistic and comforting options. Each in his own way calls on his listeners to reflect about the Kingdom of God from the still center of the juncture of the ages. For them, the apocalyptic tradition has become a way of knowing God in time in the full richness of God's mystery.

The specific impact of this way of knowing can best be described in relation to the dynamic impact of the parables and letters themselves. Epistemology at the turn of the ages is a dialectic that undermines in each new context any total confidence in knowing oneself or one's community as a 'helper' of the Kingdom of God while at the same time being known as one who is redeemed by the powers of that same Kingdom. The knowledge that is gained in these parables of Jesus, in 2 Corinthians, and in Mark is that we know ourselves and our communities at the juncture of the ages as beloved enemies of the Kingdom who are called to be storytellers, parablers and apostles of the signs of the new age hidden in the midst of the old age by the grace of God.

NOTES

1. J.L. Martyn, 'Epistemology at the Turn of the Ages: 2 Corinthians 5.16', *Christian History and Interpretation: Studies Presented to John Knox*

(ed. W.R. Farmer *et al.*; Cambridge: Cambridge University Press, 1967), pp. 269-87.

2. *Ibid.*, p. 286.

3. Stanley E. Fish, *Self-Consuming Artifacts* (Berkeley & Los Angeles: University of California Press, 1972); cited by J. Dominic Crossan, *Finding is the First Act* (Philadelphia: Fortress Press, 1979), pp. 118-19.

4. Stanley Fish, pp. 1-2.

5. *Ibid.*, p. 378.

6. E. Käsemann, 'The Beginnings of Christian Theology', in *New Testament Questions of Today* (Philadelphia: Fortress, 1969), p. 101. The problem addressed by Käsemann is the central question of the essential continuity or discontinuity of early Christianity between its founder/hero and its most generative apostle. We are thus addressing anew the problem which Käsemann cogently identifies: 'The same problem which determines all New Testament theology is being raised—namely, that of the relation of the proclamation about Jesus to the message of Jesus; and the answer arrived at here is precisely that the earthly Jesus and the *ipsissima verba* do not come out on top. We only need to substitute Gospel for prophecy, and mutatis mutandis, we are with Paul or John. Both proclaim determination by preaching, to which they ascribe revelational character as being the word of the exalted Lord' (p. 103). One way of formulating the question of this essay is whether there are other ways of approaching the relationship between Jesus and Paul than the continuity/discontinuity of either content or verbal identity.

7. The methods of rhetorical analysis used here are developed most fully in Wayne Booth, *The Rhetoric of Fiction* (Chicago: University of Chicago Press, 1961); in biblical studies, see Thomas E. Boomershine, 'Mark, the Storyteller' (unpublished dissertation, Union Theological Seminary, 1974). The categories of actantial analysis used here are taken from A.-J. Greimas *Sémantique structurale: Recherche de méthode* (Paris: Larousse, 1966) and *Du sens: Essais sémiotiques* (Paris: Seuil, 1970), who in turn developed this schema of narrative structure from the studies of V. Propp, *Morphology of the Folktale* (Austin: University of Texas, 1963). The basic actantial structure of narratives is comprised of six elements: a *sender* or primary agent who sends an *object* to a *receiver* by means of a *subject* generally the hero/heroine who has *helpers* and *enemies*. The interaction of these actantial roles in the various axes of a narrative comprise the actantial structure of the narrative.

8. For the purpose of this disccusion, I will not make any effort to discriminate between the earliest stage of the parable tradition in Jesus' ministry and its later forms in the Gospel. While there is the possible implication that a pervasive pattern may indicate that it originated with Jesus himself, the only concern here is to identify the patterns in the parable tradition.

9. Other extensive inside views occur in the parables of the prodigal son, the dishonest steward, and the servant entrusted with authority.

10. Joel Marcus, *The Mystery of the Kingdom of God* (Atlanta, Georgia: Scholars Press, 1986).

11. Joel Marcus, *Mystery*, p. 106.

12. Marcus, p. 96.

13. Marcus, p. 161.

14. Marcus rightly rejects the polemical reading of the role of the disciples in Mark.

15. See my 'Mark, the Storyteller' for an analysis of the narrative structure of the passion narrative as a series of narrative units in which the endings focus on the wrong responses of the most sympathetic characters in the narrative to the crises of Jesus' passion, death, and resurrection.

16. Paul Hanson, *The Dawn of Apocalyptic* (Philadelphia: Fortress Press, 1979).

PAUL AND JEWISH APOCALYPTIC ESCHATOLOGY

Martinus C. de Boer

1. *The Problem*

A. The importance of Jewish apocalyptic eschatology for understanding Paul's theology was first fully articulated by Albert Schweitzer in his own distinctively systematic way early in this century.[1] Rudolf Bultmann acknowledged its importance but argued that Paul had in fact begun a process of existentially reinterpreting ('demythologizing') received apocalyptic traditions with its talk of cosmological powers and future cosmic transformation, a process that Bultmann sought to bring to fruition in his own existentialist reinterpretation of Paul (and other NT writings).[2] Ernst Käsemann sought in the early sixties to refute the Bultmannian approach with a series of powerful essays reasserting the central significance of apocalyptic eschatology in the New Testament, Paul's letters in particular.[3] A vigorous debate followed the publication of Käsemann's essays,[4] one that has continued to the present day.[5]

Particularly in its early stages, this debate revolved around the terms 'anthropology' and 'cosmology', terms that acquired certain distinct, quasi-technical meanings within the context of the debate. The former, used to sum up the interpretation of Paul by Bultmann and his followers, referred to the *individual* as he or she is addressed by the gospel message in the *present* and confronted with the *decision* of faith. The latter term, shorthand for Käsemann's apocalyptic interpretation of Paul, seemed to denote *God's* destruction in the *future* of the *cosmic forces* that now enslave the creation, a creation from which the individual human being cannot be isolated. Each side, it may be noted, nevertheless sought to come to grips with the dialectic of 'already' and 'not yet' evident in Paul's thought. Both sides largely agreed that whereas 'cosmology' was properly apocalyptic, 'anthropology' (as defined above) was not.

Careful attention to the dispute between Bultmann and Käsemann over Paul's theology of justification (or rectification),[6] an aspect of Paul's thought that provided the larger debate with its focal point, causes one to begin to doubt, however, whether *only* the cosmological reading of Paul has the right to be deemed the apocalyptic one.

B. In the first volume of his *Theology of the New Testament*,[7] Bultmann had argued that there was 'complete agreement' between Paul and first-century Jews 'as to the formal meaning of *dikaiosyne*: It is a forensic-eschatological term' (p. 273).[8] The event of Christ's death and resurrection, however, caused Paul to make two key modifications in the Jewish view:

1. Present not Future: 'what for the Jews', Bultmann wrote, appealing to Rom. 5.1, 'is a *matter of hope* is for Paul a *present reality*—or, better, is also a present reality' (p. 279; emphasis original). Thus, through the Christ-event, 'God already pronounces His eschatological verdict (over the man of faith) in the present; the eschatological event is a present reality, or, rather, is beginning in the present' (p. 276). Christ's death and resurrection was 'the eschatological event by which God ended the old course of the world and introduced a new aeon [N.B.]' (p. 278). Through that event 'God's acquitting decision' (p. 279) has been declared, a verdict that becomes a reality for the individual 'hearer of the gospel' (p. 275).

2. Faith not Works: Whereas 'the pious Jew endeavors. . . to fulfill the conditions which are the presupposition' of God's eschatological justifying verdict (at the last judgment), namely, 'keeping the commandments of the Law and doing good works' (p. 273), the Christian does not seek justification by works of the Law but receives it by faith: 'Righteousness, then', Bultmann wrote, 'cannot be won by human effort, nor does any human accomplishment establish a claim to it; it is sheer gift' (pp. 280-81). The 'righteousness of God' (*dikaiosyne theou*) is thus 'God-given, God-adjudicated righteousness' (p. 285).

It is evident from this brief summary of Bultmann's views that he assumed that Paul's 'anthropological' understanding of 'the righteousness of God' was—apart from the two modifications discussed—essentially the same as that found in Jewish *apocalyptic* eschatology. The agreement pertains not only to the forensic-eschatological character of righteousness but, as the discussion of the second modification bears out, also to its concern with the *individual*.

In his essay '"The Righteousness of God" in Paul' (1961),[9] Käsemann in turn argued that the expression *dikaiosyne theou* (Rom. 1.17; 3.5, 21, 22; 10.3; 2 Cor. 5.21) was a unified one, not to be subsumed (à la Bultmann) under the general heading of 'righteousness' and furthermore not created by Paul (p. 172). It was a technical expression, derived from the Old Testament (Deut. 33.21), that found a home in Jewish apocalyptic thought (1QS 11.12; *T. Dan* 6.10) (p. 172). This unified expression denoted God's eschatological saving action and power. Paul, Käsemann argued, retained this meaning in his appropriation of the expression. For Käsemann, then, the undoubted character of righteousness as a forensic-eschatological gift (a concession to Bultmann) cannot be separated from its character as God's saving power: 'God's saving activity... is present in his gift'; the righteousness of God 'partakes of the character of power, insofar as God himself enters the arena with it' (p. 174). God's righteousness is a gift only insofar as it also signifies submissive obedience to God's saving power (p. 182).

In the process of establishing his thesis, Käsemann also attacked the two modifications Bultmann attributed to Paul:

1. According to Käsemann, what made Paul's use of the expression unique over against the Jewish apocalyptic use of it was not, as Bultmann maintained, the present reality of righteousness. The Thanksgiving Hymns from Qumran show that its present reality was also stressed in one stream of apocalyptic Judaism (p. 178). But Käsemann's basic point was not that Bultmann had misunderstood Jewish apocalyptic eschatology but that he had misunderstood *Paul*: Though Käsemann conceded that 'Paul lays the strongest stress on the present nature of salvation' (p. 178), he emphasized that Paul's 'present eschatology cannot be taken out its context of future eschatology... Paul remained an apocalyptist' (p. 181).

2. Similarly, in attacking Bultmann's second modification, Käsemann asserted that 'the righteousness of God does not, *in Paul's understanding*, refer primarily to the individual and is not to be understood exclusively in the context of a doctrine of man' (p. 180; emphasis added). The Bultmannian anthropological/individual constriction occurs when exclusive emphasis is laid on the gift-character of righteousness and the latter is interpreted in terms of the contrast between faith and works (pp. 172-73, 176). *Paul's* theology of God's

righteousness is not 'essentially concerned with anthropology' (p. 181), but with God's own redemptive action in and for the world. It is here that the uniqueness of Paul's appropriation of the expression 'the righteousness of God' lies, according to Käsemann. Over against Jewish apocalypticism as well as pre-Pauline Jewish Christianity, the disclosure of God's righteousness in Christ can no longer signify only his covenant faithfulness but also, and primarily, his faithfulness toward the whole creation. It is 'God's sovereignty over the world revealing itself eschatologically in Jesus' (p. 180) through whom, contrary to the Jewish view, God justifies not the godly but the ungodly (p. 178).[10]

Thus while Käsemann was busy claiming that his cosmological interpretation of Paul's *dikaiosyne theou* found support in Jewish apocalyptic eschatology and that Bultmann had misunderstood Paul, he did not show that Bultmann's basic assumption was unwarranted, namely, that an anthropological interpretation of Paul's *dikaiosyne theou* also finds support in Jewish apocalyptic eschatology. We may thus begin to ask—leaving aside for the moment the issue of whether Käsemann or Bultmann gave the more compelling account of *Paul's* views—on what ground it is legitimate or accurate to label Paul's thought 'apocalyptic', particularly in relation to the alternative 'cosmology' and 'anthropology'. And that question in turn prompts us to ask about the nature of the Jewish apocalyptic eschatology that is the presumed 'background' for the apostle's own views.

C. My intention in this essay is not, however, to undertake a new investigation of some discrete element in Jewish apocalyptic eschatology (least of all righteousness since that has been sufficiently done elsewhere, largely in support of Käsemann's theses)[11] in order to determine its relevance for 'apocalyptic Paul'. Rather, in the spirit of the honoree of this Festschrift, I shall be bold and seek to demonstrate that Jewish apocalyptic eschatology took two distinct forms, or 'tracks', in the New Testament period. One of these tracks, to be sure, provides support for Käsemann's 'cosmological' reading of Paul, but the other provides some measure of support for Bultmann's 'anthropological' reading of Paul.

2. The Two Tracks of Jewish Apocalyptic Eschatology

A. It is useful to begin by making explicit what has been implicit thus far, namely, that the phrase 'apocalyptic eschatology' does not occur in the literature we are about to discuss nor in the letters of Paul. It is a construct of scholars that purports to epitomize certain phenomena discernible in the sources. It has been used in Pauline scholarship because students of Paul perceive certain conceptual affinities between Paul's thought and Jewish eschatological expectations that are also labeled 'apocalyptic'.

Such eschatology is usually associated with a genre of works known as 'apocalypses' of which the canonical books of Daniel and Revelation (The Apocalypse to John) are notable examples. Recent scholars, however, such as Paul D. Hanson and John J. Collins, have sought to distinguish 'apocalyptic eschatology' from the literary genre. Thus Collins characterizes apocalyptic eschatology 'as a set of ideas and motifs that may also be found in *other literary genres...* '[12] The point is of obvious importance since it means that apocalyptic eschatology, though it may find its most vivid expression in apocalypses, is not confined to such works.[13] The point is also of particular importance for any assessment of Paul's supposed apocalyptic eschatology since the apostle wrote letters not apocalypses.[14]

Most students of Jewish apocalyptic eschatology will agree with Philipp Vielhauer's assertion that 'the essential characteristic of Apocalyptic' is what he labels 'the eschatological dualism' of the two ages, 'this age' and 'the age to come'.[15] The dualism is 'eschatological' because it concerns the final, definitive replacement of 'this age' by the new one. This basic definition of apocalyptic is presupposed by Pauline scholars as well.[16] Though Jewish apocalyptic eschatology finds, as is to be expected, its focus in God's covenantal relationship to Israel, the scope of the two ages is nevertheless cosmic in the sense that they involve two self-contained and all-embracing 'worlds'.[17]

In accordance with the etymology of the term 'apocalyptic' (from the Greek verb *apokalypto*, to unveil), apocalyptic eschatology is 'revealed' (from the Latin *revelare*, also to unveil)[18] eschatology— revealed, that is, *by God*.[19] Since it is only through the disclosure of the coming age that the present can be perceived as 'this age', the notion of revelation in fact encompasses *both* ages. The point has recently been formulated with characteristic clarity and precision by J. Louis Martyn: Apocalyptic, he writes, involves 'the conviction that *God* has now given to the elect true perception *both* of present developments (the real world) and of a wondrous transformation in the near future'.[20] As we shall see below, the perception of one age bears a complementary relationship to the perception of the other.

With these necessary introductory comments we may now outline the two tracks of Jewish apocalyptic eschatology.[21]

B. Track 1: 'This age' is characterized by the fact that evil angelic powers have, in some primeval time (namely, the time of Noah), come to rule over the world.

The story of this angelic fall is found or alluded to in much of the literature (*1 Enoch* 6–19; 64.1-2; 69.4-5; 86.1-6; 106.13-17; *Jub.* 4.15, 22; 5.1-8; 10.4-5; *T. Reub.* 5.6-7; *T. Naph.* 3.5; CD 2.17–3.1; *2 Bar.* 56.12-15; *LAB* 34.1-5; Wis. 2.23-24; cf. Jude 6; 2 Pet. 2.4). The basic story, one that also lies behind Gen. 6.1-6, is that some of God's angels descended to the earth and married beautiful women, thereby begetting giants. Though there was a preliminary judgment of the angels themselves in the time of the Flood, the giants they begot left behind a host of demonic spirits who continue to pervert the earth, primarily by leading human beings, even God's own people, astray into idolatry. Furthermore, it is evident that Satan (Mastema, Belial, the devil) and his angels continue to wreak havoc on the earth.

To illustrate this track we may turn to the first section of *1 Enoch*, the so-called 'Book of the Watchers' (chs. 1–36).[22] In this section of *1 Enoch*, all sin and evil are attributed to the fallen angels (the Watchers) and their demonic progeny (cf. 9.1, 6-9; 10.7-9; 15.8–16.2; 19.1-2): 'they', we are told, 'have transgressed the commandments of the Lord' (21.6; cf. 18.15). When they descended to the earth where human beings dwell, they led them 'astray' from God (19.1-2; cf. 5.4- 5) and 'revealed to them every (kind) of sin' (9.8; cf. 10.9; 16.3). The fallen angels imparted to human beings knowledge that is detrimental to their well being, e.g. the making of weapons of war (8.1), with the result that 'the whole earth was filled with blood and oppression' (9.9). It is thus the evil fallen angels who are actually, or at least ultimately, responsible for the multiplication of 'evil deeds upon the earth' by human beings (16.3; cf. 5.4-5). By leaving their proper heavenly abode, these angels have caused cosmic disorder (15.3, 9- 10), bringing about the pollution, corruption, and perversion of both nature and history. In the midst of 'this age', however, there is a small group, God's righteous elect, who bear witness to the Creator, the God of Israel, and who know that this situation was not intended by God and will not be tolerated by Him for very long (cf. 1.1-5).

When 'this age' is perceived in this way, in terms of subjection to suprahuman angelic powers, it is understandable that the last judgment, the juncture at which 'this age' is replaced by 'the age to come', is depicted as a cosmic confrontation, a war, between God and the Watchers. Thus we read in *1 Enoch* 1.4-5: 'The God of the universe. . . will come forth from his dwelling. And from there he will march upon Mount Sinai and appear in his camp emerging from heaven with a mighty power. And everyone shall be afraid, and Watchers shall quiver'. The arena of the coming eschatological war is the physical universe that God created to be the human habitat. The earth is to be delivered from those alien powers that have come to oppress it (cf. chs. 5, 10, 16, 19, 21). In the new age, Satan and his demonic spirits will be no more. They shall have been defeated and eternally banished from the world (cf. chs. 16, 19). The righteous elect will be vindicated and allowed to live on a purified earth (cf. 1.9; 5.7; 10.17-22).

We may label this track 'cosmological apocalyptic eschatology'.

C. Track 2: 'This age' is characterized by the fact that human beings wilfully reject or deny the Creator, who is the God of Israel, thereby bringing about death and the perversion and corruption of the world. Adam and/or Eve are the primal ancestors who set the pattern for all subsequent human beings.

The fall of Adam and/or Eve is mentioned in a number of works (see *1 Enoch* 69.6; *Jub.* 3.17-25; 4.29-30; *LAB* 13.8-9; Sir. 25.24; Wis. 10.1; cf. 2 Cor. 11.3; 1 Tim. 2.13-14; 1 Cor. 15.21-22; Rom. 5.12-21), but is particularly prominent in two apocalypses, *4 Ezra* and *2 Baruch* (*4 Ezra* 3.5-7, 20-21; 4.30-31; 7.118-119; *2 Bar.* 17.2-3; 23.4; 48.42-43; 54.14, 19; 56.6). *Evil angelic powers are absent from both works*.

To illustrate this 'track' we may refer to *2 Baruch*. In 54.14, 19, we read that while 'Adam sinned first and. . . brought death upon all. . . *each* of us has become his own Adam'. The sin of Adam (and of Eve, who is mentioned in 48.43) and each of his descendants is that they 'did not recognize you [God] as their Creator' (48.46; cf. 14.15-19). God has, however, graciously given the Law as a remedy for this situation whereby each person's ultimate destiny is in his or her own hands: 'each of them who has been born from him [Adam] has prepared for himself the coming torment. . . each of them has *chosen* for himself the coming glory' (54.15; cf. 51.16; 85.7). To choose the coming glory is to choose the Law: The righteous are those who devote themselves to God and His Law (cf. 17.4; 38.1-2; 48.22; 54.5), the wicked are those who do not (cf. 41.3; 51.3; 54.14). Thus, as W. Harnisch has suggested, while 'this age' is the all-embracing time of transgression and thus death, it is also the time of *decision*.[23]

When 'this age' is understood in this way, in terms of willful human rejection of God and of accountability vis-à-vis the Law, the turn of the ages is depicted accordingly: The final judgment is not a cosmic war against cosmological, angelic powers but a courtroom in which all humanity appears before the bar of the Judge (chs. 49–51). The righteous, those who have acknowledged the claim of God by choosing His Law, are rewarded with eternal life; the wicked are condemned to eternal punishment. The sentence of death that fell on Adam and Eve and all their descendants is reversed at the Last Judgment for those who chose the Law, and permanently confirmed for those who did not (cf. 51.16). This basis of God's judgment, not surprisingly, is 'works' (51.3, 7; cf. 14.12; 46.6; 57.2).[24]

We may label this track 'forensic apocalyptic eschatology'. Free will and individual responsibility are emphasized in this track, unlike track 1 where there is no exhortation to choose the Law. The emphasis in track 1 falls rather on God's election (see above on *1 Enoch* 1-36). The righteous are not those who have exercised free will as individuals, but those whom God has collectively elected to be His witnesses to His rightful claim on the world in the midst of the old age where evil cosmological rulers hold sway.

D. By isolating and describing two distinct 'tracks' in Jewish apocalyptic eschatology, I do not wish to suggest that the various Jewish documents that to one degree or another bear witness to the eschatological dualism of the two ages can be assigned simply to one of the two tracks. Rather, I present the two tracks as *heuristic models* that may be used as interpretive tools to understand the dynamics of the various texts, including of course the letters of Paul. Nevertheless, the two tracks *are* found in nearly 'pure' form in *1 Enoch* 1-36 and the apocalypse of *2 Baruch* and I have outlined the two tracks on the basis of these two works.

Other documents indicate that the two tracks can, like those of a railway, run side by side, crisscross, or overlap in various ways, even in the same work. In the Dead Sea Scrolls, to cite the most notable instance of this combining of the two tracks, we find both cosmological subjection and wilfull human transgression, both election and human control of personal destiny, both predestination and exhortation to observe the Law (as interpreted by the community), both God's eschatological war against Belial and his cohorts and God's judgment of human beings on the basis of their 'works' or deeds (see e.g. 1QS 1-4; 1QM; CD). According to the Scrolls, the community as a whole as well as the individual believer are under constant threat from evil cosmological powers (Belial, the Angel of Darkness, the Spirit of Falsehood or Deceit). To choose the Law is thus to choose to stand in the protected sphere of God's own power (as represented by Michael, the Angel of Light, the Spirit of Truth). The Law is God's powerful weapon whereby He enables the righteous believer to withstand the superhuman power of the demonic forces (cf. CD 16.1-3). Present existence is thus marked by a struggle between two contending groups of cosmological powers or spirits that seek to lay their claim on human beings. This struggle does not manifest itself only in the sociological separation of the righteous (the covenantal community) from the wicked (the world outside), but also in the choice that the individual, especially the member of the community, must make each day for God and His Law. The struggle penetrates the heart of the individual (cf. esp. 1QS 3-4).[25]

Much the same could be said for the book of *Jubilees* and the *Testaments of the Twelve Patriarchs*, two works that have numerous similarities to the Dead Sea Scrolls with respect to the ways in which 'cosmological' and 'forensic' (or 'anthropological') elements run side by side or overlap, though it might be argued they do not keep the same balance between the two tracks as do the Dead Sea Scrolls.[26]

E. For the purposes of the present essay, the heuristic value of the two tracks described above can perhaps best be seen not in connection with works that exhibit both tracks but in connection with those that qualify or reject, sometimes quite explicitly, track 1.

The author of *2 Baruch*, for instance, knows the myth of the fallen angels (56.11-15), but he reports that they were definitively punished in the past: 'At that time they who acted like this were tormented in chains'. Nothing is said about a demonic legacy nor about evil angelic powers in the author's present. Furthermore, according to the author of *2 Baruch*, it was in fact Adam who was responsible for the fall of these angels: 'For he who was a danger to himself was also a danger to the angels'! It is human transgression, not angelic rebellion, that has brought about and continues to bring about cosmic disorder.

The qualification or rejection of track 1 is in fact much earlier than *2 Baruch* (c. 100 CE). In the fifth section of *1 Enoch*, the so-called 'Epistle of Enoch' (chs. 91–105),[27] there is a notable polemic against cosmological apocalyptic eschatology, against blaming evil cosmological forces for human sinfulness. In 98.4, the author explicitly affirms that human beings are themselves responsible for sin:

> I have sworn to you, sinners: In the same manner that a mountain has not become a servant, nor shall a hill (ever) become a maidservant of a woman; likewise *sin has not been sent into the world. It is the people who have themselves invented it.*

Similarly, a Greek portion of 98.5 (not found in the Ethiopic text) reads: 'lawlessness was not given from above but from transgression'.[28] For the author of the 'Epistle of Enoch', then, personal accountability is central. He writes as a wise man (98.1) instructing his children to seek righteousness and walk in its paths (cf. 91.19; 94.1-4). He exhorts them to '*choose* righteousness and the elect life' (94.4) and thus to avoid 'the ways of injustice and of death' (94.2). That choice determines one's destiny at the last judgment (cf. 91.7-8; 93.3; 94.7, 9; 96.8; 97.3, 5; 98.8, 10; 99.15; 100.4, 5; 103.8; 104.3, 5). The 'Epistle of Enoch' has in effect adapted the idea of the Two Ways (cf. OT Psalm 1) to the dualism of apocalyptic eschatology, *forensic* apocalyptic eschatology.

The same is true of the *Psalms of Solomon* (first century BCE), a work which makes no mention of evil cosmological powers in opposition to God. In these Psalms, too, there is a considerable emphasis on personal accountability and choice:

> Our works (are) in the choosing (*en ekloge*) and power of our souls, to do right (*dikaiosyne*) and wrong (*adikia*) in the works of our hands... the one who does what is right (*dikaiosyne*) saves up life for himself with the Lord, and the one who does what is evil causes his own life to be destroyed (9.4-5).

Those who 'live in the righteousness of his commandments, in the Law' (14.2) shall by God's mercy receive the reward of eternal life (3.12) at the last judgment when sinners shall be eternally punished (15.12-15).

The apocalypses of *4 Ezra* (late first century CE) and *2 Baruch* also make use of the motif the Two Ways, a motif that finds its most notable expression in Deut. 30.19: '. . . I [Moses, speaking for God] have set before you life and death, blessing and curse; therefore, choose (LXX: *eklexai*) life, that you and your descendants may live. . . ' This text is paraphrased by both *4 Ezra* (7.129; cf. 7.48) and *2 Baruch* (19.1; cf. 46.3; 54.15; 84.2). In both works, the exhortation to choose life, i.e. the Law (cf. *4 Ezra* 14.30; *2 Bar.* 38.2), has an individual focus, unlike Deut. 30.19 itself, where Moses addresses 'all Israel' (29.1; 31.1) gathered for instruction as a people prior to their entry into the promised land.

4 Ezra's use of Deut. 30.19 is particularly interesting since it occurs at the end of a passage that echoes the kind of modified cosmological apocalyptic eschatology we have observed in Qumran, namely, the violent struggle in the present between two spirits (cf. also *T. Jud.* 20.1).[29] An *angelus interpres*, who probably represents the views of the author,[30] speaks to the seer, 'Ezra' (7.127-129):

> This is the meaning of the contest which every man who is born on earth shall wage, that if he is defeated he shall suffer what you have said, but if he is victorious he shall receive what I have said. For this is the way of which Moses, while he was alive, spoke to the people, saying, '*Choose* for yourself life, that you may live!'

And yet, as previously noted, there are no cosmological powers present in the apocalypse of *4 Ezra*. The creative balance between the two tracks found in the Dead Sea Scrolls has been dissolved in the direction of track 2: In *4 Ezra* the cosmological struggle between the two spirits is transmuted into a struggle in the human heart between a mysterious and unexplained 'evil root' and the Law (3.20-22).[31] And the 'evil root', though powerful, cannot serve as an excuse for evading the choice of Deut. 30.19. The angel tells the seer that though it may be difficult to observe the Law, it is possible to do so. In 8.38, the seer is told that God will not concern himself with the 'death, judgment, or damnation' of sinners since 'though they received freedom. . . they despised the Most High, and were contemptuous of his Law, and forsook his ways' (8.55-56; cf. 8.59; 9.11-12;

2 Bar. 85.7). Those who choose the Law, who will have 'a treasure of good works laid up with the Most High' (7.77; cf. 8.33, 36), will be saved (cf. 7.13, 97, 113). In *4 Ezra*, as in *2 Baruch*, the future will bring a general resurrection in which all people will be judged on the basis of their observance of the Law and thus their 'works' (7.33-39; 9.7-8).

It is worth noting that the qualification or rejection of cosmological apocalyptic eschatology need not be confined to documents that exhibit the marks of forensic apocalyptic eschatology. Sirach, a work that like the 'Epistle of Enoch' comes from the second century BCE, contains an evident polemic against attributing human sinfulness to cosmological powers. Thus in 21.28, the author writes: 'When an ungodly person curses Satan, he is actually cursing himself' (my translation). You cannot blame the devil for human transgression. For the author, sin has a human origin: 'From a woman sin had its beginning, and because of her we all die' (25.24; cf. 15.14). In this work too, then, the emphasis falls upon personal responsibility and choice: 'If you will, you can keep the commandments, and to act faithfully is a matter of your own choice (*eudokias*)' (15.15). In 15.17, Sirach echoes the Deuteronomic choice: 'Before a man are life and death and whichever he chooses (*eudokesei*) will be given to him'. In Sirach, too, a person chooses life by choosing the Law (cf. Sir. 15.1; 17.11), but, in contrast to the 'Epistle of Enoch', the *Psalms of Solomon*, *4 Ezra* and *2 Baruch*, this choice has no eschatological significance.

3. *Summary and Conclusions*

A. We may summarize the two tracks of Jewish apocalyptic eschatology outlined in the previous section as follows:

1. Cosmological-apocalyptic eschatology: The world has come under the dominion of evil, angelic powers. God's sovereign rights have been usurped and the world, including God's own people, have been led astray into idolatry. But there is a righteous remnant, chosen by God, who by their submission to the Creator, the God of Israel, bear witness to the fact that those evil cosmological powers are doomed to pass away. This remnant, the elect of God, await God's deliverance. God will invade the world under the dominion of the evil powers and defeat them in a cosmic war. Only God has the

power to defeat and to overthrow the demonic powers that have subjugated and perverted the earth. God will establish his sovereignty very soon, delivering the righteous and bringing about a new age in which He will reign unopposed.

2. Forensic-apocalyptic eschatology: This is a modified form of the first track. In this view, the notion of evil, cosmological forces is absent, recedes into the background or is even explicitly rejected. Instead, the emphasis falls on free will and decision. Thus we find a kind of legal piety in which personal responsibility and accountability are dominant. Sin is wilfull rejection of the Creator God (the First Commandment) and death is punishment for this fundamental sin. God has, however, provided the Law as a remedy for this situation and a person's posture toward this Law determines one's ultimate destiny. At the Last Judgment God will reward those who have acknowledged His claim and chosen the Law, while He will punish those who have not.[32]

B. Track 1 is consistent with Käsemann's 'cosmological' understanding of apocalyptic eschatology, track 2 with Bultmann's 'anthropological' understanding, particularly in terms of the emphasis on individual decision vis-à-vis the Law. With an eye on Bultmann, we may however observe, first, that track 2, like track 1, is cosmic in scope, in contrast to Bultmann's individualistic constriction of Paul's thought, which had arguably more in common with modern existentialism than with Paul himself or with first-century Judaism.[33] Secondly, track 2, like track 1, is theocentric not anthropocentric. Both tracks are fundamentally concerned with the revelation of God's claim on the world he has created and its rectification. Wheres track 1 underscores the human need for God's help and action, track 2 underscores human accountability to God for sin and its terrible consequences.

C. The two tracks of Jewish apocalyptic eschatology as I have outlined them are meant to be heuristic models, each one seeking to describe an internally coherent or consistent configuration of motifs. These models are, of course, based on evidence provided by the primary sources. The two tracks are found in nearly 'pure' form in *1 Enoch* 1–36 and the apocalypse of *2 Baruch*. Elements proper to one track can, and frequently do, run side by side or overlap with elements proper to the other, most notably in the Dead Sea Scrolls (see section 2 D above). Furthermore, there is considerable evidence to indicate that there were Jews who specifically rejected motifs proper to what I have labeled 'cosmological apocalyptic eschatology' in favour of what I have labeled 'forensic apocalyptic eschatology' (see section 2 E above). In addition, the evidence indicates that track 2 overtook and displaced track 1 completely after the disaster of 70 CE (cf. *4 Ezra, 2 Baruch*).[34]

D. Paul of course lived in a time when both tracks of Jewish apocalyptic eschatology were still prominent and the discussion of the debate between Bultmann and Käsemann over Paul's theology of justification (or rectification) at the beginning of this essay is a sufficient indication that the traces of both, *christologically appropriated and modified*, are present in Paul, much as in the Dead Sea Scrolls.[35] It is not possible to explore this claim in detail here; I must confine myself to a few pertinent observations in conclusion:

The letter to the Romans indicates that Paul can isolate the two tracks to some extent. In Rom. 1.1–5.11, the elements of forensic apocalyptic eschatology clearly dominate. In Rom. 6.1–8.38, however, the elements of cosmological apocalyptic eschatology are notably prominent (e.g. sin, death, righteousness, flesh, the spirit as cosmological powers). In 5.12-21, where Paul appeals to Adam, the figure prominent in track 2 Jewish apocalyptic eschatology, and sets him in contrast to Christ, the two tracks completely interpenetrate, though the passage itself marks the shift from predominantly forensic to predominantly cosmological categories in Paul's argument.[36] That shift finds its anticipation in 1.16-17 and 3.9, two texts that occur at crucial junctures in Paul's argument in the first three chapters. Thus, while such texts as 8.1 and 8.33-34 indicate that forensic categories have hardly been given up or left behind, the structure and progression of Paul's argument in Romans 1–8 suggest that motifs proper to track 1 circumscribe and, to a large extent, overtake motifs proper to track 2.

If this assessment of Romans is correct, then the question is: Why are motifs proper to track 2 present at all? The answer, we may properly assume, has something to do with what J. Louis Martyn likes to call Paul's 'conversation partners'. If one of those partners in Romans was 'Judaism' (as interpreters of Romans have often claimed), then it was also a Judaism embracing *track 2* apocalyptic eschatology. It is not without interest to note that, in 2.5-8, Paul reproduces a nearly pure specimen of Jewish forensic apocalyptic eschatology with its adaptation of the Two Ways:[37]

> But by your hard and impenitent heart you are storing up wrath for yourself on the day of wrath when God's righteous judgment will be revealed. For he will render to every man according to his works: to those who by patience in well-doing seek for glory and honor and immortality, he will give eternal life; but for those who are factious and do not obey the truth, but obey wickedness, there will be wrath and fury (cf. 2.13).

Since Paul is writing to Christians in Rome, it is also quite possible (probable, in my estimation) that these particular conversation partners, whether of Jewish or Gentile birth, had appropriated track 2 Jewish apocalyptic eschatology. For such Christians, Christ's death would have been understood as a sacrifice atoning for past sins or trespasses (Rom. 3.25-26; 4.25; cf. 1 Cor. 15.3; Gal. 1.4). This sacrificial death did not put an end to Law observance, but quite to the contrary, obligated those so forgiven to obey it all the more (cf. Mt. 5.17-20).

Throughout 1.18–3.19, Paul embraces the presuppositions of track 2 Jewish (and/or Jewish-Christian) apocalyptic eschatology, most notably its understanding of the role and function of the Law, only to claim that by the standard of the Law, through which 'the whole world may be held accountable to God' (3.19; cf. 2.12-16), the human situation is in fact hopeless (cf. 3.10-20; 4.15; 8.1). It is hopeless because, for Paul, everyone is 'under the power of sin' (3.9), a claim that presumes what is made abundantly clear later in Romans, namely, the inability of the Law to provide deliverance from sin and thus death (cf. 7.7–8.8).

Reliance on 'works of the Law' (3.20, 28), therefore, is quite literally a dead-end (cf. 4.15a) and, in any event, is ruled out of court by the justifying death of Christ (3.21-30; cf. 5.1-11), good news indeed. Faith is the appropriate human posture to this event, replacing (as Bultmann rightly claimed) 'works of the Law'. But Paul's cosmological understanding of God's righteousness (1.16-17) and of sin (3.9) indicate that faith is not, as Bultmann thought, analogous to what it replaces, i.e. it is precisely not a matter of human 'choice', 'decision', or, as Americans might say, 'action' (cf.

10.17). It is in fact a matter of being initially passive and grateful beneficiaries of God's gracious, liberating power revealed in the death and resurrection of Jesus Christ (cf. 5.11). Thus, while Paul speaks of faith (or of justification by faith) primarily when he is combatting the claim (among both Jews and Christians) that 'works of the Law' provide the righteousness that will lead to eschatological acquittal and thus to life, the meaning of faith is actually determined by the cosmological-apocalyptic disclosure of God's righteousness and of sin in the death (crucifixion) of Christ. Christ's death cannot be understood in exclusively forensic terms, since it marks God's triumphant invasion of the world 'under sin' (3.9) to liberate human beings (the ungodly) from its deadly power.

Much the same may, I think, be said about Paul's letter to the Galatians, particularly in light of the highly illuminating article of J. Louis Martyn, 'Apocalyptic Antinomies in the Letter to the Galatians'. Pointing to Paul's polemically ironical use of conversion terminology in 4.9, Martyn observes that the circumcising, Law-observant Teachers whose gospel Paul combats in Galatians believed 'that the advent of Christ introduced a new religion' (p. 423 n. 25). Paul accordingly 'causes the letter to be focused' on this issue, at least in part (*ibid.*). For Paul, however, the gospel is not 'about the better of two ways' (p. 414), nor then is the letter 'designed to convert its readers from one religion to another' (p. 420). Rather, the gospel, and the subject of Galatians, is the apocalypse of Christ and his cross (p. 421), an event that marks 'the death of one world and the advent of another' (p. 414) and inaugurates a cosmic warfare, most notably between Flesh and Spirit (Gal. 5.19-23). Thus, the world in which the Galatians now live is 'the scene of antinomous warfare on a cosmic scale' (p. 421). Paul's use of such 'pairs of opposites' as Flesh and Spirit in Galatians 'does not fall in the line of the wisdom tradition, with its marriage of the pairs to the doctrine of the Two Ways' (p. 423 n. 25) nor then is Gal. 5.19-23 'a new edition of the doctrine of the Two Ways' (p. 423 n. 25). In short, the advent of Christ is *not* about making a choice between the better of two ways, two religions, but concerns God's redemptive invasion of the human world.

Martyn labels Paul's cosmological views 'apocalyptic', and rightly so, but it seems to me that the view of the Teachers were also 'apocalyptic', albeit in a different way: In line with the forensic

Jewish apocalyptic eschatology found in such works as the 'Epistle of Enoch', the *Psalms of Solomon*, *4 Ezra* and *2 Baruch*, they had not only married pairs of opposites to the doctrine of the Two Ways but had also adapted (with their own christological slant) the latter to the dualism of the two ages.[38] Paul circumscribes the forensic apocalyptic eschatology of the Galatian Teachers with a cosmological apocalyptic eschatology of his own. If the fact that Martyn begins his argument for apocalyptic antinomies in Galatians with the epistle's final paragraph is not coincidental, it may perhaps be said that by the end of the epistle the forensic apocalyptic eschatology of the Teachers has been decisively overtaken and neutralized by Paul's cosmological apocalyptic eschatology.

NOTES

1. *Paul and His Interpreters. A Critical History* (German original, 1911; New York: Schocken, 1964); *The Mysticism of Paul the Apostle* (German original 1931; New York: Seabury, 1968). The former volume began as an introduction to the latter which was actually given a first draft in 1906 (see *ibid.*, p. vii). See also W. Wrede, *Paul* (Geman original, 1904; London: Philip Green, 1907), and, earlier, R. Kabisch, *Die Eschatologie des Paulus in ihren Zusammenhängen mit dem Gesamtbegriff des Paulinismus* (Göttingen: Vandenhoeck & Ruprecht, 1893).

2. See his programmatic essay, 'New Testament and Mythology', first published in 1941, and now available in S.M. Ogden, ed., *New Testament & Mythology and Other Basic Writings* (Philadelphia: Fortress, 1984), pp. 1-43. See also Bultmann's *Theology of the New Testament* (German original, 1948-1953; 2 vols.; New York: Scribner's, 1951, 1955), Vol. I, pp. 185-352.

3. 'The Beginnings of Christian Theology' (1960); 'On the Subject of Primitive Christian Apocalyptic' (1962); 'Paul and Early Catholicism' (1963). These essays are available in English translation in *New Testament Questions of Today* (Philadelphia: Fortress, 1969).

4. See Bultmann, 'Ist Apokalyptik die Mutter der christlichen Theologie?', in *Apophoreta: Festschrift für E. Haenchen* (BZNW, 30; Berlin: Töpelmann, 1964), pp. 64-69; Käsemann, 'On Paul's Anthropology', in *Perspectives on Paul* (Philadelphia: Fortress, 1969), pp. 1-31. Käsemann responded to many of his critics in the footnotes of the articles cited in the previous note.

5. See especially the work of J.C. Beker, *Paul the Apostle. The Triumph of God in Life & Thought* (Philadelphia: Fortress, 1980); J. Baumgarten, *Paulus und die Apokalyptik. Die Auslegung apokalyptischer Überlieferung in den*

echten Paulusbriefen (Neukirchen-Vluyn: Neukirchener Verlag, 1975); L.E. Keck, 'Paul and Apocalyptic Theology', *Int* 38 (1984), pp. 229-41; V.P. Branick, 'Apocalyptic Paul?', *CBQ* 47 (1985), pp. 664-75. Of considerable importance is the essay of J.L. Martyn, 'Apocalyptic Antinomies in the Letter to the Galatians', *NTS* 31 (1985), pp. 419-24. Roughly speaking, Beker, Keck and Martyn are in Käsemann's corner; Baumgarten and Branick in Bultmann's.

6. Whether the Greek words *dikaioō/dikaiosynē* are best translated 'justify/justification' or 'rectify/rectification' (for the latter, see L.E. Keck, *Paul and His Letters* [Philadelphia: Fortress, 1979], pp. 118-23; Martyn, 'Apocalyptic Antinomies', p. 418) is partly what is at issue: the former seems closer to Bultmann's views, the latter to Käsemann's. The Greek noun is of course also commonly translated 'righteousness'.

7. See note 2 above. The following citations are from Volume I of this work.

8. Emphasis removed. Bultmann appeals to Rom. 2.13; 4.3, 5, 6, 22; Gal. 3.6. Righteousness as a forensic term implies the imagery of the law court and thus means the 'favorable standing' one has in such a court (p. 272). It does not mean 'the ethical quality of a person' (p. 272), but 'his relation to God' (p. 277).

9. Available in *New Testament Questions of Today*, pp. 168-82.

10. Bultmann and Käsemann defended their views in subsequent publications. See Bultmann, *'DIKAIOSYNE THEOU'*, *JBL* 83 (1964), pp. 12-16. Käsemann responded to Bultmann in footnotes included in the republication of his original article; see *New Testament Questions of Today*, pp. 168, 169, 173.

11. See C. Muller, *Gottes Gerechtigkeit und Gottes Volk* (FRLANT, 86; Göttingen: Vandenhoeck & Ruprecht, 1964); K. Kertelge, *'Rechtfertigung' bei Paulus* (NTAbh 33; 2nd edn; Münster: Aschendorff, 1967); P. Stuhlmacher, *Gerechtigkeit Gottes bei Paulus* (Göttingen: Vandenhoeck & Ruprecht, 1965). These works provided support for Käsemann's position. A significant defense of Bultmann was the essay by H. Conzelmann, 'Die Rechtfertigungslehre des Paulus: Theologie oder Anthropologie?', *EvT* 28 (1968), pp. 389-404. See Käsemann's response to Conzelmann in 'Justification and Salvation History', *Perspectives*, p. 76 n. 27. See further the discussion by E.P. Sanders, *Paul and Palestinian Judaism* (Philadelphia: Fortress, 1977), pp. 474-511, and the appendix in the same work by M.T. Brauch, 'Perspectives on "God's righteousness" in recent German discussion', pp. 523-42.

12. *The Apocalyptic Imagination. An Introduction to the Jewish Matrix of Christianity* (New York: Crossroad, 1984), p. 2; emphasis added. See P.D. Hanson, 'Apocalypse, Genre' and 'Apocalypticism', *IDBSup*, pp. 27-34.

13. In any event, Collins (*Apoclayptic Imagination*, p. 3) points out that it is dubious whether we can really speak about the genre 'apocalypse' prior to the second century CE. He nevertheless proceeds as if we can.

14. For this reason Paul's apocalyptic eschatology need not necessarily be confined to the scenarios found in e.g. 1 Thess. 4.14-18 or 1 Corinthians 15. See, for instance, G. Bornkamm, *Paul* (New York: Harper & Row, 1969), p. 76, or Baumgarten, *Paulus*, p. 130.

15. 'Introduction' to 'Apocalypses and Related Subjects', in E. Hennecke, *New Testament Apocrypha* (ed. W. Schneemelcher; 2 vols.; Philadelphia: Westminster, 1964), Vol. II, pp. 588-89. Similarly, Hanson defines apocalyptic eschatology as 'a religious perspective' whose 'essential characteristics' are two ages separated by 'a great judgment' (*Dawn of Apocalyptic. The Historical and Sociological Roots of Jewish Apocalyptic Eschatology* [2nd edn; Philadelphia: Fortress, 1979], pp. 431, 440). D.S. Russell writes that the 'dualistic view of the world, which is characteristic of apocalyptic eschatology, finds expression in a doctrine of two ages' (*The Method and Message of Jewish Apocalyptic, 200 BC-AD 100* [OTL; Philadelphia: Westminster, 1964], p. 269). The specific terminology need not be used for the motif to be present.

16. See e.g. Schweitzer, *Mysticism*, p. 55; Bultmann, *Theology*, Vol. I, p. 278; Käsemann, *Commentary on Romans* (Grand Rapids: Eerdmans, 1980; German, 4th edn, 1980), p. 150; Beker, *Paul*, p. 136.

17. The two ages can thus also be labeled 'this world' and 'the world to come'. For the terminology and the motif, see *1 Enoch* 71.15; *4 Ezra* 7.50, 112, 119; *2 Bar.* 44.8-15; 83.4-9; Mk 10.30; Mt. 12.32; Lk. 18.30; Eph. 1.21; 2.7; Heb. 6.5; *m. Abot* 4.1; *m. Sanh.* 10.1; *b. Ber.* 9.5. In Paul, see Rom. 12.2; 1 Cor. 1.20; 2.6, 8, 18; 3.19; 5.10; 7.31; 2 Cor. 4.4; Gal. 1.4. Paul employs the expression 'this age' and 'this world' interchangeably. He does not employ the expression 'the age/world to come', but, as Keck ('Paul and Apocalyptic Theology', p. 234) points out, the idea is implied when the present world is characterized as '*this* age/world'. Besides, such expressions as 'the kingdom of God' (Rom. 14.17; 1 Cor. 4.20; 6.9; 15.24, 50; Gal. 5.21; 1 Thess. 2.12), 'eternal life' (Rom. 2.7; 5.21; 6.22, 23; Gal. 6.8), and 'new creation' (2 Cor. 5.17; Gal. 6.15) are surely other ways of speaking about the age to come.

18. See the discussion of Martyn, 'From Paul to Flannery O'Connor with the Power of Grace', *Katallagete* 6 (1981), pp. 10-17.

19. Apocalyptic eschatology is thus not simply the kind of eschatology found in apocalypses (contra Collins, *Apocalyptic Imagination*, p. 9), as if the genre defines the phenomenon. What joins the eschatology found in the apocalypses with the apocalyptic eschatology found in other literature is (among other things) the notion of the revelation (*apocalypsis*) of two ages.

20. 'Apocalyptic Antinomies', p. 424 n. 28; emphasis added. For this reason, as Martyn points out here, a central concern of apocalyptic is epistemology, 'the birth of a new way of knowing both present and future', one that is God-given. See already his earlier essay, 'Epistemology at the

Turn of the Ages: 2 Corinthians 5.16', in *Christian History and Interpretation: Studies Presented to John Knox* (Cambridge: Cambridge University Press, 1967), pp. 269-87. See also the comments of C. Rowland, *The Open Heaven. A Study of Apocalyptic in Judaism and Early Christianity* (New York: Crossroad, 1982), p. 113.

21. Unless otherwise noted, citations of so-called apocryphal and pseudepigraphical works are taken from the RSV translation *The Apocrypha* (New York: Thomas Nelson, 1957) and from J.H. Charlesworth, ed., *The Old Testament Pseudepigrapha* (2 vols.; Garden City, N.Y.: Doubleday, 1983, 1985).

22. J.T. Milik (*The Books of Enoch. Aramaic Fragments of Qumran Cave 4* [Oxford: Clarendon, 1976], p. 25) surmises on the basis of the Aramaic fragments from Qumran that 'the Book of the Watchers had essentially the same form as that in which it is known through the Greek and Ethiopic versions'. This 'Book of the Watchers' is but one of five major sections of *1 Enoch* and I treat it as a distinct unit because it may be doubted whether the five-book Enoch (now extant only in Ethiopic) existed as such prior to the second century CE. M. Black (*Book of Enoch or 1 Enoch* [Studia in Veteris Testamenti Pseudepigrapha 7; Leiden: Brill, 1985], pp. 10-11), for instance, believes that the idea of an Enochic Pentateuch may have been the work of Christian scribes, writing in Greek, who completed their work in the second century CE.

Milik (*Aramaic Fragments*, p. 31) has argued that the Enochic version of the fall of the angels may have influenced Gen. 6.1-6, rather than the reverse. See also Black, *The Book of Enoch*, pp. 14, 124. Collins (*Apocalyptic Imagination*, p. 34) thinks that Gen. 6.1-6 is prior.

23. *Verhängnis und Verheissung der Geschichte. Untersuchung zum Zeit- und Geschichtsverständnis im 4. Buch Esra und in der syr. Baruchapokalypse* (FRLANT, 97; Göttingen: Vandenhoeck & Ruprecht, 1969), p. 241.

24. See further, M. Desjardins, 'Law in 2 Baruch and 4 Ezra', *Stud Rel/ SciRel* 14 (1985), pp. 25-37.

25. See Sanders, *Paul and Palestinian Judaism*, pp. 237-321 (on the Dead Sea Scrolls), esp. p. 295.

26. Cf. e.g. Collins (*Apocalyptic Imagination*, p. 111): 'The Testaments lack the strong deterministic note' of the Dead Sea Scrolls. 'T. Asher emphasizes that men are free to choose between the two ways. The Qumran community Rule suggests that humanity is already divided into two lots, although in practice a choice would still seem to be required'. It needs to be acknowledged here that the dating and provenance of the *Testaments of the Twelve Patriarchs* have been and continue to be matters of debate.

27. Dated by Milik (*Enoch*, pp. 48ff.) to the second century BCE.

28. See also the argument of Milik (*ibid.*, pp. 52-53) with respect to *1 Enoch* 100.4.

29. See E. Brandenburger, *Adam und Christus. Exegetisch-religionsge-schichtliche Untersuchung zu Röm 5.12-21 (1. Kor. 15)* (Neukirchen: Neukirchener Verlag, 1962), p. 33 n. 6.

30. See Harnisch, *Verhängnis*, pp. 48ff., 60-67.

31. Numerous interpreters see in the reference to the 'evil root' (or 'the grain of evil seed' in 4.30-31 and 'evil thought' in 7.92) an analogue to the rabbinic notion of the Evil Impulse. This notion could be fruitfully discussed in terms of the two tracks I have outlined though space forbids such discussion here. See the recent study by G.H. Cohen Stuart, *The Struggle in Man Between Good and Evil. An Inquiry into the Origin of the Rabbinic Concept of the Yeser Hara'* (Kampen: Kok, 1984).

32. The two tracks as I have outlined them do not pretend to account for all that may be important in Jewish apocalyptic eschatology, e.g. messianism, national disaster and restoration, the Temple, repentance, atonement, covenant. Part 2 of this essay was presented in oral form to the 'Werkgezelschap Judaica' at the University of Leiden in the fall of 1986 and I would like to thank J.W. van Henten, M. de Jonge, and P.T. van Rooden for their helpful and stimulating comments.

33. In his essay 'New Testament and Mythology', Bultmann wrote that myth, with its talk of cosmic powers and forces controlling human life, 'does not want to be interpreted in cosmological terms but in anthropological terms—or, better, in *existentialist* terms' (p. 9; emphasis added). Bultmann's descriptive account of Jewish apocalyptic eschatology, however, is quite close to track 1. For example, he writes: 'In the apocalyptic view the individual is responsible for himself only . . . and the individual's future will be decided according to his works. And this is a judgment over the whole world' (*The Presence of Eternity. History and Eschatology* [Wesport, Connecticut: Greenwood, 1975], p. 31). In *Primitive Christianity in its Contemporary Setting* (New York: Meridian, 1956; German, 1949; pp. 80-86), Bultmann relies primarily on *4 Ezra* for his account of Jewish apocalyptic eschatology, while in his *Theology* (Vol. I, p. 230), he attributes talk of cosmological powers in Paul to the influence of 'the cosmological mythology of Gnosticism', rather than to the influence of Jewish apocalyptic traditions.

34. Track 2 finds its fruition in Rabbinic Judaism: see A.J. Saldarini, 'The Uses of Apocalyptic in the Mishna and Tosephta', *CBQ* 39 (1977), pp. 396-409; A.P. Hayman, 'The Fall, Freewill and Human Responsibility in Rabbinic Judaism', *SJT* 37 (1984), pp. 13-22; P. Schäfer, 'Die Lehre von den zwei Welten', in *Studien zur Geschichte und Theologie des rabbinischen Judentums* (Leiden: Brill, 1978), pp. 244-91.

35. I do not mean to imply that I necessarily agree with either Bultmann or Käsemann on all points.

36. I give detailed treatment of Rom. 5.12-21 and the parallel passage in 1 Cor. 15.21-28 in *The Defeat of Death. Apocalyptic Eschatology in 1*

Corinthians 15 and Romans 5 (JSNTS, 22; Sheffield: JSOT, 1988). I also give a full discussion of the Jewish texts used in this essay as well as others not mentioned here.

37. E.P. Sanders has recently argued that, apart from the 'tag' of 2.16, there is nothing in Rom. 1.18–2.29 that is peculiarly Christian (*Paul, the Law, and the Jewish People* [Philadelphia: Fortress, 1983], pp. 123-35, esp. p. 231). The passage, he maintains, is 'a synagogue sermon' whose 'point is to have its hearers become better Jews on strictly non-Christian Jewish terms. . . the entire chapter is written from a Jewish perspective' (*ibid.*, p. 129). Sanders makes this claim even though he 'can adduce no proof' for Paul' assertion in 2.12-15 that 'all humanity will be judged and either justified or condemned according to the same law' (*ibid.*, pp. 130-31). He might perhaps have considered such texts as *4 Ezra* 7.37, 72; *2 Bar.* 15.5; 48.40. The motif of a general resurrection for judgment on the basis of 'works', found in both *4 Ezra* and *2 Baruch*, is predicated on the universal applicability of the Law, the heart of which is the First Commandment (cf. *4 Ezra* 8.60; *2 Bar.* 48.46-47 with Rom. 1.19-23).

38. That the gospel of the Teachers had an eschatological component (informed by the dualism of the two ages) is implied by Martyn's account of the Teachers' gospel in 'A Law-Observant Mission to Gentiles: The Background of Galatians', *SJT* 38 (1985), pp. 307-24, esp. pp. 322-23.

'THE RIGHTEOUS ONE' AS ESCHATOLOGICAL DELIVERER: A CASE STUDY IN PAUL'S APOCALYPTIC HERMENEUTICS

Richard B. Hays

1. *Introduction: Apocalyptic and Hermeneutics*

Lou Martyn has made a signal contribution to Pauline scholarship by patiently reminding his colleagues that apocalyptic thought asserts its influence in Paul not only through images of resurrection and parousia but also through signs more subtle and pervasive: wherever Paul construes the present time as fundamentally trans-formed through God's invasive act of deliverance—which is to say everywhere—we find him employing apocalyptic categories.[1] The texture of Paul's carefully tailored language reveals that it has been cut from an apocalyptic bolt; to read him rightly we must read with sensibilities responsive to this texture. Such a reading shows that Galatians, despite its omission of references to a specific future eschatological scenario, must be understood as 'a letter fully as apocalyptic as are the other Paulines',[2] because it reveals the present as the time of 'the dawn of God's New Creation'.[3]

If Paul's temporal sensibilities are apocalyptic in character, the same must be said of his hermeneutics—if we may employ this anachronistic academic term to describe his way of understanding the message of Scripture. Because all things have been (or will be) transformed by God's redemptive action in Christ, Scripture must be read with new eyes.[4] The reader who stands at the turn of the ages can no longer believe that Scripture merely authorizes religion-as-usual for Israel; instead, it must promise the New Creation. Scripture must adumbrate, for those who have eyes to see, the coming of eschatological transformation.[5]

This approach to Scripture has direct consequences for Paul's christology. If Paul interprets Christ's death as 'the apocalypse of his cross',[6] signifying the death of the old cosmos and the birth of the new, and if that death took place 'according to the Scriptures' (cf. 1 Cor. 15.3), might we not expect to find Paul interpreting scriptural texts through a hermeneutic that would disclose the apocalyptic dimensions of Jesus' identity and mission? And, if that is so, might a careful investigation of Paul's christological language disclose hitherto unrecognized (or at least underemphasized) links with the messianic expectation and categories of early Jewish Christianity? Certainly Paul's initial presentation of Jesus in Galatians has a strongly apocalyptic shading: God 'raised him from the dead' (1.1), and he is characterized as 'Lord Jesus Christ who gave himself for our sins in order to deliver us from the present evil age' (1.3b-4a). Paul's citation of these apocalyptic formulas in his letter-opening is surely not haphazard; their construal of Jesus' death and resurrection as an event signalling eschatological deliverance from the power of an evil age must govern our reading of Paul's subsequent statements.

One of the striking things about Paul's use of Scripture is his apparent disinterest, in contrast to Matthew and later Christian apologists, in overt appeals to christological proofs based on the fulfillment of prophecy. Nonetheless, it will be the burden of this essay to argue that Paul does indeed presuppose certain apocalyptic traditions of christological exegesis, traditions that he shared with many other first-century Jewish Chrstians.

Specifically, this essay will reexamine Paul's reading of Hab. 2.4 by testing a pair of closely linked hypotheses: (1) that *ho dikaios* ('The Righteous One') was a standard epithet for the Messiah in early Jewish Christian circles, and (2) that Paul's citation (in Rom. 1.17 and Gal. 3.11) of Hab. 2.4 (*ho dikaios ek pisteōs zesetai*) presupposes an apocalyptic/messianic interpretation of that text. Each of these hypotheses has been proposed from time to time by various scholars,[7] though the second thesis remains a minority view and the first is rarely seen as a matter of much importance. I have argued elsewhere, on grounds of the internal logic of Paul's argument in Galatians 3, that Paul did indeed understand *ho dikaios* as a messianic designation.[8] However, Lou Martyn's delineation of the apocalyptic contours of Galatians provides a new perspective from which the problem must be considered: we should inquire how Paul's apocalyptic hermeneutic would have shaped his understanding of Hab. 2.4 (and vice-versa). The present essay, then, will first survey several non-Pauline texts in which *ho dikaios* appears to be used as a messianic designation and then return to consider Paul's use of the Habbakkuk citation in light of Martyn's insights, remembering that apocalyptic perceptions may be imbedded in the language and between the lines of the text.

2. *'The Righteous One' as Messianic Designation? Non-Pauline Texts*

NT scholars have for some time recognized that several first-century texts refer to a 'Righteous One' who is the eschatological agent of God.[9] A survey of these familiar passages will show not only how widespread the 'Righteous One' designation is but also how it gathers significations by echoing a variety of antecedent scriptural texts.

A. *The Evidence of 1 Enoch*
Outside the canon of Christian texts, *1 Enoch* provides the only generally acknowledged example of a Jewish document antedating or contemporary with the NT that employs 'The Righteous One' as a title for a messianic figure. This single example is, however, a very important one for our present purposes.

In *1 Enoch* 38, the visionary Enoch begins to recount his revealed wisdom by describing a scene of eschatological judgment:

> When the congregation of the righteous shall appear,
> sinners shall be judged for their sins,
> they shall be driven from the face of the earth,
> and when the Righteous One shall appear before the face of the
>   righteous,
> those elect ones, their deeds are hung upon the lord of the
>   Spirits,
> he shall reveal light to the righteous and the elect who
> dwell upon the earth. . .
> When the secrets of the Righteous One are revealed,
> he shall judge the sinners,
> and the wicked ones will be driven from the presence of the
> righteous and the elect. . .[10]

Taken alone, this text could be understood simply as a portrayal of God's activity in the final judgment, and 'the Righteous One' could be God himself. However, as the visionary description unfolds, 'the Righteous One' is clearly identified with a figure distinct from God, 'the Elect One of righteousness and of faith' (39.6; cf. Hab. 2.4!), the instrument of God's judging and saving power, who is glorified by God (see especially *1 Enoch* 61), and who is also called 'the Son of Man, to whom belongs righteousness and with whom righteousness dwells' (46.3; cf. 48.2; 62.5ff.). While the author of *1 Enoch* seems to prefer as a title 'The Elect One', the epithets can be combined, as in 53.6: 'the Righteous and Elect One'. Although this Righteous One is apparently a human figure rather than an angelic heavenly being, he appears only at the eschatological judgment, having been 'concealed' by God until that moment (62.7). He is said to be righteous primarily with respect to his role as executor of divine justice.

This portrayal of 'the Righteous One' is confined to the Similitudes of Enoch (*1 Enoch* 37–71) and does not appear elsewhere in the book. Since that portion of *1 Enoch* is not attested in the fragmentary manuscript evidence discovered at Qumran, J.T. Milik has raised the conjecture that this entire section of the book is a later Christian addition. Most scholars, however, continue to regard the Similitudes as a first-century Jewish text.[11] While a resolution of the problem of the date and origin of the Similitudes is of course important for many reasons, our present inquiry need not hinge upon the outcome of this debate. If—as is probable—this material is non-Christian it provides evidence for the existence of a Jewish tradition that identified the expected eschatological deliverer as 'the Righteous One'. If, on the other hand, the Similitudes be ascribed to Christian authorship, they provide one more piece of evidence, in addition to the NT texts cited below, that Jewish Christians characteristically and distinctively applied this designation to Jesus.[12]

B. *The Evidence of Acts*

Three passages in the Acts of the Apostles, all appearing in the speeches rather than in the narrative framework, refer directly to Jesus as 'the Righteous One'. Let us examine each in turn before drawing some conclusions.

In Peter's speech to the crowd in Solomon's portico, after the healing of a lame man, he declares that

> The God of Abraham and of Isaac and of Jacob, the God of our fathers glorified his servant (*paida*) Jesus, whom you delivered up (*paredōkate*) and denied in the presence of Pilate, when he had decided to release him. But you denied the Holy and Righteous

One (*ton hagion kai dikaion*), and asked for a murderer to be granted to you, and killed the Author of Life, whom God raised from the dead (3.13-15).

The references here to a *pais* who was 'delivered up' may echo the language of Isa. 52.13–53.12 (cf. also Acts 3.18), though the point is much disputed. Whether or not Isaiah's figure of the suffering servant stands behind this language,[13] it is certainly clear that 'the Holy and Righteous One' is Jesus the Messiah (3.18, 20), who suffered an unjust death (3.15, 18) but who has now been received into heaven until the time of universal eschatological restoration (3.21), which is prefigured palpably by the healing of the lame man before the eyes of these onlookers. Like the *1 Enoch* texts, Peter's speech depicts the Righteous One as a glorified figure whose appearance will accompany the cosmic resolution of all things; unlike the *1 Enoch* texts, Peter's speech associates the righteousness of the Righteous One with the theme of wrongful suffering and vindication through resurrection.

The next appearance of the phrase is given special emphasis by its placement in the climax of Stephen's speech before a hostile Sanhedrin.

> You stiff-necked people, uncircumcised in heart and ears, you always resist the Holy Spirit. As your fathers did, so do you. Which of the prophets did not your fathers persecute? And they killed those who announced beforehand the coming of the Righteous One (*tēs eleuseōs tou dikaiou*), whom you have now betrayed and murdered, you who received the Law as delivered by angels and did not keep it (7.51-53).

Here, 'the Righteous One' is used in an unmistakably titular fashion, and the term is presented in a strongly apocalyptic context: his 'coming' was prophesied by a whole series of Israel's prophets, and he is identified in 7.55-56 with 'the Son of Man standing at the right hand of God' (cf. Dan. 7.13-14; Ps. 110.1). Here again, as in 3.14, the ascription of heavenly glory to the Righteous One is fused with the theme of his death as a martyr, which is of course paradigmatic for Stephen's own fate as enacted in this very scene.

Four matters call for attention here: (1) Stephen's reference to the *eleusis* of the Righteous One may echo a well-established tradition of reading Hab. 2.3-4 as a messianic prophecy.[14] None of the other texts usually read as messianic prophecies corresponds as closely to the terminology of 7.52 as does Hab. 2.3-4. That Luke was familiar with such traditions may be indicated by his inclusion (without explanation) of the question of John the Baptist's disciples to Jesus: 'Are you the Coming One (*ho erchomenos*), or shall we look for another?' (Lk. 7.19; cf. Hab. 2.3 LXX; Ps. 117.26 LXX).[15] (2) The proximity of the terms Righteous One and Son of Man as titles for the same figure might suggest a common background for this passage and the *1 Enoch* texts discussed above. (3) In the narrative context of the story of Stephen's martyrdom, the reference to Jesus a *ho dikaios* in 7.52 can hardly fail to recall Luke's distinctive account of the words of the centurion at the cross in Lk. 23.47: 'Truly this man was *dikaios*'. If we assume that Luke thought of *ho dikaios* as a recognizable designation for the Messiah, the story would exemplify Luke's characteristic fondness for dramatic irony: the centurion means no more than 'this man was innocent', but his words bear testimony to a truth larger than he realizes, the truth known to Luke and the reader that Jesus is the Righteous One.[16] (4) There are several distant but cumulatively interesting connections between Acts 7.51-53 and Galatians 3. Most compelling, of course, is the reference in both texts to the tradition that the law was given through the angels (Acts 7.53: *eis diatagas aggelōn*; Gal. 3.19: *diatageis di' aggelōn*). In addition to this, however, both texts refer to the prior scriptural announcement of the gospel (Acts 7.52; Gal. 3.8) and both relate *ho dikaios* in some way to the material content of Christian proclamation (Acts 7.52; Gal. 3.11). (I deliberately formulate this last observation in the most general way possible; for further discussion see below.)

The final use of *ho dikaios* as a title in Acts appears in Paul's speech before the Jerusalem crowd, as he recounts Ananias's words to him after his 'Damascus Road' experience: 'The God of our fathers appointed you to know his will, to see the Righteous One (*ton dikaion*) and to hear a voice from his mouth; for you will be a witness for him to all men of what you have seen and heard' (Acts 22.14-15). Here, despite the absence of eschatological motifs, the context is apocalyptic in the sense that *ho dikaios* appears in a revelatory vision, and the vision entails a commissioning of the 'seer' to bear witness concerning the *apokalypsis*. What did Paul learn about the Righteous One? We are told here only that he is identified with Jesus of

Nazareth (22.8); the motifs of the Righteous One's suffering, death, resurrection, and eschatological judgment are not explicitly invoked. The 'persecution' of Jesus mentioned here is actually a reference to Paul's persecution of Christians (22.4-5); the point is an important one, because it illustrates the strong sense of identification between the Messiah and his people, an identification that is crucial for the soteriological logic of early Christian proclamation.[17]

With these passages before us, let us draw together some conclusions about the epithet *ho dikaios* in Acts. The term occurs *only* in speeches addressed to Jewish audiences—indeed, only to Jewish audiences in Jerusalem—and in every case the term is used without explanation, as though its meaning were presumed to be self-evident to the hearers. Luke does not use this title in his redactional framework or in constructive christological formulations elsewhere; there is no reason to regard it as a Lukan theologoumenon. This does not mean, however, that the language of the speeches is 'authentic' in the sense of giving a precise account of what Peter, Stephen, and Paul said on the occasions narrated by Luke. It would be a serious methodological error to assume, for example, that Acts 22.14 provides direct support for the view that Paul knew and used *ho dikaios* as a messianic title. What it does show is that Luke, with his interest in historical verisimilitude, believed that *ho dikaios* was a messianic title that would have been used by first-generation Jewish Christian preachers in speaking to Jewish audiences about the Messiah.[18] Whether Luke is actually drawing upon traditional sources or whether he is freely composing these speeches after what he believed to be the style of early Jewish Christian proclamation is very difficult to say. In either case, however, these three passages in Acts bear witness to the high probability that 'the Righteous One' was a conventional messianic designation in early Christianity, specifically in Jewish Christian circles. The term appears in these passages in direct association with apocalyptic motifs of resurrection and judgment, and it also highlights the awful injustice of Jesus' death. The use of the epithet in the speeches suggests allusions to Hab. 2.3-4 and to Isaiah 53, as well as points of contact with circles of theological ideas found in *1 Enoch* on the one hand and in Galatians on the other.

Finally, one odd silence in Acts is worth pondering. Hegesippus reports that James (whom Paul calls 'the brother of the Lord') was called 'the Just' (*dikaios*) 'by all men from the Lord's time to ours',[19] and indeed the account there given of his martyrdom repeatedly refers to him as *ho dikaios*, as though it were virtually a proper name. For instance, the climax of the account runs as follows:

> And a certain man among them, one of the laundrymen, took the club with which he used to beat out the clothes, and hit the Just on the head, and so he suffered martyrdom.[20]

Lake and Cadbury, evidently embarrassed for theological reasons by the temerity of their own suggestion, venture the guess that the title 'Righteous One' was originally applied to Jesus and later 'inherited— if the phrase may be forgiven—by his brother James'.[21] Strikingly, however, though James appears as a key character in Acts, sympathetically portrayed by Luke in the Apostolic Council of Acts 15, Luke never refers to him as *ho dikaios* or gives his readers any hint that he was known by such a title.[22] This omission seems surprising. Why is there no trace of the title applied to James in the NT, particularly in Acts? There are really only two possibilities. (1) Luke knew of no such tradition about James. Hegesippus's claim that James was universally known as *ho dikaios* is one more piece of embellishment in an account admittedly heavily embroidered with legendary hagiographic motifs. This source provides no reliable information about what James was actually called by his contemporaries. (2) Hegesippus's account is indeed reliable on this point at least, and Luke has suppressed the information for reasons that parallel Lake and Cadbury's embarrassment: *ho dikaios* is a title that rightly applies to Jesus alone. I think that there are good reasons for preferring the first of these explanations: the tradition about this epithet as a designation for James is attested neither by any of the several NT writings that mention him, including most tellingly even the Epistle of James,[23] nor by Josephus (*Ant.* 20.200). Even if the latter explanation that Luke has suppressed James's characteristic title is correct, however,—indeed, *especially* if it is correct—Luke bears witness to a stream of early tradition that reserves the epithet *ho dikaios* for the eschatological deliverer, Jesus.

C. *The Evidence of the Catholic Epistles*

A number of references to a Righteous One also turn up in the Catholic Epistles, offering further evidence of the use of the term as a christological designation. The most significant of these references is found in 1 Pet. 3.18:

> For Christ also suffered for sins once for all, the Righteous One for the unrighteous (*dikaios hyper adikōn*).[24]

Here, citing what would appear to be a traditional confessional formula, 1 Peter represents the suffering of Jesus as paradigmatic for the conduct of Christians, who are exhorted to follow his example (cf. 2.21) by suffering for doing right (3.17). Interestingly, although the confessional formula itself stresses the vicarious effect of the Righteous One's suffering, the author of 1 Peter chooses to highlight its exemplary character. These different emphases, which might appear disparate to modern critics, are evidently part of a single conceptual package for this author. The confessional formulation is almost certainly based upon Isa. 53.10b-12 (LXX):

> And the Lord wills... to justify a Righteous One (*dikaiōsai dikaion*) who serves many well, and he will bear their sins. For this reason he will inherit many things (*kleronomēsei pollous*) and he will divide the spoils of the strong, because his soul was handed over (*paredothē*) to death, and he was reckoned among the lawless. And he bore the sins of many, and he was handed over on account of their sins (*dia tas hamartias autōn paredothē*).[25]

The close resemblance of 1 Pet. 3.18 to Gal. 1.4 ('Jesus Christ who gave himself for our sins') should be observed.[26] The explicitly redemptive aspect of the Righteous One's suffering is a theme that did not appear in the Acts passages, but the other motifs associated with this figure are similar to what we have seen already: he suffered unjustly, he was vindicated by God, and now is exalted in glory 'at the right hand of God, with angels, authorities and powers subject to him' (3.22; again we may wonder whether there are echoes here of *1 Enoch*, as well as of Psalm 110). The reference to the destruction of the earth by water in the time of Noah (3.20; cf. *1 Enoch* 65-67) reminds us also that 1 Peter's exhortation to the endurance of suffering is from start to finish located in an apocalyptic perception of the present time as the hour of eschatological crisis (see especially 4.12-19).

   The last passage cited contains a quotation that is of particular interest for our investigation: 'If the righteous man (*ho dikaios*) is scarcely saved, where will the impious and sinner appear?' (4.18, quoting Prov. 11.31 LXX). Should we interpret this occurrence of *ho dikaios*, in light of 3.18, as another reference to Jesus, or should we interpret the passage as a generic reference to 'the righteous person', which is of course its original meaning in Proverbs? The parallel with 4.17b suggests that the latter exegesis is the correct one. Thus, this text demonstrates a significant point: 1 Peter (unlike Luke?) can use *ho dikaios* either as an epithet of Jesus or as a generic term, depending on context. The interpretation of Jesus as paradigmatic righteous person allows the transition between the two senses to be made easily. In short, while the allusive connection between Jesus as *ho dikaios* and the servant figure of Isaiah is more evident in 1 Peter than in Acts, the titular force of the expression is weaker.

A similar problem arises with regard to Jas 5.6: 'You have condemned (*katedikasate*), you have killed the righteous one (*ton dikaion*); he does not resist you'. Nothing in the context suggests a christological reading of the verse, which appears at the conclusion of a pronouncement of woe upon the rich for their oppression of the innocent (5.1-6). The passage does appear, however, to play off the themes and language of Wis. 2.6-20: 'Let us oppress the righteous poor man. . . Let us lie in wait for the righteous man (*ton dikaion*), because he is inconvenient to us and opposes our actions. . . . Let us condemn (*katadikasōmen*) him to a shameful death' (vv. 10, 12, 20). Once the allusion to Wisdom 2 is recognized, however, the interpretation of Jas 5.6 becomes more rather than less complicated. First of all, the nonresistance of the righteous one in Jas 5.6b has no obvious basis in Wisdom 2; where does this motif come from? Secondly, it is difficult to believe that any early Christian could read Wis. 2.10-20 without finding in it a prophetic prefiguration of the passion of Jesus:

> He professes to have knowledge of God,
> and calls himself a child (*paida*) of the Lord. . . .
> he calls the last end of the righteous happy,
> and boasts that God is his father.
> Let us see if his words are true,
> and let us test what will happen at the end of his life;
> for if the righteous one (*ho dikaios*) is God's son (*huios theou*),[27]
> he will help him,
> and will deliver him from the hand of his adversaries.
> (2.13, 16b-18; cf. also 5.1-7)

The more inclined we are to find an allusion to Wisdom 2 in Jas 5.6, the more prepared we must be to entertain the possibility that even here *ho dikaios* is an oblique reference to Jesus and that the motif of nonresistance derives from the traditions about Jesus' passion. In that case, Jas 5.6 would present a close analogy to 1 Pet. 4.18: a generic use of *ho dikaios* with Jesus as prototype of the genre. It should be reiterated that this use of the term *ho dikaios* is cognate with but distinguishable from the titular use of the same term in *1 Enoch* and Acts.

Finally, three instances of *dikaios* in 1 John must be noted. In 1 Jn 2.1b we find a turn of phrase that looks similar to 1 Pet. 3.18's use of the *dikaios* epithet: 'If anyone should sin, we have a paraclete with the Father, Jesus Messiah Righteous One (*Iēsoun Christon Dikaion*)[28]; and he is the expiation for our sins, and not for ours only but also for the sins of the whole world' (1 Jn 2.1b-2). As in 1 Peter, the Righteous One is presented as a figure who makes vicarious atonement for the unrighteous; the parenetic application, however, is slightly different here in two ways: Jesus the Righteous One is offered as reassurance for those who sin, and there is no specific reference to his exemplary *suffering*. His moral example is apparently of a more general type, as we see from the further references in 2.29 and 3.7b:

> If you know that he is righteous (*dikaios*), you may be sure that every one who does righteousness (*dikaiosynēn*) is born of him.... Whoever does righteousness (*dikaiosynēn*) is righteous (*dikaios*), as he is righteous (*dikaios*).

In these passages, *dikaios* is arguably used merely as an ascriptive adjective, its titular character virtually dissipated, or whispered into the reader's ear only through the initial appearance of the term in 2.1. There is no explicit attempt to connect this designation of Jesus to prophetic Scriptures. Furthermore, the term does not function here as a unique title for an eschatological judge and deliverer; it is rather a characterization of Jesus who stands as moral paradigm for the community of faith. Those who abide in him (2.28) will participate in the manner of life that he exemplifies. Although the tradition of describing Jesus as 'Righteous One' thus receives a distinctive Johannine interpretation, it is noteworthy that the eschatological horizon of this language is not entirely lost, as 2.28-29 demonstrates: those who abide in him and do righteousness are thereby enabled to stand with confidence before Jesus at his *parousia*.

D. *The Evidence of Hebrews*

Finally, the Letter to the Hebrews brings us back within hailing distance of Paul, because, like Paul, it quotes Habakkuk 2. The importance of this citation is such that it merits careful attention.

The writer of this *logos parakleseōs* (13.22), admonishing his readers to 'hold fast the confession of our hope without wavering' (10.23) amidst adverse circumstances, invokes Habakkuk's prophecy as a part of his appeal for *hypomonē*:

> Therefore do not throw away your confidence (*parrēsia*; cf. 10.19), which has a great reward. For you have need of endurance, so that you may do the will of God and receive what is promised (*tēn epaggelian*; cf. 10.23; Gal. 3.14-22).

> For yet a little while,
> and the Coming One (*ho erchomenos*) shall come and
>   shall not tarry;
> but my righteous one shall live by faith
> (*ho de dikaios mou ek pisteōs zēsetai*),
> and if he shrinks back,
> my soul has no pleasure in him.

> But we are not of those who shrink back and are destroyed, but of those who have faith and keep their souls (10.35-39).

The form of the Habakkuk citation here provides major clues to the interpretation assigned to it by the author of Hebrews. Though the text is close to the LXX, there are several key differences.[29] If the LXX is already 'messianic' in its rendering of the passage,[30] Hebrews removes any possible ambiguity on this point by inserting the definite article *ho* before the participle *erchomenos*. 'The Coming One' here is understood as a title, just as in Mt. 11.3=Lk. 7.19. The most crucial emendation of the text, however, occurs in 10.38, where the author of Hebrews has inverted the order of Hab. 2.4a and 2.4b,[31] thus forging a significant reinterpretation. As T.W. Manson recognized,[32] the LXX text contrasts two possible modes of action for the Coming One, who—it is affirmed—will not shrink back but will live *ek pisteōs*; thus, the most natural reading of the LXX is to treat *ho dikaios* synonymously with *ho erchomenos*, as another ascription of the Messiah. The writer of Hebrews, however, motivated by a parenetic agenda, achieves a very different reading by transposing the clauses. In light of the assurance that a Coming One will come very soon, the key issue is the response of those who wait: will it be characterized by faithful endurance or by apostasy?[33] The summarizing comment in 10.39 demonstrates the point clearly, lifting the terms *pistis* and *hypostolē* out of Hab. 2.4 as thematic catchwords that distinguish between the faithful members of the Christian community and the apostates. Thus, Heb. 10.37-38 forces a non-messianic interpretation of *ho dikaios*: 'my righteous one' in this passage means 'the faithful Christian believer during the present eschatological interval before the coming of the Coming One'.

Thus, the interpretation of Hab. 2.3-4 in Hebrews bears a striking formal similarity to the interpretation given at Qumran, as attested by 1QpHab. Because the Qumran interpreter is working from a Hebrew text rather than from the LXX, there is no trace of a messianic reading even in 2.3, which is understood as a comment on the delay of 'the appointed time'; nonetheless, both Hebrews and 1QpHab understand the passage fundamentally as an exhortation to keep the faith during trials that accompany the delay of the end.

> *If it tarries, wait for it, for it shall surely come and not be late* (ii, 3b). Interpreted, this concerns the men of truth who keep the Law, whose hands shall not slacken in the service of truth when the final age is prolonged. For all the ages of God reach their appointed end as He determines for them in the mysteries of His wisdom. . . .[*But the righteous shall live by his faith*] (ii, 4b). Interpreted, this concerns all those who observe the Law in the House of Judah, whom God will deliver from the House of Judgment because of their suffering and because of their faith in the Teacher of Righteousness.[34]

The Qumran commentary identifies 'the righteous one' (presumably following the singular reading of the Hebrew text as found in MT)[35] with 'all (plural) those who observe the Law' according to the interpretation of the Teacher of Righteousness. For Hebrews, of course, faithfulness is defined not by observing the Law but by adherence to the Christian confession; still, the parenetic construal of Hab. 2.4 is much the same in both texts, and the 'righteous one' of Habakkuk is interpreted in both places as the ideal type for steadfast obedience in the face of suffering.

If we ask ourselves, however, *who* exemplifies that ideal type for steadfast obedience in the Letter to the Hebrews, the answer is plain: Jesus, 'who was faithful to the one that appointed him' (2.2), Jesus who as the 'pioneer and perfecter of faith' (*tēs pisteōs archēgon kai teleiōtēn*, 12.2) recapitulates and culminates the testimony of the whole cloud of faithful witnesses rhetorically summoned up in ch. 11. Perhaps more clearly than any other NT writing, Hebrews presents Jesus as the paradigm for the life of faith. Thus, although the Habakkuk citation in Heb. 10.37-38 does not understand *ho dikaios* as a messianic title, it does project a vision of faithfulness for which Jesus is the prototype. Though the author of Hebrews does not think of Jesus as 'the Righteous One', he could hardly think of a 'righteous one' without thinking of Jesus. Consequently, the situation here is similar to the state of affairs already discussed above with reference to Jas 5.6: though the term *ho dikaios* is not a title, Jesus is the prototype who provides its material content.

One final observation casts further light on the apocalyptic hermeneutical context presupposed in Hebrews 10 for the reading of Hab. 2.3-4. That this passage was widely discussed in formative Judaism and in early Christianity as a *locus* crucial for theological understanding of the delay of the endtime has been amply documented by A. Strobel's extensive study of the history of interpretation of this text;[36] thus, it is no surprise to find the author of Hebrews employing it as part of a plea for eschatological *hypomonē*. However, the strongly apocalyptic coloring of the quotation is even more clearly visible in the light of a fact often noted but rarely pondered by commentators: the Habakkuk quotation is introduced in Heb. 10.37 by a fragmentary allusion to Isa. 26.20 LXX ('For yet a little while' [*eti gar mikron hoson hoson*]). Of course, when linked syntactically with Hab. 2.3, the adverbial phrase simply serves to stress the imminence of the coming of the Coming One, but a careful reader may recall the apocalyptic imagery of the original context in the LXX of Isaiah:

> The dead shall rise, and those who are in the tombs shall be raised, and those who are in the earth shall rejoice. For the dew that comes from you is a healing for them, but the land of the ungodly shall fall. Walk, my people, go into your closets, shut your door, be hidden for a little while (*mikron hoson hoson*) until the wrath of the Lord passes away. For behold, the Lord is bringing wrath from the holy place (or: Holy One? [*apo tou hagiou*]) upon those who dwell upon the earth.... (Isa. 26.19-21)

Visions of wrath and resurrection, judgment upon the ungodly and warnings to God's people to lay low for the briefest of times to await the working of God's power: is the echo of Isaiah in Heb. 10.37 a calculated evocation of these themes and images? If not, it is hard to imagine why the distinctive phrasing of Isa. 26.20 should be employed. If so, the apocalyptic matrix within which Hab. 2.3-4 was read by early Christians becomes more clearly evident.

Having completed our survey of texts that speak of an eschatological 'righteous one', we may draw some conclusions. It is difficult to make the case that 'Righteous One' was a fixed formal title for the Messiah in pre-Christian Judaism. (Of course it is notoriously difficult to make out *any* case for what may have been believed or said about 'the Messiah' in pre-Christian Judaism.) It is clear, however, that at least in some Christian circles, there was an early convention of applying the epithet *ho dikaios* to Jesus. The evidence of Acts leads us to suppose that this convention may have been characteristic of Jewish Christian communities, and the evidence of *1 Enoch* makes it likely that non-Christian Jews also entertained the expectation of an eschatological Righteous One who would appear as judge in the endtime to set things right. Expectations of this sort may well have been grounded in Hab. 2.3-4, although the specifically messianic interpretation of this text must have arisen within communities that read the prophecy in the LXX translation rather than in the Hebrew.

The linkage of the Coming/Righteous One to the righteous sufferer of Isaiah 53 is surely a distinctive Christian exegetical development. Once the linkage was made, however, several consequences followed: (1) the Isaiah text (and perhaps Wisdom 2 as well) was used apologetically to defend the innocence of Jesus and to argue the culpability of his executioners, as we see in the Acts speeches; (2) the suffering of the Righteous One was interpreted as making vicarious atonement for sin, as in 1 Peter and 1 John; (3) the Righteous One's suffering was interpreted as paradigmatic for steadfast obedience to God (=*pistis*) in the time of eschatological adversity, as in 1 Peter, Hebrews, and perhaps James. The ideas of (2) and (3) are very closely connected, because both presuppose an identification between the Righteous One and his people—indeed, the identification is so complete that it seems at times to posit an ontological bonding, as becomes apparent in texts like 1 Jn 2.29 and Hebrews (*passim*).

All of these texts, with the possible exception of *1 Enoch*, are to be dated slightly later than the Pauline epistles, but the motif of the Righteous One appears in formulations that may be traditional and therefore early. This is especially true of the relevant passages in Acts and 1 Peter. The conflated citation of Isa. 26.20 and Hab. 2.3-4 in Heb. 10.37-38 may also presuppose an existing exegetical tradition. The evidence, both within the NT itself and in the subsequent history of interpretation, makes it unlikely that the titular use *ho dikaios* in relation to Jesus is a late theological development; if anything, the evidence runs the other direction. 'The Righteous One' appears to be a designation accorded to Jesus within earliest apocalyptic Jewish Christianity but subsequently abandoned by the church, presumably because it was neither distinctive enough (cf. the discussion above of the application of the same title to James)[37] nor adequately expressive of the exalted metaphysical claims that Christians wanted to make about Jesus. Insofar as the designation continues to be ascribed to Jesus in the later Catholic epistles, it is moving away from its apocalyptic point of origin and towards an emphasis on Jesus as good moral example, though the apocalyptic connotations are never entirely surrendered in the NT.

3. *The Righteous One in Paul*

In light of these reflections, we may approach Paul's two explicit citations of Hab. 2.4 and ask how this text must have looked to him through the lenses of early Christian traditions and of his own apocalyptic hermeneutic. I leave Gal. 3.11 for last because it is by far the more difficult of the two cases.

A. *Romans 1.17*

That Paul's citation of Hab. 2.4 in Rom. 1.17 appears in an apocalyptic theological context should require no labored demonstration. The Habbakkuk text is adduced in support of Paul's proclamation that the righteousness of God is being revealed (*apokalyptetai*) in the gospel; furthermore, this revelation of the righteousness of God is accompanied by the revelation of God's wrath (1.18-32) and impending eschatological judgment (cf. 2.1-11). Thus, the programmatic declaration of Rom. 1.16-17 stands as the keynote of a gospel written in an apocalyptic key.[38] The language used in this declaration echoes numerous passages in the Psalms and Isaiah that promise a future eschatological consummation in which God's salvific intervention on behalf of Israel will bring all nations to worship Israel's God. A particularly clear example, prefiguring almost all the key terms of Rom. 1.16-17, is to be found in Ps. 97.2 (LXX): 'The Lord has made known his salvation (*sotērion*); in the presence of the nations (*ethnōn* he has revealed (*apekalypsen*) his righteousness (*dikaiosynēn*)'. (Cf. also Isa. 51.4-5; 52.10.) Though Paul does not refer explicitly to these scriptural passages, his use of their language suggests that his gospel must be understood as the fulfillment of the hope to which they point: that God's righteousness will be revealed in an act of deliverance for the Jews first and also for the Gentiles.[39] This claim stands as the foundation of the apologetic edifice constructed by the rest of the letter, which argues vigorously that God's righteousness is confirmed, not compromised, by his act of deliverance through Jesus Christ (cf. 3.5-26).[40]

How, in this context, does the citation of Hab. 2.4 serve to support the argument? Amidst all the controversy since the Reformation about how the expression *ho dikaios ek pisteōs zēsetai* should be interpreted, parties on all sides of the debate have been surprisingly content to assume that Paul employs the passage as a prooftext with complete disregard for its original setting in Habakkuk's prophecy. When we realize, however, that Paul is setting out in Romans to address the question of God's faithfulness to the covenant with Israel, the aptness of the quotation from Habakkuk immediately stands forth. In Habakkuk, the passage that Paul quotes comes as the nub of God's answer to the prophet's complaint (Hab. 2.1) against the apparent injustice of God's ways. How can God allow the wicked to oppress the righteous (1.13; cf. 1.2-4)? Has God abandoned his people? Whatever else Hab. 2.4 might be construed to mean, it is a response to the problem of theodicy, an implicit assertion of God's righteousness. The faithful community is enjoined to wait with patience for that which they do not yet see: the appearing of God's justice. This hope God will not disappoint.

Unlike 1QpHab and Hebrews, however, Paul does not appeal to the Habakkuk text in service of an exhortation to patience. Instead, he treats the passage as a prophecy now fulfilled in the revelation of the gospel. The manifestation of the righteousness of God is present reality, not merely future hope. Just as it is written (*kathōs gegraptai*) that the righteous one will live by faith, so now indeed the righteousness of God is being revealed *ek pisteōs eis pistin*. The gospel of God was 'pre-announced' through prophets in holy writings (1.2), and now the prophesied eschatological deliverance has come/is coming to pass in such a way that the correlation between prophetic word and present reality undergirds the assertion of God's righteousness. In short, Paul is claiming that Habakkuk's hope has at last received its answer through a revelation *ek pisteōs*.

It is not hard to understand such a claim if we recall that the LXX of Hab. 2.3-4 was messianic in character. It promised a Coming One, and the whole weight of Christian proclamation declared that Jesus was precisely that long-expected figure. Thus, it is entirely probable that Paul's apocalyptic exegesis of Habakkuk would have recognized in the prophecy a promise about the coming of Jesus Christ. As C.H. Dodd remarked, Paul's use of the quotation is most readily intelligible if 'he drew upon a tradition which already recognized the passage from Habakkuk as a *testimonium* to the coming of Christ'.[41]

But what about *ho dikaios*? Is there any indication that Paul understood this term as a messianic designation? Or is it more likely that, like the writer of Hebrews, he read the Habakkuk passage as messianic/apocalyptic without construing *ho dikaios* as a direct reference to Jesus? Unfortunately, the compressed formulaic character of Rom 1.17 makes this question impossible to answer definitively. The best that can be done within the compass of this essay is to suggest briefly three factors that might favor a 'messianic' interpretation of Rom. 1.17. (Readers can supply the counterarguments for themselves.)

1. What sense does it make to say, as the syntax of Rom. 1.17 requires us to do, that God's saving righteousness is revealed *out of* faith (*ek pisteōs*)? Surely it would be peculiar to suppose that the human (Christian) disposition of faith towards God should be itself the source out of which God's eschatological righteousness is now revealed in a new way. Paul has been so interpreted in some theological traditions, but the oddness of the interpretation must be marked. Have not Jews always had faith in God? Would not Paul's sentence make better sense if he meant that through the *pistis* of Jesus the Righteous One the righteousness of God is now revealed to those who believe (*eis pistin*)? (After all, in Rom. 3.25-26 Paul says that God put Jesus forward as a demonstration of his [God's]

righteousness; this looks very much like an explication of the sense in which Hab. 2.4 can be construed as a confirmation of Paul's claim [1.17] that the righteousness of God is revealed in the gospel). Since I have contended elsewhere that the logic of the argumentation in Rom. 3.21-26 requires this interpretation of 'the faith of Jesus Christ',[42] I will not try the reader's patience by repeating that argument here.

2. Paul's account of the mechanism of salvation in Rom. 5.18-19, in an antithetical parallelism to the consequences of Adam's disobedience, asserts that Jesus' 'righteous deed' (*dikaiōma*, in contrast to Adam's *paraptōma*) has resulted in the 'righteousness of life' (cf. Hab. 2.4) for all and that many shall be constituted righteous (*dikaioi*) through *Jesus'* obedience. 'Righteous One' is not used as an epithet of Jesus in this very dense passage, but the certain allusion in 5.19 to Isa. 53.11 suggests that Paul is drawing here on a tradition that describes Jesus as the *dikaios* whose righteousness is vicariously efficacious for 'many'.[43]

3. The other NT texts considered in Part 2 of this essay suggest that Paul lived and wrote in a world of discourse—i.e. early Jewish Christianity—where *ho dikaios* was a common designation for Jesus. If that is so, Paul might presuppose the christological exegesis of Hab. 2.4 without commenting on it, just as he presupposes without comment the christological exegesis of Psalm 69 in Rom. 15.3. On the other hand, if he held some idiosyncratic interpretation of the text (such as 'the one who is righteous-through-faith-not-through-works shall live'), he would certainly run the risk of being severely misunderstood in quoting the phrase to an unfamiliar Christian congregation at Rome with no more explanation than he offers in Romans 1.

None of these considerations is entirely compelling, but the strongly apocalyptic theological context of Romans 1 creates at least a presumption in favor of the messianic exegesis of Hab. 2.4 as the interpretation that would have been most readily at hand for Paul and that makes the best sense out of the letter's argument. It remains to be seen whether a similar claim can be made in relation to Gal. 3.11.

B. *Galatians 3.11*

With the aid of the observations above about the apocalyptic theology of Romans, we may identify four apocalyptic motifs in

Galatians that are especially pertinent to the interpretation of Gal.
3.11 in its context.[44]

1. As in his letter to the Romans, Paul contends in Galatians that
the Scripture promises the inclusion of the Gentiles among God's
people (3.8-9) and that the present empirical phenomenon of the
Gentiles' receiving of the gospel constitutes the eschatological
fulfillment of that promise (3.14). The (Christian) faith of the
Gentiles is not merely a nice broadening of Israel's religious
constituency; rather, it is an apocalyptic sign, a phenomenon that
bears witness to the presence of the new age (3.23-29).[45] (That is one
of the reasons behind Paul's bitter opposition to the efforts of others
to turn the Galatians into Jewish proselytes: that would turn the
calendar back by erasing the apocalyptic sign.)

2. The presence of the Spirit in the community (3.3-5) is also a sign
of the new age, a fulfillment of the eschatological promise (3.14;
4.6).

3. The Spirit is the source of *life* (5.25), not just ordinary human
existence but an eschatological life to/with God, a life lived in the
power of the new age through participation in the death of Christ
(2.19-20). Paul construes the *zēsetai* of Hab. 2.4 as a reference to this
eschatological life (cf. Rom. 1.16-17), and he is sure that the Law,
contrary to its self-advertisement (Lev. 18.5; Gal. 3.12), has no power
to give such life (3.21).

4. All of these apocalyptic blessings (faith, Spirit, life) are made
available only at one appointed time (3.23; 4.4) and only to One,
namely 'the Seed to whom it was promised' (3.19). The 'Seed', Paul
insists, is Christ alone (3.16), and others receive the abundance of
eschatological blessing only 'in Christ', (3.14) i.e. as a result of
participation in him (3.26-29). For Paul, Christ is the one to whom
God's promise is made and in whom it is fulfilled.

In light of this configuration of apocalyptic themes, which
constitute the foundation and framework of Paul's argument in
Galatians, we may ask a simple question: who is *ho dikaios*? When
Paul, operating out of this sort of apocalyptic intellectual matrix,
read Hab. 2.3-4 in the LXX, a text which already carried apocalyptic/
messianic resonances for Jews of his time, how did he understand it?
My contention remains that he understood it as a messianic
prophecy, just as he understood—in a way quite startling to us—
Gen. 17.8 as messianic prophecy (Gal. 3.16). This sort of divinatory

reading is a direct and natural consequence of the apostle's apocalyptic hermeneutical perspective: those who have experienced the apocalypse of the Son of God now find the veil taken away from Scripture so that they can perceive its witness to him, including its witness to him as the Coming/Righteous One.

There is one very simple test of this proposal: read through Gal. 3.10-18 with the working hypothesis that *ho dikaios=Christos Iēsous=to sperma*. Does Paul's exegetical argument make more or less sense on the basis of the hypothesis?

Of course, we remain much more in the dark than we would like to be. If Paul has in mind a messianic interpretation of Hab. 2.4, why does he not say so more clearly, as he does in the case of Gen. 17.8? There can be no definitive answer, of course, but we would do well to bear in mind a salutary reminder of Strobel: the way in which Paul introduces the quotation in 3.11 (*dēlon*) presupposes that his readers know all about it already,[46] a presupposition that appears entirely reasonable in light of Strobel's evidence about the status of Hab. 2.3-4 as a *locus classicus* in Jewish apocalyptic traditions. Rather than having to explain the meaning of the quotation, Paul can use it to argue a point. A similar observation could be made about the way he uses the text in Rom. 1.17: he appears to be citing a famous text that serves at once as rubric and clincher of his argument.

These reflections about the possibility that Paul understood Hab. 2.4 as an apocalyptic testimonium to the coming of an eschatological deliverer are of course not probative in their force; they represent a first attempt to think through some of the implications of Lou Martyn's deft and provocative placement of Galatians into an apocalyptic theological context.[47] Whether these suggestions about the interpretation of Rom. 1.17 and Gal. 3.11 find favor or not, a larger task lies before us as we take up Martyn's challenge to allow Galatians 'to play its own role in showing us precisely what the nature of Paul's apocalyptic was'.[48] The task is to seek an understanding of the way in which Paul's reading of *Scripture* unfolds apocalyptic perceptions of world and text.

NOTES

1. Important articulations of this insight are to be found in Martyn's essay 'Epistemology at the Turn of the Ages: 2 Corinthians 5.16' in W.R.

Farmer, C.F.D. Moule, and R.R. Niebuhr, eds., *Christian History and Interpretation: Studies Presented to John Knox* (Cambridge: Cambridge University Press, 1967), pp. 269-87, and in his recent 'Apocalyptic Antinomies in Paul's Letter to the Galatians', *NTS* 31 (1985), pp. 410-24.

2. Martyn, 'Antinomies', p. 420.

3. *Ibid.*, p. 417.

4. Martyn makes a similar point in 'Epistemology' not only about 'knowing Christ' but about knowing in general; the application of the argument to hermeneutical issues is both natural and necessary.

5. Cf. 2 Cor. 3.14-17.

6. Martyn, 'Antinomies', p. 421. '(T)hrough the whole of Galatians the focus of Paul's apocalyptic lies not on Christ's parousia but rather on his death' (p. 420).

7. For (1), see especially H. Dechent, 'Der "Gerechte"—eine Bezeichnung für den Messias', *TSK* 100 (1927-28), pp. 439-43; and H.J. Cadbury, 'The Titles of Jesus in Acts', in F.J. Foakes Jackson and K. Lake, *The Beginnings of Christianity, Part I: The Acts of the Apostles* (London: Macmillan, 1920-33), V, pp. 354-75. For (2), see A.T. Hanson, *Studies in Paul's Technique and Theology* (London: SPCK, 1974), pp. 39-45; L.T. Johnson, 'Romans 3.21-26 and the Faith of Jesus', *CBQ* 44 (1982), p. 90; further references in R.B. Hays, *The Faith of Jesus Christ: An Investigation of the Narrative Substructure of Gal. 3.1–4.11* (SBLDS, 56; Chico: Scholars, 1983), p. 183 n. 67.

8. Hays, *Faith of Jesus Christ*, pp. 151-57, 206-209. Even some of the critics who have received my book most graciously have expressed skepticism about this aspect of the argument (e.g. C. Roetzel, *JAAR* 53 [1985], p. 490: 'I remain unconvinced that Hab. 2.4 is or was a messianic text'. Cf. R.N. Longenecker, *Themelios*, 10/2 [1985], p. 38 T.L. Donaldson, 'The "Curse of the Law" and the Inclusion of the Gentiles: Gal. 3.13-14', *NTS* 32 [1986], p. 112 n. 78). Consequently, I trust that readers will not find it tedious of me to reexamine this same problem from a completely different angle.

9. In addition to the studies mentioned in note 7 above, see also L. Ruppert, *Jesus als der leidende Gerechte?* (Stuttgart: KBW, 1972); and E. Franklin, *Christ the Lord* (London: SPCK, 1975), pp. 62-63.

10. This and the following citations from *1 Enoch* are taken from the translation of E. Isaac, in J.H. Charlesworth, *The Old Testament Pseudepigrapha*, Vol. I (Garden City, NY: Doubleday, 1983). In 38.3, the older standard translation of R.H. Charles (*Apocrypha and Pseudepigrapha of the New Testament* [Oxford: Clarendon, 1913]) and the recent translation of M.A. Knibb (*The Ethiopic Book of Enoch* [Oxford: Clarendon, 1978]) following different manuscript evidence, read the plural 'secrets of the righteous', and Knibb also opts for the plural in 39.6: 'the chosen ones of

righteousness and of faith'. In the crucial passages in 38.2 and 53.6, however, the singular 'Righteous One' is unambiguously attested.

11. See J.C. Greenfield and M.E. Stone, 'The Enochic Pentateuch and the Date of the Similitudes', *HTR* 70 (1977), pp. 51-65; J.A. Fitzmyer, 'Implications of the New Enoch Literature from Qumran', *TS* 38 (1977), pp. 340-44; J.H. Charlesworth, 'The SNTS Pseudepigrapha Seminars at Tübingen and Paris on the Books of Enoch', *NTS* 25 (1978-79), pp. 315-23; M.A. Knibb, 'The Date of the Parables of Enoch: A Critical Review', *NTS* 25 (1978-79), pp. 345-59; C.L. Mearns, 'Dating the Similitudes of Enoch', *NTS* 25 (1978-79), pp. 360-69; D.W. Suter, *Tradition and Composition in the Parables of Enoch* (SBLDS, 47; Missoula, MT: Scholars Press, 1979), pp. 11-33.

12. This way of formulating the matter assumes that Milik's late dating of the Similitudes is incorrect and that, even if they should be judged to come from Christian circles, the sort of Christianity that they represent is strongly Jewish in character.

13. Cf. the discussion of 1 Pet. 3.18, below.

14. On this tradition, see A. Strobel, *Untersuchungen zum eschatologischen Verzögerungsproblem auf Grund der spätjüdisch-urchristlichen Geschichte von Habakuk 2,2 ff.* (NovTSup, 2; Leiden: Brill, 1961), especially his comments on the LXX (pp. 47-56). The position is now supported also by D.-A. Koch, 'Der Text von Hab 2.4b in der Septuaginta und im Neuen Testament', *ZNW* 76 (1985), p. 73 n. 25.

15. The title in Lk. 7.19 (=Mt. 11.3) might also be explained by appeal to Ps. 117.26 (LXX); however, once *ho erchomenos* came to be understood as a messianic title, a midrashic link between the Psalm text and Hab. 2.3 would have been in any case virtually inevitable. For a full discussion arguing for Hab. 2.3 as the background for the gospel saying, see Strobel, *Verzögerungsproblem*, pp. 265-77.

16. Lake and Cadbury comment that 'the story gains point if *ho dikaios* was a familiar title of Jesus' and draw the inference that '*ho dikaios* is less likely to be original' than Mark's *theou huios* (*Beginnings of Christianity* IV, p. 83). It is unlikely, however, that Mt. 27.19 should be similarly interpreted. Matthew is hardly capable of such ironic nuances.

17. See the discussion in Hays, *Faith of Jesus Christ*, pp. 248-56.

18. For a helpful discussion of Luke's technique in tailoring the speeches in Acts to fit the narrative setting, see B.R. Gaventa, 'The Overthrown Enemy: Luke's Portrait of Paul', *SBL Seminar Papers* (1985), pp. 439-49.

19. Cited in Eusebius, *HE* 2.23.4.

20. *Ibid.*, 2.23.18.

21. Lake and Cadbury, *Beginnings of Christianity*, IV, p. 104.

22. The same observation could be made of Paul's references to James in

Gal. 2.9, 12; Paul's reasons for omitting mention of such an honorific title, even if were known to him, would be fairly obvious.

23. What motive would a pseudepigraphist have for omitting a title that would so forthrightly commend the putative author of his work?

24. The diversity of readings in the textual tradition for 3.18a has no bearing upon the use of *dikaios* in the formula.

25. Douglas J. Moo unaccountably remarks that '*diakaios* is not used in Is. 53.11 LXX' (*The Old Testament in the Gospel Passion Narratives* [Sheffield: Almond, 1983], p. 158). This is simply an error.

26. It is also interesting to speculate about the conceptual connections between these formulations and Gal. 3.13-14.

27. In passing, it is intriguing to note that this line in Wis. 2.18 contains *both* of the epithets ascribed to Jesus by the different synoptic accounts of the centurion's 'confession' at the foot of the cross (Mt. 27.54=Mk 15.39; Lk. 23.47).

28. The translation here is mine.

29. Cf. the discussion of Koch, 'Der Text von Hab. 2.4b', pp. 75-78.

30. See the references in note 14, above, and T.W. Manson, 'The Argument from Prophecy', *JTS* 46 (1945), pp. 133-34.

31. For a clear chart and discussion, see C.H. Dodd, *According to the Scriptures* (London: Nisbet, 1952), p. 50.

32. Manson, 'Argument from Prophecy', p. 134.

33. This observation also probably explains the transposition of *mou* in the text of Heb. 10.38: if *mou* were left to modify *pisteos*, as in the LXX, the hortatory force of the point articulated in 10.39 would be blunted.

34. 1QpHab 7.9–8.3, as translated by G. Vermes, *The Dead Sea Scrolls in English* (2nd edn; Harmondsworth: Penguin, 1975), p. 239.

35. The portion of the scroll containing this part of the text has been destroyed.

36. Strobel, *Verzögerungsproblem*.

37. Cadbury ('Titles of Jesus', p. 364 n. 2) also points out parallels such as the Athenian statesman Aristides the Just and the use of Justus as a common Latin surname (cf. Acts 1.23; 18.7; Col. 4.11).

38. This point stands even if Ernst Käsemann is wrong about *dikaiosynē theou* as a technical term in apocalyptic theological discourse.

39. These observations also suggest that 'the righteousness of God' in Romans should be understood first of all in relation to the background of this language in Isaiah and the Psalms. Cf. R.B. Hays, 'Psalm 143 and the Logic of Romans 3', *JBL* 99 (1980), pp. 107-15; see also *idem*, 'Justification', in the *Anchor Bible Dictionary* (forthcoming).

40. Of course it is not possible to defend this interpretation within the present essay. A full discussion is forthcoming in my book on Paul as interpreter of Scripture, *Echoes of Scripture in the Letters of Paul* (New Haven: Yale University Press, 1989).

41. Dodd, *According to the Scriptures*, p. 51.

42. Hays, *Faith of Jesus Christ*, pp. 170-74; in addition to the references cited there, the position is now supported by B. Byrne, *Reckoning with Romans* (Wilmington: Glazier, 1986), pp. 79-80.

43. On Rom. 5.18-19, see especially the discussion of Johnson, 'Faith of Jesus', pp. 87-90.

44. Cf. the motifs enumerated by Martyn, 'Antinomies', pp. 416-18.

45. Cf. T.L. Donaldson, '"Curse"', pp. 94-112, for a helpful discussion of the centrality of this theme within Paul's theological reflection.

46. Strobel, *Verzögerungsproblem*, p. 191.

47. One of the hazards of becoming an esteemed scholar for whom *Festschriften* are written is that all the contributors seek to attribute their divers schemes and notions to the influence of the honoree. Let it be said, therefore, that Lou is hereby absolved of responsibility for anything harebrained herein and gratefully thanked for the true and useful things that I have learned from him.

48. Martyn, 'Antinomies', p. 412.

THE ARCHONS, THE SPIRIT AND
THE DEATH OF CHRIST:
DO WE NEED THE HYPOTHESIS OF
GNOSTIC OPPONENTS TO EXPLAIN 1 COR. 2.6-16?

Judith L. Kovacs

This paper argues that interpretation of 1 Cor. 2.6-16 has been hindered by the widespread assumption that Paul wrote this text in reaction to gnostic (or proto-gnostic) opponents in Corinth, and that the way to interpret it is by means of parallels in later gnostic texts.[1] The passage is frequently understood as Paul's attempt to parody his gnostic opponents or to compete with them by showing that he too has a hidden wisdom.[2] One recent interpreter has even argued that the text is an interpolation written by 'enthusiasts' at Corinth.[3] I shall attempt to show that the passage, far from being merely a response, serious or ironic, to opponents, expresses Paul's own characteristic theology, his apocalyptic interpretation of the death of Christ,[4] and that it bears a close relationship to other parts of 1 Corinthians, especially chs. 1 and 15. It is to be explicated not by later gnostic parallels but by passages in Paul's own letters which speak of Jesus' death as an apocalyptic event, as well as by Jewish apocalyptic texts which illustrate the background to Paul's thinking.[5] A translation of the first part of the text follows:

> (6) But we speak wisdom among the perfect, wisdom which does not belong to this age nor to the rulers of this age, who are being destroyed. (7) But we speak God's wisdom in a mystery, the hidden wisdom which God foreordained before the ages with a view to our glory. (8) This wisdom none of the rulers of this age knew, for if they had known it, they would not have crucified the Lord of glory. (9) But as it is written: 'Things which eye has not seen nor ear heard, which did not enter into the heart of man, things which God has prepared for those who love him'. (10) But to us God has revealed (these things) through the Spirit.

Since the work of Wilckens and Schmithals, the hermeneutical key to this text has been sought in the term *teleios* (v. 6). This is interpreted in light of terms *pneumatikos* and *psychikos* later in the passage, and these in turn are interpreted in light of the use of these terms by Christian gnostics such as the Valentinians.[6] This interpretation detects two gnostic notions in the passage, the idea of esoteric knowledge and the idea of different classes of Christians. Conzelmann's introductory summary of the passage illustrates this approach:

> The section 2.6-16 stands out from its context both in style and in content. It presents a self-contained idea, a commonplace of 'wisdom.' It is a contradiction of his previous statement when Paul now announces after all a positive, undialectical possibility of cultivating a wisdom of the 'perfect.'... The offense of the cross appears to be thrust aside in favor of the direct knowledge of spirit by spirit. Bultmann explains this break in the thought as being due to the polemical situation. He thinks that Paul, in his eagerness to refute the ideas of his opponents, allows himself to be carried away into linking up with these ideas for the sake of argument, and in so doing is himself drawn a certain distance within their orbit.[7]

I would like to explore another possibility, that the key to this text is the reference to the cross in v. 8 and that 1 Cor. 2.6-16 is not a deviation from Paul's basic kerygma but an elaboration of it. This elaboration is not a superfluous addition designed to make Paul more competitive with his opponents but a crucial preparation both for the discussions of problems in Christian living which make up the bulk of the letter and for the treatment of resurrection and parousia in ch. 15. Beker and Martyn[8] have shown that elsewhere in Paul the cross is treated in terms that owe much to Jewish apocalyptic. It is this background, and not that of a purely hypothetical Gnosticism in Corinth, that allows us to understand our passage as well.

Consider first the language of the passage. The following of its terms and phrases have parallels in Jewish apocalyptic texts: *sophia, ho aiōn houtos, archontes* used of demonic powers, *mystērion apokekrymenos, pneuma* as revealer, *doxa, kyrios tēs doxēs* and obviously, *apokalyptō*.[9] Such a list, by itself, cannot stand as an argument that the text is apocalyptic. Many of these terms— especially 'wisdom' and 'mystery' and the idea of 'hidden' wisdom— were in common use in the ancient world, for example in Jewish wisdom circles, in mystery religions, and in later Gnosticism.[10] But the use of so many of Paul's terms in apocalyptic literature suggests that we need not assume a gnostic or 'protognostic' or 'Hellenistic enthusiastic' background in order to understand our passage.

If we procede to ask *how* Paul uses these terms, we see that the closest analogue to the view of wisdom which he presents in these verses is in apocalyptic texts. The central idea here is also a key theme in many Jewish apocalyptic texts, the notion that God has a secret plan for the consummation of history which is revealed only to the apocalyptic seer and which consists of judgment on the forces of evil and salvation for the elect.[11] The hidden wisdom of which Paul speaks in 1 Cor. 2.6ff. is not, as in gnostic texts, a speculation on the origin and destiny of the elect soul, nor is it concerned to identify a Christian elite, as several interpreters suggest. It is concerned with God's plan for salvation and judgment, a plan carried out in the arena of history.

Paul speaks of God's wisdom in terms of past, present, and future. In the past lie God's determination (*prohōrisen*) and preparation (*hētoimasen*) to glorify those who love him. In the immediate past it embraces the crucial events of salvation and revelation, the crucifixion of 'the Lord of glory' (v. 8) and the sending of the Spirit (vv. 10 and 12).

The plan of God also concerns the present. Paul describes the present as 'this age', a phrase used by the authors of several Jewish apocalypses to refer to the evil character of this present and provisional period of history in contrast to the glorious new age with which God will consummate history.[12] That Paul uses this term in an apocalyptic sense is made clear by Gal. 1.3-4:

> Grace to you and peace from God the Father and our Lord Jesus Christ, who gave himself for our sins to deliver us from the present evil age, according to the will of our God and Father.

See also 2 Cor. 4.4, where Paul speaks of 'the god of this age' who has 'blinded the hearts of unbelievers'.[13] The present is a period in which demonic powers, the *archontes*,[14] have authority. But it is also a time when their authority is in the process of being destroyed, as the present tense of *katargoumenōn* indicates.

Paul points to the future dimension of God's plan through the phrase *eis doxan hēmōn* (v. 7). Conzelmann interprets this phrase against the background of gnostic ideas:

The 'present' unveiling is indicated by the expression *eis doxan hēmōn*, 'with a view to our glory.' *doxa*, 'glory,' describes our new being as supernatural. Paul is on the verge of a self-understanding in Gnostic terms of habitual disposition but avoids it by pointing to the 'extra nos' factor.[15]

In light of Paul's use of *doxa* in Rom. 8.17-18; 2.10; 1 Cor. 15.43; 2 Cor. 4.17 to refer to the exaltation of believers at the parousia, such an interpretation seems gratuitous. Paul uses *doxa* to refer to the eschatological rewards of those favored by God, a use which corresponds to the sense of 'glory' in apocalyptic texts such as *4 Ezra* 7.91ff.; *2 Bar.* 51.12; *1 Enoch* 62.15.[16]

If the general theme of 1 Cor. 2.6-16 is God's wise plan for salvation, a plan which is seen in terms of time and history, the specific focus is on how the event of Jesus' death functions in this plan and how believers come to know the meaning of the cross.

> None of the rulers of this ages knew [God's wisdom], for if they had known [it], they would not have crucified the Lord of glory (2.8).

This verse has played an important role in the gnostic interpretation of 1 Corinthians 2, as the following statement of Bultmann illustrates:

> The Gnostic idea that Christ's earthly garment of flesh was the disguise in consequence of which the world-rulers failed to recognize him—for if they had recognized him, they would not have brought about their own defeat by causing his crucifixion— lurks behind 1 Cor. 2.8.[17]

For Wilckens the gnostic redeemer myth explains not only v. 8 but also the reference to the 'rulers of this world' in v. 6:

> Der Zusatz im 2.6: *oude tōn archontōn tou aiōnos toutou* ist dabei als typisch gnostisches Element zu werten, und allein im Zusammenhang des gnostischen Erlösermythos hat er seinen Sinn: Insofern die Weisheit der herabkommende Erlöser ist, kann er mit den kosmischen Mächten gar nichts gemein haben; denn diese sind ja die vielschichtige feindliche Front, die er heimlich zu durchbrechen hat, um die zu erlösenden Pneumatiker als *teleioi* durch sie hindurch nach oben in ihre jenseitig himmlische Heimat zurückzuführen... Die Aussage 2,8 ist ... nur vom Hintergrund des gnostischen Erlöser-Mythos her verständlich.[18]

This interpretation of v. 8 continues to hold the field in the commentaries. Conzelmann says in *Hermeneia*: 'For in [Jesus'] descent through the cosmos he disguised himself'.[19] Barrett likewise views this verse as an adaptation of a gnostic myth:

> Paul's language is gnostic and recalls the myth of the redeemer who is unrecognized in his descent to earth, but the myth is thoroughly moralized.[20]

These commentators assume that Paul has taken a gnostic myth which referred to the pre-historical existence of the redeemer—the story of the trick by which the redeemer escapes the notice of the hostile heavenly rulers in order to descend to earth and save the elect—and radically altered its meaning by applying it to the historical event of the crucifixion. But is such a theory tenable?

The plausibility of this theory is considerably diminished when we note the gender of the relative pronoun in v. 8: if Paul is alluding to the failure of the archons to recognize the redeemer, we would expect him to say *hon oudeis egnōken* and not *hēn*. The parallel with gnostic texts thus becomes rather slight.[21] There is also, it should be noted, considerable difference between the gnostic descriptions of the descent of the redeemer through the heavens and the present reference to the historical event of the crucifixion.

It is more natural to assume, not that Paul has tacked the crucifixion on to a gnostic formula but that the cross is the central element in the passage around which the rest is constructed. Paul understands Jesus' death as an apocalyptic event and describes it in apocalyptic terms, such as 'mystery' and 'hidden', and through the apocalyptic ideas of victory over evil forces, of judgment, and of revelation. Paul here expresses his belief that God's plan for human salvation centers on the concrete and surprising event of the crucifixion of the 'Lord of glory'. The use of terms like 'hidden' and 'mystery' do not have to be understood as evidence of Paul's superficial and half-hearted attempt to out-mystify gnostic opponents, nor as an inorganic taking over of some earlier scheme, whether gnostic or apocalyptic,[22] but as an expression of Paul's own experience of the cross as divine wisdom at work. The cross is 'what no eye has seen nor ear heard nor ever entered the human mind' (v. 9). That God should reveal himself through a crucified messiah certainly never entered the mind of a Pharisee like Paul (cf. Gal.

3.13). The meaning of the cross as the center of God's plan of salvation is known only by the gift of divine revelation (v. 10; cf. Gal. 1.16).

In his chapter on 'The Scandal of the Cross', Beker shows how Paul adds to the interpretations of Jesus' death which he received from earlier Christian tradition his own original interpretation, one which draws on ideas common in Jewish apocalyptic:

> Although Paul and the early tradition share an apocalyptic outlook, Paul's focus on the apocalyptic dimension of the death of Christ is specifically his own.[23]

Strangely, Beker seems to pay little attention to 1 Cor. 2.6-16 even though it illustrates his thesis quite as well as the passages he considers in detail. If we compare it with passages such as Gal. 1.4, 3.13, and 6.14, emphasized by Beker, the similarities are evident. We can see here too how Paul uses several apocalyptic themes in developing his own interpretation of Jesus' death.

Paul views the crucifixion of Christ as a decisive event in history, an event which brings about the end of this age (cf. Gal. 1.4; 1 Cor. 10.11), in Martyn's phrase,[24] the 'horrifying death of the cosmos' (cf. Gal. 6.14). As in apocalyptic thought there is a plan of God and a distinction of two ages. Paul's apocalyptic, however, is centered on the cross of Christ, in which God has entered human history in a new way, asserting his power over his creation (1 Cor. 1.18, 24).

For Paul Jesus' death is the power of God for salvation and judgment. In 1 Corinthians 1, for example, he focuses on the cross as power for the salvation or condemnation of human beings (vv. 18, 21, 28). 1 Cor. 2.6ff. is an extension of this idea, for Paul moves on to the wider implications of the death of Christ. It affects not only humanity but also the superhuman powers which exercise control over human history. In apocalyptic fashion Paul views reality on two levels:[25] behind the events of human history lies the cosmic struggle of God with the forces of evil.

Paul speaks of this cosmic level of reality as a *mystērion*: see Rom. 11.25; 1 Cor. 2.1, 7; 4.1; 13.2; 14.2; 15.51. While he does not share the interest of some Jewish apocalyptic writers in classifying and describing the superhuman forces of evil, he clearly believes in the reality and importance of such powers.[26] There are references to these powers in every one of the undisputed letters except Philemon (cf. 1 Cor. 15.24; Rom. 8.3ff.; Gal. 4.3, 9; Phil. 2.10; 2 Cor. 4.4; 1 Thess. 2.18). Paul calls the powers of evil by various names: for example, *archē, exousia, dynamis* (1 Cor. 15.24) or *ta stoicheia* (Gal. 4.3, 9). Their leader is called 'the god of this world' (2 Cor. 4.4) and Satan (1 Cor. 5.5; 7.5; 2 Cor. 2.11; 11.14; 12.7; 1 Thess. 2.18).

As Beker has pointed out, Paul also describes the forces of evil through the personified terms Death, Sin, Law and Flesh:

> The major apocalyptic forces are, for him, those ontological powers that determine the human situation within the context of God's created order and that comprise the 'field' of death, sin, the law, and the flesh.[27]

This idea that the world is influenced by demonic forces is expressed in 1 Corinthians 2 through the phrase 'the rulers of this age'.[28] Verse 8 portrays the crucifixion of Jesus as a confrontation between the demonic rulers and God. There is an analogy in Gal. 3.13, where Jesus' death is interpreted as a confrontation between the Law and Christ.[29] While the Law, with its curse, seems temporarily to triumph over Christ, the crucified Christ turns back the curse upon the Law and overthrows its power (Gal. 3.13; cf. 3.25). So here the archons think they will destroy the 'Lord of glory' by causing his death, but instead the reverse happens: by killing Christ they have sealed their own destruction, a destruction alluded to in *katargoumenōn* (v. 6). (Compare Rom. 8.3, where the effect of the cross is the condemnation of another apocalyptic power, Sin.) The archons did not know the hidden wisdom of God, his surprising plan to save humanity through a crucified messiah. They could not guess that the real cause of the cross was neither their own will nor that of the human authorities who condemned Jesus but the hidden will of God. No could they foresee that the result of Jesus' death would be a change in the structure of powers which govern human existence.

The thought of 1 Cor. 2.6-8 is related to Gal. 1.4.

> [Jesus Christ] gave himself on behalf of our sins so that he might rescue us from the present evil age, in accordance with the will of our God and Father.

Like 1 Cor. 2.6ff., Gal. 1.4 interprets the cross as the apocalyptic turning point in history. In the Galatians passage this change is described as a rescue from the 'present evil age', the time dominated by evil powers, while 1 Corinthians speaks of the destruction of powers hostile to God.

Paul's description of the archons as *katargoumenoi* (v. 6) deserves close attention. It means that we should not attempt to understand the passage as a timeless speculation on epistemology or a 'commonplace of "wisdom"'.[30] The present tense of the verb points to the character of the present time as Paul experiences it, as a time in which the God is still engaged in conflict with the evil rulers.[31] The force of this verb should not be minimized, as Carr tries to do:

> It is also noteworthy that there is no hint in I Cor. ii of an ignominious end for these rulers, but only of their ignominious act—the crucifying of the Lord of Glory. Their fate is not mentioned, nor is any glorious future of the saints. In ii. 6 *katargoumenōn* refers, as elsewhere in Paul, not to destruction but to decline into unimportance.[32]

While Paul sometimes uses the term *katargeō* in the sense Carr suggests (e.g. at 1 Cor. 1.28), that this is not its meaning in 1 Cor. 2.6 is shown by the close parallel at 1 Cor. 15.24-26:

> Then [will come] the end, when [Christ] hands over the kingdom to God, the Father, when he destroys [*katargēsēi*] every rule [*archēn*] and every authority [*exousian*] and every power [*dunamin*]. For it is necessary for him to rule until he puts all enemies under his feet. As the last enemy, Death is destroyed [*katargeitai*].

Here Paul depicts the final destruction of the cosmic forces which oppose God, describing the powers of evil in both traditional, mythological terms ('every rule, authority and power': cf. the 'rulers' of 1 Cor. 2.6ff.) and as the personified Death (cf. 15.54-56: Death, Sin, Law).

At the end of ch. 15 Paul comes back to this theme of God's final battle against the forces of evil, portraying as a 'mystery' God's final defeat of Death, together with its allies Sin and Law:

> Behold I tell you a mystery. We shall not all sleep, but we shall all be changed. . . . Then the word which is written shall be [fulfilled]: 'Death is swallowed up in victory. Where, O Death, is your victory? Where, O Death, is your sting?' Now the sting of Death is Sin, and the power of Sin is the Law. Thanks be to god who gives us the victory through our Lord Jesus Christ (1 Cor. 15.51, 54-57).

These passages, coming as they do at what both Barth and Beker have called the climax of the whole letter,[33] show the importance of the theme of God's battle with cosmic forces of evil for the letter as a whole. As in ch. 2, Paul uses the term 'mystery' to describe God's plan for salvation, his battle plan. While 1 Cor. 2.6 characterizes the time between the crucifixion and the parousia as the time in which God's enemies are being destroyed (*katargoumenōn*), 1 Cor. 15.24-26 depicts the completion of the divine victory at the time of the parousia when 'God will be all in all'.

After his portrayal of the confrontation between the archons and the crucified Christ in 2.6-9, Paul turns in v. 10 to the theme of revelation through the Spirit:

> (10) But to us God has revealed [these things] through the Spirit. For the Spirit searches all things, even the depths of God. (11) For who of men knows the things of man except the spirit of man within him? In like manner, no one has known the things of God except the Spirit of God. (12) And we have not received the Spirit of the world but the Spirit that comes from God, so that we may know the things that have been graciously given to us by God. (13) These things we speak, not with words taught by human wisdom but with (words) taught by the Spirit, interpreting spiritual things to those who are spiritual. (14) Now the natural man does not receive the things of the Spirit of God, for they are folly to him, and he cannot know (them), for they are judged spiritually. (15) But the spiritual man judges all things, and himself is judged by no one. (16) 'For who has known the mind of the Lord so as to instruct him?' But we have the mind of Christ.

In this section, too, scholars have seen references to the hypothetical gnostic ideas of Paul's opponents. But there is little to encourage such speculations. It is true that the terms *pneumatikos* and *psychikos* are prominent in later gnostic writers, who use them to designate two classes of believers. But the most obvious source for these terms in gnostic writers such as the Valentinians is Paul himself,[34] and there is nothing in the passage itself which compels the conclusion that Paul borrowed the antithesis from his opponents.[35]

Verses 10-16 of ch. 2 are more naturally understood as an extension of the apocalyptic argument developed in vv. 6-9. The rulers of this age did not know the plan of God, but we know it because it has been revealed to us by the Spirit, and it is only the Spirit that allows us to apprehend what escaped the rulers and appears as foolishness to the natural man. This revelation is the necessary complement to the action of God in the cross. Just as the cross is God's power for salvation and judgment—a power which enters history at the particular point ordained in God's wise plan, so the Spirit is given at a particular point in time (*elabomen*, v. 12) to make known God's plan, in particular the meaning of the cross. The cross cannot be understood through human reason (v. 9) but is only through revelation (v. 10; cf. Gal. 1.11ff.).

Several other passage show how closely Paul connected the gift of the Spirit with the cross of Christ:

> Christ has redeemed us from the curse of the Law, having become a curse on our account . . . so that the blessing of Abraham might come to the gentiles, so that we might receive the promise of the Spirit through faith (Gal. 3.13f.).

> And hope does not cause us shame, because God's love has been poured into our hearts through the Holy Spirit who has been given to us. For when we were still weak, at the right time Christ died for the ungodly . . . But God shows his love for us in that while we were still sinners Christ died for us (Rom. 5.5-6, 8).

> For what the Law, weakened by the Flesh, could not do [God has done]: sending his own Son in the likeness of sinful flesh and as a sin offering, he condemned Sin in the flesh, so that the just requirement of the Law might be fulfilled in us, who walk not according to the Flesh but according to the Spirit (Rom. 8.3-4).

> Or do you not know that your body is a temple of the Holy Spirit who dwells in you, which you have from God, and you are not your own? For you were bought for a price (1 Cor. 6.19-20; cf. 6.11; Gal. 3.1-2).

Paul presents the crucifixion of Christ and the arrival of the Spirit as events of salvation and revelation which complement each other. It is because of the costly act of Christ's death that the Spirit comes to dwell in believers, and that the gift of the Spirit is extended even to gentiles. Only after the sacrifice of God's Son is it possible to escape the dominion of the Flesh and 'walk' according to the Spirit. The cross reveals the amazing news of God's love for the ungodly (i.e. for all people); this revelation is understood and appropriated when the Spirit is poured into the hearts of believers.[36] Just as Paul says that 'no one can say "Jesus is Lord" except by the Holy Spirit' (1 Cor. 12.3), so he says in 1 Corinthians 2 that only those who receive the revelation of the Spirit understand the meaning of the cross.

The crucial verse in 2.10-16 is v. 10, which many interpreters understand against the background of gnostic ideas. So Wilckens comments on vv. 10-12:

> Zweifellos hat man auch dies von der Gnosis her zu verstehen: In den gnostischen Texten ist der Offenbarer selbst in seinem Wesen Pneuma. Der Empfang des Pneuma verwandelt den Empfangenden in das Wesen des Pneuma hinein, so dass er als *pneumatikos* mit dem *pneuma*-Offenbarer identisch geworden und also 'sein' Erkennen in Wahrheit das des Pneuma ist, in das er hineingenommen ist.[37]

Conzelmann comments on v. 10:

> In the underlying schema of the mysteries the essential idea is precisely the identity of the power to reveal and to receive. Paul does in fact go on in this sense. In so doing he is on the verge of Gnosticism—to be sure, without developing the mythical motif of descent. He speaks in a way that takes no acount of the historical character of revelation, but solely of the illumination of the recipients. The object of knowledge is not the historic Christ, but the mystery, and only in a secondary sense the mythical background of the historic crucifixion.[38]

But here again the gnostic parallels adduced to our text are more misleading than helpful. There is no reason to read into 1 Cor. 2.10ff. the idea that the recipient of the divine Spirit becomes identical in nature with the Spirit-revealer. Paul's picture of the Spirit as agent of revelation (*apekalypsen*) is paralleled not only in the Old Testament (Isa. 61.1; Ezek. 8.3) but also in Jewish apocalyptic texts. In the fifth book of *1 Enoch*, for example, Enoch attributes his revelation about the consummation of history to the Spirit which is poured out upon him:

> Now, my son Methuselah, (please) summon all your brothers on my behalf, and gather together all the sons of your mother; for a voice calls me, and the spirit is poured over me so that I may show you everything that shall happen to you forever (*1 Enoch* 91.1).[39]

The revelation which follows this introduction, and which includes the well-known 'Apocalypse of Weeks' (91.12-17; 93.1-10) is a description of God's plans for the last days of world history—a description which treats both the acts of human beings and of God and his angels. A key feature in this description is the theme of judgment:

Then, after this matter, on the tenth week in the seventh part, there shall be the eternal judgment, and it shall be executed by the angels of the eternal heaven. ... The first heaven shall depart and pass away; a new heaven shall appear; and all the powers of heaven shall shine forever sevenfold. ... it shall be (a time) of goodness and righteousness, and sin shall no more be heard of forever (91.12-17; cf. 93.1ff.).

Another apocalyptic text which combines the ideas of the reception of the Spirit and the understanding of God's hidden plan is *4 Ezra* 14.19-20. After God's command to Ezra to instruct people that they are living during the last evil time and must repent, Ezra makes the following request:

If then I have found favor before you, send the Holy Spirit to me, and I will write everything that has happened in the world from the beginning, the things which were written in your Law, that men may be able to find the path, and that those who wish to live in the last days may live.[40]

In 1 Cor. 2.6ff. Paul presents Jesus' death as an apocalypse and thus combines two different motifs found in Jewish apocalyptic texts, the idea of a special revelation to the apocalyptic seer and the idea that specific historical events are to be understood as part of a two-level divine drama, as the carrying out of God's hidden plan. The Holy Spirit reveals the meaning of Jesus' death, but the death itself is also revelation: it makes clear that the time in which believers now find themselves is the 'end of the ages', the time of judgment and redemption, of the final battle between divine forces and the forces of evil.[41]

The cross is revelation and also an act of God's power. So the spirit is not only an agent of revelation but also a new power in history (cf. 2.4-5), a power which opposes the 'Spirit of the world' (2.12; cf. 2. Cor. 4.4 'the God of this world') and the 'rulers this age' (1 Cor. 2.6, 8).

In Galatians and Romans Paul develops the idea of the Spirit as power in conflict with the powers of evil (Flesh, Sin, Law, and Death). In Gal. 5.17-18 Paul describes the conflict between Spirit and the personified Flesh:

For the Flesh lusts against the Spirit and the Spirit against the flesh, for these are opposed to each other.

Martyn says of Spirit and Flesh in this passage:

> They are a pair of warriors, locked in combat with one another (note especially Paul's use of the term *aphormē* in 5.13). And this warfare has been started by the Spirit, sent by God into the realm of the Flesh.[42]

In Romans 8 Paul describes the conflict between the powers of Flesh and Spirit for dominion over human beings:

> For those who live according to the Flesh set their minds on the things of the Flesh, but those who live according to the Spirit set their minds on the things of the Spirit. . . . For the mind that is set on the Flesh is hostile to God; it does not submit to God's law. . . . But you are not in the Flesh, you are in the Spirit (Rom. 8.5, 7).

In Rom. 8.18-39 Paul goes to describe the fate of those who ally themselves with the Spirit and have the 'mind' of the Spirit (cf. 1 Cor. 2.11-12, 16): through suffering they will be glorified (8.17; cf. *doxa* in 1 Cor. 2.7) and will win the battle (v. 37 *hypernikōmen*) over all the forces which oppose God (vv. 38-39).

These treatments of Spirit as a divine power at war with the forces of evil tell against the idea that Paul's statements about Spirit and spiritual in 1 Cor. 2.6ff. have a predominantly anthropological sense, as if the main point of this passage were the distinction of human faculties or of classes of people. Despite the anthropological comparison in 2.11, the central focus of the section is God's wise plan for history, which is revealed and enacted in the death of his messiah and in the gift of the Holy Spirit—events which show God's power (cf. 2.4-5; 1.24, 31) and begin the 'war of liberation'[43] against the forces of evil (2.6-8). This section is concerned with epistemology, but in an apocalyptic, not a gnostic or philosophical sense.[44] The *pneumatikos* is not the person who understands that his inner self is divine but one who understands and lives in accordance with the gift of the Spirit, that is, every Christian in so far as he is true to his calling (cf. 3.16; 6.19).

This apocalyptic reading of 1 Cor. 2.6ff. allows us to understand this passage and 1 Corinthians 15 as a framework for the rest of the letter, a framework which makes clear in what light we are to consider the concrete issues of Christian life in the world discussed in the central portion of the letter. Paul takes everyday Christian experience seriously, and he reminds the Corinthians that there is another level of reality behind the events of their lives. Christian life is to be lived in light of the apocalypse of Christ's death. It is determined both by the past and by the future, by the destruction of the evil powers begun in the cross (*katargoumenōn*, 2.6) and by the completion of God's victory in the imminent future (*hotan katargēsēi*, 15.24).

Thus Paul's advice for Christian living, which forms the major part of 1 Corinthians, is not in the form of general maxims which are valid for all time, but is written for the particular time and situation in which Christians find themselves, the time of the final cosmic battle. Not only is the treatment of matters such as marriage, sexuality, relation to pagan religious practices and proper worship surrounded before and after by the references to the destruction of cosmic powers in chs. 2 and 15; in the central section itself there are also numerous references to the future consummation (e.g. 1.7-8; 3.8, 13-15, 17; 4.5; 5.5, 13; 6.2-3, 9, 13-14; 7.26, 29; 8.8, 11; 9.27; 10.9-13; 11.19, 29-34; 13.8-10; 15.1-2, 12-58; 16.21). Prominent among them is the theme of judgment, as the following texts illustrate:

> . . . so that you are not lacking in any spiritual gift, as you wait for the revealing of our Lord Jesus Christ, who will sustain you to the end, guiltless in the day of our Lord Jesus Christ (1.7-8).

> Each man's work will become manifest, for the Day will disclose it, because it will be revealed with fire, and the fire will test what sort of work each one has done. . . . If any one destroys God's temple, God will destroy him (3.13, 17).

> Therefore do not pronounce judgment before the time, before the Lord comes, who will bring to light the things now hidden in darkness and will disclose the purposes of the heart (4.5).

> Do you not know that we are to judge angels? How much more [shall we judge] matters pertaining to this life? (6.2-3)

> Now these things happened to them as a warning, but they were written down for our instruction, upon whom the end of the ages has come. Therefore let any one who thinks that he stands take heed lest he fall (10.11-12).

> For any one who eats and drinks without discerning the body eats and drinks judgment upon himself. . . But if we judged ourselves truly, we should not be judged. But when we are judged by the Lord, we are chastened so that we may not be condemned along with the world (11.29, 31-32).[45]

Paul interprets the cross of Christ as the revelation of God's final judgment, a judgment which affects the whole cosmos. In the cross God has pronounced judgment on the superhuman powers of evil and has begun their destruction (1 Cor. 2.6-8), a destruction which will be completed at the parousia (1 Cor. 15.24-28). He has also revealed his judgment of humanity, which is already at work in the present (cf. *tois apollumenois*, 1.18) and which will be confirmed and completed at the parousia. Paul reminds the Christians that they are destined for glory (1 Cor. 2.8; 15.43) and expresses confidence that they will be found blameless at the last judgment, on the 'day of the Lord' (1.7-8), but he also warns them to take care lest they fall (10.12). They are still subject to the attacks of Satan (7.5; cf. 5.5), and their everyday life is a skirmish in the cosmic battle (cf. 15.30-32, 57-58).

It is significant that Paul ends his treatment of wisdom in 1 Cor. 2.6-16 with a discussion of judgment: 'The spiritual person judges (*anakrinei*) all things, but is himself judged (*anakrinetai*) by no one' (2.15). As in 4.3-5 Paul uses the verb *anakrinō* to refer both to human judgment and to God's final judgment. The person who has received the gift of the Spirit and who lives his life in accordance with the revelation and power of the Spirit, is able to *discern* God's action in history, which is invisible to the natural man. At the same time he is subject to no human judgment and will be found blameless at God's final judgment. In 11.26-32 Paul, commenting on the celebration of the cross in Lord's Supper, says that those who fail to discern (*diakrinōn*) the Lord's body and to judge (*diakrinō*) themselves, fall under judgment (*krinō*). So too in 2.15, the possession of discernment implies freedom from judgment.

We see thus that from beginning to end 1 Cor. 2.6-16 is an expression of Paul's own theology. We need not imagine that Paul is contradicting himself or being ironic or attempting to outbid his opponents in esoteric knowledge. The practice of *Paulon ek Paulou saphēnizein* rescues the unity of the letter, showing the relevance of the eschatological frame to the ethical center, as well as the close connection of crucifixion, Spirit, and 'last things' in the thought of the apostle.

NOTES

1. According to Birger Pearson (*The Pneumatikos-Psychikos Terminology in I Corinthians* [Missoula, MT: Society of Biblical Literature, 1973], p. 1), the widely accepted thesis that Paul's opponents in 1 Corinthians were Gnostics was first proposed by W. Lütgert in *Freiheitspredigt und Schwarmgeister in Korinth* (BFCT 12/3; Gütersloh, 1908). It has been argued at length by Ulrich Wilckens (*Weisheit und Torheit* [Tübingen: J.B.C. Mohr, 1959]) and by Walter Schmithals (*Gnosticism in Corinth* [trans. J. Steely; Nashville: Abingdon, 1971]). Pearson's book is a challenge to the scholarly consensus on this point; cf. especially p. 82.

2. After his analysis of this passage on pp. 52-98, Wilckens concludes that Paul here expresses not his own ideas but those of his opponents: 'aber die entscheidende Differenz zu seiner eigenen Verkündigung eindeutig zum Ausdruck zu bringen, ist ihm offensichtlich in 2,6ff. nicht ganz gelungen, weil er sich hier bemüht, in dem Sprach- und Vorstellungsbereich der Korinther zu diskutieren. Dass es sich bei dieser von ihm hier vorgetragenen gnostischen Lehre nicht um seine eigene Lehre handelt, zeigt ein Blick auf seine sonstige Verkündigung'. Less extreme statements of this view are found in Hans Conzelmann, *1 Corinthians* (trans. James W. Leitch; Hermeneia; Philadelphia: Fortress, 1975), pp. 57ff.; Rudolf Bultmann, *Faith and Understanding*, vol. I (trans. Louis Pettibone Smith, ed. Robert W. Funk; New York: Harper & Row, 1969), pp. 71f.; Dieter Lührmann, *Das Offenbarungsverständnis bei Paulus und in paulinischen Gemeinden* (Neukirchen: Neukirchener Verlag, 1965), p. 113. Cf. also Ernst Käsemann, 'Meditation zu 1 Kor 2.6-16', *Exegetische Versuche und Besinnungen*', Vol. I (Göttingen: Vandenhoeck & Ruprecht, 1964), p. 267: 'Der Apostel bekämpft die christlichen Enthusiasten gleichsam mit ihren eigenen Waffen und auf dem von ihnen gewählten Felde'.

3. Martin Widmann, 'I Kor 2.6-16: Ein Einspruch gegen Paulus', *ZNW* 70 (1979), pp. 44-53. Widmann states his thesis on p. 46: 'Die ungezwungenste Lösung der Frage, wie sich dieses befremdliche Stück zum paulinischen Kontext verhalte, ist, hier eine längere Glosse anzunehmen, welche die enthusiastische Gruppe in der korinthischen Gemeinde als Entgegnung zum Brieforiginal dazuschrieb und die dann beim späteren Abschreiben in den Paulustext eingeführt wurde'.

4. On Paul's apocalyptic interpretation of the death of Christ see J. Christiaan Beker, *Paul the Apostle* (Philadelphia: Fortress, 1980), pp. 182-212, and J. Louis Martyn, 'Apocalyptic Antinomies in Paul's Letter to the Galatians', *NTS* 31 (1985), pp. 410-24.

5. On Paul as an apocalyptic theologian see the works cited in n. 4; Ernst Käsemann, 'The Beginnings of Christian Theology', *New Testament Questions of Today* (Philadelphia: Fortress, 1969), pp. 82-107; *idem*, 'On the

Subject of Primitive Christian Apocalyptic', *op. cit.*, pp. 108-37; Leander E. Keck, 'Paul and Apocalyptic Theology', *Interpretation* 38 (1984), pp. 229-41; Jorg Baumgarten, *Paulus und die Apokalyptik* (Neukirchen: Neukirchener Verlag, 1975).

6. The distinction between the *psychikos* and the *pneumatikos*, and the description of the latter as *teleios*, occurs frequently in Valentinian texts, cf. e.g. Clement of Alexandria, *Exc. Theod.* 56.3; Irenaeus, *Adv. Haer.* I 6.1-4.

7. Page 57. Conzelmann refers to the article of Bultmann cited in note 2 above.

8. See note 4.

9. Various interpreters—including those who argue that 1 Cor 2.6ff. is thoroughly gnostic—have pointed out parallels to these terms in Jewish apocalyptic texts. Wilckens adduces parallels to the following terms: *archontes* (p. 63), *mystērion* (p. 64 n. 1 and p. 65), *apokekrymenos* (p. 65), *doxa* (p. 66), *sophia* in the sense of the 'Heilsplan Gottes' (p. 69, reference to *2 Bar.* 14.8ff.). In addition Wilckens describes the quotation in 2.9 as 'eine typisch apokalyptische Aussage' (p. 66). On apocalyptic parallels to Paul's terminology in 2.6ff. see further Lührmann, pp. 99f., 115ff.; Pearson, p. 33 (*kyrios tēs doxēs*) and notes 12, 16, 28, and 39 below.

10. For parallels in Jewish wisdom literature, especially Philo, see Conzelmann, p. 59; Pearson, pp. 27ff.

11. Compare for example the first chapter of *1 Enoch*, in which the sage receives a revelation of the God's future judgment on both men and superhuman powers of evil ('the Watchers'); cf. *1 Enoch* 91 cited below. See also D.S. Russell, *The Method and Message of Jewish Apocalyptic* (Philadelphia: Westminster, 1964), pp. 230ff.; Christopher Rowland, *The Open Heaven* (New York: Crossroad, 1982), pp. 160ff. Rowland and others have called into question the tendency of earlier scholars to define apocalyptic solely in terms of eschatology; nonetheless it cannot be denied that the revelation of the divine plan for the consummation of history is a prominent theme in many Jewish apocalypses—e.g. Dan. 7-12; the 'Animal Apocalypse' (*1 Enoch* 83-90), the 'Apocalypse of Weeks' (*1 Enoch* 93.1-10; 91.11-17), *4 Ezra*; *2 Baruch*. Compare the moderating view of J.J. Collins in *Apocalypse: The Morphology of a Genre. Semeia* 14 (Missoula, MT: Scholars Press, 1979), p. 14, and in *The Apocalyptic Imagination* (New York: Crossroad, 1984), pp. 9ff.

12. The 'doctrine of two ages', which Philipp Vielhauer puts at the beginning of his definition of 'apocalyptic' (in *New Testament Apocrypha*, Vol. II [ed. E. Hennecke and W. Schneemelcher, trans. R. McL. Wilson; Philadelphia: Westminster, 1964], pp. 588f.) is explicitly stated in only one text, *4 Ezra* 7.50, but the phrase 'this age' is common, as is the general idea of historical dualism; cf. Russell, pp. 266ff.; Rowland, pp. 27-28.

13. Paul also speaks of 'this age' in 1 Cor. 1.20; 3.18; Rom. 12.2. Cf. Beker, p. 384 n. 44; Baumgarten, pp. 181-89.

14. For further discussion of the *archontes* as demonic powers and of the verb *katargeō* see below, especially note 28.

15. Page 62. Compare the interpretation of Wilckens, who notes apocalyptic parallels to Paul's use of the term *doxa* in 2.7 but nonetheless finds the key to the text in gnostic ideas: 'Ist in 2,7 mit der 'Weisheit Gottes' Christus gemeint, so ist hier die geläufige apokalyptische Vorstellung von der zukünftigen Verherrlichung der Gerechten mit der gnostischen Vorstellung einer gegenwärtigen Verwandlung des Gnostikers in die *doxa* des Erlösers verschmolzen. In diesem spezifisch gnostischen Sinn ist das folgende christologische Prädikat *kyrios tēs doxēs* gemeint'.

16. On the use of 'glory' in apocalyptic texts and in Paul cf. Beker, pp. 136, 148, 167; Wilckens, p. 66; Lührmann, p. 115; cf. also Klaus Koch, *The Rediscovery of Apocalyptic* (trans. Margaret Kohl; London: SCM, 1972), p. 32: 'The catchword *glory* is used wherever the final state of affairs is set apart from the present and whenever a final amalgamation of the earthly and heavenly spheres is prophesied. Glory is the portion of those who have been raised from the dead, who will thus become as the angels or the stars of heaven (Dan 12.3; I Enoch 50.1; 51.4)'.

17. Rudolf Bultmann, *Theology of the New Testament*, Vol. I (trans. Kendrick Grobel; New York: Scribners, 1951), p. 175.

18. Wilckens, p. 206. Wilckens adds to the received tradition that there is a gnostic redeemer myth behind 1 Cor. 2 the further thesis that *sophia* is here a title for Christ—a theory which has not found general acceptance; cf. Schmithals, pp. 138ff.; Pearson, p. 34.

19. Conzelmann, p. 63. He points out in note 65 that this motif also 'has a part to play in Gnosticism'. Conzelmann's treatment of v. 8 is surprisingly brief and focuses mainly on its 'contradictions'.

20. C.K. Barrett, *A Commentary on the First Epistle to the Corinthians* (New York: Harper and Row, 1968), pp. 71-72. It is perhaps significant that none of the four commentators cited here refers to specific gnostic texts where the motif of the redeemer's deception of the powers during his descent to earth is clearly attested. Hans Lietzmann (*An die Korinther I/II* [Tübingen: J.C.B. Mohr, 1969], p. 12), who also follows this interpretation of the background of 2.8, refers to several primary texts, e.g. the reports of Irenaeus in *Adv. Haer.* I 30.12; 24.5f.; 23.3. On this motif see further Kurt Rudolf, *Gnosis* (ed. R.McL. Wilson; San Francisco: Harper and Row, 1983), p. 139.

21. This point has also been noticed by Pearson, p. 34.

22. Cf. Lührmann, pp. 113ff., 133ff. and the criticism of Lührmann by Conzelmann, pp. 58f., and Pearson, p. 31.

23. Beker, p. 191. Cf. the whole of ch. 9, 'The Scandal of the Cross' (pp. 182-212, esp. p. 189).

24. Martyn, p. 420.

25. Compare Collins's description of the apocalyptic genre (*Apocalypse*, pp. 10-11): 'Both the manner of revelation and the eschatological content point beyond this world to another, which is at once the source of revelation and of future salvation'. Cf. also Rowland, pp. 2f.

26. Jewish apocalyptic texts which exhibit this interest include *1 Enoch* 6ff.; 53ff.; 69.4-12; cf. Russell, pp. 235-62 and Rowland, pp. 93ff. On Paul's view of superhuman powers see Martin Dibelius, *Die Geisterwelt im Glauben des Paulus* (Göttingen: Vandenhoeck & Ruprecht, 1909), especially pp. 88-99, 181; Clinton Morrison, *The Powers that Be* (Naperville, IL: Allenson, 1960), pp. 17-24 and bibliography cited in note on p. 17; Barrett, p. 70; Pearson, p. 33.

27. Beker, p. 189. There is a certain inconsistency in Beker's argument. While his argument as a whole serves to emphasize the importance of superhuman powers of evil in Paul—especially the powers of Death, Sin, Law, and Flesh—Beker tends to minimize the more mythological references to evil powers: 'Paul uses traditional apocalyptic terminology sparingly and interprets it anthropologically . . . so that words such as 'powers,' 'rulers,' 'lordships,' 'thrones,' 'world rulers of darkness in the heavens' (cf. Eph. 6.12; Col. 1.16) are primarily restricted to the apocalyptic sections of 1 Cor. 15.24-28 and Rom. 8.38-39 (cf. 1 Cor. 2.6-9)'. Thus he gives short shrift to 1 Cor. 2.6ff. Cf. his remark on p. 273: 'How can anyone after reading 1 Cor. 2.6-16, with its theme of our already perfected spiritual wisdom, expect the future apocalyptic of 1 Cor. 4.4-5, 13.8-10, or 15.12-58?'

28. This is the only use which Paul make of this phrase; cf. Jn 12.31; 14.30; 16.11 where Satan is called the 'ruler of this world'. For discussion of the meaning of *archontes* in Paul see Wesley Carr, 'The Rulers of This Age—I Corinthians II.6-8', *NTS* 23 (1976), pp. 20-35, and the literature cited there. Carr outlines three different interpretations of the 'rulers', with the most usual view being 'that it refers to demonic beings, those archons who rule the world'. (Among those who subscribe to this view are Dibelius, pp. 89ff.; Barrett, p. 70; Conzelmann, p. 61, Beker, p. 189; Pearson, p. 33.) Carr's attempt to show that the *archontes* are not demonic powers but the human authorities who crucified Jesus is not convincing.

29. Cf. Beker, pp. 184ff.

30. Contra Conzelmann, p. 57.

31. Beker, pp. 159f., following Oscar Cullmann, *Christ and Time* (Philadelphia: Westminster, 1950), p. 145, describes this situation through the analogy of D-Day and V-Day.

32. Carr, p. 32.

33. Beker, p. 164; Beker refers to Barth's argument in *The Resurrection of the Dead* (New York: Fleming H. Revell, 1933), pp. 13-124.

34. See Elaine H. Pagels, *The Gnostic Paul* (Philadelphia: Fortress Press, 1975), especially pp. 6ff., 57ff.

35. Pearson assumes that Paul took over the *psychikos/pneumatikos* antithesis from his Corinthian opponents (p. 38), but he disputes the idea that the opponents were gnostics (p. 82).

36. Compare Martyn's comment on the role of the Spirit in Galatians (p. 417): 'The advent of the Son and of his Spirit is also the coming of faith, an event that Paul explicitly calls an apocalypse (note the parallel expressions "to come" and "to be apocalypsed" in 3. 23)'.

37. Wilckens, p. 81.

38. Conzelmann, p. 65.

39. Translation of passages from *1 Enoch* are by E. Isaac in *The Old Testament Pseudepigrapha*, Vol. I (ed. James H. Charlesworth; New York: Doubleday, 1983), pp. 13ff. This text is found on p. 72.

40. Translation of *4 Ezra* is by Bruce M. Metzger in Charlesworth, Vol. I, p. 554. Cf. also *4 Ezra* 5.21-22; Dan. 5.12; 6.3.

41. Compare Martyn's remark (p. 418) that the crucial question addressed in Galatians is 'What time is it?'

42. Martyn, p. 416.

43. Martyn, p. 418.

44. Cf. Martyn, p. 424 n. 28, for a discussion of epistemology in Jewish apocalyptic and in Paul: 'The new way of knowing, granted by God, is focused first of all on the cross, and also on the parousia, these two being, then, the parents of that new manner of perception'.

45. Translations are from the Revised Standard Version (1971). Further references to judgment are found in 1 Cor. 5.12-13; 6.9, 13-14; 8.8, 11; 11.19; 16.21.

SEEKING (ZĒTEIN) AND SINNING (HAMARTŌLOS & HAMARTIA) ACCORDING TO GALATIANS 2.17

Marion L. Soards

Writing in the Festschrift for John Knox, J. Louis Martyn said, 'Daily experience in the reading of Paul's letters teaches us ... that the apostle's most important statements often, present the greatest ambiguity. That is nowhere more obviously true than in 2 Cor. 5.16'.[1] Exactly the same may be said of Gal. 2.17, which reads in the Nestle-Aland 26th edition: *ei de zētountes dikaiōthēnai en christō heurethēmen kai autoi hamartōloi, ara christos hamartias diakonos; mē genoito.* Recognizing the importance of this difficult verse commentators have offered different translations and various interpretations of Paul's words. This essay will ultimately strike a new direction in terms of both translation and interpretation of Gal. 2.17. But that the differences between the new understanding of the verse argued for below and those previously articulated by commenatators may be clear, the first portion of this study provides a synthetic overview (with some critique) of portions of previous scholarship on this verse.

The State of the Question

Gal. 2.17 is generally understood to fall into two parts:

17a = *ei de zētountes dikaiōthēnai en christō*
      heurethēmen kai autoi hamartōloi
17b = *ara christos hamartias diakonos* and *mē genoito.*

Translation

There is only minor debate about the translation of 17a. KJV reads, 'But if, while we seek to be justified by Christ, we ourselves also are found sinners'; RSV renders the line, 'But if, in our endeavor to be justified in Christ, we ourselves were found to be sinners'; NAS translates, 'But if, while seeking to be justified in Christ, we ourselves have also been found sinners'; NAB has, 'But if, in seeking to be justified in Christ, we are shown to be sinners'; NIV reads, 'If, while we seek to be justified in Christ, it becomes evident that we ourselves are sinners'; and New JB translates, 'Now if we too are found to be sinners on the grounds that we seek our justification in Christ'.

The translations differ chiefly in the ways they have read the participle *zētountes* and the verb *heurethēmen*. *zētountes* is sometimes rendered as a participle ('seeking', as in NAS and NAB), sometimes as a verb ('we seek', as in KJV, NIV, and New JB), and sometimes as a substantive ('our endeavor', as in RSV). But, in all cases, as the accompanying, preceding words and phrases ('while', 'in', and 'on the grounds that') indicate, the participle is understood to be a circumstantial use 'denoting some attendant circumstance and qualifying the main verb like an adverbial phrase or clause'.[3]

The main verb, *heurethēmen*, is also translated variously: 'we are found', 'we were found', 'we have been found', 'we are shown', and 'it becomes evident'. But all these translations make an effort to recognize the passive voice of the verb, and they demonstrate reservation about pressing meaning from this form.[4] The translations do demonstrate an odd variety in handling the aorist tense of the verb. Clearly the readings that reflect the past tense are correct ('were found' and 'have been found'); whereas those rendering in the present tense are incorrect ('are found', 'are shown', and 'becomes evident'). Yet, more importantly, the translations above (and all others of which I am aware, in all languages) agree that *heurethēmen kai autoi hamartōloi* is a coherent phrase. Thus, despite some differences over the precise manner in which Gal. 2.17a should be rendered, the verse is not a problem for interpreters at the level of translation.

The debate of commentators concerning the translation of 17b is reflected in the versions under consideration. KJV reads, 'is therefore Christ the minister of sin? God forbid'; RSV translates, 'is Christ then an agent of sin? Certainly not!'; NAS has, 'is Christ then a minister of sin? May it never be!'; NAB reads, 'does that mean that Christ is encouraging sin? Unthinkable'; NIV renders, 'does that mean that Christ promotes sin? Absolutely not!'; and New JB translates, 'it would surely follow that Christ was at the service of sin. Out of the question!'

The variety of translation of *mē genoito* is remarkable but unimportant, for it primarily attests to the stylistic sensibilities of the translators and reflects no actual difference in understandings.[5] The real issue here is whether one should read *ara* as the interrogative particle, accented with a circumflex, or as the illative/inferential/ concluding particle, accented with the acute as a paroxytone. For some translators the difference is understood as whether *ara christos hamartias diakonos* is a question (as in NAB and NIV, 'does that mean') or a statement (as in New JB, 'it would surely follow that').[6] But, the difference is not as great as that. From the *mē genoito* which follows, it is clear that *ara christos hamartias diakonos* is a question; for in every use of the objection, *mē genoito*, Paul states the point which he protests in the form of a rhetorical question.[7] But, it is possible that *ara* in 17b is the illative particle, meaning 'then, consequently', and introduces an inferential question; so that translations like RSV and NAS that preserve the ambiguity with 'then' are the best solution to the problem.[8]

In general, the issues of translation for this verse are not regarded by commentators as being complex, despite occasional remarks about there being 'complications involved in understanding the first part of this verse' because of 'the embedding of a clause of attendant circumstances' (*zētountes kikaiōthēnai en christǭ*) 'within a conditional clause' (*ei de . . . heurethēmen kai autoi hamartōloi*).[9] Thus, it is fair to conclude that, independent of matters of exegetical interpretation, the formal equivalence style translation of NAS summarizes the basic manner in which commentators judge Gal. 2.17 should be rendered:

> But if, while seeking to be justified in Christ, we ourselves have also been found sinners, is Christ then a minister of sin? May it never be!

Interpretation

Commentators disagree over the meaning of Gal. 2.17. For the present discussion consideration of the radically different understandings of *hamartōloi* in 17a gives one entrée into the broader issues of interpretation of this verse. Scholars fall into two camps concerning *hamartōloi*. One group, which includes W.F. Arndt,[10] F.F. Bruce,[11] and J.D.G. Dunn,[12] reads the word in 17a in parallel to its use in Jewish circles contemporary to Paul. Thus Dunn examines *hamartōlos* in the LXX, including the Apocrypha (1 Maccabees, Tobit, and *4 Ezra*); apocryphal writings (esp. *Psalms of Solomon* and *Jubilees*); Q material; other Gospels ministry material; and the Mishnah.[13] The claim of this group of interpreters is that *hamartōlos* is 'more and more a technical term for someone who either broke the law or did not know the law'.[14] As confirmation of this interpretation these scholars frequently point to Gal. 2.15, which they translate with RSV, 'We ourselves, who are Jews by birth and not Gentile sinners', and claim Gal. 2.15 and 2.17 are parallel instances of Paul's use of *hamartōloi* to indicate those who do not observe the law.[15] The other group, following Luther, J. Calvin, and J. Wesley, reads *hamartōloi* in 17a in relation to *hamartia* in 17b, where *hamartia* clearly means 'going against God's will' or 'living outside the realm of God's salvation'. In favor of this interpretation one notices that *hamartōlos* is a rare word in Paul's writings, occurring outside of Gal. 2.15, 17 only four times in Romans (3.7; 5.8, 19; 7.13).[16] In each of the uses in Romans, the word seems to designate one who is set against God, not merely one who is outside the law. Moreover, it is possible, perhaps preferable, to render Gal. 2.15 as Luther did in his earlier commentary on Galatians, 'We are sinners of Jewish, not Gentile origin'.[17]

Working with these different understandings of *hamartōloi*, commentators propose at least four lines of interpretation of Gal. 2.17. For clarity and simplicity of presentation I will offer paraphrases of the lines of interpretation.

First, taking the word to mean 'those outside the law' some interpreters[18] argue that Paul is saying this: 'While it is true that Christ leads the Christian outside the law (17a), it is not true that Christ is an agent of sin (17b); and so, it is not a sin for Christians not to observe the law'. There are several weakness in this interpretation. The meaning attributed to *hamartōloi* upon which this understanding is based 'goes too far afield for its explanation of the word',[19] by surveying everything but that which is most crucial, viz. the meaning implied by Paul's own use of *hamartōlos*. Moreover, commentators holding this position usually understand that up to *mē genoito* in v. 17 (*ei de zētountes dikaiōthēnai en christō heurethēmen kai autoi hamartōloi, ara christos hamartias diakonos?*) Paul is probably quoting or employing the language of those who objected to his law-free gospel. This is what is known as a 'mirror-reading' of the passage, and there are times when Paul's letters give the interpreter cues to employ such a method for understanding the text, e.g. 1 Cor. 7.1, 25; 8.1; 12.1; 16.1; Rom. 3.8; and perhaps 6.1. But, recent work by G. Lyons shows the interpreter should not take for granted that antithetical formulations in Paul's argumentation presume the apostle's opponents;[20] so mirror-readings should be done only when the text directs such interpretation and occasionally, with reservation, when no other interpretative solution is available for making sense of a passage. That is not the case in Gal. 2.17. In fact, the particular mirror-reading under consideration makes strange sense of the text, for it requires one to postulate two distinct senses for *hamartōloi* and *hamartia*. Furthermore, it misconstrues the issue Paul is discussing in Galatians. The problem he is facing is the activity of *putting on the law 'in Christ'* (as Peter did in Antioch and as the Galatians are doing in accepting another gospel) not *putting off the law for Christ* (as one is to suppose Paul's critics must have said he had done). At issue in Galatians is the interpretation of Christian freedom, whether the Christian is bound to observe the law, not whether it is a sin for Christians to cease to be law-observant.

Second, understanding *hamartōloi* to mean 'those going against God's will' or 'those outside the realm of God's salvation', other commentators interpret v. 17 to mean, 'since it is true that Christians are justified in Christ, then it is impossible for Christians to be sinners, for if they are sinners then Christ is an agent of sin; but Christ is not the agent of sin, but of justification, and so Christians are not sinners'.[21] In this reading the interpreter takes 17a in two parts: (1) 'But if, while seeking to be justified in Christ', and (2) 'we ourselves have also been found sinners'.[22] This interpretation argues that Paul approves of part one and denies part two through the rhetorical question and answer in 17b. Thus, interpreters deem the logic in 17a to be that of Paul's opponents. This logic is faulty, though not absurd; for it is easy to misunderstand Paul's position 'that those who believe in Christ and are justified are not sinners, since no man is without sin'. But what Paul means, according to these interpreters is that 'everyone who believes in Christ is righteous, not yet fully in point of fact, but in hope'.[23] This interpretation of 2.17 has several liabilities. It depends upon a hypothetical mirror-reading of the verse, but then artificially abstracts the issue, *Christ versus the Law*, from the context in the letter and treats the verse as a dictum on Christian justification. The logic is contorted, replete with rationalizations, and it is unbelievable that any first-century reader would have been able to understand the verse in the manner proposed by this exposition.

Third, also understanding *hamartōloi* to mean 'those going against God's will', some interpreters of 2.17 hear Paul say, 'while it is true that the grace of Christ places Jews on the same level as Gentiles, i.e., reckoned guilty and polluted, in order to redeem both through the righteousness of faith, Christ did not bring sin but unveiled it, stripping the Jew of a false disguise; and so it is absurd to conclude that Christ is an agent of sin'.[24] The advantages of this interpretation are that it avoids a mirror-reading of the verse and that it attributes only one sense to both *hamartōloi* in 2.15, 17a and *hamartia* in 2.17b. But, as Calvin, who is the major proponent of this exposition recognized, understood this way 'it [the verse] certainly has very little, if anything, to do with the speech' Paul is making in Galatians.[25]

Fourth, again understanding *hamartōloi* to mean 'those going against God's will', other commentators relate 2.17 to the issue of 'whether it necessarily follows that Christ is the *countenancer* of sin because the Christian continues in sin. Paul denies this'. Wesley[26] read the verse this way, and thereby related it to his own thinking about sanctification. This interpretation turns the verse into a statement about Christian piety and suggests a meaning that again has little, if anything, to do with the situation Paul was addressing in Galatia.

Frequently contemporary treatments of Galatians merely rehearse one or another of these now traditional interpretations, though difficulties and ambiguities are admitted. Yet, a few recent studies recognize the liabilities of these interpretations and propose solutions different from those which have become customary. R. Bultmann devoted an essay to the study of Gal. 2.15-18 and, in it, suggested new interpretations of *heurethēmen kai autoi hamartōloi* and *ara christos hamartias diakonos* that related the phrases to the situations in Antioch and, in turn, Galatia.[27] Others followed his lead with further studies. The most radical work is that of J.C. O'Neill[28] who contends that when the verse is read for its own sake one finds it means something like what Wesley proposed. Therefore, O'Neill insists that 2.17 is irrelevant and is probably a later scribal gloss, so he recommends omitting 2.17 from the text altogether. Others, including G. Wagner,[29] J. Lambrecht,[30] and H. Neitzel,[31] attempt less reckless solutions. Their efforts are different from one another in methods and conclusions, but they are alike in that they seek new, less dogmatically determined ways to read the verse as a coherent part of the section in which it occurs. In what follows my methods and conclusions will again be different from those of interpreters who have previously worked on this verse, but I join Bultmann, Wagner, Lambrecht, and Neitzel in the attempt to read these lines in their context, as was surely the case with the first readers and hearers of the text.

A New Reading of Gal. 2.17

Regardless of the modest diversity in translations of Gal. 2.17, translators and interpreters of Gal. 2.17 are in complete agreement about the basic grammar of this verse: It comprises two broad parts, referred to as 17a and 17b and schematized as we have seen:

17a =   *ei de zētountes dikaiōthēnai en christǭ*
        heurethēmen kai autoi hamartōloi
17b =   *ara christos hamartias diakonos* and *mē genoito.*

17a is universally read as a conditional clause (*ei de . . . heurethēmen kai autoi hamartōloi*) containing a circumstantial participal phrase modifying the main verb by articulating attendant circumstances contemporaneous with the action of the main verb (*zētountes dikaiōthēnai en christǭ*). Moreover, *heurethēmen kai autoi hamartōloi* is universally taken as a coherent phrase. The only grammatical debate is minor, viz. whether *ara christos hamartias diakonos* is a statement or a question.

Yet despite the unanimity of interpreters in their grammatical analysis, there is another way to construe this verse that makes sense of the words, and more important, of the text in its context. Gal. 2.17 may be translated:

> But if we were found seeking to be justified in Christ, indeed we ourselves are sinners—then is Christ an agent of sin? Certainly not!

I shall defend this translation and the sense I understand it to imply from the vantage points of grammar, vocabulary, context, and Pauline theology.

The grammar
Interpreters have regarded 17a as an instance where '*heuriskein* is complemented by an unexpressed *einai* and a predicate nominative or adjective . . . "to find (someone) to be (something)"'.[32] But BDF (§416) and H.W. Smyth's *Greek Grammar*[33] describe *heuriskein* as a verb of cognition often occurring with a supplementary participle in either direct or indirect discourse. In 2.17 the form would be that of indirect discourse, 'of the fact that a person or thing is found in an act or state'.[34] When *heuriskein* is in this construction and it is passive (*heuriskesthai*), as it is in 2.17, the verb occurs with a nominative participle in agreement with the subject of the verb, as it does in 2.17. BDF states that this form is preserved in the NT, though Gal. 2.17 is not cited as an instance of the pattern.

In distinction from the circumstantial participle, the supplementary participle completes the verbal predicate. Thus, understood in this fashion, in 2.17a the participle and the phrase it governs (*zētountes dikaiōthēnai en christǭ*) should be read as completing the 'idea of the verb by showing that to which its action relates';[35] and so, the verbal sense of 17a is 'we were found seeking to be justified in Christ', not the usual rendering, 'we ourselves have also been found sinners' which takes *heurethēmen kai autoi hamartōloi* as a coherent phrase. Admittedly this is not the syntax one might expect, for in the conventional pattern of this construction one finds the main verb (of cognition) at the beginning of the phrase in which it is modified by the supplementary participle. But, the form that seems to occur in 2.17a is exactly like that in Acts 24.10 where in indirect discourse the main verb (of cognition), *epistasthai*, follows its supplementary participle, *onta*, and the phrase that the participle governs (*onta se kritēn tǭ ethnei toutǭ epistamenos*). Indeed from observing these parallels and noticing the intensity of expression in the statements one suspects that Paul and Luke varied the more normal word order that they might lay emphasis on the participial phrase.[36]

The vocabulary
From a survey of Pauline texts one finds confirmation for the sense of the translation of 2.17 proposed above in the meaning denoted in Paul's use of four key words in this verse:

1. *Zētein.* Paul uses this verb in Romans (2.7; 3.11; 10.3, 20; 11.3), 1 Corinthians (1.22; 4.2; 7.27 [2×]; 10.24, 33; 13.5; 14.12), 2

Corinthians (12.14; 13.3), Galatians (1.10; 2.17), Philippians (2.21), and 1 Thessalonians (2.6). His usage denotes 'seeking' in the sense of 'to look for', 'to try to get', and 'to make an effort'. *Zētein* expresses the idea of *striving to attain something that one presently does not have*, as is clear, for example, from the mention in Rom. 2.7 of seeking 'glory and honor and immortality'. In passages with a religious sense, like Gal. 2.17, one finds that the term denotes humanity's 'general philosophical search or quest',[37] again for something that humanity does not understand itself to possess.

Most commentators read *zētein* here as if it were a synonym for *pisteuein*, and therefore understand *zētountes dikaiōthēnai en christǭ* in 2.17 to be synonymous with *episteusamen, hina dikaiōthōmen ek pisteōs christou* in Gal. 2.16. For Paul 'believing' or 'having faith' is clearly appropriate activity, but it is not something humans do of their own accord. *Pistis* is an active force that *came* into the human realm; in fact it *was revealed* (Gal. 3.23). *Pistis* is a *fruit of the spirit* (Gal. 5.22) that in the human context *hears* (*hē akoē pisteōs*, Gal. 3.2, 5). Thus humans *believe* (*pisteuein*) as the spirit grows faith in their lives and that faith hears [the gospel]. Paul uses *zētein* in a variety of ways, sometimes viewing it positively (*agathou doxan kai timēn kai aphtharsian zētousin*, Rom. 2.7), sometimes negatively (*Hellēnes sophian zētousin*, 1 Cor. 1.22), and sometimes neutrally (*zēteitai en tois oikonomois*, 1 Cor. 4.2). But as the full range of Paul's usages shows, *zētein* is an activity generated completely by humans that ultimately does not extend from the activity of God. Thus it seems unnecessary, even unwise, to view *zētein dikaiōthēnai en christǭ* as an expression synonymous with *pisteuein en christǭ*, for the former describes a human endeavor and the latter is ultimately the result of divine activity.

2. *Dikaioun*. Paul uses this verb in Romans (2.13; 3.4, 20, 24, 26, 28, 30; 4.2, 5; 5.1, 9; 6.7; 8.30, 33), 1 Corinthians (4.4; 6.11), and Galatians (2.15 [3×], 17; 3.8, 11, 24; 5.4). His usage consistently denotes the idea 'to set right'. Human beings are never named as the subject of this verb, rather they are the objects of the action, themselves 'being set right' (Rom. 3.24; 1 Cor. 6.11; Gal. 3.24). According to Paul *God is the one who justifies humanity* (Rom. 8.33; Gal. 3.8), and God does this by grace through the redemption which is in Christ Jesus (Rom. 3.24), in/by Christ's blood (Rom. 5.9), and through the faith of Jesus Christ (Rom. 3.26; Gal. 2.16).[38] Space

prohibits the exploration here of the meaning of these phrases in Paul's writings, but one must at least recognize that according to Paul humans do not justify, they are justified. This is an old point, but it bears being repeated.

Moreover, in the coupling of *dikaioun* with *zētein* one observes a remarkable concept, viz. humans endeavoring to be justified in Christ. It is of course possible to understand this idea positively or negatively, but in the light of Rom. 10.3, 20 it seems best to view *zētountes dikaiōthēnai en christǭ* as behavior that Paul understands to be inappropriate. Rom. 10.3 is the only other place where Paul uses *zētein* in relationship to the *dikaio-* word group. There Paul uses *zētein* to name what Jews did who were ignorant of the righteousness of God—they *sought* to establish their own righteousness and did not submit to God's (*zētountes stēsai, tę dikaiosynē tou theou ouch hypetagēsan*). Then in Rom. 10.20 Paul declares (quoting Isa. 65.1[39])

> *heurethēn [en] tois eme mē zētousin,*
> *emphanēs egenomēn tois eme mē eperōtōsin.*

In other words God breaks into the lives, not of those seeking God, but of the very ones not seeking. Divine initiative does not produce seeking that results in humans having an encounter with God; in fact, this verse may mean that seeking is antithetical to God's self-revelation to humans.

3. *Hamartōlos.* We saw above that this word is rare in Paul's letters, but in the occurrences other than in Galatians Paul clearly uses the word to designate 'one who is set against the will of God'; for example, Rom. 5.19 refers to Adam's 'disobedience' which made 'many sinners'. In Gal. 2.15,[40] 17 there is no reason to understand the word to mean anything other than what it does outside Galatians.[41]

4. *Diakonos.* Paul uses this word in Romans (13.4 [2×]; 15.8; 16.1), 1 Corinthians (3.5), 2 Corinthians (3.6; 6.4; 11.15, 23), Galatians (2.17), Philippians (1.1), and possibly 1 Thessalonians (3.2). The word is frequently coupled with a genitive, as it is in Gal. 2.17, and in these instances denotes 'one who renders service to' or 'one who advances the cause of'—as in Rom. 13.4, where 'authority' is 'the agent of God . . . for good' or that 'brings wrath'. In a religious sense, as the word is used in Gal. 2.17, *diakonos* denotes 'the servant of a spiritual power'.[42]

The text in its context and in the light of Pauline theology
Paul penned Galatians because the churches in Galatia were, according to Paul, deserting their calling in grace and turning to a different gospel (1.6). Paul describes this reorientation of the Galatians as a move from 'spirit' to 'flesh' (3.3), from 'the hearing of faith' to 'the works of the law' (3.2, 5). From references in 4.10 to the festal calendar, in 5.2 to 'circumcision', and in 5.3 to 'the whole law', it seems clear that under the influence of some persons who have come among the Galatians after Paul founded the churches there (these people are mentioned in 1.6-7; 5.12; 6.13), the Galatians were moving toward law-observance.

Paul attempts to stay this mutiny by writing the letter to the Galatians. Paul explains the difference between the law-free gospel he preaches and the gospel of law-observance preached by the newcomers in Galatià by describing the origins of his proclamation: Paul's gospel came directly from God by revelation; he did not get it or learn it from any human being (1.11-17). Paul proves the divine origin of his gospel by illustrating his independence from those who were apostles before him (1.18-24), and he shows that his gospel has always been recognized to be different, but valid, by recounting how James, Cephas, and John received him and Barnabas in Jerusalem (2.1-10). Yet, Paul goes on to show that this reception was not a coopting of himself and his gospel by telling the Galatians about his having rebuked Cephas in Antioch (2.11-14).

At this point in his letter, Paul brings his argument home to the situation in Galatia; for what Cephas did in Antioch is exactly what the Galatians were doing, viz. adding the law to the gospel of Christ as if Christians were somehow obliged to observe the law. But, Paul says that Cephas' behavior was hypocritical and wrong-headed (2.14), for Christians are justified *ek pisteōs christou*,[44] not *ex ergōn nomou*. Because Christians are justified by God's work in Christ and not by the law, Paul declares in 2.17a what Cephas' activity in Antioch and the Galatians' recent behavior amounts to: *sin*. Why? Because Cephas and the Galatians were not relying upon the work of God for justification. To use language borrowed from E.P. Sanders,[45] in 'seeking to be justified in Christ', both Cephas and the Galatians manifested a 'pattern of religion' that demonstrates that they understood Christianity to be a new form of 'covenantal nomism'. Theirs is a two-step religion:[46] God in Christ has acted to save humankind, and now those who believe are obligate to do certain things themselves in order to sustain the relationship that God has established. Cephas and the Galatians are possibility-thinkers who believe that God in Christ created a potentially significant relationship between God and humanity, and now, Cephas and the Galatians are cashing in on that new possibility as they seek to be justified in Christ. But, for Paul, in 'seeking to be justified in Christ' human beings declare that justification is not the work of God alone and that God needs or requires human assistance in order to actualize justification. According to this line of thought the Creator is not in full command of the creation and is unable to redeem a creation in bondage to sin. Moreover, once again the creature raises him- or herself up to the level of the Creator by throwing human effort in with the work of the divine in an attempt to complete what, it is implied, God is incapable of doing alone. Thus Paul declares that if one is found, as Cephas was and as the Galatians are, 'seeking to be justified in Christ', then, one is a sinner.

Having declared that 'seeking to be justified in Christ' is a sin, Paul explains this verdict in relation to the shocking inference he draws from such activity. He says that if such seeking is necessary then Christ has furthered sin's cause; he has not redeemed humanity from its plight. Paul boldly denies this inference: *mē genoito* (2.17b). Indeed, if Christians need to seek to be justified in Christ, then Christ has not fully dealt with sin;[47] rather, he has advanced the causes of sin exactly the way Paul, in Rom. 7, says the law has served sin's purposes—by deceiving the believer. Ultimately, seeking to be justified in Christ amounts to putting oneself in the context of the law, which according to Paul was itself a tool in the hands of sin (Rom. 7). Yet, Paul the Christian knows this: The law has no power to effect salvation through maintenance of status before God (Gal. 3.19-21; Phil. 3.6-11), and human beings only deceive themselves if they think they are keeping the law (Gal. 6.13; Rom. 7.7-20). Moreover, it is God who justifies, not humans by their seeking; so either God is capable or incapable of justification.

To summarize: Gal. 2.17 states Paul's understanding of the efforts of some Christians (Cephas, by illustration; and the Galatians, by application) to observe the law: one doing this is a sinner. Gal. 2.17b registers Paul's theological objection to this behavior: it implies that, rather than having dealt with sin, Christ advanced sin's cause. Thus

2.17 critiques and rejects the Galatians' turning from the law-free gospel Paul preached to the gospel of law-observance.

Paul continues by explaining his position from his own point of view in 2.18.[48] He tells the Galatians what it would amount to if he were to preach and practice the gospel of law-observance. In structure the explanation in v. 18, signaled by the *gar*, is patterned exactly like 17a:

17a   But if we were found seeking to be justified in Christ
17a'   indeed we ourselves are sinners

18a   For if I build up again the things that I tore down
18b'   I prove myself a transgressor.

For Paul, whose gospel is law-free, a return to law-observance would amount to an admission that he was incorrect when he earlier abandoned the law, with its program of self-maintained righteousness, in order to be justified by the faith of Christ. In 2.19-21 Paul continues his explanation, as is signaled by the second *gar* (v. 19). According to these verses such an admission is set out of the question, for Paul now lives *in the realm of Christ*, not *in the realm of the law*. He is justified in Christ, but if he could have been, or was, justified in the law, then Christ died for absolutely nothing. What follows in Gal. 3–6 are Paul's more fully developed arguments of the issue he raises in these verses: Humans are either justified by Christ or they are justified by the law, and they live in one context or the other. But, above all, they are not justified by Christ + the law. In such a formula, Paul says, Christ is irrelevant (Gal. 2.21).

To understand Paul's thinking, it is necessary to take into account what lies behind his statements. After his revelatory encounter with the risen Son of God, Paul had a different perspective on the world from the one he had prior to this *apokalypsis*. He viewed reality from the perspective of an apocalyptically structured temporal dualism, thinking in terms of two ages:[49] 'the present evil age' (1 Cor. 2.6-8; Gal. 1.4) and the 'new creation' (2 Cor. 5.17; Gal. 6.15). In the present evil age Satan (1 Cor. 5.5; 2 Cor. 4.4) and the elemental spirits of the universe (1 Cor. 2.8; Gal. 4.3) rule over human beings, and humanity is in bondage to the power of sin (Rom. 3.9). But God acted in Christ to deliver humanity from the present evil age (Gal. 1.4), reconciling humans to God (2 Cor. 5.19) by justifying them (Rom. 8.33) and bringing them into the context of the new creation

(2 Cor. 5.17). As a result of this activity of God, the present evil age is already passing away (1 Cor. 7.31b) and the new creation has already begun (2 Cor. 5.17); though the present evil age has not yet fully passed away and the new creation has not yet full come (1 Cor. 7.31b; 15.25-26; 1 Thess. 4.13-18). Thus, for Paul, the present exists as a juncture of the ages (see esp. 1 Cor. 10.11, *eis hous ta telē tōn aiōnōn katentēken*).[50] In this time between the whiles, humans live either still in the context of the present evil age or already in the context of the new creation. Where they are depends not upon what they do or what they know,[51] but rather upon whether they have been saved by the power of God which invaded the present evil age in the most unexpected of places, the cross of Christ (1 Cor. 1.18).[52] Those still in the present evil age are currently experiencing the wrath of God, while those already in the new creation are experiencing God's mercy, or grace. Those redeemed, or justified, by the power of God are 'in Christ'.

The work of Lou Martyn has helped the reader of Paul's letters, esp. Galatians, to see that the apostle's thought in relation to this temporally dualistic world view is expressed in a variety of antinomies[53] which characterize or are characteristic of the two ages. Throughout Galatians one encounters these antinomies in pairs of words, like 'circumcision/uncircumcision', 'Jew/Gentile', 'slave/free', 'male/female', 'flesh/spirit', 'law/faith', 'law/promise', and in pairs of phrases like 'works of the law/the faith of Jesus Christ', 'works of the flesh/fruit of the spirit', 'under the law/*in Christ*'.

At issue in Gal. 2.17 is what constitutes appropriate behavior 'in Christ'. In this verse and throughout this letter Paul rejects the idea that those 'in Christ' are obliged to act in pursuit of their own justification, for according to the apostle those 'in Christ' are justified by God and are being justified by God alone. In other words, 'in Christ' one does not seek to be justified, for 'seeking to be justified' is activity characteristic of those 'under the law'. Living 'in Christ' one relates to God in faith (or trust) and is no longer driven by sin's deception, 'seeking to be justified', as are those living in the present evil age. Paul's gospel is this: One who lives by the gracious power of God 'in Christ' is free—*free from* the endless endeavors of the self-maintained righteousness of the law ('seeking to be justified') and *free for* living in the spirit, walking in the spirit, waiting for the hope of justification which is the work of God. As Paul says, in Gal.

5.5, 'In the spirit, out of faith, we await the hope of justification'—nothing more, nothing less.[54]

NOTES

1. 'Epistemology at the Turn of the Ages: 2 Corinthians 5.16', in W.R. Farmer, C.F.D. Moule, and R.R. Niebuhr, eds., *Christian History and Interpretation: Studies Presented to John Knox* (Cambridge: Cambridge University Press, 1967), p. 269.

2. The RSV translators apparently judged that a special shift in translation was necessary at this point, though whatever logic motivated this decision is not immediately clear given the realities of Greek grammar. Consult, for example, H.W. Smyth, *Greek Grammar* (rev. edn by G.M. Messing: Cambridge, MA: Harvard University Press, 1956—original 1920) §§2039-48 (hereafter, referred to as Smyth with section numbers).

3. Smyth §2046.

4. E.D. Burton (*A Critical and Exegetical Commentary on the Epistle to the Galatians* [ICC; Edinburgh: T. & T. Clark, 1921] p. 125) advises against pressing this form for too much content. His advice is ignored by several well-known translations that pour paraphrase into the text here in order to interpret rather than translate. E.g.

Moffatt:	If it is discovered that in our quest for justification in Christ we are 'sinners' as well as the Gentiles, does that make Christ an agent of sin? Never!
JB:	Now if we were to admit that the result of looking to Christ to justify us is to make us sinners like the rest, it would follow that Christ had induced us to sin, which would be absurd.
NEB:	If now, in seeking to be justified in Christ, we ourselves no less than the Gentiles turn out to be sinners against the law, does that mean that Christ is an abettor of sin? No, never!

5. There is no difference unless one wishes to suggest that the reading, 'God forbid', understands the non-specific optative to indicate divine agency whereas other translations do not share this understanding.

6. See the explanation by J.B. Lightfoot (*St. Paul's Epistle to the Galatians* [10th edn; London, 1890—reprinted Lynn, MA: Hendrickson Publishers, 1982], p. 116) that delineates the interpretative options with clarity, though Lightfoot overdrew the contrast saying that the interrogative 'hesitates' and the illative 'concludes'.

7. For the most recent work on *mē genoito* as a dialogical element typical of Stoic and Cynic argumentations, see A.J. Malherbe ('*MĒ GENOITO* in the Diatribe and Paul', *HTR* 73 [1980], pp. 231-40) and S.K. Stowers (*The Diatribe and Paul's Letter to the Romans* [SBLDS 57; Chico, CA: Scholars Press, 1981]).

8. H.N. Ridderbos, *The Epistle of Paul to the Churches of Galatia* (Grand Rapids, MI: Eerdmans, 1953), p. 101; BDF, §440 (2).

9. D.C. Arichea, Jr and E.A. Nida, *A Translator's Handbook on Paul's Letter to the Galatians* (Stuttgart: United Bible Societies, 1976), p. 47.

10. W.F. Arndt, 'On Gal. 2.17-19', *CTM* 27 (1956), pp. 128-29.

11. F.F. Bruce, *The Epistle to the Galatians* (New International Greek Testament Commentary; Grand Rapids, MI: Eerdmans, 1982), p. 140.

12. J.D.G. Dunn, 'The Incident at Antioch (Gal. 2.11-18)', *JSNT* 18 (1983), pp. 3-57, esp. pp. 27-28.

13. Dunn, 'Incident', pp. 27-28.

14. Dunn, 'Incident', pp. 27-28.

15. Against this translation, see M. Barth ('Justification: From Text to Sermon on Galatians 2.11-21', *Int* 22 [1968], pp. 147-57, esp. p. 155).

16. 1 Tim. 1.9, 15 are not included here since I do not regard 1 Timothy as a Pauline letter. But if one accepts this text (as does the recent major work by L.T. Johnson, *The Writings of the New Testament: An Interpretation* [Philadelphia: Fortress, 1986], pp. 381-407) the case seems even clearer that for Paul *hamartōlos* only describes one who is set against God, not merely one outside the law.

17. M. Luther, *Lectures on Galatians, 1519*, in J. Pelikan, ed., *Luther's Works*, vol. XXVII (St. Louis: Concordia Publishing House, 1963). Luther changed his mind about this translation as is seen in his *Lectures on Galatians, 1535* in Pelikan, ed., *Luther's Works*, vol. XXVI.

18. Bruce, *Epistle*, p. 141; Dunn, 'Incident', pp. 27-28.

19. Burton, *Commentary*, p. 129.

20. *Pauline Autobiography, Toward a New Understanding* (SBLDS 73; Atlanta: Scholars Press, 1985), esp. p. 80.

21. This is largely a paraphrase using the language of Luther—see *Lectures, 1519*, p. 227 or *Lectures, 1535*, pp. 144-51.

22. H.D. Betz (*Galatians* [Hermeneia; Philadelphia: Fortress, 1979], pp. 119-20) follows Luther exactly here and refines the argument in relation to a reading of Galatians as an example the proposed genre of 'apologetic' letters. Thus he labels 2.15-21 *propositio*. On this genre and understanding of Galatians, see Betz's article, 'The Literary Composition and Function of Paul's Letter to the Galatians', *NTS* 21 (1975), pp. 353-79.

23. Luther, *Lectures, 1519*, p. 227.

24. This is a paraphrase using the language of J. Calvin (*Commentaries on the Epistles of Paul to the Galatians and Ephesians* [Grand Rapids, MI: Eerdmans, 1948], p. 71—trans. from the Latin original of 1548 by W. Pringle).

25. *Commentaries*, p. 70.

26. This is a paraphrase using the language of J. Wesley (*Explanatory Notes on the New Testament* [London: Epworth, 1977—original 1754], p. 685).

27. 'Zur Auslegung von Galater 2,15-18', in *Exegetica: Aufsätze zur Erforschung des Neuen Testaments* (Tübingen: J.C.B. Mohr, 1967—original 1952), pp. 394-99.

28. *The Recovery of Paul's Letter to the Galatians* (London: SPCK, 1972), esp. pp. 42-43.

29. 'Le repas du Seigneur et la justification par la foi. Exégèse de Galates 2-17', *ETR* 36 (1961), pp. 245-54.

30. 'The Line of Thought in Gal. 2.14b-21', *NTS* 24 (1978), pp. 484-95.

31. 'Zur Interpretation von Galater 2.11-21. Teil 1', *ThQ* 163 (1983), pp. 15-39.

32. R.B. Hays, '"Have we found Abraham to be our forefather according to the flesh?" A Reconsideration of Rom. 4.1', *NovT* 27 (1985), p. 82.

33. Smyth, §2113.

34. Smyth, §2113.

35. Smyth, §2089.

36. One sees that Paul alters the syntax in relation to *heuriskein* even in the construction where the verb is complemented by an unexpressed *einai* and a predicate nominative or adjective. There are instances where the complement (unstated *einai* + pred. nom. or adj.) follow the main verb: 1 Cor. 15.15; 2 Cor. 9.4; and there are instances where the complement precedes *heuriskein*: 1 Cor. 4.2; 2 Cor. 5.3; 12.20.

37. H. Greeven, '*zēteō*', *TDNT* II, pp. 892-93.

38. G. Schrenk, '*dikaioō*', *TDNT* II, pp. 211-19.

39. Rom. 10.20 reverses the clauses in which the verbs *zētousin* and *eperōtōsin* occur, but preserves the original order of the final verb in each line. This variation may be simply a casual error, but even so, it reveals that Paul understands that God's being found (through revelation) is not the result of human seeking.

40. Barth, 'Justification', p. 155.

41. K.H. Rengstorf, '*hamartōlos*', *TDNT* I, pp. 317-33, esp. p. 328. Rengstorf understands *hamartōloi* in Gal. 2.17 to refer to 'guilty humanity', though he see the world in 2.15 expressing the Jewish view of one outside the *nomos* (p. 328).

42. H.W. Beyer, '*diakonos*', *TDNT* II, pp. 88-89.

43. See J.L. Martyn, 'A Law-Observant Mission to Gentiles: The Background of Galatians', *Michigan Quarterly Review* 22 (1983), pp. 221-36 (reprinted in *SJT* 38 [1985], pp. 307-24) and M.L. Soards, *The Apostle Paul: An Introduction to His Writings and Teaching* (New York: Paulist, 1987), pp. 57-67.

44. With G. Howard ('On the "Faith of Christ"', *HTR* 61 [1967], pp. 459-65; 'The "Faith of Christ"', *ExpT* 85 [1973-74], pp. 212-14; and *Paul: Crisis in Galatia* [SNTSMS 35; Cambridge: Cambridge University Press, 1979], esp. pp. 57-58), M. Barth ('The Faith of the Messiah', *HeyJ* 19 [1969], pp. 363-

70), and R.B. Hays (*The Faith of Jesus Christ* [SBLDS 56; Chico, CA: Scholars Press, 1983], *passim*), I take this phrase to mean the 'faith that Jesus Christ had'.

45.   *Paul and Palestinian Judaism* (Philadelphia: Fortress, 1977), *passim*.

46.   See J.L. Martyn's review of L.E. Keck's *Paul and His Letters* in *Reflection* 27 (1980).

47.   Somewhat similarly Bultmann ('Auslegung', p. 396) takes *heurethēmen kai autoi hamartōloi* as a *realis* describing the behavior of Peter in Antioch. Thus he takes 'Christ is a servant of sin' to be an objection from Paul's opponent, who having observed Peter's activity, concluded that Christ's work of justification was not fully effective in removing sin.

48.   Arndt, 'On Gal. 2.17-19', pp. 129-31.

49.   For a fuller explanation of Paul's apocalyptic perspective, see M.L. Soards ('Paul: Apostle and Apocalyptic Visionary', *BTB* 16 [1986], pp. 148-50; and *The Apostle Paul*, *passim*, esp. pp. 37-41).

50.   The phrase is correctly translated 'upon whom the ends of the ages have met', see J.A. Fitzmyer ('Paul and the Law' in *To Advance the Gospel: New Testament Studies* [New York: Crossroad, 1981], pp. 186-201, esp. p. 188).

51.   See Martyn's 'Epistemology' on this point.

52.   Especially instructive on this point is U. Wilckens (*Weisheit und Torheit: Eine exegetisch-religionsgeschichtliche Untersuchung zu 1 Kor. 1 und 2* [Tübingen: J.C.B. Mohr, 1959], esp. pp. 214-24).

53.   'Apocalyptic Antinomies in Paul's Letter to the Galatians', *NTS* 31 (1985), pp. 410-24.

54.   In examining Gal. 2.17 in the broad context of Paul's theology, one finds troubling questions raised that simply are not answered and that cannot be answered from Paul's letters. This is a frustration with which every interpreter of Paul must learn to live, though the more one studies the letters the more one is tempted to infer what the apostle would likely say about this or that. Yet, some restraint is necessary in formulating such 'probable' answers; and, here again, Lou Martyn offers helpful advice, 'It has occurred to me that it would be a valuable practice for the historian [read 'exegete'] to rise each morning saying to himself three times slowly and with emphasis, "I do not know"' ('Glimpses into the History of the Johannine Community', in Martyn's *The Gospel of John in Christian History* [New York: Paulist, 1979], pp. 90-121, esp. p. 92—originally published in M. de Jonge, ed., *L'Evangile de Jean* [BETL 44; Leuven: Leuven University Press, 1977], pp. 149-75).

WHO ARE THE HEIRS OF THE NEW AGE
IN THE EPISTLE TO THE HEBREWS?

Charles P. Anderson

In recent decades the rich and diverse heritage behind the Epistle to the Hebrews has begun to emerge. Lines have now been traced between this writing and various currents of first-century thought, including apocalyptic,[1] Philo,[2] Platonism,[3] Qumran[4] and Gnosticism.[5] It is no longer possible to claim an exclusive dependence of Hebrews on any single tradition, though debate continues over primary affinities.[6]

Yet, the importance, even centrality, of apocalyptic assumptions in the argument of Hebrews remains secure, however much they may be modified by the author. No NT writing more systematically and thoroughly embodies the conception of the two ages and the conviction that the transition between them is now in process. The old covenant has been decisively declared obsolete and 'ready to vanish away' (8.13), having been replaced by a new covenant 'enacted on better promises'.[7] The author shared with other early Christians the belief that his generation would see the 'age (or world) to come' (*tēn oikoumenēn tēn mellousan*, 2.5; *mellontos aiōnos*, 6.5). The day of judgment, part of the elementary teaching assumed by the author (6.1-2; see also 10.26-31; 2.3; 12.29), was not far away (10.25). The present time was the 'last days' (*ep eschatou tōn hēmerōn toutōn*, 1.2) which would conclude this age (*sunteleia tōn aiōnōn*, 9.26) and lead immediately into the coming age or world or 'rest'.

'Today' as an Apocalyptic Category

One of the most important terms in Hebrews, uniting the epistle's conceptual and paraenetic components, is 'today' (*sēmeron*). The apocalyptic significance assigned to 'today' appears to owe nothing to early Christian (nor, as far as I am aware, Jewish) tradition but is the author's own interpretation of this term as he finds it in two biblical psalms. Ps. 2.7, 'My Son, today I have begotten thee', is twice employed in Hebrews in Christological contexts, first to prove Jesus' superiority to the angels (1.5) and then to demonstrate his divine appointment as high priest (5.5). Quotations from Ps. 95.7-11 (LXX Ps. 94) form part of the epistle's paraenesis as the author emphasizes the gravity of the present time in which God is once again speaking to his people, offering salvation but prepared to judge those who ignore his words (3.7, 13, 15; 4.7).[8] In all these cases, 'today' designates a time inaugurated by Jesus, of undetermined but limited duration, and terminating in 'the Day' which is drawing near (10.25). The same apocalyptic periodization of time is also evident in the opening line of the epistle in which the time of revelation through prophets is sharply distinguished from the time of revelation through a Son, who is begotten 'today' (1.5).

In Hebrews, 'today' is the name of this contemporary period in which the voice of God is heard once again offering access to his 'rest' and cautioning the present generation to avoid the *apistia* ('faithlessness') of the wilderness generation. 'Today' is not the 'eternally present moment' available to anyone at any time. Neither does it extend from the time of the psalmist to the present and beyond.[9] It never existed prior to the age of the new covenant, to the time of Christ whose sacrificial offering opened a 'new and living way' (10.20) of access to the eternal world. 'Today' is identical to the 'last days', that relatively brief period between the two appearances of Jesus (9.28) in which the opportunity of salvation is offered.

Thus the reader of Hebrews is left in no doubt that, whatever else Hebrews is, it is an *apocalyptic* 'word of exhortation' (13.22), written from the conviction that the present generation was experiencing the fundamental apocalyptic event, the transition to the new age.

However, apocalyptic conviction and ideology are not the whole story in Hebrews. There is a practical side to apocalyptic in this work, a facet which might be called 'applied apocalyptic'. Those who believe in an apocalyptically delineated world do more than observe the signs of the times and wait in hope for the concluding apocalyptic events. They also act, and some of their activity necessarily flows from convictions derived from their apocalyptic beliefs. This essay addresses one such practical concern which Hebrews shared with every early Christian community, namely, whom should they try to convert? Or to put the question more apocalyptically, who is deemed eligible for participation in the world to come?

Ethnicity and the People of God

In order to put the issue in its simplest and at the same time in its broadest possible form, let us reduce it to this: what is the assumed *ethnic* identity of those who are regarded in Hebrews as heirs of the new age, the descendants of Abraham? Are they Jews or gentiles or both? Granted the emphasis in this writing on the sharp distinction between the two covenants, what are the nature and limits of that distinction and how do they relate to the practical matter of mission? This is not intended as a sociological question. The issue is not the closely related but distinct question of the actual ethnic composition of the Hebrews community, but rather the assumptions of the author concerning the ethnic identity of the people of God.

Since there are no 'missionary' passages in Hebrews as there are in the Gospels,[10] it is necessary to approach the matter indirectly, through analysis of certain arguments in which assumptions relevant to the question here posed may be uncovered.[11] This procedure will also involve analysis of supporting quotations drawn from the OT, which we shall set alongside comparable quotations in the Pauline letters to clarify the issues involved.

It may also be helpful to formulate the question in different ways. For example, does the new covenant imply a new people of God in Hebrews, totally discontinuous from those of the first covenant? Alternatively, does Hebrews stay within the limits of a radical but still 'in-house' critique of the cult, as found at Qumran? Does 'today' imply continuity with the Jewish people and its Torah? Or is there a total and irrevocable separation between the past when the Mosaic Law was the standard of observance for the people of God and 'today' when the Torah is rejected by a community which does not consider itself part of traditional Israel? Are gentiles now eligible as gentiles, as in Paul's gospel? Has ethnicity become irrelevant?

In a recent article devoted to the formulation of a typology of various groups in early Christianity on the basis of their stance toward the Jewish Law, Raymond E. Brown assigns Hebrews along with the Fourth Gospel to a 'radicalized variety of. . . Christianity. . . so that Judaism has become another religion belonging to the old covenant'.[12] Brown is concerned to clear up a confusion in terminology in which the legitimate distinction between Jewish Christianity and Gentile Christianity on grounds of ethnicity is extended 'to differentiate theological and/or ecclesiological stances *in NT times*'.[13] Toward that goal he posits four types of Jewish/Gentile Christianity, ranging from full observance of the Jewish Law (type one) to complete rejection of the Law, including circumcision, food laws and the temple cult (type four). Hebrews is regarded as a radical version of type four. Brown's position probably reflects the majority view among Hebrews scholars, whether they hold that Hebrews addresses a community of Jewish background,[14] or that the intended readers were predominantly if not exclusively gentile.[15] Scholarly works on Hebrews characteristically see in it the gospel of Christ set over against the Law of Moses, and the church against Judaism.[16]

However, it is my conviction that Hebrews neither makes nor assumes a wholesale onslaught against the Law as such, nor against Judaism as such. Further, to place Hebrews and the Fourth Gospel in the same class confuses the issue. It is significant that Hebrews not only lacks the polemical language of the Fourth Gospel where 'the Jews' are targeted as an opposing group, but does not even contain that term. Likewise, it is not simply fortuitous that gentiles are never mentioned in Hebrews. The terms of opposition, in my view, do not follow the lines of gospel versus Law, nor Christianity versus Judaism. In this paper a different case will be argued. Rather than 'Judaism' being considered a foreign religion in Hebrews, the epistle testifies to a type of 'Christianity' which is oriented primarily if not exclusively toward Jews. This form of Christianity, while opposing cultic or temple Judaism[17] in the strongest possible terms, nevertheless considers itself Jewish, not just in a metaphorical but in a quite literal sense. Two questions will form the framework of the argument. First and foremost, who are the 'seed of Abraham' (Heb. 2.16) who inherit the age to come, and second, what is the Law that is changed (7.12) with the coming of the new age?

Abraham and his Descendants

The author of Hebrews assures his readers that Christ is not concerned with angels but with 'the descendants of Abraham' (*spermatos Abraam*, 2.16). Commentators have interpreted this passage in diametrically opposite ways. For some, the seed of Abraham is meant in its traditional Jewish sense, as referring to Israel.[18] For others, the author shares Paul's view that this phrase designates all who have faith regardless of their 'fleshly', i.e. ethnic, identity (Rom. 4; Gal. 3.7, 9, 29).[19] Any consideration of this issue requires taking into account the role Abraham plays in Hebrews.

In addition to the initial reference in 2.16, Abraham appears in four places in Hebrews. The first (6.13-15) follows a paraenetic section in which the readers are severely reprimanded for their lack of maturity (5.11–6.8). This section concludes with softer and more encouraging words (6.9-12), which come to a head in the transition to the Abrahamic passage: 'So that you may not be sluggish, but imitators of those who through faith and patience inherit the promises' (6.12). Abraham is then considered as an example of one whose patience or endurance under testing led to his receiving the promises.

As a glance at a concordance shows, apart from Paul's letters, Hebrews contains the larges number of references to God's promises of any NT writing. As for Paul (Rom. 4.13-21; Gal. 3.16),[20] two promises to Abraham are of special interest to the author of Hebrews. One concerns Abraham's progeny (Gen. 15.4-5), the other involves inheriting the land (Gen. 15.7). Whether our author believes the first has been fulfilled is a matter of debate,[21] but there can be no doubt that in his view the second is pending. 'Land', 'sabbath', 'rest', 'inheritance', 'homeland' (*patris*), a 'better and abiding possession' (10.34), and 'the things not seen' (11.1) all point to the one object of hope.[22]

The author, of course, is aware that, according to Josh. 22.4, the Israelites had been given 'rest', as God had promised (Deut. 3.20). But, so the argument goes (4.6-10), the land (of Canaan) was not the genuine rest, as is demonstrated by Psalm 95. Otherwise, David, who came later than Moses, would not refer to another opportunity for Israel to enter the rest by using the term 'today' (Heb. 4.7-8). Therefore, the true 'rest' remains an unfulfilled promise (4.9). At the same time, the 'rest' has existed ever since creation was completed (4.4), since it is the sabbath rest of Gen. 2.2-3. At the opposite end of time, it is the 'unshakeable' kingdom (12.27-28) which remains after earth and heaven are removed.[23] The 'rest' of God is also presented under the image of a sanctuary, in both senses of the word, a place of worship and a refuge (6.18-20).

Thus, the promise of the land—the 'heavenly country' (11.16)—has yet to be fulfilled. Abraham looked forward to dwelling in God's city which has foundations not found under tents (11.9-10). It is this promise that he and all those who 'died in faith' saw from afar and yearned for, but which was not fulfilled. It is this promise that is of special interest for the author of Hebrews, for its fulfilment is imminent and open once again to those who hear and obey the voice of God.

Dominated by the author's paraenetic motive to persuade his readers to maintain their faith, Heb. 6.13-15 is concerned especially with demonstrating the significance that Gen. 22.17 has for their situation: 'Surely I will bless you and multiply you'. Of all Abrahamic texts, only Gen. 22.16-17 mentions an oath of God: 'By myself I have sworn, says the Lord, because you have done this and have not withheld your son, your only son, I will indeed bless you and multiply your descendants. . . . ' For the author of Hebrews, the addition of the oath should increase the readers' confidence in God's promise, that 'through two unchangeable things. . . we might have strong encouragement to seize the hope set before us' (6.18).

Obviously an article of major importance for our author, the oath of God appears in two other biblical passages quoted in Hebrews. The oath in Ps. 95.11 ('As I swore in my wrath, "They shall never enter my rest"') gives a second and incontrovertible assurance that entry into the 'rest', the 'promised land', is not an event of the past. Therefore, it is open for those addressed in the 'today' of verse seven of that psalm. Psalm 110 not only provides the capstone of the seven quotations demonstrating the superiority of the son to the angels (1.5-13),[24] but also supplies the proof text for the superiority of Jesus' priesthood over the Levitical: 'The Lord has sworn and will not change his mind, "Thou art a priest for ever after the order of Melchizedek"' (7.17, 21, 28).

Thus God's oath is associated with three of the key teachings of the epistle: the blessing of Abraham regarding progeny, the priesthood and cultic activity of Jesus, and the availability of entrance into the 'rest'.

The second and third Abrahamic passages constitute part of the list of Israel's examples of faith in ch. 11 (11.8-10, 17-19). Each of the two biblical stories in view here, like the one treated above, contains a promise. The first (11.8-10) centers on the land and Abraham's obedience to God's call to go out to it. From this story the author derives a lesson not only about faith but also about the identity of the real promised land, the city of God (11.10).

The second passage (11.17-19) involves the sacrifice of Isaac and its presupposition, God's promise of descendants through him ('through Isaac shall your descendants be named', Gen. 21.12). Swetnam's detailed study of the influence of the Aqedah on Hebrews[25] demonstrates the important role this story played both in Jewish and early Christian instruction and interpretation. Unequivocal NT references to the sacrifice of Isaac appear only here and in Jas 2.21-23. Although Rom. 8.32 employs the phrase *ouk epheisato* ('did not spare'), perhaps derived from LXX Gen. 22.16, it is only in Hebrews and James that explicit lessons regarding faith are drawn from Abraham's deed. Confronted with a divine command which appeared to contradict God's promise,[26] Abraham proves able both to maintain his faith in the promise and to obey the command, although he is aware that nothing short of a resurrection would be required (Heb. 11.19) to resolve the contradiction.

The same promise regarding descendants, derived in this case not from Gen. 21.12 but from 22.17 following Abraham's successful response to this test of faith, appears in Heb. 11.12. That the reference here is to Gen. 22.17 is apparent from the fact that only in this passage do both stars (cf. Gen. 15.5) and sand of the seashore (cf. Gen. 32.12) appear together as metaphors of Abraham's innumerable descendants. The earlier reference to Abraham in 6.13-15 also relies on Genesis 22. Abraham's patient endurance, despite the most formidable of obstacles, qualifies him as the preeminent model for the readers to emulate. The single reference to Sarah (11.11; cf. Gen. 17.15-21; 18.9-15; 21.1-7) considers her also an example of faith and leads into the fulfilment of that promise in the followng verse.

What is particularly interesting, and I believe, indicative, is that despite the importance given the story of the sacrifice of Isaac, nowhere in Hebrews is any interest shown in that part of Genesis 22 which refers to gentiles: 'By your descendants shall all the nations of the earth bless themselves, because you have obeyed my voice' (22.18). If Paul had quoted this passage (which he does not), surely that is one part he would have quoted—with emphasis added!—after pointing out of course that *sperma* ('seed') is singular and therefore refers to Christ (Gal. 3.16). Paul would likely also have omitted the final clause since it could be understood to diminish the emphasis on God's grace. A priori, one would assume that any first century Christian concerned with a gentile mission would not leave out the one part of this passage connecting the blessing of Abraham with non-Jews. Although an argument from silence, this argument nevertheless raises doubts about the author's presumed gentile orientation.

The significance of the selective use of Gen. 22.16-18 in Hebrews may become clearer when compared with the choice and interpretation of Abrahamic texts found in the Pauline tradition. This way of approaching the problem has merit for the reason that in Paul we have as close to a 'control' as can reasonably be expected. Paul's arguments for the inclusion of gentiles among the people of God rely heavily on Abrahamic texts. These passages provide Paul with an important resource in his attempt to justify the opening of the gospel to the gentiles on a law-free basis. Since there is no doubt about Paul's conception of the appropriate ethnic composition of the saints, a comparison of his arguments regarding Abraham and his descendants with those of Hebrews should shed light on the latter's conception of the ethnic identity of the heirs of the new age.

Paul's favorite Abrahamic text, as is well known, is Gen. 15.6: 'And he believed the Lord; and he reckoned it to him as righteousness'. Paul's doctrine of faith has its primary biblical foundation in this passage, as is amply illustrated in Romans 4 and Galatians 3. The cornerstone of Paul's gospel to the gentiles is that they are included among God's people through justification 'by faith apart from works of Law' (Rom. 3.28). Paul's argument that faith is consistent with Torah is supported by reference to Gen. 15.6, where Abraham's faith is the basis of his being reckoned righteous (Rom. 4.3). But a second Abrahamic text clinches Paul's argument. Against the counter argument that Genesis 15 has nothing to do with gentiles since they are not mentioned there, Paul introduces Gen. 17.1-14 (the institution of circumcision) into the discussion. The important point is the chronological relationship of the two passages. Since Abraham was 'justified' prior to being circumcised, righteousness must precede circumcision (Rom. 4.10) and be independent of it. The force of this argument is to break any connection between righteousness and

Abraham's obedience of a commandment, whether it be the commandment to be circumcised or the one to sacrifice his son. Righteousness is pronounced solely on the basis of his trust (*pistis*) in God's promise. Circumcision, on the other hand, depends on a prior righteousness by faith of which it is a 'sign or seal' (Rom. 4.11). Abraham's faith, therefore, was originally that of an uncircumcised man, in effect, a gentile, and thus he was the 'father' of all gentiles who believe. His subsequent circumcision made him also the father of all believing Jews.

It is crucial for Paul to establish this point, and it is significant that he has chosen precisely those Abrahamic texts from which supporting arguments could be drawn. On the surface, it would appear that Gen. 22.17-18 would have been of assistance also, since in contrast to both chs. 15 and 17, gentiles are mentioned there. However, Paul avoids the entire story of the sacrifice of Isaac which is, on the whole, damaging to his position. Unlike Hebrews, therefore, Paul looks to Genesis 15 rather than Genesis 22 for the promise of descendants to Abraham. But for Paul, the point is not the promise of physical descendants to Abraham but justification or forgiveness apart from 'works' (Rom. 4.5-8). The promise has become spiritualized and individualized so as to apply to anyone. Its ethnic dimension is eliminated. To be sure, Abraham remains an example of faith for the Jew (Rom. 4.12). But Abraham is also the father of 'many nations' (Rom. 4.17; Gen. 17.5) who believe. For Paul, faith is an essential quality of religious experience as such, trust in God 'who justifies the ungodly' (Rom. 4.5), whereas in Hebrews the justification element is absent. Indeed, the verb *dikaioō* is not found in Hebrews. Righteousness is a quality which may or may not be present in the lives of individual persons. When present, it is recognized by God and rewarded accordingly, as in the case of the blessing of Abraham in Genesis 22. But righteousness is not a gift from God. On this matter, Paul and the author of Hebrews hold different views.

Likewise, there is a signficantly different interpretation of 'promise' in Hebrews and Paul. For Paul, the promise to Abraham concerns both those who have faith, regardless of their physical relationship to Abraham, and Christ, the 'seed' of Abraham who would inherit the world (no longer 'land' [*gē*], but *kosmos*; Rom. 4.13). In both cases Paul gives an interpretation of the promise of descendants to Abraham which was undoubtedly very controversial in Jewish and

Jewish Christian circles of that time. In Hebrews, on the other hand, no Abrahamic promise is given either a gentile or a christological interpretation. Gentiles are never mentioned in Hebrews, and Jesus' redemptive work is traced to Ps. 110.4 rather than being made the object of a promise which could otherwise be interpreted to refer to Israel as a whole. In Hebrews the distinction between Jesus and Israel is never blurred. It is the land, not the seed, which is given a spiritual reinterpretation.[27] Paul, on the other hand, shows little interest in the land. Indeed, the word *gē* appears in the Pauline letters only in the general sense of the earth, e.g. as contrasted to heaven. On the whole, Paul ignores the Abrahamic passages concerning the promised land[28] and spiritualizes those texts regarding Abraham's descendants so that refer to gentiles as well as Jews. The author of Hebrews spiritualizes the passages about the promised land, but does not extend the passages about descendants to gentiles. This suggests that the missionary horizon of the author of Hebrews is quite different from Paul's, and that in contrast to Paul's does not extend beyond the Jewish community.

As mentioned above, nowhere in the Pauline letters is an appeal made to what was probably the most commonly known and utilized Abrahamic story, the sacrifice of Isaac.[29] The verbal allusion to Isaac in Rom. 8.32 is minimal, to say the least. If in fact it is an allusion, it points to nothing more than an existing tradition in which a comparison was made between Abraham and God, each of whom did not spare his respective son.[30] Otherwise, Paul is completely silent about the test of Abraham. Why? Swetnam's comment regarding Romans 4 applies to Paul generally—Paul deliberately avoids mentioning this popular story because it 'had too many associations as an example of faith demanding a reward'.[31] Appeal to this passage potentially would weaken Paul's emphasis on God's graciousness—and on justification of gentiles who do not have the Law.

But there is a second reason for Paul's aversion to the story of the sacrifice of Isaac. God's blessing, i.e. the promise of (spiritual) descendants to Abraham, intended for gentiles as well as Jews, must precede the institution of the critical distinguishing mark between the two, namely, circumcision. But this sign of the covenant had already been established in Genesis 17, prior to the testing of Abraham. Therefore, for his purpose of constructing a biblical base for a principle which could accommodate non-circumcision of gentiles and circumcision of Jews, while relativizing both, Paul must either turn to a statement of the blessing of Abraham prior to ch. 17 or create a non-specific, generalized formulation of the blessing. He does both. Justification on the basis of faith is now considered the primary blessing of Abraham, who is regarded as the father of all who believe (in Christ) and are thereby 'reckoned righteous'. In addition, Paul's reference to the blessing of the gentiles has been generalized; it cannot be identified with any specific text.[32] The same is true of his use of the phrase 'seed of Abraham'. Paul is keenly aware that the Abrahamic texts, which are on the one hand the biblical cornerstone of his gentile gospel, can also be turned against him. His careful selection as well as his interpretation of those texts therefore is quite understandable.

In Hebrews, the argument proceeds along different lines. The blessing of Abraham comes in response not to his faith as stated in Genesis 15 but to his faith as evidenced in his obedience to the command of God as documented in Genesis 22. Unlike Paul, the author of Hebrews is not deterred by the fact that the story of Abraham successfully passing his test *follows* his circumcision. Within the context of an argument in which Abraham is the father of gentile as well as Jewish believers, Paul's lack of interest in a post-circumcision Abrahamic faith-text makes good sense. But the author of Hebrews does not share Paul's concern to extend Abraham's role as a faith model to gentile believers. The oath which validates the promise comes after Abraham's circumcision (which is left unmentioned since it is not relevant to the argument in Hebrews) in response to his demonstration of faith. In short, that form of the promise of descendants which is of interest in Hebrews is the one found not in Genesis 15 but in Genesis 22. There the blessing is validated by an absolutely dependable oath, sworn by God upon himself (Heb. 6.13-18). In Hebrews the promise comes only after Abraham has demonstrated his faithfulness, in other words, as a reward.

The author of Hebrews has no difficulty in picturing God as a rewarder of faithful deeds. The image of wage-payer is applied to God twice, positively in 11.6 to indicate that God is a rewarder (*misthapodotēs*) of those who seek him, and negatively in 2.2 where the passive verb points to the divine hand behind the 'just retribution' (*endikon misthapodosian*) of transgressions and disobedience. Paul, on the other hand, reveals some ambivalence about the wage image. In 1 Cor. 3.8, 14 and 9.17-18, *misthos* ('wages') appears in a positive light, first as a reward given (by God) to Apollos and himself for their work on behalf of the church at Corinth, and second as a reward he enjoys for preaching the gospel without pay. But when it comes to the question of Abraham and justification, Paul considers the wage image to be theologically inappropriate (Rom. 4.1-5). Drawing on support from Ps. 31.1-2, Paul states that blessedness comes not from receiving one's due, but from *not* receiving it, i.e. by having one's sins forgiven rather than punished (Rom. 4.6-8). Justification is a gift, not a reward or wage for service performed.

In contrast to both Paul and Hebrews, Jas 2.21-24 interprets Genesis 15 and 22 in the light of each other. Like Paul, James addresses the righteousness issue for which Genesis 15 is the basic biblical source. But in James, as in traditional Jewish exegesis, Abraham is not considered a '"justified" sinner, but a righteous man who is recognized and rewarded by God'.[33] The righteousness of Abraham which is recognized in Genesis 15 is validated and the reward bestowed in Genesis 22. As the greatest of the (ten traditional) tests of Abraham,[34] the sacrifice of Isaac demonstrated and exemplified Abraham's faith. In 1 Macc. 2.52, the 'reckoning righteousness' to Abraham is even transposed from its original context in Genesis 15 to Genesis 22: 'Was not Abraham found faithful when tested, and it was reckoned to him as righteousness?'

No hint of the faith/works controversy evident in both Paul and James[35] is present in Hebrews, where 'work(s)' has a very different set of meanings. All but two of the eight instances of 'works' (*erga*) in Hebrews regard them in a thoroughly positive light, i.e., the good work(s) of the readers, both past (6.10) and future (10.24), and God's works (mostly in quotations: 1.10; 3.9; 4.3-4). Works and faith are never contrasted in Hebrews, nor is there any suggestion that their separation is a possibility to be opposed, as in the case of James. The Pauline phrase 'works of the Law' does not appear in Hebrews. In the two negative cases, 'works' (*erga*) is modified by the adjective 'dead' (*nekra*). The dead works from which repentance is required (6.1) and from which the conscience is cleansed by the blood of Christ (9.14) have nothing to do with the debates in which Paul and James were engaged, nor with 'works of the Law'. Dead works are manifestations of that manner of life which leads to death in contrast to life.[36] They signify all that is opposed to faith in God or the true cult.[37]

While faith and righteousness are closely connected in Hebrews 11, Gen. 15.6 is never introduced into the discussion. Indeed, Gen. 15.6 seems to play no role at all in Hebrews. The statement that Noah became 'an heir of the righteousness which comes by faith' (11.7) is not connected to Gen. 15.6 but, insofar as it goes beyond the story of Gen. 6.9–9.29, is advanced as an illustration of the quotation from Habakkuk ('my righteous one shall live by faith') in Heb. 10.38. In 11.33 we read of those 'who through faith. . . worked righteousness' (RSV reads 'enforced justice'), but, as in 11.7, this is no more than a truism. The basic Pauline text for a theology of mission which includes gentiles as well as Jews is not included among the Abrahamic passages in Hebrews.

The final Abrahamic passage referred to in Hebrews (7.1-10) could also be classified as Melchizedekian. No other NT writer quotes or refers to Gen. 14.17-20 where Melchizedek meets the victorious Abraham as he returns from battle, serves him bread and wine, blesses him, and in turn, receives from him a tenth of the spoils. As the only biblical reference to Melchizedek outside Ps. 110.4, the attraction of this story for the author of Hebrews requires no further explanation. A substantial portion of chapter seven is devoted to Melchizedek as a type of Jesus' priesthood. Of particular interest for our purpose is the relationship between Melchizedek and Abraham. From the dual fact of the blessing bestowed by Melchizedek upon Abraham, and the tithe paid by Abraham to his host, plus the august titles and functions of the latter and his lack of a genealogy, the author of Hebrews infers Melchizedek's superiority to Abraham (7.7). But that conclusion is only a means to the more important goal of demonstrating the superiority of Melchizedek's priesthood over the Levitical (7.9-10). That being established, the author can then argue that Jesus is the one addressed in Ps. 110.4 as 'priest forever, after the order of Melchizedek' (7.17).

Thus in this passage Abraham plays a significantly different role than elsewhere in Hebrews. He is still the recipient of a blessing, but no longer a faith model, nor the recipient of a reward. Only a single action of his is considered, the tithe he paid to Melchizedek. This, combined with the blessing (only God and Melchizedek bless Abraham), establishes a hierarchy between the two. However, even in this context, the descendants of Abraham appear once again. Although emphasis is placed on a single tribe, the Levitical, as (an inferior) part of the hierarchical structure established in chapter seven, the rest of Abraham's descendants are also mentioned (7.5). In this context, there can be no question of these being other than Abraham's physical descendants, i.e. Jews.

This brief consideration of the Abrahamic passages in Hebrews turns up no case where Abraham appears as a generalized type of faith, applicable to gentiles as well as Jews. He is placed consistently within Jewish history, and no inferences for gentiles are ever drawn from his faith. Even when interpreting a passage in which the nations are mentioned, such as Genesis 22, the author of Hebrews ignores that aspect of it. Abraham is nothing else than the faithful, enduring, righteous father of the Jewish people. The question of election *within* the Jewish people is not directly addressed in Hebrews, though one might infer the author's position from, for example, the distinction he makes between those who serve the earthly tent and those whose altar is in the true tent (13.10). Swetnam[38] argues for a 'spiritual' meaning of the 'seed of Abraham' in Hebrews, similar to that found in Rom. 9.7 in which he sees the 'seed' denoting 'persons constantly chosen by God on an individual basis'.[39] Even so, these 'spiritual seed' are Jews, as Swetnam recognizes.

When compared with the selection and intepretation of Abrahamic passages by Paul, the implication of the Abrahamic passages in Hebrews for our question is clear: the appropriate object of mission is Israel. Israelites or Jews are the 'seed of Abraham' (2.16) with whom Christ is concerned; they are his 'brothers' (2.11), the 'sons' (2.10) and 'children' (2.14) whose transgressions under the first covenant are expiated by his sacrifice (9.15; cf. 2.17). Paul's concern with gentiles is conspicuously absent from Hebrews. The two writers focus on different Abrahamic texts, Paul on Genesis 15 and 17, the author of Hebrews on Genesis 22. Whereas Paul finds in his selected texts warrant for his gentile gospel, the author of Hebrews gives not a hint that his gospel was directed to other than the children of Abraham in the traditional sense.

A 'Change in the Law'

This leads us back to our starting point. If 'today' signifies a radical or 'apocalyptic' departure from earlier times, precisely what structures are changed, and to what extent? What are the areas of continuity and discontinuity? If, as I have argued, there is no evidence in Hebrews of ethnic discontinuity, what about the Torah? Does the community envisaged in Hebrews keep the whole Torah or any part of it? What is the relationship in Hebrews between covenant, the people, and the Torah?

We may begin with Heb. 7.12: 'For when there is a change in the priesthood, there is necessarily a change in the Law as well'. The second part of this sentence has often been interepreted as a rejection of the Jewish Law as such. This understanding seems to be largely due—or at least related—to a similar understanding of the previous verse: 'Now if perfection had been attainable through the Levitical priesthood (for under it the people received the Law), what further need would there have been for another priest. . . . ' The RSV is not alone in seeing in *nenomothetētai* ('received the law', according to the RSV) a reference to the giving of the Torah at Sinai. A perusal of a few other modern translations reveals that this is a common view ('given the law'—NEB; 'the law was given'—NIV; 'the Law given'—JB). But such translations create a serious difficulty of interpretation. What would it mean to say that the Torah was given 'under' the Levitical priesthood? What has the priesthood to do with the giving of the Torah at Sinai? And how would such a statement cohere with its context?

Two things need to be pointed out here. First, the verb *nomotheteō* simply means 'to legislate', and in the passive, as used here, 'to be instituted by Law'.[40] In and of itself, it does not refer to the giving of *the* Law, and apart from Heb. 7.11 it is never taken to mean that. Second, the same passive verb followed by the preposition *epi* ('upon' or 'on the basis of'), is found in 8.6, where it expresses the basis upon which the new covenant rests ('it is enacted on better promises'). None of the translations mentioned above finds any association with the giving of the Torah at Sinai in the use of *nenomothetētai* in 8.6. Neither should they in 7.11. Rather, 7.11 refers to specific commandments concerning the Levitical priesthood and their sacrificial service to the people, nothing more. Harm W. Hollander's translation accurately expresses the meaning of 7.11: 'The people of Israel received regulations concerning the levitical priesthood'.[41] This translation makes good sense of the sentence in its context, while the others do not. The meaning is not that the Torah was given on the basis of or under the Levitical priesthood, but rather that the people

received commandments regarding the priesthood. Those commandments were of course part of the Torah, but not its totality. The
author is simply stating an obvious fact as a basis for the next stage in
his argument legitimating the priesthood of Jesus. Having demonstrated
the superiority of Melchizedek to Abraham and therefore to Levi and
his descendants (7.1-10), the author now deals with the question of
priestly laws. The Torah as such never enters the picture.

The 'change in the Law' in 7.12, therefore, refers to priestly law.
The argument is that a change in priesthood, from the order of Aaron
to the order of Melchizedek (7.11), is paralleled by and requires a
change in the laws governing the priestly order as such. Priesthood
itself is not in question. Indeed, it is essential to the teaching that
leads to maturity. What has been changed is the order or type and
therefore the effectiveness of priesthood and the priestly act. Since
Torah contains specific commandments and regulations regarding
sacrifice, including priests, materials and site, it is obvious to the
author that those parts of Torah have been changed by God. What is
referred to in 7.12 is the one elemental discontinuity permeating the
epistle, the cultic life of Israel. If Jesus is the one true, effective
sacrifice for the cleansing of the conscience, opening the way to God,
then other sacrifices are no longer valid. It is 'liturgical' law (8.2, 6),
and only liturgical law, that is changed in Hebrews. Inferences
concerning other aspects of Torah or the Torah as such are
unwarranted.

This interpretation is supported by the clarification of 7.12 which
immediately follows in 7.13-14. The author now meets the logical
objection that the application of the title of priest to Jesus, who is
known to be of the tribe of Judah, is inconsistent with Mosaic
legislation regarding priests (Moses said nothing about priests of the
tribe of Judah). Yet the entire soteriology of Hebrews depends on the
fundamental affirmation, derived from Ps. 110.4, that Jesus is the
priest of the new age. Moses' legislation regarding priests, and by
implication other aspects of the sacrificial arrangements, applied
only to the old age (the 'former days'). But those parts of the Torah,
including the laws concerning the appointment of Levitical priests,
proved ineffectual; they did not 'perfect' (7.11) since they did not
address the central problem, the conscience. Consequently, a new
arrangement was required. This new arrangement is articulated and
validated with an oath in Ps. 110.4. But there cannot be two different

priesthoods under the same divine arrangement, during the same age. Therefore, as it is put in Hebrews, a 'change' (*metathesis*, 7.12) in the Law (i.e. those regulations dealing with priesthood) was required.

The transition from the Levitical to the Melchizedekian order is, for our author, implied by Ps. 110.4. The law appointing Levitical priests (the 'former commandment', *proagousēs entolēs*), having proved itself useless, is now withdrawn (7.18). That 'the law' (*ho nomos*) of 7.19 does not refer to Torah as such but only to those aspects of it regarding the appointment of the Levitical priests, is verified in 7.28, which summarizes the basic argument of this portion of Hebrews: 'Indeed, the law appoints men in their weakness as high priests, but the word of the oath [i.e., Ps. 110.4], which came later than the law, appoints a Son who has been made perfect for ever'. In this context, 'law' is used in a way similar to commandment (*entolē*), but in a generalized sense to cover all specific commandments dealing with or assuming the legitimacy of the Levitical priesthood. It does not refer to the Torah as such, the totality of Jewish law and teaching governing all aspects of life, but to those laws specifically concerned with the prevailing Jewish priestly order.

Just as the 'word of the oath' of Ps. 110.4 implies a change in the commandment(s) concerning the appointment of priests from the tribe of Levi, likewise other elements of the sacrificial arrangements established in the Torah have now been changed. The overall term employed in Hebrews to designate the totality of those arrangements is 'covenant'. In Hebrews, 'covenant' designates a divinely instituted soteriological order or arrangement. Whereas it includes the entire sweep of Mosaic legislation (9.19-20), the regulations governing the sacrificial system, especially priesthood, sacrifice, and tabernacle are the author's primary interest.

For the author of Hebrews, Ps. 110.4 not only declares Jesus' appointment as priest; it also implies a new, 'better covenant' (7.22), mediated by Jesus (8.6; 9.15; 12.24). This is the same covenant foretold for Israel in Jer. 31.31-34, a passage from which the author infers several things. First, the very mention of a new covenant implies the removal of the first (8.13), which in these last days, is on the verge of disappearing. Second, the essence of both covenants is their concern with the removal of sin. It is instructive that the quotation from Jeremiah begins with the establishment of the new covenant and ends with 'I will remember their sins no more' (8.12). Third, and closely related to the second, each covenant involves a sacrificial ritual whose goal is the removal of sins. For both covenants, the Day of Atonement ritual of Leviticus 16 provides the basic model. But under the new covenant, based on better promises (8.6) and with its better priesthood, better sacrifice, and better tabernacle, the goal not reached under the first covenant is now attainable.

While the Torah as a whole has not been replaced, only 'changed' in the sense that its parts dealing with sacrifice required relegislation, the same cannot be said about the covenant. This is partly due to the fact that there is only one Torah but two covenants. Further, covenant is not law, but the framework in which law has its significance. But both covenants are given by God to Israel, and while they point to two different religious systems, there is considerable overlap between them, despite the antithetical position they are given in Hebrews. In particular, the 'new' covenant does not imply a new people. But it does imply a 'change in the law' because the new covenant brings perfection of the conscience and all that requires, while the first covenant failed in purifying the conscience from sins.

The arguments in Hebrews could be extended to cover gentiles as well as Jews, as they have been by most modern interpreters of this writing. But the author himself does not do so, and such an extension requires considerable readjustment of his tightly woven logic and scriptural interpretation.

Summary

Whereas discontinuity between the former and the present times is vigorously affirmed in Hebrews, it must not be extended beyond the limits set for it there. Rather than covering the entirety of Torah, it applies only to cultic legislation.[42] And rather than proclaiming, as Paul did, a new ethnic principle inherent in the new covenant which constitutes a fundamental departure from the first covenant, Hebrews contains no evidence of an envisaged rupture between traditional Israel and the heirs of the new age. In Israel then and now are found both those whose *apistia* ('unfaithfulness') barred them from inheriting the rest and those whose faith qualified them for it.

The 'seed of Abraham' (2.16), whose salvation is at stake, is 'Israel'.

The arguments in Hebrews regarding Law and covenant are misunderstood if confused with Paul's argument concerning the incorporation of the gentiles into faithful Israel. The religious world of Hebrews is narrower and more traditional than Paul's. With the one fundamental exception relating to the cult, the Torah is still valid for those to whom it was given by Moses. No break with Jewish tradition apart from priesthood, sacrifice and temple is assumed in Hebrews. Discontinuity centers upon cult, not Torah. Of course, cult implicates Torah. But Torah is a larger category, and apart from priesthood and other cultic aspects, is left untouched by the critique of Hebrews. The new covenant does not imply a new Torah, but a 'changed' Torah in which earlier cultic legislation is replaced. What distinguishes the two covenants is their relative efficacy to purify the conscience from sin. Thus there is a close relationship between the 'change in the law' and the transition to the new covenant. Jesus is the mediator of both.

The choice of Israel as the recipient of the new as well as the first covenant is nowhere questioned; on the contrary, it is assumed throughout. Rather than Hebrews being at or near the end of the process of disengagement from Judaism, it seems to me that, as far as its assumptions regarding the people and the Law are concerned, it belongs to an early stage of the process.

The author of Hebrews goes much further than the Qumran community in his critique of the sacrificial cult.[43] It is not just the current administration of sacrificial practices that is rejected, but the 'earthly' sacrificial cult itself. In this sense, Hebrews is radical. But Judaism was more than the temple cult, as it demonstrated following the destruction of the temple and the cessation of its services. In Hebrews we encounter a set of arguments designed, among other things, to justify transfer of support and commitment from the sacrificial system to this new sect[44] which believed that a new set of sacrificial rules had been divinely instituted. For its members, the death of Jesus had replaced all other sacrifices concerned with sin.

Who are those to whom missionary activity should be directed according to Hebrews? Ethnically, they are the same as those indicated in Mt. 10.6: 'Go nowhere among the Gentiles, and enter no town of the Samaritans, but go rather to the lost sheep of the house of

Israel'. The heirs of the new age envisaged in Hebrews are among those 'lost sheep' (cf. Heb. 13.20). They have no need to use the term 'seed of Abraham' metaphorically, nor to be blessed through Abraham's descendants. They *are* descendants of Abraham and are therefore the primary heirs of the promise.

NOTES

1. E.g. C.K. Barrett, 'The Eschatology of the Epistle to the Hebrews', *The Background of the New Testament and its Eschatology* (ed. W.D. Davies and D. Daube; Cambridge: Cambridge University Press, 1964), pp. 363-93; Otfried Hofius, *Katapausis, Die Vorstellung vom endzeitlichen Ruheort im Hebräerbrief* (WUNT; Tübingen: J.C.B. Mohr, 1970).

2. C. Spicq, *L'Epitre aux Hébreux* (2 vols.; 3rd edn; Paris: Librairie Lecoffre, 1952), Vol. I, pp. 39-91. See the critique by Ronald Williamson, *Philo and the Epistle to the Hebrews* (Leiden: E.J. Brill, 1970).

3. James W. Thompson, *The Beginnings of Christian Philosophy: The Epistle to the Hebrews* (CBQMS 13; Washington, DC: The Catholic Biblical Association of America, 1982).

4. Hans Kosmala, *Hebräer—Essener—Christen; Studien zur Vorgeschichte der frühchristlichen Verkündigung* (Leiden: E.J. Brill, 1959); Yigael Yadin, 'The Dead Sea Scrolls and the Epistle to the Hebrews', *Aspects of the Dead Sea Scrolls* (ed. Chaim Rabin and Yigael Yadin; Scripta Hierosolymitana 4; Jerusalem: Magnes, 1958), pp. 36-65.

5. Ernst Käsemann, *Das wandernde Gottesvolk: Eine Untersuchung zum Hebräerbrief* (FRLANT; 4th edn; Göttingen: Vandenhoeck & Ruprecht, 1961; ET *The Wandering People of God, an Investigation of the Letter to the Hebrews* (Minneapolis: Augsburg Publishing House, 1984). See further Thompson, pp. 2-5.

6. E.g. the debate over the relationship between Hebrews and Philo (Williamson and Thompson) or the primacy of the eschatological (Barrett) or the Platonic (Thompson). George W. MacRae ('Heavenly Temple and Eschatology in the Letter to the Hebrews', *Semeia* 12 [1978], pp. 179-99) proposes a resolution of the Alexandrian/apocalyptic debate: the Alexandrian temple imagery of Hebrews is assigned to the author while the apocalyptic aspects of the letter reflect the author's concessions to his readers' assumptions.

7. All biblical quotations are given according to the RSV.

8. Hebrews and Acts (13.33) are the only NT writings to quote Ps. 2.7.

9. *Contra* Simon Kistemaker, *The Psalm Citations in the Epistle to the Hebrews* (Amsterdam: Soest, 1961), p. 113: 'For the *today* in not limited to

the time of the psalmist, nor is it bound to the OT period, but it extends beyond this to the day of salvation. . . . ' See also Calvin's commentary on Heb. 3.13: 'He tells us that the word today. . . ought not to be confined to the age of David, but that it embraces all time in which God accosts us' (*Calvin's Commentaries; The Epistle of Paul the Apostle to the Hebrews* [Edinburgh: Tweeddale Court, 1963], p. 41).

10. The nearest to a missionary text is 2.3 ('. . . it was attested to us by those who heard him').

11. In connection with the eschatology of Hebrews, Harold Attridge ('"Let us Strive to Enter That Rest", The Logic of Hebrews 4.1-11', *HTR* 73 [1980], pp. 279-88; see p. 280) has reminded us that 'concentration on these [gnostic or apocalyptic] parallels may obscure the dynamics of Hebrews' argument, which should serve as the fundamental criterion by which to assess the work's eschatology'. This paper concentrates on those arguments of Hebrews in which Abraham plays a role.

12. 'Not Jewish Christianity and Gentile Christianity but Types of Jewish/Gentile Christianity', *CBQ* 45 (1983), pp. 74-79. See also Raymond E. Brown and John P. Meier, *Antioch and Rome, New Testament Cradles of Catholic Christianity* (New York: Paulist Press, 1983), pp. 1-9.

13. Brown, 'Not Jewish Christianity', p. 74.

14. E.g. George Wesley Buchanan, *To the Hebrews* (AB; Garden City, New York: Doubleday, 1972); Otto Michel, *Der Brief an die Hebräer* (MeyerK; 12th edn; Göttingen: Vandenhoeck & Ruprecht, 1966); Spicq; William Manson, *The Epistle to the Hebrews* (London: Hodder and Stoughton, 1951); Kosmala; F.F. Bruce, *Commentary on the Epistle to the Hebrews* (The New International Commentary on the New Testament; London: Marshall, Morgan & Scott, 1964).

15. E.g. Barrett; James Moffatt, *A Critical and Exegetical Commentary on the Epistle to the Hebrews* (Edinburgh: T. & T. Clark, 1924); Käsemann; Herbert Braun, *An die Hebräer* (HNT; Tübingen: J.C.B. Mohr, 1984).

16. E.g. Thompson (p. 99) commenting on 4.3-11: 'The main statement contrasts the situation of the new people of God with Israel. The fact that the church 'enters' (*eiserchometha*) is contrasted to Israel's failure to enter (3.19). . . . ' 'Church' and 'Israel' are Thompson's interpretation of 'we' and 'they'.

17. Samuel Sandmel's distinction between 'Synagogue Judaism' and that of the temple is useful here (*Judaism and Christian Beginnings* [New York: Oxford University Press, 1978], pp. 4-5).

18. E.g. Buchanan, p. 36.

19. E.g. Braun, p. 68.

20. Brendan Byrne, *'Sons of God'—'Seed of Abraham', A Study of the Idea of the Sonship of God of All Christians in Paul against the Jewish Background* (AnBib 83; Rome: Biblical Institute Press, 1979), p. 160; James Swetnam,

Jesus and Isaac, A Study of the Epistle to the Hebrews in the Light of the Aqedah (AnBib 94; Rome: Biblical Institute Press, 1982), p. 90.

21. Swetnam (p. 90 n. 22) takes the view that Abraham receives only promises of a vast progeny and of the land, but not the fulfilment of either. However, who could deny that in fact the promise of numerous offspring had been fulfilled, if the promise is taken in a literal sense? Further, without some evidence that God keeps his promises, the argument in Hebrews regarding the land would be greatly weakened.

22. Among contemporary Hebrews scholars, Buchanan (p. 65) seems to be alone in denying an eschatological significance to 'land': 'The author expected the promised heritage of the land of Canaan under the rule of the Messiah to be fulfilled for Jesus and his followers'.

23. On the importance of 'stability' in Hebrews, see Thompson, pp. 143-50.

24. And therefore the superiority of his revelation to theirs; see Graham Hughes, *Hebrews and Hermeneutics, The Epistle to the Hebrews as a New Testament Example of Biblical Interpretation* (SNTSMS 36; Cambridge: Cambridge University Press, 1979), pp. 7-8.

25. See above, note 20.

26. Swetnam, p. 88.

27. *Contra* Buchanan regarding the land and Swetnam regarding seed.

28. Byrne (p. 160) claims that Gal. 3.16 refers to the promise of the land (Gen. 17.5) which is understood by Paul as it is in Hebrews, i.e. as the inheritance (Gal. 3.18) of the final age.

29. Swetnam, pp. 23-80. Swetnam (p. 77) concludes: 'Much more probably than not, the Aqedah seems to have been considered as a part of the living tradition of what being a Jew meant'.

30. *Ibid.*, pp. 80-81.

31. *Ibid.*, pp. 82-83.

32. Hans Dieter Betz, *Galatians, A Commentary on Paul's Letter to the Churches in Galatia* (Hermeneia; Philadelphia: Fortress Press, 1979), p. 142.

33. Martin Dibelius, *James, A Commentary on the Epistle of James*, rev. by Heinrich Greeven (Hermeneia; Philadelphia: Fortress Press, 1976), p. 162.

34. See *Gen. R.* 56.11; *Jub.* 19.8 identifies the burial of Sarah as the tenth test. See Swetnam, p. 81 n. 470.

35. On the faith/works issue in Paul and James, see John G. Lodge, 'James and Paul at Cross-Purposes? James 2,22', *Bib* 62 (1981), pp. 195-213.

36. Bruce, pp. 113-14.

37. Braun, pp. 160, 271. Braun rejects the view that Heb. 6.1 points to the readers having been Jews. Curiously, Buchanan (p. 103), contrary to what he says elsewhere, apparently agrees, suggesting that the readers had been gentiles 'living as other pagans'.

38. Swetnam, p. 100.

39. *Ibid.*, p. 105.

40. BAG, p. 544.

41. 'Hebrews 7.11 and 8.6: a suggestion for the translation of *nenomothetētai epi*', *BT* 30 (1979), pp. 244-47; see p. 247.

42. In an otherwise enlightening study, it is unfortunate that Frances M. Young ('Temple Cult and Law in Early Christianity', *NTS* 19 [1983], pp. 325-38) lumps together law, temple and cult and identifies the conflict between Jews and Christians as between a 'legalist, ritualist tradition' and a 'prophetic, moralizing tradition'. This pattern simply does not apply to Hebrews. The critique in Hebrews concerns sacrificial ritual, not ritual in general.

43. Elisabeth Schüssler Fiorenza, 'Cultic Language in Qumran and in the NT', *CBQ* 38 (1976), pp. 159-77.

44. Hebrews readily fits into the Jewish sectarian pattern proposed by Shaye J.D. Cohen, 'The Significance of Yavneh: Pharisees, Rabbis, and the End of Jewish Sectarianism', *HUCA* 55 (1984), pp. 27-53. For his definition of sect, see pp. 29-30. Interestingly, Cohen identifies laws concerning the temple as being at the center of sectarian disputes: 'The sects debated many different laws, but the specific halakhot which always stood at the heart of Jewish sectarianism were the laws related to the temple: purity, cult, and priestly offerings. The sects advanced different theories of self-legitimation but the authority figures against whom they always defined themselves were the priests of the temple. Hence a common feature of Jewish sectarianism is the polemic against the temple of Jerusalem: its precincts are impure, its cult profane, and its priests illegitimate' (p. 43). While Hebrews speaks of ineffectiveness rather than impurity, the temple, the priesthood and the temple ritual legitimated under the former covenant constitute the anthithesis of the new and 'true' temple, priesthood and cultic activity.

THE SIGNIFICANCE OF PAULINE APOCALYPTIC FOR THEOLOGICAL ETHICS

Nancy J. Duff

'There are two ways', begins the *Didache*, 'one of life and one of death; and great is the difference between the two ways'.[1] As a seminarian taking a course in the history of Christian doctrine I found myself struck by the wisdom and beauty of the doctrine of the two ways offered by this second-century document. For me its wisdom lay in its rigorous distinction between Christian and non-Christian behavior and its beauty in its simple presentation of the truth. I believed it offered a clear description of the choice we face in moral decision-making—the way of life or the way of death, the way of God or the way of evil—a choice, moreover, wedded to the New Testament idea of 'working out your own salvation'.[2] Furthermore, the doctrine implies that the two ways are readily recognizable and accessible to all humanity, and that we are equipped with the vision necessary to see the alternatives that stretch before us and the power necessary to choose between them. On first studying the *Didache* I resented the fact that the Church had not seen its way to include it in the canon.

I was not alone in my admiration for the doctrine of the two ways. Although the doctrine officially lost the battle with Christian 'orthodoxy' because of its affirmation of human free will, in practice it has won the day.[3] I would venture to say that it expresses the position of the majority of confessing Christians. God, we often hear, has set two possibilities before us: salvation in Jesus Christ or condemnation apart from Christ. All that is required to gain salvation and to fulfill the standards of Christian morality is to choose the way of life offered by God in Jesus Christ.

Hence, the doctrine of the two ways interprets the Gospel as an invitation which calls for human response. This interpretation has influenced a popular style of preaching which makes frequent use of the phrase 'if only': 'If only you will accept Jesus as your personal Lord and Savior. . . '; 'If only you will ask God to forgive you. . . ' The conclusion to these conditional clauses is: 'then you will be saved'. The 'if' implies the condition and the 'only' suggests the simplicity of the action required.

Adherents to the doctrine of the two ways believe they have found the avenue by which to affirm God's freely given grace as the foundation of salvation *and* to preserve human free will at the same time. On the one hand, we do not earn salvation through good works, but through God's free offer of salvation. On the other hand, we are not human puppets conscripted into God's service, but independent beings who have the freedom and capacity to choose our destiny, i.e. to follow the way offered by God or to reject it.

In spite of the seeming beauty, wisdom, and popularity of the doctrine of the two ways, J. Louis Martyn has persisted in teaching his students that the doctrine is *not* true to the Gospel. Calling it the 'theological two-step', whereby God offers grace to humanity (first step) and humanity offers a 'faith response' to God (second step), he believes it is foreign to the Gospel, and, particularly for our purposes here, foreign to the Gospel proclaimed by the apostle Paul. According to Prof. Martyn, the concepts 'faith-response' and 'choice' are incorrect identifications of the nature of Pauline theology.

> In the literal crucifixion of Jesus of Nazareth God invades without a single 'if'. Not 'if' you repent. Not 'if' you learn. Not even 'if' you believe. The absence of the little word, 'if', the uncontingent, prevenient, invading nature of God's grace shows God to be the power and victorious Advocate of the entire race of human beings.[4]

Paul does *not* speak of two alternatives or two possibilities between which we choose, but of two worlds that are in conflict with one another.[5] Paul does not describe 'timeless doctrines' to which we should subscribe nor the *summum bonum* toward which we should strive. Instead he describes a conflict between two orbs of power and calls us to portray by our actions which sphere of power directs our lives. Professor Martyn claims, therefore, that to converse with Paul we must come to terms not with the doctrine of the two ways but 'with the strange world of Pauline apocalyptic'.[6]

If, however, we are to come to terms with the strange apocalyptic world of Paul we first have to understand what is meant by 'apocalyptic'.[7] Lou Martyn has taught his students to begin to untangle this slippery word by expanding the definition of it offered by Ernst Käsemann, i.e. 'expectation of an imminent parousia'.[8] Such expectation certainly forms a portion of Paul's perspective. Like the apocalyptic writers of his time Paul expected the end to come soon (1 Thess. 4.13–5.11). Unlike the other apocalyptic writers, however, Paul believed that the turning of the ages had already begun.[9] We do not now live completely in the New Age, but the New Age (or New Creation) has already been inaugurated in Jesus Christ. Hence, we live at the *juncture* of the ages. As a result of the clashing of the New Age with the Old a great conflict has arisen between the reality embraced by the Old Age and that which is acknowledged as real in the New Age.

Pauline apocalyptic, therefore, has to do with a particular understanding of the revelation of that reality. In fact 'revelation' is the English word most frequently used to translate the Greek word 'apocalypse'. According to Professor Martyn, however, it provides only an inadequate translation.[10] 'Apocalypse' does not just mean the unveiling of something already existing but heretofore unknown, as the word 'revelation' indicates. Apocalypse also means the 'invasion' of God's grace into the world, an invasion which brings into existence that which was not there before (Rom. 4.17).[11] Revelation, therefore, understood as apocalypse, points to the ideas of both incarnation and knowledge. On the one hand, revelation is incarnation, i.e. God's apocalypse of God's self in the cross and resurrection. Furthermore, God's incarnation or invasion of this world in the form of Jesus Christ's life, death and resurrection changes the very structure of reality in the world. Hence, revelation *is* the transformation of the world.[12] On the other hand, revelation is knowledge, i.e. the knowledge of both existing yet hidden truth and the knowledge of that which has been brought newly upon the scene. Both aspects of revelation as apocalypse (incarnation and knowledge) are centered for Paul in the Cross. The Cross is *the* apocalyptic event which has changed the world and our way of perceiving it.

Convinced that Professor Martyn correctly replaces the doctrine of the two ways with Paul's apocalyptic perspective, it is my intention here to examine the implications of Pauline apocalyptic for the discipline of Christian theological ethics. I will argue that apocalyptic themes in Paul challenge descriptions of responsible

Christian action as autonomous choices between alternatives and instead describe responsible action as anticipatory reflections of the New Age inaugurated and promised by Jesus Christ.

We will explore the significance of three aspects of Pauline apocalyptic for theological ethics: (1) the lordship of Christ (2) the revelation or apocalypse of the New Creation already inaugurated by Jesus Christ at the turn of the ages, and (3) the expectation of the imminent parousia.[13]

1. *Lordship*

According to Ernst Käsemann the fundamental apocalyptic question is 'To whom does the sovereignty of the world belong?'[14] This is true of the theology of Paul no less than that of other apocalyptic writers. Paul's theology includes a limited dualism in which the powers and principalities vie for lordship over creation. Borrowing a phrase from Flannery O'Connor, Professor Martyn believes that Paul's apocalyptic proclaims 'the action of grace in territory held largely by the devil'.[15] According to Paul, human beings always have a lord—either the demonic powers or the Spirit of Jesus Christ. Human identity and action, therefore, are determined by anwering the question, 'Who is the lord of our existence?' or 'Whose slave are we?'

For Paul this question of lordship is decisively answered in the apocalypse of Jesus Christ. There is no image of freedom in Paul apart from the reality of lordship. We are either in bondage to Sin or we are freed by being slaves to Christ.[16] Hence the question 'Who is our Lord?' becomes for Paul *the* ethical question.

Examining how the question of lordship affects Paul's definition of sin will illuminate how Pauline apocalyptic challenges the doctrine of the two ways. Sin for Paul can no longer be understood simply as a list of wrong acts. More often Paul speaks of 'Sin' in the singular and describes it as a sphere of influence, a cosmic force, or a personified power. Sin is not simply something that we do; Sin itself acts. Sin has 'come into the world' (Rom. 5.2) and 'achieved dominion' (Rom. 5.21). It is a power that enslaves (Gal. 5.15) and that exacts its wages in death (Rom. 6.23).[17]

There is, therefore, no such thing as a totally autonomous human decision. Here we find the initial and most significant challenge to the doctrine of the two ways and the Pelagian position on freedom of the will. Human responsibility cannot be understood in and of itself but only in relation to the powers that vie for lordship over human existence. There are no human actions apart from the powers that rule us. This does not mean that human beings are reduced to marionettes with no will of their own. It does mean that the self always acts in relation to a power beyond itself. Thus Paul can describe his own frustration at setting out to do the good and yet doing the very evil he seeks to avoid. He describes the self as enslaved to a power beyond its control, i.e. a self 'sold under sin' (Rom. 7.14b). Clearly Paul speaks of the self doing the action here: '*I* do what I do not want'. At the same time there is another actor on the scene as Sin directs the self's action: 'It is no longer I that do it, but sin which dwells within me' (Rom. 7.17). 'I, yet not I', Paul says, 'commit sinful acts'.

Just as Paul has this understanding of the idea of 'I, but not I' of human action regarding Sin, we also find this idea when Paul refers to grace. He claims that he has worked hard, and yet it is not he who has done the work, but Christ (1 Cor. 15.10). Our actions are directed by the one who is our Lord, i.e. either by Sin or by Christ. What makes us responsible, i.e. 'able to respond', is either the Sin that dwells in us or the Christ who sets us free.[18]

This concept of lordship removes ethics from the realm of choosing between possibilities and into the realm of power. In exhorting Christians to choose between two ways—the way of life or the way of death, the way of the spirit or the way of the flesh, the way of sin or the way of grace—we have simply reduced the Gospel to a list of New Year's resolutions which we will try hard to live up to. The devastating fact of our moral lives, however, is that we often fail to do the good we set out with such great resolution to do. The Gospel does not just leave us to our own initiative, giving us a list of good things to do and wicked things to avoid. Such admonitions carry with them no power to fulfill them.

The result of Christ's victory over the demonic powers is not that we now have the freedom to choose between good and evil. Rather, it is that we now have the freedom and therefore the power to obey the One whose lordship over us sets us free. Ethics is not centered in knowing what is the good, but in knowing who is our Lord.[19] It is not a matter of choice, but a matter of apocalyptic perspective, i.e. knowing who is the Lord of our existence and whose side we are on.

By destroying the powers that enslave us Christ gives us the power to live as new creatures freed from the tyranny of illegitimate lords.

Paul's apocalyptic view, therefore, calls us to resist the powers and principalities which claim illegitimate lordship in the world. In recent years feminist theology has rightly claimed that the Church too often believes that the concept of Christ's lordship over us permits a parallel human structure whereby some persons exercise lordship over others, e.g. Christians over non-Christians, men over women, or white persons over persons of color. It is true, of course, that this is the stance that the Church often takes. Affirmation of the lordship of Christ does not, however, justify such a turn. God's action toward us liberates human beings, enabling them to act like human beings, *not* to act like gods. Human action is not necessarily parallel to divine action. The lordship of Christ declares all other claims to lordship illegitimate. God does not call us to be lords over our neighbors; only Jesus Christ is Lord.

It follows, then, that the lordship of Christ prohibits any confusion between Christ's lordship and human political movements. At a time when the Christian right is raising its voice in matters concerning the relationship between church and state we must be particularly alert to the dangers of confusing the two. The cover of a recent theological journal on religious toleration displayed an image of the American flag in which the usual stars representing the states were replaced with Christian crosses and Jewish stars of David. Surely the emblem was nothing more than a symbol of religious toleration in America. Such a mixture of the symbols of church and state, however, inadvertently moves toward an ever-present danger for the Church, i.e. the attempted coalition between the lordship of Christ and the lords of this world. It is indeed a long way from that collated symbol of church and state to the transformation of the Greek cross into the state's emblem in Nazi Germany.[20] Nevertheless, in light of President Reagan's reference to the Gospel of Luke in defense of arms buildup, the Pentagon's attempt to name a nuclear submarine *Corpus Christi*, and Christian prayers for the death of supreme court justices, we need to be reminded that our symbols as well as our actions should signify that Christ alone is Lord of the world.

If we are not to confuse Christ's lordship with the lords of the world, neither are we to separate Christ from the concerns of the world. Christ does not defeat the powers and principalities solely for the sake of the Church, but for the sake of the whole world as well. Visser t' Hooft once rightly claimed:

> God thinks and plans in terms of humanity and of the universe... Church and world have, therefore, a great deal in common. Both have the same Lord. Both live in the light of the same victory of Christ over the power of sin and death... Both together are the realm over which Christ is lord.[21]

In radical distinction from the theology of the apocalypses the Lordship of Christ leads us to understand that 'both believer and unbeliever belong to Christ'.[22] 'For as in Adam all die, so also in Christ shall *all* be made alive' (1 Cor. 15.22). That Christ is Lord of the world as well as of the Church indicates that the Church has no room to boast of special privilege. If we seek to lord ourselves over others we have not accurately answered the ethical question 'Who is our Lord?' nor have we yet recognized our apocalyptic vocation which calls us to live in the New Age inaugurated by Jesus Christ.

2. New Creation: Old Age/New Age

While Paul fights the enthusiasts who believe that the New Age has fully arrived, he nevertheless believes that the turning of the ages has already begun. He stands among those 'upon whom the end of the ages has come' (1 Cor. 10.11) and among those who know that 'the form of this world is passing away' (1 Cor. 7.31). According to Paul a 'new space' within the world has been created by the death and resurrection of Jesus Christ.[23] Professor Martyn explains that according to Paul certain distinctions that had always existed in the world have with the advent, death and resurrection, and expected return of Christ, been destroyed:

> There was a world whose fundamental structures were certain pairs of opposites: circumcision/uncircumcision; Jew/Gentile; slave/free; male/female... Those who have been baptized into Christ, however, know that, in Christ, that world does not any longer have real existence.[24]

In contrast to the Old Age distinctions, unity marks the New World created by Christ: 'You are all of you, one in Christ Jesus' (Gal. 3.27-29). With Christ's life, death and resurrection a new reality enters the world and all reality is fundamentally changed. Hence, one begins to understand what is meant by the claim that for Paul God's revelation *is* the transformation of the world. The turning of the ages indicates (to borrow a phrase from Paul Lehmann) that the 'transfiguration of the world is underway'.[25]

Signs of the New Age, however, are presently hidden in the Old Age, and, therefore, require new vision in order to be seen. It is not true, as the doctrine of the two ways suggests, that we are naturally equipped with the vision necessary to see and therefore choose the way of life in the world. Standing at the turn of the ages, Paul speaks of a new way of knowing that is not ours by nature but ours as a gift of the Spirit.[26] He does not, however, speak of knowing according to the New Age, but of knowing according to the cross.[27]

Using the image of the two lenses of bi-focals, one to sharpen 'near vision' and the other to sharpen 'far vision', Professor Martyn suggests that apocalyptic vision enables us to see 'near things and far things'.[28] Such 'bi-focal vision' helps us to understand what it means to have inherited both 'the suffering world' and 'the triumphant Hallelujah Chorus'.[29] There are people in the world who actually cannot see suffering around them. By knowing according to the cross, however, we look at the world and see the suffering. 'Who is weak and I am not weak? Who is made to fall, and I am not indignant?' (2 Cor. 11.29). Our near vision enables us to see that a war is raging between God and the powers of death. There are other people in the world who cannot see anything but suffering. By knowing according to the cross, however, we look at the world and see hope. 'The sufferings of this present time are not worth comparing with the glory that is to be revealed to us' (Rom. 8.18). Our 'far vision' enables us to see the outcome of the battle, i.e. to see the resurrection. By knowing the world according to the cross we see both suffering and hope.

Through apocalyptic vision we are enabled to see both the war and the outcome of the battle. Paul is not, however, proposing an 'interim ethic' showing us how to live in the Old Age before the New Age arrives. Although we must be alert to the dangers of enthusiasm, we nevertheless live *now* in that new space created by the powerful invasion of Christ. Living within that new space we can no longer tolerate Old Age distinctions in the social and political order which oppress and destroy. We refuse to allow the political order which has foundations in the Old Age to operate under the slogan 'business as usual', because we do not recognize its legitimacy in God's world. It is in that new space created in Christ that the Church is called into being and action.

J. Christiaan Beker rightly describes the Church as 'the blueprint of a new eschatological order'.[30] Thus in the midst of a society which lives according to Old Age distinctions, the Church provides 'pockets' of a new life. The members of the Church are to be 'blameless and innocent children of God in the midst of a crooked and perverse generation, among whom [they] shine as lights in the world' (Phil. 2.14-16). The Church fights the powers and principalities by refusing to live according to their ways. Paul's view on mutuality in marriage (1 Cor. 7.3-5) and his eradication of racial, social, and sexual distinctions in the Church (Gal. 3.28) run counter to the society in which he lives. The Church is to live in a different way, in a different and yet overlapping sphere and age. Old Age distinctions are not allowed as the Church fulfills its apocalyptic vocation in the world.

Examples of this apocalyptic rendering of the Church as the 'blueprint of the New Age' can be found in two images of the black Church, one from the nineteenth century, the other from the twentieth. The first image comes from James Theodore Holly, the first black bishop of the Anglican Church. While insisting that the Church could not take up arms against the state's oppressive structures such as slavery, he claimed that within the Church distinctions between slave and free, landowner and sharecropper, rich and poor, royalty and subject would not be recognized. Refusing to acknowledge the distinctions that the world so loves would in itself, he believed, constitute subversive activity by providing a visible indictment of this world which is passing away and an anticipatory image of the world that is to come in Jesus Christ.[31]

The second image of the Church as 'the blueprint of the New Age' comes from James Cone's description of the black Church as 'an eschatological community that lives as if the end of time is already at hand'.[32] According to Cone black congregations know when they gather to worship that the Spirit of Jesus Christ 'bestows upon them a new vision of their future humanity'. It is now the Spirit rather than the world which gives them their identity:

> The Holy Spirit's presence with the people is a liberating experience. Black people who have been humiliated and oppressed

by the structures of white society six days of the week, gather together each Sunday morning in order to experience a new definition of their humanity. The transition from Saturday to Sunday is not just a chronological change from the seventh to the first day of the week. It is rather a rupture in time, a kairos-event which produces a radical transformation in the people's identity. The janitor becomes the chairperson of the Deacon Board; the maid becomes the president of the Stewardess Board. . . Everybody becomes Mr. and Mrs., or Brother and Sister. The last becomes first, making a radical change in the perception of self and one's calling in the society. Every person becomes somebody. . .[33]

If the Church truly refused to tolerate the accepted social and political principles based on Old Age distinctions, all Christians would meet united as brothers and sisters, worshipping one Lord. Within the Church there would be no relation of master and slave, rich and poor, king and subject. Whether or not Paul allowed active resistance against the state requires further study; nevertheless, we can claim that *at least* this much is required. The Church will recognize no Old Age distinctions in rank, wealth, race, social position or caste. Such refusal would in itself be subversive activity against the powers and principalities.

If, however, we begin to speak about the conflict between the Old Age and the New Age, or God's invasion into the world which creates a new space in which we live, does it follow that all who do not recognize the lordship of Christ are condemned by Christ? Some people are rightly fearful that the war imagery essential to apocalyptic thinking will lead to the image of 'Christian soldiers marching off to war' and proclaiming: 'If you refuse to live within this new space created by Christ we will destroy you, or at least we will pronounce you eternally damned'. Does apocalyptic by definition lead to the mentality of the Crusades?

By no means! If Christ is the defender of life, how can we possibly believe that we are called upon to pronounce death and damnation?[34] Our apocalyptic vocation does not lead us to say: 'If you refuse to live in this space we will destroy you in the name of Christ', but rather: 'We will struggle to defy the powers of darkness that seek to destroy and oppress, no matter who the victim is'. According to Lou Martyn, God is 'the Passionate Advocate' of each one of us, and it is this God who calls us 'to fight the only good fight in the world'.[35] The battle is not one of Christians against non-Christians. We struggle on behalf of those who are perishing at the hands of the powers and principalities, no matter who those persons might be.

3. *Imminent Parousia*

It is this third characteristic of Pauline apocalyptic—the expectation of an imminent parousia—that we would most expect to hear about in a lecture on apocalyptic. However ambiguous the term 'apocalyptic' is, the expectation of the end of the world has long been associated with it and even classified as its key characteristic.

While the expectation of the imminent end of the world may be apocalyptic, it is not without qualification Pauline, that is to say, Christian apocalyptic. Apocalyptic expectation is used in the secular and the pseudo-Christian realm to refer exclusively to the destruction of the world. Thus, the movie 'Apocalypse Now' portrays the apocalyptic end of the civilized world in the context of the atrocities of war. In like manner apocalyptic passages in the Bible are often equated with the threat of nuclear destruction. The use of the word 'apocalypse' or 'apocalyptic' in these instances carries the message that the end of the world is imminent and that the revelation regarding the end is clearly given to all who have eyes to see. These passages, however, cannot be equated with Pauline apocalyptic, for they are utterly divorced from the proclamation of Christ's death, resurrection, and future advent.

While Paul clearly expects an imminent parousia (1 Thess. 4.13–5.10; 1 Cor. 15.24), at no point in Paul's thought can we find the expectation of the end divorced from the destiny of Jesus Christ. Unlike these other apocalyptic expectations, Paul regards the end of the ages not with despair but with hope. For that reason, we can never equate the apocalyptic passages in the Bible with the threat of nuclear war or with any human destruction of creation. For Paul, the imminent parousia is not brought on by human foolishness or error but is determined solely by God.

How, though, do we deal with the fact that the end of the ages did not occur according to expectations? The ongoing experience of time and history probably serves as a stronger hindrance to the appropriation of apocalyptic thought than any other problem we might have with the concept. How can we possibly take seriously Paul's admonition to 'stay awake' and to be alert with anticipation when 1900 years have passed since Paul spoke them?

The most popular solution to this dilemma comes from Bultmann's proposal for 'demythologizing'. We can reinterpret Paul's mythological understanding of the parousia by moving its reference from the cosmic to the internal, existential realm. While the Kingdom of God did not occur in history, it can be encountered in each successive moment by the individual who is to remain always open to the promises of God. In similar fashion we can admit that while Paul was wrong about the approaching parousia, we encounter the truth behind his expectation when we contemplate our own impending death. The threat of individual death serves, so it is claimed, the same purpose as Paul's expectation of the imminent Day of the Lord. Our death calls each of us to be decisive and repentant in the present while God promises us future glory in our own resurrection to the next world.

The problem with such interpretations is that they undercut the *cosmic* force of the gospel Paul preaches. Paul was indeed mistaken about the nearness of the end, but Paul himself said that we cannot know the time or the season (1 Thess. 5.1-2). The ethical significance of the second advent of Christ is not destroyed by its delay. We can in fact identify at least two major consequences of the expectation of the second advent for theological ethics.

First, the significance of Paul's image of the Second Coming lies in our inheritance of an ethic of hope. Hope, not guilt or fear, defines who we are and what we are to do. The promise held out by the second advent of Christ is, in the words of Rubem Alves, that the 'overwhelming brutality of facts that oppress' us in this present age does not have the last word, has not said all there is to say.[36] Hope reminds us that although we know the darkness of this evil age, we are not *of* the darkness. Living in the present we, nevertheless, live as children of tomorrow, i.e. children of hope. Our lives are now bound up with the destiny of Jesus Christ. That does not mean that we do not have to worry about the future because God is in charge of it. Because we have hope in the promises of God's future which is transfiguring the present age, we 'give an account of the hope that is in us' by what we do.[37]

One does not, therefore, motivate Christians to action by activating guilt. While confession of guilt is required for true repentance, guilt itself cripples rather than liberates one to action. One also does not motivate Christians to action by activating fear. Constant fear that God's grace will be snatched from us if we do not fulfill the right conditions turns the Gospel into a burden. Those who interpret the apocalyptic images of the imminent parousia as the individual's salvation into heaven have also missed the point. Neither the fear of losing the heavenly life nor the hope of achieving it motivate Christian action. The heavenly life is our given. The context in which we 'live and move and have our being' is one which acknowledges the reality of Christ's ultimate victory over the powers and principalities.[38]

Second, the significance of Paul's image of the Second Coming lies in a reinterpretation of the *imitatio Christi*, the imitation of Christ. This interpretation begins with the understanding that Pauline ethics is not based on a Platonic ideal by which everything else is judged. Human behavior, according to Paul, is not judged by some perfect image that stands above us, out of reach. Rather, human action is defined by a power that draws us into its realm. Therefore, as Paul Lehmann reminds us 'behavior is ethically defined not by perfections but by parabolic power'. Our behavior becomes a 'fragmentary foretaste' and living parable of the 'fulfillment which is alrady on its way'.[39] The promise of the Second Coming calls us to signify our hope by our behavior. This behavior, however, signifies not only our individual hope for salvation, but hope for the world. As we have 'groaned with the whole creation which has been subjected to futility' our actions are to signify the fact that 'the creation itself will be set free from its bondage to decay and obtain the glorious liberty of the children of God' (Rom. 8.21). We cannot simply advocate a private ethic that emphasizes only personal salvation. Pauline apocalyptic leads us to an ethic of solidarity with all creation and humankind. Hence, Pauline apocalyptic pushes us to redefine the traditional interpretation of the imitation of Christ.

We do not imitate Christ by basing our actions on the teachings of Jesus that have been abstracted from the biblical story of God's dealing with the world in Jesus Christ. In other words we cannot formulate universal ethical principles or ideals by which we regulate human behavior. Christ is not a static ideal or principle. Christ is the living Lord who draws us into a new orbit of power. In Paul's perception of the powers that vie for lordship over the world, the

Law has become impotent before the power of sin and death. It is the Spirit of Christ, not the Law, which breaks the power of sin.

From Paul's apocalyptic theology we understand that to imitate Christ means to become a living parable of God's action on behalf of creation. All human action symbolizes the One we recognize as the Lord of the world. As Käsemann reminded us, each life 'mirrors the cosmic contention for the lordship of the world'.[40]

Given the conflict now raging between the Old Age and the New Age we must confess that our actions are often parables signifying our recognition of the lordship of the powers and principalities of the Old Age. We often act in recognition of the Old Age distinctions between slave and free such as we find in South Africa, as well as in our own segregated schools, neighborhoods, places of work, and places of worship. We often act in recognition of the Old Age distinctions between male and female such as we find in churches which refuse to value the ministry of women. In such ways as these we signify that the lords of our existence are the Old Age powers and principalities.

Our actions, however, can become parables signifying the lordship of Christ. This means, on the one hand, that we recognize that the New Age is not fully consummated and so we act in solidarity with the groaning creation, 'weeping with those who weep'. We can stand with those whose lives are threatened and devastated by the powers of death. This means, on the other hand, that our actions can signify the New Age that has been inaugurated by Christ. Refusing to live by Old Age distinctions, refusing to recognize the legitimacy of the powers that oppress and destroy, we given an account of the hope that comes to us from the future.

Rubem Alves describes this parabolic character of Christian behavior:

> Living is like dancing. As you dance you move your body according to a rhythm and a harmony which fill the space. The complexity of our human predicament is due to the fact that a number of conflicting rhythms and harmonies are being played at the same time... You may dance the tune played by the present reality. Your style of life will be realistic and pragmatic. Or you may choose to move your body under the spell of a mysterious tune and rhythm which come from a world we do not fully see, the world of our hopes and apsirations. *Hope is hearing the melody of the future. Faith is to dance it.* You risk your life, and you take your risk to its

ultimate conclusion, even the cross, because you detect a strange odor of death mixed with the fascinating music of Mephisto, lord of the 'present evil world'. The rhythms of the future, on the other hand, contain promises of freedom, love and life.[41]

With Rubem Alves, J. Louis Martyn, and the apostle Paul we can proclaim that it is worth the risk to dance to such a tune.

NOTES

1. *The Didache*. Reprinted in *Christian Ethics: Sources of the Living Tradition* (ed. Waldo Beach and H. Richard Niebuhr; New York: Ronald Press, 1973), p. 58.

2. See Phil. 2.12.

3. The reference here is to Augustine's victory in debate with Pelagius. 'Orthodoxy' is, however, a very slippery word. Many Christian traditions would claim the affirmation of free will as the 'orthodox' doctrine.

4. J. Louis Martyn, 'From Paul to Flannery O'Connor With the Power of Grace', *Katallagete* 7.4 (Winter, 1981), p. 15.

5. According to Lou Martyn, the Gospel is not 'a matter of opening up new possibilities for human beings, so that humanity is encouraged, as we say, to 'realize their potentials'. In the apocalyptic war as Paul sees it, the focus is not on options and possibilities. Rather, as in all wars, the focus is on power, and in the first instance the power question is posed because, as we have seen, the coming of Christ, the apocalypse of Christ, is the powerful invasion of Christ' ('From Paul to Flannery O'Connor', p. 12).

6. J. Louis Martyn, 'From Paul to Flannery O'Connor with the Power of Grace', p. 11.

7. In defining Pauline apocalyptic one must keep in mind that Paul's theology does not agree in every respect with the theology found in the apocalyptic literature of his day. As Leander Keck ('Paul and Apocalyptic Theology', *Int* 38/3 [July, 1984], p. 231) claims, Paul 'rethought everything in light of Christ's death and resurrection'. Therefore, 'if we find apocalyptic theology in Paul, it will have been transformed'.

8. Ernst Käsemann, 'On the Subject of Primitive Christian Apocalyptic', in *New Testament Questions of Today* (Philadelphia: Fortress Press, 1969), p. 109.

9. Vincent Branick ('Apocalyptic Paul?', *CBQ* 47 [1985], p. 666) gives supporting evidence that Paul believed that the end time had already begun by telling us that 'Paul differs from traditional apocalyptic. . . in his faith that the end time has begun with the resurrection of Christ. Christ's resurrection for Paul is above all 'the first fruits' of the general resurrection (1 Cor. 15.20).

The Spirit already given is the 'down payment' of eschatological blessings (2 Cor. 1.22). Paul's apocalyptic, therefore, exhibits the paradoxical tension of the 'already' and the 'not yet.' Existence according to the Spirit takes place fully only at the resurrection (1 Cor. 15.42-44), yet the resurrection of Christ has already taken place.'

10. Martyn, 'From Paul to Flannery O'Connor', p. 11.

11. See also 1 Cor. 1.28-29.

12. This understanding of revelation has been suggested to me by both Christopher Morse and Paul Lehmann. See Christopher L. Morse, *The Logic of Promise in Moltmann's Theology* (Philadelphia: Fortress, 1979) and Paul Lehmann, *The Transfiguration of Politics: The Presence and Power of Jesus of Nazareth in and over Human Affairs* (New York: Harper & Row, 1975).

13. Two presuppositions of my position regarding Christian ethics should be mentioned briefly. First, in order for ethics to be Christian ethics it must have its basis in the Bible. Therefore, my understanding of the significance of apocalyptic for theological ethics is based on an interpretation of scripture, particularly an interpretation of the apostle Paul. My second presupposition is that ethics as a discipline of the Church is always related to Christian doctrine. Although apocalyptic is not a doctrine, its implications are initially for systematic theology and only then for theological ethics. Putting these two presuppositions together it should become clear that in my understanding Christian ethics is a derivative discipline with its foundation in biblical studies and its immediate context in systematic theology. I am grateful to Lou Martyn for furthering my understanding of this relationship.

14. Ernst Käsemann, 'Primitive Christian Apocalyptic', pp. 135-36.

15. Martyn, 'From Paul to Flannery O'Connor', p. 15.

16. According to Käsemann, 'man for Paul is never just on his own. He is always a specific piece of world and therefore becomes what in the last resort he is by determination from outside, i.e., by the power which takes possession of him and the lordship to which he surrenders himself. His life is from the beginning a stake in the confrontation between God and the principalities of this world. In other words, it mirrors the cosmic contention for the lordship of the world and is its concretion' ('Primitive Christian Apocalyptic', p. 136).

17. Günther Bornkamm, *Paul* (New York: Harper & Row, 1971), p. 133.

18. Approaching the question of responsibility by asking 'What makes us able to respond?' was suggested by Christopher L. Morse, Union Theological Seminary, New York.

19. This claim is consistent with Karl Barth's and Paul Lehmann's understanding that ethics begins with 'divine praxis' (Barth) and 'the political character of divine activity' (Lehmann), not with an independent search for the good. See Karl Barth, *Church Dogmatics*, Vol. II 2: *The*

Doctrine of God (Edinburgh: T. & T. Clark, 1957); Paul Lehmann, *Ethics in a Christian Context* (New York: Harper & Row, 1963).

20. The German *swastika* was a Greek cross which meant peace and prosperity.

21. W.A. Visser t'Hooft, *The Kingship of Christ* (New York: Harper & Row, 1948), pp. 19 and 20. Quoted in Paul Lehmann, *Ethics in a Christian Context* (New York: Harper & Row, 1963), pp. 115-16.

22. Lehmann, *Ethics*, p. 117.

23. The use of the image of 'new space' to describe this aspect of Paul's thought comes from Professor Martyn.

24. J. Louis Martyn, 'Apocalyptic Antinomies in Paul's Letter to the Galatians', *NTS* 31 (1985), p. 415.

25. Paul Lehmann, *Transfiguration of Politics* (New York: Harper & Row, 1975). According to Lehmann 'transfiguration means the ingression of "things that are not" into the "things that are," so that man may come abreast of God's next move in giving human shape to human life' (p. 76). The turning of the ages does not simply mean that the world will be experienced or perceived differently, though it certainly does mean that. More importantly, it means that history, nature, society, culture and humanity 'will not be as before'. There is, according to Lehmann, an ontological shifting of the structures that make up the world. Jesus Christ's presence in the human story means that things will never be the same again.

26. Martyn, 'Epistemology at the Turn of the Ages', p. 279.

27. *Ibid.*, p. 285.

28. Martyn, 'From Paul to Flannery O'Connor', p. 12.

29. *Ibid.*, p. 10.

30. J. Christiaan Beker, *Paul the Apostle: The Triumph of God in Life and Thought* (Philadelphia: Fortress, 1980), p. 326.

31. James Theodore Holly, 'Musings On the Kingdom of Christ: First Paper', *The Anglo-African Magazine* II/2 (February, 1860) and 'Musings On the Kingdom of Christ: Second Paper', *Anglo-African Magazine* II/3 (March, 1860).

32. James Cone, 'Sanctification, Liberation, and Black Worship', *Theology Today* 35 (1978-79), pp. 139-52. This article was first brought to my attention by Geoffrey Wainwright, *Doxology: The Praise of God in Worship, Doctrine, and Life* (New York: Oxford University Press, 1980), pp. 418-19 n. 1018.

33. *Ibid.*, p. 140.

34. James Cone, *God of the Oppressed* (New York: The Seabury Press, 1975), p. 104.

35. Martyn, 'From Paul to Flannery O'Connor', p. 17.

36. Rubem Alves, *Tomorrow's Child: Imagination, Creativity, and the Rebirth of Culture* (New York: Harper & Row, 1972), p. 194.

37. See 1 Pet. 3.15. Christopher Morse has brought the significance of this passage to my attention.

38. The reference is to Acts 17.28.

39. Paul Lehmann, *Ethics*, p. 122.

40. Käsemann, 'Primitive Christian Apocalyptic', p. 133. See note 16 of this paper.

41. Rubem Alves, *Tomorrow's Child*, pp. 195-96.

BARMEN AND THE CHURCH'S CALL
TO FAITHFULNESS AND SOCIAL RESPONSIBILITY

Paul Lehmann

This chapter is adapted from an address that was delivered at the opening session of the International Symposium in Commemoration of the Fiftieth Anniversary of the Theological Declaration of Barmen, 29-31 May 1934, at the Graduate School of Public Affairs, University of Washington, Seattle, Washington, 25-29 April 1984.* It relates to the topic 'apocalyptic and the New Testament' because its central concern is the church's apocalyptic vision of the world as *theatrum Dei gloriae*, and its consquent call to be the church in the world for the sake of the world.

I wish to dedicate the written form of this address to J. Louis Martyn, a friend of many years, a sharer in the church's apocalyptic vision, and a person from whom I have learned much about the New Testament expressions of that vision. I am especially grateful to him for the help he has given me in understanding Paul's use of the term *stoicheia tou kosmou*, upon which I comment in what follows.

1. *Of Faithfulness, Responsibility and the Confessional State of the Church*

The confessional state of the church and the church *in statu confessionis* are interrelated but not identical ways of taking responsibility for the faithfulness of the church to what the church is called to be, to believe, to think about, and to do in the world. The confessional state of the church may be recognized by the church's seriousness about, acceptance of, and obedience to the confessional statements, which ever and again take form and utterance in the course of the church's response to its calling to faithfulness and responsibility. The confessional statements of the church express the faith, authority, meaning and nurture by which the church lives and bears witness in word and action in the world to what God has purposed the church and the world to be. These statements summarily formulate, inform and guide what it means to belong to Jesus Christ. Accordingly, the confessional state of the church is the sign and seal of the church's *faithfulness* to the fact that the church has been called into existence in the world by Jesus Christ for the sake of the world.

The church *in statu confessionis*, on the other hand, is the church in the act of stating and doing what it means to belong to the church of Jesus Christ in the world—on the critical boundary on which the presence and purposes of the church in and for the world and the cross-purposes of the world not only co-exist but intersect. These cross-purposes not only disregard and endanger the witness and life of the church in the world. They also disregard and endanger the meaning and purpose of the world and of living meaningfully in it. Accordingly, the church *in statu confessionis* is the sign and seal of the *responsibility* intrinsic to the church's faithfulness to the fact that the church has been called into the world by Jesus Christ for the sake of the world, and not only for the sake of the church. Responsibility for the faithfulness of the church to its calling to be in the world for the sake of the world and faithfulness to the confessional integrity of the church's presence and purpose in the world are, thus, correlative but not identical marks of the church's confessional situation.

A major—if not *the* major—significance of *The Theological Declaration of Barmen* is its documentation of the church on the way from confessional faithfulness to confessional responsibility. On the record, it seems that the confessional story—from Nicea, Chalcedon and the *Symbolum Romanum* to Trent; and from Trent, via Augsburg and the Formula of Concord, on the one hand, and the Geneva, Scots and Westminster Confessions, on the other, to the Catechisms: Roman, Lutheran and Reformed, and the unexcelled irenic tonalities of Heidelberg—seems more pre-occupied with the responsibility of the faithfulness of the church to its calling to be the church than with the faithfulness of the church to the responsibility intrinsic to being the church in the world for the sake of the world. The watchwords of responsibility for faithfulness have been the formative and authoritative bearing of Holy Scripture upon the content and witness of the Confessions, the proclamation of the Word and the celebration of the Sacraments, the grace, faith and obedience by which individual believers receive and express their salvation in this world and the next. The world—for the sake of which the church is called to be the church—was largely left to its own devices, under the custodial watchfulness of a power settlement which neatly, if not always smoothly, divided responsibility between things spiritual and things temporal. This arrangement, dubiously ascribed to divine appointment, managed, with less than unexceptional operational effectiveness, to keep the world in tow and on course until the unfailingly anticipated Second Advent, which seemed to have fallen into the awkward habit of continual postponement.

Meanwhile, faithfulness to the responsibility intrinsic to being the church in the world for the sake of the world seems to have been reserved—at least, confessionally—to that strange assortment of communities and pieties identified by Ernst Troeltsch as 'the sect type' and as 'mysticism'; and among whom may be counted Baptists and Methodists, Mennonites, Moravians and Quakers, and their precursors, the Waldensians and the Czech Brethren.[1] Here too, responsibility for the world fell more than short of Calvin's daring and still inadequately appropriated vision of a '*theatrum Dei gloriae*'.[2] The practice of this responsibility was carefully restricted and restrained. Troeltsch calls it 'Ascetic Protestantism'; and compares it favorably with medieval Catholicism. An instructive passage, two-thirds of the way through the second volume of *The Social Teaching of the Christian Churches*, is worth noting in the context of this Symposium Commemoration because of its succinct account of the dialectics and the dynamics of the church's responsibility in the world for the world. Indeed, it is not too much to regard this account as a formulation of the occasion for and the pertinence of the Barmen Declaration.

> The great problem of Christian supernaturalism,—that of uniting and adapting itself to the practical life of society—was solved . . . in Catholicism, by means of a universal Church, which regulates, supervises, and finally itself effects the ascent of Nature to Grace; in ascetic Protestantism, by a highly individualistic congregational system which was in harmony with modern individualism, and through the ascetic self-control of individuals who reduce the whole of secular and social life to the level of a mere method of glorifying God and proving the state of grace. Thus there are certain points of contact between the two systems, since both express the Christian hostility to the world in a systematic discipline and in asceticism.

The ideal of the radical sects, on the contrary, was never developed out of the purely inward dialectic of Christian thought. In its primitive form, Christian thought left all such matters too much to a future which was to be brought about by God, ... and it left all details in God's Hands, and not to the consideration and organization of man. After the Christian faith had adjusted itself to the present world and had become a Church, *the expectation of a complete world-renewal could only be introduced into Christianity from outside through the pressure of intolerable conditions;* and, somehow or other, that inevitably implied human thought and human organization. *Particularly threatening social and political conditions were then held to be signs of world-renewals which were about to come,* as a challenge to prepare the way of the Lord for the Kingdom of God; *it was a mingled attitude of believing expectation of the Kingdom, and an actual effort to cause new conditions.*[3]

Troeltsch goes on to point out that 'Christianity does not breed social revolution'. It aims rather to adjust itself to 'the modern social revolution' which recognizes that 'spiritual values are intimately connected with the material social basis of life' and that this connection 'must always be stressed very strongly, if it is to lead to a thorough social reform, or even to the revolution of Society'. Nevertheless, 'the social influence of Ascetic Protestantism upon the history of civilization has been penetrating and comprehensive'.[4]

Which brings us to the pertinence and the dialectics of *The Theological Declaration of Barmen.* We commemorate this Declaration—sooner rather than later in and for our time—in faithfulness and thankfulness for Barmen, which barely made it—in its time—in time.

I am indebted to Eberhard Bethge for drawing my attention to two current German reflections upon Barmen which tend to affirm the move from faithfulness to responsibility; and at the same time, to invite a warning. Christoph Barth's informative paperback bears the title: 'Confession in the Making', and gives some account of newly found sources of the emergence of the Barmen Declaration. Some of these sources had long been known but were missing. Others however, are a notable tribute to the prescience of a sixteen-year-old son who rescued them from his father's waste basket, carefully preserved them, only later to discover their significance, and to regret that he had neglected to record the precise date in May of 1934 on which he had retrieved them from permanent oblivion.[5] A companion paperback undertakes to provide an introduction and interpretation of Barmen for contemporary readers, and includes a particularly valuable appendix, in which the unfolding form of the six Barmen Theses is carefully set down.[6]

Of particular pertinence to the present discussion, however, is the circumstance that each of these recent interpretations hints at the question of responsibility for faithfulness to the church's calling to be the church in and for the world. The more recent of the two little books expressly uses the word, *responsibility*, in praise of the Barmen Declaration. The Foreword by Bishop Edward Lohse declares that 'through the strength and clarity of its language, the Theological Declaration of Barmen understands exactly what is involved by making clear the decisive bases (*Grundlagen*) of our faith in a particular situation. We can all learn from this achievement—and the texts of Barmen still help us today to take positions on the many questions of our time because of our Christian responsibility' (BWL, p. 6; translation mine).

Christoph Barth, on the other hand, is at once implicit about the word, *responsibility*, and explicit about what the responsibility is. About this responsibility, there was an intense struggle. Alluding to a radio interview of Karl Barth, on 9 May 1966, in which Barth used the phrase 'political undertone' with reference to Barmen, Christoph Barth notes, with respect to Thesis 4, that the tensions over this 'political undertone' were directed more against the substance of the paragraph than against its actual formulation (CB, pp. 34-35). At issue was the language of the '*damnamus* clause'. Two earlier drafts (Bonn, 13.5.34; and Frankfurt, three days later) declared that: 'We reject the falsehood, as though the church apart from this ministry (i.e. the church's own scripturally warranted ministry), could and were permitted to give or allow itself to be given particular 'leaders' in accordance with the example of the state today' (CB, pp. 34-35; parentheses added). The final draft deleted the quotation marks surrounding the word, 'leaders'; deleted the reference to the state and substituted the phrase: 'special leaders vested with ruling powers' (Barmen, 30.5.34). The Lutherans found the deletion to involve no great matter. The Calvinists in part, and others, also in part, were troubled by the ambiguity of the reference to the state, as though the thrust were against the political authorities rather than the church government of the German Christians. Still others felt that the rejection of the state wavered between theological and secular meanings (CB, p. 34). If Christoph Barth is correct, the adopted text as amended still echoed the 'political undertone', so that its adoption may still be regarded as 'an astonishing fact' (CB, p. 35; translation mine). As Troeltsch had almost clairvoyantly discerned, in the instructive passage already cited: 'After the Christian faith had adjusted itself to the present world and had become a Church, the expectation of a complete world-renewal could only be introduced into Christianity from the outside through the pressure of intolerable conditions. . .'[7]

That was, of course, two decades and three years before Barmen (i.e. 1911). But reflecting upon Barmen in the light of Troeltsch's assessment, and upon Troeltsch in the light of Barmen, a haunting line from a widely received play by Tom Stoppard, acclaimed in the United States three decades after Barmen (1967), kept inserting itself into this context. Stoppard's play is called, 'Rosenkrantz and Guildenstern Are Dead'. It concerns the struggles, tensions and musings of Hamlet's two University friends—for Shakespeare as for Stoppard, more than coincidentally German. Towards the end of the play, these friends find themselves en route to England bearing letters to the King which, unknown to them, order their execution upon arrival, as traitors to the Danish realm. Musing over their strange odyssey—'from their calling to their destiny'[8]—Guildenstern wistfully remarks to his companion, Rosenkrantz: 'There must have been a moment, at the beginning, when we could have said—"No!" But somehow we missed it'.[9] But 'the gate is wide and the way is easy that leads to destruction, and those who enter by it are many. For the gate is narrow and the way is hard that leads to life, and those who find it are few' (Mt. 7.13-14).

The move from confessional faithfulness to confessional responsibility is a move which draws the confessional state of the church across the boundary which summons the church to a state of confession (*status confessionis*). As regards the *Theological Declaration of Barmen*, the dialectics and dynamics of this move inevitably put Thesis 1 and Theses 4–6 either in complementarity or in contradiction. The critical issue was and is: whether the unmistakeable and inviolable *solus Christus* of Thesis 1, is confined *to* and confined *by* the *sola gratia: sola fide* affirmations and rejections of Theses 2 and 3; or whether the *solus Christus* of Barmen 1 inexorably and insistently draws the *sola gratia: sola fide* toward and into the tensions, turmoil and risks of Barmen 4-6. These Theses, especially 4 and 5, are the 'sticky wickets' of the Barmen Declaration—then and now. For they involve the ministry of Word and Sacrament (4) and the unity of believers (6) *expressis verbis* in the question: whose task it is to take up the task of safeguarding and furthering justice and peace? Thesis 5 declares:

> 'Fear God, Honor the Emperor' (1 Pet. 2.17). Scripture tells us that, in an as yet unredeemed world in which the Church also exists, the State has by divine appointment *the task of providing for justice and peace*. (It fulfills this task) by means of the threat and exercise of force, according to the measure of human judgment and human possibility. In gratitude and reverence before God, the Church acknowledges the benevolence (*Wohltat*) of this divine *ordination* (*Anordnung*). The Church calls to mind God's Kingdom, Command and Righteousness, and thereby the responsibility both of rulers and of the ruled. It trusts and obeys the power of the Word by which God upholds all things.
>
> We reject, the false doctrine, as though the State, over and beyond its special commission, should and could become the single and totalitarian order of human life, thus fulfilling the Church's vocation as well.
>
> We reject the false doctrine, as though the Church, over and beyond its special commission, should and could appropriate the characteristics, the tasks, and the dignity of the State, thus itself becoming an organ of the State'.[10]

The question which Thesis 5 urgently presses upon us now is this: Is the *solus Christus* to be understood, accepted, interpreted and implemented as forging a link between *sola gratia: sola fide* and *sola iustitiaque pace*, or is it not? If 'yes'—the *confitemur* and the *damnamus* clauses of Thesis 5 are congruent; and the 'No!' of Barmen 5 signals an unequivocal calling of the church to faithfulness and reponsibility by calling into question both itself and the state, under which and against which, the church is called to be the church in the world for the sake of the world. If the answer is 'No', the *confitemur* and the *damnamus* clauses of Barmen 5 are at best asymmetrical, at worst, euphoric. Their sequence fails of the faithfulness and responsibility in the freedom of which the church is called and empowered to call into question both itself and the state.

The 'No!' of Barmen 5 is, then, at cross-purposes with itself because the 'Yes!', which occasions, guides and sustains that 'No!', has been 'bound in shallows and in miseries'.[11] Over the 'No!' *of* Barmen 5, there looms the prospect of an emerging 'No!' *to* Barmen 5. That the unequivocal 'No!' *of* Barmen 5 was the intention of the Declaration and of the Synod which adopted it, is confirmed by the concluding Thesis 6, which expressly grounds the church's freedom in its calling.[12]

'There must have been a moment at the beginning, when we could have said—"No!"'. But somehow we missed it'. The *solus Christus*, distinct, but inseparable from, and incessantly conjoining the *sola gratia* with the *iustitiaque pace*, is the 'Yes!' which called the Confessional Synod of the German Evangelical Church, assembled at Barmen, 29-31 May 1934, to say the 'No!', sustained, guided and nurtured by that 'Yes!'. If Barmen did not miss *that* moment to say, 'No!', will we, following after, seize it, or somehow miss it?

At least among us here in the United States, in the church and in the world, there are those increasingly vocal ones who give lip service to the dialectic and dynamics of the church's calling to faithfulness and responsibility, while displacing it with a logamachy of 'Yes!' and 'No!' of their own contrivance. Like those in the church in Sardis, they 'have the name of being alive, and, are dead' (Rev. 3.1). Like those in their sister church in Laodicea, their works are known as 'neither cold nor hot! So, because (they) are neither cold nor hot', they will be spewed out of the mouth. 'For (they) say, I am rich, I have prospered, and I need nothing; not knowing that (they) are wretched, pitiable, poor, blind, and naked' (Rev. 3.15-17; adapted). The record is that they have their reward. They will continue to confuse self-justification with justification by faith, the 'view from above' with the 'view from below', and self-righteousness with the righteousness of faith. But if we have seized the moment from Barmen for our present times, we shall be open to the *solus Christus* and its liberating and fulfilling conjunction of the *sola gratia: sola fide* with the *iustitiaque pace*. In and through that openness, we shall be alert to a *damnamus* of the unholy and inhumane collusion of Presbyterian passions and plans for a second 'Great Awakening' in January 1985, to the emerging training operations for incipient 'German Christians', American-style, in centers of theological inquiry and institutes for religion and democracy, complete with

Manichean mind-sets, with assets tax-sheltered in Caribbean sunlight, or in the darkness of the CIA, and theological gurus, preoccupied with the move from nature to grace as the frontier on which 'the foundations of theological and scientific knowledge, the origins and growth of specific faith traditions, and historical and contemporary manifestations of the religious consciousness' are to be advanced.[13] Under the guise of 'creation science and faith', these pre-occupations commend themselves—ostrich-like, as 'safety nets' of advance—in astonishing disregard of the technology of communications, which a recent issue of the *Harvard Alumni Magazine* headlines with the lead: 'He's Got the Whole Wired World in His Hands'. 'He' is not God, of course, but a brilliant Professor of Information Technology in Harvard University.[14] There are also quasi-theological gurus who specialize in rumors of angels and in whisperings of transcendence, and who bewitch the contemporary descendants of the churches in Sardis and Laodicea with sophisticated sociological wisdom. This wisdom, born of a disillusionment with the ineptitude, weakness and collapse of the Weimar Republic, offers the dubious promise of the human prospect of a politics which never makes a political move without a demonstrable policy alternative.[15] It is as though the canon of Scripture, which warrants, informs and guides the calling of the church to faithfulness and responsibility, had been excised of Lot's wife, of Amos and Jeremiah, of the Kingdom Parables, of the Transfiguration, and of the seventh angel (Rev. 10.7) and made no mention of those passages upon which the six theses of the Barmen Declaration drew.[16] 'There must have been a moment, at the beginning, when we could have said—"No!". But somehow we missed it.' Whether we have or not may be tested now—as then—by the fact and the integrity of the move from the confessional state of the church to the church in a state of confession (*in statu confessionis.*

2. *The Power of Justice and the Justice of Power*

The church on the move from confessional faithfulness to confessional responsibility intrinsically and inevitably converges upon the power of justice and the justice of power. Justice—as Professor Dorothy Soelle explains—is 'the true name of peace'. Meanwhile, our own concentration upon the relation between justice and power may be aided by a semantic clarification.

As regards the meaning and praxis of justice, a distinction must be made between the prophets of Israel and Jesus, on the one hand; and Cicero, on the other. For Cicero, whose definition of justice permeated the canon law of the church, as well as the jurisprudence of western culture, taught that justice is the recognition and application of the principle of the *suum cuique* (to each his own) in the relations between individuals as citizens and among states. This Ciceronian view has undergone a brilliant re-examination and amplification by Professor John Rawls of Harvard University.[17] In his widely discussed book *A Theory of Justice*, Rawls endeavors to explore anew the conception of 'Justice as Fairness', and to show how this conception applies to 'the basic structure of society' (p. 61). Justice, understood as fairness, moves the interpretation and practice of justice beyond arbitrariness and relativism. Understood as fairness, justice frees us from preoccupation with such abstractions as virtue, equality, liberty, right; and from utilitarian attempts to give concrete significance to these aspects of justice on the basis of the social contract (Locke, Rousseau, Kant; Preface). In short, justice as fairness is rescued from both utilitarianism and intuitionism (ch. 1). For Rawls, the key to a rational interpretation and validation of justice is provided by 'an original position'. This position is that conception of justice which 'rational persons in the initial situation would choose ... '. Thus, the theory of justice and the theory of rational choice are connected.[17]

Winsome, cogent and influential as this understanding of justice is;—it is, at best, tangential to what the prophets of Israel and Jesus had on their minds when they put forward *righteousness* as the test case of the obedience of faith and the key to power at the service of responsibility. In the context of the Scriptures, righteousness and justice are interchangeable words. Either word points to and points up God's way of being true to the purposes for which human life and human living in this world were covenanted. This *righteousness* or *justice* is—in word and deed—the making room in the world for the faithfulness of God in being present to and in the midst of human life as help and salvation. The righteousness of God so practiced is the power of justice to initiate and to give effect to the justice of power which is the taking of responsibility for setting right what is not right in the world. Thus, justice is the critical link between power and responsibility because justice is the righteousness of God in action displacing self-justification by the responsive discernment of the neighbor's good, enmity by reconciliation, and oppression by the freedom which being human takes. The praxis of justice exposes the human reality of enmity as the concrete point of entry for the primacy of responsibility for the healing of human alienation, so that caring may take priority over competition, trust take priority over domination in human relations and interrelations, and covenant displace contract as the foundation, bond, and promise of human society. To adapt Immanuel Kant's familiar and illuminating aphorism: Responsibility without power is empty; power without responsibility is blind.[18] In a covenantal society, anchored in a covenanted world, the justice of power is its commitment and power to effect the power of justice to make room for and to further what God is doing in the world to make and to keep human life human.

3. *Faithfulness, Responsibility and Resistance*

Resistance is the *ultima ratio* of the church's call to faithfulness and responsibility in which justice is the cutting edge of the relation between power and responsibility. Resistance is the *actualization—* not the *negation—*of the faithfulness and responsibility of the church called to take responsibility for power in the world for the sake of which the church is *there*. To put it another way—in remembrance of *The Theological Declaration of Barmen—*we could say that resistance is the obedient conjunction of the *confitemur* and the *damnamus* dimensions of the obedience of faith. In consequence of this conjunction, a saving distinction between confession and ratification is exposed and resistance becomes the threshold of justice in putting power at the service of responsibility. At stake is the witness in word and deed to the intrinsic link between the *solus Christus: sola gratia: sola fide* and the *justitiaque pace*. So we come in conclusion to a brief indication of the difference between ratification and resistance as modes of confessional faithfulness and responsibility.

A. *Ratification*

Turning first to ratification, let me note that ratification is the unreadiness or unwillingness to say, 'No!', on the part of a church, deprived by its calling of the possibility of being in the world *for the sake of the church*, and called instead to be a church and ministry *in* the world *for the sake of the world*. Ratification is the nurture of the obedience of faith in the unrecognized disobedience of taking it for granted that being on the Lord's side is a foolproof guarantee that the Lord is on the side of those who 'say or meditate or do' (Calvin), as though they were on His. Ratification is the defensive surprise that erupts in the midst of the household of faith when the beliefs, commitments, values and ways of being in church and ministry in the world for the sake of the church are called into question by the calling of the church to be in the world for the sake of the world, and not for the sake of the church. *Ratification* is the pattern of thought and life and judgment in church and ministry which basically affirms the prevailing patterns of thought and life and value in the world as congruent with the obedience of faith; which calls the world into question without calling into question the obedience of the church; which nurtures the pious complacency which practices the tithing of mint and dill and cummin while neglecting the weightier matters of the law: justice and mercy and faith (Mt. 23.23; Lk. 11.42); which sanctifies the world in sanctifying the church. In short, *ratification* is the cultivation in church and ministry of the self-justifying surprise at being found by the Lord of the church as being goats and not sheep (Mt. 25.44).

I venture to think that each of us could readily draw up his or her own list of ratification items. Let me, however, note for the present purpose two instances. One points to and points up the world in the church; the other, the church in the world. The first indicates the accommodation of the church *to* the world; the second indicates the co-optation of the church *by* the world. The first instance concerns a Presbyterian Church in the center of a town which, as I was to learn, is also the bedroom of two thirds of the corporate power structure of this country. The church was in some liturgical disarray. The ministers had begun to vary the familiar order of worship from time to time by substituting for the General Confession one or another contemporary form. A murmur arose among the members of the congregation strongly dissenting from these contemporary forms and urging the Session to rule in favor of the General Confession. A clear reason for this discontent seemed to have been the disinclination to acknowledge specific determinations of personal and social sinfulness expressed in the variant confessional forms. The acknowledged elegance of the cadences of the General Confession was put forward as a further ground for the alleged inappropriateness of the language in which the concreteness of contemporary departures from the will and the ways of God was expressed. After all, 'All we, like sheep, have gone astray', makes the point without convicting anybody of wife-swapping or of specific complicity in economic and social injustice.

How is it that baptized and even ordained members of the household of faith have so learned to bring every thought into captivity to the obedience of Christ (2 Cor. 10.5), as to expect 'the Word rightly preached' and 'the Sacraments rightly administered' to ratify our ways of being *who* we are, *where* and *as* we are; and evidence surprise that such preaching and administration should call us radically into question?

As for the co-optation of the church by the world: in the week of 5 April 1981, the New York Times carried a full page ad bearing the banner headline, 'Intellectuals and Religious Leaders in Support of the Administration's Foreign Policy Aid to El Salvador'. Among the signatories I found the name of eminent colleagues, and in many other respects, friends of whom I should have expected more. *The Committee on Freedom* which sponsored the ad seemed to me to be ominously reminiscent of an earlier *American Committee on Cultural Freedom* in which not a few eminent divines joined, thereby furthering the anti-communist hysteria—now emerging again—but then fostered by the then lamentable Junior Senator from Wisconsin, Joseph B. McCarthy. *Quem Deus perdere vult, dementat prius* (those whom God would destroy, He first makes mad).[19]

B. *Resistance*

So much for the *ratification* factor, as a still too widely practiced mode of confessional faithfulness and responsibility. What about the factor of *resistance?*

As *ratification* tends to desensitize the confessional state of the church of its openness to and movement towards a *status confessionis*, *resistance* tends—by reason of the complexity and ambiguity of the confessional situation—to imperil the church by intensifying mistrust within and persecution from without. As *ratification* spawns heresies, *resistance* spawns schisms. There must indeed have been a time when we could have said, *'No!'* But this very retrospective discovery is companioned by another. This is that more often than not we discover too late what is the *'Yes!'* which is the bearer of that *'No!'* to the world from a church called to confessional faithfulness and responsibility in the world for the sake of the world. Except for the 'Yes!' which bears the 'No!', *resistance* is vulnerable to the self-righteous negativism which confuses resistance *in* the world with resistance *of* the world. Except for the *'Yes!'* which bears the 'No!', the refusal of the world would be desensitized of ambiguity and thus vulnerable to ascetic or perfectionist surrogates for the faithfulness and responsibility of the church for the world. Except for the 'Yes!' which bears the 'No!', *ratification* would carry the day, *any* day, against *resistance*. 'Evil be thou my good!', which Milton said was Satan's self-identifying watchword, would then become the order of *every* day.[20]

The *stoicheia tou kosmou* (principalities and powers of the world), of which the New Testament variously speaks,[21] have been winning one for the Gipper on *that* front since long before Bonzo ever set foot in Death Valley. And since worse than *doing* evil is *being* evil (Bonhoeffer), these same *stoicheia* are possessed of an unerring instinct for the jugular. They know when and where their doom has been sealed (Mk 1.21-27). Second only to their adroitness in converting evil into good is their adroitness in converting dissent into disloyalty, poverty into irresponsibility, property into privilege, security into weaponry, and justice into power. Thus, the *No-sayers* are identified *not* by what they affirm but by what they call into question. *Resistance* is called that which endangers the security of the state and *resisting resistance* goes unrecognized as the state's way of absolutizing itself. A politics of power, second to none in a nuclear age, and fuelled by a passion for the free market as the safest harbinger of productivity—whereby the good of each is the good of all—inevitably exalts material over human values, private over public liberty, freedom over justice, injustice over compassion, and accelerates its self-destruction. This dénouement is inevitable because—as the inscription from the Lithuanian-born and Polish Nobel Laureate (1980), Czeslaw Milosz, at the base of the workers' monument in Gdansk, tellingly puts it—'You who harm a simple human being, do not feel secure. A poet remembers'.

The Church, on the way from confessional faithfulness to confessional responsibility also remembers—and hopes. In the power of the church's hope-fashioned memories, the church discerns the dénouement of the appointed authorities already under way and the shape of the 'No!' required by the 'Yes!' of the church's calling to be in the world for the sake of the world. In the power of the church's hope-fashioned memories, the church does not resist the appointed authorities. The authorities—divinely appointed or otherwise, duly constituted or otherwise—resist the church. In the words of *The Theological Declaration of Barmen*:

> In opposition to attempts to establish the unity of the German Evangelical Church by means of false doctrine, by the use of force and insincere practices, the Confessional Synod insists that the unity of the Evangelical Church in Germany can come only from the Word of God in faith through the Holy Spirit. Thus alone is the Church renewed . . .
>
> Be not deceived by loose talk, as if we meant to oppose the unity of the German nation! Do not listen to the seducers who pervert our intentions, as if we wanted to break up the unity of the German Evangelical Church or to forsake the Confesssions of the Fathers!
>
> Try the Spirits whether they are of God! . . . If you find that we are speaking contrary to Scripture, then do not listen to us! But if you find that we are taking our stand upon Scripture, then let no fear or temptation keep you from treading with us the path of faith and obedience to the Word of God, in order that God's people be of one mind upon earth and that we in faith experience what he himself has said: "I will never leave you, nor forsake you!" Therefore, "Fear not little flock, for it is your Father's good pleasure to give you the kingdom!"[22]

The Resisted—you see—are the Resisters! Accordingly, the church, on the way from confessional faithfulness to confessional responsibility, is summoned to break the conspiracy of sound and silence which spells out *ratification*; and to take shape in a congeries of comradeships—within and among congregations, and within and among its Judicatories—identified by the Resisted as *resistance*![23]

It could be that in these days of a rising tide of military, moral and legislative madness, such comradeships of resistance would find themselves drawn together and towards an agenda of 'Yes!' and 'No!', that would include, at the very least, the following:

1. A 'Yes!' to the conviction that the global unification of the world requires a re-shaping of sovereignties and a re-distribution of natural, cultural and economic resources, so

that the security of all peoples may be anchored in the trust of all peoples! This 'Yes!' is correlative with a 'No!' to be said to the passions, policies, and values which exalt military strength and supremacy as the guarantee of security, further the disequilibrium which defense establishments impose upon the livelihood of the peoples, and, in so doing, court the risk of a totalitarian imposition of order, in violation of justice, upon the common life;

2. A 'Yes!' to the primacy of persons over property is correlative with a 'No!' to a politics of productivity designed to encourage and reward enterprise above public trust and responsibility;

3. A 'Yes!' to the conviction that the human good of each depends upon the human good of all is correlative with a 'No!' to persuasions and policies that promote the human good of each as the harbinger of the human good of all;

4. A 'Yes!' to the conviction that the freedom which being human takes is guaranteed and furthered by an unswerving commitment to certain inviolable rights, guaranteeing that the just powers of government shall be drawn from the consent of the governed, is correlative with a 'No!' to every legislative and/or executive and/or judicial encroachment upon a *Bill of Rights*, as the charter of the liberties of the people;

5. A 'Yes!' to the primacy of responsibility for life over the right-to-life is correlative with a 'No!' to constitutional or legislative attempts to define when a human life is human, while at the same time exhibiting a callous indifference to conditions which deny a human prospect to a human life born;

6. A 'Yes!' to the primacy and priority of human rights over all other considerations in the determination of foreign and domestic policies of states is correlative with a 'No!' to governments—whether foreign or domestic, and to those to whom governments entrust the administration of the affairs and the lives of the people—which conceal their commitment to the pre-eminence of power beneath sophistries seeking to distinguish between totalitarian and authoritarian forms of power;

7. A 'Yes!' to the conviction that the environment which nature provides for human societies and the resources of the earth belong to all peoples of the earth, and that their responsible trusteeship *includes* limits and *excludes* private ownership is correlative with a 'No!' to values, policies and warrants which convert availability into development, development into possession, possession into privilege, and privilege into private gain—in disregard of nature's own rhythm of replenishment and of the vulnerability to exploitation, intrinsic to technological mastery of and dominion over nature.

From Micah to the Magnificat, the church, called to be in the world for the sake of the world, has been shown what is good. And 'what doth the Lord require of you but to do justly, to love mercy, and to walk humbly with your God' (Mic. 6.8) . . . 'He hath scattered the proud in the imagination of their hearts, he has put down the mighty from their thrones, and exalted those of low degree; he has filled the hungry with good things and the rich he has sent empty away' (Lk 1.51-52).

'Who knows whether it is not for such a time as this that we (together with Barmen) have come to the kingdom?' (Esth. 4.14). Or, to borrow an apostolic phrase, 'as certain of (our) own poets have said' (Acts 17.28b):

> King Christ this world is all aleak
> and life preservers there are none:
> and waves which only they may walk
> Who dare to call themselves human.[24]

Let it not be said of us that 'there was a moment, at the beginning, when we could have said, "No!". But somehow we missed it.'

NOTES

*This address was originally submitted for inclusion in a Barmen Commemorative Symposium volume. Since my own conviction is that the Press to which that volume has been entrusted is in violation of Thesis 1 of the Barmen Declaration, I have formally requested the return of my chapter to me for the present purpose.

1. Ernst Troeltsch, *The Social Teaching of the Christian Churches* (trans. Olive Wyon; London: Allen and Unwin, Vol. II, 1931; orig. 1912), ch. III, Section 4, pp. 691-990. Troeltsch's *Preface* is dated 1911. Troeltsch does not mention the Czech Brethren.

2. John Calvin, *Institutes of the Christian Religion* (trans. J. Allen; Philadelphia: The Board of Christian Education, 1960), Vol. I. Bk I, ch. 5, 5.

3. Ernst Troeltsch, *op. cit.*, pp. 815, 817. Emphasis mine.

4. *Ibid.*, p. 818.

5. So Christoph Barth, *Bekenntnis im Werden, Neue Quellen zur Entstehung der Barmer Erklärung* (Neukirchen-Vluyn: Neukirchener Verlag), pp. 6-9. Further references will be identified by the abbreviation CB.

6. Alfred Burgsmiller und Rudolf Wethe, *Die Barmer Theologische Erklärung, mit Vorwort von Edward Lohse* (Neukirchen-Vluyn: Neukirchener Verlag, 1983). Further references will be identified by the abbreviation BWL. I have translated *Anordnung* as *Ordination*. Barmen says: 'Appointment', which is better than 'Order' but weaker than 'Ordination'. See note 10, below.

7. See above, at note 3.

8. The phrase is Eberhard Bethge's about Dietrich Bonhoeffer in the context of his conversations with Colonel Oster and others in the early days of the conspiracy which led to the failed assassination attempt upon Adolf Hitler of 20 July 1944. See Eberhard Bethge, *Dietrich Bonhoeffer: Theologe, Christ, Zeitgenosse* (München: Chr. Kaiser, 1967), pp. 744-60. English translation, by Edward Robertson: *Dietrich Bonhoeffer, Man of Vision, Man of Courage* (New York: Harper and Row, 1970), pp. 579-80. The phrase about 'calling and destiny' is on p. 761 of the German text and on p. 581 of the English text.

9. Tom Stoppard, *Rosenkrantz and Guildenstern Are Dead* (New York: Grove Press, 1967), p. 125.

10. *The Theological Declaration of Barmen*, Thesis 5. Emphasis and parentheses mine. I have compared the English text, as translated and published in *The Constitution of the Presbyterian Church (USA)*, Bk I, *The Book of Confessions* (New York, 1983), pars. 8.06–8.28, at p. 147, with the German text of the Six Barmen Theses in the appendix of the volume by Christoph Barth, CB, pp. 61-63. At certain points, I have altered the English translation in favor of a translation of my own. Particular attention is called here to the substitution of the word 'ordination' for 'appointment'. In the German discussions, a lively controversy surrounded the distinction between 'Ordnung' and 'Anordnung'; i.e. between *order* and *ordination*, i.e. between the State as an '*order* of Cration' and the State as a providentially purposed divine mandate (Bonhoeffer) or arrangement for the furtherance of the creation towards its fulfillment. It is *this* purpose to which the word 'ordination' refers. See note 6 above.

11. William Shakespeare, *Julius Caesar*, IV, 3.

12. Not in its 'commission', as my Presbyterian translation says, but in its constitutive 'calling' (*Auftrag*), as the original text declares. So, *op. cit.*, 8.26 and CB, p. 63.

13. See 'The Religious Case Against Creation Science' by Roland Mushat Frye (Report from the Center, No. 1, 1983, with a preface by James I. McCord, Chancellor of the Center of Advanced Theological Inquiry, Princeton, New Jersey), where the passage quoted may be found.

14. *The Harvard Magazine*, 84 5 (May-June 1982). The article is by Gretchen Friesinger and entitled, 'The Wired World of Anthony Oettinger', pp. 36-42.

15. See 'The Religion and Society Report' of the Rockford Institute/New York and the Center on Religion and Society (Richard A. Vaughan, Publisher, Richard John Neuhaus, Director, Peter L. Berger, Senior Consultant, P.O. Box 800, Rockford, Illinois 61105).

16. These passages are, in the order of the theses: (1) Jn 14.6; 10.1, 9; (2) 1 Cor. 1.30; (3) Eph. 4.15, 16; (4) Mt. 20.25, 26; (5) 1 Pet. 2.17; (6) Mt. 28.20; 2 Tim. 2.9. Happily, at least *some* Presbyterians are beginning to listen again to *The Seventh Angel*. Volume I, No. 1, of this 'independent new magazine for Presbyterian and Reformed People', was published on Sunday, 15 January 1984, under the editorship of James Gittings, Box 334, Pottstown, Pennsylvania, 29464. So Pottstown is possessed both of a house divided against itself and of a house built upon a rock.

17. John Rawls, *A Theory of Justice* (Cambridge: Harvard University Press, 1971). Specific references to Rawls's work are given in parentheses following.

18. Immanuel Kant, *Kritik der reinen Vernunft* (Riga: Johann Friedrich Hartknoch, 1781), I. 'Transcendentale Elementarlehre', Zweiter Theil : 'Die Transcendentale Logik', 1, 'Von der Logik Ueberhaupt', p. 77. For an English text, see *Kant Selections* (ed. Theodore Meyer Greene, New York: Charles Scribner's Sons, 1929), p. 57.

19. The maxim is a Latin adaptation of a scholion to Sophocles' *Antigone*, V. 620, by an unknown Greek tragedian.

20. The phrase is part of John Milton's description of Satan. See *The Poetical Works of John Milton*, Vol. I (ed. Helen Darbishire; Oxford: Clarendon, 1952, 1973), Bk IV, 1.110.

21. *Inter alia*, Romans, Galatians, Ephesians, Colossians.

22. *Part I. The Appeal*. For the text, see note 10, above.

23. For an instructive and challenging indication of possibilities, well-grounded in the Church's calling to be in the world for the sake of the world, see Wallace M. Alston, Jr, *The Reformed Doctrine of the Church* (Atlanta: John Knox Press, 1984). See also, Richard Shaull, *Heralds of a New Reformation* (Maryknoll: New York, Orbis Books, 1984).

24. E.E. Cummings, *Complete Poems* (New York: Harcourt, Brace, Jovanovich, 1972), p. 438 n. 54. The last two lines have been altered in the interest of inclusive language. The original reads:

> and waves which only he may walk
> who dares to call himself a man

A CHILD AND ADAM:
A PARABLE OF THE TWO AGES*

Dorothy W. Martyn

Introduction: Two Pictures

A child at play

A little girl of nine years comes into the play-therapy room and begins to play with the dolls. The ensuing drama is predictable, as it has been enacted over and over in the same pattern. She prepares a meal for her babies, sets the table, and invites the therapist to join her. In the middle of the play-like meal, after a blessing has been earnestly voiced and while the little girl seems to be happily feeding her babies, there is a sudden disjuncture. The tea begins to get spilled, apparently quite by accident; the atmosphere is charged with excitement; the doll's head is thrust ruthlessly into a plate of food; a flood of rage breaks loose. Until the child can be physically restrained, she engages in a rampage of destruction. With a wide sweep of her arm, she knocks over the tea dishes and attempts to throw the play food all over the room, while kicking the table over. She also attempts to hit, bite, spit at, tear at, and curse the therapist, whom a few minutes earlier she had greeted as a friend. The therapist helps her back into control—for the time being—and that siege is past. In a quieter moment the little girl will say, ostensibly of her doll, though actually of herself, 'She has a spell on her'.

Man at war

A Swiss Red Cross worker, on a day in April of 1948, arrived on the scene of the massacre of the village of Deir Yassin. He described the spectacle in his diary as follows:

> The first thing I saw were people running everywhere, rushing in and out of houses, carrying Sten guns, rifles, pistols, and long ornate Arab knives. . . . They seemed half mad. I saw a beautiful girl carrying a dagger still covered with blood. I heard screams. I saw a young woman stab an elderly man and woman cowering on the doorsteps of their hut. . . . Everything had been ripped apart

and torn upside down. . . . There were bodies strewn about. They had done their 'cleaning up' with guns and grenades and finished their work with knives, anyone could see that'. Moving in the shadows, he discovered 'a little foot, still warm'. It belonged to a child of ten years, who had been wounded. Among the corpses was that of 'a woman who must have been eight months pregnant, hit in the stomach, with powder burns on her dress indicating she'd been shot point blank.[1]

The same Red Cross worker viewed a scene from the opposite side of the conflict, the massacre at Nebi Daniel:

> At Nebi Daniel, the firing was still going on. As the column rounded a curve, Jacques de Reynier of the Red Cross suddenly saw the house 'small and alone in the middle of hell'. On the road leading up to it, he noted 'a sprawl of shattered, blackened vehicles and burned bodies, their heads and sexual organs carefully mutilated'.[2]

Other versions of these scenes could no doubt be drawn from the history of any country in any age.

1. *'In Adam all die' (1 Cor. 15.22; Rom. 5.18)*
The human situation: microcosm and macrocosm
The play-therapy room as mirror of the larger world

The child introduced above accurately reveals in her play, as children invariably do in their secret language, her situation in the larger world.[3] The words used here, microcosm and macrocosm, draw on a formulation reintroduced by Erikson, who spoke of the microsphere, the small world of manageable toys in a child's play, as representing the macrosphere, the larger world shared with others. The child in question is in a psychiatric hospital, not because she is mentally incapacitated, but because her ego is intermittently overrun by a malign, destructive rage, which leaves her helpless in its throes. During the ordinary routine of her school day or at home with her family, she may suddenly be triggered into a rampage of destructive behavior. When truly angry, she may viciously attack another child, stab her teacher with her pencil, or throw scissors at her sister.

What is striking in the case of the child, as well as in the accounts of the massacres, is the impression that something 'other' is at work here, some mighty, destructive power, which 'deranges the spirit, violently possesses a soul, throws a person out of himself. . . '[4] and brings disastrous consequences in its wake. It appears that the child in the playroom, and humankind collectively, find themselves repeatedly overrun by some malignant force, some irrational drive of evil, 'too powerful to be overcome by the conscious mind's approval of the good and hatred of the evil'.[5]

There are, of course, many perspectives from which attempts have been made to shed light on this human situation. For the present undertaking, the framework that will guide our observations is Romans 5-8, with special attention to 5.12-21:

> Therefore as sin came into the world through one man and death through sin, and so death spread to all men because all men sinned—sin indeed was in the world before the law was given, but sin is not counted where there is no law. Yet death reigned from Adam to Moses, even over those whose sins were not like the transgression of Adam, who was a type of the one who was to come.

> But the free gift is not like the trespass. For if many died through one man's trespass, much more have the grace of God and the free gift in the grace of that one man Jesus Christ abounded for many. And the free gift is not like the effect of that one man's sin. For the judgment following one trespass brought condemnation, but the free gift following many trespasses brings justification. If, because of one man's trespass, death reigned through that one man, much more will those who receive the abundance of grace and the free gift of righteousness reign in life through the one man Jesus Christ.

> Then as one man's trespass led to condemnation for all men, so one man's act of righteousness leads to acquittal and life for all men. For as by one man's disobedience many were made sinners, so by one man's obedience many will be made righteous. Law came in, to increase the trespass; but where sin increased, grace abounded all the more, so that, as sin reigned in death, grace also might reign through righteousness to eternal life through Jesus Christ our Lord.

A brief statement of the same thought can be found in 1 Cor. 15.22: 'For as in Adam all die, so also in Christ shall all be made alive'.

A. *Paul's anthropological perspective*

The study of these texts reveals, first of all, that Paul does not seem to be interested in matters that concern modern psychologists, such as personal fulfillment, individuation, self-actualization, or a process of inner maturing.[6] Here, at least, Paul is not talking about growth. He does not concern himself greatly with feelings, though it is true that those verses at the end of ch. 7 that deal with conflict between willing and doing invite psychological interpretation, provided both Barth and Käsemann are ignored. Emphasis is given, rather, to the objective realities of man's status and condition.[7] Paul does not appear to consider the individual, as such, to be a suitable focus of investigation, and there is no question of human autonomy.[8] Rather, he sees man[9] as defined in terms of his interrelatedness, or corporate existence.

B. *Man's corporate existence*

Corporate personality, as contrasted with our own tradition of individualism, was fundamental in Paul's thinking, as it was characteristic of classic Hebraic thought and the first century of rabbinic exegesis.[10] Examples of this collective understanding of anthropology are familiar to us: e.g. if Achan broke taboo (Joshua 7), his clan fell under a curse; the blessing to Abraham and his offspring is a *collective* concept. Ernst Käsemann and C.K. Barrett have emphasized that the world for Paul is simply not the sphere of being of the individual.[11] As over against any idea of a human being as a separable ego, he understands man to be identifiable only as a representative, a crystallization of a corporate existence, which is embodied in a lord or family head.

> Paul sees history gathering at nodal points, and crystallizing upon outstanding figures—men who are notable in themselves as individual persons, but even more notable as representative figures. These men, as it were, incorporate the human race, or sections of it, within themselves, and the dealings they have with God they have representatively on behalf of their fellows.[12]

One may assume that such collective anthropology is the opposite of that embraced by modern psychotherapy, for which the individual psyche is the apparent focus. However, relational interdependence is also fundamental to psychoanalytic theory and is taken as the foundation of the present investigation.

To develop this statement, let us return to the child of whom we have had a glimpse. What is wrong with her? We can name the problem, clinically, as a severe impulse control disorder, but the name does not tell us very much. If we read her history and study her Rorschach responses and other clinical data, we find, rather readily, that the etiology of the difficulty is a *relational* matter. For a variety of reasons, the child was deprived in earliest infancy of what D.W. Winnicott calls 'good-enough mothering', and virtually all fathering.[13] Parenthetically, it cannot be far from accurate to state that at least nine out of ten children who are hospitalized with psychic disorders of an emotional nature, that is, excluding organic disorders, have experienced insufficient or nonexistent parental relationship in early childhood. Either there was no caring person accessible to them or there was present some condition, not fully understood by any of the various schools of psychiatry, that caused the child biologically or psychically to be unable to appropriate the caring presence.

The stark reality of emotional impoverishment is vividly illustrated in a Rorschach response of the child under discussion. In contemplating a configuration that suggests to most people some semblance of active, human-like figures (Card III) this child's reponse was, 'It is two skeletons, with a third skeleton in between', thus referring to her own relationship with her two parents and the cold, lifeless, death-like quality of that relationship. How could such a crippling deprivation of a child's emotional needs happen in a human family?

It is of course tempting to blame the mother and father, as both professionals and nonprofessionals, at some level, are prone to do. But if one spends a bit of time with the mother, in an attitude of listening, it becomes quickly manifest that the mother did not willfully deprive her child; the difficulty lay in the fact that she, too, for various reasons, was deprived, in her turn, of 'good-enough' mothering and fathering. She herself had not found nurture at a mother's breast and therefore had little nurture to offer her child. She also was brought up by a mother and father who likewise had little to give because they also had been brought up by parents who had little to give. It is a small step from this situation to Paul's discussion in Rom. 5.12, where he talks about the Adamic situation in which all are blighted:

> Therefore as sin came into the world through one man and death through sin, and so death spread to all men because all men sinned. . .

The radical nature of man's situation was never more clearly presented. Psychological distress in itself is not erasable because there is no way to start over. We are caught in an infinite series of mirrors in which repetition of human error is inevitable because internalization from one's relational matrix is axiomatic. As Barth wrote in his Dogmatics:

> The name of Adam sums up the meaning or meaninglessness of this [human] history. It is Adamic history, and—this is the Word and judgment of God on it, this is the explanation of its staggering monotony, this is the reason why there can never be any progress— it continually corresponds to his history. It is continually like it. With innumerable variations it constantly repeats it. It constantly re-enacts the little scene in the garden of Eden. There never was a golden age. There is no point in looking back to one. The first man was immediately the first sinner.[14]

C. *Humanity corporate in Adam: Sin*

The child with her image of skeletons in her relational world reminds us of Paul's startling assertion: 'In Adam all die'. For Paul, this statement is a description of the situation in which man finds himself inextricably caught, a situation of corporate wrongness,[15] the personal and cosmic disaster that has been drawn from Adam and summed up in 'death'. The emphasis is on what Paul considers to be the dragging of humanity as a whole into a state of bondage and corruption, a state of anthropological and cosmic malaise,[16] which human beings on their own have no means of setting right.

There is a very interesting treatment in Barrett in which 'the rebellious beasts', no longer in subjection to man as in the original order of creation, became in time the source of the beast-like figures of the apocalypse, where animals represent spiritual powers.[17] There are intriguing analogies implicit here to what psychoanalysis unveils in the deep reaches of the unconscious, where the bestial forces of the id may invade also the sphere of conscience (superego) and ruthlessly oppress the ego from two directions. The child of our story magnifies for us this situation: the instinctual urges, which should be subject to the authority of her ego, have instead come to have dominion over her, both from the standpoint of impulses that she cannot control and from the standpoint of a cruel and punitive superego, against which the ego is in a position of weakness.

That this child specifically and humanity collectively is under the sway of powers beyond the ability of the rational mind to control is as evident to the psychoanalyst as it is to Paul. Just as Paul sees that it would be useless to call to holy life those who are still under the dominion of the old age, an analyst sees that it would be useless to exhort a patient to change his behavior when he is besieged with unconscious forces over which he has little control. While the analyst, however, focuses on the origin of conditions within the immediate relational matrix of his patient, particularly on the effects of the earliest familial influences on the unconscious, Paul does not hesitate to make a global analysis, in which Sin, or the repudiation of God by man from the very beginning, set in motion in the world a force that came to have dominion over man.

In fact, both Sin and Righteousness in Paul are not so much conceived of in terms of man's actions as in terms of powers over him.[18] Sin is seen as beginning with man's self-deification, or his wanting to extend his rightful lordship over creation into being God himself. (For an analytic treatment of this idea, see Reik's *Myth and Guilt*.[18]) This denial of his creaturehood and rebellion against implication of inferiority to his creator is seen to result in moral wickedness and imitation of the beasts, over which he was to have had dominion. This understanding of human history, which regarded immorality as a secondary consequence of idolatry, was not original with Paul, but was in keeping with rabbinic thought.[20]

The special emphasis that concerns us here, however, is Paul's treatment of Sin as 'a living, active, almost a personal agency', which, once it had entered, was inescapable to all.[21] 'Just as a child picks up the words and gestures of those among whom it is reared, so it picks up the Sin that is already in the world.'[22] 'Once this [entrance] was found, it did not need to be propagated—by sexual relations, or descent in any other way; it propagated itself.'[23]

In summary, then, both the picture in the playroom and the picture of man at war place in bold relief the corporate portrait of a humanity overrun by forces over which it has insufficient control, and both illustrate for us Paul's assertion that in Adam all die. In this corporate family of man—which, of course, is the meaning of the Hebrew word Adam—there is a radical disability, an anthropological and cosmic disorder that is universally manifest in each of its representatives. 'Death spread to all men, as all men sinned.'[24]

2. *'In Christ shall all be made alive' (1 Cor. 15.22; Rom. 5.18)*
The new age and the order of grace

> For if many died through one man's trespass, much more have the grace of God and the free gift in the grace of that one man Jesus Christ abounded for many.

This assertion of Paul's assaults the mind. After the apparently hopeless picture of humankind under the dominion of alien powers, here Paul claims that God's act in Jesus Christ has more than defeated these powers. It is not simply that a new Adam has come along to balance out the old one. Paul states unequivocally that the death and resurrection of Jesus Christ have reversed and annulled the old order in such a manner as absolutely to outweigh it. The two orders, as Barth clarifies, are radically unequal and are more to be considered in their difference than in their likeness:

> If he juxtaposes here right and wrong, truth and falsehood, power and powerlessness—it is in such a way that wrong must witness in favor of the right, falsehood in favor of truth, weakness in favor of power, sinful man in favor of God who gives grace—...[25]

> It is Christ first, and Adam seen in retrospect as a similitude, as a 'head of a race', but not comparable in substance.... The former [Adam] is like the rainbow in relation to the sun. It is only a reflection of it. It has no independent existence. It cannot stand against it. It does not balance it. When weighed in the scales, it is only like a feather.[26]

Justice cannot be done here to the wealth of exegetical material that illuminates Paul's account of the overthrow of the old order, the cutting at the root of the corporate wrongness in which man has been enslaved in the Adamic family, and the grafting of mankind onto a new head.[27] Instead, I will emphasize, with the help of the child, two aspects of the new age to which I believe psychotherapy bears witness as parable.

A. *New relationship*

The idea of two ages, old and new, comes out of Jewish thought, in which the old age of man, Adam, was contrasted with new age, with

Messiah, which would bring life and righteousness.[28] What Paul is claiming is that God has indeed ushered in the new age through the death and resurrection of Jesus Christ, through which man is brought into a new status and condition: a redemptive relationship with a new family head in whom humanity is incorporated.

Paul requires the apparently innocent preposition 'in' to bear a heavy load. He speaks of our being *in Christ*—incorporated into this new family head, who is therefore *both* a person and a realm. 'If any man is *in* Christ he is a new creature'. But he also uses this same pregnant preposition in the opposite way. The new family head is spoken of as being internalized—to use a psychoanalytic expression—by man: 'It is not I but Christ who liveth in me'. This double-directional use of the preposition 'in' is the kind of language that describes human relatedness in the most elemental sense of the word. Comparable psychoanalytic language is found in such concepts as 'incorporation' and 'identification', which refer to inseparable processes lying at the very earliest and deepest layers of personality formation.[29] To use a very concrete image, a child's first mode of relationship is simply to 'swallow' his parents; he carries his parents around with him forever after as a kind of inner image. It would be interesting to pursue this language in connection with the Christian practice of the Eucharist, but it is beyond my purposes here. The process of 'swallowing' one's parents is axiomatic. It is, as a matter of fact, the absence of parent figures who can thus be internalized that produces some of the most severe mental disorders.

In the case of the child we have met, the process of internalization of her parents happened, of course, since it always does if there are parents. The problem here had to do with the distorted condition of the psyche of the parents who were incorporated, stemming, as we have seen, from the same etiology in their own childhood. Now, if we can stay with this psychoanalytic language briefly without losing Paul, it would seem that it is precisely this internalization of the new family head, Jesus Christ, by men—who in turn exist only in union with him—that gives them their new identity.

The inevitable interrelatedness of the familial nexus is involved here. When Paul speaks in Rom. 8.9 about the Spirit of God *dwelling in* you, he is clearly referring to an objective condition that exists, not some sort of feeling or idea of devotion or some willing or striving after the right. It is something much more radical, much more factual, and, if I may add, much more commensurate with what Freud learned about the ratio of unconscious to conscious mental life in man. Consciousness, 'which once was so omnipotent and hid all else from view',[30] is known in the present day to play only a partial role in the psyche's mental activities; in every human relationship, unconscious factors are at least as significant as conscious ones. Paul is speaking here about an incorporated personage, simultaneously identified with—since these are inseparable ideas—who alters the inner nature of personality. It is as though a child, tormented by the internalization of blighted and corrupt images, could by some miracle be grafted onto a new parental situation, where the old inner images could be mitigated and a new internalization with a different kind of parent could take place, altering his intrapsychic situation. This is precisely one way of conceptualizing the process of psychoanalysis and, to the extent that it is successful, such a miracle has taken place.

B. *The free gift*

Paul hardly makes it possible for us to miss this aspect of the new order God has brought into being, this idea of the 'free gift'. These words keep standing out; in Rom. 5.15-17 we see the words 'free gift' no less than six times. While the words are simple, their implications are elusive and therefore require some development. The idea of the free gift is, of course, not separable from the new relatedness we have talked about, but is rather the characteristic quality of that new kind of relatedness.

The idea of the free gift is elusive because it is offensive to the natural way of thinking, a kind of moral scandal. 'Something for nothing' is not considered to be a worthy goal for a man. The parable of equal pay for unequal work in the vineyard, the judgment of 'acquittal' on any criminal thought to be guilty, a child who 'gets away with it'—these aberrations seem to violate something in the universe that is basic to any understanding of justice and of the sequence of cause and effect. One gets what he earns, he must reap what he sows, he must suffer for his wrongdoing. It is not only that these tenets seem to promise some kind of order; it is also true that they represent the remnants of the primitive *lex talionis* to which we are all heirs and which we retain in the unconscious—that primordial layer in which a wrong throws the world out of kilter and must be righted by punishment. The assault Paul makes on this approach to things, to my understanding, lies at the heart of both Christian theology and all genuine psychotherapy: namely the simple, unconditional statement that 'our misdeeds are not laid against us'.

The child in the playroom can teach us a great deal about the old-age way of thinking and about its inversion by the attack—if you will—of the free gift. Her misdeeds had always been counted very heavily against her; the 'reap what you sow' mode of existence had caught her inextricably in a predictable sequence: bad behavior was followed by punishment, good behavior by reward. She had 'gotten what she deserved', which was generally punishment. The punishment, of course, served only to generate more anger, which produced more punishment. Such is the order under Law.

Psychotherapy for the child had to consist in a new relationship wherein there was a radical reversal of this sequence. Prevenient acceptance, uncontingent on her behavior, in a word, a 'free gift', which is the whole meaning of grace, had to be made available to her through another person. This statement, of course, does not mean that the child was to be abandoned to her destructive impulses, which would have been the cruelest kind of rejection. It does mean that no action of hers resulted in an attitude or action of punishment. What cut into her predicament was not punishment, but rather the offering of the person of the therapist in a free-gift alliance *with* the child *against* the destructive impulse. The destructive impulse must be seen as essentially alien to the child's deepest self and deepest desire, from which she yearns to be delivered. This fact reminds us of Rom. 7.20, where Paul says, 'Now if I do what I do not want, it is no longer I that do it, but sin which dwells within me'. If a child senses the prevenient grace, the uncontingent acceptance of his personhood, he will most gratefully accept the alliance with the therapist in the battle against the destructive impulse.

That the acceptance—the free gift—must be both prevenient and uncontingent is at the very heart of the matter. This stance is exactly opposite to that of the school of thought in the field of psychology according to which a patient is manipulated by rewards based on his behavior; such a position forfeits the unique stance—of grace—from which deep change can be wrought and embraces the impotence of old-age power. To tell a child who is at the mercy of his impulses that you will reward him for certain behavior is about as effective psychologically, in terms of actual transformation, as it would have been theologically efficacious for God to tell mankind that if he would forego murder, envy, malice, and strife for one week, He would give him a savior.

The child speaks more eloquently here, however, than exposition of theory. After many months of therapy—that is to say, after many months of the free gift of prevenient and uncontingent acceptance, of alliance with the child against the destructive impulse—the playroom offers us a different scene from the one we observed before. While the child is feeding her dolls, she says thoughtfully, 'This is a new recipe for my babies; they haven't had it before'. In the same hour while cleaning the floor with her toy broom and mop: 'The old wax is coming up; the new wax is going down'.

These are sacred words, spoken from the lips of a child who is telling us about grace, though she does not know the word. She is telling us about the new age, though the concept is far beyond her cognitive level. She speaks of regeneration, though her way of putting it is to say, on picking up a toy rattle from the floor, 'Don't tell me there's a new-born baby in here'.

The words she brought to my mind when she said these things were: 'This is the new covenant in my blood', and these words from Isaiah:

> Behold I do a new thing;
> Even now it breaks from the bud,
> Can you not perceive it?

3. *Psychotherapy as an eschatological sign*

> For the creation waits with eager longing for the revealing of the sons of God (Rom. 8.19ff.).

Questions in regard to the significance of new age and old age in reality might well be raised at this point. Namely, is the child now cured? Is she free from the oppression of her impulses? Can she control herself? In these questions from the microcosm of the child in the playroom, of course, lies the same question in the macrocosm of the world: If Christ's death and resurrection have triumphed over the old order of cosmic wrong, is man now free from the oppression of his destructive impulses?

The answer to the first may shed some light on the second. The child is indeed still oppressed by her impulses. It was, in fact, just minutes before one of her explosive outbreaks that she said earnestly to me, 'I ain't going to have that control problem no more; I was baptized last night'.

She had been baptized. She had also had many months of psychotherapy, and the impulse problem was still there. However, we can say that her situation is not at all the same as it was, as new powers that substantially alter the force field have been brought into play. In psychological terms, one could state that the new relationship has strengthened the ego, enabling her to struggle better against the oppressive instinctual forces. The child's symbolic language of play expressed it another way: the room that had been the scene of so many storms was carefully straightened and tidied by the little girl, and the toy kitchen was scrubbed until it shone, while she repeatedly said to me, 'Can you *see* how much dirt is coming off?'

The new condition of the room, of course, represents the new situation she sensed within herself. Theologically, we would speak of the 'empowering quality of grace', which has transformed the 'I must' to the 'I may and I can'.[31]

Another remark of the child brings me to my final focus. She was making play-like bread one day and, since communication seemed to be good, I took advantage of the situation to attempt to give her, verbally, some insights on her progress that I thought might help her. She looked disapprovingly at me and said, with characteristic incisiveness, 'Just put the bread on the table—don't you know it has to rise?'

Thus the child has suggested to us in very simple language something analogous to the eschatological tension that we encounter in Paul's writing, the 'already—not yet'. It is clear from Rom. 8.19-23, which speaks of the whole creation longing and groaning in travail for final deliverance, that for Paul, Christ's victory over the cosmic powers of evil is decisive, but not yet complete.

> The demonic elements. . . are still at work. . . the historic work of Jesus thus requires extension and completion. . . . for the running battle that follows a decisive action to be completed in the final overthrow and subjugation of the demonic forces who, since the fall of Adam, have dominated not only the human scene but the cosmos as a whole, which sighs inarticulately for the day when it

shall be released from bondage to Vanity, the No-God, and resume the freedom of service to Man.[32]

In the Christian faith, *then*, we stand in a dialectic between something already realized—it is not as it was before, as Jesus Christ has broken into the old age and ushered in the new—and something 'not yet', which is not only chronologically futuristic, but which impinges on us now by God's eschatological signs.[32] The witness of the church lies in this in-between sphere, and all the gifts of the spirit that are manifest in the church, whether they be prophecy, teaching, healing, or some other gift, must be seen in this light, that they are tokens that God has begun powerfully to realize his promises. The Holy Spirit 'is the agency and mark of the eschatological situation of the church... the first installment of the blessed life.... Spiritual gifts are no more than a parable of the truth'.[34]

'A parable of the truth'. It was this phrase of C.K. Barrett's that provided for me a way to conceptualize the psychotherapeutic journey, which might be called the recapitulative miracle. It is an astounding but predictable fact that a child—also an adult, for that matter—on finding himself in the kind of therapeutic relationship described above, will embark on a recapitulation, which he himself unconsciously unfolds, of his infancy and childhood. He re-enacts, symbolically, the drama of his family, in partnership with the therapist, who offers to him, also in symbolic form, the good-enough parental nurture of which he has been to whatever degree or for whatever reason deprived. A force is set in motion operating through the therapist, though he is not its prime cause; it is a force that might be analogous to the process of healing in a surgical wound, which a surgeon may facilitate, but which he can in no wise initiate or provide from his own resources. Harold Searles, in speaking of the therapeutic reworking of early ego development in the treatment of schizophrenia, says:

> ... not only the patient but [the therapist] also is in the grip of a process, the therapeutic process, which is comparable in its strength to the maturational process in the child—which is, indeed, this same process in a particular context.... The more experienced and confident the therapist becomes in this work, the more deeply does he realize that this process if far too powerful for either the patient or himself to be able at all easily to deflect it, consciously and willfully and singlehandedly, away from the confluent channel

which it is tending—with irresistible power, if we can give ourselves up to the current—to form for itself. . . .[35]

Clinically, we are speaking of what is possible within the phenomenon of transference, the discovery and use of which were Freud's greatest contribution to psychotherapy. That a patient will unconsciously replay the old, in conjunction with a new parent, in such a way that there can be substantive alteration in the deepest reaches of his personality is the foundation on which all psychoanalytic treatment rests.

In this context, however, what is most significant is the picture of a drama with a second act, which seems to offer itself as a parable, a sign, of the replay of man's story in the new Adam. One thinks especially of Irenaeus at this point, for whom the doctrine of 'recapitulation' underlay all theology: 'God recapitulated in himself the ancient formation of man, that he might kill sin, deprive death of its power, and vivify man'.[36] Or, as the hymn writer felt it:

Oh loving wisdom of our God, when all was sin and shame
A second Adam to the fight and to the rescue came.
Oh wisest love! that flesh and blood which did in Adam fail
Should strive afresh against their foe
Should strive and should prevail.

It appears, then, that the manifestation of God's empowering grace in the experience of this child may be understood as one of those signs, those tokens, 'that God is regrasping the world for himself' in this present age, where we stand in the interpenetration of this age and the age to come. Like the work of the church in all its forms, the child's experience bears witness to the 'universal validity of the might [power] of Christ's resurrection. . . already breaking into the present out of the future'.[37] We are pointed by Käsemann to this conclusion:

Man cannot be defined from within his own limits, but he is eschatologically defined in the light of the name of Christ, just as Adam once received his name from God, thereby acquiring a definition as creature. It is true of both that they are unable to give themselves being and existence, but remain dependent on grace, which is new every morning and never finds an end.[38]

NOTES

*This article was first published in *Journal of Religion and Health* 16/4 (1977) and is used by permission of the Editors.

1. Collins, L., and Lapierre, D., *Oh, Jerusalem* (New York: Simon and Schuster, 1972), p. 278.
2. *Ibid.*, p. 238.
3. Freud, S., *Beyond the Pleasure Principle* (1920) (New York: W.W. Norton, 1961); Erikson, E., 'Toys and Reasons' (1950), in *Childhood and Society* (New York: W.W. Norton, 1963).
4. Ulanov, A.B., 'The Psychological Reality of the Demonic', in Olson, A., ed., *Disguises of the Demonic* (New York, Association Press, 1974), p. 559.
5. Beare, F.W., 'The Letter to the Romans', *Interpreter's Dictionary of the Bible* (New York: Abingdon Press, 1962).
6. Käsemann, E., 'The Righteousness of God in Paul', *New Testament Questions of Today* (London: SCM, 1965); *idem*, 'On Paul's Anthropology', *Perspectives on Paul* (London: SCM, 1971).
7. Beare, *op. cit.*; Barrett, C.K., *A Commentary on the Epistle to the Romans* (London: Adam and Charles Black, 1962); *idem*, *From First Adam to Last* (London: Adam and Charles Black, 1962); Barth, K., *A Shorter Commentary on Romans* (London: SCM, 1959); Best, E., *The Letter of Paul to the Romans* (Cambridge: Cambridge University Press, 1967).
8. Best, *op. cit.*
9. The word 'man' as used throughout the paper is a translation of the Greek *anthropos* and includes both man and woman.
10. Dodd, C.H., *The Epistle of Paul to the Romans* (Moffatt Series; London: Hodder and Stoughton, 1932).
11. Käsemann, 'On Paul's Anthropology', *op. cit.*; Barrett, *A Commentary on the Epistle to the Romans*; *idem*, *From First Adam to Last*.
12. Barrett, *From First Adam to Last*, p. 5.
13. Winnicott, D.W., *Playing and Reality* (New York: Basic Books, 1971).
14. Barth, *Church Dogmatics* (Edinburgh, T. & T. Clark, 1961), Vol. 41, pp. 508ff.
15. Dodd, *op. cit.*
16. Barrett, *From First Adam to Last*.
17. *Ibid.*, pp. 10ff.
18. Barth, *A Shorter Commentary on Romans*, p. 72.
19. Reik, T., *Myth and Guilt* (New York: George Braziller, 1957).
20. Barrett, *From First Adam to Last*, p. 18.
21. *Ibid.*, p. 20.
22. Best, *op. cit.*, p. 60.

23. Barrett, *From First Adam to Last*, p. 20.

24. For the purposes of this paper, I shall not attempt to deal with the difficult and complex question of the relation of the Law to Paul's picture, except to say that it also, in the final analysis, according to Paul, bears witness only to the incapacity of any instrument to free men from the hold of sin. 'If this sytem, which came from God himself, could in this age lead only to condemnation and death, no other could possibly be effective. The way forward must be a way beyond religion, and beyond morals. . . . The effect of the law was to demonstrate beyond all doubt that those who lived under it belonged to a world which was under the authority of sin rather than the authority of God. It belonged to Adam's world; everything in this world, dominated by evil spirits, was liable to corruption, and *corruptio optimi pessima* [The corruption of the best is the worst possible corruption]' (Barrett, *ibid.*, pp. 63ff.).

25. Barth, *A Shorter Commentary on Romans*, p. 62.

26. Barth, *Church Dogmatics*, p. 513.

27. Barth, *A Shorter Commentary on Romans*; Barrett, *A Commentary on the Epistle to the Romans*; *idem, From First Adam to Last*; Beare, *op. cit.*; Best, *op. cit.*; Dodd, *op. cit.*; Käsemann, 'The Righteousness of God in Paul'; *idem*, 'On Paul's Anthropology'; *idem, An die Römer* (Tübingen: J.C.B. Mohr [Paul Siebeck], 1973).

28. Best, *op. cit.*, p. 61.

29. Fenichel, O., *The Psychoanalytic Theory of Neurosis* (New York: W.W. Norton, 1945).

30. Freud, *The Interpretation of Dreams* (1900) (New York: Basic Books, 1965).

31. Käsemann, 'The Righteousness of God in Paul'.

32. Barrett, *From First Adam to Last*, pp. 93ff.

33. *Ibid.*, pp. 92ff.; Käsemann, *An die Römer*, p. 147.

34. Barrett, from *First Adam to Last*, pp. 110ff.

35. Searles, H.F., 'Patient-therapist Interaction', *Collected Papers on Schizophrenia and Related Subjects* (New York: International Universities Press, 1965), p. 559.

36. Cross, F.L., ed., *The Oxford Dictionary of the Christian Church* (London: Oxford University Press, 1974); Irenaeus, *Against Heresies* 3.18.7.

37. Käsemann, *An die Römer*, p. 147 (author's translation).

38. Käsemann, 'On Paul's Anthropology', p. 31.

INDEX

INDEX OF BIBLICAL AND OTHER REFERENCES

OLD TESTAMENT

APOCRYPHA

NEW TESTAMENT

QUMRAN LITERATURE

CD		7	64	4.19-21	66
2.17-3.1	174	7.1-2	53	6.2	111
14.20	111	7.2	53, 64	11.12	171
16.1-3	177	7.7-8	63		
		7.7	64	*4QpNah*	
1QH	75	7.9-8.3	214	3.3	53
		7.13	64		
1QM	36			*4QpPss*[b]	
		1QS		1.51.5	53
1QpHab		1-4	177		
2.3	203	3-4	177		

OLD TESTAMENT PSEUDEPIGRAPHA

Apocalypse of Abraham		23.4	175	1.1-5	175
17	83	29.3	63	1.4-5	175
19.5	75	30.1, 3	63	1.9	175
		38.1-2	176	5	175
Apocalypse of Elijah		38.2	179	5.4-5	174
37.3-4	78	41.3	176	5.7	175
		44.8-15	187	6-19	174
Apocalypse of Moses		46.3	179	6ff.	235
	77	46.4	79	8.1	174
33.34	79	46.6	176	9.1	174
36.3	79	48.22	176	9.6-9	174
37.3	79	48.40	190	9.8	174
		48.42-43	175	9.9	174
		48.46-47	190	10	175
Assumption of Moses		48.46	175	10.7-9	174
10.7-10	151	49-51	176	10.9	174
		51.3	176	10.17-22	175
		51.12	220	14	91
Ascension of Isaiah		51.16	176	14.8-9	79
7.21-22	78	54.5	176	15.3	174
9.9	78	54.14	175, 176	15.8-16.2	174
9.13	78	54.15	176, 179	15.9-10	174
9.18	78	54.19	175	16	175
10.14	89	56.6	175	16.3	174
		56.11-15	177	18.6	76
2 Baruch	77	56.12-15	174	18.15	174
14.8ff.	233	57.2	176	19	175
14.12	176	83.4-9	187	19.1-2	174
14.15-19	175	84.2	179	21	175
15.5	190	85.7	176, 180	21.6	174
17.2-3	175			25.3	76
17.4	176	*1 Enoch*		37-71	194
19.1	179	1-36	174, 176, 181	38	193

RABBINIC LITERATURE

Babylonian Talmud

Jerusalem Talmud

Tosefta

Midrash

INDEX OF AUTHORS

Wrede, W. 68, 185

Yadin, Y. 274

Young, F.M. 277

Zimmerli, W. 90

MEANS TO AN END

John Rowan Wilson

MEANS TO
AN END

DOUBLEDAY & COMPANY, INC., GARDEN CITY, NEW YORK, 1959

All of the characters in this book are fictitious, and any resemblance
to actual persons, living or dead, is purely coincidental.

PART I

CHAPTER I

MARSHALL GLANCED at his watch and said for the third time, "I'm afraid I have to go now." He tried to sound regretful, but the effort was wasted since in any case the girl hardly seemed to hear him. She was deeply involved in some complex and mildly slanderous theatrical anecdote of which he had long since lost the point. He wondered, as so often on similar occasions, what on earth had attracted him to her in the first place. Boredom? Loneliness? A mistaken idea that she might be interesting to talk to? In the middle of the day, fully clad, at a distance of only three or four feet, she was not even especially desirable.

He scribbled his name across the bottom of the bill and managed to move her, still talking, out of the restaurant into Fifty-third Street. There was spring in the air, fighting with the gas fumes, the grit and wastepaper, the blasts of sooty air coming up the gratings from the subways. Possibly because of the spring, possibly those two extra manhattans which had seemed justifiable under the circumstances, Marshall felt a resurgence of optimism, a vague hope that, contrary to all experience, something exciting and unusual might be waiting for him just around some corner or other. He tried to crush the feeling immediately, recognizing it as a danger sign, a prelude to some spontaneous action which he might afterward regret. It was an impulse of a similar kind which had resulted in this abominable luncheon today.

The girl looked back at him as he almost pushed her into a cab. He had been a good audience and she was sorry to lose him.

"You wouldn't like to come and watch me rehearse?"

"I'd like to very much. But I have to be somewhere——"

"Okay. Well, some other time——"

"I'll call you up," he promised. It was what you said to people you were never going to see again. He watched the taxi out of sight and began to walk the two blocks to his office.

The spring (or the manhattans) lasted him along Fifty-third Street and quite a distance down Sixth Avenue. He carried it with him, in diminished form, through the lobby of the office building, up the express elevator, past the door which said "Marshall Corporation—International Department." But as he made his way through the high-pitched voices and clattering typewriters of the outer offices, it suddenly left him, to be succeeded by a mood of thoughtful melancholy. He became conscious that he was more than usually late for the meeting.

Miss Curran, Kingham's secretary, was in her usual place, sitting on guard over the entrance to the Holy of Holies. He asked her, "Have they started?"

"They started fifteen minutes ago, Mr. Marshall." Her voice was quite devoid of expression. She was neither amused nor reproachful, she merely stated facts. She had known the company since the early days, when there was no International Department and Kingham was no more than a keen goggle-eyed salesman. She looked at Marshall with a merciless, dead-pan stare which he always found disconcerting. Was she noting the flush on his cheeks, the slightly alcoholic brightness of his eye? Was she comparing him unfavorably with his brother or his dead father? Was she sympathetic, contemptuous, envious—or perhaps simply totally uninterested? There was no means of knowing.

"I don't suppose they've really missed me," he said with an attempt at joviality. "If it's going to be anything like this morning——"

If it was going to be anything like the morning, he thought, he might as well not have turned up at all. Uneasily conscious of the discourtesy of being late, he consoled himself with the reflection

that Kingham need never have called him in the first place. Occasionally, for some reason unexplainable except by sheer perversity, he would do this; men would be kept sitting, sometimes for days on end, in conferences about subjects with which they were not concerned, their presence unregarded, their opinion never asked. This morning had been taken up entirely with a report from Wilcox, the European representative, who had just flown home from London. It had been a long and complicated report and the discussion following it would be even worse. The European interests of the company were a tangled web of holding companies, distributorships, agencies, subsidiaries, and cross-licensing agreements—it was a perfect field for argument, for new angles and fresh concepts, for the throwing out of ideas. . . . The meeting might go on indefinitely.

But it was too late to go home now. Accepting the inevitable, he opened the door of the conference room and slipped into the vacant seat at the end of the table. There was not even a pause in the discussion as he entered the room; nobody so much as bothered to look around.

Now spring was no more than a memory. In the conference room there was neither time nor place nor season of the year. Poised, windowless, two hundred feet above street level, it might well have been some cavern quarried deep within the bowels of the earth. Here, night and day were one. A sickly, shadowless light was diffused through the room from a series of opaque panels on the wall. The atmosphere, ingeniously held uniform in temperature and humidity by the air-conditioning system, was curiously tasteless and soporific, a constant invitation to sleep.

On the long table there were jugs of ice water, paper cups, cigarettes, books of matches, memo pads, all discreetly labeled with the emblem of the company. Almost everybody was smoking. The voices droned on through the heavy afternoon, sometimes fluent, sometimes halting, sometimes aggressively confident, sometimes heavily deferential. Issues were raised and disposed of, problems were considered, results were analyzed, recommendations were made. Opinions rose with the cigarette smoke, to be sucked out

by the fan and eventually dispersed in merciful dilution through the air of midtown Manhattan.

Marshall felt his eyelids beginning to droop. Alarmed, he wriggled in his seat, took a sip of water, and lit a cigarette. It would never do for him to fall asleep; inattention might be concealed and even under certain circumstances excused, but actual slumber . . . It had happened once before, he remembered, after a late night with some friends in the Village. He had recollections of Kingham's sharp, nasal voice making some point about the supplies of insulation material in Bolivia and then a stab of pain in his right ankle where Richardson had kicked him awake.

Kingham had said nothing. This did not mean, as Marshall well knew, that the incident had passed unnoticed or been regarded lightly. Kingham was not that kind of man. And it was well known that he took these meetings very seriously. They were his own conception, the first innovation he had made on taking over the International. "An informal get-together," he would explain, "to give the department heads a chance to kick their ideas around and really get to know each other. Nothing too formal, you understand. I head the meeting, of course, because somebody has to get the thing started. But from then on it's strictly up to the boys themselves. They can relax, bring up any subject they're interested in, shoot at each other if they want to, shoot at *me* if they want to. That particular day, nobody's the boss, and we can all take our hair down." And he would add, "It's been a most rewarding experiment."

For Kingham himself it was, perhaps, rewarding. By the others the meeting was regarded as an extra Management conference rendered more complex and tedious by the necessity of acting out an elaborate charade of informality. This had to be done with discretion; there were still vivid memories of the early days of the experiment when various individuals (no longer employed by the company), had taken Kingham's instructions a little too literally. But it was necessary to put up a show, and experienced members of the committee, those who knew how far to go, would often engage in spirited little arguments with each other, though always on a friendly, Christian-name basis. Kingham would watch these benignly, like a schoolmaster refereeing a boy's boxing match. His

job, as he saw it, was to see fair play without spoiling the fun. Occasionally, but not too often, somebody started an argument with Kingham himself. For that, you had to pick your day.

Today was not one of them. It was soon plain that the men closest to Kingham had sensed that this was no occasion for departmental shadow-boxing, however good-natured. Gradually even Marshall, through a fog of smoke and boredom, became aware that events were not following their usual course. Somehow, things were not going well for Wilcox. His facts were subjected to query, his conclusions disputed. Nobody went so far as to criticize him openly; it was more a matter of an impatient wrinkling of Kingham's forehead, a testy inflection in his voice when pointing out the inadequacy of an answer. It was hard to resist the conclusion that Wilcox had briefed himself inadequately, had not given sufficient coverage to the territory, had spent his energies on nonentities while missing out on the important people altogether. A question would be asked about some point of detail—the sales figures for Sweden, the new currency restrictions recently introduced by the Portuguese Government. No doubt Mr. Wilcox would have the figures with him? Well, no, he didn't have them with him right now, he was afraid, but they were in the file, he could easily . . . No, no, it was all right. As it happened, John Richardson had got them out just before the meeting, having anticipated that the matter might be raised. Well, then, John, perhaps you'd like to tell us what your thinking is about this one. . . .

Marshall looked down at the table and began to doodle absent-mindedly on his memo pad. This, he reminded himself as his pencil moved in a series of elaborate, vaguely Freudian patterns, was no concern of his. If they were out to crucify Wilcox, there was nothing he could do to stop them. He had been present at such spectacles before and knew the uselessness of intervention. It was best to preserve the attitude of the naturalist, to watch them like fish through the glass wall of a tank, fighting, rutting, making their messes in front of his eyes—so near, yet never quite near enough to touch him. Kingham, it seemed, would eat Wilcox; perhaps, with luck, someone in due time would eat Kingham. Who? he wondered. Richardson? Livera? Or more likely some larger fish alto-

gether, from outside the International, some savage razor-toothed vice-president, some hypertensive pike in bifocals. It was possible. In this world anyone might get eaten, even Mr. Bernstein himself, if he relaxed his concentration for a moment. Nobody was immortal—except perhaps himself. Too unimportant to fear, yet too dangerous to attack, he alone carried pretensions to immunity.

Weary of whorls and rectangles, he began to draw caricatures—the easy way. That is to say, he would draw the faces first and then decide who they were meant to be. It was a pleasant and unexacting way of whiling away a dull afternoon. After a few minutes of earnest concentration he was left with a sketch of a cross-eyed old harridan with bushy eyebrows and a hatful of wax fruit. Obviously, he decided without hesitation, a lady novelist. But which one? Colette? Willa Cather? Mrs. Humphry Ward?

Unable to reach a satisfactory decision, he dropped his pencil on the table and turned his attention back to the meeting. Wilcox was taking it well, all things considered. Occasionally he would give a thin little smile and a nod of agreement, just to show that he was not the sort of man who turned sulky under criticism. He had obviously understood and accepted the process which was now going on. Perhaps he had indeed, as was continually being implied, fallen down on the job. Or it might be that this was merely a demonstration, that certain private and personal scores had to be paid off, that some policy decision had been made which required that Wilcox should, in this particular instance at least, be discredited.

If that was the case, the outlook for Wilcox would be more hopeful than it superficially appeared. There was always a good chance that some reversal of policy, some reshuffling of personalities might restore him to favor. The only thing which would be fatal to him would be a loss of self-control at the present moment, a surrender to the temptation to hit back. It seemed that Wilcox was well aware of this danger. At certain crucial points he had developed a tendency to gaze fixedly at the ceiling through half-closed eyes. His lips would move slightly, as if repeating something silently to himself.

Repeating what? Marshall wondered. Some maxim from Dale Carnegie or the *Reader's Digest*, some fragment of Kipling's *If*? More likely he was repeating figures. How much would he be earn-

ing? Fifteen thousand, probably. Not bad for a man just over thirty. More than he was worth. The old man had said: "Always pay your executives more than they are worth. That way you get loyalty."

And so you did. Because when a man was pulling down fifteen thousand a year he got into the habit of living that way, with a couple of cars and the right sort of house with the right sort of mortgage on it. He had an expensive wife and two or three kids and a country-club subscription and quite a load of insurance. And the nearer his commitments approached the amount of money he had left after taxes, the more scared he became of losing his job and the more loyal he became. . . .

On this basis everyone around the table was loyal—everyone, that is to say, except himself, doodling subversively on a piece of company paper. He could see that his behavior was annoying Kingham and could almost imagine the fatal word of condemnation forming in the other man's mind—Marshall was disloyal. With his family name and private fortune, with his minor but not insignificant shareholding and a brother on the Board, disloyalty was a luxury he could afford. If he performed no other function in the organization, he could at least be independent and unafraid. Inherited wealth, he thought as he absently added a pair of pince-nez and an incipient mustache to his portrait, was one of the few remaining defenses against the tyranny of vulgar ability.

Kingham stopped in the middle of a review of some sales figures. "Did you say something, Chris?"

Could he possibly have spoken aloud? "No," he said, "I didn't say anything."

He spoke carelessly, but the disturbing fact was that it needed a deliberate effort, he had to work to keep the respect out of his voice. Kingham regarded him impassively, the schoolmaster who is quite confident of his power to enforce discipline but prepared to be indulgent on this occasion. Then he resumed his speech. He was a slight, birdlike man. His nose was pointed, his eyes dark and bright behind the horn-rimmed spectacles, his thin hair slicked back over his scalp like the feathers of a starling. His mouth was tight and small; his chin, though slightly receding, gave no impression of

vacuity or weakness. He was dressed, as always, with great care. Two triangular points of a white handkerchief, one monogrammed, peeped above the aperture of his breast pocket. As he spoke he rested his small hands, palms downward, on either side of his notes. His voice was crisp and confident. Every now and then he would glance swiftly down with a sharp pecking movement, pick up a fact from the sheet of paper in front of him, and incorporate it into his argument.

It was after five when the conference broke up. Afterward the members of the committee stood around in groups, chatting. The ash trays were crammed with the butts of half-smoked cigarettes. Marshall watched Wilcox slip unobtrusively out of the room. He was preparing to leave himself when he felt an arm on his shoulder. He looked up to see Kingham smiling down at him.

Kingham pointed down at the drawing. "Who's that supposed to be?"

"Nobody special. Have you any suggestions?"

Kingham shook his head. The smile remained, fixed and patronizing. "It shows talent," he said.

"Thank you."

"Almost professional, I'd say. But then I'm no judge." Marshall made a noncommittal noise. Was there hidden malice behind these remarks, or was it merely a heavy-handed attempt at amiability? Kingham went on, "Didn't you spend a couple of years in Paris or something? I seem to remember your father telling me——"

"Yes," said Marshall shortly. Naturally, he thought with some bitterness, his father would have told Kingham. He had told everybody. It was the sort of story that appealed to him—a victory for himself. "My father thought I was crazy. And it so happened he was right."

"He often was," said Kingham, "about a lot of things. He was a smart old man."

"I don't give him any credit in this case. He would have thought Michelangelo was crazy."

Kingham laughed. "I guess he would, at that." He lit a cigarette and said pensively, "There are a lot of things about art that I don't get at all. I mean, how did you know in the end that"—he hesitated,

searching for some more delicate way of describing failure—"well, that he was right and you were wrong?"

"People tell you—people who are supposed to know. You tell yourself they don't know, that nobody really knows. And then one day you look at something you've done and you find yourself agreeing with them. After that——" He shrugged his shoulders.

Kingham wrinkled his brows. He was a man who prided himself on his interest in people. He liked, he often said, to be able to get inside another man's problems. "But if you went on working? If you really wanted to succeed badly enough——"

Marshall made a grimace. How had he been fool enough to let the conversation get as far as this? "We're talking about two different things," he said abruptly. "Don't ever let them tell you that genius is an infinite capacity for taking pains." He folded the sheet of paper into four, tore it up, and dropped the fragments into an ash tray. Perhaps Kingham would take the hint and leave him alone. But the hand remained on his shoulder.

"There was something else," said Kingham, "that I wanted to talk to you about."

Marshall looked at him with interest. What could be going on? He had not received as much attention as this in years. He was not Kingham's type of man. Kingham liked the bright boys, the keen boys, the Richardsons, the Wilcoxes, clear of eye and clean of limb, bursting with ideals. "Go right ahead," he said.

Kingham looked around the room. There were still one or two other people left. "Not here, I think."

"Is it important?"

Kingham nodded. "We might discuss it over a drink. Perhaps you could meet me at the Phoenix in about half an hour's time."

CHAPTER II

THERE WAS just time to call in at his office and sign the day's correspondence. As he walked down the corridor he was conscious once more of the world outside. Shafts of April sunlight splashed, like searchlight beams, across the main corridor, giving patchy illumination to the pale green walls, lighting up the colored maps and photographs of factories, the bronze plaque which had been affixed in honor of his father (recalling that memorable day, three years ago, when the old man had succumbed to a fatal apoplexy after failing to bribe a senator over some government contracts). The executive offices of the International opened off one side of the corridor—Sales, Technical Direction, Production, Advertising, Market Research. He opened a door labeled "Publicity Co-ordination" and went in. In the outer office there were two stenographers and Rose Bauer, his assistant.

Rose was a plump, almost pretty blonde of about his own age, married to a trombonist in the New York Philharmonic.

"Anything new?" he asked.

"Well . . ." She flipped over some papers. "There're some figures about the production potentialities of the new plant in Montreal —a picture of Mr. Bernstein receiving the Order of the Golden Fleece, third class, in some South American republic——"

"Christ."

"Some information on the use of precision instruments in guided missiles, with particular reference to our K 702——"

"That sounds good."

"We probably can't use it. There's some question of secrecy. One of our people in Japan has won a lottery——"

"How much?"

"Sixty thousand yen. So far as I can gather, that's about fifty dollars. But I've circulated it, anyway."

"That's the girl. Anything else come up?"

"Charlie Parker called. He wants a cover for the house magazine."

"Give him Mr. Bernstein and the Golden Fleece."

She looked doubtful. "Last issue we had Mr. Bernstein and the Chamber of Commerce."

"Never mind. We can't get too much of Mr. Bernstein."

He was conscious of a querulous presence at his elbow. It was his secretary, Miss Tracy.

"Mr. Marshall, your office is full of letters for signing. If you don't come in right now I shall miss the afternoon mail."

"Okay."

He walked through with her into the inner office. The letters were filed neatly on his blotter; as usual, they were monotonously accurate, without even so much as a spelling mistake to enliven them. As he read through the drab, shopworn, repetitive phrases he was filled with distaste. This sort of thing was all very well for Rose—distributing handouts, buying drinks for journalists, replying to inquiries from shareholders. She might pretend to be cynical about it, but in fact she enjoyed it. Also, the job was valuable to her—Fred Bauer was an unstable personality even for a musician. Only last week he had got drunk in Cincinnati and came in four bars too soon on the Sibelius. . . .

Yes, for Rose it made some sense. But for him—the whole outfit stank of a sinecure, a nice warm place for the old man's son, where he couldn't do much harm. He turned over the letters irritably, at increasing speed, and handed them back to Miss Tracy.

"Is that all?"

"There are these as well."

She handed him a sheaf of typed memoranda on the pale blue paper used for inter-office communications. They were the fruit of a recent burst of reorganization put through by Kingham at the in-

stigation of a firm of management consultants. Memoranda which had once been dealt with individually by department heads were now circulated among all the members of the board of management of the International. There was a special sheet attached for comments and signatures. Most of the memoranda were quite trivial. Since they circulated in order of descending importance, it was almost unknown for anybody to disagree with the first opinion expressed.

"Hell," said Marshall, "I haven't time to read all these."

As the most junior and insignificant of the departmental heads, he was the last to receive the memoranda. He noticed that all the present collection had been approved by the others before reaching him. Without bothering to read them he scribbled "Agreed" on each one, added his signature, and handed them back to his secretary.

By New York standards, the Phoenix Hotel was something in the nature of an ancient monument. In a city where progress was king, it remained as one of the few reminders of the luxury which was fashionable in the early years of the century. Marble floors, high decorated ceilings, extravagantly wasteful in space, endowed it with a cavernous distinction. Always, even when all the rooms were occupied, it appeared to the casual visitor half empty. The bar opened like a small private chapel off the cathedral bulk of the main hall. Here the tables were spaced well apart, the waiters alert but soft-footed, the charges frequently capricious and invariably extortionate.

Marshall ordered a drink for himself and lit a cigarette. Kingham would be late. A scrupulously punctual man, it was his custom to keep his juniors waiting, as a matter of prestige. The length of time varied with the status of the person concerned—it was regarded as a useful method of gauging one's current rating in the company.

It was just on a quarter past six when Kingham entered the bar. Marshall recorded the fact with interest—up till now he had been a twenty-minute man. Could it be that by some mysterious process he had gained in favor? It seemed unlikely. He watched the sleek head turn quickly to right and left, scanning the room for acquaint-

ances. The barman nodded respectfully, and Kingham nodded back with an assured smile which came up from deep in the recesses of his expense account. Then he walked over to the table.

"Sorry to keep you waiting, Chris," he said. "I was just getting ready to leave when Bernie called up."

"That's all right."

There was a slight pause. Marshall had the feeling that something was demanded of him. Did Kingham expect him to be impressed by his intimacy with the president of the company, this casual use of nicknames? If so, he was ready to play in, up to a point. But he could never be sure of such things. He felt his own inadequacy in this particular world. Any of the others—Richardson, Livera, Wilcox—would have known instinctively how to react.

"Had Mr. Bernstein anything special to say?" he asked finally, conscious of the stiffness of the question but unable to do anything to improve it.

"No. He just likes to toss the ball around—let us know he's alive." Kingham picked up a handful of salted nuts and swallowed them. "What's that you're drinking?"

"Scotch."

He called the waiter. "Two scotch—on the rocks." He looked round at the pillars and the palms. "You know, this place has something."

"Yes," agreed Chris. "Of course it shouldn't be in America at all. It's more like a spa hotel in Aix or Baden-Baden. You can practically see the dowagers knitting behind the potted palms."

Kingham laughed perfunctorily. After a pause he said, "How long did you say you were in Europe?"

"Four years. First at Cambridge, then in Paris."

"Do you speak French?"

"Not well." He explained, "At the art schools the foreign students used to stick together. Most of my friends were American or English."

"You liked it over there?"

"Yes." His voice was careless, noncommittal. He was not to be caught again. Even after several years the memory of this particular episode in his life had the power to raise emotions in him which

he found it almost impossible to control. The way to handle it was to prevent it from getting hold, to think of something else, pretend that you were talking about a thing that had happened to some other person, someone you hardly knew.

"Would you like to go back?"

"It depends."

He was doing fine. Kingham was looking at him in a puzzled way, surprised that he was showing so little animation. Suddenly he changed the subject.

"How do you think the meeting went today?"

Marshall regarded him warily. What was he up to now? "All right. Pretty much as usual."

"What did you think of Wilcox?"

"Wilcox?"

"Yes. You know what I mean. How did you think he was measuring up to the job?"

Marshall floundered. "That's a difficult question. Unless one knows all the circumstances——"

Kingham held up a hand. "That's okay. You don't have to say any more. Maybe I shouldn't have asked." He paused. "Just the same, I wanted your reaction. My guess is that if you'd felt completely confident in him you'd have come out with considerably more enthusiasm. Right?"

"No," Marshall protested, "that's not so. I genuinely meant——"

"Forget it," Kingham cut in. "Forget I ever asked you. Whatever you think about Wilcox, I know what *I* think—and I feel badly about it. You see, Wilcox was my boy—I pushed him all the way. And what it amounts to is that I pushed him too far and too fast. If there's been a mistake," he asserted handsomely, "I take the blame for it. But we can't run a business like this successfully unless we face up to the facts. Personal feelings have to take second place. The truth is, Wilcox hasn't measured up to the job."

Awkwardly Marshall began to protest. He had the feeling of being present at an assassination, with no very clear idea as to what he ought to do about it. He had not been involved in the attack on Wilcox and he could not understand what Kingham's object was in dragging him into the matter. As a rule he was told

nothing about what was happening until afterward, and sometimes not even then. Frequently the stenographers knew more about what was going on in the office than he did. He was not accustomed to confidential talks of this kind.

Kingham brushed the protests aside. In spite of disagreeable necessities he was, he conveyed, fundamentally benevolent.

"One has to remember," he said, "that Wilcox is still young. I haven't lost faith in him. I still think he's a fine guy and we're lucky to have him. He just wasn't ready for what I gave him. He was short on background." He shook his head regretfully and went on with some solemnity, "It's clear to me now that what we need is someone with a broader approach. Not just a keen boy like Wilcox who's never been out of the United States in his life. Someone more sophisticated, if you get me." He paused for a moment to let the idea make its mark and then said, "How'd you like to go to Europe for a spell, Chris?"

So *that* was what it was all about.

"In Wilcox's place?" he asked.

"Yes. I'm going to move him to another area where he'll feel more at home."

"You think," asked Marshall with a touch of irony, "that I'd be a success?"

"I wouldn't offer it otherwise."

"I haven't so very much business experience."

"I thought of that. But it doesn't matter too much. Your position would be more liaison than executive. Primarily, what we want is character and personality. You'll pick up the rest fast enough as you go along. You know," he said thoughtfully, "I've been thinking for some time that you weren't very happy in your present job. Am I right?"

"I haven't complained," said Marshall.

"No. But I just had the idea. . . . And I don't blame you. It's a department, I know. But not really a top-line one. It always seemed to me that you were a little wasted there. I've been looking for a way to use you, to build you up. And I'm convinced that this is it." He sat back. "Well, what do you say?"

Marshall hesitated. It was, on the face of it, a considerable op-

portunity. If nothing else, it would get him out of public relations and away from the New York office. The job sounded interesting, and he would be working in a country he had always liked. He would have some degree of independence. . . .

And yet the offer was puzzling. He could not persuade himself that Kingham liked him or had any regard for his abilities. Why then should he wish to "build him up"? There were plenty of other young men, enthusiastic, loyal young men who would jump at the opportunity. There must be *something* wrong with it.

Cautiously he said, "It sounds attractive. Could I have a couple of days to think it over?"

Kingham frowned. He was not accustomed to having his favors treated in this cavalier fashion.

"Is that necessary?" he said.

"I'm afraid so." All Marshall's dislike of Kingham flared up. The bastard could wait. "I have," he said meaninglessly, "personal reasons."

"Very well," said Kingham reluctantly. "But we've got to get things rolling. I'd like your answer by first thing Monday morning." There was a slight pause. Having carried out his purpose, he was left with nothing more to say. "How about another drink?" he asked without enthusiasm.

"No, thanks," Marshall said, taking his cue. He was no more anxious to prolong the conversation himself. "I ought to be leaving. I have a date for dinner."

CHAPTER III

HE JOINED the stream of traffic on the parkway, easing his car into the more sluggish outside lane. He was in no hurry. Past him, in an endless procession, nose to tail, drove the more ambitious commuters; each evening they poured out of Manhattan like a defeated army, bolting for refuge in the suburbs. In a score of neat, prosperous, ever-growing villages, a hundred thousand wives in a hundred thousand houses waited, and wondered whether it was time to start fixing a martini. Twice that number of children played on the lawns behind the houses or poised themselves in a cataleptic trance before the mystery of television. Soon Dad would be home. And Dad, all tensed up after a hard day at the office, took one hand off the wheel of his new two-hundred-horsepower sedan and fumbled for the last remaining cigarette in his coat pocket. The sun was setting on another American day.

As he drove along, Marshall thought again about Kingham's offer. Why had he been so hesitant about accepting it? Had he, after all, so much to lose? There was a danger that his personal dislike of Kingham might be turning into an obsession, so that everything that came from him, no matter how superficially desirable, was treated as a matter of course with suspicion. It was important to see Kingham's point of view, to visualize yourself as a man in authority, plagued by a useless, unco-operative subordinate whom circumstances made it impossible to remove. You did your best to keep him away from real responsibility, but so long as he

was around he remained a stone in your shoe, a bad example to others. What more obvious approach to the problem than to send him abroad?

It seemed the most likely explanation and one that he would be unreasonable to resent. Yet still he found himself unwilling to make a decision. Why? Could it be that he was afraid of returning to Paris? But surely that was over and done with. He had admitted his failure as a man might eat some nauseating meal, managing somehow to keep it down, hoping that at least he might absorb from it some benefit for the future. His father had, characteristically, spared him nothing, offered him no consolation. And he had asked for none. He had accepted his present position with resignation, because it was the logical thing to do, once you had lost, to accept the terms of the victor. He had even once hoped that in due time he might come, not perhaps to enjoy it, but at least to regard it without active disgust. Now he knew that this was an illusion. After five years he still hated New York, he hated the business, he hated Kingham. It was hard to see how any change could possibly be for the worse.

It was almost half-past eight when he reached the house. It was a rambling Dutch-colonial mansion which had been far too big even when his father was alive. The old man had seen it going cheaply during the depression and had snapped it up on a quick deal. He had had very little feeling for it except in so far as it had been a bargain, and he always felt affectionately toward a bargain. He had taken a pride in keeping it in good shape, though he had spent little of his time there. Since his death, his widow had lived there constantly, loving the house, and done practically nothing to keep it in repair; she seemed to prefer an atmosphere of mild dilapidation. The garden was overgrown, and some of the window frames needed painting. As he got out of the car an old great Dane lumbered reluctantly from his place on the porch, walked over, and nuzzled his hand. He was growing fat and sleepy. Very soon he would be just watching from the porch, too lazy to get up.

Marshall walked through the hall to the living room. His mother was sitting at a card table, playing solitaire. It was as he had expected to find her.

"Hello, Mother."

"Hello, Chris." Though she had lived in the North for years, she still bore traces of the accent she had brought with her from Petersburg as a bride. Nowadays it seemed to him, if anything, more noticeable, possibly because she went around so little and spent so much time talking to the servants.

She put down her pack of cards and allowed him to kiss her on the cheek. "How's everything?"

"Oh, fine, fine." He looked out of the open french doors. The shadows on the lawns were warm and scented. "The country certainly is wonderful at this time of year."

"Yes." Her face was handsome even now, her voice pleasant, her smile charming, her movements graceful. Yet somehow she had always been slightly unsatisfactory as a mother. There was a certain vagueness about her affection for her two children which seemed at times, particularly in Jeff's case, almost to amount to indifference. Though interested in their affairs, she was primarily occupied by her own. As boys they had been grateful for her lack of possessiveness, and yet at the same time they had felt vaguely cheated, as if they had missed some warm maternal experience which they had a right to expect. "You should come out here more often," she said casually, as if talking to an old friend, some near but not very intimate relation. "We're not as cut off as we used to be. It's only an hour on the parkway."

"An hour and a half."

"Your father used to say he could make it in an hour."

"He was a liar."

"Chris——" she protested mildly.

"Well, he was, wasn't he?"

"He might perhaps have exaggerated a little . . ."

"That nonsense about doing New York in an hour was typical of him. He liked to show off, like a child. When you pointed out to him that he wasn't telling the truth, he got mad and tried to shout you down." And then of course he wasn't like a child any more. Marshall remembered those rages (who could have forgotten them?), the flushed face, the glaring pale blue eyes, the short stocky figure rigid with determination. That determination had been his

most lavish asset; he had had it to burn, as another man might have intelligence or imagination. And he had burned it. He had used it to compensate for a dozen other disadvantages—impulsiveness, lack of education, deficiencies in charm. Like any man with an abundance of something, he had almost seemed to take pleasure in wasting it. The smallest disputes within the family were enough to call out the utmost violence of his nature. The recalcitrance of a golf ball could arouse within him agonies of frustration.

"I don't think," said Mrs. Marshall mildly, "that you should talk about your father like that."

"I don't know why not." He began to mix himself a drink. "He always said what he liked about me."

She turned on him reproachfully. "He thought the world of you, Chris."

It was true, of course. As a boy he had been the smart one and his father had worshiped smartness—up to a point. "Oh, sure. So long as he thought I'd do what he wanted, we were great pals. When he found I wouldn't, he hated the sight of me."

"No, he didn't. He——"

"I'm not complaining. It's just that he had to do everything a hundred per cent. Or rather more if possible."

"It made him what he was."

"Yes, by God." There didn't seem to be anything more to say about that. After a short silence his mother said, "Are you staying for the weekend?"

"Until Sunday night—if that's all right with you."

"Of course." A transient sense of social obligation came over her. "Perhaps you'd like to invite some friends over one afternoon. We could mark out the tennis court . . ."

The tennis court had not been weeded or marked out since his father died. He said: "Don't worry, Mother. There's no one around I want to ask."

"As you say, dear." She could not disguise her relief. At least she had made the gesture. "It probably would be better for you to take a rest. I'm sure you lead a very hectic and unhealthy life in New York."

"Not really."

"No? Somehow I always think of young men in service apartments living on cigarettes and highballs. And you look so thin——"

"I always was, you know."

"That's true. Well, perhaps I'm completely wrong. And when a man's getting near thirty he has to lead his own life—there's no object in trying to influence him any more," she said. She was obviously glad to be released of any obligation to do so. "Shall we go in for dinner?"

"I thought Jeff and Paula were coming."

"Not until afterward. Paula called up to say they'd had some trouble with baby-sitters. But they'll be over for coffee." With unconcealed satisfaction she added: "So we can have an hour on our own." Getting up from her chair, she suddenly raised her voice and called, "Virgie!"

"Yes'm," came a voice from the kitchen.

"Is dinner ready?"

"Been ready for some while now."

"We'll be coming right in then."

The big dining-room table was laid for two places only and lit by an enormous silver candelabrum, one of whose arms had fractured in the middle and had been temporarily splinted with wire. The meal was served by Virgie, the colored woman who had come North with his mother from Petersburg. Now aged and almost entirely toothless, she shuffled to and from the kitchen with the dishes, humming snatches of some old song and occasionally talking to herself in a low voice. Her husband, Joe, acted as chauffeur-gardener, driving Mrs. Marshall around the district in an old Cadillac almost as gaunt and dilapidated as himself. As they all grew older, the tempo of life at Falls Ridge was running down. Gradually in her old age Mrs. Marshall was returning to the old, sleepy, sunny, careless way of life of her childhood.

The food, however, was still good. There was fried chicken for Marshall; his mother, who had taken to vegetarianism and bridge as hobbies suitable to her widowhood, was served an avocado-pear salad.

During the meal he said, "There's some possibility that I may go to Europe fairly soon."

"On a trip?"

"No. I've been offered a job. As European representative."

"When was this?"

"About an hour or two ago. Kingham—do you know him?"

"No. Should I?"

"He's head of the International. He occasionally asks after you."

She thought and then shook her head. "I don't know him. Perhaps he came here to one of your father's parties in the old days. So many of them did. I could never remember . . ." She asked plaintively, "What exactly *is* a European representative?"

He waited for Virgie to take away his empty plate and then said, "Well, as you may know, we deal with Europe mainly through agencies and distributors. They sell our goods for us and take a percentage. Theoretically they're separate firms, but most of them are in some degree or other dependent on the corporation. The British one, and that's the largest, is a subsidiary in everything but name. The European representative of Marshall's is based in London and acts as a liaison between these firms and the main office in New York. It used to be a man called Wilcox, but he's due for transfer. Today Kingham asked me if I'd like to go in his place."

She paused for a moment, as if searching for a means of interpretation. "And what did you say?"

"I said I'd like to think about it."

She looked at him more sharply. In spite of her vagueness she was by no means an unperceptive woman. "You have some doubts about it?"

"Yes." He was hesitant. They were doubts he hardly felt able to express.

Fortunately she did not ask him for details. "I wish I could help you," she said after a pause, "but I know so little of what goes on in the company nowadays. This person Kingham, for instance——" In her world, thought Chris, everything was seen in terms of personalities. He had at one time laughed at this naïve type of approach. As he grew older he was not so sure. "What does Mr. Bernstein say?" she asked.

He smiled. She was certainly a little out of touch. "The company's much bigger nowadays, Mother. I hardly ever see Mr. Bernstein."

She shook her head in wonderment. "It seems funny, Alfred Bernstein being so important. I remember him from the old days when he and Sarah used to come round for a game of bridge in the evening. He could never make up his mind what to call and your father used to get so impatient that we had to stop inviting them. Poor man, he had no card sense. I think he only played to be agreeable." She was silent for a moment and then suddenly asked, "Is this European job an advancement?"

He was momentarily disconcerted. This was an aspect which he had hardly considered. "Oh yes. I'd say so——"

"What's the salary?"

"I'm afraid I forgot to ask."

She looked at him in surprise. "*Really*, Chris."

"But, hell," he protested, "the money doesn't matter. It only goes in taxes anyway."

"I know that." She went on patiently, as if to a child, "But it's still important. The more they pay you, the more you count for. If you're prepared to work for nothing, they'll think of you as a nobody—you've got to keep up your prestige."

"Oh, sure," he said ironically. "I'm loaded with prestige right now. Co-ordinator of publicity."

"What's wrong with that?"

"It doesn't mean anything, that's all." She opened her mouth to speak, but he went on quickly, "Now don't get the idea that I'm beefing about it. It's really very kind of them to have me around at all."

"You can do anything that Jeff can," she said with spirit. "And now he's on the Board."

"I know." His voice was tired. This was an old argument. "Jeff's no ball of fire, we'll agree on that. But he works hard and he believes like hell in his job. And that's what matters."

"Your father used to say——"

"Please, Mother—please!" He got up from the table in his agitation. "Don't quote Father to me. It just makes me mad."

"I don't know why——"

"Because I'm not prepared to accept anything he said—or anything he did, for that matter——"

"He did a lot for us."

"He made money—that's what you mean."

"Is that nothing?"

"It isn't enough."

She sighed. "Nothing's ever quite enough, you know. We have to do the best we can."

"Okay, I'll agree with that." He sat down again. "But he didn't. He was a liar and a cheat and a bully. And, what was worse, he was proud of it." He said with disgust, "Anything to win a trick."

"No." She shook her head. "You're not being fair to him. He could be like that, I know—he made me very unhappy, especially when I was younger. In those days I didn't understand the sort of problems he had to face." She explained slowly, "Your father had a great deal to do in the world. He was a man who couldn't stand still—he had always to be acting, moving, fighting. He couldn't help that—it was his nature. To keep up his self-confidence he had to win as often as possible. And to win——"

"He had to cheat."

"Sometimes," she admitted. "Sometimes he behaved very badly. And naturally it was a great shock to him when you wanted to go to Paris and paint pictures——"

"I wasn't talking about that. I was talking generally." Seeing the look of disbelief on her face, he added irritably, "You never seem to understand that people can be talking generally."

"Perhaps not." She was undisturbed by his annoyance. It was impossible to quarrel with her; in the world she inhabited now, nothing was sufficiently serious. She smiled. "Your father used to complain about that too."

The tension between them was relaxed. Soon she changed the subject and began to talk about her health. She was a mild hypochondriac and at the present moment under the sway of a certain Dr. Aronson, who claimed to be a specialist in allergies. She had a long list of various substances, any one of which might do her irreparable harm if inadvertently eaten or inhaled, and carried it with her everywhere. It made her whole life a sort of gigantic obstacle race. A copy of the list had also been posted in the kitchen, but Virgie, she complained, was proving unco-operative.

"I can't imagine why she's so awkward," said Mrs. Marshall, peering suspiciously into her fruit cup. "It's impossible to trust her any more. I must have told her a hundred times that I'm sensitive to pineapples."

Jeff and Paula arrived in time for coffee. Their entrance was always an impressive ceremony, as if Jeff, instead of living ten miles away, had been off on safari for at least a year. He was a large, heavily built man in his middle thirties. At college he had been a footballer of distinction, but since then he had put on some weight. The dark, smooth-shaven chin had lost a good deal of its sharpness. His wife was small, fair, and very pretty.

"Hi, Chris."

"Hi, Jeff." Marshall moved forward and allowed his hand to be gripped. Extricating his bruised fingers, he said, "Hello, Paula. I hardly saw you."

This got a laugh, as he knew it would. The contrast in their sizes was an endless source of delight to them both. "How are the kids?" he said.

"Terrible!" shrieked Paula proudly. "They're driving me crazy. First they want fur hats, then space helmets and death-ray guns. Now they're all steamed up about some sort of a mouse. I don't get it at all."

"She spoils them," said Jeff. "They get too many gadgets nowadays. Why, when I was a kid——"

"But, honey, what can you do? All the other kids have them."

"Yeah, I guess so," he agreed indulgently. As they went into the living room he said, "Congratulations on the new job, Chris."

"Oh—you heard?"

"Yes, Harry Kingham just called me up."

"I haven't officially accepted yet."

"Oh, but you will, won't you?"

Mrs. Marshall was pouring the coffee. "Do you think he should, Jeff?"

"Why, surely." He added earnestly, "This is tailored for you, Chris. Wilcox was all right, but he just didn't have the necessary class."

"You think I can make something of it?"

"Sure I do. And so does Kingham."

"I wouldn't have thought I was his type."

Jeff shook his head knowingly. "That's where you're wrong. Kingham's a smart guy—he's not so conventional as some. I'm telling you—you rate higher than you think."

"Well—that's encouraging."

"I know you won't take it wrong if I say this, Chris—but, the way I look at it, all you lack is self-confidence."

Chris looked at him, taking in the smooth, solemn face, the Rotary Club voice, the dull, tenacious, satisfied mouth. "You think so?"

"Sure. Just because Dad——"

"Never mind about Dad," he cut in sharply. "In fact, never mind about Kingham, or Bernstein, or Handley, or Lewis, or all the rest of the vice-presidents. They're all great guys and as smart as whips. There isn't a finer board of management in the whole of American industry. Am I right?"

Jeff eyed him doggedly. "I believe so."

Suddenly he was tired, not of Jeff, but of himself. Who was he to be getting so smart and cynical about everything? The clever younger brother who never grew up, who hadn't managed to make anything of his own life but consoled himself by sneering at the beliefs and enthusiasms of other people. It was easy enough to do—too easy—especially when the people you were sneering at were your own family and too kindhearted to hit back where they knew it would really hurt. . . . What he really needed, he thought, was to get away. Away from the people who knew his history, and remembered his father, and had formed preconceived ideas about everything concerning him. Somewhere else he could start afresh with a different set of people. They would look at him with new eyes and perhaps he would see himself differently too. Perhaps for once spring was right, there *was* something round the corner. . . .

He put his arm affectionately on Jeff's shoulder. "Don't worry," he said. "I was only kidding you. I'm going to accept."

CHAPTER IV

ON THE MONDAY MORNING he called Kingham as soon as he reached the office.

"Yes?"

"This is Chris Marshall. I called you to say I'd like to take the job."

"The job? Oh yes——" He was expected to draw the inference that Kingham had so many things on his mind that he had momentarily forgotten about the job altogether. "Good. That's fine. Now, wait a moment—I'd like to talk to you but I'm busy right now. What about lunch?"

"I'm free."

"Okay. Twelve forty-five?"

He rang off sharply. Marshall started to go through the morning's mail. It was a fairly average sample—the usual proofs of public relations handouts, foreign press cuttings, some advertising material, an invitation to a trade function. It was pleasant to think that he would not be doing this kind of work much longer. When Rose came in he handed the correspondence to her.

"You'd better handle this," he said. "I'm leaving."

She raised her eyebrows. "To do what?"

"Wilcox's job."

"Congratulations," she said. "You'll like it, won't you?"

"I hope so."

"It sounds like a lot more fun than this. Traveling around . . . Though I'm sorry you're going."

Looking at her, he realized with surprise and gratitude that she was genuinely sorry. "You won't notice much difference," he said. "You always did all the work anyway."

She didn't bother to deny it. "Just the same, we've had some good times."

"They may even promote you."

"I doubt it. More likely they'll push in some eager beaver who wants to make a reputation for himself by running us all ragged. Or even wash up the department altogether." She sighed. "No. I'm happy as I am. I just want to be left alone. But there's no sense in hoping for that in this outfit."

Over lunch Kingham said, "I felt sure you'd take it."

"You did?"

"Certainly. I couldn't see any ambitious man of your age passing up an opportunity like this. It's more than just an ordinary job," he said in an approach to lyricism. "It's a challenge." He popped an olive into his mouth. "And I know you're going to meet it."

"That's very kind of you——"

Kingham waved away gratitude. "The hell with that. I say what I think. And that's my guess about you. I may be wrong—but I don't think so." His mistake about Wilcox, thought Marshall, had evidently not affected his faith in his own judgment. "And now—perhaps I'd better give you some details about the setup over there."

The setup in Europe, he explained, was by no means as tidy as the company liked. Most of the trading arrangements had been made just after the war, when conditions were very confused and there was a shortage of reliable information. The essential thing had been to get into the new markets quickly. There were difficulties to overcome concerning the importation of materials and the remission of dollars.

"Those were difficult days," said Kingham reminiscently. "When your father went over there in 1946 everything was in chaos. The ordinary rules of business didn't apply. You couldn't look for a

reputable, long-established firm to handle your goods. They didn't exist any more. Or if they did you probably found that the managing director had bolted for the Argentine or been put in prison as a collaborator or something. You couldn't have a standard form of agreement, because what might be accepted in one country wouldn't work in another. You had to improvise, to pick your men and take a chance on them, to make what arrangements seemed possible at the time. That was the sort of situation where your father scored. He was prepared to jump in and gamble on his own judgment. He met with a good deal of criticism in certain quarters. But in the end he proved himself right. He sure was a great judge of men." Kingham paused reverently and then went on, "You never met any of the distributors?"

"No. They're just names to me."

"The countries that matter most are England and France. Gilbertson in London will be your nearest contact—he may seem a little formal and British at first, but underneath it all he's a very fine guy and a pretty shrewd businessman. I'm confident that he'll help you right up to the limit. But the really brilliant person over there is Furac, the Paris distributor. He's done miracles in building up business under extremely difficult conditions. Believe me, he's a really smart man. And very cultured too."

He went on to speak of others of lesser importance. Most of them received a build-up of one kind or another. They were either very sound or very smart or had unusual experience or first-rate connections. Marshall began to feel restless. No individual characters could be discerned through this fog of superlatives, no clear picture of his own place in the scene.

Kingham paused for a moment. He had finally come to the end of his list of significant personalities. It was time for the summing up. "Now," he said carefully, "what I want to emphasize is this. These are men we have confidence in, because they've produced results. I believe, as your father believed, that results are what matter. You'll pick up knowledge gradually as you go along—that's the only way. Don't get the idea that you're expected to reorganize the whole continent in a month. Take it slowly and be tactful.

Over there, they're only too ready to believe that Americans want to push them around. If their methods are different from ours, don't immediately assume they're crazy. What goes in one place doesn't necessarily go in another. Do you get me?"

"Yes, of course." The advice was sensible, if somewhat obvious. The implication was, presumably, that Wilcox had been overenthusiastic, had interfered, had trodden on influential toes in some fatal but unexplained fashion.

"Then that's fine." Kingham gave a satisfied smile. "I hope I've made everything clear?"

Marshall hesitated. "There's just one thing——"

"What's that?"

He asked rather diffidently, "Well, what do I actually *do?*"

"Do?" Kingham frowned, as if he were beginning to have doubts of Marshall's intelligence. "Well, you're there to look after the interests of the company. You'll report periodically, as Wilcox did. You'll receive instructions from here and act as liaison with the European distributors, especially with the English subsidiary. . . ." He added reassuringly, "You'll soon get into it. As regards the ordinary day-to-day routine, Gilbertson will be able to give you all the information you want. You'll find him most helpful."

"Yes, I'm sure I will," said Marshall. He was still not entirely clear about the position. For instance, what was to be his precise relationship with Gilbertson? However, there seemed little chance of getting any clarification from Kingham. "I suppose," he said, "I shall have a chance to talk to Wilcox before I go?"

"Oh, sure, sure. There should be lots of time for that," Kingham said. "He's being transferred to Domestic, you know."

"I didn't know."

"We think he'll fit in better that way. He'll have a few months' training out in the field, then they'll probably give him an area." He added: "He's going off to Detroit for a couple of days, but he should be back before you go."

"When would you like me to leave?"

"The beginning of next week would be early enough, I guess." Kingham added generously, "I always like to give people time to make arrangements."

It was almost three o'clock when he returned to the office, heavy with rich food and brandy. He had only a week to clear up all outstanding work, arrange his affairs in New York, and see about letting his apartment. He felt excited but confused; events were beginning to march more quickly than he was used to. He telephoned the travel agency to book his passage. The girl was dubious. The notice was short, and first-class berths were not easy to come by. However, she would make inquiries and perhaps call back later in the afternoon.

At half-past five she had still not phoned. He picked up the telephone and then put it down again. Personal contact was always more effective. He decided to call in at the agency on his way out.

The girl behind the counter was apologetic.

"I'm very sorry, Mr. Marshall. I had a note to phone you, but the reservation only came through a matter of ten minutes ago. Yes, it's okay. You were so lucky, just one stateroom left, a cancellation——"

"Well, that's fine. Thank you very much."

"You're welcome." As she made out the ticket, she said: "I really feel badly about not calling you up, but we've been so busy . . ."

"That's quite all right."

"Mostly from your office too. It's really one person's work just looking after the Marshall reservations. And always at the last minute. They think we can work miracles. It's not so difficult on some of the routes. But it's a busy service to Los Angeles——"

To make conversation he asked, "Who's going to Los Angeles?"

"Mr. Wilcox."

"Wilcox? I thought he was going to Detroit."

"Well, yes he is. He had a Detroit return and then we were told this afternoon that it was to be changed to a through ticket to Los Angeles with a forty-eight-hour stopover at Detroit. I've managed it for him in the end, but I practically had to go on my *knees* to the airline——"

"So he won't be coming back to New York?"

"Well, no. At least that's how it stands at the moment. But don't quote me on that. For all I know, he may change his mind again. . . ."

She continued to chatter, but Marshall was no longer listening. The company was given to these sudden and unpredictable postings to distant areas; they gave an impression of urgency and drama, but this was carrying things to absurdity. Presumably the Domestic Division had changed Wilcox's itinerary without bothering to notify Kingham about it. It was a typical piece of administrative muddle. By the time Wilcox returned Marshall would have left for Europe.

He turned back to the girl. "When does Mr. Wilcox leave?" he asked.

"You mean his plane for Detroit?"

"Yes."

"The bus leaves the air terminal at six-thirty, but I gathered from Mr. Wilcox that he wasn't taking it. He said he'd take a cab from his home directly to La Guardia."

"When does the plane actually leave?"

"At eight o'clock. But of course you have to check in twenty minutes earlier."

"Thanks." There was time to drive out to La Guardia if he wanted to. There might be nothing to be gained, but it seemed crazy to go out on a new job without at least having a talk with the man who had been doing it for the past two years. There might be some useful advice he could pick up. He turned away from the desk.

"Mr. Marshall, your tickets." The travel clerk's voice was plaintive. She was having a difficult afternoon. "And here are the baggage tags——"

"Send them up to my office."

He took his car out of the garage and drove to the airport. At first he found himself hurrying and then slowed down, realizing that it was pointless. Even so, he arrived much too early. He lit a cigarette and sat down by the gate for the Detroit flight. It was nearly half an hour before he noticed Wilcox threading his way through the crowd.

"Why, hello!" Wilcox looked at him in surprise. "I didn't figure on a send-off," he added, not too pleasantly.

"I just wanted to have a talk with you before you left."

"Sure. Glad to. Though I haven't much time. . . . I'd better check in first."

When he had checked in they went upstairs to the bar.

"I only just heard," said Marshall, "that you were going through to Los Angeles. It occurred to me that we wouldn't have a chance to talk——"

Wilcox nodded. "It was a rush decision." His speech was a little faster, his face pinker, his whole manner a little less guarded than usual. "I wasn't any too pleased with it myself, but what the hell can you do? There's no sense in arguing."

"It was stupid of them not to tell Kingham."

Wilcox looked at him skeptically. "He didn't know?"

"No. He told me at lunch that you'd be back from Detroit in a day or two."

"Well, what do you know," he said. He gave an unsuccessful little smile and said: "What can I do for you?"

"I was hoping to hear something from you about the European job."

"Were you?" Wilcox picked up a cocktail stick and prodded moodily at the ice in his glass. "There's not much I can tell you in a quarter of an hour. Besides," he added obscurely, "you may know more about what goes on than I do."

"Meaning what?"

Wilcox looked at Marshall as if wondering whether to be wise or to forget about discretion for a change. There was more than one whisky on his breath. He said: "Maybe I was wrong. I had the idea that all this was being arranged for your benefit. Isn't that right?"

"You mean that you were moved out to make a place for me?" Wilcox nodded. "No," said Marshall, "I don't think so. If it was, I knew nothing about it, I can promise you that."

Wilcox regarded him for a moment with the unembarrassed stare of the slightly drunk. "All right," he said eventually. "I believe you. Though God knows why I should." Almost to himself he said: "I guess it must've been the other business. . . ."

"What other business?"

Wilcox paused and then rubbed a hand across his face. He

yawned. "Nothing," he said indifferently. "Nothing that you have to worry about anyway. God," he went on with apparent irrelevance, "I won't be sorry to get back to working on American soil. No, sir."

"You didn't like it over there?" asked Marshall, seeing a possible opportunity of getting back to the point.

"No." Wilcox was suddenly assailed with melancholy and self-doubt. "Maybe Kingham was right—I just don't connect with Europeans. I don't speak their language. All I want to do is to go ahead and get a job done. But it seems that's not enough," he said bitterly, "not for those boys. Have you met Gilbertson?"

"No."

Wilcox shrugged his shoulders. "You may get along all right with him. To me he's just a stuffed shirt."

"Kingham said he was a good businessman."

"He's not such a fool as he looks, I'll give him that."

"What about the other countries?"

"Well, as you probably know, the agencies in Scandinavia and Italy aren't worth much. Nor are the Germans—they can make instruments just as good as ours, and cheaper. Apart from England, France is the only place that counts." He was silent for a moment. "You've heard of Furac?"

"Yes."

"You'll like him," he said sarcastically. "He'll give you a wonderful time. But when you shake hands with him, just count your fingers afterward, that's all." He added with feeling, "Boy, I hope I never see France again."

He drained his glass and looked at Marshall.

"All right," he said sourly, "I know what you're thinking. Poor old Wilcox—he flopped out, and now he's blaming the rest of the team. Correct?"

"No, not at all. I——"

"I didn't look so good at the meeting—I know that. But, brother, you wait till they want to fix you the same way. You just have to sit there and take it—there isn't a goddamn thing you can do. They made it look as if I fell down all along the line. But there was only one thing I did wrong. Do you know what that was?"

He leaned toward Marshall, tapping him on the chest. "Do you know what it was?" he repeated.

"What?"

"I tried to play it the straight way, the American way——" he said in a maudlin voice. "Yes sir, that was my mistake."

This obscurity was maddening. "Tried to play what?" Marshall asked impatiently.

Wilcox withdrew, shaking his head. "Let's leave it there. I've got my future to think of." He was suddenly cautious. "My old man didn't leave me a million dollars, you know."

It was fifteen minutes to eight. Urgently the loud-speakers began to call passengers for the plane to Detroit. Wilcox picked up his brief case from the floor with an air of relief. Obviously he was determined to say no more. Nor did Marshall feel like pressing him. He was out of patience with Wilcox, with his mysterious allusions and his drunken self-pity. Obviously he had antagonized the distributors in Europe and they had used their influence with Kingham to have him replaced. Looking at him now, Marshall found it possible to sympathize with them. Coldly he shook hands and then watched Wilcox disappear through the door toward his plane. Then he went out of the building to look for his car. It had been hardly worth while making the journey.

PART II

CHAPTER I

HIS FIRST SIGHT of Europe was at Cherbourg. The town was a gray, jagged pattern in the misty evening light, with that air of shabby abandonment so characteristic of the ports of northern France since World War II. A few new blocks of concrete flats had appeared, standing on plots of waste ground like skittles in an alley, waiting despondently for the next invader to come and knock them down. The harbor seemed almost deserted as the great ship moved in. Ashore, a few pale lights twinkled sparsely in the main streets of the town. Marshall could visualize the narrow streets, the cafés, the indomitable old women in shiny black clothes poking about for bargains in the shops. He could see the walls covered with tattered posters and scrawled with slogans, the dockside bars in which men sat for hours in political argument or playing belote with greasy packs of cards. The ship drew into the quay, a puff of wind blew from the shore, and he smelled once again the odor of France—something vaguely compounded of coffee and old furniture and dubious sanitation, and the baking of bread in basement kitchens. . . . A few bronzed figures stood lounging on the quay, picturesque in their berets and fishermen's linen trousers, scowling into the clicking cameras of the tourists. A gangway went down and a handful of passengers hurried ashore to catch the train to Paris. The gong for second dinner boomed up from the saloon. Marshall stayed on deck for a little while, feasting on nostalgia. But the air was cold, the diet thin and lacking in sustenance. Presently he left the rail and went down to dinner with the rest.

A few hours later they were in Southampton. Here it was just as he remembered it, only rather smaller. After New York, the houses, the streets, the trains, the automobiles were like a collection of miniatures, delightful in their tidy completeness but hardly to be taken seriously. Even the polite formality of the people seemed to be somehow related to this smallness—the necessary courtesy of individuals compelled to live together in a confined space. He watched them in the train as it traveled toward London, seated within inches of each other in the narrow carriages but carefully avoiding each other's eyes, taking elaborate steps to avoid being drawn into conversation. Outside in the darkness was the tame, trim countryside of Hampshire, punctuated now and then by a flash of lights from an occasional market town. The food in the dining car was cheap but bad, and they were running late; no one knew why. He felt himself growing attuned once more to the rhythm of British life.

It was after midnight when the train drew into Waterloo. He was standing on the platform looking for a porter to collect his luggage when he noticed someone pushing his way through the crowds toward him. It was a young man of between twenty and thirty, wearing a loose tweed suit and a small mustache of a vaguely military appearance. He leaped over a pair of suitcases and presented himself with the satisfied air of a man breasting the tape at the end of an obstacle race.

"Mr. Marshall?"

"Yes?"

"How do you do, sir?"

Marshall was about to say, "Fine—fine" and then remembered in time. "How do you do?"

The young man shot out an arm and shook hands with him, squeezing quite unnecessarily hard, as if he had once been advised to cultivate a strong, positive handshake. "My name's Travers. I'm Mr. Gilbertson's personal assistant."

"I'm very glad to meet you."

"Mr. Gilbertson asked me to apologize for him. He had a dinner engagement outside London which he couldn't very well skip. . . ."

"Please don't apologize," said Marshall. "I never expected him to be here. Or anyone, for that matter. It was very good of you to come along."

"Delighted. Delighted." He spoke with apparent sincerity. Perhaps he was the sort of person who enjoyed meeting trains at midnight. "I'll just see about your luggage." Travers waved to a porter who had been waiting some ten yards away, deaf to all other requests. The disposal of the luggage was arranged with ostentatious briskness and efficiency. Plainly, Travers was out to make an impression. It occurred to Marshall for the first time that over here they might have the mistaken idea that he was a person of importance in the organization. He had the feeling of gaining attention under false pretenses.

Outside the station there was a hired car with a chauffeur. As they drove away Travers said: "We fixed a room for you at the Savoy, sir. I hope that's all right?"

"Oh, sure." He wished Travers would stop calling him "sir." It made him feel foolish—and rather old. On the other hand, this was the better of the two extremes. In New York, Travers would have been calling him "Chris."

"I took a look at the room myself. It's quite a good one, facing on to the river."

"It sounds fine."

"I wasn't sure whether you might not prefer a suite. But then I thought, well, you could always change——"

"Sure. That's right. Thanks a lot." He was beginning to feel suffocated with so much thoughtfulness. He looked out of the window. It was raining—as it should be, he thought, on one's first night in London. They were crossing Waterloo Bridge, with the lights of the Embankment stretched in a great arc before them, outlining the north bank of the river. Somerset House, the Shell-Mex Building, the Houses of Parliament, covered with scaffolding as usual, damp, shining streets, so silent after midnight. The river was high —a tug passing upstream with a string of coal barges seemed to be sitting on the same level as the road. . . . He turned back reluctantly to his companion.

"Have you been with the organization long?" he asked.

"Two years only." Travers gave a brisk and rather meaningless smile.

"And before that?"

"Before that I was"—he paused and then went on rather obscurely—"connected with the motor industry." Selling cars? wondered Marshall. It seemed rather likely. "It was quite fun, but rather a dead end, you know. Then this chance of a job at Marshall's came up and naturally I jumped at it. Enormous piece of luck, really."

"You like the work?"

"Oh, rather." He added earnestly, "I mean—I do feel there's an enormous excitement in working for a really alive, *growing* concern. Some of the English firms are pretty stick-in-the-mud, you know."

"Oh, I wouldn't exactly say that——"

"Yes, I'm afraid we have to admit it. We have certain virtues, it's true, over here, but we haven't the energy, the streamlined efficiency, the sense of dedication, if you know what I mean——"

"Yes, I know what you mean." The frightening thing was, there was some truth in it. Not about the efficiency so much—the New York office seemed to spend most of its time in a state of bureaucratic confusion—but about the dedication. His father had been a dedicated man. But dedicated to what?

"And the other thing is, I'm glad to be dealing in something important, something really new, not just soap powders or vacuum cleaners—those are all very well in their way, but these instruments of ours are things of the future. Nobody knows what their eventual implications may be——"

He went on to give his views on possible developments in the use of transistors. It sounded like a speech he had made often before.

Marshall yawned. Faith, he thought, faith and loyalty in another country and another language. He had traveled four thousand miles to be confronted once again with his own isolation. His first pleasure at being in England began to leave him.

Travers stopped quite abruptly, sensing a failure of response. Had he laid it on a bit too thick? Was he talking too much? After a short pause he looked out of the window and said: "This is the

Strand we're turning into now. But perhaps you know London?"

"Fairly well. I was over here in the Army Air Force for a little while. Then after I was released I spent a year or two at Cambridge."

"Oh, really?" Travers sighed fondly. "Wonderful place, Cambridge. I was there for some time myself."

"Is that so?" Marshall's interest was momentarily aroused. "Which college?"

"Well, I wasn't exactly at the *university* . . ."

The car drew up in front of the Savoy. As Travers made a move to get out behind him, Marshall said, "Don't bother to come in. I can manage."

"Oh, but——"

"No, I insist. It's late and you must be very tired. I know I am." He could feel Travers' disappointment. He had been looking forward to a late-night drink, a little chat. This was his chance to get on easy terms with a supposedly influential American, perhaps to strike up a personal friendship. You never knew, it might lead to anything—one of these days Marshall might be talking to some nameless demi-god in Rockefeller Plaza and say casually, "I know just the man you want. I met him in London—young, keen, smart as a whip." That was how big careers were made, by attracting attention, making the right sorts of contacts. . . .

Marshall was not attracted to Travers but he felt a moment of sympathy for him. He was probably as able as Wilcox or Richardson if the truth were known. But nobody had ever heard of him and nobody would, except through a lucky chance. One could hardly blame him for doing his best. Just the same, there was no obligation to sit up all night with him.

Marshall held out his hand. "Good night," he said, "and thanks a lot."

"It's been a pleasure," said Travers. He sank back, thwarted, into his hired limousine. "Will you be in at the office in the morning?"

"Sure."

"You have the address?"

"Yes."

"I'll tell Mr. Gilbertson. He's looking forward to seeing you."

CHAPTER II

GILBERTSON AND COWLES, the partly owned British subsidiary of the Marshall Corporation, occupied a pleasing Georgian house in a square about midway between Oxford Street and Piccadilly. These, at one time, had been the town residences of the great people of a vanished age. Now not a single one remained in private occupation. The cold winds of the twentieth century had blown with devastating effect through these magnificent double reception rooms, up the elegant staircases and tall, drafty corridors. Supertax and death duties, high wages, inflation, and rent-restriction acts had succeeded in beating the ancient aristocracy to its knees. Social change, more ruthless than any foreign invader, was gradually stripping the great families of their possessions. One by one they had fled, to country houses half closed down, to "amusing" converted stables in Kensington, to farms in Kenya or tax-free villas on the shores of the Caribbean.

Their homes had been taken by various forms of national or commercial enterprise. In parts, wholesale destruction, either speculative or bureaucratic, had led to replacement by concrete office blocks. In more fortunate areas, such as in this particular square, there had been determined efforts at preservation. With a delicacy that was almost oppressive, façades had been repainted, chandeliers cleaned and replaced, rooms repapered in the style of the appropriate period. Window boxes flourished. Furniture hardly distinguishable from real Sheraton added dignity to waiting rooms and

executive offices. Many of the houses had not looked so well cared for in years.

The only thing that gave the game away from outside was the metal plates on the doors. Although unobtrusive and in the best of taste, they could not avoid generating a certain disillusion. Or so it seemed to Marshall, glancing idly at the names of the occupants as he passed by. Accrington Jute Spinners, Susie Gay Modes Ltd. (K. Schumberger), Ministry of Agriculture and Fisheries (Cattle Cake Section)—they were all doing first-rate work, no doubt, the sort of work that needed doing in this modern world. And yet, somehow . . .

Gilbertson and Cowles, he was pleased to find, had one of the best houses, with a front elevation rather strikingly picked out in gray paint. Inside the hall an attractive receptionist was standing behind a desk, putting the finishing touches to a bowl of daffodils. He introduced himself.

"Mr. Marshall?" She threw him a brilliant smile. "Please come this way. Mr. Gilbertson is expecting you."

She led him upstairs to a room on the first floor and knocked on the door. There was an indefinable sound from within. She opened the door.

"Mr. Marshall."

Gilbertson rose to his feet as Marshall entered the room. He was a man in his forties, very tall and thin, with a kind of languid, whiskery distinction. His trousers were narrow, his coat full-skirted, his shoes almost certainly handmade. His hair was thick and dark and brushed back over his ears in a faintly theatrical fashion.

"Marshall?" He loped forward, extending a thin hairy hand. It was curiously dry to the touch, like that of one of the higher primates.

"Delighted to see you. You found the office without any trouble?"

"Yes, thanks."

"Excellent. Now do sit down." He gripped Marshall's shoulder and impelled him into a chair. "Cigarette?" He snapped open a case. "I hope young Travers looked after you properly last night?"

"Oh, certainly. It was most kind of him. But there was really no need——"

"My dear fellow, he was delighted to do it. I was sorry I couldn't be there myself, but I live rather far out and my wife had a dinner party arranged sometime before, you understand." He sat down behind the desk and folded one spidery leg over the other. "Otherwise, of course——"

"I quite understand," said Marshall. As Gilbertson lit a cigarette for himself, Marshall glanced around the room. It was large and high-ceilinged, with an Adam fireplace along one wall and two sets of french windows leading out on to a wrought-iron balcony.

"Quite a place you have here," he remarked.

"You like it?" Gilbertson grinned delightedly. "I'm so glad. We got it for a song—by your standards, that is. They wanted a good tenant on a long lease and I happened to be a friend of Charlie Porteous, the owner. Naturally he didn't want to let it go to a somebody who'd turn it into a corset factory or something." He sighed. "Impossible to run as a house any longer, I'm afraid. Charlie was heartbroken. His family had lived here for two hundred years."

"That's pretty tough."

"Yes. But he doesn't feel too badly about it now. He looked in the other day, as a matter of fact. He told me it was the first time it had been properly decorated since the First World War. They couldn't afford it, you see."

"I suppose not."

"And it suits us perfectly. A little chilly in winter on the upper floors, perhaps, but the girls don't seem to mind. And they love the address. It gives them cachet in some extraordinary way, to work in Mayfair. It means that we can get a good class of girl." He paused, as if seeking an illustration. "You met Miss Carvill-Sykes, our receptionist?"

"Momentarily."

"Charming, don't you think?" With a significance which Marshall failed to grasp he added: "She's a vicar's daughter." He suddenly swung around in his swivel chair and recrossed his legs. Then he grinned again at Marshall. His whole behavior somehow gave the impression of being a performance, as if he was always rather amused at the idea of himself sitting behind a desk, playing the

part of a businessman and had to be careful not to let the performance degenerate into burlesque.

"Did you have a good crossing?" he asked.

"Very good, thanks."

"I'm so glad. You know," he said reflectively, "I think you were most sensible to come by boat. Between ourselves, there's far too much chasing about in airplanes nowadays. There's a tendency to work oneself into a premature grave. . . ." It was a tendency, Marshall imagined, which Gilbertson himself had so far managed to resist. "I hope you're going to enjoy yourself over here."

"I hope so too." Not to be outdone in courtesy, he added: "I fully expect to."

"Good. Naturally we'll do everything we can . . ." Gilbertson suddenly rose from his chair. "I expect the first thing you'd like to do is to have a look at your office. I'll take you along and introduce you to some of the boys and girls. You'll find them all very anxious to help you. We're a pretty happy family here, on the whole."

His own office was on the floor above Gilbertson's, not quite so grand, but with a view of the square—presumably it had been one of the better bedrooms of the house. When the tour of the building was over, Gilbertson deposited him there, having first invited him to lunch.

"I'll give you a chance to settle down," he said. "If there's anything you particularly want, just shout for it." He indicated a buzzer on the telephone table. "This calls your secretary, Miss Lancing. She works in a room just across the hall. A very experienced girl. I'm sure she'll be a great help to you."

When Gilbertson had left, Marshall sat down behind the mahogany desk and tried to fit himself, as it were, into his new part. There was a palatial emptiness about the office which he found intimidating. The desk was completely bare, the drawers empty; there were no filing cabinets in the room, though one corner held a bookcase filled with trade journals and almanacs and a copy of last year's *Who's Who*. There was not a trace of anything personal. Nothing to remind him of Wilcox. Of course it was a little while now since Wilcox had left London, but he had somehow expected

some degree of continuity, a feeling of taking over rather than starting afresh. . . .

He was just engaged in wondering who had been doing Wilcox's work during the last two months, when there was a knock on the door.

"Yes?"

"Mr. Marshall? I'm Miss Lancing."

The girl who came in was small and slight, her thin oval face moderately and somehow discreetly good-looking. Her hair was cleverly arranged to make the most of her face, her blouse and skirt suitable and becoming to her trim, tight-waisted figure. Her eyes were smiling, but sharply interested, making only a formal effort to disguise their curiosity.

"Glad to meet you, Miss Lancing." They shook hands. "Do sit down."

"I don't want to interrupt——"

"That's all right." He waved a hand over the naked desk. "As you see, I'm not very busy right now. Perhaps this is a good time for us to get to know each other. You used to work for Mr. Wilcox, I take it?"

"Yes."

"I saw him just before I left. He's got a new assignment in the Domestic Division, you know."

She nodded, showing respectful interest. Then she asked innocently, "A promotion?"

"Why, yes——" He was slightly off guard. His voice, he realized, sounded confused; almost, for no logical reason, guilty. "Yes—I imagine so. Though of course I don't know too much about that end of the business——"

"I suppose not." Her interest in Wilcox's future seemed to have been no more than perfunctory. She glanced around the room. "I hope everything's all right for you," she said. "Mr. Gilbertson told me to be sure to see you had everything you wanted."

"That was kind of him."

"He's a very kind man," she said demurely. She looked down at her notebook, the merest trace of a smile on her lips. He had the feeling that beneath the façade of respect she was secretly laughing

at something or somebody. Himself? Gilbertson? The whole organization?

"Is there nothing," she asked, "that I can get for you? Please don't hesitate to ask for it if there is. Most of the executives," she explained almost reproachfully, "have certain little peculiarities of their own."

Already, thought Marshall, before he had been much more than an hour in the building, he was beginning to disappoint people. It was true enough that he found his working quarters lacking in something, but he could not immediately put his finger on what it was. The successful man of affairs did not accept everything, as he was tempted to do—he made demands, demonstrated his own methods, set up a form of organization, stamped any new environment immediately with the mark of a distinctive personality. Even the secretaries knew it and expected it.

On the defensive, he searched his mind furiously for something to ask for, some memorable but not too outrageous demand.

"Since you ask," he said, "there are one or two matters——"

"Yes?" Miss Lancing's pencil hovered expectantly over her notebook.

"I like a box of cigarettes on my desk. One of those leather ones —you know the kind? And fill it with Chesterfields. You'll need about a hundred a week. Can you arrange that?"

She made a few squiggles in her notebook.

"And some English cigarettes for visitors."

"The charwomen will pinch them."

"Never mind." This was something, but hardly enough. Another idea came to him. "And it seems to me that the offices in this building are hard to find. Why don't we have name plates?"

She looked serious. "Mr. Gilbertson doesn't like them. He says they disfigure the doors."

"Well, I like them." He was determined to be decisive. "Fix one for me, will you?"

"I don't think I could, not unless you would clear it with Mr. Gilbertson first. I believe he promised Sir Charles Porteous——"

"The hell with Sir Charles Porteous."

"Yes, sir." She made another squiggle in the notebook. Once

again a secret trace of a smile, little more than a movement of the lips, crossed her face. He wondered if she had seen through his bluff. Suddenly he was tired of this childish game.

"No, I don't mean that. Forget it." He looked around him. "I guess he has a point of view, at that."

"You like the house?" she asked.

"Yes indeed." He contemplated the fireplace, the high, carved ceiling. "It's certainly a change from New York."

She put down her pencil and relaxed in her chair. She became suddenly less prim and more human. "You wait until the cold weather sets in. Though it's nice at Christmas, I have to admit that. Mr. Gilbertson gives a party to the staff in that great office of his— it used to be the drawing room, of course, in the old days——"

She was interrupted by a knock on the door. The receptionist came in, carrying a tray of coffee. She gave a cup to Marshall and then turned to Miss Lancing questioningly.

"Shall I take yours through to the back room, Jane?"

Miss Lancing did not immediately reply. It was as if she had misheard or misunderstood. It was a few seconds before Marshall realized that the question had been silently transferred to him. Presumably this was a matter for his own discretion.

He had no wish to seem undemocratic. "Why not drink it here?" he said.

When the receptionist had left, Miss Lancing looked at him over the top of her cup.

"That," she said, "was Miss Carvill-Sykes."

"So I understand."

"Our receptionist." With a touch of malice she added, "She's a vicar's daughter."

"Mr. Gilbertson told me."

She raised her eyebrows, and once again he saw the faint, secret, mocking smile. But this time it was not quite so secret and it occurred to him that he was invited to share in the joke if he chose. Unfortunately he was not quite clear what the joke was, except that it was at Gilbertson's expense. Whatever it was, it seemed a good thing to ignore it. He decided to move the conversation back to business.

"Have you done this job for long?" he asked.

"About eighteen months."

"Then you probably know the routine better than I do at the moment." This, he thought, was putting it mildly. So far he had only the haziest idea of what he was supposed to be doing. He sought for a way of obtaining information from her without exposing his ignorance too nakedly. "Is there anything I ought to be attending to right now? Anything urgent?"

"Not really. There's a certain amount of mail. Would you like to see it?"

"Yes, please."

She went out, taking the empty coffee cups with her. A few minutes later she came back with a pile of letters and trade journals. He looked casually through the letters. There was about a dozen of them, mostly routine inquiries.

"Not much here," he said.

"No."

"Surely this isn't all since Mr. Wilcox left?"

"Oh no. The rest are dealt with. Mr. Gilbertson told me to answer as many as I could myself and pass the rest over to him."

"Oh—I see."

"Mr. Wilcox was often away on business trips," she explained. "He left a good deal to my discretion in the matter of correspondence. Of course it's up to you now. If you just tell me how you want things done——"

She spoke without a trace of officiousness, as if prepared to take responsibility if he wished it but not in the least concerned if he didn't. Nevertheless, he was cautious. It would probably be a tactical mistake to hand over too much at this early stage.

"Well," he said amiably, "perhaps we'd better see how it shakes down, shall we? In the meantime"—he picked up the letters—"I think I'll take care of these myself."

CHAPTER III

"I ALWAYS SAY," said Gilbertson, looking at his plate with appreciation, "that here they have the best cold beef in London."

"Is that so?" Marshall tried to make the phrase express not skepticism but rather gratitude for a useful piece of local knowledge. He himself, in a rash attempt to be thoroughly English, had ordered steak-and-kidney pie and was now regretting it.

"Yes. Of course the secret is to cook it and let it go cold. Once you cut into it——" He smiled in acknowledgment to an acquaintance who passed their table. "That's Tom Phillipson, the Q.C., most interesting fellow, perhaps you'd like to meet him later on." He took an exploratory sip from his glass of burgundy. "I hope you'll like this. I've always considered it a really first-rate Chambertin."

Fortunately it was. It was also a wine of high alcoholic content, and a couple of glasses of it had the effect of generating a certain warmth of spirit to counteract the forbidding effect of the club itself. Marshall found himself able to look around the cavernous dining room with something approaching equanimity. It was, even now, not exactly friendly—but it was rather less sepulchral than the nave of Westminster Abbey.

Having declared his support for the food and wine, Gilbertson began to explore a series of conversational gambits. He spoke in a high-pitched, slightly exhausted voice, with prolonged, strangled

vowels, and he had a tendency to drop his voice into a weary mumble at the end of each sentence. This, together with his clothes, his club, even his walk, had the effect of placing him, to anyone familiar with English social distinctions, as a member of a certain economic and cultural caste. It was a caste with which Marshall had never felt entirely at home, since he had always sensed within it an atmosphere of patronage. He was repelled by the complacent lack of curiosity about strangers, the evasion of any attempt to build up a relationship on a personal basis. At this moment, for instance, he had the impression that Gilbertson was carrying out a mere performance; he had a certain routine for visiting Americans, appropriate topics of conversation, a little flattery because they were simple people and known to like it, a joke or two . . . The needle was put into the groove and the record was played—it bore no relation to himself at all.

Nor did it give any clue about Gilbertson's own attitudes. His formality of manner was effective in concealing not only his personal reaction to Marshall but his views on the system of European representatives as a whole. It seemed important to get a clear picture of this as soon as possible. Marshall was wondering how to move the conversation politely back to business when Gilbertson made the change himself.

Raising his wineglass, he said, "To success in your new job."

"Thank you very much."

"I'm sure we shall be able to work together very smoothly," he said. "Naturally it will take you a little while to settle down. I don't want to interfere in your affairs, but it may be that I can help you over some matters——"

"I was hoping you might. When I spoke with Mr. Kingham in New York before I left, he told me that you would be able to explain a good many things to me."

"Glad to." Gilbertson added appreciatively, "A very capable fellow, Kingham, don't you think?"

"Oh yes."

"I was most impressed by him the last time I was over there. A very acute mind."

They remained silent for a moment, meditating on the acuity of

Kingham's mind. Suddenly Gilbertson became more confidential in manner. The record had been switched off; even his voice had lost some of its affectations. For the first time he appeared to address Marshall as an individual. "He wrote me a personal letter about you, as a matter of fact. Gave you an enormous build-up."

"That was good of him."

"I must say that when I read it I was relieved. It encouraged me to hope that we might be getting just the sort of person we needed."

"I hope I shan't disappoint you."

"I'm sure you won't."

"You hardly know me yet," Marshall pointed out. He felt a little uneasy at so much approbation.

"Perhaps not." Gilbertson smiled at him benignly. "But one feels these things. And you've lived in Europe before. That's an enormous help—far more than you probably think."

"Are we Americans quite so foreign as all that?"

"I used not to think so. But recently . . ." He sighed, as if remembering a regrettable episode. "You take young Wilcox, for instance. A charming fellow—keen as mustard—excellent businessman. He'll be a big success in the States. But, let's be honest, he didn't really fit in over here."

"No?" Marshall waited expectantly.

"No. Of course he was—young."

Gilbertson almost whispered the last word, as if youth were a disease one didn't mention in public. "I was sorry for him, really. He often seemed rather bewildered."

"By what?"

"Oh—conditions generally. I'm not saying it's anything against him—much more probably something wrong with us." He grinned to make it clear that this was a joke. "But there you are. In an organization of this kind, one of the most important things is to be able to adapt oneself to varying conditions. Flexibility," he said with the air of a man summing up a complex situation in a single word. "Flexibility, above all things, is what is required here."

Marshall nodded in a dazed way. Gilbertson's words, though delivered with the utmost solemnity, seemed to him to mean prac-

tically nothing at all. Perhaps, he thought, the wine was responsible for some degree of failure in communication.

"You see," Gilbertson went on after a pause, "business here isn't quite the same as it is in the States. Over there it's a fairly straightforward problem. You make a good article, fix your price in relation to the competition, and then use your sales organization to get as much of the market as you can. Correct?"

"Yes." It was not only correct, it was elementary.

"And if you know your job and put your back to it, you make money, and society applauds you for it?"

"More or less."

"Well, here," said Gilbertson, "it's not quite so simple. In England, business, and particularly American business, is regarded with suspicion by a large part of the community. If you manage to make money, the assumption is that you've stolen it from somebody. Most of your profits go in taxation, and as for the rest, it's extremely difficult to get it out of the country owing to the Exchange Control. Politics come into everything, even when they don't immediately appear to." He paused to allow the waiter to clear away the cheese and serve them with coffee and brandy. Then he went on, "So you see, the main problems here are ones that don't exist for you at home. You may think they shouldn't exist here either, but there's nothing we can do about it. Personally, I've long since lost interest in discussing the rights and wrongs of a situation which I can't change. But"—he leaned forward earnestly; his eyes were hard and the languid note had left his voice—"the main point I want to emphasize is that you have to accept it. It's no use getting exasperated and saying it couldn't happen at home."

Marshall nodded. So this, presumably, was where Wilcox had gone wrong. He had refused to accept local customs and had been punished for it. The situation was becoming to some extent clarified. The rather curious aspect of the affair was that officially the European representative was supposed to be supervising the subsidiaries on behalf of New York, but evidently it was dangerous to supervise them too closely. It seemed likely that Wilcox and Gilbertson had disagreed on some matter of policy, that the matter had been taken to New York for arbitration, and that Gilbertson

had won. That would explain everything, including Wilcox's attitude when they had talked together at La Guardia. Only the details of the struggle were still obscure.

"You'll find," said Gilbertson, reverting to a more relaxed manner, "that it isn't easy to do anything here in a hurry. Before you make any sort of move you have to consider the possible reactions of various influential bodies—government departments, business associations, trades unions—we can't afford to get across any of them."

"You make it sound tough going."

"One gets used to it. It's largely a question of getting accustomed to a more"—he searched for a word—"a more *deliberate* approach. There isn't, in any case, the same incentive toward developing absolutely maximum efficiency under present circumstances."

"Not worth the effort, you mean?"

"Well—not worth killing yourself, shall we say? After all, life is there to be lived, to be enjoyed . . ." He looked fondly at his brandy glass, at the spring sunshine pouring in through the tall windows. "When you get to my age you begin to have some idea of what's worth while, of what's possible and what isn't. It's hard sometimes to be patient with people who want to go through the whole process again, just to find out for themselves. It's very satisfying to come across somebody who can grasp not only the possibilities of an enterprise but the necessary limitations." He added reminiscently: "Your father was a man like that."

"Was he?" Marshall looked at him skeptically. This conception of his father was new to him. "That wasn't how I saw him."

"Oh yes," said Gilbertson with assurance, "of course he was very forceful and energetic, and he liked to play that side of himself up —he was a bit of an actor, I think you'll admit. But when it came to the point, you could always make him see reason. He had no taste for beating his head against a brick wall."

There was a silence. As so often when he listened to the opinions of other people about his father, he found himself withdrawing, like some threatened crustacean, into the confines of a shell which was not quite large enough to give him complete protection. Gilbertson was wrong, of course, just as his mother and Kingham and

Jeff were wrong—the vivid, colorful personality of the old man had been too strong for them. Like a conjurer, he had so succeeded in dominating their attention that he could attract it at will in any direction which suited him, while at the same time diverting it from other activities which he wished to conceal. He had been able, at various times, to pass himself off as the bluff, honest, jovial self-made man; the rough go-getter with a heart of gold beneath all his toughness; the shrewd operator; the capable administrator conscious of his lack of education but with a talent for picking up technical knowledge as he went along; the sympathetic listener; the loyal friend; the lost child sitting lonely and forlorn in the midst of all his possessions. . . . And the curious thing was that those closest to him were deceived along with the rest, perhaps even more than the rest. They found him out and still continued to believe, as if the belief had become as necessary for themselves as for him. Only a few, thought Marshall with a certain pride, were incapable of such easy forgiveness.

But there was no question of explaining this to Gilbertson. Marshall was more interested in trying to get a clear picture of the present situation. These obscure hints were beginning to get on his nerves.

"I follow your point in general," he said. "But I'd appreciate it if you could give me a little more detail. I presume you must have some particular problems in mind—some specific examples——"

Gilbertson flapped his hand in a gesture almost of panic. "No, no, I can assure you I had nothing specific in mind—nothing." He appeared quite horrified at the suggestion. "I was speaking purely generally. My advice is simply this—settle down here. Get to know us. Make the necessary contacts, see how the land lies, and don't be in too much of a hurry to change everything. Rome wasn't built in a day, you know." He looked up at Marshall through his bushy eyebrows and said with significance, "I'm sure Mr. Kingham agrees with me."

"I guess so." So, he thought, Gilbertson knew what the line was, knew what Kingham had said to him in New York. The line was: Plenty of tact, no interference, and remember what happened to Wilcox. He was to be what he had been in the past—nothing. And

Gilbertson knew it. It was only on the Travers level that there remained any illusions about his significance in the company.

He told himself, not for the first time, that he must expect nothing else. He was the unbeliever at the séance whose very presence was a threat to those assumptions on which the whole performance was based. They could not be blamed for distrusting him, for trying to hide him away in some unimportant corner of the organization where he would have no reponsibilities and be the least possible nuisance. Nevertheless, he felt a fierce, illogical blaze of anger at being held so cheaply.

Gilbertson had moved on to firm ground. "How do you like the idea of living in England?"

"Very much."

"Of course you were here before, weren't you? But that was not long after the war. You'll find everything greatly changed. Do you know many people in London?"

"A few."

"Excellent. I feel sure you'll enjoy yourself enormously. This is quite the best time of year, you know. There's everything—cricket, tennis, golf, the theater——" He waved his hand expansively. "I really envy you. And if I can be of any help with introductions——"

"That's very kind of you."

"Not a bit, my dear fellow, just say the word. I suppose you'll be living in town?"

"I imagine so."

"Quite the best thing for a bachelor. Though for a family man like myself there's a lot to be said for the country. I have a house in Sussex—not a large place, you know, that's quite impossible nowadays—but it's very pleasant out there. You might like to come and spend a weekend with us sometime."

"Very much."

"Excellent. I'll have a talk with my wife and then we can fix a date."

Gilbertson looked up at the clock. "Good God—it's three o'clock. If you'll excuse me I think I ought to get back to the office." He added with solemnity, "I don't like to set a bad example."

CHAPTER IV

AFTER THE RAIN which had greeted his arrival the skies had suddenly cleared, and London was enjoying a period of spring weather of unexpected magnificence. The air was crisp and fresh, the trees in the squares were coming into leaf, and the parks at midday were crowded with office girls in summer frocks, eating picnic lunches on the grass. It was not difficult, in these first few weeks, to take Gilbertson's advice, to let things go and enjoy himself. He was happy to explore the labyrinth of narrow streets, to visit the curbside market of Soho, to eat alone in the taverns of Fleet Street or the chophouses of the City. It was at first pleasant to be unknown after the compulsive sociability of New York.

He rented a furnished apartment in a small old-fashioned block in St. James's. The narrow, twisting stairs, the manservant he shared with another bachelor, even the eccentric arrangements for heating the water generated an atmosphere pleasantly reminiscent of Cambridge. He bought a few pictures and a great many books. Now at last, he persuaded himself, he would have time, in these placid solitary evenings, to catch up on his reading. *Madame Bovary, David Copperfield, The Brothers Karamazov* . . .

But shortly he grew restless with his own company. He began to look up old friends. He was surprised to find how many of the people he knew were no longer traceable. Those who were still in London were delighted to hear from him. They were mostly married by now, with small children, and lived out in the suburbs. Evenings

in town were not easy to arrange, but he must certainly come out
one evening for dinner. Potluck, of course . . .

The dinners always turned out to be unnecessarily elaborate, the
wives harassed, servantless, and mildly resentful of university reminiscence. The men seemed to Marshall to have aged to a quite unreasonable extent under the pressure of family responsibilities.
Conversation would flourish gallantly for the first hour or so as they
talked of old times, then quite suddenly it would wither and die,
to be replaced by an atmosphere of mutual dissatisfaction. He
found them stodgy and began to suspect that they in turn looked
upon him as frivolous and immature. There was no longer any point
of contact.

He had known loneliness in New York, but it had been a loneliness of the spirit; there had been almost an excess of physical com-
panionship. Now for the first time he began to find it difficult to
fill in his days. There was little to do at the office, and it seemed to
be a matter of indifference to everybody whether he went there
or not, but it was at least an anchor, a place where he felt, however
insignificantly, a part of something. And there was always Miss
Lancing to talk to. She was, he found, one of the few people in
London with as much time to spare as himself.

"Don't you find this work boring?" he asked her once. She raised
her eyebrows. "After all, there isn't very much to interest you."

"That's true," she admitted. "But then all work's pretty boring,
isn't it? And at least it's better than living at home."

She was, she told him, a fugitive from the provinces, the daughter of a solicitor in Stoke-on-Trent. She lived alone in a bed-sitting-
room in South Kensington.

"I used to share rooms with a girl friend, but she left to get married," she explained.

"And you're not lonely?"

"I'm used to it now. At first I didn't like it much. I have quite a
few friends. Among the other girls here, for instance . . ."

She made no mention of men friends. It was likely that she had
them—she was undeniably attractive in a curiously detached, independent way. Perhaps that might explain her cheerful acceptance
of what seemed a fairly depressing and uneventful existence. She
was also, he found out, extremely curious. Almost imperceptibly she

managed to lead him into disclosing a good deal of information about himself. In exchange she handed out titbits of gossip about the various inhabitants of the London office. At times he felt guilty about these conversations. It was, when all was said and done, none of his business if Travers was in the habit of padding his expense sheet or if Gilbertson had been seen dining tête-à-tête at a restaurant in Charlotte Street with Miss Carvill-Sykes. He should be above taking an interest in such matters.

But (one had to face facts) he *was* interested. And Miss Lancing knew he was interested. She also knew that in this field he was like some timid virgin, ashamed of the force of his own curiosity. She never told him very much at a time. When he showed signs of being shocked she would withdraw, like an expert seducer, biding her time, waiting confidently for him to invite further advances.

But gradually his idleness began to get on his nerves. He could not contemplate an existence so utterly futile as this. Whether Gilbertson liked it or not, he would find some kind of work to do. How, for instance, had Wilcox managed to spend his time? He decided to ask Miss Lancing.

"Oh, he was always on the go," she said in a voice which combined admiration and amusement. "Conferences with Mr. Gilbertson, sales estimates, memoranda on this and that, visiting the distributors on the Continent—we had a high old time, I can tell you." She shook her head reminiscently. "You couldn't keep Mr. Wilcox out of anything."

That, Marshall thought uneasily, was how it ought to be. He, Marshall, was obviously considered to be a man who could be left out of anything and everything. It was true that Wilcox's energy appeared to have done him more harm than good. On the other hand, he had at least achieved a kind of respect.

A few days later he approached Gilbertson.

"I've been here a month now," he said, briskly businesslike, "and I'm quite settled in. I feel completely at home. Now I think it's time I did something."

Gilbertson stroked the hair back over his right ear in an exasperated way. "I'm not quite sure that I follow you. What exactly——"

Marshall was prepared for this. "I'm anxious to get a complete

picture of the business over here. I'd like to go through the books, see the sales records for the last few years and the estimates for the coming year. Also the production reports, the proportion of turnover due to re-exportation, and so on. After that I can go up to Lancashire and visit the plant. And then . . ."

It sounded good, he thought. Gilbertson was visibly disconcerted.

"Yes, yes, of course. Naturally we'll be delighted for you to see anything you wish, my dear fellow." He spoke as if Marshall were some distinguished but rather tiresome visitor. "Though I don't know that you'll get very much out of it. Still, if that's what you'd like . . . I'll get Travers to make you out a summary." He sighed. "He's fairly busy at the moment, but I imagine he'll be able to fix it within the next week or two."

"You don't have to bother Mr. Travers," Marshall said firmly. "Just send down the original figures. I'll make my own summary."

"You'll find it heavy going, I'm afraid."

"Never mind. I'll have a try. If I get stuck I can always call on you or Mr. Travers."

"Oh, definitely—definitely."

Even after this there was an inexplicable delay. When the figures failed to appear, Marshall telephoned Gilbertson's office, only to be told that the managing director had gone away on some unspecified business trip and omitted to leave any instructions with the Accounts Department. When Gilbertson returned he seemed slightly exasperated to find the matter still under discussion.

"Of course—I'm so sorry. Most annoying for you. I'm sure I left instructions with somebody, but there it is. One can't be everywhere oneself, more's the pity. One has to delegate responsibility."

When the books were finally brought to his office Marshall regarded them with the satisfaction due the trophies of a minor victory. He did not suppose there would be anything very exciting or unusual in the figures themselves, copies of which would have been long since sent to New York for analysis. He imagined that Gilbertson's passive resistance to showing them to him had been largely a matter of principle.

Nevertheless, on going through them he discovered one thing which surprised him. He made some notes in longhand and went back to see Gilbertson.

"I don't know whether you'll agree with my interpretation, but as I see it, the figures show that on the sales in this country and the Commonwealth we hardly pay our way. The profits only just cover the fixed overheads."

"Oh, come." Gilbertson smiled uneasily. "I think you'll agree that our final returns are excellent."

"Certainly. But that's almost entirely due to the sale of instruments assembled here and re-exported to France. Without that, we should be nowhere."

Gilbertson thought for a moment and then nodded. Marshall, he conveyed, had been a clever boy and should not be denied his appreciation. "Yes," he said, "you're quite right—though, as you can imagine, we don't go around advertising the fact. The truth is, our things are too expensive. They can't really compete in the sterling area." He added cheerfully, "I've pointed that out to New York on innumerable occasions."

"You don't seem very concerned."

"Well, there's no point in making ourselves miserable about it, is there? And the business is doing all right on the over-all figures. The great thing is to judge by results—don't worry too much about the details. As your father used to say, let's take the broad approach."

"But," said Marshall, "supposing you lost the French business?"

"Time enough to worry about that if and when it happens." He gave an unexpected guffaw. "Perhaps you chaps in New York would have to cut down your prices a bit, eh? But don't worry," he said reassuringly, "old Furac's a first-rate man. He's got the Paris connection very nicely sewn up."

"You don't think there's any risk of our being priced out of the market in France?"

Gilbertson gave a confident shake of the head. Then he said with aristocratic tolerance, "The French are a queer lot. I don't profess to understand them myself. Personal connections seem to count for a lot over there."

It seemed to Marshall as he pondered this conversation afterward that here at last was an opportunity for him to take some part in affairs. However casually Gilbertson might regard it, the position was plainly unsatisfactory and should be called to New York's attention. It would have to be done tactfully, not in the form of a criticism of any particular person, but as a review of the trading difficulties peculiar to the area. After that it would be up to Kingham to decide whether anything should be done.

He rang for Miss Lancing.

"I want you to take a memorandum," he said. "It's to Mr. Kingham. Head it: 'Trading Position in Western Europe.'" He hesitated. Did that sound pretentious? Never mind. "'An analysis of the records for the past two years, together with a breakdown of present sales estimates, appears to indicate the following . . .'"

He began to dictate slowly, referring now and then to his notes for the relevant figures. He was just warming to his thesis when he looked up and noticed that Miss Lancing had stopped writing. She was regarding him in a faintly apologetic way.

"What's the matter?" he asked. "Is there something you can't follow?"

"Oh no. It's just that—I don't really know whether I ought to say this—but I think you should know——" She stopped, waiting for encouragement.

"What is it?"

"Well, Mr. Wilcox already did a memorandum saying all this, soon after he came here. He made more or less the same points as you have."

"I see." He slumped back in his chair, unable to conceal his frustration. It was hard to resist the conviction that there was something like a conspiracy in the company to make his every action appear futile and ridiculous. His anger, foiled of any other object, directed itself toward Miss Lancing.

"It might have been a good idea," he said acidly, "to have shown it to me before this. Don't you think so?"

"Yes, I'm sorry, but——"

"I distinctly remember asking to see any important letters or memoranda from Mr. Wilcox's back correspondence. Naturally I

assumed that any documents of this kind would be included. Otherwise I'm simply wasting my time going over old ground." She tried to speak again, but he was too angry to listen. "Now, before we go any further, would you mind getting for me the *complete* files, with all the copies of the Wilcox correspondence, memoranda, and so on—just so I can get some idea of what happened here before I came?"

"I'm awfully sorry, Mr. Marshall, but I'm afraid I can't——"

"Why not?"

"Because it isn't there. The memoranda to New York were in a different file. I went through all the records when you arrived, but I couldn't find that one anywhere."

"You mean you lost it?"

"No. I'm sure I put it in the right place in the cabinet. It just wasn't there when I went back for it."

"You'd better have another look." He got up impatiently from his chair. "I'll come along and help you."

As they passed the general office the clerks were covering their typewriters and putting on their coats preparatory to leaving. It was half-past five. They went on to the filing room on an upper floor, a dark room with flowered wallpaper and two small windows which looked out on to a bombed site.

Silently they began to go through the filing cabinets in an atmosphere rendered oppressive with dust and resentment. He read through old letters, desperate, staccato cables about long-forgotten crises, tedious, inflated reports about unimportant problems—but nothing from Wilcox. After half an hour he slammed the last drawer of the last cabinet and said irritably:

"All right, then, I agree—it isn't there. But where is it?"

"Mr. Wilcox may have taken it away with him."

"Is that likely?"

"It's possible. Or Mr. Gilbertson may have taken it." She shrugged her shoulders. "I don't know," she said coldly. "It's really nothing to do with me."

She sat down and looked at him, waiting for orders. Her expression said plainly that since he had decided to act like a boss he had better tell her what to do next. Suddenly he felt ashamed of

himself. He had done what he had so often criticized others for doing—vented his personal chagrin and annoyance on a subordinate. It was particularly despicable after he had encouraged her to treat him as a friend.

"I'm sorry," he said. "I shouldn't have bawled you out like that. It wasn't your fault."

Immediately her expression changed. She was evidently not a girl who liked to bear a grudge. "I should have told you before that the file was gone."

"I don't think so." One could hardly expect her to have done that, he realized, particularly if she thought Gilbertson had taken it—not unless she was looking for trouble. He heard the clock strike in the square. "I'm afraid I've kept you late."

"It doesn't matter."

"I hope you didn't have a date or anything——"

"Oh no."

He was persuading himself that he owed her something for putting up with his ill temper, for keeping her almost an hour after the others had gone. It was hardly fair to send her home now. Also, she was a woman and attractive, and he was lonely.

"It's almost half-past six," he said. "Would you care to join me for dinner?"

Anticipation flashed for a moment in her eyes. Then she looked down at her blouse and skirt. "I'm not dressed."

"Don't worry about that. We'll go to some small place."

Suddenly he realized how close they were together in the narrow space between the filing cabinets. High up in this silent, deserted house, every word, every movement seemed to carry a heightened significance. She raised her right arm to push back a lock of hair which had fallen across her face while she was working. Her faint, feminine scent hung in the still, dusty air of the room. She smiled at him in a way slightly but indescribably different from before, as if she were adjusting her conception of him, trying to evaluate him for the first time, not as a man across a desk, but as a possible friend, even a possible lover. . . .

"I'd love to come," she said.

CHAPTER V

It was a curious and slightly awkward sensation at first. His relations with women usually started off according to a fairly conventional routine. There was the process of exchanging confidences, discussing attitudes and tastes, becoming gradually more intimate if things went favorably, and signing off at a fairly early stage if they did not. But on this occasion a great deal of the preliminary spadework had already been done. They had learned a good deal about each other, but without considering that this knowledge might ever be a preliminary to anything. It was like watching rehearsals of a play and then suddenly being expected to take a leading part in the first act.

She was, or at least appeared to be, a good deal less ill at ease than he was. She was also noticeably less discreet than she had been during their conversation at the office.

"You know," she said, "between ourselves, I think it was pretty certainly Gilbertson who pinched that memorandum."

"Why? After all, it was only a copy. New York must have received the original."

"Perhaps he didn't want you to see it."

"I don't know why. I'm not so important. Anyhow," he said impatiently, "it doesn't matter. If New York has the information, that's all that concerns me. If Gilbertson wants to act like a screwball . . ." He added uncomfortably, "It made me a little sore at the time. I feel very badly about speaking to you the way I did."

She smiled. "That was nothing. I'm really far tougher than you

think." After a pause she said, "Do you mind if I say something rather personal?"

"Go ahead."

"I think you worry too much."

"About what?"

"All sorts of things. That was just an example. You were momentarily rude to me—well, what of it? Nobody behaves well all the time. I never thought you were St. Francis of Assisi."

"Now you make me feel silly."

"I didn't mean to. I just didn't want you to set yourself too high a standard, that was all. People are more at ease with you if you behave badly now and then. Don't you think so?"

"It depends who you are. Some people can get away with it. My father, for instance, behaved abominably most of the time. He insulted his friends or his business associates or members of his family whenever he felt inclined. Then an hour or two afterward he would see them again, tell them a joke, offer them a drink, just as if nothing had happened. And he got away with it. They made excuses for him. They used to say he didn't mean it. But he did mean it. I know he did. How do you explain that?"

"He was a powerful man, wasn't he? Everybody wants to think powerful men are good—it's less frightening that way."

"Nobody makes excuses for me," he said. "If I insult them they take it for granted that I mean it. You think I'd be more popular if I were more powerful?"

"Yes, of course. Do you want that?"

He shook his head. "No, thanks. That's not for me."

When they left the restaurant she said, "Thank you very much for the dinner. I enjoyed it enormously."

He was reluctant to end the evening but did not know quite how to prolong it. In New York it would have been easy, but here —what did one do after dinner?

"Shall we go someplace for a drink? Or dance, perhaps? I don't know exactly where——"

"No, really, I'd sooner go home if you don't mind. I can catch the tube just around this corner——"

"The hell with that. I'm certainly going to insist on taking you home. Let's see if we can find a cab."

The taxi stopped outside a big terrace house in South Kensington.

"This is where I live," she said. "Would you like to come in?"

He was not sure what he ought to reply. Was her invitation merely a polite formality which he was expected to refuse? The house looked shabby and depressing—a sort of rooming house. He noticed the movement of a curtain, the suspicion of a face peering out of a ground-floor window. He was curious to know what sort of life went on within.

Noticing his hesitation, she said, "It's not very luxurious, I'm afraid." Her tone was amused rather than defensive. She had contrived to solve his problem for him. A refusal now would seem snobbish.

"Well, thanks very much. If that's okay. . . ."

She opened the door with a latchkey. As soon as they were inside the hall, a small white-haired woman poked her head out of a door on one side of it.

"Oh, hello, Jane dear. I'm sorry—I thought it might be Mrs. Venables." Her eyes were on Marshall, devouring him with ferocious curiosity. "You haven't seen her, have you?"

"I'm afraid not."

"She went to a séance at that place in Lancaster Gate. I hope nothing's happened to her." She said to Marshall, "Excuse my impertinence, young man, but are you any relation to Miss Bellamy's fiancé?"

"Not so far as I know."

"No? You have quite a look of him, you know. Where are you from?"

"New York."

"Oh, that's quite impossible then. He was from Cardiff." With a sharp, disappointed nod she popped back into her room.

"Who was she?" asked Marshall as they climbed the stairs.

"Just a woman who lives here. She's lonely, and I feel sorry for her. Mind you, it's a mistake to give her too much encouragement." She added reflectively, "London's full of old girls like that. They live in bed-sitters on a little capital and every year sell out a few more shares to cover the increase in the cost of living. They haven't anything to do but peep out of windows and quarrel with each

other and complain to the landlady about the hot water. With any luck they die before they go broke." She stopped outside a door on the top floor where a card read: "Miss Jane Lancing." "Could you hold this for a moment?"

She handed him a leather bucket-bag containing a novel, a rolled-up plastic raincoat, a small soft parcel from Swan and Edgar's, and two more solid ones from Selfridge's. She took another key out of her handbag and unlocked the door. The bed-sitting-room was a fairly large one, with a curtain drawn across the bed and a screen to hide the washbasin—two pairs of stockings were hanging over the top of it. There was a cheap sofa and an armchair, a threadbare carpet which covered little more than half the floor, and a gas fire serviced by a shilling in the slot meter. A dormer window looked out on to the glistening wet roof of an adjoining house.

She waved at the armchair. "Make yourself at home." She took off her coat, whisked the drying stockings into a drawer, dropped a coin in the meter, and turned on the gas fire. The boards creaked as she walked about the room.

"I've got some gin and orange squash, but there's no ice and I really wouldn't recommend it. The usual thing round these parts is coffee and biscuits."

"That's fine with me."

She made two cups of instant coffee and opened a tin of biscuits.

"How long have you lived here?" he said.

"Two years. Ever since my girl friend got married." There was mockery in the smile she gave him. "I expect it looks a bit gruesome after the Savoy."

"I don't know," said Marshall awkwardly. "You seem to have——"

"You think I've made it nice and homey?" She shook her head. "I did have a try once, but the wallpaper beat me. There seemed so much of it somehow." There was a short silence. Then she said, "But I don't really mind. If you have to be badly off, London's the place to live in."

"Why?"

"Because nobody cares. The city's so crammed with decayed gentility that you don't have to keep up with the Joneses—the

Joneses are in the same mess as you are. It's a nice, restful feeling."

"Does everyone feel like that?"

"No." Her voice hardened. "It would be better if they did. This country's poisoned with self-pity. Old people who do nothing but look back to the days before the war, young men who've had things too easy since the war and sit around bellyaching because life isn't exciting enough. I'm sick to death of people complaining about things they can't alter."

"That makes you sound pretty tough."

"I'm not really. It's just that—it's in the air. I suppose I'm afraid it might get me too. Have another biscuit?"

"No, thanks."

"They're not very nice, are they? I think the damp must have got at them." She put the tin away. "Do you like this job you're doing?"

"Not much."

"I didn't think you did. You find it a bit pointless perhaps?"

"Yes."

"You mustn't let it get you down. So far as I can see, the way to be popular is to do as little as possible. You'll soon get the hang of it."

"You seem to know a lot about what goes on."

"I keep my eyes open. And I see most of the correspondence, you know. And I talk to the other girls. You'd be surprised how much the secretaries know."

"I suppose so." He was silent for a moment. Then he said: "It's not just this particular job as far as I'm concerned. I've always felt completely out of place in the organization."

"Then why don't you leave?" she asked bluntly.

"I don't know quite what I'd do. I never wanted to go into the business. I tried to paint once, but I was a failure. Somehow I can't bring myself just to do nothing."

"What you're doing now makes a pretty close approach."

"I know. Naturally they realize I haven't got my heart in the game, so they won't give me anything worth while to do. You can hardly blame them."

"Why are you so against it—the business, I mean?"

"I just don't feel identified with it. Do you?"

"On my salary you don't feel identified with anything. But it should be different for you. You can get somewhere."

"Pushing people around," he said bitterly. "That's all it amounts to. That's what they get their fun out of. They call it administration."

"I suppose it has to be somebody's job."

"Not mine. I've seen enough of it."

"So what are you going to do? Stay as you are?"

"I don't know," he said wearily. "Sometimes I try to think it out, but I get nowhere. I suppose you think I'm hopelessly confused——"

"Just a crazy mixed-up millionaire?"

"I guess I asked for that."

"No, please." She sat down beside him on the sofa. "Really, I'm terribly sorry. Please don't be angry."

"That's okay. You were right."

"No, it was unforgivable. I invited your confidence and then sneered at you. I didn't even mean it. I just put on an act—pretending to be hard-boiled. I'm not really that sort of person at all."

"No?"

"No. Really, I suppose I'm frightened—scared stiff, just like so many of us, but I daren't admit it to myself. Once you do"—she looked at the dingy yellow walls, the spluttering gas fire, and shivered slightly—"in a place like this——"

"So in fact," he said, "you're just as weak as I am?"

She looked up at him, her eyes suddenly dark and sad, her defenses abandoned. She said: "If you only knew . . ."

It was then that he kissed her. She made no attempt to resist. Compliantly she turned her face upward and pressed her lips against his. Her eyes were shut, her body immobile—she seemed hardly to be breathing. There was something curiously exciting to him in the strangeness of the situation—the bare room, silent above the roof tops, the bed behind the curtain, the washbasin behind the screen. Here in this room her whole life was laid out in front of him. Here she dressed and undressed, brewed her solitary cup of coffee, read her novel, and entertained her friends. All her intimate possessions were around him, open to his gaze. There was

something almost indecent, to his eyes, in such a lack of privacy. But to her there was nothing extraordinary about it. In her world it was not considered in any way unusual to entertain a man in your bedroom. As a rule, it was the only room you had.

Presently she got up and began to tidy away the cups and saucers.

She said, "Shall we pretend that didn't happen?"

"Why?"

She was determinedly matter-of-fact. "Because if I'm any judge you're going to feel like hell going home. Once you get into your taxi, you'll break out into a cold sweat and wonder how things are going to be in the morning. Am I going to be saucy and knowing and difficult to handle? Am I going to blow the works to the other girls?" She went on reassuringly, "Don't think I blame you. I hate women myself. But, honestly, you don't have to worry."

"I wasn't worrying," he said angrily. "You can tell anyone you damn well please."

He walked over to her and kissed her again, furiously this time, as if to avenge the insult she had thrown at him. But as he held her, his resentment faded and was lost in tenderness. He was suddenly conscious of the supreme importance of this moment, struggling against the force of his own emotions to record it and preserve it in his memory. The scent of her hair, the touch of her silk blouse against his fingers, her back slightly arched under the pressure of his hand. Never again would her flesh seem quite so warm or her lips so moist. In that first surrender she was mystery, she was desire, she was consolation, she was danger and opportunity, she was life. At one time he would have pressed impatiently on, eager to possess her that very night. He would have destroyed the moment—or tried to. But in this one respect at least he was wiser than he had been at twenty. When she made a gentle effort to move away from him, he let her go. As he did so, he heard the sound of footsteps on the stairs. A door opened and closed on the landing, and the footsteps continued in the next room, clearly audible through the wall, succeeded by the noise of water running. A high cracked voice began to sing "Abide with Me." Mrs. Venables had returned home safely.

CHAPTER VI

OUTSIDE, in St. James's Square, the gas lamps began to go on one by one, casting shadows on the ceiling of his living room.

"Darling Jane . . ."

"Darling Chris . . ." Suddenly she said, "Damn, I shall have to move, my arm's gone to sleep." She got up and began to massage the fingers of her left hand. "Shall I draw the curtains?"

"What about going out for dinner?" he said.

"I'm not hungry just yet. Are you?"

"No."

"I'll make you an omelet later on."

She drew the curtains and switched on the lights. Looking around the room, she said, "You're so lucky."

"Why?"

"To have this little flat. I suppose it costs the earth."

"Well . . ." He was uncomfortably aware that the rent he paid was considerably more than her weekly salary. "It's only really fun when you're here."

"You don't have to say that, you know."

"It's true. Nothing's quite the same when I'm on my own. I used to sit here in the evenings and wonder what to do. Or I'd go out to restaurants and read a book with my dinner. Often I used to wish I were back in New York."

"You told me you liked Europe."

"When I was here before I did. I had lots of fun—until the last part. . . ."

"In Paris?"

"Yes. I think the very fact that I loved Paris so much made it worse when I found that I hadn't any place there."

"But are you sure——"

"Sure enough. You see, my father made a bargain with me. At first, when I wanted to paint, he shouted and swore and tried to ridicule me. Then, when he saw it wasn't working, he suddenly became reasonable. He said, 'Okay, if you're set on it, I won't stop you. But knowing you, I'd say you want to be good. You don't want to just sit around in a beard and velvet pants playing at it. Am I right?' I told him he was right. So he made me a typical businessman's proposition." He made a helpless gesture. "And it sounded reasonable enough. By his standards—and by mine, too, at that time, I guess. He would finance me for two years at the best art school in Paris, then at the end I was to show my work to the best art teacher in Paris—everything had to be the best, you notice, he could afford it—and then accept his opinion. We chose a man called Mayer."

"And what did he say?"

"Mayer?" He laughed, as he had trained himself to laugh when telling this story. "I can see him now—a little bald-headed man in a linen jacket covered with grease spots. He had false teeth and he kept pushing his upper plate back with his thumb the way people do when they don't fit very well. But he knew about pictures all right. I explained what I wanted and he told me to bring along what I thought were my ten best pictures to his studio. He asked an extortionate fee, of course."

"And he didn't like them?"

"He let me put them up, one after another. He didn't say a word —just nodded when he'd finished looking and wanted me to put up the next one. When he'd seen them all he said, 'Tell me, Monsieur Marshall—have you ever contemplated any alternative career?'"

"And then?"

"That was all. He didn't need to say any more."

"But he might have been wrong. They don't always know——"

"Let's not talk about it, shall we?"

"Sorry."

"That's all right. It's just that—well, I've thought about all those things myself, and it gets me nowhere. I was beaten. I gave up. Let's leave it at that."

"Even so, you needn't have come back into the business."

"I thought I might as well keep my side of the bargain. Not that it mattered, as it happened. My father died soon afterward."

"But you still carried on?"

"Why not?" he asked indifferently.

"Why not?" She was incredulous. "Because you hate it—because it doesn't mean anything to you. Surely there's every reason in the world for packing it up and doing something else. What you have now isn't a life at all——"

"There was only one sort of life that mattered to me and I failed at it." When she said nothing, he went on: "What do you suggest I should do?"

"Anything!" She looked at him desperately, in furious impatience at his inactivity. "Surely you must see that anything's better than what you're doing now. You can't just throw your hand in at your age and admit you're beaten. What you're saying is that if you can't have the thing you wanted most you're going to stop trying. Isn't that it?"

"In a sense, yes."

"Well, I think you're crazy." She got up and walked away from him. "You never stop criticizing your father, but at least he had some fight in him——"

Was even *she* on the side of the old man? "You think that's all that matters?" he said. "To fight—no matter what you're fighting for? At least I'm doing no harm——"

"It might almost be better if you did. Better for yourself, anyway." She turned on him. "Anything rather than sit here inert, doing nothing—suffering——"

The impatience in her voice was surprisingly painful to him. So this, he thought, is how I appear. Without ever admitting it, he had held in the back of his mind a picture of himself as a Byronic

figure, withdrawn in a tragic and dignified isolation. With this image he had comforted himself for years. Now, in a few words, she had destroyed it.

"I shouldn't have said that," she said. Her voice was so unhappy that it was hardly audible. "I don't know what it is. There's something about you which seems to force me into hurting you."

"Perhaps," he said bitterly, "you see in me a natural victim."

"No, I don't." She shook her head. "Not in the least. I just think you're behaving not as yourself at all, but as a sort of idea of yourself built up on the basis of a lot of things that happened years ago. Don't you see what I mean?"

"Everybody does that to some extent."

"Yes, I know. But with you it's such a—well, such a *negative* idea, isn't it?"

He laughed. When everything else failed it was always possible to take refuge in a joke. "It's a little hard to come four thousand miles to be told about the Power of Positive Thinking."

Later she said, "You don't hate me, darling, do you? Tell me you don't hate me."

"For what?"

"For saying what I did."

"Of course I don't hate you. You may even be right."

"You're happy now?"

"Yes. As happy as I've ever been."

"You'll get tired of me. We see too much of each other." He smiled at the stereotyped, woman's-magazine wisdom. "Yes, we do. Every day. Almost every evening." She shook her head. "It can't last."

"Don't you enjoy it?"

"Yes, of course——"

"Then why go looking for trouble? Are you so afraid of being happy?"

"In a way." Now it was her own experience speaking. "Nothing's all that good in this world."

He pulled her gently onto the sofa. He kissed her and said, "I love you, Jane."

"Don't say that."

"Why not?"

"We've known each other such a short time."

"A moment ago you were saying——"

"You know what I mean. Give yourself time. It's best to be cautious."

"I don't feel cautious. I feel proud. I want to tell people. Though I don't know why one should feel so proud of being in love. It's the one thing any fool can do."

He meant it as a joke, but she answered him quite seriously. "Yes," she said. "That's true, isn't it?" She moved suddenly away from him, frowning a little. It came to him that she would want more from a man than mere devotion, just as she in her turn would wish to give more. There were other things as important as love—respect, admiration, the promise of adventure. She seemed about to explain some of this and then changed her mind. "I'm hungry now," she said. "Why don't we have something to eat?"

She made omelets and laid the table in front of the fire. As they were eating she said, "By the way, I forgot to tell you. Gilbertson was looking for you this afternoon."

"Yes, I saw him just before I left the office. He was unusually friendly. The ice seems to have thawed a bit." Ever since the incident of the accounts there had been a noticeable coldness between himself and Gilbertson. "He asked me out to his place in the country next weekend."

"Did you accept?"

"Why not? We have to work together, don't we?"

"Have you ever spoken to him about that memorandum of Wilcox's? The one that was missing from the files?"

"No. I decided there wasn't anything to be gained——"

"You're going to let him get away with it?"

He frowned. "I haven't much alternative. If that's the way New York wants it——"

"You have to be a good boy and do as they tell you?"

"Up to a point." He rebelled against the implication. "No, that isn't entirely true. I have a certain amount of discretion. But ob-

viously only within limits. And it's not easy to see what's to be done right now. I get the feeling that things are being kept from me and that Wilcox was moved out because he got too nosy—all right. But it's all very insubstantial. . . ." He could hear his own voice as he felt she must hear it—excuses, excuses for doing nothing. She thought he was afraid of action. Could it be true? he wondered with his always fatal readiness to see the other person's point of view. This Olympian detachment of his, which affected to despise the squalid personal feuds, the petty jealousies, the constant struggle for advancement, for money, for power—was it, when it came to the point, no more than an excuse for laziness and cowardice? "It might be different," he added defensively, "if I had some facts."

She looked at him questioningly. Her eyes seemed to be asking him, "Do you really mean it or is it just part of the act?" In business, she knew, it wasn't always advisable to take statements at their face value. Promises were made, plans were outlined, more as a pious hope for the future than as a definite undertaking; they were easily forgotten and it was considered tactless to remind anybody of them at a later date. But he looked back at her defiantly, daring her to disbelieve him. It was as if, without saying anything, an agreement had been made between them, a contract signed.

She lit a cigarette. "If you're interested, I could tell you some other things," she said slowly, "about Wilcox. . . ."

"Such as?"

"He used to send confidential reports to New York. Did you know that?"

"No."

"He didn't even let me type them. He would stay behind in the evening and use my typewriter. Then in the morning he'd hand me a sealed envelope marked 'Private and Confidential.'"

"Who were they addressed to?"

"Kingham, usually. He kept the copies himself, of course."

Marshall felt a spasm of envy for Wilcox. Nobody had ever asked him to send confidential letters. Ever since his childhood he had experienced this feeling of being excluded from certain inner circles of trust. He had always comforted himself with the conviction

that the secrets involved were for the most part unimportant as well as frequently ridiculous. It had, after all, done little good to Wilcox, being so confidential. Nevertheless, he was piqued.

"So you don't know what he said?"

"No."

"Then where does that lead us?"

She hesitated for a moment. Then she picked up her bag and took out a notecase. Behind the few pound notes she carried was a piece of paper folded into four. She handed it to Marshall.

It was a typed list consisting mainly of dates, with various odd words and code letters opposite each one. Most of the words were quite simple—"Budget," "Estimates," "Pricing," "Production," and so on. Many of the dates had the letter K next to them. A few were marked K(C).

Marshall looked at it in perplexity. "I don't understand. What *is* this?"

"It's a record Wilcox made of his letters to New York."

"He gave this to you?"

"No. After he left I was cleaning out and I——" Seeing the look on his face, she said, "All right, I know I should have torn it up. You can, now, if you want."

He should, of course. It was undoubtedly the correct thing to do, as well as the easiest. For a moment, unknown to him, the lives of not only himself and Jane but of Gilbertson, Furac, Kingham, Jeff, Bernstein, and some thousands of men he had never even seen or heard of stood suspended, waiting for his decision on this minor ethical point. It was mainly curiosity which decided him.

"What do these letters mean?" he asked.

"I can only guess. But some of them are obvious. Those without the C are the ones he dictated to me. K refers to Kingham. The ones marked K(C) are almost certainly the confidential memoranda. As you see, they got more frequent toward the end."

"Yes." His attention was attracted by the last three entries. They referred to letters written only a few weeks before Wilcox was recalled to New York. The first two were marked "A.V." The last, two weeks later, "A.V.—immediate action."

He looked up at Jane. "Have you any idea what A.V. refers to?"

"No. That's one of the things I wondered about. All I know is that he'd just returned from Paris about that time. It might refer to something there—or some person. I don't know."

There was a silence. He turned the piece of paper over. There was nothing on the other side.

"This is all there is to it?"

She nodded.

"Well, I don't see where it gets us, frankly," he said. "He wrote some confidential letters—so what?"

"Toward the end he and Gilbertson were always quarreling. We could hear them through the door sometimes. It was worse after he came back from Paris the last time. Then he wrote that last letter, calling for immediate action. A few days later he was recalled." She added with significance, "Don't you think there's anything in that?"

"Maybe," he admitted. "Maybe. But I still can't see anything I can do about it. There's nothing to go on." After a pause he added, "If we had any idea what A.V. referred to, it might be different."

CHAPTER VII

"MY IDEA," said Gilbertson, "was to have a quiet, restful weekend. Completely informal. I hope that's all right with you."

"Surely."

"We can get up when we want to. Lounge about in old clothes. I'll introduce you to some of the local people. . . . My wife's looking forward enormously to meeting you."

Marshall made a suitably appreciative noise. It was Friday evening and they were driving down to Sussex in Gilbertson's 1936 Rolls-Royce, color maroon, coachwork by Hooper. Gilbertson himself made a fine sight at the wheel, with his long bloodhound face, his Homburg and lemon-yellow wash-leather gloves. They traveled slowly but in style.

"It's a grand old bus," said Gilbertson with obvious affection. "Never lets you down. A bit heavy on petrol, but I don't do a big mileage. Most days I take the train into town—it works out rather quicker."

"I see you have commuting problems here too."

"Yes indeed, my dear fellow." He went on to describe in somewhat tedious detail the traffic congestion on the Southern Region. It seemed to Marshall that the weekend was likely to turn out a little dull. On the other hand, it was pleasant to be on good terms with Gilbertson again. He seemed to be taking the view that Marshall, after a short phase when he had shown signs of being "diffi-

cult," was now settling down to behave in a suitable fashion. Did he know about Jane? Marshall wondered. Probably—people always knew more than you thought. No doubt he regarded the affair indulgently, in view of his own efforts with Miss Carvill-Sykes, or even with active support, as a healthy method of keeping Marshall's mind off more serious matters. . . .

"It takes me well over an hour to get to the office every morning," Gilbertson was saying, "but it's worth it—for me, at any rate. I have to work in London, but I'd always want to make my home in the country." He meditated for a moment. "Of course that's where you Americans have it over us. You actually *enjoy* business."

Marshall looked at him with interest. "Don't you?"

"Between ourselves," said Gilbertson, "it bores me to death. One has to make a living, of course, so there's nothing else for it. But if I were in your position, for instance——"

"You'd give it up?"

"My dear boy, you wouldn't see me for dust."

"Do you think you'd be able to enjoy life without an occupation?" Marshall asked doubtfully. "Just doing nothing?"

"I don't see why not," said Gilbertson almost peevishly, "my father did." He went on, "The trouble with you people is that you've accumulated enormous wealth without creating a proper leisured class to spend it. The upshot is that you become richer and richer all the time, and nobody knows what the hell to do with you. Most inconsiderate."

They were well out of London now, driving across the Downs. As they drove over a hill Gilbertson pointed to a large house partly hidden by a clump of trees. "You see that house?"

"Yes."

"I was born there. It's a beautiful place—sixteenth century. We had to sell it when my father died, to pay the death duties." He said regretfully, "The house we have now is pleasant enough, but when you were brought up in the old place . . . Do you know what I'd really like to do?"

"What?"

"I'd like to make enough money to buy it back and retire there— end up my days as I started. God knows if I shall ever be able to

pull it off, what with the inflation and one damn thing and another, but still, there's no harm in hoping." With some defiance he added: "I suppose you think that's absurd?"

"No." Marshall was taken by surprise. He had never thought of Gilbertson as a passionate man. Plainly, beneath his desiccated exterior there lay unsuspected depths of romanticism. On the face of it, in this highly taxed, servantless post-war world, it was a mad ambition. Yet there was a certain gallantry about it which prevented it from being entirely ridiculous.

The house in which the Gilbertsons now lived was only a few miles away and was fairly imposing in its own right. It was an ivy-covered Georgian mansion with an acre of garden and a small paddock. Mrs. Gilbertson was almost as tall as her husband, angular, harsh of voice, and with an abruptness of manner which attempted unsuccessfully to conceal her natural shyness. As she showed Marshall to his room she told him once again that it was to be an informal weekend. There were to be no other guests. The two children, a girl of seventeen and a boy of fourteen, were away at school.

Dinner was a protracted and unappetizing meal, served by a gloomy, semi-moronic village girl who had been dressed up unconvincingly for the occasion in a cap and apron. There was a multitude of tiny courses—soup, fish, meat, dessert, savory, cheese—the changing of plates was punctuated by unexplained delays and the sound of voices raised in argument from the kitchen. The lamb was overcooked, there was a skin on the egg sauce, and some unspeakable disaster had occurred to the summer pudding. Mrs. Gilbertson sat on the edge of her chair, following the maid constantly with her eyes and occasionally hissing furious instructions through her teeth; her response to any form of conversation was no more than fragmentary. Every now and then an expression of despair would flit transiently across her face. Marshall felt sorry for her. He wanted to tell her that he understood all about the servant problem and the impossibility of maintaining pre-war standards—he would have been quite happy to serve himself and dry the dishes afterward. Was she, he wondered, going through this rigmarole to please her husband? Or were they partners in self-delusion? Did she, too,

feel the necessity of preserving this ritual of the Good Old Days?

When the cheese was cleared, she got up from the table and left the two men alone. They sat dutifully for some time over port and cigars, trying to find something to say to each other. Marshall grew bored and sleepy. It seemed to him that he was taking part in some tedious game which Gilbertson was staging to appease his own nostalgia. Perhaps he could find other Englishmen who were happy to play with him, to pretend that the income tax was only five shillings in the pound and the landed gentry still relatively secure in their possessions, and that in the servants' quarters were a cook and two housemaids instead of a half-witted girl and a daily woman who stayed late once in a while as a special favor. Marshall felt himself miscast. He did not know the rules and he found the game without interest. He was beginning to lose sympathy with this obvious yearning for the past, and he suspected that Gilbertson was finding him equally unsatisfactory. He refused a second glass of port and they went to join Mrs. Gilbertson, but when they looked in the drawing room she was not there. Marshall had a shrewd suspicion that she was in the kitchen, helping with the washing up. As soon as was decently possible, he excused himself and went to bed.

The next morning they breakfasted late and went for a walk through the village. Marshall was relieved to find that his sports coat and trousers were sufficiently shabby to be acceptable—his stock went up slightly when he appeared in them. They lunched at the local pub, spent the afternoon at a cricket match, and dined with a retired stockbroker who was endeavoring to adjust his tax position by breeding pedigree cattle at a loss. As they left the stockbroker's house Gilbertson said to him, "We'll see you tomorrow evening then, Charles? Any time after you've finished dinner." To Marshall he said, "We're having a few friends in—I'd like you to meet some of the people around here. Nothing elaborate, of course."

Elaborate or not, it appeared to entail a good deal of preparation. Mrs. Gilbertson was hardly to be seen on the Sunday. In the afternoon Travers drove up. His position at the party seemed to be

something between guest and part-time butler. He prepared drinks, moved furniture, flattered Mrs. Gilbertson, and made brightly predictable remarks on general subjects.

They dined lightly off cold ham and salad. Soon afterward the guests began to arrive. Apart from the vicar and the doctor and the land agent of a local nobleman, they were mostly men like Gilbertson. They spent five days of the week in town, banking or underwriting or sitting on boards of directors, in order to earn the money to play at being country gentlemen on Saturday and Sunday. The talk was mainly of gardens and horses and church bazaars—any mention of business was an obvious social blunder.

By eleven o'clock it seemed to Marshall that the party had been going on for several days. He found himself in the grip of a determined matron who had once spent a week in New York and was counted in consequence as an authority on American social customs.

"In our view," she said, baring her dentures and adroitly intercepting an attempt at escape, "the women over there get far too much of their own way. It isn't good for them. Basically, as a sex, we need to be dominated. Don't you agree?"

"Perhaps. I——"

Ignoring what she appeared to regard as an interruption, she went on to illustrate her point with an anecdote about a prize-winning Labrador bitch, now unhappily deceased. Above the hubbub of conversation, the telephone rang.

Gilbertson motioned to Travers. "Take it in the dining room, would you, Travers?" Travers disappeared. Gilbertson, suddenly conscious of Marshall's predicament, walked over to rescue him.

"Marcia, I believe Henry wants to ask you about the next meeting of the R.S.P.C.A." As she moved hurriedly away he said apologetically, "Rather a bore, I'm afraid—but a wonderful hand with Labradors. I remember—— Yes?"

Travers was standing at his elbow. "It's from Paris, sir. Monsieur Furac."

"Oh—excuse me, would you?" He left the room.

Marshall carried on a desultory conversation with Travers. After a while Gilbertson returned, his manner noticeably abstracted.

"Anything serious?" Marshall asked.

"Oh no, not really." He looked down at Marshall's glass. "But you're not drinking, my dear fellow. Travers . . ."

"I don't want any more, thanks." He put the glass on the mantelpiece behind him. "Was it about business?"

"Yes——" Gilbertson hesitated. "In a way . . ."

"Does he often ring up on Sunday nights?"

"Oh no—quite unusual really." Gilbertson half turned away, with the obvious intention of terminating the conversation. He had administered a snub, and if Marshall was to behave like a well-conducted Englishman he would blush and regret his own inquisitiveness. But Marshall had suddenly grown tired of Gilbertson's conception of good behavior. He was bored and irritable. His resentment at the atmosphere of concealment and delay at the office flooded back. He would not be treated like an inquisitive child.

"I'm sorry if I sound intrusive," he said sharply, "but if it was a matter of business I am naturally interested. You must appreciate that I have a direct responsibility to New York for the Paris agency."

The determination in his tone surprised even himself. Gilbertson turned back toward him, startled at this unexpected attack. Travers had disappeared.

"Have you?" Gilbertson was undecided. His instinct was to question Marshall's authority to demand information. On the other hand, one could not be sure. Kingham was not the only powerful man in New York. And there was the magic of the name. Cipher though he was reputed to be, this was still Marcus Marshall's son. It might not be safe to go too far.

"Yes." Marshall spoke firmly, conscious of the other man's indecision. "So, naturally, I want to be kept abreast of what happens there."

"I see." Gilbertson acknowledged defeat. He went on coldly, "Well, I don't know whether you'll find this particular piece of news of great significance. It's mainly personal." He went on in a voice of exaggerated casualness, as if describing the sort of trivial incident which was always happening. "It seems that one of Furac's

employees has gone off his head and taken a shot at him with a revolver."

Marshall looked at him in astonishment. "That doesn't sound exactly insignificant to me. Is he seriously hurt?"

"No, no, just a flesh wound." Gilbertson assumed an expression of distaste. These excitable Americans . . . "The chap was evidently quite mad. Afterward he turned the gun on himself and tried to blow his brains out. With only partial success, apparently."

"He's still alive?"

"Yes. He's unconscious in hospital. They say he probably won't survive."

"Does anybody know why he did it?"

Gilbertson shrugged his shoulders. "He just went crazy. Furac says he always was what he calls an introspective type."

There was a silence. Gilbertson was regarding him with hostility, as if to say: "Well then, what now?" Marshall suddenly began to feel ashamed of his curiosity. It was true—the information meant nothing to him. A tragic, sensational accident involving two people he had never met; no more than that. He found himself trying to justify himself in his own mind. It was a consequence of this absurd secrecy. If so much had not been kept from him previously he would never have been so insistent. And why had Gilbertson been so unwilling to tell him?

"Are you satisfied?" said Gilbertson ironically. "Or is there anything else you'd like to know?"

Marshall flushed. He was being put hopelessly in the wrong. In a final burst of obstinacy he said, "What's the man's name?"

"Nobody you've ever heard of. He was a salesman called André Verrier."

PART III

CHAPTER I

THE PLANE climbed through the uppermost layer of fleecy cloud into a world of limitless blue sky and glittering sunlight. It was like suddenly going into heaven through a trap door. The note of the engines changed slightly as they leveled off. The stewardess began to pass up the aisle with coffee and biscuits. In less than an hour they would be in Paris.

Gilbertson said, "I still think it's a little unnecessary for us both to go chasing over like this."

"I told you," said Marshall, "that I didn't mind going by myself."

"Oh no." Gilbertson sounded shocked. "I couldn't let you do that—not the first time. It wouldn't be the thing at all. Much better for me to take you over, introduce you—and so forth. I'd intended to do that later on in the year," he added reproachfully.

"I'm sorry if I upset your program."

"That's all right. One must be flexible, I suppose." He sighed. If one was condemned to deal with lunatics, he managed to suggest, flexibility was the only answer. But there was no object in pretending to enjoy it. "It's just—at such short notice—rather inconvenient. . . ."

These, Marshall realized, were hard words. In Gilbertson's world it was a very serious matter to be accused of causing inconvenience. Marshall was given to understand that he had failed dismally to live up to the advance publicity he had received from Kingham.

Instead of accepting things as he found them, in an appropriately man-of-the-world fashion, he had been tactless and interfering.

Marshall was a man who, on the whole, liked to be popular. He had never achieved any satisfaction from arousing dislike, nor had he been able, in the way of most successful men, to accept it with either indifference or resignation as the necessary price of action. But over the past few months he had been tried too hard. Too often he had been reminded of his own insignificance, told (by inference, if not in so many words) to mind his own business. Now he was weary of being tactful and no longer cared whether Gilbertson liked him or not. Kingham's instructions were forgotten. His own pride demanded satisfaction. And his curiosity also. For he felt certain that André Verrier must be the A.V. referred to in the list of Wilcox's confidential correspondence. Wilcox had written three letters to New York about him, letters which he preferred to type himself and of which no copies had ever been filed. Shortly before his return to New York he had made a visit to Paris, quarreled with Gilbertson on his return, written a last letter about A.V. demanding action—and then been immediately recalled. Now Wilcox was in California and Verrier had tried to kill himself. Marshall could not imagine what the explanation might be. But he was certain of one thing, that it was his duty to talk to Verrier if it was humanly possible.

"If we'd waited till it was convenient," he pointed out, "it might have been too late."

"Too late for what?"

"You tell me Verrier's critically ill. I am particularly anxious to speak to him."

"I can't imagine why," said Gilbertson testily. "You don't know him, do you?"

"Not personally—no."

Gilbertson glanced sharply at him. Deliberately he had tried to put as much significance as he could into his last remark. With luck, Gilbertson might suspect that Wilcox had confided in him or that he had, while in New York, read the confidential memoranda. Without doubt, his bluff had had some effect. Gilbertson dropped the subject immediately.

"Furac will be meeting us at the airport," he said. "I told him it wasn't necessary, but he insisted. He's a very hospitable person. Almost overwhelming at times."

Once again Marshall felt the desire to shock, to push a vulgar finger through this veil of discretion.

"Do you like him?" he asked bluntly.

"Like him?" Gilbertson floundered for a moment. "I don't really know him very well—I mean, ours is just a business relationship, you understand. He's a shrewd man, there's no doubt of that. And very cultured, too, I believe—speaks several languages." He added obscurely: "Not perhaps everybody's cup of tea . . ."

"In what way?"

Gilbertson fluttered his fingers. "It's not easy to explain." He paused and then said carefully, "He's a bit of a law unto himself, if you see what I mean."

"I don't, quite."

"You will when you've met him, I think."

Furac was waiting for them at the customs barrier. He was a tall man with a bald head and a long reptilian neck. At a distance he could be easily mistaken for a relatively young man, but on closer inspection his real age became apparent. Above the neat, dapper body the face was old, with anxious, vertical wrinkles; it seemed to look down on his elegant gray suit, the handmade shoes, the pale manicured hands, and derive from them nothing more than a grim satisfaction. He smiled perfunctorily and apologized for not shaking hands. His right arm was in a sling.

"It's very kind of you to meet us," said Gilbertson. "There was really no need——"

"Not at all." He spoke English with only a very slight accent. "I have been looking forward very much to meeting Mr. Marshall."

"But your arm——"

"Oh, that is nothing," said Furac positively. "A mere scratch. It causes only slight inconvenience, nothing more." He added, "Fortunately Verrier was unused to firearms. He was a poor shot."

"How is he?" asked Marshall.

"Still alive—but unconscious, I believe." He added with indifference, "The doctors say his condition is extremely serious."

Gilbertson shook his head solemnly. "A shocking business."

"Yes. Most unfortunate."

"Have you any idea why he did it?" said Marshall.

"How does one account for the actions of a madman?" Furac accompanied his words with short, sharp gesticulations. It was plain that, for all his protestations, he had been badly shaken up by his experience. "You must understand that Verrier was always a man of unstable personality. We've had trouble with him frequently before."

"What sort of trouble?"

"Oh—hysterical outbursts, paranoid delusions. He brooded a great deal and fancied that people were against him. I myself am an amateur student of psychology and I did my best to help him, but without success unfortunately. In fact, it seems that I turned his delusions to some extent against myself. That sometimes happens, you know."

"He thought he had a grievance against you?"

"Presumably. I cannot imagine what it was, since he made no attempt to explain himself. He simply took out this revolver and shot at me." Furac shook his head and frowned; a diagnostician confronted with a difficult problem. "The whole case is extremely complex. He had, I know, certain other troubles—private difficulties, you understand. . . . No doubt under the circumstances it was foolish of me to continue to employ him, but I was sorry for him. He would have had difficulty in finding another job. So"—he gave a curious nervous wriggle, as if dislodging a fly from one of his shoulder blades—"I have been punished for my foolishness. It is perhaps a lesson to me."

Outside the airport was a large chauffeur-driven Mercedes. As they drove away, Marshall said, "I'd like to see Verrier if I could."

Furac's eyes regarded him questioningly. Beneath his grim, humorless self-possession there were signs of strain.

"Certainly," he said. "Though, as I said, he is unconscious at the present time. You would not be able to speak to him."

"Just the same——"

"I will try to arrange it for you. Meanwhile, my wife is expecting us all to lunch at our apartment. I hope this will be convenient?"

"Of course," said Gilbertson. "We shall be delighted. I hope we haven't put Madame Furac to too much trouble?"

"On the contrary, it will be a great pleasure," he said with formal, toneless courtesy. "My wife is most anxious to meet Mr. Marshall."

If that was so, Marshall reflected later, it was certainly not immediately apparent. Madame Furac was a woman many years younger than her husband, with white-blond hair, a Riviera tan, and an appearance of exhausted boredom with her surroundings which was curiously infectious. Having dressed and groomed herself with considerable care for her luncheon party, she obviously considered that she had done all that could possibly be expected of her. She made little attempt to conceal the fact that she found them all, Furac included, extremely dull company.

The apartment was large and luxuriously furnished, the meal served in a magnificent dining room overlooking the Bois. There was a great deal of food and wine. By the time they had finished drinking their coffee it was after three o'clock. Gilbertson just managed to suppress a yawn.

"Perhaps we should be checking in at our hotel," he suggested to Marshall.

Furac stood up. "Of course. There are rooms for you at the Plaza-Athenée—I will drive you there." He paused. "This evening I would very much like you to meet a friend of mine, Monsieur Patou. He is a deputy." He turned back to Gilbertson. "Patou is an extremely influential man."

"Naturally," said Gilbertson formally, "we shall be delighted. . . ."

"Excellent. I have a reservation at eight o'clock at the Tour d'Argent. I could perhaps pick you up at the hotel a quarter of an hour before that." He looked at Gilbertson's flushed, sleepy face, at the sun pouring down on the street outside. "In the meantime you will probably wish to rest a little."

The thought of a few hours on a bed in a luxury hotel was undeniably seductive. Marshall had to force himself to intervene.

"What about visiting the hospital?" he said.

There was a silence. Furac regarded him sourly, Gilbertson half closed his eyes as if in pain. It was as if some appalling social indiscretion had been committed which they hoped he would at least have the decency to retract. But he said nothing. Finally Furac said reluctantly, "I will try to find out what can be arranged."

"Is it necessary to arrange anything? Couldn't we just go along there?"

"I am afraid not. You would almost certainly be refused admission. Not being a relative or, for that matter, even an acquaintance of the patient, you would have no standing. On the other hand, I, as his employer, might be able to persuade the hospital to admit you. If you would care to wait another few minutes I will make a telephone call now."

He went out, leaving the two men alone. Gilbertson said: "Of course, I'm sorry for the poor fellow and all that, but if he's unconscious——"

"He may not be unconscious when we get there."

"Perhaps not. But even so—I mean, we don't even know the fellow."

Gilbertson's embarrassment was genuine, if slightly absurd. Even in these circumstances it seemed he recoiled from the idea of an interview with a person to whom he had not been introduced.

"You haven't met Verrier before?"

"Never in my life. I've heard Furac mention his name occasionally."

"If that's how you feel," said Marshall, "why don't you stay and rest in the hotel? I'll go alone."

"No, no," said Gilbertson hurriedly. "I wouldn't hear of it. If you're set on going, of course I'll go with you." He added in a discouraging voice, "Let's hope it isn't a complete waste of time."

In a few minutes Furac returned.

"Nothing is possible until six o'clock," he said. "Then we may see him for a short while."

"How is he?" asked Marshall.

"His condition is very serious."

"But hell——" He grew angry. He was being stalled again. This supercilious old camel was stringing him along. And not knowing

the language well enough, there was nothing much he could do about it. "That's nonsense! He may be dead by six."

Furac waved his hands, palms upward, fingers outspread, to indicate his own impotence in the matter. "The rules of the hospital are very strict." Seeing that Marshall was once again preparing to protest, he added with absolute finality, "My chauffeur is waiting to take you to the hotel. I will call for you there at five-thirty."

CHAPTER II

THE HOSPITAL was a massive structure built entirely of dark gray stone. It consisted of a series of parallel rectangular blocks six stories high leading off a central administration building; running around the buildings and between the blocks were graveled paths and a few ill-kept flower beds. The whole was enclosed within a protective circle of high spiked railings.

They drove along beside it for almost half a mile before arriving at the entrance. The huge double gates were surmounted with barbed wire and securely locked. "This is a very poor district," explained Furac. "There are many criminals . . ." He and the chauffeur became involved in an argument with an aged concierge—apparently the instructions for their reception had not been passed sufficiently far down the scale of authority. After a good deal of talk and gesticulation, terminating in the furtive passage of money, they were finally allowed in.

"This is not the normal visiting hour, you understand," said Furac. "One has to make special arrangements."

Inside the hospital there was a dank, tomblike atmosphere. Their footsteps echoed on the stone flags of the main corridor. There was none of the bustle which Marshall had always associated with hospitals at home. The sunlight struggled hopelessly through high dusty windows, illuminating strips of wall from which the paint was peeling and Gothic archways like those of an old seminary. Nobody interfered with them or asked who they were. It seemed

that, once past the barrier of the main gate, their presence was accepted without question.

They found the ward with some difficulty. It was on the third floor of one of the side blocks, up a narrow stone staircase with different smells, ranging from carbolic acid to stew, on each landing. By this time they had all begun to feel much less important than they had felt a quarter of an hour ago. Effortlessly this gaunt, archaic building had cut them down to size. Here nobody cared for them. Their bank accounts and expensive cars and homes and clothes meant nothing. The hospital was not impressed; it saw them merely as men, like all the others. It seemed to be awaiting with grim expectancy the day when it might see them again under less favorable circumstances.

They were in a small corridor with doors opening off it on either side. At the far end were large swing doors leading into the ward proper. The corridor was deserted. More than ever, they felt like intruders.

"What do we do now?" asked Gilbertson.

Furac looked about, exasperated. The lack of interest in their arrival was like a personal insult to him. It reflected on the efficiency of his organization and the importance of his contacts. Marshall was slightly amused. In international business it was a point of prestige to demonstrate to foreign visitors the extent of one's influence. Furac had lost face.

"I cannot understand it," he said. "The superintendent assured me that we would be expected. He promised to notify the sister of the ward. No doubt she is in her office." He approached one of the doors and stood before it indecisively. Suddenly it opened and a tiny, aged man in a flannel nightgown shuffled out and walked past them toward the ward. There was the sound of rushing water, stifled as the door sprang shut again.

"I can't help feeling," said Gilbertson, "that it was perhaps a mistake to come at this time. It may be rather inconvenient. . . ."

He looked longingly at his lines of retreat, which were, his voice reminded them, still open. A quick change of plan and they could be drinking champagne cocktails in the Tour d'Argent, with this ridiculous escapade completely forgotten. . . . Marshall's own con-

fidence was beginning to ebb. After all, what was he really trying to do? What conceivable object was there in this visit to the sick-bed of an unconscious man whom he had never met and whose existence had been unknown to him until a week or two ago? Supposing Verrier did regain consciousness, what then? What questions could he ask? Would the two of them be left alone? Most unlikely, he decided, especially if Furac had anything to hide. And, in any case, would Verrier be able to understand English?

The ward door opened and a tall woman of about thirty-five in a blue uniform came out. She looked at them questioningly.

"Excuse me," said Furac. "That is the sister."

He hurried up to her and engaged her in conversation. Marshall and Gilbertson followed. After they had listened uncomprehendingly for a while to the rapid conversation, Furac turned to them.

"He is still unconscious," he explained. "It is impossible to speak to him."

The sister nodded sharply two or three times and led them to the ward door. She pushed it open to show a long row of beds, one of which was encircled by screens.

"She says he has been screened off because he is seriously ill. Also, his wife is with him. He cannot receive any visitors at the moment."

Marshall nodded despondently. That certainly seemed to settle the matter. It was hard to see what more he could do. Would Jane understand? he wondered. He remembered her excitement when he had spoken to her on the telephone just before leaving for Paris, her unconcealed delight at the knowledge that he had roused himself from his inertia and decided to take the initiative. The thought of her confidence in him had given him strength to withstand the hostility of Gilbertson and Furac. It would be hard to tell her that it had all come to nothing. It was no fault of his, of course, he had every excuse. But there came a time when no excuse was good enough.

He summoned together the last remnants of his determination.

"Perhaps," he said, "we could wait a little while——"

Furac frowned. "But there is no object——"

"We don't want to make ourselves a nuisance," put in Gilbertson.

"That's for Sister to decide." Marshall was conscious of the weakness of his position. He could not himself give any reason for staying, except that to go now would be to admit that he was beaten. "Will she allow us to wait?" he asked Furac.

Furac, with a sigh of exasperation, spoke again to the sister. She gave a shrug. "*Si vous voulez . . .*"

"Okay," said Marshall. "Let's do that."

She opened a door on the left-hand side of the corridor and showed them into a small bare office. Marshall was conscious of being the focal point in an atmosphere of disapproval to which the other three contributed in some degree. It varied from the impersonal irritation of the sister to downright disgust on the part of Furac. When the sister had left, Gilbertson arranged himself in a chair and offered cigarettes.

"We might as well be as comfortable as possible," he said. "Goodness knows how long we shall have to wait."

"Our dinner engagement," said Furac pointedly, "is in one hour's time."

Marshall said nothing. It seemed to him that anything he might say would only make matters worse. His chair was beside a desk on which the sister presumably did her clerical work. There was a litter of memoranda and half-completed temperature charts, a pile of case sheets. He glanced over them idly. They were meaningless to him, but at least it was better to look at them than to meet the eyes of his two companions. Suddenly he noticed the name on the top case sheet.

André Verrier, age 32. Occupation: Salesman. Address: 49C rue Zurbaran; married; no children; next of kin—wife, Louise Verrier, same address. Date of admission to hospital: . . . . Date of discharge: . . . . Mode of discharge: . . . .

That was all, on the front sheet. Presumably the details of his medical condition were on the other side. Marshall was tempted to turn over the page in search of further information but could not bring himself to do so. As he looked away, he saw Furac's eyes upon him. He also had seen the case sheet.

They had been sitting there for almost half an hour in complete silence when they heard the sound of voices in the corridor outside. Then, without warning, the door was thrown open and a young man in a white coat, with a stethoscope round his neck, came into the room. He looked at them in surprise, muttered excuses, and walked over to the desk. Picking up Verrier's case sheet from the desk, he took a fountain pen out of the pocket of his coat and in the column labeled "Mode of discharge" he scribbled: "Mort." Then he tossed the case notes into a wire tray for disposal.

Furac said: "You are the doctor in charge of André Verrier?"

"Yes." The doctor raised his eyebrows questioningly. He could not have been more than twenty-five or so; his clothes were cheap, his collar soiled and crumpled. Even in death Verrier was in no position to demand the best.

"Are you friends of his?"

"Yes. I am his employer."

With a spark of interest the doctor looked at the sling on Furac's right arm. "The one he . . . ?"

"That is so."

"You were lucky. It was a dangerous weapon——"

"He was mad. I knew it as soon as he came into the room."

"Really?" The doctor was only mildly impressed. "That may be so. For myself, I had no chance to speak to him. You understand, I suppose, that he is dead?"

Furac nodded, his long bony face composed in an expression of solemnity. "It is very tragic."

"Yes." The doctor made no attempt to be anything other than perfunctory. He looked at Gilbertson and Marshall as if wondering whether to ask who they were and what they were doing here. Then he seemed to decide against it—he was too busy and too indifferent to care. He gave them all a thin, tired smile and left the room.

"I guess we might as well leave now," said Marshall. Despite himself, he was conscious of an apologetic note in his voice. The affair was finished; Verrier was dead, wiped off the face of the earth with a stroke of red ink. . . . With the air of a man in retreat, he walked out into the corridor.

As they stood there, waiting to take their leave of the sister, a woman came out of the ward. The light was poor, and Marshall formed no more impression of her than that she was fair and slight in build, with a pale, oval face. As she passed by them Furac nodded at her, smiling uncertainly, like a man who remembers a snub on some previous occasion. The woman showed no sign of recognition.

Marshall looked at him sharply. "Is that his wife?"

"Yes. I have met her once before." His tone was disparaging. "She is not a bad girl—though somewhat provincial——"

"Excuse me."

She had almost reached the outer pair of swing doors when Marshall overtook her. Hearing his footsteps, she half turned to meet him.

"Madame Verrier?"

"Yes."

She regarded him coldly, without welcome or encouragement. He found himself at a loss for words. It was necessary to make some contact, some show of human sympathy. Whatever the truth about Verrier or the meaning of his dealings with Wilcox, he had nevertheless died in horrible circumstances, perhaps in madness, perhaps in despair. It was not possible to go out to dinner and forget about it, to allow his widow to walk past in a corridor without a word. But he was discouraged by her lack of response. Everywhere he found himself surrounded by suspicion and hostility—even in the eyes of the person he was trying to befriend.

"I would like to say——" he began in his halting French. As he searched for words, he cursed himself for his own idleness, his failure to learn the language. How was it possible to gain understanding or express sympathy under such conditions? He started again. "*Je veux offrir*——" What was the French for condolences? But even that was too cold, a card on a wreath, black-edged. "*Je suis triste*——" he began again.

She had no mercy for his embarrassment. "Perhaps," she said coldly in English, "you should speak your own language."

"Oh, I'm sorry. I didn't realize——" He added with relief, "That will be much easier——"

"You are a friend of Monsieur Furac?"

"Yes. Of course, how stupid of me, you don't know who I am. I should introduce myself. My name is Marshall—Christopher Marshall. I'm from the New York office of the corporation. I was in London and as soon as I heard——"

"You are Marshall?"

She spoke softly, but it seemed to him that at that moment her attitude of indifference had changed to something much more positive. She looked at him almost with loathing.

"Yes. This has been a terrible tragedy. I wonder if there is anything I can do to help."

"To help? In what way?"

He floundered. He had not intended to discuss details. Nor, he began to realize, had he any clear idea of what his intentions were. "Well, I don't know exactly just now. Perhaps we could have a talk——"

She shook her head. "No." The eyes that regarded him were red-rimmed, shadowed, implacable. In her voice there was hate, not only for him, but for his organization, his country, everything he might be taken to represent. "There is nothing I want from you —nothing whatever."

She turned and walked hurriedly away, her footsteps echoing along the stone walls of the corridor. He thought of following her and then stopped himself. He would only expose himself to further humiliation, and at this time, at least, she had the right to be alone if she wished.

In the silence that followed, Furac was the first to speak. "Perhaps we should go now," he said. "It would be impolite to keep Monsieur Patou waiting."

CHAPTER III

WHEN HE AWOKE next morning his head was throbbing and his mouth was dry and sore from innumerable cigarettes. Memories of the night before came back to him, combining with his physical condition to induce a mood of extreme pessimism. He had gone to bed late, and after the first hour or two of heavy sleep owing to the wine, he had passed a restless night. He looked at his watch on the bedside table. It was after nine o'clock.

It had been a dreadful, nightmarish evening. Monsieur Patou had turned out to be a florid, middle-aged man with a thick, coarse voice and an uncertain temper. He spoke no English. When they first met him he was in a bad mood for some reason which was never clearly explained, but began to thaw a little under the influence of alcohol. Gilbertson and Marshall, after the first introductions, he practically ignored. He ate and drank on a Rabelaisian scale, stopping only to shout at the waiters or wipe the sweat from his forehead with the napkin he wore tucked in his collar. Every now and then he would laugh harshly, explosively, for no obvious reason. Marshall watched with mounting indignation as he ordered bottle after bottle of champagne without consultation with the other members of the party. As the wine took hold of him, his voice rose and he banged on the table with his fist to emphasize his points. Furac smiled and nodded agreement; occasionally he would translate snatches of Patou's conversation into English in the patient but patronizing manner of a professor of psychiatry

showing off a mental case. As Patou sank farther into drunkenness, Furac amused himself by making contemptuous remarks about him in English to Marshall and Gilbertson. It was as if in this way he was somehow able to disclaim responsibility for his own part in the spectacle.

The entertainment had ended at a night club in Montmartre, where Patou had capsized among the bottles and glasses which littered the table, to be eventually borne home unconscious.

Marshall heaved himself wearily out of bed, drank a glass of Perrier to clear his mouth, and opened the shutters. The sunlight hurt his eyes. The bedroom was magnificent, with a balcony facing on to a courtyard and a fountain—it was part of a two-bedroom suite which he was sharing with Gilbertson. He put on his dressing gown and walked into the sitting room.

Gilbertson was already up, eating croissants and reading the *Continental Daily Mail*. He looked as neat as ever and none the worse for the previous night. His coldness of manner had now entirely disappeared. He seemed to be taking the attitude that Marshall had behaved badly yesterday but had, after all, been punished for it by being made to look foolish. It was not for him to kick a man when he was down. He waved a hand in greeting.

"Good morning," he said. "Help yourself to breakfast. Wonderful day, isn't it?"

"Yes." Marshall poured coffee for himself. He looked at the food and decided against it. Instead, he lit a cigarette. "How do you feel after last night?"

"Fair," Gilbertson said judicially. "But I couldn't stand it very often. I'm not much of a man for the night life, myself. I suppose," he added with large tolerance, "the French have more stamina for that sort of thing."

"What I can't understand is what we were doing there at all."

"Prestige, my dear boy, prestige. These distributors like to show you around. It convinces chaps like Patou that there *is* such a thing as the Marshall Corporation and that Furac isn't just knocking those machines of yours up himself in a converted garage at Passy. I suppose it's of some value," he added dubiously.

"Where does this Patou come in, anyway? Government contracts?"

"I shouldn't be surprised. Though I don't know much detail of what goes on over here. He was certainly a dreadful bore."

"You said it." But he didn't want to sound too holier-than-thou. It was the kind of attitude that got Americans disliked abroad. "Mind you, we have them like that at home. I guess it's pretty much the same everywhere."

Gilbertson nodded noncommittally. Evidently he was not prepared to speak for England in the matter. Marshall went over to the window and looked out into the courtyard. He found he could manage to stand the light a little better now. "What goes on today?" he asked.

"I had a ring from Furac a little while ago. He's tied up this morning, it seems. That's understandable, since we came at such short notice. But he's going to send his assistant, Colbert, round in the car. He thought you'd like a little drive around the city. You know the sort of thing—the Champs Elysées, the Bois——"

Marshall shook his head. "I'm sorry." An idea that had been lying around in the back of his mind since they had left the hospital the previous afternoon was beginning to take shape. "I'm afraid you'll have to give him my apologies. I can't come for a drive this morning."

"Oh dear." Gilbertson was perturbed. "Are you sure? I mean —it's really very kind of Furac to offer—— He may be rather offended——"

"He should have asked me personally."

"You were asleep."

"Well, that's too bad. Tell him I'm sorry," he repeated. "I've got something else to do."

He waited for Gilbertson to ask him what it was. But of course an Englishman couldn't ask that sort of question, no matter how curious he might be, no matter how much he might raise one bushy eyebrow, waiting for you to volunteer the information. . . .

"Perhaps," said Gilbertson finally, "you could manage to meet us later?" He picked up a napkin and carefully dried the coffee out of his mustache. "We shall be at the office at one o'clock."

Marshall glanced at his watch. There should be enough time, provided it was not too far away. "I guess so."

"We'll expect to see you then."

Marshall went back to his room and bathed and dressed hurriedly. He took an aspirin for his headache and a benzedrine for the depression which usually accompanied it on these occasions—he was a poor drinker. Shortly afterward he imagined he felt better. As he passed through the lobby on his way out of the hotel he saw an anxious-looking olive-skinned young man at the reception desk, asking for Mr. Gilbertson. Colbert? The Mercedes was waiting outside, but the chauffeur seemed not to recognize him. He called a taxi.

"Forty-nine rue Zurbaran."

The driver took out a tattered street guide and leafed through it. After a while he gave an ill-tempered grunt and started off.

They crossed the river and headed south. At first they were in the Montparnasse area, where Marshall had lived and worked—many years ago, it seemed to him.

He remembered the excitement with which he had first explored the quarter. There, on the right of the Boulevard St. Germain, was the café where he had spent so many of his evenings. He had sat drinking cognac with Ken Pearson and Rafael da Silva, wearing berets and linen trousers and hoping people would take them for Frenchmen. Nobody ever did. Now Rafael was an insurance assessor in São Paulo and Ken was an executive in an advertising agency, drawing women with forty-inch busts for the glossy magazines. Neither of them had minded very much. It had been fun while it lasted, but when the fun was over you went back home and married and got down to a real job of work. When they had got themselves enough money they would come back for a vacation with their wives, hinting (as would be expected of them) of wild, unspecified adventures, of mistresses casually shared by impecunious students. Except that they hadn't been impecunious, and, no matter how you tried to kid yourself, Paris in the 1950s wasn't really very much like *la vie de Bohème*. Perhaps it never had been.

But soon they were beyond the area he knew. The streets were narrower, the stucco was cracking on the walls of the tall gray build-

ings, pieces of washing hung out from the windows of the apartment houses. Even the sun seemed to lose its brilliance, filtered through a cloud of poverty.

He felt obscurely intimidated. It was like making his way into a jungle peopled with savages he could never understand. He began to regret the impulse which had led him into making this expedition, the quirk of memory which had held in his mind the address he had seen on Verrier's case sheet. Why, after all, was he doing this? By any ordinary standards he had no longer any obligation to Madame Verrier. He had offered to help her and his offer had been rudely rejected. And yet, somehow, remembering her eyes in that last moment before she had turned away from him down the hospital corridor, he could not find within himself any genuine resentment against her.

Forty-nine rue Zurbaran was a house like all the others in the quarter. Inside the doorway there were slots containing four cards, one of which said "Verrier." Marshall paid off his taxi and then regretted that he had not asked the man to wait. There was, after all, no more than an even chance that she would be there.

The concierge's lodge was empty. He walked up the stairs. The building seemed quite uninhabited—probably all the tenants were out at work. His footsteps echoed on the carpetless stairs.

On the third floor there was a door marked "49C." The silence was such that he felt sure she was not at home. When he rang the bell he thought at first that he heard the sound of movement, but when it was not repeated he decided he had been mistaken. He rang again to make sure and was just about to turn and go down the stairs when she opened the door. She was wearing an apron over the same black dress she had worn at the hospital.

"Good morning," he said.

She seemed surprised to see him and at a loss to know what to say or do. At the hospital she had shown herself completely in command of the situation; now her assurance had deserted her. In the middle of her housework, her hair uncombed, her face not completely made up, she was unprepared for battle.

"What are you doing here?" she asked finally.

"I came to have a talk with you."

"About what?"

They were still standing in the doorway. He said, "Do you mind if I come in?"

She said nothing, but moved aside and allowed him to enter the apartment. It seemed to consist of no more than three rooms. The living room was small and cheaply furnished. She motioned toward a chair.

"You will excuse me for one moment?"

While she was away he looked around the room. The furniture was of light pine, highly polished, thinly upholstered with imitation leather. You could almost see the store where it had been sold on such accommodatingly easy terms. Part of the suite was a glass-fronted bookcase, fitted mainly with back numbers of *Paris-Match*. On top of the bookcase was a photograph. Madame Verrier was on the deck of a *bateau mouche*, arm in arm with a man, presumably Verrier himself. He was a delicate-looking man, dandified in the ready-made way of the traveling salesman. Behind the smile which the photograph had demanded there was a lingering trace of anxiety which he had found it impossible to conceal. He was rather smaller than his wife.

He had picked up the photograph and was looking at it when she came into the room.

"Your husband?" he asked.

"Yes." She had discarded her apron and made up her face. Her moment of confusion was over. She sat down in one of the shoddy chairs and regarded him uncompromisingly. When he hesitated, wondering how to begin, she grew impatient.

"Well?" she asked sharply. "What is it you wish to say?"

"Yesterday," he said slowly, "I offered to help you and you refused. I'd like to know why."

She sighed irritably. "I was very upset, you must understand."

"I understand and sympathize. Just the same——"

"I am sorry if I have offended you." She was offhand and perfunctory. If his vanity was hurt, she was prepared to make amends as the price of getting rid of him. "I apologize. Now please go."

"I didn't come here for an apology."

"What for, then?"

"An explanation. You appear to have something against me—or my company——"

The word "company" seemed to spark her into aggression. "Mr. Marshall, my husband is dead. I have no connection with your company any more."

"You prefer it that way?"

"Yes."

"Why? I may be able to help you——"

She shook her head, as if he were trying to sell her something. "This is a waste of time. I am busy."

"Listen." He was suddenly exasperated with her. Pride was all very well, but she was carrying it to the point of affectation. He would make one more attempt, and if she wasn't interested he would wrap up the whole Verrier affair and forget it. "I don't know what the situation was with your husband. But I got an idea from Wilcox——"

At that moment the doorbell rang. He stopped, waiting for her to answer it. But she did not move. The bell rang again, insistently.

"Aren't you going to answer?"

"No. It will not be important." She nibbled nervously at her upper lip. The person outside grew tired of ringing and began to bang on the door. The noise reverberated throughout the house.

Suddenly her endurance gave way. She got up and went to open the door. From the living room Marshall could hear her engaged in bitter argument with a man outside. The conversation was in French far too rapid for him to follow. It continued for a surprisingly long time, with the constant repetition of certain phrases. It sounded like a dispute in which neither side was prepared to give way.

Finally he got up and walked out into the hall.

"Anything I can do?"

She turned round. "No—it is nothing."

"It doesn't sound like nothing."

The man at the door slapped an account book he held in his hand, and pointed to one of the columns. "*Dix mille,*" he said violently. "*Dix mille six cents quarante.*"

"You owe him money?"

"Please—you must not interfere——"

Conscious of the cheapness of his gesture, he took some notes out of his wallet and handed them to the collector. Her efforts seemed to have exhausted her; she made no attempt to stop him. When the collector had gone he said: "I hope you didn't mind. It seemed the only way of carrying on our conversation."

She shook her head and sat down. It occurred to him that she was close to tears.

"Was it the rent?" he asked.

"No—the furniture. I had to pay the rent yesterday." She shrugged her shoulders. "Naturally they are all afraid I shall leave without paying them."

"You're going to leave here?"

"I think so."

"Where will you go?"

"I don't know yet. Somewhere smaller."

It was difficult to imagine anything much smaller. He said wonderingly, "Have you no money at all?"

In her unhappiness she had forgotten her bitterness against him. Now it was suddenly revived.

"I have enough, thank you."

"Enough for what?"

"To pay for the funeral. After that I shall get a job. Then I will pay you back your eleven thousand francs."

If his action in paying the money had been theatrical, her intention to repay it was even more so. He said, "Don't be silly."

"I am not silly!" She flushed indignantly. Her aloofness was gone; she was an unhappy little girl insisting on her right to be treated as an adult. "You do not want me to pay you back, I know. The money is nothing to you and you would like me to be grateful. In America you can buy anything—even people. But not here."

"You can't buy a hell of a lot of gratitude for thirty dollars, even in the States. And some people are for sale everywhere. Isn't that so?"

"Yes, that is so." Her voice was suddenly tired. "After all, you bought my husband, didn't you—so very cheaply."

"I don't quite know what you mean by that."

"No?"

"No. Your husband was employed by Furac."

"On your business."

"That's true. And of course indirectly I suppose we paid his salary." He looked round the room uneasily. "Incidentally, what was his salary?"

"Fifty thousand francs a month."

"Fifty thousand?" About four hundred to the dollar. "That——"

"A hundred and twenty-five dollars," she said bitterly. "Thirty dollars a week. Not very much, is it? Even for a poor country."

He strove to remember—there was some arrangement about salaries in the International. Money was paid from New York to the distributors to cover payment of staff, but he could not recollect the details.

"That can't be right. Why, my secretary——" Miss Tracy had earned a hundred a week and was not oversatisfied at that. "Do they know about this in New York?"

"I don't know. I think so. André didn't tell me much. But I know he spoke to Mr. Wilcox."

"And what did Wilcox say?"

"He said it was quite wrong. He told André that Furac received money from New York to cover his expenses and that it was sufficient to pay his staff very well. He promised to raise the matter with your head office. André was very hopeful. Then Wilcox left Paris and we never saw him again." She added with boundless cynicism, "I think perhaps he forgot."

"He didn't forget. He tried."

"You have spoken to him?"

"Not about that. But I happen to know he wrote to New York several times about your husband——" He had to admit to a feeling of disappointment. He had hoped for something more dramatic. Was this all there was to it—a sordid, petty swindle involving a few thousand francs a week?

She seemed to read his mind. Perhaps she had seen the same expression on the face of others. "Yes," she said, "that's all it is. Hardly worth your trouble, is it?"

"I didn't say that."

"You were thinking it. I could see you. That's why I didn't want to talk to you in the first place. I knew it would be like this." She sighed hopelessly. "But to us it was important."

"Of course it's important." He spoke violently, angry with himself. He had almost fallen into the same trap as the others. Human injustice was never trivial. The smallness of the sum involved made the affair more rather than less serious, since it could have been so easily put right. Why, he wondered incredulously, had it not been? Why, if she was telling the truth, had nothing been done?

"So you think Furac was cheating you?" he asked.

"Of course."

Her acceptance of it as a matter of course was more painful to him than any reproach. "And us too?"

"How should I know? André didn't tell me everything about his job." She hesitated, as if struggling with the impulse to confide in him. "He was not always an easy man to understand. He had a tendency to brood, to make secrets. He would say sometimes that he would not accept such treatment forever, that Furac should be careful, he would drive him too far, he could make trouble if he wished, and so on and so forth. I must confess I didn't take him too seriously. Furac had become something of an obsession with him. He talked of him all the time."

"Did he ever go direct to Furac about the money?"

"Oh yes. They had many arguments. But André always lost. He hated Furac but he was afraid of him too. Eventually he decided the only thing to do was to go over Furac's head. After he had spoken to Mr. Wilcox he had great faith that everything would be all right. He was very simple in some ways." She glanced at the photograph. The delicate face, fixed forever in a nervous half-smile, gazed uncertainly back to her, eager for reassurance. "I told him not to trust the Americans."

Half an hour ago she could have made him angry. Now he felt only pity for her. He said, "You don't like us much."

She shook her head. "I don't understand you."

"We're not so difficult."

"Oh yes. With people like Furac it is easy. They take everything

and give nothing. One knows what to expect. But the Americans are so anxious to be fair and generous and for everyone to love them. But, in the end, somehow we are still poor and they are even richer than before."

"Look," he said desperately, "you've got to understand about Wilcox. He was on the level. It wasn't his fault. I know he felt very badly——"

"Very well," she said impatiently. "It was not his fault. But my husband is dead. And Mr. Wilcox is—where?"

"In California. They put him on a job——"

"California—that must be a very nice place."

"He was sent there. He didn't want to go."

She said nothing for a moment. Then almost to herself she said, "He never even wrote a letter."

"He didn't? I can't understand that."

"The first we knew was when André heard from Furac that Wilcox had been replaced. After that he knew there was nothing to hope for any more."

"Surely that wasn't the reason——" But, after all, why not? He looked around at the pitiful little room, the mortgaged furniture. In this world he was a stranger. Here a man's home, his self-respect, the fidelity of his wife could hang on the same amount of money as you tipped the headwaiter at your hotel. You paid him five dollars a week less than he could live on, and he killed himself. He asked her, turning to her experience, "Is it possible?"

"How can I say? He didn't tell me he was going to do it." She stood up, dismissing the subject and Marshall with it. There was no hatred in her voice now, only a dignified finality less possible to ignore than hatred. "But, after all, it is done and there is no use to go on talking about it. You have heard everything I have to tell you. I do not dislike you any more. This was not your fault, I see now. You have been kind." She prolonged the word, with no more than a trace of irony. "Now you should go back to the Georges Cinq and drink your cocktails."

"No." He shook his head. "I didn't come here just to give myself a good conscience." Though perhaps he had—he could not be sure.

Certainly, now, there was no possibility of such an easy solution. "I'm going to do something. . . ."

"I do not know what there is to do."

He was not very sure himself, he realized. If Varrier had still been alive it would have been different. He could make trouble, insist on an inquiry into the whole of Furac's dealings with his staff—that would help certain other people, but what about her? Some form of compensation, perhaps? On the other hand, he had heard only her side of the story. It was necessary to be cautious.

"It's early to talk about that. But I won't let it go. You can rely on that."

"Thank you."

The clock above the mantelpiece showed half-past twelve. There was nothing else to say, no reason to stay any longer. He got up to go.

"You can find your way back?" She gave him a thin smile. It was suddenly clear to him that she had believed nothing. He would find his way back, as Wilcox had done; into his own world, the world of big deals and important men and large sums of money. In the comfort of his hotel her problem would seem less important. A good meal, a bottle of wine, a word of reassurance from Furac or Gilbertson, and he would begin to wonder whether it had ever existed. Helpless though she was, she could at least take pride in being undeceived; she had learned the value of promises. With a dignity born of total disillusion she was waiting calmly for him to betray her.

CHAPTER IV

Out in the street there was no sign of a taxi. An old woman at a tobacco stand on the corner directed him to the nearest Métro station, but the walk was longer than he expected. He saw, to his relief, that there was no chance of his being able to reach Furac's office by one o'clock. Instead, he took the Métro to the Champs Elysées and had lunch by himself in a small café. Over his coffee he asked the waiter for some paper and envelopes and wrote a letter to Jane.

Toward the end he said:

. . . So, as you see, this isn't going to be exactly a simple affair. Verrier may have been out of his mind, as they say— even his wife seemed to admit it as a possibility, though she suggests that anxiety may have made it worse. In any case, it seems that he had a genuine grievance, and I think the company should do something about it, even if it does mean antagonizing important people. I am going to collect any information I can in Paris and also possibly raise the matter point-blank with Furac—there has been too much politeness and covering up so far. It will be interesting to see what he has to say.

Good-by, darling, and look after yourself. I think of you all the time. You were right in what you said about me—it isn't really enough to spend my life as a spectator. I am much happier now that I feel I have something worth while to do. It may not seem very important, but I think this is the sort of thing I am particularly fitted for. Fortunately it doesn't matter very much to me if I make myself unpopular. . . .

When the letter was finished, he posted it and took a taxi back to the hotel. He found Gilbertson and Furac in the suite, drinking whisky.

"Hello, Marshall." The friendliness in Gilbertson's voice was noticeably strained. "Where on earth did you get to? We waited for you at the office——"

"I'm sorry. I got tied up."

"Why didn't you telephone?"

"I'm afraid there wasn't one at hand."

His answers were perfunctory. His eyes were on Furac, who had so far said nothing. The Frenchman showed no sign of resentment or even of curiosity. His left hand mechanically stroked at the bald area on the top of his head, as if searching for something long since lost.

"I hope I didn't spoil your lunch," said Marshall.

"Not at all." Speech seemed to relax Furac. His hand dropped to his side. Three parallel red lines on the top of his head showed where he had been scratching with his fingernail. "Though naturally we missed you." He paused for a moment and then said, "How was Madame Verrier?"

For a moment Marshall was disconcerted. Surely he had not told anyone where he was going. . . . Then he remembered Furac's chauffeur—the man had been only a few feet away from him when he had given her address to the cab driver. He sat down and lit a cigarette. On reflection, he was encouraged by the fact that Furac had chosen to raise the question. It showed a certain anxiety.

"Not so bad," he said, "taking everything into consideration."

Furac nodded. "She has, of course, experienced a great tragedy. One has to remember that." His sympathy was perfunctory. "I trust you found her more co-operative this morning?"

"Definitely."

"She confided in you?"

"To a certain extent."

Furac looked at his fingernails. "Perhaps I should warn you," he said, "in your own interests not to set too much value on everything she tells you. She has the reputation of being"—he hesitated—"a little unreliable."

"'That wasn't my impression."

"No?" The pale, watery eyes opened wide, politely astonished at Marshall's simplicity. "I suppose it might not be so obvious to somebody who did not know her very well."

"Perhaps you'd explain what you mean."

Furac gave a small exasperated sigh. "You place me in an embarrassing position, Mr. Marshall. Naturally one doesn't wish to say unpleasant things about a person who is in such unfortunate circumstances. However, since you seem so interested in her . . ." He shrugged his shoulders, disclaiming responsibility. "She caused poor Verrier a great deal of trouble at one time or another."

"What sort of trouble?"

"She worried him. She was persistent and ambitious—also somewhat extravagant. Always she tried to drive him into doing things which were beyond his abilities. She made him feel a failure—you know what I mean? Well, maybe he was a failure, but no man likes his wife to think so. I think it was partly because of this that he ended up the way he did." He shook his head regretfully. "He was not a man of strong character."

"You think it was because of her that he tried to shoot you?"

"I would not be so specific." He became slightly patronizing, the lecturer too experienced to be caught out by a bright student. "But it is by no means impossible. The human mind is very complex. Have you ever studied psychology, Mr. Marshall?"

"Not seriously."

"You would find it well worth while. To a businessman I would say it is indispensable. I have no claims to be anything more than an amateur," he said modestly, "yet I have gained from it more than I can say. So many of the obscurities of human behavior are clarified by psychology." He returned suddenly to more specific matters. "You appreciate, of course, that Madame Verrier did not care for her husband?"

"No."

"It is so, I can assure you."

"Then why did she——?"

"Why did she behave so strangely yesterday? Why is she unhappy? Why does she feel resentment against me—against you even,

whom she has never met before? I will tell you why." He paused oratorically, his index finger raised in the air. "Guilt."

"Nonsense."

Furac was not put out. "That is what people always say when first confronted with the truths of psychology," he said complacently. "Nevertheless——"

"What reason would she have to feel guilty?"

"She did not love him. She cannot help this, but she is ashamed just the same. She reproaches herself. If she had loved him more he might not have killed himself. She cannot face this—she must reassure herself—she makes a parade of sorrow—she blames others——"

Marshall got up and walked toward the windows. There were shadows in the courtyard now, but a few people were still sitting about in cane chairs, drinking afternoon tea to the music of the fountain. There was a waiter with a trolley of cream cakes. One woman was trying to feed pieces of chocolate éclair to a satiated and indifferent poodle. He turned away from the window and looked at Furac.

"How much did you pay Verrier?" he asked.

The harshness of his voice cut violently across the silence of the room. It was as if anger had taken hold of him against his will, giving him, temporarily at least, a new personality of which he had little experience. It had happened to him on occasions before, and always afterward he had felt ashamed. It was so easy to lose control—and to enjoy it. Also to profit from it, on occasion. He remembered the purposeful, calculated rages of his father, so often invoked with no other purpose than to gain time, to prevent logical discussion of a matter about which he was in the wrong. . . .

The two men were looking at him in surprise. Furac blinked and began to stroke his head again. He was like a nervous lion tamer confronted by a disagreeable interruption in the rhythm of his act. He regarded Marshall indecisively, wondering what was required. A touch of the whip? Or a lump of sugar?

Eventually it was Gilbertson who spoke.

"I'm not quite sure what your object is in asking that question, Marshall," he said.

"Furac knows."

Furac shook his head. "I assure you I don't. Nor—and you must forgive me for saying this—do I consider it any of your business——"

"I seem to recollect an arrangement by which you have financial support from New York for payment of staff. Isn't that so?"

Furac rose from his chair. "Mr. Marshall, I don't wish to quarrel with you, but if I am to speak frankly——"

"Speak as frankly as you like."

"I consider your whole attitude offensive in the extreme——"

"I can understand that." He added grimly, "I know what you paid Verrier. I heard about it today."

"From his wife?"

"Yes." When Furac made a gesture of impatience he said, "All right, don't tell me—she's unreliable. Then prove it to me. Show me your books. Show me what you got from New York and how much you passed on to your men. And how much you took for yourself, and that apartment of yours, and your car and chauffeur——"

"Marshall, for God's sake!" Gilbertson's voice was sharp and determined, like a slap in the face to a hysteric. "Take a hold on yourself, man. You can't make accusations of that sort without proof."

This attack from the flank was slightly sobering. But he said stubbornly, "If it's untrue, let him prove it. I'd like to see his books."

"Now look here——"

"Please." At some point while the other two had been arguing, Furac had recovered his confidence. He spoke quietly and with dignity. "If I may be allowed an occasional word, I would like to clarify certain points. I think Mr. Marshall has become a little emotional under the influence of Madame Verrier and has lost touch with the realities of the situation." He turned to Marshall. "I should perhaps remind you that I am an independent man of business. I have close agreements with your corporation, but I am not employed by them. I cannot be easily bullied, or shouted at, or accused of theft or embezzlement merely on the unsupported word of a hysterical woman—no matter how attractive she may be——"

As Marshall opened his mouth to speak Furac went on quickly: "That is my position, Mr. Marshall. Now—tell me—what is yours?"

"You know what my position is."

"You are the European representative—that I know. Are you any-

thing more?" When Marshall did not speak, he went on with satisfaction: "Evidently not. Now, I have had dealings with quite a few
European representatives in my time, as has Mr. Gilbertson. We
have a fairly clear idea of the duties and responsibilities involved.
It may be that you consider yourself in a special position because
of your name and family connections, but I must tell you that these
mean nothing to me. In my opinion you have grossly exceeded your
authority." He picked up his hat. "I am prepared to overlook your
behavior this afternoon on the supposition that you are in an un-
balanced state of mind and have been influenced by an extremely
plausible and deceitful woman. On the other hand, I certainly do
not intend to discuss this question with you any further."

He bowed formally to both of them and left the room. When he
had gone, Gilbertson said:

"You put your foot in it there, I'm afraid."

"He's a crook."

"Very probably," said Gilbertson without emotion. "But just the
same——"

"He underpaid that poor bastard until he drove him off his head."

"Well—rather a strong reaction to a grievance about salary, don't
you think?"

"You didn't see the way they were living. Why——" He began
to describe the apartment, the sleazy, poverty-stricken district, the
debt collector. Gilbertson was still dubious.

"It was ghastly by your standards, I can see. No fridge or dish-
washer, sharing a bathroom, gold watch up the spout, and so on.
But a lot of people live like that, you know. And if they all went
round taking potshots at their employers——"

"Hell, this isn't a joke. I wish it were." He glared resentfully at
Gilbertson. "You think the way he does, don't you? That she made
a goat out of me?"

"I don't know. It's really not my affair. . . ."

"You have a sense of justice, don't you?"

"Of course. But I have to limit it to my own field of responsibility." The indifference dropped out of his voice. He leaned forward and spoke with unaccustomed intensity. "Let me tell you
something, Marshall. I'm an older man than you, and I've seen a

great deal of suffering and injustice in my time. I was a prisoner of war in Java for three years. When you were amusing yourself in college I was watching my friends being tortured and beaten and dying of starvation and dysentery. There was nothing I could do about it. I learned then that you can't go around feeling for everybody. A man has only so much sympathy to give. He has to ration it. Spread it too thin and it isn't worth a damn to anybody."

Marshall was taken aback. He realized that he hardly knew Gilbertson at all. He had tended to think of him almost as a caricature, a symbol of reaction, rather than as a separate individual subject to all the ordinary human emotions. He said defensively, "So you say—just let things go on as they are?"

Gilbertson relaxed into his old manner. "I wouldn't presume to advise you—especially since I'm quite sure you wouldn't take any notice. But, as a matter of interest, what's your alternative?"

"Take the matter to New York. Ask for an investigation. They won't like it when they find that they've been taken for a ride, I can promise you that."

"You'll need some facts."

"I can get them. There's Verrier's bank account for a start. And I'm going to get hold of some of Furac's other employees. I shall be surprised if he isn't playing the same game with them. What was the name of that man who took you around this morning?"

"Colbert."

Marshall wrote the name down in his diary. "I'll start with him."

"Are you sure," said Gilbertson dubiously, "that you have authority——"

"Perhaps not officially. But facts are facts. Once I give this story to New York, it'll be too late to ask about authority."

He put his diary away and smiled at Gilbertson. He felt suddenly very happy and very confident. The sense of malaise and boredom that had troubled him for so long had left him. He was invigorated by a sense of purpose. "I'm sorry," he said cheerfully, "that you're finding me such a nuisance."

"A nuisance?" Gilbertson raised his bushy eyebrows. "Not to me, my dear fellow—not to me."

CHAPTER V

THE NEXT MORNING he was awakened at eight o'clock by the bellboy with a cable. It read:

PLEASE RETURN NEW YORK WITHOUT DELAY   REGARDS   KINGHAM

As soon as he read it he was angry with himself for not having anticipated something of the kind. Furac was not the man to wait passively to be attacked without taking some form of counteraction. He would use the same method which had proved so successful with Wilcox, except that now there was more urgency. No doubt he had cabled, or more likely telephoned, New York as soon as he had left the hotel on the previous afternoon. He would have told Kingham that Marshall was making a fool of himself in Paris and ought to be recalled immediately, before he did serious harm. It was a warning which Kingham could hardly afford to ignore.

Marshall was conscious that he had been outmaneuvered. In matters of this kind it was important to get one's word in before the other man. *He* should have made the first telephone call. It was not too late, however, to hit back. If he moved fast he might still be able to redress the balance in his favor. He picked up his bedside telephone. "I want to make a personal call to New York." He gave Kingham's number. There would be half an hour's delay, they said. "And send me up some breakfast, would you?"

He had just finished dressing when the telephone rang again. "I am sorry, sir, we are unable to put through your call."

"Can't you find him?"

"We got through to Mr. Kingham, sir, but he refused to accept the call."

"Did he say why?"

"I gather it was because of the time."

"The time?"

"Yes." The voice was still bland and respectful, but with an undertone of amusement. "There is five hours' difference, you understand."

"Yes—yes, of course." He tried to sound unconcerned. "Thank you very much."

He put down the receiver. He had blundered again. In New York, he remembered too late, it was still only four o'clock in the morning. And Kingham had a particular objection to being called in the middle of the night, as he never ceased to remind people. He had a favorite story about a distributor who had conceived the idea of wishing him a merry Christmas, just after lunch in Manila. . . .

What was he to do now? he wondered. Certainly he had made the worst possible start. He could wait for five hours and call again —but somehow the idea of a telephone conversation with Kingham had lost its attraction. It might be better to cable. Using one of the cable forms on the desk, he wrote:

URGENT BUSINESS HERE REQUIRING SEVERAL MORE DAYS TO COMPLETE STOP WILL EXPLAIN ON RETURN   REGARDS   MARSHALL

That seemed fairly satisfactory. It was in any case impossible to give details of what was happening. A point-blank refusal would cripple his case from the outset. The best he could hope for was to gain time. The showdown could wait till he got back to New York.

He handed the cable to the waiter who brought in his breakfast. A little later, when he was reading the papers over his coffee, Gilbertson came in. "I don't know about you," he said, "but I really ought to get back to London today. There are probably all kinds of problems waiting for me——"

"Sure, I understand. Why don't you do that?"

"What about you?"

"Don't worry about me. I'm staying here just for the moment. Then I'll probably fly straight to New York."

"You won't be coming back to London?"

"Not immediately."

"I see." Gilbertson's eyes flickered momentarily over the cable on the dressing table. "I hope everything's all right. No bad news or anything like that?"

"Nothing I didn't expect."

"Good. That's fine." He seemed a little ill at ease. He lit a cigarette and puffed at it with exaggerated concentration. "You still intend to go on with this—business?"

"Yes."

"I can't help feeling you're making too much of it."

"I don't know why you should care. After all, it doesn't really concern you," Marshall said with slight malice.

"Of course not," said Gilbertson sharply. "Nevertheless, I know from experience how easy it is to get involved in a great deal of unpleasantness without really knowing what you're doing. If you go around looking for trouble there may be—unforeseen consequences." He added heavily, "Since you came over from New York I felt we were getting to know each other pretty well—it seemed to me that you were going to fit in. In fact, I said to my wife only the other day . . ." He paused for a moment. "I wouldn't like to see you run into difficulties."

"You think that's likely?"

The creases in his bloodhound face seemed to deepen. He said in a melancholy voice, "Furac can be an awkward man to cross, I should imagine." When Marshall gave no signs of replying, Gilbertson got up from his chair and held out a hairy hand. "But of course it's entirely your affair. I shall be leaving on the midday plane, so I'll say good-by now." He added, not very hopefully, "I look forward to seeing you in London."

When he had left, Marshall rang up Furac's office.

"I wish to speak to Monsieur Colbert."

"Who is that, please?" said a female voice.

"My name is Marshall."

"Ah, Mr. Marshall. Good morning, sir."

"Good morning. Could you put me through to——"

"You wish to speak to Monsieur Furac? Yes. I will arrange——"

"Not Monsieur Furac—Monsieur Colbert. You understand? Colbert—C-o-l——"

"Yes. Yes. Very well. One moment." The line went dead. Then a new voice came on.

"Good morning, Mr. Marshall."

"Good morning. Is that Monsieur Colbert?"

"No, this is Furac speaking. How are you this morning?"

"Very well, thank you. But the operator must have made a mistake. I wanted to speak to——"

"Colbert. Yes, so I gathered. But unfortunately, you see, he is not in the office today. He has gone out——"

"Can you tell me where he is?"

"I am afraid not. He may be one of several places. He will not be back for two or three days at least, I am afraid. Can I give him any message?"

"No, thanks. Could you give me his home telephone number?"

"He is not on the telephone at home. Nor do I know his address. He has just moved. Most unfortunate——"

"Yes."

"So it seems you may miss him," said Furac. After a slight pause he added: "Did I hear that you might be going to New York very soon?"

"Who told you that?"

"I don't know. Perhaps I was mistaken. Shall I be seeing you again before you leave Paris?"

"I doubt it."

"Then I wish you a pleasant journey. And—one more thing——"

"Yes?"

His voice became suddenly openly unpleasant. "If you wish to interrogate any other members of my staff, you will please have the courtesy to notify me first. Thank you so much."

He rang off. So that hole had been stopped up, thought Marshall. At this rate his investigations were not going to get very far. He was not sure what to do now. He did not want to leave the hotel until he had heard from Kingham.

He read a novel until lunch time and then went down to the restaurant. At around two o'clock the cables started again.

> REGRET CANNOT GRANT YOUR REQUEST TO STAY LONGER IN PARIS STOP YOUR PRESENCE REQUIRED HERE RIGHT NOW STOP DONT CALL UP IN THE MIDDLE OF THE NIGHT DAMN YOU   REGARDS   KINGHAM

The pressure was getting strong. It was true, of course, that he wasn't going to do much good here, now that he had failed to see Colbert. Just the same, it was important to talk to Madame Verrier again, if only to convince her that he intended to keep his promise. And Verrier's funeral was tomorrow. He would stay for that, at the very least. He wrote:

> RATHER EXCEPTIONAL CIRCUMSTANCES HERE IMPOSSIBLE TO EXPLAIN ADEQUATELY BY CABLE STOP WILL LEAVE PARIS SOONEST CONSISTENT WITH CERTAIN OBLIGATIONS STOP SORRY ABOUT TELEPHONE CALL   REGARDS   MARSHALL

The reply came rapidly.

> RETURN IMMEDIATELY REPEAT IMMEDIATELY WITHOUT FURTHER ARGUMENT CONFIRM FLIGHT   KINGHAM

This time there were not even any regards—a serious sign. Kingham must be very angry indeed. Well, there was nothing to be done about it. Marshall went to the travel agency in the lobby and booked a seat on a plane for the following afternoon. Then he went to the hall porter and wrote out another cable. It simply gave the flight number and his time of arrival.

"Don't send it now," he said. "Hold it."

"Till when, sir?"

"Let me see." He wanted it to arrive just after Kingham had left the office. Then he would not pick it up till he came in the following morning—which would be early afternoon in Paris. That would stall things along for eighteen hours or so. He said: "Send it off about eleven o'clock tonight."

Marshall dropped a five-hundred franc note on the counter. The hall porter raised his eyebrows, but only momentarily. Americans were notoriously mad—but it was a profitable lunacy. He picked

up the note in an absent-minded way, like a good housewife removing a speck of dust. "*Merci, monsieur.*"

Marshall went back to his room. There was something else he had to do. He picked up the telephone and said: "I want to make a call to London. Berkeley 4848."

He waited a few minutes. There was some crackling and snatches of muttered conversation in two languages. Then an English voice which Marshall recognized said:

"Gilbertson and Cowles speaking. Who is that, please?"

"Mr. Marshall."

"Oh yes, Mr. Marshall. You want to speak to Mr. Gilbertson?"

"No, thanks. He's back already?"

"He got in about an hour ago. Whom would you like to speak to?"

"Get me Miss Lancing, please."

"Very well, Mr. Marshall. Just one moment——"

A few seconds later he heard Jane's voice.

"Is that you, Jane?"

"Yes. Where are you?"

"I'm still in Paris. I didn't come back with Gilbertson. Did you get my letter?"

"No."

Of course, he thought, it was too soon, he had only posted it yesterday. It made explanation considerably more difficult. He heard a click on the line and the background noise sounded slightly different. Could somebody, say the switchboard girl, be listening to their conversation? Perhaps he was growing morbidly suspicious. But even the outside chance of being overheard made confidences impossible.

"You should get it within the next day or two. It explains most of what's been happening over here up to yesterday afternoon——"

"Did you see—the man you wanted to see?"

"No. I was too late. But I had a talk with his wife. She told me most of what I wanted to know." He went on hurriedly, before she could ask any more questions: "But you'll find all that in my letter, together with quite a few other things I can't tell you over the phone."

"Yes, I understand."

"But since I wrote to you, things have advanced a little——"

"Favorably?"

"Not entirely. There are certain interested parties I have to deal with—some degree of competition, if you understand me. It means I shall have to go to New York to straighten it out."

"I see." She was silent for a moment. "When are you leaving?"

"Tomorrow afternoon. In the morning I—I promised to attend the funeral. As soon as it's over I shall catch the plane from Paris. I'll write to you in detail. I just thought I'd let you know what was happening."

"Thank you. When you didn't come back with Mr. Gilbertson, I wondered——" Her voice was admirably casual. Anyone listening would learn nothing about them from her.

"Is everything all right in the office?"

"Yes." She paused momentarily. "When will you be back?"

"I can't say definitely. Soon, I hope. I'll keep in touch with you."

"I'll be looking forward to seeing you." Just for a second a trace of anxiety seemed to come through into her voice. "Come back as soon as you can."

"I will, don't worry." There was a short silence. There was so much to say but no possible channel of communication except on this prosaic, meaningless level.

"Good-by," he said.

"Good-by."

CHAPTER VI

THERE WAS nobody very much at the funeral—just himself and Madame Verrier and a few nondescript people from the neighborhood. The priest gabbled his lines and hurried off, like a man working on a tight schedule. Marshall could see another coffin, another seedy little group of mourners, waiting around a corner. Nobody, he thought, had ever had very much time to spare for Verrier.

Afterward they went to a little café by the cemetery. The waiter brought them two filters and they sat for a while watching the tepid liquid dribbling through the strainer. The air was stale and dusty. Someone in a back room was frying onions to the sound of a radio. There was a smell of onions and dust and sweet liqueurs. Everywhere in France, he thought, there was a smell of something.

"It was kind of you to come," she said.

"I wanted to."

Across the perfunctory phrases, the stilted, tea-table conversation, he regarded her anxiously, wondering what she really thought and felt. Unconsciously he found himself searching for a sign, something he could put a label on. In each country there were certain conventional ways of demonstrating emotion, a code of communication to which only those who had been brought up within that same community could hold the key. The language of words was one thing—but the language of sincerity, of courage and faith and sense of humor—what could the stranger know of that? If she had

been an American woman, her reaction to her husband's funeral would have told him something about her feeling for him. Not much, perhaps, but enough for a starting point. Here, he knew nothing. He realized that she could tell him anything and he had no means of checking it. How could one recognize a lie in a foreign language?

"You must be glad it's over," he said. He searched for some way to console her and found only the old, tired phrases of a ready letter writer. Death was like love—everything had been said before, long ago. "It won't be quite so bad from now on."

"Because he's gone—put away? I can begin to forget him, you mean?" As he tried to protest, she went on: "But you're quite right. That's what will happen. Even now . . ." Always her eyes were away from his, regarding the table top, her cup of coffee. "He was a man, you know, who never made a strong impression. As you saw today, he had few friends."

"He was—shy?"

"Perhaps. He was afraid."

"Of what?"

"Of everything. Of being laughed at, of poverty, of losing his job. And of people too. Furac, of course. Even me." She suddenly looked up. "That sounds bad, doesn't it? As if I were cruel to him— but I wasn't. I was simply stronger, and he was afraid of strength. You can't do anything about that."

"Of course not." He was reminded of Furac's words—"She is ashamed." Anybody could be right sometimes about people. No matter how calculating or dishonest, no matter how addicted to cheap, secondhand psychology—they could still be right. He asked, "Did you love him?"

She was silent for a long time. "Why do you ask me that?"

"I'm sorry." They were always apologizing to each other, he thought. "I had no right to ask. It was a most personal question. . . ."

"I don't mind." She looked at him with a thin half-smile. "I am not so fragile, you know. I have not traveled through the world as you have, but I have experienced a great deal in some ways. When I first married André I was a silly young girl. I loved him then, I

think. Of course I always understood that he was a little weak, but I was convinced that when we were married . . . Well, I was prepared to have strength enough for two, you understand?"

Marshall nodded. He remembered the photograph, the strong sunburned hand of the girl clutching the arm of the cheap gabardine jacket. She said, excusing herself, "I was only eighteen at that time. I did not understand very much."

"It didn't work out?"

"My parents were very angry with me. André earned very little money, and because my father disliked him he refused to help us. We were always poor. But that was not so important—when you are young and you are living in Paris, it is not so bad as all that to be poor. No—there is only one thing that is really bad in this world." She leaned her head forward and rested her chin on the palm of her hand. She was looking, not at him, not at the café or the anonymous, deserted street, but at some secret source of unhappiness within herself. "To be a failure."

"Maybe"—he spoke hesitantly—"some people just don't get the breaks——"

"*Comment?*"

"I mean—they just don't have any luck."

"You think that?"

"It happens, I guess."

She shook her head. "When you live with somebody, you know. André was a failure. He knew it. I knew it. Furac, even the people who lived in the other apartments of the house . . . And there was nothing I could do about it. I could not even go on loving him in the same way. Because, you see, when a man is a failure, failure is the most important thing about him. To love him, you have to love that."

When you had a wound, he thought, you might forget it for years, but there was no knowing when a chance knock might reopen it.

She was talking of Verrier, but she might just as easily have been referring to himself. He, too, when all was said and done, was a failure. He had thought of it as a private thing which he alone had to come to terms with. Now he realized for the first time that it

was a problem which involved everyone he cared for or who cared for him. Failure was a disease with which he infected the ones he loved.

He thought of Jane, her fear of being committed, the urgency with which she had tried to persuade him to action, any action. Was she, too, conscious of the same danger? Was he the only one who was unaware of it?

Anxious to learn, he asked: "And you found you couldn't love —failure?"

"No." Beneath her shame he could feel the full impact of her determination. It was possible to sympathize with Verrier, conscious of his own weakness, ground between his wife on one hand and a hostile, merciless world on the other. "Not in the way I wanted—or he wanted. I was too sorry for him." She was silent for a moment. "I suppose it was Furac who told you?"

"About what?"

"About André and me. That is one of the reasons why he does so well—he takes great trouble to find out things about people. He has probably already found out a great deal about you."

"I wouldn't be surprised. Obviously he's prepared to fight me with everything he has. I might as well tell you," he said with an attempt at lightness, "that I've been recalled."

"Recalled? To New York?"

"Yes. Of course there may be no connection, but I think we can take it as Furac's doing." He described their conversation in the hotel. "Then, within a matter of hours, I got the cable."

"And this means you have to go?"

"I'm afraid so. I made one or two attempts to stall them, but——" He took the cables out of his pocket and showed them to her. "As you see, I didn't have much success."

When she had read them she said, "Who is this man Kingham?"

"He's my boss—the head of the International."

"What sort of a man is he?"

"Well—he's okay, I guess." Some half-forgotten loyalty to the organization prevented him from speaking freely about Kingham to an outsider. "Everyone thinks he's a pretty smart man."

"You don't like him?"

He shifted uncomfortably in his seat. "I wouldn't exactly say that——"

"Is he honest?"

"If you mean," said Marshall, "would he be a party to a piece of cheap chiseling on your husband's salary?" He shook his head. "I can't really see it. Even if he was prepared to do it, it would hardly seem worth his while."

"Then," she said with a persistence he was beginning to recognize as a characteristic of hers, "what about Mr. Wilcox?"

"You mean why was he taken away?" He shrugged his shoulders. "I don't know. I shall have to see what I can find out when I get to New York."

She pondered for a moment. "There is one thing," she said, "which I do not quite understand. Kingham is your boss, you say. Yet you are Marshall . . ."

He smiled. "A lot of people get mixed up that way. The company was my father's. He built it up. But when he died, the management passed away from the family. My brother's on the Board and we hold a certain amount of stock, naturally. But that's as far as it goes. Don't run away with the idea that I'm somebody very important."

"Oh."

He could sense her disappointment. "But don't worry," he said. "I'm not entirely without influence. They'll listen to what I have to say, all right."

"They will also listen to Furac," she said dubiously.

"Sure they will. But he's got a bad case and he knows it. He can't beat the facts. And incidentally—if you don't mind, I'd like to take some documentary proof with me, to show what your husband was paid. Have you anything—a bank statement, for instance?"

She hesitated. "I am not sure. I think that this will be required by the notary—for the will, you understand——"

"A copy would do."

She was still doubtful. "Perhaps we should look in the apartment. There may be something similar."

He paid for the coffee and they went back to the apartment. Eventually she found a few slips of paper on which Verrier had

made records of his salary checks. Marshall put them in his wallet, then said, "I have to go now."

"You are flying this afternoon?"

"Yes." He looked around the tiny living room of the apartment. Each tasteless chair, each patch of damp on the corner of the ceiling was something he must remember. With some embarrassment he added, "I've put a sum of money to your credit in the Banque du Nord. That's on account of what you're owed by the organization."

She frowned, suspecting charity. "I do not know——"

"It's a purely business arrangement. You're obviously entitled to some form of compensation. But knowing our accountants, it may take some time to arrive. When it does you can refund my advance if it makes you happier."

"Very well. On those terms——" She suddenly laughed. "The bank will be pleased. They will think I am being kept by a rich American."

He was concerned. The idea had not occurred to him. "Would that be embarrassing? We can think of some other way——"

"No, of course not." It was the first time he had seen her at ease. At last she seemed to be able to talk to him in a casual, comradely way, even to laugh at him a little. "It is most considerate of you."

He got up to go. "I have to get back to the hotel and see about my luggage. My plane leaves in a couple of hours."

"I hope you have a pleasant journey."

"Thank you." As they shook hands he said, "Don't worry. I promise I'll do everything I can for you."

"I am not worrying."

She smiled confidently. That was why her manner had changed, he realized. She believed in him. Her cynicism had been no more than skin-deep after all. He was proud and yet a little frightened to feel the weight of her faith settling like a load on his back. These were the kinds of commitments he had avoided for so long. Gradually he was beginning to accumulate responsibilities.

PART IV

CHAPTER I

NEW YORK was a city in its shirt sleeves. Down the long avenues the July sunlight glittered in the still, heavy air, reflected from the sidewalks, the multitude of windows, the paint of a hundred thousand crawling automobiles. As always here, the heat seemed to arouse resentment rather than lassitude. The crowds jostled angrily, the taxi drivers blasted their horns and poked beefy faces out of their cabs, yelling abuse. The cops sweltered on traffic duty, their shirts sticking to their backs. The small, crowded island of Manhattan heaved, grumbled, sweated, like a man with a temperature.

Marshall, sitting in the back of a cab, wiped the palms of his hands on his handkerchief. He was nervous as well as hot. Ever since the plane left Paris he had been trying to prepare himself for the situation which lay before him. He had already rehearsed a dozen conversations with Kingham, but all of them had shared a certain lack of plausibility. He had no very clear idea what his reception would be, except that it was likely to be a cold one, judging by the cables he had received in Paris. It was just possible that Kingham might change his tune on hearing the facts of the case. He hoped so. He had no desire for trouble if it could be avoided. It occurred to him that, however bravely he might pretend, he was to some extent afraid of Kingham.

He paid the cabdriver and walked into the office building. Inside, the heat was less oppressive. He went through the glass doors

marked "Marshall Corporation" and nodded to the girl at the reception desk.

"Why, it's Mr. Marshall." She smiled at him. "How was Europe?"

"Oh, fine—fine." She must make quite a game of it, he thought —remembering where everybody had gone. It was always the same —"How was Detroit?" "How was Johannesburg?" "How was Tokyo?" And the reply was always "Fine—fine." He said, "Is Mr. Kingham in?"

"I haven't seen him come in yet this morning."

He was ashamed of his own feeling of relief. But it was a breathing space.

"I expect he'll be in later. Would you like to check with Miss Curran?"

He nodded and walked along to Kingham's office. In the outer office Miss Curran sat at her typewriter. She didn't look surprised to see him and she didn't ask him how Europe was. But the look she gave him was rather alarming. It was almost compassionate.

"They tell me the boss hasn't arrived?"

"No."

"I suppose he got my cable from Paris, did he? I sent it off as soon as I knew the flight number. As a matter of fact, I was damned lucky to get on, it's pretty crowded this time of year——" He was talking too much. He pulled himself up. "When will he be in?"

She turned away and twisted a piece of paper out of the typewriter with a brisk, meaningless little gesture. "He won't be in, I'm afraid. He's gone away."

"Gone away? Where to?"

"Mexico."

"Mexico!" He looked at her in mounting exasperation. It seemed to him that whenever he wanted to talk to somebody that person took a plane to the other side of the world. "How was that? Was he called away unexpectedly?"

"I don't know. I don't think so."

"Well, that's most extraordinary. We must have got our wires crossed somewhere. He certainly gave me the impression that he was in a great hurry to see me. When will he be back?"

"He didn't say."

"Did he mention me at all?"

"Yes. He wanted you to see Mr. Richardson. I guess he must have left some instructions with him." As he turned to go she said: "Just a moment—I'll see if he's free."

Marshall watched her as she dialed Richardson's number on the inter-office telephone. She knew everything, of course. She knew how Kingham felt and why he had gone to Mexico and, in all probability, when he was coming back. But if you tried to get any information out of her you would merely cause an embarrassing situation and get nowhere. Nobody ever knew quite what she thought about anything, but even if someone did know, it wouldn't make any difference. She might think you were a hero and Kingham was a louse—but she was paid to keep her mouth shut, and there it was. She said, "Mr. Richardson *is* free."

"Thanks." He hesitated for a moment before leaving. He had the feeling that, in the most muted possible way, she was trying to tell him things. To be careful, perhaps? To watch his step? He knew that.

"Things pretty much the same here as when I went away?" he asked tentatively.

"No big changes," she said. "There's been a certain amount of—reorganization." She gave one of her rare smiles. They had a reorganization every few months, of some kind or another.

"Anything special?"

"Not really. Some go down—some go up. You know how it is."

"Yes." Richardson, for instance, was evidently up a little. You couldn't just knock on his door and stick your head around any more. Somebody had to telephone and see if he was "free." In a world where one man was supposed to be as good as another, little things like that took on an unusual significance.

If Richardson's rating had increased, he showed no obvious sign of it. When Marshall walked in he jumped up and wrung him by the hand, his pale blue eyes bulging with good will.

"Good to see you, Chris. Sit down and relax." He regarded Marshall appreciatively. "My, you certainly look fit—Europe seems to agree with you. Did you have a good flight?"

"Pretty comfortable. I got in last night an hour before schedule. We had a tail wind."

"Is that so? It certainly makes a difference when you get a tail wind." He shook his head in wonderment. "An hour early—can you beat that?"

He couldn't be *that* interested, Marshall thought, wondering why he had mentioned the tail wind in the first place. It was just the sort of tedious conversation one always tried to avoid—flight schedules, hotels, the advantages of the new Oldsmobile over last year's Mercury. And what was Richardson's Christian name? This was no time to sound high hat.

He remembered with relief. "You're looking pretty good yourself, John."

"I get along. Though—this heat . . ." He leaned back in his swivel chair. The superficial courtesies were over; it was time for business. "Miss Curran told you that Mr. Kingham was away?"

"Yes."

"Certainly keeps moving, doesn't he?" said Richardson admiringly. "Has his hand on everything—all over the world. He never seems to rest. I don't think there are many men of our age who'd care to take on his job."

Like hell you don't, thought Marshall. "And when will he be back?"

"Nobody knows exactly. I doubt whether he knows himself. You remember what he's like—finishes what he has to do and then grabs the next plane." He said, "I'm sure he was sorry to have missed you."

Richardson had spoken as if Marshall were making a routine visit of no special significance. It was possible that he knew nothing of the circumstances, and it would be foolish to tell him. Marshall said, "Did he leave any message for me?"

"Yes. He said he looked forward to seeing you when he got back. In the meantime . . ." He pressed a button on the intercom. "Could you bring in those surveys for Mr. Marshall?" Turning back to Marshall, he went on, "There are some market surveys we've had made for various countries. Kingham said he'd like you to go through them and write a report on the prospects for possible trad-

ing in the areas concerned. Some of them are pretty exotic, but the boss doesn't believe in missing a trick anywhere if he can help it." The secretary came in and handed a file of reports to Marshall. "Well—there you are. I guess that should keep you busy."

Nice of Kingham to think of something for him to do. "Shall I use my old office? Or is that taken?"

"I'm afraid it is. Rose Bauer's in there."

Good old Rose, he thought, she was up too. "Is she publicity co-ordinator now?"

"Well, not exactly." Richardson was almost apologetic. "That post doesn't exist any more as such." Marshall nodded understandingly. They hadn't wasted any time in throwing that useless department out of the window once they had packed him off to Europe. "She's supervisor of technical advertising."

"She's a fine girl. She'll do a wonderful job." This was to show he wasn't jealous of Rose. Besides, it was true.

"Oh, sure." Richardson darted a glance at his watch. Until this moment he had seemed to have time to burn. Now suddenly he was in a hurry, waiting for Marshall to leave. It was an executive's trick to establish an ascendancy—your time was more valuable than the other man's. He stood up. "If you'll excuse me, Chris, I'm pretty tied up this morning. Perhaps we could have a talk about things later—over a drink or something." Before Marshall could suggest an actual time he went on, "We have managed to find an office for you temporarily. It's three floors down, on the twenty-fourth—you know how crowded we are for space up here." They were almost out of the door now. "Gladys will show you where it is—won't you, Gladys? Well"—he patted Marshall affectionately on the arm and began to move back into the office—"see you, Chris."

The office on the twenty-fourth was small and ill furnished; it had no air conditioning, and its one window looked out on to a ventilation shaft. The rest of the floor was taken by Accountancy and Statistics. Marshall was to share a secretary with one of the junior accountants.

He opened the file and began to go through the market surveys. There were a great many of them and they were extremely detailed —the firm which had made them had plainly been in no mood to

save either trouble or expense. Some of them were quite absurdly out of date. There were three pages of optimistic forecasts about the economic future of a country which had now been engaged in civil war for at least six months. Other areas were rendered inoperative by reason of industrial backwardness, currency restrictions, or unfriendly governments. The surveys were, in fact, quite useless and not worth the time and energy required to report on them. Marshall could imagine how they had come to be made. Somebody in one of those grandiose moods which so often took possession of people at management conferences had suggested them. The idea sounded efficient, the sort of project a go-ahead business firm ought to engage in. There would be a persuasive customers' man from the agency—"a complete survey of world markets, Mr. X, specially tailored to your requirements, with all the benefits of our world-wide service"—and Mr. X himself, anxious to be up to the minute, to "think big." And at the end of it the corporation exchanged a check for ten thousand dollars for a sackful of beautifully printed junk.

Mr. X, whoever he was, had by this time long since forgotten all about it. When he got the reports he found them too boring to read and passed them to the man below him, who passed them on down the line, until eventually they ended up in a filing cabinet somewhere. Some men might have thrown them away, but not Kingham. He had thought of a use for them.

It was, Marshall realized, the business equivalent of moving a heap of stones from one spot to another and back again. His report would probably never be read, and if it was read it would be of no value. That Kingham had left instructions for him to do it made the suspicions that had been growing within him all morning crystallize into certainty. He had watched this happen before with others. The offhand treatment, the slight but perceptible change in attitude of subordinates who knew which way the wind was blowing, the withdrawal of prestige symbols such as a comfortable office and a private secretary, the handing out of pointless and unimportant tasks . . .

He picked up the telephone and dialed.

"Rose?"

"Who's that?"

"This is Chris Marshall. I just got back."

"Why, that's wonderful. And how was——"

"Europe was fine." He realized his voice sounded curt, but it was too late to do anything about it. "I'd like to talk to you, Rose. What about meeting me for lunch?"

"Just a minute. I'll look at my book."

Things had certainly changed. Now Rose had got so important that she couldn't remember with whom she was lunching. He waited impatiently. It didn't surprise him when she said, "I'm sorry, Chris. It seems I'm tied up today."

"Tomorrow?" he asked, just to make sure.

"I honestly doubt if I could make it. There's some sort of a conference——"

He put the telephone down. For a few minutes he stared at the papers in front of him. The telephone rang twice, but he ignored it. Then he picked up his jacket from the back of a chair, mopped the sweat from his face, and made his way up to the twenty-seventh.

Rose was dictating letters. When he walked in she nodded to the stenographer, who slipped out and closed the door. He looked round at the office. It seemed larger and lighter than he remembered. There was a bowl of roses, a photograph of Bauer looking like a musician, a couple of prints on the walls. She had moved the desk to a better position. There was a feminine scent about the place.

"You've made it nice in here," he said.

"Thank you very much."

He sat down in the chair the stenographer had left. Neither of them mentioned the fact that he had hung up on her.

"How's Fred?"

She shook her head sadly. "He got fired."

"You don't say?" Suddenly his anger had left him. It was hard to be anything but sympathetic with Rose.

"Yes. He got high one night on tour and gave them a couple of riffs in the middle of Tchaikovsky's Fourth. I guess it had to happen sometime."

"What's he doing now?"

"Looking around. It's not too easy, as you can imagine. . . ."

"I'm sorry to hear that."

"Things could be worse," she said brightly. "About money, I mean. Since I got this job——"

"Sure." He smiled. "You're moving along fast. I should congratulate you."

He said it fondly, without irony. She replied simply, "Thank you. It was very lucky for me, coming when it did. Though of course . . ."

Though of course it wasn't the same as having a husband with sufficient sense to stay sober and keep himself out of trouble, her tone implied. Poor Rose . . . He asked abruptly, "You knew I was coming back?"

"Yes." She looked at him with obvious sincerity. "I was on the level, Chris—about not being able to meet you for lunch."

"Yes, I know that now. I'm sorry." He laughed shortly. "This place doesn't seem to suit me. I haven't been back twenty-four hours and I get delusions of persecution——"

"Who have you met?"

"Richardson." He added after a pause, "He seems to be a big boy now."

"That's right."

"He'll end up with an electric typewriter one of these days if he's not careful."

She frowned. "What's so wrong with that?"

"Nothing, I guess."

"He's got a right to be ambitious, hasn't he? If you want to stand out of it yourself, that's your own affair. But don't blame other people." She added, "I like Richardson."

"Yes, he's a nice guy." After all, he was a good husband and father, kind to animals, paid his club dues on time—what more could you ask? There was nothing wrong with Richardson.

She said hesitantly, "If they *are* putting the freeze on you——"

He sprang on the remark. "You think they are?"

"You should know better than I." She seemed to be wondering

how much to say. "The rumor round here is that Kingham is after your hide for something or other."

"He hasn't heard what I have to say yet." Suddenly his resentment became so strong that he could no longer sit still. He got up and began to walk about the room. "If he goes on like this he's going to get too smart for his own good. He seems to think the International belongs to him."

"I don't know about that. So far as I'm concerned——"

"He's the boss. Okay, I can see how you feel. But he's not God, you know. There are limits to what he can do."

Rose looked doubtful. To her, for all practical purposes, Kingham *was* God. She knew, of course, that there was a Board, and a chairman, and several vice-presidents, but they meant nothing to her; so far as she knew, they had never affected her in any way. Whereas Kingham affected her all the time. Every decision he made, every new idea, every mood and caprice had to be considered and minutely analyzed because of the momentous consequences they might have on her personal life.

That was all very well for Rose. But there had to be somebody who was different, some outpost of independence. Kingham had tried unsuccessfully to remove this outpost by diplomatic measures. What would be his next move. Siege? Open warfare?

"You should watch him," said Rose. "Whatever you think of him, he's no fool. And it looks to me as if he's out to show you what he can do."

"I can do something too, if it comes to that."

"Such as?"

"I can——" He halted, wondering whether he was talking too much, even if this *was* Rose. But she cut in before he had time to say anything more.

"You can go over his head. But I'd think carefully about it first. Maybe that's what he wants you to do."

He sat down again. "Why do you say that?"

"It just occurred to me. He calls you back in a hurry to see him, goes away for a while and leaves you to sit around waiting. Everything's fixed up to annoy you as much as possible. Obviously you'll

be tempted to go to somebody high up and complain. Why does he give you the opportunity?"

"You tell me."

"To show that you think you have special privileges because of your family. He may have complained beforehand that you're difficult to handle on that account. This would prove it for him."

He said nothing. The nightmarish quality which had permeated all his experiences since he entered the building that morning was increasing in intensity. He had been away only a few months, but everything was changed. He was suddenly a kind of outlaw, a person from whom things were hidden. He could trust nobody. He had imagined that while he was in Europe he had been forgotten. But it might be that he had been sent away deliberately so that his position might be damaged in his absence, by a word here and there, a shrug of the shoulders when his name was mentioned, a routine reorganization which omitted to take him into account. Then, on his return, he was to be provoked into doing something foolish, to confirm the rumors and present his own head for the chopping block. . . .

"It isn't possible," he said.

"Why not?"

"He's bastard enough to do it, I'll agree. But to take so much trouble——"

"It might be trouble to you. But it would interest him. To Kingham, a person like you presents a special problem. To solve it might become a point of honor."

He thought it over. Bewilderment and disgust were giving way to a cold rage. He wished no harm to anybody. Why wouldn't they leave him alone?

"I don't like that," he said.

"But why should you worry? You never liked this work anyway. If you left——" Like all women, having aroused him, she felt the necessity to calm him down.

"That's not the point."

She looked at him questioningly, but he made no attempt to explain. There was no sense in dragging Rose into it. She had enough problems of her own. Verrier meant nothing to her, and

Paris was a long way away, a strange foreign city you sometimes saw in the movies, full of cafés and boulevards and nude shows and Maurice Chevalier. Nothing serious ever happened there. The things that really mattered were that Richardson had an increase in salary or that Bob Gross had been in trouble with the accountants or that Bernstein had invited Flack up to his house for dinner three times in the last two months. Even for him, it took an effort in this place to remember the apartment in the rue Zurbaran, the hospital, the man lying in a cheap grave in the cemetery at Père Lachaise with an ugly hole in the top of his skull. . . . It took an effort, but it could be done.

He said, as much to himself as to Rose, "I made a promise. . . ."

CHAPTER II

FOR THE NEXT WEEK he arrived at the office punctually at nine and left at five, working, or pretending to work, at his report. He would not give them any opportunity to accuse him of slackness. There was no news of Kingham's return, and after a few days he stopped ringing up to ask. Each day some minor incident reminded him of his own isolation. He knew nobody on the twenty-fourth floor and all his former friends on the twenty-seventh had become unaccountably busy. Evidently the word had got around. The only cheering event was a letter from Jane.

Dear Chris,
   I hope things are going well in New York. I was so glad to receive your letter and feel sure you are doing the right thing. Furac sounds quite *unspeakable* (which I had always suspected anyway, from the way Mr. Wilcox talked about him). Gilbertson arrived back from Paris in a very bad temper and even snapped at Miss Carvill-Sykes—vicar's daughter or not! —so that evidently the trip hadn't been a great success as far as he was concerned. I am doing my best to cope with your correspondence unaided (3 letters yesterday!). There is also some personal correspondence, mostly bills. Do you want me to hold onto them or post them to you? I suppose it will rather depend on how soon you are likely to return.
   I don't suppose what you are doing now will be easy, but after all you are in the right and that is a good deal. Try not to be too discouraged if you run into difficulties. I am think-

ing of you all the time and looking forward always to your return. . . .

He smiled. It was like a clear, crisp breeze in this humid atmosphere. It was almost as if she were the older, more responsible one of the two. Each word she wrote, even the forward-sloping, unfeminine shape of her handwriting, reminded him of her presence. Affectionate, yet without possessiveness, irreverent, unafraid. Here at least was someone who could be neither bought nor intimidated. Just as there was no man as dependent as the Wilcoxes, the Richardsons, with their mediocre abilities and large salaries, so there were few people as free as a competent, intelligent secretary earning the equivalent of thirty to forty dollars a week. At that rate she owed nothing to anybody—no gratitude, no loyalty, no respect. She had no obligation to feel part of the system or to fool herself that there was something mystically important about it. To her, Gilbertson, Furac, Kingham, perhaps even the great Bernstein himself, were no more than a group of balding dyspeptic men talking solemnly about markets and trading conditions, dictating pompous letters to each other—playing a ridiculous but also rather pathetic middle-aged game they referred to reverently as Business.

He wrote a reply to the letter, tossed it into his out tray, and wondered what to do. It was several days since he had been up to the twenty-seventh—he had been kept away by an obscure fear of embarrassing people. He decided he might as well try Miss Curran again—she might just possibly have some news.

When the elevator stopped at the twenty-seventh floor there were several people waiting outside the doors. In the middle of them, no more than a yard away, was Furac. For a moment they stood face to face. There was no time, for Marshall at least, to decide on an attitude to take up toward such an unexpected meeting. Furac, though surely he must have at least regarded it as a possibility, seemed equally at a loss. His eyes blinked anxiously; his shoulders wriggled a little. It was easy, seeing his nervousness, to underestimate him, until one remembered the determination and intelligence which lay beneath it. The reminder of his ability was doubly disconcerting when it came.

Furac's lips moved in a thin half-smile. In it there was neither friendship nor enmity, nothing but a desire to escape as quickly as possible from an awkward predicament. Then he was past, shielded once more by the intervening bodies of his companions. The elevator doors closed behind him.

Miss Curran was sitting in the outer office. She swung around from her typewriter and regarded Marshall warily. Before she had time to speak he said, "I want to see Kingham."

He had intended to sound coldly businesslike, with perhaps an undertone of menace. But from her expression he realized that his anger must be a great deal more apparent than he had thought. He tried to tone it down a little.

"He *is* back, isn't he?" he asked.

"Yes."

"I thought you were going to let me know——"

"I said," she corrected him, "that I'd tell him you wanted to see him the moment he got back. And I did. After that it was up to him." Seeing his expression, she added, "I'm sorry, Mr. Marshall——"

"Yes—all right." This wasn't the time to discuss Miss Curran's ethics. "How long has he been here?"

"Since the day before yesterday."

"He's seen Furac?"

"Yes. They had a dinner for him—last night——" She opened a drawer in her desk, picked out a sheet of paper, and handed it to him. It was a list of guests for the dinner. They were all members of the International with one exception.

"Bernstein was there?"

"Yes." She took the list and replaced it in the desk. For her, it had been quite an indiscretion. No doubt she would regret it later.

He looked toward the door of the inner office. "Is he by himself?"

"Yes, but——"

"You tried to keep me out," he said, "but I pushed past you." He walked to the door, knocked lightly, and without waiting for an answer walked in.

Kingham looked even smaller than usual sitting behind the large desk. His chair seemed somehow too high for him; he had to point

his toes a little to reach the floor. The sunlight glinted off his spectacles as he looked up. His face showed neither surprise nor annoyance.

"Hello, Chris," he said. Then he frowned. "I don't remember making any appointment——"

"You didn't. But I want to talk to you."

"Yes, of course. There are several matters . . . However, I'm pretty busy right now——"

Marshall advanced into the room. "I'd like to talk to you," he repeated.

Kingham looked at him for a moment. Then he seemed to make up his mind. "Okay," he said. "Sit down. I'll just sign these letters." He went through a pile of letters, made corrections on one or two, signed his name neatly and carefully on the others, and rang for Miss Curran. As she went out with the letters he said: "And cancel that call to Washington. I'll let you know later." He swung around and said, "Now, Chris, what is it that needs telling about in such a hurry?"

"Why did you call me back from Europe?"

Kingham paused before replying. He seemed to be wondering whether it would be beneath his dignity to answer the question at all. "Because I thought it was time," he said eventually. "Next question?"

"Why did you so suddenly think it was time?"

"Chris, I want to remind you of something. I'm the head of this division. I don't have to account to you for the way I run things."

Marshall made a gesture of impatience.

"This is fine. Nobody has to account to anybody for anything. Furac said much the same thing to me in Paris."

"Did he?" Kingham's lips tightened.

"Yes. Hasn't he told you?" Marshall knew he was attacking recklessly, ignoring the conventions, making an amicable settlement of the matter almost out of the question. But his experiences of the past weeks had damaged his self-control. Perhaps that was the object of the technique—a softening-up process designed to destroy

a man's judgment. He said, "I hear you had a long talk with him last night."

"So what?" It was difficult to know whether Kingham's rising anger was genuine or simulated. "What business is it of yours who I talk to?" He leaned forward in his chair. "I'm an easy man to get along with, as you know, but you're beginning to try my patience pretty hard. I don't know who the hell you think you are, pushing your way in here when I'm busy——"

Marshall could see the game moving away from him. He counter-attacked desperately. "Don't you know that Furac's a crook? Or don't you care?"

There was a moment's silence. Kingham regarded him impassively, his brow furrowed, his anger seemingly replaced by mystification.

"A crook? What are you talking about?"

"He's cheating his staff—and us too, for that matter. You remember a man called Verrier?"

"This person who shot himself? I gather he was out of his mind."

"That's the story. However, I got talking to his wife——" He opened his wallet and took out two folded sheets of paper. "While I was waiting for you, I prepared a report about him—with figures."

Kingham read it through without any change of expression. Then he put it down on his blotter.

"I should like to check on this," he said.

"Naturally."

"Though I must say, even if it proves to be correct——" He looked up in perplexity. "Is this all? You mean this is what you're getting so steamed up about?"

"Verrier killed himself," said Marshall.

"But not over this. For God's sake, the whole claim can't add up to more than a couple of hundred dollars."

Marshall leaned forward and said earnestly, "But that's the terrible thing about it, don't you see? It means nothing to us, next to nothing to Furac. But to a man like that, it was the difference between life and death." In his agitation he got up from his chair and began to pace the room. "Whether you like it or not, Verrier worked for us. He sold our merchandise and was paid with our

money. He hadn't a house or a piece of furniture of his own; when he died he left his wife just enough to pay for his funeral; he was cheated and exploited and underpaid, and he knew it. He protested to us, and nobody took a damn bit of notice. So finally he took a gun and blew his brains out." He halted at the end of the desk, looking down at Kingham. "Now, I contend we have a responsibility here——"

"To do what?"

"To offer compensation, for one thing. To make sure that it isn't happening in other cases, and won't happen again. And to get rid of people like Furac."

Kingham nodded thoughtfully. "You think we should just shoot off our mouths and tell them how to handle things—or else. Is that it?"

"In a case like this—yes."

Kingham said nothing. Instead he lit a cigarette and threw the pack across the desk. Marshall, suddenly self-conscious about his standing position, went back to his chair.

Kingham blew out a cloud of smoke. "I'll tell you something, Chris," he said confidentially. "I was mad with you. The way I saw it was this: I picked you out for a real opportunity, one that most of the boys around here would have given their eyes for. You went off to Europe and what did you do? For the first month or so, so far as I could see—nothing." He cut short Marshall's protest. "Okay, I reminded myself, give him time, you told him to take it slowly at the beginning. He's getting himself settled in, learning to handle the people, and so on. Better that than going off half cocked—at least he isn't annoying the distributors. So I waited. And then— boom! What do I find? Not only have you done nothing useful. Not only have you gone over to Paris without notifying me. But after only three days there you have insulted one of our most important business associates, called him a crook and a racketeer, tried to cross-examine his staff——" He asked reasonably, "Are you really surprised that I recalled you?"

"It might have been a good idea to hear my side——"

"I've heard it now. If I heard Furac first, it's because I've known him a lot longer than you. Like me, he's been in this business for the

last twenty years. He's a smart man, and he's done wonderful work for the company. He knows conditions in France like no one else. He's an associate of ours, not an employee. I wouldn't feel like trying to interfere in his relations with his staff."

"So you won't do anything?" Marshall said bitterly. He was not surprised; he had not really expected Kingham to do anything, but nevertheless he felt his heart sinking. There was no prospect now of an easy way out.

"I shall go into the matter—check the facts——"

"And then?"

"Then you'll have to leave it to me." He put his palm down on the report and said, "You've done your part now—you've turned in your report. You can forget it."

Marshall shook his head. "I'm sorry. I can't take it like that."

Kingham looked at him and said softly, "I'm afraid you'll have to, Chris."

"We'll see."

"No." He snapped out the word. "We won't see—we'll have it out right now. I don't give a damn who your father was, you're in my division and under my orders. You have no special privileges."

"I don't want anything for myself——"

"That's not the point. The point is that I'm in charge and you must accept my decision or get out. Is that clear?"

His body was rigid; his face peered forward as if to emphasize the determination behind his words. It occurred to Marshall that Kingham could have stalled had he wanted to. He could have promised an investigation, a discussion with Furac which would drag on and eventually come to nothing. In his position he had so many advantages; he could have won easily enough by guile. He must know that. And his rejection of the easier course could mean only one thing—that he had decided that this was suitable ground for an issue of principle, a test of strength between the two of them. From this moment there was no possibility of compromise.

Nor was there anything further to say at the moment. Without replying to the challenge, he got up and walked out of the room.

CHAPTER III

"I DIDN'T COME to you before," Marshall said to his brother, "because I wanted to do things the right way."

"Uh-huh." Jeff took a cigar out of a box on the sideboard, crackled it against his ear, and cut the end off. "You don't use these, do you?"

"No, thanks."

He lit, puffed, inspected the burning end. It glowed symmetrically; the ritual was completed. "Why don't we go out in the garden?"

Outside, the heat of the day was fading. The trees made long shadows on the lawns; the water from the sprinklers glittered in the last rays of the setting sun. Behind them, through the open upstairs windows, they could hear the voices of the children as they were put to bed. Jeff looked around him and sniffed the scent of the summer evening. He thought of his new Buick and the Dodge station wagon, the lake at the end of the garden where his cabin cruiser rode at its moorings, and sighed with happiness.

"Pretty nice out here," he observed.

"Yes."

"Wonderful relaxation after the city. The way I look at it, even if you only get an hour or so each evening, it's worth it. Gets back your sense of proportion somehow. And as for the kids—— You know, Chris, you ought to settle down." He frowned, to show he

wanted to be taken seriously. "No, I mean it. You'd be surprised the difference it would make to you."

"Only a few months ago you were advising me to pack up and go to Europe."

Jeff laughed disarmingly. "Yes, that's right. Well, maybe I was mistaken about that."

"Maybe you're mistaken now."

"I don't know." He was thoughtful again. "I'm a great hand for giving people advice, I guess. When things go pretty well for you, you want them to go well for others too." He would have liked his brother to have a cigar and a wife and a house and three kids and two automobiles and a cabin cruiser. There was, after all, no real difficulty in obtaining them. It seemed mysterious to him that a man could perversely reject happiness when it was so closely within his reach. "But perhaps," he said without any real conviction, "what suits me might not suit you." When Marshall said nothing, he went on, "You had something on your mind?"

"Yes. As I was saying, I thought I ought to take it to Kingham first, because it concerns the International——"

"That's right." Jeff nodded energetically. "Can't be too careful about things like that."

"However, I didn't get anywhere with him, so I thought I'd have a talk with you about it."

"I don't have any authority over Kingham, you know."

"Who has?"

"Only Bernstein. And the Board, officially—but in practice that means Bernstein again."

"But, as a member of the Board, you are in a position to raise any question that's of importance to the company——"

"Yes, I suppose so." He spoke with slight impatience. Like many rather slow-thinking men, he was always in fear of being driven into a corner and disliked talking of hypothetical cases. "But why don't you tell me what it's all about?"

He was, Marshall thought as he told the story, a good listener. He had no temptation to interrupt or to see ahead to a later point in the narrative and lose concentration until it was reached. Thought, for him, was full-time work and he liked to devote all

his energies to it. When Marshall had finished, Jeff was silent for a while, puffing at his cigar.

Finally he said, "It seems to me there are two separate issues here. One is Furac and this guy—what was his name?"

"Verrier."

"Right. Maybe there was a racket going on in a small way. The question is whether it's any of our business, and if so, what we ought to do about it. Agreed?"

"I think we *have* to do something."

"Kingham doesn't agree?"

"No."

"The second point concerns your own position. You contend that as soon as you found out about this Kingham called you home, put the freeze on you, and generally kicked you around——"

"That's not so important in itself. But just the same, it shouldn't happen. And it hasn't happened just to me. You knew Wilcox?"

"Just slightly."

"I'm pretty sure the same thing happened to him, for the same reason. You could talk to him——"

"I doubt it." He looked at the end of his cigar regretfully. "Cigars," he observed, "are like a lot of other things. If you want to get the full enjoyment, you have to stop just that little bit too soon." He threw the butt away into some bushes. "No, Wilcox isn't going to be any use to you, I'm afraid. He's left the company."

The announcement was like a sudden withdrawal of support. Marshall was shaken. To some extent, at least, he had been counting on Wilcox.

"When?"

"A few weeks ago. I don't know any details. I just heard. I don't even know where he went."

At least he might be able to make something out of it. "Well, there you are, you see how it is. Why should Wilcox walk out? He was a promising man——"

"Lots of people are promising until somebody decides they're not. Maybe he was dissatisfied. Maybe he had reason, I don't know. But either way, he's gone now and that's it. He wasn't even fired— he walked out."

"He was squeezed out."

"That's possible." Jeff shrugged his great footballer's shoulders. "Don't let's be naïve, Chris. It happens all the time. Sometimes it has to be done that way. A man may be no good. He may be good but his face doesn't fit with the boss. Nobody likes to fire him outright, but he's not going to get anywhere sticking around. If he's smart, he sees it himself. If not, he gets a hint. It may be rough on him, but in a competitive game like ours you have to do it, otherwise you get loaded down with dead wood."

"All right, then." The point was reasonable in general. Nobody could run a business or any other organization efficiently on the basis of absolute fairness. If a man was to be given authority, he must be allowed to choose his subordinates and get rid of others. The methods by which the selection was carried out might vary; the process itself would always be painful and frequently unjust. It was the price of action. "I agree that if Kingham doesn't want somebody, he has a right to squeeze him out. But not simply because he complains about racketeering."

Jeff looked at him with slow disapproval. "It seems to me that there are a lot of assumptions there that you wouldn't like to be asked to prove."

"I can prove that Furac's a crook."

"To the tune of about a hundred and eighty dollars."

"That's all we know about. There may be other things."

"We can only talk about what we know. All the rest doesn't amount to a row of beans." Jeff frowned. "The thing I can't figure out is this. You say you're pretty sure Wilcox must have brought this matter up before?"

"I'm certain. That's why he was moved."

"Then there should be some record. If Kingham concealed his report or destroyed it, that would certainly put him in the wrong. For one thing, he has an obligation on financial matters to notify the accountants." He said dubiously, "I suppose I could raise that point with him. Would you like me to?"

"Yes. Do it whatever way you think best. But I think he should answer—to somebody." An idea came to him. "Would it be worth telling Bernstein?"

Jeff shook his head decisively. "No. He doesn't have anything to do with details of administration. He's too busy buying and selling companies, making stock issues, and so on. You couldn't interest him in a small thing like this. He might even take it the wrong way. And talking of that——" He hesitated. "I suppose you understand that, whichever way this turns out, it isn't going to do any good to your personal position?"

"Yes, of course." Kingham would never forgive him. But that hardly seemed to matter. "Just the same, I'd like you to see him."

Jeff was silent for a little while. Marshall realized that, for all the sympathetic reception Jeff had given to the story, he had little appreciation of the issues at stake. To him, the matter was a small one. Of more importance was the fact that his younger brother had been badly treated, and he felt a family obligation to come to his support, just as he had done when Marshall had been set upon by other boys at school. The obligation was a nuisance but carried a certain satisfaction of its own. Jeff knew that his family had always thought him stupid and unimaginative. In a household dominated by his father, only the flashier virtues had been thought worthy of consideration. But in the long run he had proved them wrong— patience and stability had prevailed. Now his brother had to come and beg for his assistance.

"Okay then," he said heavily. "I'll see what I can do." It was quite dark now, and the lights were on in the house. Paula had come downstairs after bathing the children and was watching television. They could hear the muffled boom of voices, interspersed with an occasional snatch of music. Jeff turned toward the house. "I'll see him tomorrow morning. Now let's go in and see how Paula's getting along."

Inside, Jeff mixed drinks for the three of them and they sat watching television. After a while Marshall grew tired of the program and began to watch Jeff and Paula instead. Their chairs were together, and Paula's hand was resting on her husband's arm. On occasions like this it seemed to give her pleasure to be in physical contact with him, no matter how slight the contact might be. She was like a dog who cannot sleep soundly without one paw on his master's boot.

Whatever Jeff might be to anyone else, to Paula at least he was

a personage. She pushed him around in many ways, of course. She was demanding and possessive, not only on her own behalf but also on behalf of the children. She was jealous, too, without any obvious cause. But Jeff did not seem to mind. He had always longed to be loved and respected. As a boy he had seen the love of his mother and the hopes of his father fixed on his younger brother. Even later, when Chris had proved a disappointment, he had only been accepted reluctantly, as a second best—he had worshiped his father and never received anything but indifference in return. But with his marriage to Paula everything had changed. He was suddenly a person of importance. At home his desires were studied, his views treated with as much reverence as if he were Marcus Marshall himself. Each night his self-confidence was replenished; each morning he took it with him to the office like the papers in his brief case. He was able to believe in his own ability and, now that his father was dead, others were prepared to believe in them too.

The corporation, under the direction of Bernstein, had moved into a quieter and more prudent phase. The days of wild, brilliant growth had given way to a process of consolidation. Unprofitable subsidiaries were closed down, the more speculative ventures sold at a loss. Into this atmosphere Jeff had fitted perfectly. His ponderous approach had given him the reputation of being a safe, thoughtful man. Success had come to him as a pleasing surprise; he had accepted it with dignity and a certain complacency.

The program faded out, the announcer came forward, bright-eyed, anxiously seductive, like an old man trying to entice a schoolgirl into a back alley. He was halfway through a commercial about somebody's beer when Jeff snapped off the set.

He yawned and looked at his watch. "Guess it's about time for us working people to get to bed," he said.

CHAPTER IV

THE NEXT MORNING his office seemed even hotter than ever. The electric fan he had obtained with so much difficulty made no noticeable difference; it did no more than move around the same stale, humid air grimed with the smoke of innumerable cigarettes. He tried to concentrate on his report, but work was impossible. Three floors up, Jeff and Kingham were talking about him; relaxed and reasonable, no doubt, in large leather armchairs suitable for men of consequence. Never before had he resented so bitterly his own inferior position. He could not blame anybody else—it had been his own doing. He had defied authority, and authority had struck back by depriving him of the gifts it had to offer—power, prestige, the privilege of access to those higher circles where decisions were made. He had never wanted them before. Now, when something needed to be done, he craved them desperately. This was the result of his policy of detachment—that in a matter of the greatest importance to him he was reduced to relying on Jeff to put his case.

It was nearly twelve o'clock when Jeff finally appeared. He walked into the office, nodded curtly, and seated himself in a chair on the other side of the desk. The expression on his face was somber. Marshall felt his hands grow clammy. Jeff was a man who enjoyed bringing good news. He would almost certainly have been smiling if things had gone well.

"Did you see him?" Marshall asked anxiously.

"Yes."

"Well—how did it go?"

"How did it go?" Jeff's voice rose in indignation. He said hopelessly, "God, Chris, I don't understand you. I really don't."

"What do you mean?"

Marshall was bewildered. However things had gone, he could see no reason for such bitterness against himself. "What happened?"

Jeff ignored the question. "I'm going to speak frankly to you," he said. "I feel I have a right to do that. You'll admit that I've always played square with you, no matter how we might have differed sometimes——"

"Of course."

"And I had the idea that it was the same with you. To my way of thinking, you did some goddamn stupid things, but you were always on the level. It honestly never entered my head that you'd try to put something like this over on me."

"I still don't understand——"

"No?" He looked closely at Marshall for a moment. "You really don't? Then maybe Kingham's right."

"About what?"

Jeff said curtly, "He says you're nuts."

"And you believed him?"

"I might as well. I can't believe you any more." Suddenly he seemed to become aware of what he had said. Half a lifetime of trust had been cut across. As if stretching out a hand in a wild effort to restore it, he said helplessly, "I don't know what to say. I trusted you. I never even bothered to confirm your story."

"For God's sake, what is this all about? My story was true. I can substantiate any part of it."

Jeff shook his head. "You told me you knew nothing about this business until you went to Paris."

"That's so."

"And that Kingham must have heard about it from Wilcox and deliberately concealed it."

"There's no other explanation."

"That's what I told him. He sat there without saying anything

and let me accuse him of covering up a fraud. Then he showed me this."

He zipped open his dispatch case and took a memorandum file out of it. He tossed it across the desk. It was in the usual form for internal correspondence, with the names of the department heads to whom it should be circulated on the cover, the memorandum itself bound inside. It was headed: "Financial Arrangements concerning Foreign Agencies." It was dated February of that year.

Marshall looked inside. The memorandum was closely printed and several pages long. He began to skim through. As usual, the style was turgid, the prose almost unreadable, the meaning in many places hard to follow. The first page was concerned mainly with office equipment. He was halfway down page two before he found anything which applied to his own problem.

". . . Notice has also been received that in some cases there is a lack of exact correspondence between sums paid by distributors to employers on account of direct compensation . . . certain complexities of accountancy varying in nature in different territories. . . . Particular taxation systems liable to influence the use of variable ratios between direct compensation and expense accounting . . ." (In other words, thought Marshall, some of the boys would sooner get part of their wages in the form of expenses and avoid tax. Well, okay.)

". . . It is felt that any attempt to enforce a rigid uniformity in this respect would not only create difficulties for the distributors but also put an additional burden on the Finance Department which it is not at present equipped to handle. Also, lacking special knowledge of local conditions, it might be that decisions made in the U.S.A. would be found impossible to implement in certain foreign territories. . . ."

He began to skip. Old familiar phrases appeared. ". . . avoid unnecessary interference . . . excellent relations with foreign associates . . . complete confidence . . . no reason to abandon certain fundamental principles . . .

". . . It is therefore recommended," said the memorandum with sudden brevity, "that the details of implementation of such finan-

cial agreements be left, as heretofore, in the hands of the agents concerned."

Marshall looked up, frowning. "Well, so what? This is just a lot of gobbledygook. They put it in general terms, mix it up with a lot of other stuff, make it as difficult to understand as they can, then stick it in the file. It's just a cover-up."

"You can understand it, can't you?"

"Sure, but——"

"The English may not be so good, but it's clear enough to me what it means. They discussed the whole thing in February, and a collective decision was made to do nothing about it."

"Collective, hell! You mean Kingham decided to do nothing about it."

"Others were consulted," said Jeff coldly. He added, "Look on the outside of the folder."

Marshall turned back to the cover sheet. On it were the names of most of the department heads in the International. The memorandum had been widely circulated. Opposite each name were the scribbled initials of the person concerned, and in the space for comments, always the single word: "Agreed."

The last signature on the list was his own.

It seemed a long time before they spoke again. Marshall looked down at the sheet of paper on which was written, as clearly as if it had been expressed in words, his own defeat. The pain was violent, sickening, but not unfamiliar. He remembered the school examinations failed because of laziness and overconfidence, the voice of Mayer saying: "Have you considered any alternative occupation?" In each case the possibility of failure had been contemplated beforehand yet never fully believed. It was unthinkable, it couldn't happen. You would fall down dead, the world would explode, you would wake up and find you had been dreaming. But when the time came, nothing like that occurred to let you out. You had to stand there and face the moment, dumb, suffering, letting it hit you. It couldn't last forever. Every second took it a little farther away.

"Well?" said Jeff finally.

"I don't know——" He tried hopelessly to arrange his thoughts, to think of a new approach.

"That's your signature? You're not trying to tell me he forged it?"

"Of course not." The sickening truth was that there was no need for forgery, as Kingham probably knew. Marshall had always regarded the endless circulation of memoranda as mere bureaucratic stupidity. But perhaps he had underrated his enemies. Perhaps this was a deliberate method of securing assent to dubious propositions, by sandwiching them in between a mass of verbiage. He explained weakly, "I must have signed it without reading it very carefully. There are so many of these darned things—you get half a dozen on your desk at the same time. You know how it is."

He looked up, hoping for some sign of understanding or sympathy, but Jeff was untouched. Plainly, this excuse meant nothing to him. It occurred to Marshall that his brother was probably the only man in the organization who went through all the memoranda before signing them.

"I can't say I do. It seems to me there isn't much point in circulating things unless people read them."

At least, thought Marshall, he believed the excuse even if he was unable to understand it. It was more acceptable to Jeff to think of him as a careless incompetent than as a liar. More plausible, too.

Though he was now without any real hope, he felt the necessity to try again, to salvage something from the wreckage.

"Okay, I was sloppy. I should have read it, I know. But that doesn't alter the facts about Verrier——"

Jeff interrupted him impatiently. "Chris, be your age. This stuff about Verrier is dead, stone cold dead—you must see that. It never amounted to much anyway. Even last night I was doubtful whether you could make it stick."

"You didn't say so."

"I didn't want to hurt your feelings. And I thought you had a point of view. But it so happens that Kingham's one of the best men we've got, as far as efficiency goes. Whether he's in the right or in the wrong, nobody's going to be fighting for the chance to slap him down over a matter of a hundred and eighty dollars."

"I keep telling you, it's not the amount of money that matters. It's the principle——"

"I heard you. And I was prepared to buy that—last night. Now" —he pointed to the file on the desk—"it's just ridiculous."

"I don't think so."

"If you can't see that——"

"Listen, Jeff," he said desperately. "I want you, for my sake, to try to understand about this. The point is that, even if I had read that memorandum in February, I should still probably have signed it. It would have looked to me, as it looked to all the others, like the sensible thing to do. But since then I've seen the people, I know what it really means. You can kill a man with a signature, Jeff."

Jeff looked at him with some disgust. He was being melodramatic.

"I don't think this is getting us anywhere."

"Let's forget about ourselves for a moment. You're mad at me, I know, and I sympathize. But this isn't about me. The fact that I've made a fool of myself shouldn't mean that a man like Verrier should have to suffer."

Like someone teaching a lesson to a child, Jeff said, "But it does. That's what responsibility means. You always thought I wasn't very smart, but at least I have brains enough to know that." He leaned forward, attacking. "You took the attitude that business was a kid's game, not big enough for somebody of your intelligence. It had to be like that, if fools like me could succeed in it. You couldn't bother your head with a lot of routine jobs, like reading reports and attending conferences. The reports were badly written; at the conferences everybody talked too much, they hadn't got your incisive brain, they couldn't express their ideas—isn't that so?"

"Yes." His head was aching; his unhappiness was so great that he felt no resentment against Jeff. "Yes, I said all those things. It was tactless, I suppose."

"You're damn right it was tactless. It doesn't matter so much with me. I know you and I make allowances. But other people take it differently."

"You mean Kingham?"

"Not just Kingham. You've made plenty of people sore, talking like that."

It was like being back at school. The same thing had happened there. Innocently he had opened his mouth too wide, spoken his thought aloud, questioned authority; and suddenly found himself, to his utter astonishment, suspect and unpopular. It had never occurred to him that his opinions would cause such general hostility. He had always imagined that the great majority, secure in their own world, would regard him with tolerance, as a licensed eccentric. It was always a shock to him to discover how superficial that tolerance was, to have his own familiar world turned upside down and suddenly filled with strange and menacing faces.

All these years, he realized now, Jeff had been defending him, making excuses for him. He said unhappily, "I'm afraid I put you on the spot."

"You surely did." The recollection was painful. It would remain so for a long time. "I had to apologize to Kingham."

"I'm sorry. I mean it—I can't tell you how sorry I am."

"Okay—well—it's done now, let's forget it." He meant, Let's say no more about it. Neither of them would ever forget it. Jeff hesitated. There was another awkward question to dispose of. "The important thing is, what happens now?"

"To me?"

"That's right. You appreciate, don't you, that you can't go on just as if nothing had happened?"

"I suppose not." He waited. When his brother said nothing, he went on with a touch of irony, "Well, come on. You've got some ideas, I imagine. You discussed it with Kingham, didn't you?"

"Yes, I did. Do you object?"

"I'm in no position to object to anything. What's your proposition?"

Jeff settled back in his chair. He was on more comfortable ground now, dealing with what was essentially an administrative problem. "In the first place, you obviously won't want to go on working in the International. Correct?"

Marshall almost smiled. Such crude, pathetic courtesy, the pre-

tense that the choice was his. But it was kindly meant. "Correct," he said.

"On the other hand, it would be a pity if you decided to leave the company altogether. After all, you have a special interest in it, just as I have. . . ."

Jeff was almost coaxing. Marshall was aware that his brother was anxious for him to stay on, in spite of everything. Why? Family loyalty? Or was it, perhaps, the block of shares he held, which indirectly strengthened Jeff's own position?

"I don't know——" he said indifferently.

"If you do want to stay, I'm sure I could fix something for you."

"Such as?"

"I'm not sure yet. Something in Domestic Sales, probably."

"In New York?"

Jeff was doubtful. "I'm not so sure about that. We've a pretty full team here and I wouldn't like to break it up. Maybe, when we have a move sometime, you could come in——"

"From where?"

"I can't tell you right away." He became vague. "Chicago—Kansas City—New Orleans—somewhere like that."

It was, Marshall realized, too much to expect that they would not punish him in some way. A job out of New York would be obvious to everyone as a demotion.

"I'd sooner stay here."

Jeff frowned. "Maybe. But as it happens, there's nothing free." With a trace of exasperation he added, "I'm doing my very best for you, Chris——"

"Okay, okay." Arguing at such a hopeless disadvantage was tiring him out. He knew that Jeff was trying to restrain himself from saying that the whole affair was his own fault and that he was in no position to pick and choose—he ought to be very grateful that someone was taking the trouble to help at all. "Whatever you say."

"That's the boy." Now that Jeff had his way, his joviality returned. "You'll probably enjoy it, you know. You'll have more freedom out there, be able to develop your own ideas. In the New York office we're too close on top of each other. Everybody's driving himself at ninety miles an hour to push ahead of the next man.

It has to be like that, otherwise we go soft. But just the same, it's a strain." He smiled ruefully. "It's a rat race."

Marshall nodded. Jeff was a great man for seeing the advantages of the inevitable. He was reminded of a similar conversation after Kingham had offered him the job in London. He wondered how Jeff would feel if it was proposed that he, too, needed a rest from the rat race, in New Orleans or Kansas City.

"When do I start?" he asked.

"I can't say exactly. I shall have to make some arrangements first. A week or two—something like that."

"I have some affairs in Europe that I want to tie up——"

"Yes, of course—I imagined you would have. That was another thing I talked over with Kingham." Jeff hesitated and then said delicately, "Between ourselves, he was a little against it. He was all for"—he searched for a tactful word—"for making a clean break as far as Europe was concerned. But I didn't think that was reasonable. After all, I reminded him, you were called over here without any expectation of its being permanent. You were bound to have personal affairs to settle. And also, I wouldn't be able to find anything for you to do in the next week or two anyway. So he finally agreed."

"That was generous of him."

Jeff missed the sarcasm. There was something on his mind and he liked to think of one thing at a time. "There was one stipulation he made, though."

"What was that?"

"On the whole, I think it's reasonable, considering what's happened." Nevertheless, he was awkward. "He wanted me to make it clear to you that you are no longer accredited by the company and have no authority to engage in any business dealings over there. He doesn't want you to make any contact with our representatives in the area."

"Anything else?"

"No. That was all."

There was a silence. Marshall tossed the pencil he was holding onto the blotting pad. Unconsciously, throughout the conversation he had been doodling on the thick white paper, drawing wild,

bizarre shapes whose meaning was obscure even to himself. As so often in times of crises, they had formed themselves into a pattern of interlocking shadows of increasing darkness and complexity. He saw his brother's disapproving glance and wanted to explain that it was an unconscious activity, a sort of nervous spasm; he wasn't as frivolous as he appeared.

Instead he said, "Well, there we are. Everything seems to be settled." And after a pause, partly because it was expected and partly because he really did feel under an obligation, "Thanks for everything."

Jeff smiled as he rose from his seat, a hearty, big-brother smile. "Forget it," he said.

CHAPTER I

THERE WAS NOBODY to meet him this time, no bright scrubbed young man in a double-breasted blue suit with a triangle of white handkerchief showing at the breast pocket; no hired limousine. That, at least, was something. He sat in a corner seat in the airport bus, looking out at the characterless suburbs of northwest London. The semi-detached houses stretched for miles along the arterial road in a belt of uniform, featureless gentility. Between the housing developments were model factories, equally prim and house-proud, manufacturers of vacuum cleaners, razor blades, lipstick; each with its piece of lawn, its ornamental flower beds. Most of them were closed today—it was Saturday morning.

At Waterloo he took a taxi and drove to the flat. When he opened the door he noticed that there was no heap of letters behind it. Nor was there that curious, still, dusty smell which speaks of closed windows and lack of habitation. He put down his suitcases and went into the living room.

The room was unusually tidy. There was a fire in the grate and Jane was sitting beside it in a high-backed chair, reading. When he came in, she carefully marked her place, put the book down on the radio, and then stood up.

"Jane—darling!"

Instead of moving toward him, she stood there, unusually shy, waiting for him to make the first move. "Surprised to see me?"

"Why, yes——" He went up to her and took her in his arms. Even as he was kissing her, she seemed a little more reserved than usual.

"You didn't mind?"

"Why should I?" He looked round at the room. The furniture was polished, the carpet newly swept, the books on their shelves dusted and placed in alphabetical order. "This is wonderful. The old place never looked like this in its life. You must have been working——"

"When I got your cable I thought it would be nice to have things ready for you." She added with disapproval: "The place was in a dreadful mess."

"I left in rather a hurry. I wrote a message for the daily woman——"

"She obviously hadn't bothered her head. I wondered what to do and then decided I couldn't just leave it; it would be very cheerless for you when you got back——"

He smiled at her affectionately. "It was very thoughtful of you."

"There wasn't much to do when you come down to it." She paused and then said rather awkwardly, "Well, that's all really. I think I ought to go now——"

"Go?" he said, puzzled. "Why? Have you got a date or something?"

"Not exactly. But you'll want to get settled in. I should only be in the way."

He put his arms round her shoulders. "Now why would I ever think you were in the way?"

"You might." She was very serious. "While I was sitting here waiting I wondered whether perhaps it wasn't a mistake. I was only intending to be friendly, but I thought you might see it differently." She added with emphasis, "I can't bear women who *impose* themselves on men."

A thought occurred to him. "How long were you waiting?"

"Oh, not so very long. An hour or two."

He said apologetically, "The plane was a little late. I'm sorry about that. Waiting for people is a little like lying awake at night. After a time the craziest thoughts come into your mind."

"This isn't crazy," she persisted. "I'm serious. I still think——"

"It's always crazy when you start thinking about 'men' and 'women' in quotes. This is you and me—an entirely different mat-

ter. It never occurred to me that you were imposing on me—and furthermore, I wouldn't mind if you did."

She began to relax. "You're very nice to me. Nobody was ever as nice to me as you are."

"Perhaps nobody was in love with you before."

"They said they were. Perhaps they even meant it. It's not always easy to tell, is it—even with yourself?" She went on, "That was what I was worried about. When you've been apart for a while you get things more in perspective. This would have been a good moment for you to change the tempo, to start off on a different footing if you wanted to. And by being here waiting for you, I was spoiling it for you." She smiled precariously. "That was what I was afraid of."

"You were silly, weren't you?"

"Was I? I hope so." She walked over to the sofa and sat down, closing the subject. "Now tell me about New York."

In a second the feeling of unreasonable happiness, of homecoming, was gone. Love was like a sort of sleep in which you could immerse yourself for a time, forgetting your troubles in vague, irresponsible dreams. But always in the morning there remained the business of living.

"It was a flop," he said painfully. "They beat me."

Her face fell. "But, darling, how? What happened?"

"The worst thing was, it was my own fault. I ran right into it. . . ."

As he told the story he found that it was not quite so bad as he had expected. Perhaps there was a relief in unburdening himself to her. Or perhaps it was simply a fatigue of emotion. You could not stimulate a nerve at maximum intensity forever.

At the end she said, "You say what really finished you was the fact that you had put your signature on the report?"

"In a way, yes."

"That sounds absurd to me." She had a feminine scorn for formalities. "Why, half the time businessmen sign things without reading them. It was just bad luck."

"No." He was ready for this one. It was too easy—dangerously easy. "I won't accept that. Whenever I flopped out before, there

was always somebody to say, 'Bad luck.'" He turned to her desperately. "Don't you see that I'd sooner be anything—stupid, ridiculous, ineffective—anything but unlucky? That's the one thing you can't beat."

She said gently, in an attempt at consolation, "You mustn't make too much of this. It isn't the earth——"

"It mattered a lot to me. More than I would have thought. Not just because of Verrier, though that was important. But because I'd gone on for years saying to myself that this was the kind of thing I could do if I had to. Then, when it came to the point, I was useless. I let everybody down, Madame Verrier, myself, you——"

"In a way it was my fault. It was I who persuaded you——"

"You gave me a chance and I made a mess of it. You can't blame yourself."

She was silent for a while, no longer looking at him. It was as if her thoughts were turned inward, searching her mind for a decision on a problem which was worrying her. Eventually she said, "Have you made any plans?"

"I shall have to be back in New York fairly soon. There are various things to arrange here. I have to see about disposing of the flat, for one thing. And I left some stuff at the office——"

She pointed to a large package in one corner of the room. "I brought everything of yours over here."

"Then you knew I wasn't coming back?"

"Gilbertson told me. From the way he said it, I guessed you must have run into trouble over there. Naturally I asked who would be succeeding you. He looked very pleased and said, so far as he knew, nobody. The job hadn't ever served very much purpose anyway. He made it pretty clear that, so far as he was concerned, you didn't exist any more."

"Did he advise you not to see me when I came over?"

"Not in so many words. He just said you wouldn't be coming near the office and that presumably none of us would be seeing you again. He isn't fool enough to try to tell me what to do out of office hours."

"No." He looked at her loyal, stubborn little face. "I can see that."

"The next morning when I came in, your room had been com-

pletely cleared. The desk drawers were empty, and Travers moved in."

He frowned. There had been nothing of any significance in the desk, but even so he was affronted by this invasion of his privacy. So far as Gilbertson was concerned, she had said, he no longer existed. . . . Suddenly he thought of another aspect of the matter. "But what about you? Are you working for Travers now?"

"No. I've been promoted," she explained. "Miss Barraclough gave notice while you were away—she's going to get married. Mr. Gilbertson asked me to work for him."

He felt unreasonably that in some way she had betrayed him. "And you agreed?"

"Why not?" Seeing the reproach in his eyes, she reminded him, "I'm a working girl, you know. I can't be too particular."

"I suppose not."

He struggled to be understanding. It was the same with everybody—Jeff, Richardson, Rose, Gilbertson, even Jane—they had a job to hold down and they couldn't be too particular. Only he had thought of himself as able to afford a romantic gesture—and where had it got him? But he must be a good loser, he remembered. The British were said to admire good losers.

"Well, there it is," he said with as much cheerful gallantry as he could muster. "I did my best, but it wasn't good enough. There's no use crying about it."

"You're going to leave it there?"

"More or less. There's Madame Verrier, of course. I'll have to make some sort of personal settlement with her. Maybe I can manage to fool her into thinking the money comes from the company."

"That's not very satisfactory, is it?"

"Of course it isn't. But what else can I do? I've tried to think of some other way of going about it, but so far as I can see there isn't any. I'm at a dead end."

She was silent for a moment, then said, "Is this thing so very important to you?"

"You know it is. I'd do anything——"

"Anything?"

"Well, you know what I mean—anything within reason." He

looked at her questioningly. "Why? What is it? What are you getting at?"

She paused again, then said with obvious reluctance, "There's something I haven't told you."

"What's that?"

"You said you didn't know where Wilcox was." He nodded. "Well, he's in London. He wants to meet you."

Astonishment held him silent for a moment. Then he felt a surge of hope. Perhaps this was a break. Perhaps he was in the game again.

"I met him a few days ago," Jane went on. "Or rather, he met me. He was waiting for me at the Bond Street tube station when I went home from the office. It was quite a surprise."

"I can imagine."

"He said he wanted to talk about something important and had I time for a drink. Naturally I was curious, so I went. He told me that he'd left the company about a month ago."

"Yes," said Marshall. "I heard that in New York. But nobody seemed to know where he'd gone. It certainly never occurred to me that he would have come back here. Who's he working for now?"

"I don't know," she said. "He didn't say and I didn't ask him." She added a little oddly, "Himself, perhaps."

"What did he want?"

"I told you. He wanted to get in touch with you. He picked on me as the best way of doing it."

"He knew I was coming back to London?"

"Yes. But he didn't know when."

"So you told him?"

She shook her head.

Puzzled, he asked, "But why not? I'd like to meet Wilcox."

"I'm not so sure," she said doubtfully.

"Why not?" He looked at her with concern. "What's worrying you? You talk as though there was something wrong with him."

It was as though she found it difficult to put her feelings into words. "I didn't like his attitude——"

"What about his attitude?"

"Well, it was too—personal, somehow. He wants to get his own back on the company for what they did to him. He has a grievance."

"I can understand that."

"Oh, so can I. But—just the same—as you know, I'm not very attracted to people with grievances. And he drank too much."

"Well, maybe." She was being a little intolerant, he thought. Surely it was possible to sympathize with Wilcox, even if he was hitting the bottle a little. "What else did he tell you?"

"Not a lot." She made a grimace. "He was talking big—about what he was going to do to various people, and so on. But all very vague—you know how drunks are. I don't know how much it really meant."

"You weren't impressed?"

"No."

"You think he's just a soak?"

"Not quite. But—well—I suppose it was a shock to me. I hadn't seen him since he was working here. I wouldn't say he was ever my type—he was shallow and pleased with himself and he often irritated me—but at least he had vitality. That was how I saw him, anyway."

"And now?"

"Now I can see how precarious it was. It all depended on everybody else thinking he was a coming young man. Once that was knocked away, he just fell to pieces. He hasn't any normal, decent ambitions any more. All he wants is trouble."

"What sort of trouble?"

Once again she did not answer him. She said, "You really want to meet him?"

"What can I lose?"

"A lot, I think." She added obscurely, "We might all lose a lot."

"What's that—woman's instinct?" He smiled, but she did not smile back. "I wish you'd explain."

"No," she said definitely. "He can do the explaining." From her attitude it was plain that Wilcox had said more to her than she was prepared to repeat. She opened her bag and took out a slip of paper. "This is the telephone number he gave me."

CHAPTER II

IT WAS a Museum number. He picked up the telephone and called it. A sharp female voice said, "Drax Hotel."

"I'd like to speak to Mr. Wilcox."

"Staying in the hotel?"

"I've no idea. I presume so——"

"You don't know his room number?"

"No."

"One moment, please."

There was silence for several minutes, then Wilcox's voice.

"Hullo—Marshall?"

"Yes."

"How are you?"

"Pretty good, thanks."

"I hoped you'd be calling." His eagerness was obvious even over the telephone. "Are you in London for long?"

"Not very long."

"Why don't we have a drink together? Can you find your way around here?"

"Tonight?"

"The sooner the better. There's something important I want to discuss with you."

"Okay." Wilcox sounded sober enough at the moment. His voice was a little nervous and aggressive, but that was nothing new. It had never been very easy to make satisfactory contact with him.

Marshall wondered whether everybody found him difficult—or was it just himself? Even now, when they were both allies in misfortune, there was no real feeling of sympathy—only an artificial good-fellowship thinly disguising suspicion. "I have a dinner engagement," he said, "but I can come along afterward. Will nine o'clock suit you?"

"Fine. See you then."

After dinner he took Jane home and then directed his taxi to Bloomsbury. The Drax Hotel was a very large building with a multitude of tiny windows and a façade which seemed to have been made out of enormous slices of some patent non-fattening biscuit—a long-discredited experiment in synthetic construction. A large yellow sign above the main entrance announced: ONE PRICE: BED AND BREAKFAST 25/-. There were indications that this figure had been changed on several occasions to keep abreast of inflation.

There was a crowd at the reception desk. Marshall found himself jostling for position with individuals more accustomed than he was to the struggle for existence in cheap hotels. There were notices everywhere: "The Management regrets that it can take no responsibility for valuables left in rooms." "Guests are respectfully reminded that all accommodation must be paid for in advance." Guests were also respectfully told that rooms had to be vacated by noon on the day of departure, that breakfast would under no circumstances be served after 10 A.M., that no alcohol could be consumed in the main lounge.

At last he reached the front of the queue. A young man in a shiny black suit regarded him with undisguised hostility.

"Yes?" he asked sharply.

"I've come to see a Mr. Wilcox."

"Initial?"

"M., I think."

"We may have several Wilcoxes, you understand." He picked a series of cards out of his filing system and flipped through them. "M. F. Wilcox, 513."

"Thank you. Do you suppose——"

The receptionist had already turned his attention to the next person in line. He looked back at Marshall with a frown.

"Yes, what is it?"

"I'd like to speak to him."

By way of reply the man pointed silently to two telephone booths in a corner of the hall. One was marked "Internal," the other "External." There were people waiting outside each one. Nothing, it seemed, was easy at the Drax. He walked to the lift and pressed the button for the fifth floor.

There was a long way to go down a dark corridor floored with linoleum. He knocked at 513. Wilcox opened the door almost immediately.

"I couldn't get to the internal telephone," Marshall explained, "so I came up."

"Sure. Come right in." The room was small and ill furnished. There was a bed, a wardrobe, a couple of cheap modern chairs, and a dressing table. The window looked out on to the gray blank wall of a block of offices.

Marshall sat down on one of the chairs. Wilcox regarded him for a moment without speaking.

"A drink?" he said anxiously, as if he were afraid of a refusal. It occurred to Marshall that Wilcox was already showing signs of an alcoholic's oversensitivity—he didn't like people to see him drinking alone.

"Thanks."

Wilcox took a bottle of scotch out of the wardrobe. On the writing table there was a carafe of water and two glasses. There was no ice.

"Plenty of water for me."

They sat opposite each other. Wilcox took a large gulp of his drink and gave again his brisk, uncertain smile, the smile of a man with something to sell. His lightweight American suit had a crumpled appearance. The hotel valeting service was not very good, perhaps. Marshall wondered why he had been so insistent that they should meet here. To demonstrate his poverty and attract sympathy? But he had never thought of Wilcox as that kind of man. He was the type, surely, who would try to keep up an appearance of

prosperity to the last. He had been brought up in a world where appeals to sympathy paid few dividends.

For a little while neither of them spoke. Wilcox seemed to be wondering how best to make his approach. Finally he said, "So they fixed you up too, uh?"

Marshall hesitated. "You might call it that."

"What else is there to call it?" Like all salesmen, he was more confident once he had started talking. "Of course I don't know all the details, but I have one or two connections in New York who keep me informed. . . . I believe you were asking after me?"

"Yes. They told me you'd quit."

"That's right. I walked out on them," he said with satisfaction. "I was smart enough for that, at any rate." He took another drink and said, "It didn't take me long to realize that Kingham had played me for a sucker."

"Oh?"

"Yes. When he transferred me he gave me a lot of stuff about the big opportunities there were in the Domestic Division. When I got there, I found there wasn't a damned thing. They'd only taken me to oblige Kingham. They were just looking for a nice suitable opportunity to get rid of me. But I didn't wait that long." He offered Marshall a cigarette. As he leaned forward to light it, he said, "It could happen to you, you know."

Marshall was noncommittal. "It's possible."

"Brother or no brother."

"I'm not counting on that."

"No?" said Wilcox skeptically. Suddenly he laughed. "Kingham must have been sore about you. He certainly never thought of you as an eager beaver. I'll be honest with you—it surprised me too." The laugh died. He had never really thought it very funny. It was all part of a build-up. A curious build-up—mainly man-to-man, confidential, both-in-the-same-spot, why-don't-we-take-our-hair-down-and-get-together—but shot through all the time with these hostile, needling remarks. Suddenly Marshall knew that Wilcox hated him, had always hated him.

"You told me over the phone you wanted to discuss something," he said.

"Yes." Wilcox paused for a moment, then said, "I was interested to know how serious you were."

He frowned. Hadn't Jane said something rather similar? "About what?"

"This whole affair."

"Of course I'm serious."

"You mightn't be. You might be just playing at it. After all, nobody enjoys being beaten——"

"It isn't just a question of"—the words were distasteful to him—"being beaten." Yet he had to admit to himself that to some extent it was. As time went on it became increasingly difficult to distinguish between the claims of abstract justice and personal pride. He said, "There's such a thing as a matter of principle. Verrier was just a little man——"

"Sure." As Wilcox lifted his drink his hand trembled a little. "We're all little men—Verrier—me—you too—— The hell with us."

Marshall waited for him to say something more, but he simply emptied his glass and stared in front of him, shaking his head gloomily. Surely there was going to be more to it than this; he had not been invited simply to take part in a crying jag?

"Jane told me you had some sort of a proposition," he said.

Wilcox nodded solemnly. But instead of answering he asked, "Has it occurred to you to wonder why I came back to Europe?"

"Up to a point. I presumed it was your own business——"

Wilcox went on as if he had not spoken. "I came here at great personal sacrifice—and expense too, if it comes to that. I had jobs offered to me in the United States—plenty of jobs. I turned them down. I came here—on my own money——" Was it, perhaps, Marshall wondered momentarily, no more than an elaborate prelude to a request for a loan? Wilcox, not yet too far gone in whisky to observe the expression on his face, waved a hand impatiently. "But that's not the point. I came back because I was mad at the way I'd been treated—I wasn't prepared to just let it go. Also, I was convinced that there was something wrong."

"In what way?"

Wilcox flopped back in his chair. "Well," he said, "when you look at it, there was always something phony about this particular deal.

So much fuss and trouble over a few hundred dollars. Didn't that occur to you?"

"Why, yes. In a way that was one of the worst features——"

"Oh, sure. But why is Kingham prepared to put himself in the wrong over so little? Just obstinacy?" He shook his head. "He's not that obstinate."

"Furac——"

"Exactly. The important thing is to lay off Furac. Furac is a genius. Everybody should be kind to him at all costs. And, after all, when you consider the business situation, you can see their point of view. In England and Germany and Scandinavia we can hardly break even. But in France we can sell all we want—at our own price. How do you explain that?"

"I don't know. It was one of the things I couldn't understand. I asked Gilbertson——"

"Yes. So did I. And I couldn't get any sense out of him." Wilcox said triumphantly, "Now I know why. I discovered recently that those instruments we sell in France don't stay there very long. They're re-exported."

"Where to?"

Wilcox hesitated. It was as if at the last moment he was reluctant to part with his secret. Finally he said, "Eastern Germany."

There was a long silence.

Wilcox threw away his half-smoked cigarette and lit another. The air was heavy with smoke. They could hear movements through the thin wall separating them from the next room. A motor bicycle coughed its way noisily up Southampton Row. Marshall said, "I take it you have some proof of this?"

"Of course." Wilcox regarded him with slight amusement. Then he walked toward the bed and picked up the telephone.

"Five-fifteen," he said.

A moment later Marshall could hear the telephone ring in the next room—the wall was little more than a plywood partition.

"Okay, honey," Wilcox said into the telephone, "you can come in now."

CHAPTER III

SHE WAS much the same as he had remembered her from their meeting in Paris. If anything, her face was a little paler, her expression even less trusting. Wilcox closed the door and showed her to a chair with exaggerated courtliness, like a lawyer with a star witness. He himself sat down on the bed.

"You've met Louise Verrier before, I think."

"Yes." To her, Marshall said, "I was planning to visit you in Paris in a few days' time. Though not with very good news, I'm afraid."

She was not surprised. "I did not expect it. Mr. Wilcox told me you had been unsuccessful."

"I'm afraid so. I can assure you," Marshall said earnestly, "that I tried my very best——"

"Yes." Her acknowledgment was perfunctory. She had never, at the best of times, been a very gracious person. "Thank you so much."

"Louise understands," Wilcox cut in. "I explained the position to her." He touched her reassuringly on the shoulder. His attitude was curiously proprietary—did the adjacent rooms have any special significance? "As I told her, this is a tough fight. You have to use everything you've got, otherwise you don't stand a chance. Isn't that so?" He looked challengingly at Marshall, as if trying to lead him toward some sort of admission. When he received no answer he went on, "It was Louise who put me onto this. I found that she had, without knowing it, a piece of very valuable information."

"What was that?"

In a dull voice, as if repeating a lesson, Louise said, "It was after you left. They sent André's clothes and belongings back in a parcel from the hospital. In his wallet I found a bill from a hotel in Zurich, made out to someone called Girard. I couldn't understand it because we knew nobody called Girard, and so far as I knew André had never been to Zurich. I checked on the date and found that it was at a time when he had told me he was going to Bordeaux." She said dispassionately, "Naturally I thought at first it was a woman. . . . But the hotel was most expensive, far more than he could ever have afforded, and there was a charge of sixty Swiss francs for dinner. Across it, in André's handwriting, was scribbled—'Wenner.' I thought about it for a while, but I still couldn't think of an explanation. So when Mr. Wilcox came I showed it to him."

"It didn't make much sense to me either, at first," said Wilcox, "but I thought it worth while going to Zurich to find out. We took a photograph of Verrier with us, and the hotel people identified him straightaway as Girard. So then we made some inquiries about Wenner."

"He was an agent?"

Wilcox nodded. "It was too easy really. One of our boys from the American consulate told me over a few drinks that they'd been watching him for years on account of this kind of thing, but they couldn't get the Swiss to co-operate." He explained cheerfully, "He told me it's a pretty well-known game. Quite a lot of prohibited materials are going across that way. You pass it through several different companies. Most of them have big-sounding names, but they're just dummies when you come down to it. They change the packing and labels and hand it over to an exporting agency with connections in Switzerland. Of course if it comes out—you're horrified. You didn't know a thing about that."

"And Verrier?"

"You have to have *some* direct connection—to make arrangements about advance shipments, methods of payment, and so on. You can do it yourself—or you may think it safer, for routine messages anyway, to use a runner."

"So Verrier was the runner?"

"He must have been."

"And did he know——"

"I am sure he knew," Louise broke in. "I noticed he grew more depressed after each time he went away. He was brooding about it." She added with conviction, "That was why he killed himself."

Wilcox said, "It sounds reasonable, doesn't it? After all, he was that kind of person——"

"Was he?" Marshall asked, almost to himself. "I never knew him."

So this, he thought, was Verrier, the little man, the victim . . . He looked up and saw that Wilcox was holding out a slip of paper toward him.

"The hotel bill." When Marshall had looked at it, Wilcox said, "Are you convinced?"

"I suppose so."

"Good," he said with satisfaction. The first phase of his project had been accomplished. "The next thing is—are you prepared to do something about it?"

Marshall frowned. There was something rather odd in the way Wilcox had expressed himself. "But this is your discovery—don't you want to handle it yourself?"

Wilcox shook his head. "It wouldn't be too easy for me," he explained. "For one thing, I've left the company. An affair like this has to be handled at top level, and I haven't the contacts." He seemed to realize himself that this was a lame excuse. "Also, there's something else——"

"What?" Marshall was immediately wary.

"You'll notice that this hotel bill connects Wenner with Verrier, not Furac. That was the whole point of sending Verrier. Furac will obviously say that he knows nothing about the deals, that Verrier was fixing them himself on a commission basis or something. Everybody else who's been implicated will want to blame Verrier too, especially since he's dead. They might easily get away with it."

Marshall thought for a moment. "Maybe," he agreed. "But that's a risk we have to take. There seems to be no alternative."

"There is," Wilcox said, leaning forward. When Marshall made no reply, he went on, "On the second of every month a letter comes

through from Paris to Gilbertson marked 'Private and Confidential.' Nobody else has ever looked at one of those letters and nobody knows where they're filed. It's reasonable to suppose that they contain details about trading in France which Gilbertson doesn't want anyone else to see." He paused. "I'd very much like to have a look at one of those reports."

"Well, so would I, but——"

"Next Friday," went on Wilcox, "is the second of the month. The mail arrives at nine-thirty and Gilbertson doesn't get in until ten. It would be very easy for somebody with access to the correspondence to remove that letter." He said deliberately, "And Jane Lancing is now Gilbertson's secretary."

Marshall recoiled. "Oh no, for God's sake——"

Wilcox shrugged his shoulders. "That's your proof. It's not the nicest way to get it, I'll agree, but it's the only way. After all," he said persuasively, "you've got to remember how serious this is. These people are practically traitors. Do you suppose the FBI would hesitate to open this mail?"

"I'm not the FBI."

"No. But you have certain duties as a citizen."

He was repelled by Wilcox's obvious insincerity. "Don't let's get too damn virtuous about it."

"All right." The appeal to patriotism, Wilcox realized, had been a mistake. "Then don't do it," he said. "Hold onto your virginity. Let them beat you again."

There was a silence. Marshall could feel the tension as Wilcox waited for him to speak. Madame Verrier looked at him with a detached, almost contemptuous interest. Eventually he said, "Did you speak to Jane about this the night you met her outside the subway?"

"Yes."

So that was why she had seemed to be holding something back. "What did she say?"

"She wouldn't do it."

"Well, then——"

"Not for me, that is." He added significantly, "But she'd do it for you."

"Did she say so?"

"No. But I could tell."

He knew now why Wilcox needed him so badly. He said, partly to gain time, partly because he needed to know, "Tell me something. What are you hoping to get out of this?"

"Nothing unreasonable." He said with sudden passion, "All I want is to be back where I was before this thing began—with a good job, some prospects, money in the bank. Why, I've spent two thousand dollars already on this trip alone——"

"I'll cover that."

"I don't want it from you. I want it from the company. Can't you understand that?"

"Yes."

In this, at least, he realized, Wilcox was sincere—he wanted more than money. It was something harder to get than money, something that required more than a signature on the bottom of a check. A form of rough justice—that right should prevail and the wicked be defeated. It was what he himself wanted too, to be justified, to taste victory, just this once. But there was a price to pay. He knew in his heart that Wilcox was correct—if he asked her, Jane would take the letter. But he could not bring himself to take the step.

"I don't know," he said after a little thought. "I'm not sure that I'm justified——"

"Now don't get things out of proportion," said Wilcox with obvious anxiety. "After all, it's only a letter——"

"No, it's not just a letter." He was not certain whether he would do it or not, but at least he wouldn't fool himself. It might be necessary perhaps. He could not persuade himself it was unimportant.

"I agree that nobody likes to open another man's mail. But surely, in the circumstances——"

Marshall looked at him. Was it any use to try to explain? Wilcox had been educated in the same school as the rest of them. When you had a chance, you took it. When you gained an advantage, you exploited it. When you scored a victory, you looked around for a way to extend it. There was no other law. The only difference was that Wilcox was down while the others were up.

He said slowly: "This isn't simply a question of opening mail.

Gilbertson treated me as his friend. He entertained me at his house. Now I'm asked to steal his private correspondence and use it as evidence to destroy him. Worse still, I'm to use somebody else——" He stopped, unable to speak to Wilcox of his feelings for Jane. But the question was insistent within him. Was he prepared to make use of her love for him to corrupt her loyalty, to persuade her to violate a trust? Could the circumstances justify that? So far, his hands were clean. It was the advantage he had over Furac, Gilbertson, Kingham, all of them. It was not an easy thing to throw it away. If he refused, he could tell himself that he had retained his integrity. But what else would he retain?

He got up from his chair. He had a sudden conviction that it would be impossible to make any sane decision in this small fetid room. He needed to make contact with the world outside, to talk to ordinary people who led sensible, balanced lives, free of ambition and bitterness and revenge. From them he might be able to absorb some fragment of simple knowledge, some sense of the prosaic decencies of life. It might become plain to him what was right and virtuous; he might be able to recognize his own motives, to distinguish scruples from cowardice, a genuine desire for justice from mere pugnacity.

"I can't make up my mind just now," he said. "I'll let you know tomorrow."

CHAPTER IV

WHEN HE LEFT THE HOTEL he began to walk in what he vaguely presumed was the right direction. The fresh air cleared his head without giving him any clue to the solution of his problems.

There was, it seemed to him, no solution which did not involve some form of debasement. They said power corrupted. If that was all, it would not matter; he had little desire for power. But there was more to it than that. He realized now that a sacrifice of integrity could be demanded not merely by ambition but by even the simplest and most well-meaning course of effective action. If he was to defeat corruption he must be prepared, to some degree at any rate, to become corrupt himself, to cheat and steal and exploit the affection of those who cared for him. Yet the alternative was to refuse all action, to do nothing and be nothing, to accept a life of idleness and futility. Was there much virtue in that?

He passed through streets he didn't know, narrow clefts between lines of seedy houses, coffee bars, Indian restaurants, bookshops overflowing onto the pavement. Every so often the sound of jazz would come bursting out of a basement—Nick's Club—Late-night Jiving—Skiffle Alley—the buildings above seemed to shiver and vibrate, but resignedly, like an old person with an uncontrollable tremor in one limb. Outside the doors the fat, corseted prostitutes stood and gossiped, the barrow boys shouted the price of oranges, the three-card men sold packets which might contain pound notes

for half-a-crown a time. On a corner an old woman peddled wilted violets out of a basket.

This was not New York, where a simple exercise in mathematics could always tell you where you were and how far from home. Sometimes the streets here curved almost imperceptibly, so that you started going south and came out facing west; sometimes they ended unexpectedly against a blank wall or in a large deserted square, as a river might suddenly widen into a lake with islands and half a dozen confusing exits. He was lost. He could ask some-one—they were always ready to tell you the way—but somehow he could not bring himself to do so. They seemed so utterly oc-cupied in their own pursuits. He felt that if he spoke they would not hear him; they might pass by, unconscious of his existence, leaving him even more alone than before.

He halted on a corner, a little tired from so much walking, un-certain which way to go. Someone opened the door of a public house. Inside he saw a long bar, bright lights, a haze of smoke. Bursts of conversation and laughter came to him through the open door. It sounded warm and companionable—he felt a longing for human society. People walked into these places, ordered a glass of beer or spirits, got talking to others, and made friends; for a time, at least, they had a place in life, they were no longer alone. On impulse he walked in to the bar and ordered a whisky. It tasted sickly and lukewarm. Did one give a tip to the barman in a place like this? he wondered. Americans were always in trouble abroad—either they gave too much, in an effort to be popular, or else they turned morbidly suspicious and got into arguments about pennies.

A small man in a greasy hat and a threadbare overcoat stood be-side him at the bar. He took his face out of a pint glass and said, "American?"

"Yes."

"You haven't much of an accent." It was presumably intended to be a compliment.

"I was educated partly over here."

"Ah!" Everything was clear now. "I had a cousin who married a GI. Went to live in Chicago. You been there?"

"Once or twice."

"Finkel, his name was. I don't suppose you've ever run across him?"

"I'm afraid not."

"We used to pull her leg about it. Mrs. Finkel." He laughed reminiscently. It was obviously a treasured family joke. "But not in any unpleasant way, mind you. What I say is, we're all brothers under the skin, no matter who our fathers may be. Isn't that right?"

It was always the same, he thought. You had the idea that it would be nice to talk to somebody, and then when it happened they bored you to death. It was like those animated conversations the French and Italians went in for. If you didn't understand them they sounded vivacious and exciting and you envied them. When it came down to it they were probably just discussing the stock market or the price of vegetables.

"I said to her, 'You watch out you don't get mixed up with any of them gangsters out there——'"

Now he was stuck with this little guy. But you couldn't be rude and walk out on him. Perhaps buy him a drink and then say you had to be somewhere in a hurry. . . .

"What are you drinking?"

The little man looked distastefully at his glass. "I was having mild-and-bitter—but it's poor stuff here." He repeated his eager, shifty smile. It was worth a try-on. "To be sociable, I'll have the same as you."

"Two large whiskies."

The barman put the drinks in front of them.

"Well," said the little man, "here's to the Star-Spangled Banner."

When they put their glasses down, Marshall saw the barman regarding them sardonically. Another American sucker taken for a free drink. So much for life, for the good, simple, human folks with their instinctive courtesy and sense of values. So much for the good-fellowship of the English pub. It had been a mistake to come into the place at all.

"Going already?" said the little man with obvious disappointment.

"I'm afraid so." He tossed a ten-shilling note on the counter. "Have another one on me."

By the time he got back to the flat it was almost midnight. But the thought of going to bed was intolerable to him; certainly there would be no chance of sleep for the next hour or two. On an impulse he picked up the phone and asked for his mother's number. While he waited he poured himself a drink but didn't finish it; the taste reminded him of his experience in the bar. He chain-smoked cigarettes and tried to get his ideas into perspective. But the same propositions, the same alternatives presented themselves. There was nothing further to argue about with himself. He needed some new internal voice, beyond argument, to give him the conviction of what he must do.

The telephone rang.

"Is that you, Mother?"

"Yes, dear. Is everything all right?"

"Yes, fine. I just thought I'd like to speak to you, that's all."

"That was very sweet of you, dear." She was pleased, but obviously puzzled. "It's good to hear your voice. How are things in London?"

"Pretty much the same."

"When will you be coming back home?"

"I'm not sure."

"Jeff said——"

The mention of his brother's name made him irritable. It was a reminder of the bad days in New York. "Never mind about Jeff."

"I think he was only trying to be helpful. He's anxious that you shouldn't get involved in any more trouble——"

"Oh, is he?" Had Jeff known? he suddenly wondered. Had they all known about Furac and Wenner and the rest of it when he was allowing them to walk all over him in New York? God, if they had . . .

There must have been something odd about his tone of voice. His mother said, "Chris, are you *sure* everything's all right?"

"Why do you keep asking that?"

"I don't know. You sound so strange——"

"Strange?"

"Yes. Not like yourself at all." He waited for her to say more,

but she said, "I can't explain on the telephone. Come and see me as soon as you get back, won't you?"

"Of course."

There was nothing more to say, except how was Jeff and how was Paula and the children, and was Virgie's rheumatism acting up again? He hadn't made the call for that. He wondered, when it came down to it, why he *had* made it. Some vague instinctive hope of support, perhaps an absurd reversion to the days when he had clutched at his mother's hand in a crowd for fear of being swept away.

As if she had read his thought, she said, "Chris darling."

"Yes."

"Don't worry too much about what happened in New York. Jeff told me all about it." Trust Jeff, he thought. "I know it must have been terrible for you——"

"I'm over it now."

"That's good." Vaguely she said, "After all, success isn't everything——"

She continued talking, trying to reassure him with platitudes of which he heard nothing. He had heard them so often, the excuses, the consolations for failure. He remembered Madame Verrier talking of her husband. He remembered her voice, a mixture of pity and contempt. "André was a failure. And when a man is a failure, failure is the most important thing about him. To love him, you have to love that."

He was there now. He had reached the end point of the reaction, the stage when judgment had grown tired and one emotional truth was stronger than a whole world of logic. He was in the grip of inevitability, of the thing that must be done.

He waited impatiently for his mother to ring off. As soon as she had done so, he picked up the telephone again and dialed Jane's number. It was late, but he had no doubt that she would answer.

CHAPTER V

"So THIS is where you live?"

"Yes."

Wilcox walked over to the window and looked out at the view over St. James's Square. "Better than the Drax."

"Yes." Marshall wanted to forget the Drax. "Why don't you move somewhere else?"

"It's cheap."

"Send the bill to me. I'm financing the operation from now on." Before Wilcox could say anything, he went on, "And you don't have to feel indebted. I shall get it back from the company."

"What about Louise?"

"Take her with you. Unless she's in a hurry to go back to Paris."

"I think she'd rather stay here—for the moment——"

"That's fine." So his suspicions had been correct—Wilcox was playing around with her. Marshall was, if anything, pleased at the discovery. From this point onward Wilcox was likely to be more of a liability than an asset—his drunken quarrelsome presence would be an embarrassment in New York. If he could be persuaded to stay in Europe with his mistress on a generous expense account, that would be an ideal arrangement.

Wilcox looked at his watch. "How soon will Jane be here?"

"Soon, I hope. She should have arrived at the office now. The first thing she does is to sort the mail. There may be nothing from Paris, of course, though she tells me it's pretty well invariable. If

the letter's there she'll get out as soon as she can and bring it to us here."

"Supposing it isn't?"

"She'll get through on the telephone."

"In that case, if she doesn't telephone within five or ten minutes, we know she's got it."

"Not necessarily. Sometimes the mail comes late. Or she may have difficulty getting privacy for the call. We shall have to be patient."

It was curious how, once the decision had been taken, his relations with Wilcox had changed. Now he was in charge. Wilcox did not resent his leadership; indeed, he seemed actually to welcome it as a relief from responsibility. It was as if the effort of having carried the project so far had exhausted him. The more Marshall saw of him, the more obvious it became that Wilcox could have gone no farther without help. That night at the Drax he had emptied his pockets and thrown everything he had left onto the board.

Now he had the air, not of the initiator of the scheme, but of a nervous and not exceptionally reliable supporter. Looking at the tremulous, nicotine-stained fingers, the slightly bloodshot eyes, Marshall knew he was committed, if successful, to restoring Wilcox to a place of responsibility in the company equivalent to the one he had held. In fairness, he was entitled to it. Who could tell whether his present state was a consequence of the treatment he had received or whether it would have been inevitable anyway? You had to give him the benefit of the doubt—he might improve when his grievance was removed. If he didn't, that would be too bad. No firm could be expected to carry him forever.

"You think we can rely on her?"

"Yes."

"So do I." Wilcox clenched his hands together. "She's a wonderful girl. I have the greatest confidence—— She'll fix it all right, don't worry."

To whom was he talking, thought Marshall—himself? Some imaginary prospect? That was the way it was if you were a salesman. Selling wasn't just talking to a man about a thing you wanted to

buy, it was a state of mind, a form of prayer. "Sell yourself first. Be convinced. Believe in yourself—and believe in the product. Then you can start talking." Being convinced could become a sort of habit, an end in itself, so that the object of your convictions could be changed conveniently from day to day as circumstances demanded. Marshall had always been a little baffled by salesmen—he tended to overestimate their transient enthusiasms. They stalked their objectives with the ferocious intensity of a kitten attacking a ball of wool—but, like the kitten, they were easily distracted.

Wilcox went on, "Did she make much difficulty about doing it?"

Marshall shook his head. He did not want to discuss Jane with Wilcox. She had made what Wilcox would have considered no difficulty at all. She had required no persuasion. But that did not mean that she was in favor of the act. It meant simply that she knew he was likely to ask her and had decided beforehand what her answer would be. It had not occurred to her to bargain with her acquiescence. She had not waited to be coaxed or bribed or reassured. She had simply said, "You want me to do it?"

"I don't want to put pressure on you. Only if you feel justified——"

"No," she had said decisively. "That's not for me—I don't know anything about justification. I don't know about law or politics or anything like that. I wouldn't do it for anyone else. If I do it," she had said, echoing Wilcox's words, "I'll do it for you. But you'll have to ask me."

He was ashamed of his attempt to retreat from responsibility, to involve her in his decision.

"I'm asking you," he had said.

He heard footsteps on the stairs which he recognized as hers. A moment later she walked into the room. She was wearing her neat secretary's clothes, the black skirt, the white crisply laundered blouse—it was the way he had first seen her. She was carrying the leather hold-all she usually took to the office. Without a word she picked an envelope out of her handbag and handed it to him.

He looked at the Paris stamp, the label "Personal and Confidential." He had imagined the situation and had known it must be like this, but even so, it seemed a terrible thing to open another

man's private correspondence. This, more than cruelty or jobbery or fraud, was a breach of all the conventions, a resort to the law of the jungle.

Wilcox was watching him intently but, with unusual tact, said nothing. Marshall hesitated slightly, holding onto the moment, the last seconds of a life which would never return to him. At least, he thought, he owed it this much, to remember exactly how it ended. Then he tore across the flap of the envelope.

Now he was a professional, like the others. He had lost something, it was true, but he consoled himself that the loss was inevitable. This was merely the final stage in a process of growing up which had taken away from him, one after the other, his childhood hopes, his confidence in his artistic genius, his respect for his father, his belief in God. Now his personal honor had been discarded, like an old handsome suitcase, admirable in its way, but too heavy for a fast flight.

He read the letter and passed it over. On Wilcox's face anxiety turned to relief, then to triumph.

"This is it, all right."

"Yes."

"Just what we want. He mentions Wenner's name three times—did you notice? That should take some explaining——"

Excitement had made him voluble. Marshall heard the sound of his voice without listening to the words. He asked himself, what did he feel? This was a big moment, after all—but he seemed to feel nothing. He had the means to win now, the weapon of destruction. It had been necessary and he did not regret it. Yet when Wilcox returned the letter to him he had to brace himself to touch it.

He felt an absolute necessity to get rid of Wilcox as soon as possible.

"I think the first thing we must do," he said, "is to make some copies of this as quickly as possible. Then we can put the original away in a safe-deposit." He took the cover off the portable typewriter on the desk. "Jane could do that now. The other thing is to notify Madame Verrier——"

"She's back at the hotel," said Wilcox. "I can ring her there."

As he moved toward the telephone Marshall said, "I thought you might prefer to tell her personally. . . ."

Wilcox put the telephone down. He looked from Marshall to Jane and said easily, "Okay, I can take a hint. We can talk about the details later. I'll ring you from my new hotel." He picked up his hat and nodded to Jane. "You did a wonderful job, honey." She said nothing. "See you."

When he had gone she said without expression, "I'll do those copies for you now."

"There's no hurry. I only said that to get rid of Wilcox."

"Oh, I see." She looked down at the letter lying on the desk where he had dropped it. "Well, that's it, isn't it? You've got what you needed. Everything's wonderful." With a rather forced cheerfulness she asked, "What will you do now?"

"Go back to New York. With this, they'll have to take notice of me."

"And Madame Verrier will get her money and Wilcox will get his job back—— Do you think it will do him any good, in the end?"

"He'll have his chance. He may be able to straighten himself out once this is over." He said impatiently, "Let's forget about Wilcox for the moment."

"All right." She picked up her hold-all from the floor and began to fumble in it for a packet of cigarettes. The bag was bulging with assorted objects—shoes, boxes of face powder, a tin of coffee, a brush and comb. "I had to bring all my stuff from the office," she explained. "I can hardly go back there."

"Of course not. But don't worry about that——"

"I wasn't worrying. I was tired of Gilbertson anyway." She lit her cigarette and sat down. "Don't look so solemn," she said. "You're wearing a face like a funeral."

"I hated myself for asking you to do this," he said unhappily.

"You mustn't let it get you down." She was determinedly cheerful. "I didn't enjoy it much myself. In fact, I felt worse about it than almost anything I've ever done. But it's done now—no use worrying about it any more."

"I *used* you," he said bitterly. It was, he remembered, the one fault he had never been able to forgive his father. It was just pos-

sible to accept the others—the lies, the tricks, the bluster and bragging, the bogus good-fellowship. Only this had seemed to him unforgivable—that love and loyalty should be treated as expendable assets, to be cashed as the occasion demanded.

She took his hand in hers, squeezing it gently in an effort at consolation. Her fingers were small, the nails neat and sensible. She wore a small ring, an onyx in the center of a circle of tiny diamonds. The onyx was chipped, the setting a little out of date. "Of course you used me," she said. "We always use the people who are fond of us. We're right to do so."

"No——" he protested.

"Yes. Because they ask for it. They want it. It gives them the sense of being needed." She looked up at him, as if perplexed by his simplicity. "Surely you understand that?"

He knew that she was wrong—his sense of having betrayed her remained. He said, excusing himself, "It had to be done. There was no other way. You do see that, don't you? With this letter we can't lose. It means the end of Furac—and Kingham as well, for that matter. We can wrap up the whole affair——"

"And then?"

Then, he thought, he would really have earned his freedom. He would be able to escape at last from those constant personal struggles, the detestable expedients. For five years he had stayed with the organization as a man might cling to a stick for fear of being unable to walk without it. When this affair was concluded he would have discharged all obligations, to himself or others. He could carry on alone. "That'll be the end as far as I'm concerned," he said. "I've had enough of them all. I shall walk out."

"Ahead of the game?" she said with slight irony.

"Yes. I suppose that's what I mean."

"And do what?"

"I'm not sure. I'll think of something." Perhaps he might go back to Paris and try painting again. Perhaps—— Now there seemed to be a hundred possibilities. "But first we'll take it easy for a while—go away for a holiday——"

"We?"

"Yes." He stopped walking and looked at her. "I want you to marry me, Jane."

There was a silence. She regarded him gravely and then shook her head. "No."

Her reply astonished him. It had never occurred to him that there was any chance of a refusal. "Why not?"

"Because—well——" She seemed to search desperately for some way of expressing herself. "Because I don't really know what sort of a person you are."

"But you must know me pretty well by now——"

"No, I don't really. Sometimes I haven't the least idea of how you're thinking or why you do things. Though I've grown to like you very much and I suppose I can even say that I'm in love with you, the idea of marriage frightens me somehow. You're still a foreigner to me in some ways, and I have a feeling that in America you might seem even more so."

"America isn't so different from here."

"Isn't it?" she said unbelievingly.

"No. People are pretty much the same wherever you go."

"I don't even believe that," she said sadly. "You see how it is, we disagree already."

"You said you were in love with me," he pointed out. He was almost pleading—the idea of going back home without her was unthinkable. "That must mean something. Why don't you give yourself some time to think about it? Come over with me when I go to New York. You can see how things are over there. If it doesn't work out, you can either get a job in the States or come back to England, whichever suits you." When she hesitated, he said, "For God's sake, what can you lose?"

"Nothing I haven't as good as lost already, I suppose," she admitted.

"So there you are. You can have a good time; get around. We could go and stay with my mother in Connecticut. She'd love to have you."

She laughed. "Getting the once-over from Mom. It sounds frightening. What is she like?"

"It's difficult for me to say." He became hesitant. How to de-

scribe his mother? He said inadequately, "I think she should appeal to you. She's very unpossessive. When I was younger I used to resent that sometimes. I wanted her to be more dependent on me. If she had been, of course, I should have spent my time struggling to get free."

"Yes, of course." A man never changed, she thought, in his attitude toward women—mother, mistress, wife, it was always the same. She asked, "Does she live alone?"

"Yes, except for an old colored couple and a local girl——"

She laughed. "In one of the big white colonial houses made of timber, with a paddock and a little lake——"

"Something like that. How did you know?"

"I go to the pictures. But it's no use trying to persuade me that those houses really exist. I'm fully prepared to find you're lying. When I get there I shall find it's just a tin shanty on the wrong side of the tracks. That's what happens to young girls who marry Americans."

He smiled. "So you'll come—if only to show me up?"

"All right."

He put his arms around her and was just about to kiss her when the telephone rang.

"Damn!" He picked up the receiver. "Who is it?"

"Mr. Marshall?" It was a girl's voice. "One moment, please." There was a click. "You're through now, Mr. Gilbertson."

"Is that you Marshall?" The well-known, languid voice carried more authority on the telephone when one couldn't actually see him. Marshall felt a spasm of nausea.

"Yes. How are you?"

"Excellent, thank you." There was a slight pause. The voice went on, bland as ever, "Excuse my asking, but you don't have my secretary with you by any chance, do you?"

He felt himself blushing. He was a child again, caught in the act of some petty but humiliating crime. He tried to answer casually.

"Yes, she's here."

"Would you mind asking her to come to the phone?"

He hesitated. He had not fully prepared himself for this situation.

He glanced at Jane's face—her eyes were bright with alarm. "I'm sorry, that's not possible."

"Why not?" Gilbertson's voice was suddenly curt, military. "Is she afraid to speak to me?"

"If you have anything to say, you can say it to me. She acted under my instructions."

"She did *what*—under your instructions?"

"You must know, or you wouldn't have called me up."

"Naturally I know. I just wondered," said Gilbertson contemptuously, "whether you would have the courage to admit it. You told her to steal my confidential correspondence?"

"One letter only."

"On what authority?" When Marshall did not reply he went on, "Does Miss Lancing realize I can prosecute her for theft?"

"She realizes you won't." Marshall made an effort to pull himself together. He was getting the worst of this. "My recommendation is that you forget about your secretary's position and think about your own."

"Meaning what?"

"For God's sake, you don't want me to talk about it on the telephone, do you?"

There was quite a long silence. He could imagine Gilbertson at the other end of the line struggling to control his anger, to remember his wife, his country house, his son who in a year or two would be going up to Oxford. When he spoke at last, it was obvious that self-discipline had triumphed.

"Perhaps," he said with only slight distaste, "the best thing would be for us to meet and discuss the matter."

"If you like. Though I wouldn't like you to think that you can influence me in any way——"

"Perhaps not. But at least you'll be able to give me an explanation of your behavior. I think I'm entitled to that."

He would have to meet Gilbertson, if only because the prospect was so repellent to him; it was necessary to prove his own courage and determination before facing the storm which awaited him in New York.

"All right, I'll meet you. When will be convenient?"

"Not today, I'm afraid. I'm extremely busy." Not too busy for this, surely. But time was needed. Time to ring Furac, Kingham, to give the advance news of the attack, the fall of the first outpost, to confer on methods of defense. "Tomorrow I'm free."

"That's Saturday," said Marshall.

"Yes. Could you manage to come out to my place? We can talk in peace there."

He was about to insist that Gilbertson come and see him. Then he rejected the idea. The strength was his, and he must be generous. The least he could do was to allow his opponent the choice of ground.

"Very well. I'll come out tomorrow evening."

"We could manage," said Gilbertson with obvious reluctance, "to give you some dinner."

"No, thanks." He was definite. The thought of a meal with the Gilbertsons under present circumstances was unbearable. "I'll come out afterward."

Gilbertson did not press the invitation.

"Good. There's an excellent train from Waterloo at eight o'clock. Will that be convenient?"

"Yes—fine."

"I'll arrange to have you met at the station. . . ."

CHAPTER VI

THE LITTLE STATION was almost deserted when he got off the train. Down at the other end of the platform there was a woman waiting. As she approached him in the gathering twilight he saw that it was Mrs. Gilbertson.

"Charles asked me to apologize for him," she said. "He would have come himself but he had to go over and see one of our neighbors. Some argument about a fence and some cows."

"You shouldn't have bothered. I could have got a taxi."

"I doubt it. We have only one and he's usually drunk on Saturday nights." She gave her nervous, abrupt laugh. He suspected that the drunken taxi driver was a source of satisfaction rather than annoyance to her; these bucolic inconveniences made her feel closer to the realities of country life. "What a pity," she said rapidly as they got into the car, "that you can't stay over the weekend. Perhaps another time . . ."

"I'm afraid I shall be going back very soon."

"Yes, of course." The invitation, he realized, had not been seriously meant. It was just the sort of thing one always said, the reflex of a hostess. How much had Gilbertson told her? he wondered. He noticed no difference in her manner from the last time they had met—if anything, it was a little less formal, because now he was no longer a stranger. But that might mean nothing with people of this kind. She might be hating him, despising him, fearing him. He would not know.

They drove in silence for some time. Occasionally he glanced at her face. It was tense and strained, but that might be due to the effort of guiding the big car down the narrow country lanes. She drove erratically, crouching over the wheel and occasionally having trouble with the gears. Eventually, as if feeling her social obligations again, she said:

"I don't think you met either of my children when you visited us before."

"No. They were at school."

"James is away at some camp or other, playing at soldiers. But Gillian's home from school." She made a harassed gesture. "Now, of course, we haven't the remotest idea what to do with her."

"Has she no ideas herself?"

"Well, you know what girls are at that age—heads full of nonsense. They all want to be fashion models."

She stopped the car in front of the house. There was a young girl standing on the terrace, fresh and attractive in a shirt and tan-colored slacks.

"This is Mr. Marshall, dear."

"How do you do, Mr. Marshall." She shook hands dutifully, but her eyes were impatient. Parents were exasperating. They insisted on keeping you hanging about to meet their friends, people you didn't care about and who couldn't possibly care about you—business friends, Americans, usually about a hundred years old and as dull as ditchwater. She had done her bit. Then she turned back to her mother.

"Mummy," she said eagerly, "the Dawsons just rang up. They're going to a dance in Guildford. Can I go with them?"

"Well, I don't know——"

"Oh, Mummy, *please* . . ."

She stood there, fidgeting impatiently. Plainly, both Marshall and her mother existed in her mind merely as obstacles to her pleasure. Marshall remembered the old rule that to establish ascendancy one should always seem to be in more of a hurry than the other fellow. The young did it without effort or intention. Who has less time to spare than a girl of seventeen waiting to go out on a date?"

"Have you asked your father?"

"He's not back yet. I said I thought it would be all right."

"Well, I suppose so. But you can't go in those clothes."

"I can change in a second." She was already halfway up the stairs.

"Well, don't be too late. . . ." Mrs. Gilbertson looked apologetically at Marshall. "They're always chasing off here and there."

He smiled back, the sort of smile that older people gave. But the smile was false, and he was aware of a stab of wounded vanity because the girl had so obviously found him uninteresting. Could he really seem so old to her? he asked himself. He wanted to tell her that at least he was on her side. To him, too, most of the pretensions of adult life appeared as nothing better than an elaborate fraud. The young were right, he thought, in their instinctive distrust of authority. They watched the antics of their elders like savages confronted with the white man's magic—powerless, bored, suspicious without knowing why. Well, soon they would know why, as he did now. In time they would become part of the fraud themselves.

"You'll have a drink?" said Mrs. Gilbertson.

Always the drink, the scotch, the glass of sherry, the apéritif, the martini (very, very dry, you said, and the barman understood—he gave you straight gin with a twist of lemon floating in it). Nothing could be done without a drink, without the spurious air of friendliness that went with it. He accepted because he was afraid to alarm her; everybody knew that Americans drank all the time, and Mrs. Gilbertson might read something sinister into his refusal. And, indeed, his acceptance seemed to reassure her. She knew something was wrong, but it could not be as bad as all that if you could sit in friendly conversation over a drink on the terrace on a summer evening. She talked about her children. The boy was clever, he had won a scholarship, but shy and slow to make friends. Gillian was popular but scatterbrained. She had almost too many friends. Some of the boys were much older than she was. . . .

"So long as they don't get drunk and go driving around in cars . . . That's what worries me most. But she's a sensible girl at heart," she added with more faith than conviction. "It's no use denying it, children are a great responsibility—as well as a great expense." She had not talked of her children so much on his pre-

vious visit. Was this, he wondered, a roundabout way of appealing for sympathy, of throwing herself on his mercy? "You're not married, Mr. Marshall?"

"No."

"No, of course not." It was as if somehow she had held an irrational hope that he might be. "I remember you told us . . ."

Gilbertson came round the side of the house. He was dressed in the dilapidated tweeds he affected for weekends. What would happen, Marshall wondered, when they wore out completely? He could hardly wear new ones. Perhaps he arranged for them to be broken in by the gardener.

"Sorry I couldn't meet you, Marshall. I got caught up in an argument with a farmer——" He went into some detail about a minor boundary dispute which had been brought to a head by the incursion of a Jersey cow into his kitchen garden. It was a dull story, and even Gilbertson himself seemed to get bored with it after a while. But his code of manners obviously demanded that some pretense of general conversation should be made, even on an occasion like this. It would have been hard to say which of the three was the most ill at ease. Eventually Gilbertson said, "So there we are. Not that I suppose I shall be able to get a penny out of him when it comes down to it. . . ." He seemed suddenly weary of this pantomime of normal behavior. It was impossible for him to keep the anxiety out of his eyes, the deepened furrows of his face. "But perhaps we'd better get down to business. Would you like to come into my study?"

The study was quite a small room, rather dark and smelling of dust. In one corner there was a set of golf clubs, in another a pair of fishing rods. On the bookshelves were mainly sets of bound volumes—*Country Life, Chambers' Encyclopaedia* (1935), the *Waverley Novels*. Gilbertson cleared the front of the desk and then half sat, half leaned against it. He motioned Marshall to a leather club chair. The chair was deep, and when he sat down he found Gilbertson towering almost directly above him, looking down at him with his melancholy bloodhound face. Always before, he had thought of Gilbertson almost as a caricature, a man whose every action carried a slight touch of exaggeration and absurdity. But

now he was no longer ridiculous; in this moment of crisis he had acquired a sort of desperate dignity, an air bordering on menace.

They regarded each other in silence for a little while. Then Gilbertson said curtly:

"How is Miss Lancing?"

"Fine, thanks."

"I hope you're looking after her properly. She's deserved well of you." He added sourly, "I imagine the rates of pay are pretty high for work of that kind?"

Now that they were alone, it was evidently permissible to be offensive. Marshall could not help feeling sympathy for him. It was always a terrible thing to find oneself betrayed. He said with careful moderation, "Is that why you asked me to come here—to make cracks about Miss Lancing?"

Gilbertson shook his head, then half closed his eyes like a man who had felt a spasm of physical pain. "I trusted her," he said.

"I'm sorry." Marshall looked away. "Believe me, I'm sorry it had to be done."

"Is that considered enough?"

"I believe my action was justified by what I found in the letter," said Marshall stubbornly.

"Do you? I'm afraid you wouldn't find many people in this country to agree with you. By British law nobody has a right to open confidential letters—not even the police——"

"I know, I know," Marshall said wearily. "But let's be realistic. I've got the letter now, and you can't do a thing about it. You have to face the present situation." To save Gilbertson the indignity of asking, he added, "I should tell you that I know all about Furac's methods of doing business. We have a good deal of other information——"

"We?"

"Myself and Wilcox. Wilcox went to Zurich and made inquiries."

"I see." Gilbertson was silent for a moment. "Have you spoken to your superiors in New York about this?"

"Not yet."

"But you propose to do so, I take it?"

"Naturally."

"Did they know you were making these—investigations?"

"No. In fact, they've been doing their best to keep me in the States. But you know all this," he said impatiently. "There's a telephone line to New York. You must have spoken to Kingham yesterday."

After a moment's hesitation Gilbertson said, "We had a short conversation. He used some harsh words about you, as you can imagine."

"And what instructions did he give you?"

Marshall was ashamed as soon as he had spoken. It was a cheap taunt, but Gilbertson took no offense. He appeared to regard it rather as a fortunate opening for something he had to say.

"I'm interested," he said, "that you should put it like that. It confirms my suspicion that you have an oversimplified approach to this very complex situation." He spoke coldly and slightly patronizingly, master to pupil. "Please try to realize that I am not a puppet of Mr. Kingham's. Nor," he added, "have I the slightest desire to become involved in any of your faction fights in New York."

"Do you really think this is just a personal feud between myself and Kingham?"

"In that direction," said Gilbertson with feeling, "nothing would surprise me."

"I can assure you it isn't. And I'm afraid it's impossible for you to shrug your way out of it. This letter definitely shows you to be involved——"

"Have I denied it?" His voice held more exasperation than guilt. "Certainly I knew of these transactions. But I don't take responsibility for them. Why should I? They weren't my idea."

"Whose idea were they then?"

"Your father's."

Gilbertson was regarding him closely for his reaction. This, no doubt, was a shot he had been saving up. Don't fire till you see the whites of their eyes—then give it to them. . . . But he had misjudged his effect. Marshall was neither disconcerted nor even, on reflection, particularly surprised. He had not thought of his father as the initiator of the scheme, but once it was suggested to him, he was only too ready to believe it.

"That sounds plausible," he said. He felt the necessity to make his position clearer. "I should perhaps inform you that I have no great admiration for my father. So far as I was concerned——" He stopped himself. His family problems were no concern of Gilbertson's. "How did it start?" he asked.

Gilbertson levered himself off the desk, walked around it, and sat down in the chair behind. It was as if he had abandoned his first idea of dominating Marshall and was now prepared to try reason and explanation.

"It was after the war," he said, "that I first met him. I was trying to build up a business again. It wasn't easy—my old office had been destroyed by bombs and I'd been in the Far East for several years. But the people I used to know before I joined the Army were very helpful and I picked up a few small agencies, enough to pay my rent, but that was about all. Then one day your father walked in. He'd heard of me from a friend of mine in New York and he was looking for a distributor in England. We met a few times and he took a fancy to me. That was how he put it, anyway. He liked to think of himself as having an instinctive judgment of men. He was the sort of person——"

Marshall cut in, "I know what sort of a person he was."

There had been no pain, or practically none, on hearing that his father was dishonest. But this description of his petty vanities aroused a trace of some old, unsuspected loyalty. You could never completely eradicate the emotions of your youth. They remained within you like the germs of a forgotten sickness, dormant, walled off, yet still carrying a primitive flicker of life, ready to awake and return to the attack if the opportunity arose.

Gilbertson was saying, ". . . and, as you can imagine, the agency was attractive to me. We did very well at first. European industry hadn't had time to change over to peacetime production and we had a clear field. In fact, we did so well that I hadn't really time for the other agencies, and when your father suggested I should give them up I agreed. That made me dependent on Marshall's, of course, but it was obviously a decision one had to take sometime and I wasn't too worried. But a year later we ran into trouble. The wheels were beginning to turn again in Europe. And their costs

were lower than ours. They were prepared to do anything to get back into the market again. They cut down the price until we couldn't get anywhere near them. It seemed as if the only sensible thing for Marshall's to do was to pull out of the European market altogether. I wouldn't have been surprised. After all, they were making plenty at home and in other parts of the world. But your father wouldn't give up. Not because he gave a damn about me but because he'd gone into Europe against the advice of his Board. It seems they'd told him this would happen and he wouldn't take any notice. He was determined not to be proved wrong. He came over here and told me that he was going to find a way of making the European area pay—somehow. And he did. He found Furac."

He paused, remembering, and then went on, "Perhaps you can imagine the awkwardness of my own position when he told me what he was proposing to do. I was tied to him completely by this time and he knew it. If he withdrew the agency I was broke. You may think I should have done the big thing and told him to go to hell, but I didn't. It was an underhand proposition and I didn't like it, but I had my wife and children to think of. If it had been a British regulation we were breaking, I should probably have acted differently, but the way I looked at it, this was an American law and, if the Americans wanted to get around it, it was up to them. I wasn't the keeper of your father's conscience."

"So it didn't worry you?"

He said sharply, "I told you I didn't like it. But I don't feel ashamed." He showed his long teeth in the trace of a smile. "Not nearly so much as you do, I should imagine, for stealing my correspondence." He went on before Marshall had time to protest, "And don't tell me this might make all the difference in the next war. I know a great deal more about war than you do. I gave up six years of my life to the last one—while you people were making money."

"We fought too, you know."

"Eventually. Eventually. But please don't think I resent your good fortune. I'm just trying to point out your approach to this question is to some extent a function of your income. You can indulge in moral attitudes which I can't afford."

"That doesn't make the attitudes wrong."

Gilbertson did not reply. Suddenly Marshall grew impatient. This was getting them nowhere. "Hell," he said, "I can see your point of view. I'm not blaming you for what you did. But that's not the point. I just can't leave things to go on as they are."

Gilbertson hesitated for a moment, as if wondering whether, in spite of his inner convictions, there might be something to be gained from making one last attempt. When he spoke, the sour, contemptuous note had left his voice; he had decided to throw away the advantage given to him by Marshall's theft of the letter.

"Why not?" he said. "After all, who's losing by this? Ask yourself that." He leaned forward. "Marshall, I think I can talk sensibly to you. Many of your countrymen, if you don't mind my saying so, have a tendency to wrap up the facts of life in a cocoon of pompous verbiage and idealistic fluff. It's a vice of conquering nations—we went in for it a great deal in the days of Victoria. But when you're up against it you have to look at things as they are. Supposing some of these instruments *are* getting to Russia or China or wherever it is. Is that going to start a war? Is it going to affect the result of a war if one does start? Does it, in fact, make a damn bit of difference to the balance of power in the world? You know as well as I do that at any moment there might be a diplomatic shuffle or a lessening in tension or whatever they call it, and these things would be taken off the prohibited list. It just doesn't make sense."

"Not to us, maybe. But it's not for us to decide. If it's the law——"

"Your law—not mine."

"Sure. So it's for me to carry it out." When Gilbertson said nothing he added, "Believe me, I wish this didn't have to happen. I can see it means a great deal to you."

"It's my livelihood. Naturally"—he picked his words carefully; even now it would never do to sound melodramatic—"I'm deeply involved. I've spent twenty-five years trying to get back into the world I was born into. . . ."

In Marshall, sympathy struggled with incomprehension. This futile, obsessive attempt to put the clock back . . . Gilbertson was

a man of intelligence and ability, in spite of his affectations. How could he fail to realize the unreality of his ambition?

"Do you really think it was worth it?"

"My dear boy," said Gilbertson pityingly, "you don't do things because you think they are worth it. You don't estimate profit and loss in these matters. The future's a mystery—life is a jump in the dark. You jump in the direction you do, not because it's the sensible thing, but because you must. If you break your neck as a consequence, there's nothing to be done about it." It came to Marshall that Gilbertson knew perfectly well that his own ambitions were impractical and, to others, absurd. To him, it was Marshall who was childish in his demand for common sense in a world which had never been even remotely sensible. "Now it's your turn to jump. Do so by all means. But don't think that things will turn out as you expect. They never do."

There was a silence. Outside now it was quite dark. They could hear the sound of a train in the distance, puffing its way across the green fields toward the south coast. Gilbertson gave the impression of searching his mind for some other avenue of persuasion worth exploring. Finally he seemed to decide that there was none.

"You're quite determined to go ahead with this?" he said.

"Yes."

"Then there's no point in wasting time." He got up from his seat. He had retained his dignity, if nothing else. From now on, for him, there was no security in possessions, no pride of ownership, no confidence in the future; he had lost, but at least he had not abased himself unnecessarily. "No doubt you'd like to get back to London."

As they went into the hall, Mrs. Gilbertson came out of the drawing room. She was carrying a pair of spectacles in one hand and a book in the other. Marshall suddenly had a picture of her sitting alone, pretending to read, as she waited for the sound of their footsteps.

"All finished?" she said anxiously.

"Yes," said Gilbertson.

It was dark in the hall. She snapped on the light and looked at their faces. Then something seemed to happen quite suddenly

to her personality. She was no longer awkward and self-conscious, tortured by the desire to be correct. It was as if despair had made her drunk.

"And what are you going to do, Mr. Marshall?" she asked.

He had been asked this question so often before, sometimes with impatience, more often with a lukewarm, perfunctory interest, but never, until now, with fear. Always in the past the question had meant what was he going to do with himself? Now he disposed of the lives of others.

Before he could think of a tactful answer Gilbertson cut in, "I think Mr. Marshall's in rather a hurry for his train, Hilda. I can explain to you later——"

"There are plenty of trains," she said. Then she turned to Marshall. "Before you go I'd like to be sure you understand the situation. My husband may not have made it entirely clear to you because——" She hesitated. "Because he's too proud—he doesn't like to make a scene. And no more do I, but then somebody has to, don't they, if they see their whole life going——"

"Hilda!"

"Please let me speak." Her eyes were still on Marshall. "I don't understand you people. You come here, expecting to be liked—you visit our houses, we behave to you as we would toward anyone else, and then——" The tears were beginning to run down her cheeks. She was almost incoherent with grief. "I want you to know what you're doing to us. My husband and I had to start again from nothing at the end of the war. Gradually we built up something for ourselves—now you want to take it away again. Your father made him do it—do you know that? You don't suppose he wanted to, do you? But he hadn't any choice. And now you come here, sitting in judgment on him——" She shouted at him, "Who do you think you are, for heaven's sake?"

He felt no resentment toward her, only pity. He would have liked to promise her hope, but there was no turning back now. He had paid for his victory with Jane's honor and his own—it was not thinkable that at this stage he should change his mind and refuse it. Somebody must suffer. If you accepted action, you accepted with it suffering, corruption, betrayal, shame. You did not will them,

except in so far as you willed the thing that caused them. For the first time he felt for his father the faint stirrings of understanding, almost of sympathy.

"I'm sorry," he said.

She looked at him as Madame Verrier had looked at him in the hospital corridor on the night of her husband's death.

"You're sorry," she said bitterly. Then, quite quietly: "I've finished what I had to say. You can leave now—go and catch your train. I never want to set eyes on you again."

She turned around and went back into the drawing room, slamming the door behind her. It was just possible to hear her sobbing from behind the door. Gilbertson made as if to follow her and then changed his mind. His face wore the baffled, weary expression of a man growing old in a world he has ceased to understand.

"It's best to leave her for the moment," he said. "I'll drive you down to the station."

PART VI

CHAPTER I

HE LOOKED AT HIS FACE closely in the mirror fixed behind the door of his cabin. It seemed to him that a man ought to do this periodically, just as he ought to review his financial position, estimating profit and loss, capital expended, reserves for the future. A face, of course, could never be as encouraging as a balance sheet. You never made a profit, you never grew richer—the triumph lay in keeping down the inevitable drain on your resources, in postponing for as long as possible the day when you looked and saw that you had nothing left.

In his early twenties there had been little enough to read. Youth, in those days, was like an enormous fortune which you spent freely since you could not imagine that any extravagance could diminish it. But recently, each year, his face had begun to tell him something. He could see, not exactly wrinkles—it was not as bad as that yet—but a slight coarsening of the skin on close inspection, a darkening of the beard area, a fixity of the creases of expression. By most standards he looked young for his age (and why not? He had been rich and idle and cared for; he had never worked very hard or had great responsibilities; he was no more than a moderate drinker) and yet, when he looked at himself very closely, in this particular light, the secret was out. He was no longer a young man.

And so what? Did he have to be young, if it came to that? There were plenty of his friends in their late twenties who were fathers of families, were putting on weight and growing bald and had

accepted readily—indeed almost eagerly—a comfortable, canasta-playing, carpet-slipper life-in-death. They were not discontented; they did not watch the years going by with an uneasiness which at any moment might mount into panic. They had decided on the future they wanted; they had set a course and were sailing it, would go on sailing it with all the skill and strength they could muster. The end was decided. Only the means remained as a preoccupation.

When you are moving in the right direction, he thought, time is not too important. Life is really too long for most of us, anyway—it gives us a plentiful margin to realize what gifts we have. If we are making any progress at all we shall get there in the end. But what of the man who is making no progress, who has not even decided on a course, who may be drifting, for all he knows, in the wrong direction, toward disaster? Who sees the years of decision passing by him, knowing that a day will soon come when he is too old, not so much to accomplish something new as to have the mental resilience to attempt it?

He snapped off the cabin light. In the twilight his own image looked more reassuring. He was once again as most people must see him, a youngish man of pleasant, prosperous appearance on whom so far life had sat lightly—a man of fortunate background and considerable opportunity. This insistent conviction that time was running out and that he must decide to set the course of his life before it was too late—this was his own secret. Only Jane knew him well enough to share it.

The engines had quietened as the ship reduced speed. They must be moving into the channel at the mouth of the Hudson. When he went up on deck he found that most of the passengers had moved forward to the bow, eager to catch their first sight of Manhattan. There were a great many unfamiliar faces, an unusual amount of noise, a profusion of children. In these last few hours the barriers between first class and tourist had been relaxed.

He found Jane standing at the rail. She squeezed to one side to make room for him. There was land on either side now. The ship had been delayed by storms and it was already dark—the lights were glittering on Long Island and the Jersey shore. Apartment and office buildings, ugly and featureless in the daylight, were converted by

darkness into a row of glittering jewels, rendered doubly brilliant by their reflections in the dark mirror of the waterfront. Car headlights streamed along the parkways like tracer bullets.

"Can we see it?" said Jane.

"Manhattan? Not yet. In a moment or two——"

Over the whole harbor there was hanging a shimmering incandescent glow from some source as yet unseen. Then the ship veered slightly, the channel curved, a tongue of land moved away on the starboard bow, and there it was; very small at first, the brilliant focal point of the glow which lit the sky, then gradually discernible as a mass of separate units. A red searchlight stabbed intermittently at the clouds with enormous urgency.

"There it is," he said.

She squeezed his hand and said nothing. The traffic in the channel was increasing. They heard the loud, hollow boom of a siren.

"What's that?"

"The Staten Island ferry."

He looked across the water at the people leaning against the rail of the ferryboat and knew he was home. Until that moment Manhattan had been a façade, a view, a picture postcard. Now it was the old, familiar, teeming ant heap, the home of express elevators and up-to-the-minute air-conditioned funeral parlors and the hamburger with the college education. Not to speak of Miss Rheingold and nobody (but nobody) underselling Gimbels. . . .

The buildings of Wall Street were discernible now.

"This beats getting in by plane," said Marshall. "You get the sense of an event."

"Even for you?"

"Yes, even for me." He waved a hand at the familiar yet ever-startling skyline. "What do you think of it?"

"It's amazing, of course." Her voice was tentative, as if she had difficulty in interpreting her own feelings. "But—at the same time —intimidating——"

"Because it's so big?"

"Not only that. It's not a friendly approach; somehow it's indifferent. You can come if you like or you can stay away. It doesn't seem to care."

He tightened his grip on her hand. She was right, of course. Manhattan, he thought, was like a wealthy and fashionable woman waiting to have a photograph taken. It was used to being rich and important and admired; it quite enjoyed showing off but in a casual, almost contemptuous way. At heart it was totally preoccupied with itself.

"But then," she added, "I'm a foreigner. After all, why should it speak to me? It doesn't know me. Perhaps with you it's different."

He shook his head. "It's the same with everybody. You have to take it as you find it."

Shortly afterward they docked at the Cunard pier. They had just finished with the immigration authorities when Marshall saw a tall, bulky figure striding toward him across the lounge.

"Jeff!"

"Hello, boy! Is this a surprise!" As hearty as usual, thought Marshall, perhaps even more than usual. And what the hell was Jeff doing here anyway? He had deliberately told no one when he was coming or by which route. Had the company resorted to using detectives? It was by no means impossible.

Jane was standing behind him. "Jane, this is my brother Jeff. Jane Lancing."

"Glad to meet you, Miss Lancing."

"How do you do." She smiled. "You're just exactly as I imagined you." She explained, "Chris has told me a lot about you."

"Nothing bad, I hope." He laughed, too loudly. His uncertainty was obvious. Evidently nobody had told him anything at all about Miss Lancing. The detective agency had slipped up on that one. He turned back to Marshall.

"Well, you're certainly looking fit, Chris."

"Thanks."

"Did you have a good crossing? Plenty of sun—good food—that's the way to do it." They began to move with the crowd toward the gangway. "And you, Miss Lancing—you enjoyed your trip? Fine, fine. Believe me, if I had my way I'd travel everywhere by sea. You get some time to think; you can get your problems into perspective. Don't you think so, Chris?"

"It's a point of view," said Marshall absently. His cabin steward had collected his suitcases and was signaling to him. "If you don't mind, I'd better just make arrangements about the baggage."

"Don't worry about a thing." Jeff put a reassuring arm around his shoulder. "Just relax. There's a guy I know who manages shipments for us and he's promised to fix it so that you won't have any unnecessary delays. He knows the customs boys and they're prepared to do him a little favor now and then. . . . So we should be able to whip you through pretty fast. Then I've got a car waiting outside to take you to your hotel——"

"Jane will be coming with us. She's also staying at the Plaza."

"Well, that's wonderful—wonderful." His eyes searched Marshall's face for some clue to the situation but found none. He turned to Jane. "Are you staying long in New York, Miss Lancing?"

"I'm not sure."

"You're from London?"

Marshall cut in restlessly, "You know, I think we ought to be getting off the boat." He smiled. "You two can play Twenty Questions later."

For all Jeff's influence, it took them over half an hour to get through customs. Down the street a company limousine was waiting.

"Do you always do things in such style?" said Jane admiringly.

"By no means. In fact, this is quite unusual." Marshall looked pointedly at his brother. "Isn't that so, Jeff?"

"Well, I don't know." Jeff wriggled in his seat. "After all, you don't come back from Europe every day."

"That's true."

The car pulled up at the Fifty-ninth Street entrance to the hotel, and he was really home. Even the doorman recognized him—or pretended to. After they had registered, Jane said, "If you'll excuse me, I'm tired. I'll go straight to bed."

"Sleep well," said Marshall. "I'll see you in the morning."

When they had seen her into the elevator, Jeff said, "Are you in a hurry to go to bed?"

"Not particularly."

"I thought we might have a little talk——"

"Sure. Why not come up to my room? I'll tell room service to send up a bottle of scotch——"

"I think you'll find that's been done." Jeff's voice showed embarrassment. It had seemed a good idea at the time, but now he was not so sure.

"Well——" Marshall looked at him with amusement. "We'd better go up right away and see what else Santa Claus has brought."

Up in the room there were two bottles of scotch, some soda, and a bowl of ice. Marshall poured out the drinks. There was a short silence.

Eventually Jeff said, "Seems a nice girl."

"Jane? Yes—she's a very nice girl."

"You met her on the boat?"

"No, I met her in London." It was time to put Jeff out of his misery. "She used to work for Gilbertson." After a slight pause to let Jeff take in the implications of this, he added, "We're thinking of getting married."

"Married!" Astonishment was mixed with something like relief. So far Jeff had given the impression of improvising, without confidence, in a situation which was strange to him and more than a little distasteful. But now at last he felt firm ground beneath his feet. He knew how to act when people got married. "Well, congratulations! I'm delighted. But why so secretive? Why didn't you let me know earlier? I was talking to her as if she was someone you'd just met casually. I didn't know she was liable to become one of the family." He shook his head ruefully. "Hell, what she must think of me——"

"I shouldn't worry about that."

"It's all very well for you to say, but you don't understand women like I do. These things matter to them. For God's sake, you never even wrote or anything! Does Mother know?"

"No," said Marshall. "Nobody knows. Anyway, it's not definite yet—that's really the reason I didn't write to you. Jane has to look around here, meet Mother, see if she likes America, and so on. She has to get herself adjusted. After all, we haven't known each other so very long."

"Oh, sure—I understand."

"So if you don't mind, I'd rather you didn't mention it to anyone."

"Don't worry about that. I'll be as tight as a clam." He became solemn. "Chris, I'm sure she's a wonderful girl and you'll be very happy."

"You hardly know her," Marshall pointed out.

"No, but I know you. You've taken plenty of time to make your choice, but now you have, I'm confident that it'll be a good one. And, as you know, it's always been my conviction that what you really needed to stabilize you and give you a sense of purpose was a wife—the right kind of wife. Why, I remember the last time we spoke together——"

Marshall ceased to listen. He was accustomed to Jeff, on occasions like this, saying with an air of discovery all the correct, conventional things that had been said a million times before. He not only failed to add to one's enjoyment of an experience by talking about it—he managed positively to destroy it. In his hands marriage became no longer an adventure but a sound measure of mental and physical hygiene, an expression of conformity with the collective outlook of Nice Girls and Regular Guys, a vote of confidence in the American way of life. Behind all his genuine good will there was an unmistakable note of satisfaction. He was going to be proved right after all. Chris would soon forget all his egghead nonsense and settle down like anyone else—some people just matured late, that was all.

The flow dried up momentarily. Jeff paused and then said, "Of course this explains a lot. I was wondering why you stopped over in England so long."

"Were you?" Marshall looked at him without expression. The courtesies were over now—they were moving toward business.

"Why, yes. You were expected back sooner."

"So everyone was anxious about me?" It was impossible to refrain from teasing him a little, if only as a reprisal for being so dull.

"Well, not exactly anxious——"

Marshall smiled maliciously. "That's the way it looks. The company pulling wires at Cunard to find out which sailing I was com-

ing on. Calling up all the hotels to check my booking. Little presents in my room. And you—down to meet me at the dock in a big black Cadillac. . . . Quite touching, it was. Especially since by rights I ought to be in the doghouse for overstaying my leave."

"Hell," said Jeff awkwardly, "if I'd known you'd take it like this—— I mean—well, if a man can't meet his own brother off the boat without arousing a lot of suspicions——"

Jeff made a halfhearted attempt to take offense. But his uneasiness was too great to make it convincing, even to himself. Marshall got up and poured more whisky into his glass. He looked at the sulky, anxious face and said, "Poor Jeff. They certainly give you some lousy jobs, don't they?"

He replied weakly, "I don't get you."

"You shouldn't let them do it, you know. After all, you don't have to do what Kingham tells you." Marshall's voice hardened. It was the thought of Kingham which made the difference. It was possible to play it almost as a game up to a certain point. A vicious, dangerous game, of course, one in which he had to make certain of winning, but nevertheless something without too much passion —he could, for instance, spare a little time to amuse himself with Jeff. But with the mention of Kingham his hands began to tremble and there was no possibility of taking a light, civilized attitude any more. There was something almost frightening to him in the realization of how much he hated Kingham. With sudden viciousness he said, "Why don't you try telling him to do his own dirty work?"

"Honest, Chris, I don't know what's got into you," Jeff said plaintively.

"You know damn well what's got into me. You can't be as dumb as that. The last time we spoke together I was right on the bottom —a piece of nothing. Remember? You were practically doing me a favor saving my job for me. And then what happens? I go back to Europe and I do everything wrong. I stay too long, I talk to all the people I was told to avoid as if they had smallpox, I notify nobody of my movements—and what do I get? Practically a ticker-tape reception. Do you think I don't know why?"

Jeff's face had become contorted into a characteristic expression.

His brow was wrinkled, his eyes slightly narrowed, as if he were suffering from some internal pain which he was too manly to complain about in words. Ever since childhood it had been his way of reacting to a situation which he had discovered himself incapable of handling.

"I can imagine just how it happened," said Marshall. "Kingham came to you and said, 'Jeff, my boy, I want to confide in you. The truth is, I'm very worried about your brother. He's been talking to some very peculiar people in Europe and they've filled him up with all sorts of crazy ideas. Now I'm fond of Chris and I don't want him to do anything foolish. For the sake of the organization, I think somebody ought to meet him the moment he arrives in New York and straighten him out a little. As you can imagine, it's difficult for me, in my position, but you, as his brother——'" He stopped for a moment. "Wasn't that it?"

Sulkily Jeff replied, "Well, if it was, I can't see anything so terrible in that."

"Not so far as I'm concerned. But it doesn't look so good for you, if that's the sort of job they hand you." The wrinkles on Jeff's forehead deepened, as if his initial agony had suddenly become intensified. Really, thought Marshall, there was no satisfaction in this—it was like hitting a man who lay helpless on the ropes, silently pleading with his eyes for mercy. In a softer voice he asked, "How much did Kingham tell you—about this particular episode, I mean?"

"He wasn't very definite. Naturally I asked him, but he didn't seem to want to say too much. He said there was a certain suspicion that some of the French consignments might have fallen into the wrong hands."

"I see." Marshall hesitated. The question now was, what to do with Jeff? Throw him out with an offensive message to take back to Kingham, use him as the first show of strength? He deserved it for allowing himself to be placed in such a humiliating position, and yet . . . For all his weakness and stupidity, for all his pompous moralizing, he was essentially a decent, kindly man who would sooner do good than harm if it was not too costly or dangerous. And they were, after all, brothers. In the moment that Marshall

made his decision he suddenly knew that it was not only the right one, it was also the wisest.

"I'd better let you have the whole story," he said.

As he told it he watched Jeff's face with considerable care. It was important to know how far the knowledge went. He had never really thought it possible that Jeff was in on the secret, and now he was certain. His brother's astonishment was genuine enough. They had told him nothing. He was just the office boy, to be fed with as much information as was suitable for him to hear.

"But that's terrible—terrible," he stammered. "Hell, it really is." He looked up pleadingly. "Can you be certain? I mean—have you any proof?"

"Yes." Marshall hesitated, but there was no point in turning back now. "We have a letter."

"Can I see it?"

Marshall opened his brief case and took out a sheet of paper. "This is a photostat."

Jeff rubbed his fingers on the stiff texture of the paper. For a moment he did not look at what was printed on it. Reproachfully he said, "You could have trusted me with the original."

Marshall said nothing. The original letter was in the file with the photostats and he could just as easily have handed it to his brother to read. There was, he knew well, no danger that Jeff would steal it or destroy it. Then why the photostat? He could find no very clear reason in his own mind. A month ago, he thought with shame, he would not have done it. Now distrust was becoming a habit.

"Read it," he said sharply.

Jeff read through the letter.

"How did you get this?" he said.

It was something you couldn't be delicate about, and certainly it would be a mistake to strike an apologetic note. Marshall realized that this was one of the things he would have to face all through the struggle—that, once he produced the letter, his moral initiative was gone. He no longer represented virtue against evil. The best way was to attack. It was necessary, and he had done it. They could think what they liked.

"I stole it," he said. The effort was painful, but he would make

it more painful still. He would leave no secret vulnerable point for his enemies to attack. "Or, to be more accurate, I got Jane to steal it for me. She was Gilbertson's secretary."

He waited, searching Jeff's face for any sign of censure or protest, ready to hit back immediately with every weapon at his command. But Jeff merely said, "So she comes into this too?"

"Yes."

So far as one could see, Jane's involvement made little impact on Jeff. The enormity of the main situation filled his mind to the exclusion of any side issues. He ran a hand over his forehead. "Christ, I don't know what to say," he said. And then, in a voice reminiscent of the days when they had got into scrapes together as children: "What are we going to do, Chris?"

His helplessness was complete. He had given up any claim to leadership. The claim had never been convincing anyway. "You don't have to do anything," said Marshall. "This is my affair."

"Well, yes." There was relief in Jeff's eyes. "But in a way it affects both of us." He said incredulously, "You say it was Dad who started this?"

"Gilbertson said so, and I've no reason to disbelieve him."

"He might have just said it as a get-out for himself."

"I don't think so."

"I just can't believe Dad would do a thing like that."

"Can't you?" said Marshall indifferently. "To me it seems just the sort of thing he would have done."

With a flash of resentment Jeff said, "You always hated him."

"No." Somehow it was very important that he should be clear on this point. He said, "It's not as simple as that. At first I admired him, I was proud of him. Then I found he was a liar and a cheat and I despised him—I despised myself, too, for having been taken in by him." He struggled to explain. "It wasn't him I hated—it was what he did——"

"That's the same thing."

"No, it isn't. I used to think so, but it isn't. It's not always easy to do things the way you want to do them." Who was he now to condemn the old man? He too had betrayed a trust and pleaded the justification of events. If his father had lived he could have gone to

him now and said, "I am grown up at last, I am a man as you are, you can talk to me and I will understand." But the time for that had long since gone. He heard Jeff saying:

"You sound as if you were making excuses for him."

He smiled. Jeff, the believer, would not find it easy to reconcile himself to the betrayal of his faith. It was to those who expected nothing that forgiveness came most easily.

"Why not? He probably thought at the time that the law was stupid and couldn't see why he should sacrifice his business to it. He had a point of view."

"I can't see it."

Marshall stopped himself from saying anything more. You could not explain a thing like that to Jeff, who lived in a world where everything was black or white. The two brothers sat for a moment in silence. Then Jeff said, "Are you going to see Kingham?"

"No." He had thought about this on the boat. "I'm not interested in Kingham."

Jeff said resentfully, "He put me in a hell of a spot. Asking me to come and meet you like this. Not even telling——" He squared his great shoulders. "I think I'm going to go and ask him for an explanation——"

Marshall shook his head. "I wouldn't." He had no faith in Jeff's ability to cope with Kingham. Even with all the cards in his hand he was certain to be outmaneuvered in some way. No, the way to handle Kingham was not to give him a chance of a straight fight at all. "I should leave Kingham right out of it." He said carefully, "This is an important matter. It needs to be taken right up to the top."

Jeff ran a finger around the inside of his collar. "Bernstein?" he said.

"Who else?"

"Do you think he knows——" Jeff stopped, frowning at the possible implications of the question.

"If he doesn't, it's certainly time he heard."

"I guess so," said Jeff unhappily. He was silent for a moment. "And what about you?"

Marshall pretended to misunderstand the question. "I plan to

stay in New York for two or three days—show Jane the sights and so on. Then we both might go out to Falls Ridge. Mother's at home, I suppose?"

"Oh, sure. She'll be there," said Jeff abstractedly. He put his question again, more specifically this time: "What I really meant was—aren't you coming with me to see Bernstein?"

Marshall shook his head. He hardly knew Bernstein; he had no personal feelings about him one way or the other. But when you were in a strong position it was always worth while emphasizing it from the very beginning. "This time people are coming to see me."

CHAPTER II

HE WOKE UP next morning with a feeling of unusual contentment. It was good to be off the ship, to sleep on a bed of adequate size, even to hear the traffic rumbling and hooting below the window. It was pleasant to be finished with waiting. The meeting with Jeff had gone well last night; the right atmosphere had been established from the start. It had really been a mistake on their part, he decided, thinking it over, to send Jeff at all. Kingham had shown his anxiety without gaining any compensating advantage.

After a while the telephone rang. It was Jane.

"Are you up yet?" she asked.

"Just thinking about it."

"I awoke at seven o'clock and I haven't been able to get to sleep since. Everything's far too noisy and exciting. And now I'm hungry. What about some breakfast?"

"I'll meet you down in the restaurant in half an hour."

He bathed and dressed hurriedly. When he got to the restaurant she had not yet arrived. The sunshine was streaming through the windows—an exhilarating change after the rain of London and the surly dullness of the North Atlantic. He ordered a large orange juice, bacon and eggs, and coffee.

Shortly afterward Jane came down to join him. When she had ordered breakfast he said, "Did they give you a good room?"

"Wonderful, thanks. But enormously expensive, I'm sure."

"Well, of course," he said cheerfully. "It's all part of the plan. I'm trying to spoil you so that you won't want to go home."

"Ah, very crafty—I hadn't thought of that." She smiled at him. "You're looking very pleased with yourself today. Any special reason?"

"Not exactly. I guess I'm much more glad to be back than I thought I would be." He could not be certain what the difference was this time, but there *was* a difference. For some reason New York appeared to him as an easier, more amiable place. It was as if it accepted him as a man of its own kind. Why was that? he wondered. Was it because for the first time he entered it as a person of consequence? Was his sense of well-being due to nothing more than the knowledge that, a few blocks away, men who had once ignored his very existence were now waiting anxiously on his word?

The idea repelled him. He hastened to change the subject.

"I rang up Falls Ridge this morning," he said. "Mother's looking forward to seeing us on Saturday. That gives us two or three days here. I imagine you'd like to have a quick look around Manhattan."

"Yes, of course——"

"We could go up the Empire State, spend an evening in the Village, hear some real jazz——"

"Won't it be boring for you?"

"No." He went on thoughtfully, "It's difficult to explain. I don't approve of New York. Nobody does. Everyone agrees it's noisy and dirty and hot and crowded and ridiculously expensive. And yet . . ."

"I know," she said. "Places get a claim on you in some way. I was born in a little town near Stoke-on-Trent—a dreadful place. Nothing to be said for it at all. Not so long ago I went back there and walked along the street where my parents' house was. It looked very small and old and ugly. Nobody on the street knew me any more. But somehow it almost frightened me. It was as if it could draw me in and take hold of me, put me back where I was as a child—and this time it would see that I wouldn't break away again." She spoke with unusual intensity. "Nothing else is quite as real as the things which happened to you as a child."

He looked at her, thinking how right she had been in London

when she had said they knew so little of each other. To know people it was not enough to know them alone—you had to know also their home, their family, the whole pattern of influences which had made them what they were. Otherwise they were like a phrase read out of context. They might mean anything—or nothing.

He spread some marmalade on a piece of toast. "I spoke to Jeff last night."

"Yes? What happened?"

He gave her an account of their conversation. She listened attentively but somehow without animation. It was as if other matters were uppermost in her mind. He found himself cutting the story short for fear of boring her. At the end he said, "So, as you see, that leaves the next move to them."

After a slight pause she said, "Supposing they do nothing?"

"They daren't. I can pull the company to pieces tomorrow, and they know it. They have to come to me."

"What's the advantage of doing it this way?"

"It's better psychologically." He hesitated. It was not too easy to explain. It was one of those things one instinctively knew. "It emphasizes the strength of my position."

She sighed rather impatiently. "I suppose you must be right. Personally, I wouldn't have the patience. I hate the whole business so much that I'd want to get it over. I'd probably burst into Bernstein's office tomorrow morning, have a tremendous fight with him, and settle everything there and then. Then I'd rush out and take a deep breath and think: Now I can start living!" She smiled at him. "Don't you feel like that at all?"

He thought about it and then shook his head. "It would be a mistake. I know just how you feel. I hate all these politics just as much as you do——"

She looked at him doubtfully. "Do you?"

"Well, of course."

"It just occurred to me," she said, "that perhaps you were rather enjoying it."

There was a moment's awkwardness between them. He found it difficult to meet her eyes.

"It's not a question of enjoying it," he said. "This is a job I have

to do. It's important, not only to me, but to a lot of other people. Surely you can understand that."

She said, as if she had made an accusation which he had refused to answer, "I understand perfectly."

"Very well then." She had a way, he thought, of questioning everything. Nothing could be accepted, every attitude and enthusiasm was automatically suspect. It was one of the things which had attracted him to her in the first place, this stern independence and refusal to take anything for granted. But it was slightly disconcerting to see it applied to himself. "I have to do it my own way," he said stiffly.

"Well, of course, if that's how you feel about it," she said. "I only said——"

"It wasn't just what you said." What else was it? Something about her voice, the lift of her eyebrows when asking a question? "You must understand that this is going to be a difficult time for me," he said in a slightly aggrieved voice. "I shall need all the support I can get."

"Yes, I know." She smiled at him and touched his hand. "I didn't mean to sound disloyal." She picked up her handbag and pushed back her chair. "Now I'm ready to go and have a look at Fifth Avenue."

It was two days before Jeff telephoned.

"Is that you, Chris?"

"Yes."

"I only just got to see Bernie this morning. He's been out of town. I've just come from talking to him now——"

"How did it go?"

"Well . . ." He sounded a little dubious, as if he could not be sure how it had gone till he received an opinion on it. "Listen, I can't talk about this over the telephone——"

"Then come over to the hotel."

"No, that's not too good either." Had they told him to keep away? Marshall wondered. "I tell you what. You're spending the weekend at Falls Ridge, aren't you?"

"Yes."

"Then why don't you and Jane drive over to my place for supper Saturday evening? Paula would love to meet her, and you and I could have a little talk about things. How about that?"

"Fine. I'll see you then. Give my love to Paula and the kids," he added as an afterthought.

It was the usual Saturday-morning crowd, he thought as he packed his car into the northbound procession on the Merritt Parkway. Mom and Dad in the front seat, the kids in the back, shouting, making faces, smearing the windows; teen-agers in secondhand convertibles, the radio going full volume. America was having fun.

He said to Jane, "I hope you'll like Falls Ridge."

"I hope so."

"It's a little phony in some ways—but it has a sort of charm. Just like my mother herself, really." After a slight pause he continued, "I should explain that she's from the South—they export charm just like Detroit exports automobiles. She likes to run the house as if it were a broken-down cotton plantation with the mortgage liable to run out at any moment. In fact, she has plenty of money. It's a sort of game——"

"It sounds as if she just likes to pretend. That's not the same as being a phony."

"Perhaps not." He laughed. "It used to annoy my father. He thought it was bad for business."

She was the one person, he thought, who had finally beaten his father. She had employed a technique which the old man was simply not equipped to understand. She would smile gently and agree—and do nothing. Shouting, blustering, threats had no effect on her. Sometimes she would appear to make an attempt to carry out his wishes, but always in the end, almost imperceptibly, her good intentions would lapse, and they were back where they started. Gradually his father had become baffled. In his family affairs (in contrast with his business dealings) he usually felt that he had right on his side, but he had consistently failed to impose his moral convictions on his wife. Eventually he had accepted defeat. "It's essential," he had once said to Marshall with unusual resignation, "not to waste your strength against something you can't

beat. Your mother has a unique talent for putting other people in the wrong."

At Falls Ridge everything was much as usual. The dirt road was a little more overgrown, the house still needed painting. Virgie was waiting for them on the porch, toothless, grinning, shy in the presence of the strange foreign woman. His mother came in from the garden, pulling off a pair of thick leather gloves.

"I was trying to tidy up the rosebushes," she explained. "Virgie says they're a disgrace. But it's hopeless—the place has become a wilderness. At one time we used to have two men to handle that garden. And now look at it. There was a young man came up here the other day who wanted to lease part of it from me—that piece down by the highway where the fruit trees are. He wanted to put up a gas station. Imagine—a gas station . . ."

"Mother, this is Jane Lancing."

She smiled sweetly at Jane. "My dear, I'm so glad to meet you. And so pretty—why didn't you tell me she was so pretty, Chris?" She turned back to Jane. "These two boys of mine, they tell me nothing. I have to find out everything for myself. Well, as I was saying, this person came to my door and offered me ten thousand dollars to build a gas station. 'Young man,' I said to him——"

She led them into the house, still talking. Marshall and Virgie carried the suitcases up to the bedrooms. Later Marshall came down and found his mother alone.

"Jane's up in her room," she said. "She wanted to unpack for this evening."

He sat down and lit a cigarette. "Do you like her?"

"She seems like a very sweet girl."

"We're thinking of getting married," he said abruptly. His mother nodded, showing mild interest. In spite of his knowledge of her, he was a little piqued at her lack of reaction. "You don't seem very surprised."

"Naturally, since you'd brought her all this way, I assumed something of the kind," she said. "Besides, I could tell by the way you looked at her. . . ."

"It's not definite yet. She wanted to come over here and see how she liked it before making up her mind." When his mother said

nothing, he added, on the defensive, "It's reasonable, after all. She's never been to America before——"

"Perhaps things are different nowadays," Mrs. Marshall said vaguely. "I remember when I married your father we never thought of where we were going to live. My parents were against it, of course—they said he was unstable," she went on, wandering effortlessly into reminiscence, "and of course they were right. He *was* unstable. But then he was living in an unstable world, and it suited him. It's never possible to give anybody advice about the future." She reflected for a moment. "Perhaps it's you that she hasn't quite made up her mind about."

"Well—maybe—I don't know——"

She made one of her sudden butterfly changes of subject. "Why did you call me up that night from London?"

Should he tell her? he wondered. But the effort of explaining it all was too great. Nor had he sufficient confidence in her ability to respond. It was only too likely that her mind would wander while he was talking and he would find at the end that she had understood only half of what he had said. "It was just an impulse," he said. "Nothing in particular."

He suddenly realized that she did not believe him. Yet at the same time she accepted the lie she apparently did not resent it. Her expression seemed to imply that she was used to being shut out of other people's lives and regarded it as a reasonable price to pay for maintaining the privacy of her own.

"Ah well," she said. "I expect you're old enough . . ." Her relief was apparent. She had offered contact and it had been refused. There was nothing more she was obliged to do. She was silent for a moment and then said, "Do you mind fish?"

"Fish?"

"Yes, for lunch." She said earnestly, "I eat practically nothing else now."

"Why?"

At last he felt that her attention was really concentrated on something. "For my blood cholesterol. Do you know it's up to two hundred and sixty?"

"Is that bad?"

"Bad? It's terrible. Dr. Aronson says that if you get over two-seventy you might just as well go out and shoot yourself. It seems that I was slowly poisoning myself with all those eggs. So now it's fish, fish, fish—nearly all the time. Virgie can't stand the stuff," she added with quiet satisfaction.

That evening Marshall and Jane drove over to see Jeff.

"Paula, I want you to meet Jane Lancing."

"Glad to know you, Jane. Jeff's been talking about nothing else ever since he met you off the boat. How do you like America?"

"Give her a chance, honey," said Jeff, "she's only just arrived——"

"So far I think it's wonderful. But then, as your husband says——"

Since Marshall last visited the house a square brick extension had been added to one side of it. It was rare that Jeff and Paula left the place alone for very long. There was usually something new whenever he visited them—a car, a color television set, a baby, a piece of domestic equipment. They liked to be asked to show them off. (They would show them off anyway, but it was more fun for them to be asked.) "I see you have some new construction over there, Jeff."

"Oh sure." Jeff's face lit up with simple pleasure. "I forgot you didn't know about it. We've extended the kitchen—it was kind of unsatisfactory. And there's a room up above for the boys, where they can racket around without getting in Paula's hair all the time. We've got electric heating up there—wonderful system, it runs around under the floor somewhere——"

"Why don't you show Chris around," Paula suggested, "while Jane and I go and take a look at the baby?"

"Sure, sure." As they walked away there was a sound of crashing glass. Two small boys came running around the side of the house, one behind the other, the larger slashing purposefully at the smaller with a baseball bat. "Paul! Paul!" Jeff cried plaintively. "Son, you mustn't do that. Now listen here——" The boys disappeared in the distance. Jeff said, "That kid's becoming quite a worry to me. The psychiatrist says he has cross dominance—his right hand doesn't work with his left eye or something, so he gets all mixed up. No

wonder he raises hell all the time. Paula worries a lot, but the way I look at it, we shall just have to be extra understanding——"

Marshall said, "Did you speak to Bernstein?"

Jeff blinked, as if he had received a sharp blow between the eyes. "Yes." He hesitated. "He was pretty mad," he said solemnly.

"Because I didn't approach him direct?"

Jeff nodded, retaining his funereal face. Obviously Mr. Bernstein's indignation had impressed him. "You're certain this is the right way to do it?" he asked.

Marshall did not answer the question. "Did he look surprised? Do you think it was news to him?"

"Oh, sure. He looked very shocked."

Marshall tried to control his exasperation. It was, of course, impossible to hope for any valuable impression on such a matter from Jeff. Any child could deceive him. That had always been one of the drawbacks of playing it this way. He had thrown away the advantage of surprise. He might never know how much Bernstein himself was aware of what was going on. Curiously enough, he knew very little about the man. Bernstein was too high, too remote to be appreciated as a person by anybody as junior as himself.

"How smart is he?" he asked.

"Bernie?" Jeff laughed shortly. "Hell, he's president of the corporation. That doesn't make him exactly a dope——"

"If he's smart," said Marshall, "surely he must have known——"

"Not necessarily. It's pretty far away from his direct responsibility."

Marshall nodded. Perhaps that was true. Perhaps Bernstein had vaguely suspected and done nothing. Perhaps it didn't matter very much anyway. After a while one grew weary of trying to apportion guilt.

Jeff said, a little breathless at his own courage, "I told Bernie that something would have to be done. I said that otherwise I couldn't carry on with the company——"

"If something isn't done there won't *be* any company," said Marshall. "But leave it to me. I'll fix it. You won't have to resign."

"Yes, but how? I mean, I have to know——"

"For God's sake, Jeff. I said leave it to me."

Jeff became agitated.

"But I want to know you're not going to do anything wild. I've been thinking about this. Whatever you do, you can't get the stuff back from the Reds. It has to be stopped, of course, but who gains from making a song and dance about it?"

"You think I haven't thought about that too?" He felt a disinclination to discuss anything in detail at the moment. There was no way in which Jeff was competent to help, and he was liable to get frightened and raise difficulties. Marshall repeated, "I said leave it to me."

There was a silence. They were standing outside the new wing, but Jeff had completely forgotten about showing it to him. Eventually he shook his head and said solemnly, "I notice a big change in you, Chris."

"Yes?"

"You must know it yourself." He looked at Marshall with concern and a certain bewilderment. It was like his children. He went on thinking he had them taped, they respected him and looked up to him, and then suddenly he had lost them—they were out of control. "What happened?" he asked.

What happened? thought Marshall. Perhaps it was quite simple. "I got tired of being beaten."

"By whom?"

"By everybody. I was beaten by my father, by Kingham, by Gilbertson, by Furac, by Bernstein—even by you. Up to a point I tried to pretend it didn't matter, they weren't worth the trouble of fighting." He smiled sourly. "Then I got tired. I said to myself, 'Just this once I would win.'"

Could it be true, he wondered, that this was all there was left? What had happened to all the rest, to the fight for justice, the championship of the small man crushed by the machine, the hatred of lying and cheap swindling and hypocrisy? Had that all really gone, been lost in the heat and the sweat, the bitter expedients of the battle? He heard Jeff saying anxiously, "And what happens afterward?"

"I don't know." He had instinctively refrained from planning too far ahead. There were too many variable factors to make it

worth while. When the time came he would know what to do. "It depends on how things pan out. I won't rock the boat too much if they're prepared to be reasonable. But there are going to be some changes." After a pause he said, "That should be good for you. You're the one person who's definitely in the clear over this business. You'll be in a strong position from now on."

Jeff shook his head dubiously. "I don't know. It ought to be like that, maybe, but—you see, Chris," he said confidentially, "my job looks good on paper and it carries a high salary but—well, I don't know why, but somehow it doesn't seem to have the weight it should."

You mean, thought Marshall, you don't have the weight. Only physically. Behind those footballer's muscles of yours lurks a wretched, frightened little boy.

"You have to make them take notice of you," he said. "Tread on their toes and wait for them to apologize." That was a thing his father used to say. And then laugh triumphantly when he saw the disgust on the face of his younger son. "Make it so that it's less trouble for them to agree with you than to fight you."

"I've tried sometimes." Jeff made a helpless motion of his head. "I guess you have to be born to it, though. And it's not so easy when you're on your own." He added tentatively, "Now, if the two of us could work together——"

Marshall shook his head.

"No? But why not, Chris?" Jeff said eagerly. "I've been thinking about this. Between us, we can really amount to something. We have the shareholding and the background. And this present business gives us something to push with. Just now you can ask for what you want from Bernie, and he has to give it to you. If Kingham leaves the International——"

"He'll have to."

"Well, then——" Jeff looked at him. "Who comes in in his place?"

"I hadn't thought of that. I don't know. Maybe Richardson, Livera—someone like that."

"Why not you?"

Marshall laughed. "Can you see them offering it to me?"

"They might," said Jeff knowingly. "This business makes you

important. It might be considered policy to offer you something."
Before Marshall could protest, he went on, "Hell, Chris, why not?
You're as good as Richardson or Livera, you know you are——"

Marshall shook his head. It was the sort of stupid, half-smart
idea that you had to expect from a person like Jeff. It took for
granted that everyone wanted the same things he wanted himself
and would use the same methods to get them. "I'm not interested,"
he said. "All I care about is to fix this one thing. After that I'm
getting out."

Jeff was bewildered. "But, Chris, why? At a time like this——"

"This is the right time. I'd have got out before but I'd had too
many failures—I couldn't bring myself to admit to another one.
But when this is over I shall have done something. I shan't owe
any more obligations to myself or anybody else. From then on I
can do as I please."

Was that it? Something like that, anyway. You got so that you
were too busy to remember why you were doing things; just doing
them took everything you had. Plans were things that never worked
out; the best ones were those you made up afterward, like those
caricatures he had drawn so long ago in the conference room the
day they fixed Wilcox. You drew the picture first—then you put a
name to it. . . .

He turned away abruptly. "Let's go back and talk to the girls," he
said.

When they were driving back to his mother's house he said to
Jane, "What do you think of them?" Seeing her hesitate, he added,
"You can be as frank as you like."

"I wasn't being delicate. I found it difficult to answer because
I honestly don't know. They don't seem real to me somehow."

"Neither of them?"

"The whole household. It's just the Young Executive Family
Group, isn't it? Everything so shiny and glossy and prosperous.
It's like some ghastly advertisement. You know what I mean."

He was suddenly, surprisingly, defending his brother.

"It's always the same when you first visit a foreign country. A lot
of the people seem like something out of a comic strip. Stage Ameri-

cans or Englishmen or Irishmen or whatever it is." He searched for an example. "Gilbertson, for instance. He was never a real person to me somehow. Not until recently, that is." He said, hoping it was true, "You'll soon get used to the people over here. . . ."

When they arrived home he was surprised to find his mother downstairs. Usually she went to bed early.

"Did you enjoy yourselves?"

"Yes—very well."

"Any news from Jeff and Paula?"

"Not really."

"Well, I have some news," she said. "You'll never guess who called me up while you were out."

"Who?"

She shot an unusually acute glance at him. "Mr. Bernstein. Now wasn't that surprising? I haven't heard from him in years. He asked if he could come to dinner tomorrow night."

CHAPTER III

WITH SOME DIFFICULTY Bernstein steered the big black Continental off the highway and onto the road leading to the house. It was a long time since he had been there and the road seemed much narrower nowadays. Or perhaps his car had grown wider. He had never been very happy with the Continental. It was altogether too long and low and powerful; he was a nervous driver and didn't have any use for three-hundred (or was it four?) horse-power, but, after all, a man owed something to his position.

He stopped the car in front of the house. Even that looked smaller, he thought, than it had when Marcus Marshall was alive. Or then again, perhaps it was he who had grown bigger. Like an actor about to go on the stage for the first time in an unfamiliar part, he took a deep breath, swallowed, moistened his lips, and took a quick glance at himself in the rear-view mirror. He was not dis-satisfied with what he saw. Time and the painstaking effort of forty years had managed finally to give him the sort of appearance he considered appropriate to his achievements and ambitions. The face was sallow and fine-drawn, the mouth humorous and sensitive, the silky hair now almost completely white. Though never hand-some, he had succeeded in becoming distinguished in a casual, un-pretentious way. He had always resisted any temptation to flamboy-ance. Restraint was implicit in everything he did, in the clothes he wore, the unobtrusive signet ring on his little finger, the gray worsted suit tailored so delicately to conceal the tiny residue of

paunch which even the most rigid dieting could never entirely eradicate. The total effect was as he had always wished it to be, complete and satisfying, a cover picture from *Time*.

He saw Mrs. Marshall coming out of the house and extricated himself from the car. It was bound to be a slightly embarrassing moment. He had neglected her since the old man died—there had been so many other important things. . . . But she would play along, he consoled himself, whatever she might think about him. By now she must surely be accustomed to the realities of business.

He went straight into his prepared entrance, taking both her hands in his. "Mary!" He looked into her face with an expression of delighted wonderment. "You haven't changed a bit."

"I should have," she said. "It's quite a time since we met."

"It certainly is." He contrived to suggest that circumstances completely beyond his control had kept them apart. "And nobody regrets it more than I do. Still, I always say, the best friends are those you don't have to see all the time—isn't that so?" He turned away. "And, Chris—I suppose I can call you Chris?"

"Sure."

"We're pretty old acquaintances, after all. In fact, you may not know this, but your father wanted me to be your godfather. It's the truth. Even when I pointed out to him that I was a Jew he couldn't see why not." He chuckled. "Theology was never his strong suit."

Marshall smiled thinly. He was trying to get used to the idea of Bernstein at close quarters. So far, apart from a few vague childhood memories, he had seen him only as a shadowy, remote personage, a maker of after-dinner speeches, a collection of photographs for the house journal. He strove to eradicate from his mind any traces of awe which might remain as a result of those earlier impressions. Bernstein was simply a man, a man his father had made and whom his mother principally remembered because he played such a bad game of bridge. All the rest was an act, just as his present performance was an act. Though, he admitted, you couldn't help admiring it purely as a demonstration of technique. The family stuff, the semi-paternal manner, the references, so lightly dropped, to old times. And the Jewishness, not concealed, but not pushed in your face either. . . .

He was at work on Jane now. "Don't be afraid, Miss Lancing. I'm not going to ask you what you think of America. When I first came to New York from Hamburg with my father I was nine years old and couldn't speak a word of English. And within twenty-four hours three people asked me what I thought of America. I got so that I was afraid to go out of the house." Swinging back to Mrs. Marshall, he said, "It's wonderful here, Mary. You haven't changed a thing."

"We let the tennis court go," said Mrs. Marshall, literal as ever. "No one wanted to play on it any more."

"Yes, that's right." Bernstein look around vaguely. Plainly his memories of Falls Ridge were not as detailed as all that. "But the essentials haven't changed. The atmosphere of the place——"

"It's a nice house," she said shortly. She loved it too much to listen to insincerity about it. "Now let's go inside and have a drink before dinner." She looked aggressively at Bernstein. "I hope you like fish."

During dinner he laughed and joked, paid compliments, told stories, and commented appropriately on the food and wine. He seemed determined to make the party a success. Marshall wondered whether he was especially anxious on this occasion. Very probably he was always the same, one of those men who, whatever the nature of the social gathering, always felt the responsibilities of a host. But what sort of person was he? What lay beneath the big hand-shake, the phony bonhomie? He had come a long way. There must be something which had carried him along—something which would need watching.

When the meal was over, Mrs. Marshall said, "Jane and I are going to have our coffee outside. Bring it out into the garden, will you, Virgie? The two men can stay in here." She smiled maliciously at Bernstein. "It's all right, Alfred, you don't have to pretend—I didn't really think you came to see me. If you like cigars there are some on the sideboard. I don't know whether they're fit to smoke or not—we've had them ever since Marcus died. . . . Come and join us when you've finished talking."

The two of them were left alone. Bernstein examined one of

the cigars, shook his head, and dropped it back in the box. He lit a cigarette instead and then said with surprising directness, "Well, here I am, Chris."

Marshall was slightly disconcerted. While he was trying to think of the right thing to say, Bernstein went on, "Your brother told me you had a problem you wanted to discuss with me." An acid note appeared in his voice. "Though why you didn't do me the courtesy of walking into my office when you were in New York, I'm not very clear."

Marshall shook his head. "I tried it that way once before."

"With Kingham?"

"Yes." The memory of his humiliation succeeded, as always, in rousing his anger against not only Kingham but all of them. "He kept me waiting for two weeks before he'd even speak to me."

"Perhaps you should have come to me."

"You wouldn't have listened to me either."

"I'm listening to you now."

"Because you have to. And that was why I wanted you to come here—to make the position quite clear to everybody. You aren't doing me a favor by listening to me. There isn't any question of saying, 'Thanks a lot, Chris. Nice of you to call around. I'll certainly see the matter gets looked into. Now you just go along and have a nice vacation and forget all about it.' "

Bernstein pursed his lips with the expression of a man who was used to keeping his temper however trying the circumstances. "Why not take the chip off your shoulder," he said, "and get down to business?"

"All right—just so long as we know where we stand." He paused for a moment. "Jeff gave you the story?"

"Yes." He said heavily, "Naturally it came as a great shock to me."

"Did it?"

Bernstein looked up sharply. He had almost forgotten what it was like to have his word questioned. "You don't believe me?"

"How should I know?"

"Would it be of any help to you," said Bernstein with considerable deliberation, "if I swore to you that I knew nothing about it?"

"Not much, I'm afraid." Marshall forced himself to be crude about it. He was afraid that if the discussion was allowed to proceed on a polite, gentlemanly plane Bernstein would use his advantages of age and position and experience to establish an ascendancy over him. "After all," he said, "if you were prepared to do it, you'd be equally prepared to lie about it, wouldn't you?"

"Listen here, Chris." An exasperated note crept into his voice. The façade of self-control was beginning to crack. "I'm a man twice your age and I've come a long way to see you. For that reason alone I guess I'm entitled to some consideration."

"Consideration?" said Marshall. "Who ever gave me consideration? Kingham——"

"Yes, I know about Kingham." Bernstein threw his cigarette butt, half smoked, into the fireplace. "And I'm sorry if you were badly treated. From what I hear, he has a tendency to play God occasionally——"

"But you never did anything about it?"

"You have to allow a man some latitude as the head of a department. You can't always be breathing down his neck—especially if he's turning in good results. Hell, I'm only one man, I can't watch everything, you know."

His voice was almost plaintive. It was the voice of a man who had managed for some years now to believe in his own pretense of being in control of the situation. You had a system of management, a chain of command, and it was supposed to work like a piece of machinery. The first queasy sense of impotence which took hold of you when you first assumed power became gradually no more than an amusing memory as you got used to your position. You began to think that you were really in charge. You had all the symbols and paraphernalia to support you and give you confidence —the limousines and private planes, the suites at Claridges and the Waldorf and the Georges Cinq, the secretaries, the penthouse apartments, the offices high, high up in the air, fifty floors above the street where ordinary people walked and lived and suffered. . . .

It was a good life. And then, to spoil it all, something happened to show you that it was a fraud. You were not in charge at all. Had

you really seriously thought you were in control of all those millions of dollars, the shareholders, employees, the unions, the agents and distributors, the government departments, the foreign branches in countries whose language you didn't understand, whose customs were a mystery to you? High up in your eagle's nest, in your mountain fastness, you formulated policies that meant nothing, made plans that were never carried out. And all the time the organization moved, amoeboid, like a stream of lava, in whatever direction chance and circumstance might decree. . . . He repeated, "It's impossible to keep track of everything."

"Well, there it is," said Marshall. "If you don't interfere, one of these days somebody else will have to." He looked at Bernstein unsympathetically. "Have you spoken to Kingham?"

"No. I thought it best to see you first." He explained, "This is going to be an awkward business to handle. No use going off half cocked." The old soothing phrases of management came comfortingly to mind, giving him a feeling that as soon as he had mentioned them some preliminary step had been taken. "We must get together—exchange ideas—formulate a policy——"

"What sort of a policy?"

"Ah well, of course," said Bernstein cautiously, "that's the point, isn't it?" He hesitated for a moment and then said, feeling his ground, "Am I right in supposing that, if we can clear the matter up within the organization, it will be good enough for you?"

"Yes. I don't see much advantage in making it public——"

"Neither do I. Especially since it would ruin us all financially— you included. Now," he said, "I haven't had too much time to work out all the details, but there are certain obvious steps we shall have to take. For a start, all sales of instruments abroad will have to be checked, to make sure that none are going to questionable sources. Agreed?"

"Of course." Marshall waited for a moment. "What else?"

Bernstein lit another cigarette and puffed hard at it several times, as if to extract wisdom from it. "Then," he said, "there's the Paris agency. I don't know quite what we should do about that. So far as I can gather, they've been doing hardly any legitimate business at all. And this man Furac——"

"Furac," said Marshall definitely, "has to go."

"Well, maybe. But we shall need to go cautiously. We have a contract with him, you understand."

"I don't give a damn about his contract."

Bernstein nodded. "Yes, I can see your point," he said reasonably. "If you feel as strongly about it as that——"

"I do."

"Okay then—I'll have a word with the lawyers. I don't know the terms of his contract, but it's possible we may be able to shake free of him without too much trouble." He touched Marshall paternally on the shoulder. "Don't worry about that. Just leave it to me."

It seemed to Marshall that all his life men in influential positions had been putting their hands on his shoulder and telling him to leave it to them, they would look after his interests for him. It was a confidence trick which was extraordinarily difficult to resist. But this time he was prepared for it. "So long as something gets done," he said.

"I promise you that." Bernstein had the air of a man making an important concession. It occurred to Marshall that he had already decided to get rid of Furac but, according to the general principles of bargaining, was making a favor of it.

"Then that takes care of Furac," he said. He moved out of shoulder-patting range. "What about Kingham?"

"Kingham?" An expression of pain passed over Bernstein's face. It was as if this was a problem he had hoped might in some way be avoided. "Well—obviously I shall have to discuss the whole question with him——"

"What is there to discuss? He knew what was going on."

Bernstein held up his hand. "Oh, now, let's be reasonable. I know you don't like the man, but we have no evidence that he was personally concerned."

"Of course he was," said Marshall. "Every time anybody asked a question about the French business Kingham tried to fire him or push him off to California or something." He glared at Bernstein. "What's the matter? Are you afraid of him?"

Bernstein swallowed. By God, thought Marshall, you learn something every minute; he *is* afraid of him—but right now he is even

more afraid of me. Otherwise he would simply walk out—he wouldn't stand for this.

The same idea seemed to occur to Bernstein. He adopted the tone of a man at the end of his patience. "Listen, Chris," he said. "I've done my best to keep my temper with you—under considerable provocation—but if you speak to me like that I'm going to walk right out of here."

He had succeeded in making Marshall feel slightly ashamed. "Hell, I'm sorry," he said. And then irritation rose in him again. "But what else do you expect? I know damn well you won't shift Kingham unless you have to."

"Kingham's one of the best men we have," said Bernstein stubbornly. "Even if he was in on this, you've got to admit there were extenuating circumstances."

"You mean my father?"

"Yes. He started the whole thing, after all. Kingham was a young man at the time. Your father was pushing him along. When the International was formed, your father handed it over to him. You know what the old man was like——"

"Yes, I know," said Marshall. He felt suddenly tired. "If Kingham had complained he would have been fired." He shrugged his shoulders. "So it seems he's just out of luck. Now he's going to get fired for not complaining."

"Chris, I don't think you quite understand. It's not so easy with a man in his position——"

"I don't care whether it's easy or not. You've got to get him out."

There was a long silence. Bernstein regarded him with dark speculative eyes, like a dealer preparing to put a final price on a piece of merchandise.

"Can I ask you something?" he said.

"Sure."

"Why is it so important to you that Kingham should go? Is it just a matter of personal dislike?"

"Of course not."

"Then why make such an issue of it?"

"Surely that should be obvious."

Once again Bernstein was silent, as if contemplating a whole series of possibilities. "Supposing I refuse?" he said.

"Let's stop pretending. You can't refuse." He felt a certain pity for Bernstein. It was tough on a man who had worked his way up from a tenement in Brooklyn to become a respected public figure, president of the Chamber of Commerce, a sound Republican. "I have only to drop two sentences to the newspapers and they'll fry you."

"I didn't know anything about this."

"Do you suppose that's going to make any difference?"

"It wouldn't only harm me, you know. You may not care about your father's reputation, but what about your mother and your brother—and yourself, for that matter? After all, you're a fairly large shareholder——"

"You think perhaps I wouldn't do it?" Marshall smiled at him. "But you daren't take a chance on it, dare you?" He had suddenly had enough of the situation. Blackmail was no fun, even in a good cause. "Well, what are you going to do?"

"It's impossible to make a decision on the spot about a matter like this," said Bernstein. He made a feeble attempt to regain his executive manner. "I shall have to consider——"

He could have his face-saver, thought Marshall. He was entitled to that, at least. "All right," he said. "How long would you like? Till Tuesday morning—eleven o'clock?" He patted Bernstein gently on the shoulder. It was his turn now. "I'll come into your office this time."

Sometime later, when he was alone with Jane, she said, "How did it go?"

"Not so bad." Virgie had left a tray on the table with drinks. He put some ice into a glass and poured scotch over it. "A drink?"

"No, thanks."

He came back and sat beside her. She was wearing a plain black dress with very little jewelry. Her dark hair was swept neatly behind her ears. Her body was like a small, tight, perfectly proportioned machine—he could imagine it in ten years' time, hardly changed.

He said, "You look beautiful tonight."

She shook her head. "I'm not beautiful." It was a statement of fact. Her attraction was not beauty. It was somehow too trim and compact. She would never have the compelling, irresponsible brilliance of his mother, for instance. But there was an unimpassioned strength in her which his mother had never had. She was dependable, he thought.

"My mother's crazy about you," he said.

"I like her too." She said seriously, "We were talking quite a lot this evening. You know, she's not nearly so scatterbrained as she likes to pretend. It's a sort of defense—she's afraid of being committed. Don't you think so?"

"Committed to what?"

"Anything. Anybody. Perhaps once she committed herself too much and got hurt, I don't know." She looked at him thoughtfully. "I can understand her. The more you feel, the more careful you have to be. There comes a time when there's no turning back."

"You mean marriage?"

"It happens before marriage. It happens in your mind. And not only with marriage either. With everything important, there's a point of no return. The difficulty is to know when you've reached it."

In some way he could not explain, her manner made him feel uneasy, as if there were some particular and slightly disturbing implication behind her remarks. To change the subject he said, "How did you like Bernstein?"

"All right," she said indifferently. "I'm really not very sure. A lot depends on whether he's a nice old man or just acting the part, doesn't it? If he were an Englishman I think I should know. But here conditions are so different. I might take something as a sign of insincerity which is just a normal way of behavior." She paused for a moment. "Do you trust him?"

"God, no." He spoke casually, as if it were a matter of no particular importance. "But if you're only going to do business with people you can trust, where are you going to get?" He added, "The important thing is that I'm in the stronger position."

"He's going to do what you want?"

"Yes. He stalled, of course. But that's just routine. I made it clear that he hadn't any choice."

She frowned. "He's going to hate you for this, isn't he?"

"Maybe," he said uncomfortably. "But I can't help it, can I? Perhaps he may even respect me for getting tough with him. But in any case I never got anywhere by being nice to people. I can't lose much by trying it the other way."

"No?" She looked at him dubiously, then said, "When will it be finished?"

"Tuesday morning. I have a meeting with Bernstein in his office. Once we've agreed about Kingham, the rest shouldn't be too difficult."

"Who will replace Kingham?"

"I don't know." His laugh was slightly forced. "Jeff was trying to persuade me to put in for it."

She looked at him steadily. "Are you interested?"

"Of course not. In any case, can you imagine them suggesting such a thing?"

It was ridiculous, of course. And yet Jeff had seemed very serious about it, almost as if he had received some sort of hint. And Bernstein had asked very deliberately why it was so important that Kingham should go, as if he suspected that Marshall had some particular reason for wanting him removed. Was it possible that they had decided that this was the motive behind his actions, the price he intended to demand for silence?

Jane seemed to be following his thoughts.

"It would be a good way to keep you quiet," she said. She added without expression, "You ought to be prepared——"

"I told you—long ago in London—I don't want to stay. Not under any circumstances."

"That was some time ago," she said seriously. "Don't think you have to stick to it. You can change your mind if you want to."

"Do you want me to?"

"That's nothing to do with it. It's your own decision."

"I know that," he said sharply. "And I'm going to make it. But I want your opinion. I have a right to know."

"Very well, then I'll tell you. I've always been behind you so

far. Right from the very beginning I thought you were right to go on with this, and even later when it meant that—that dreadful business with the letter, I told myself that it was necessary, one had to make sacrifices, there was something worth while at the end of it. But now I begin to wonder." He said nothing. It would have been foolish to pretend he didn't understand. It was what he had thought himself. "As time goes on, it seems to me, you begin to care less and less about anything but just winning. If you go on much longer there'll be nothing else." She said urgently, "You still have time—if you can go out now they'll remember afterward that there was one man they couldn't buy with money or power or anything else they had to offer. But if you stay"—there was something close to despair in her voice—"then it was all for nothing."

There was a long silence. Then he went up to her and kissed her. "Don't worry," he said. "I'm not going to stay."

CHAPTER IV

THIS WAS unknown country. Here the carpets were thick and pastel-shaded, the secretaries soft of voice, the doors closed automatically with a sigh, faint as the breath of a patient under heavy anesthesia. In the reception room there were only the deepest of chairs, the glossiest of magazines. Here a man might wait for hours, inhaling the scented air, soothing his ears with the silence, his eyes with the sumptuous charms of the receptionist. On the walls he would see no advertising slogans, no vulgar photographs of factories, no ill-painted oil paintings of bespectacled tycoons. A Degas reproduction, a bowl of roses, an enigmatic piece of pottery, part man, part fish, part interplanetary rocket, and that was all. Here a man might wait all afternoon and in the end be sent home, without resentment. To have been admitted to Mr. Bernstein's personal waiting room was an achievement in itself.

Marshall did not have to wait very long. There had to be some delay, he recognized, otherwise the whole act would fall to pieces; it was like the ritual coffee drinking which always precedes the discussion of business in Arab countries. Even if a man was tired of it himself, he had to keep it up, if only to retain the respect of his servants.

"Mr. Bernstein will see you now." The girl smiled at him, the doll-like smile of an air hostess, a ballerina. A few moments later he was in Bernstein's office. The door hissed gently shut behind him.

Bernstein was sitting behind the desk. In a chair to the left of him was a man Marshall had never seen before. He was fat and middle-aged, with a domed, balding head and practically no neck. His eyes bulged slightly; his face was gray and expressionless, frog-like.

"This is Mr. Flack, Chris, from the Legal Department. I don't believe you two have met before." As they shook hands Bernstein said, "I hope you don't mind Mr. Flack being present?"

"If *you* don't mind, I don't."

"Good. So far he's the only person I've consulted about this—unfortunate affair. I thought it essential to have a legal opinion before making any move at all. But Flack and I both feel very strongly that the fewer people who know about it, the better. We shall have to be very careful to prevent any leakage. Don't you agree?"

"Up to a point," said Marshall. "Until you've told me what you're going to do."

"You don't need to worry about that." Bernstein paused and then said, "You'll be glad to hear that we've considered your proposals and decided to accept them."

He gave the announcement as much weight as it would carry, perhaps rather more. Certainly it fell flat. Marshall crossed his legs and nodded amiably. Flack exchanged glances with Bernstein and picked up a file from the table beside his chair.

"We can break out of our contract with Furac without much difficulty," he said in a flat, nasal, indifferent voice. "There is a provision for unilateral termination on the payment of certain agreed sums, worked out on a basis of annual average turnover. It shouldn't even cost too much. There was only another two years to run anyhow."

Marshall frowned. "We have to compensate him?"

"Surely. He may have broken his contract by selling to unauthorized people, but that doesn't help us. We're in no position to take him to law." In a slightly patronizing tone he added, "You must see that."

"Yes, but——" He stopped, unable to express what he had to say. The protest in his heart was too simple, too juvenile to be

expressed in the world of half-lights and expedients in which all management was carried on. It was useless here to talk of justice, of reward for virtue and punishment for evil. When so many lives were interlocked there were no simple moral decisions any longer, only decisions of policy—and even those were mostly improvisations, an attempt to keep the ship afloat at any cost.

"And Kingham?" he asked bitterly. "Is he to be compensated too?"

Flack nodded. "We can't just fire him out of hand."

"Why not?"

"Because he might make trouble."

"How? He couldn't damage the company without damaging himself."

Bernstein leaned forward over the desk, the elder statesman. "Chris," he said seriously, "let me give you a word of advice. In this life it never pays to squeeze a man too hard. He's liable to get desperate and then you never know what he's going to do. If Kingham had been easier on you he wouldn't be in the trouble he's in today." He sat back and continued on a more reflective note. It was not enough to do what had to be done. It must also be enshrined as policy. "Now, I've come round to agree with you that he ought to go. He's a fine man in his way, but—well, between ourselves, quite apart from this, he's been worrying us a little lately. You see, for a really big post you need something more than a good administrator—you need a really *big* man—you know what I mean? Someone who can keep his head and always remember that he's a member of the team. In an outfit like this we all have to pull together; when somebody gets out of step you begin to notice it." He went on confidentially, "Just recently some of us have been getting a little worried about Kingham. He's shown a tendency to behave as if the International belonged to him. Isn't that so, Sidney?"

"That's right," said Flack in the same nasal, colorless voice.

"So you see——" said Bernstein. Marshall nodded wearily. He understood—now he was a person of experience. He knew all about men who weren't shaping up to the job, who were a little short on drive or background, who got out of step. First Wilcox, then him-

self, now it was Kingham's turn. But Kingham would not get hurt as much as some. It was a useful insurance to know where the body was buried. . . .

"We reckon," Bernstein was saying, "that it would be a good thing to have some new blood in there. But it can't be done just like that. Kingham's very popular with the Board."

"That's your problem," said Marshall, "handling the Board."

"I can handle them," said Bernstein, "so long as Kingham goes quietly and doesn't start looking for trouble."

"So you want to buy him? Is that it?"

"We have to buy him." Bernstein looked down at the pencil he was absent-mindedly playing with. "We squeeze him a bit as well, of course. We make him realize that this is a generous offer, considering the circumstances."

There was a silence. Then Marshall said, "How much?"

"Can't you leave that to us?"

"I want to know."

"I haven't decided yet. It has to be carefully worked out." He was speaking now with more confidence, the confidence of an expert on his own subject. "If we give too much he'll think we're scared of him. If we give too little he may think it worth while to fight. I'd suggest," he said thoughtfully, "something around a hundred thousand."

"Christ!" His outrage at the magnitude of the sum reminded him that he had already accepted, almost without protest, the advisability of paying Kingham *something*. He said, "That sounds a hell of a lot to me."

"It's not much to keep the company clean. And I have to get it passed by the Board, remember—not you."

"Can you do that?"

"I think so." It was against his practice to commit himself in advance, but his voice carried conviction. This was the sort of thing he was good at. Not the rough-and-tumble of the arena, but the quiet whisperings over drinks in select bars, the gentle flatteries, the final unobtrusive triumph in the conference room. "If you'll leave it to me . . . ?"

Marshall hesitated. But why not? If Kingham was to be bought, did it really matter for how much? "All right," he said.

"Good." Bernstein relaxed. The most difficult problem of all had been dealt with. "Now, there are one or two other people we have to think about." He looked down at a piece of paper on the blotter of his desk. There was a list of names. "Gilbertson."

It was partly a statement, partly a query. Plainly Gilbertson was neither here nor there to Bernstein. He had never met the man and Gilbertson was not a vital part of the machinery of the organization. If it would give Marshall any satisfaction to ruin him, that was all right with everybody present. It occurred to Marshall that for the first time he was being offered a man's life to do with as he pleased. This was not like Furac or Kingham—the situation had demanded that they should be dealt with, and he was no more than its agent. Here there was a choice, a personal choice. He had but to say the word and everything that Gilbertson valued—the house in Sussex, the small farm, the clubs, the whole elaborate charade of his existence—would be blown to pieces as if by a charge of dynamite. He contemplated the possibility with fascination mixed with horror. He looked at Bernstein impatiently waiting for his answer, and Flack, who gave the appearance of being more than usually bored by the whole proceedings. At least, he thought defensively, I have the imagination to take it seriously, I have the grace to be ashamed.

"Gilbertson can stay," he said.

Bernstein regarded him with approval. "It would certainly save a lot of trouble. We don't want to have to rebuild the whole European organization from zero." He looked down again at the list of names. "Wilcox? Now you've seen him recently, I believe?"

"Yes. He wants his job back—or its equivalent. And some expenses."

"That shouldn't be too difficult."

Flack looked up sharply. He was a man who prided himself on speaking only when he had something to say. "I've never met this man Wilcox. Is he any good?"

It was necessary to be fair to Wilcox, even though one didn't

like him—perhaps even more so because of that. And yet the truth was the truth. They would find out soon enough.

"Not much at the moment," Marshall said reluctantly. "He's drinking pretty heavily. But he's been under a big strain, remember. He may straighten out when he gets back."

"I certainly hope so," said Flack. "We can't afford to carry drunks."

Marshall glared at him angrily. He was beginning to dislike Flack. For a lawyer called in to give advice, he took too much on himself. "We've carried worse than drunks for plenty of time," he said. "In any case, you know damn well we've got to take him back, drunk or sober. So what's the use of arguing about it?"

Bernstein looked from one to the other with a sort of complacent interest. He was not too displeased to see Flack snubbed and Marshall lose his temper. On general principles it was a good thing to have subordinates who were at each other's throats. "All right," he said, "that takes care of Wilcox. Now—is that everybody?"

"There is someone else," said Marshall. "Madame Verrier."

"Madame who?"

Marshall broke into laughter. It was funny, he told himself. It had to be funny, otherwise . . . Bernstein and Flack were not faking—they had genuinely no idea who she was. They looked at him in perplexity.

"What's the joke?" asked Bernstein.

"Nothing. You wouldn't understand." He controlled himself. "She was the wife of a man who killed himself in Paris. Do you remember?"

"Oh yes—yes." A vague memory seemed to return to him. "You think she needs squaring too?"

"Yes."

Bernstein sighed impatiently. "Well, what does *she* want?"

"Money. What else is there?"

"How much?"

"I don't know." When it came to matters of this kind, he realized, he was an amateur. The two professionals regarded him disparagingly. He took refuge in sarcasm. "Not so much that she

thinks we're scared of her, and not so little that she'll go looking for trouble. You know what I mean?"

Flack said dispassionately to Bernstein, "Don't forget, she's a Frenchwoman. Whatever you offer her, she'll ask for fifty per cent more, on principle."

Bernstein tapped his teeth with the pencil. "Five thousand?"

"That sounds about right."

"After all, Verrier was only——"

"Yes," said Marshall, "he was only a little crook."

He heard the bitterness in his voice and wondered against whom it was directed. Bernstein? Himself? The situation seemed designed to destroy all moral attitudes. It had led him, step by step, into positions where no clear-cut stand could ever be taken. The problems were so complex that it was no longer a question of a correct solution—but of *any* solution. Some decision had to be taken in a hurry to stave off disaster. An end had to be attained. If it could be attained only by bribery, by treachery, by blackmail, then they had to be accepted.

Bernstein ignored his last remark. He made a tick on his piece of paper and said, "That seems to take care of most of our outstanding problems." He smiled at the other two, the smile of a man who has turned yet another awkward corner in a harassing career. Then he glanced at his watch. "It's getting very near one o'clock——"

Almost as if this were a prearranged signal, Flack squeezed himself out of his chair. "Do you need me any more just at the moment, Bernie? I made an appointment with Kelsey from the Patent Office——"

"Sure." Bernstein sprang cheerfully to his feet. "Don't let me hold you up. Good of you to come along at all at such short notice —I know how tied up you are." When he had ushered Flack out of the room he turned to Marshall and smiled indulgently. "Now," he said, "I think we've earned a drink. Anything else we can talk about over lunch."

CHAPTER V

BERNSTEIN STUDIED THE MENU with considerable care and ordered half a dozen Blue Points and a filet mignon. "No potatoes," he said, patting his miniature, hardly discernible paunch. "You have to watch yourself when you get to my age."

He lit a cigarette. The doctors were taking all the fun out of that, too, he thought resentfully. You could fool yourself with those filter tips, but it still left the nagging fear at the back of your mind. There were too many things to worry about these days; he was getting old, he couldn't take it any more. But the first martini cheered him up a little. He said, "I think we did pretty well this morning, all things considered." When Marshall said nothing, he went on, "You should be satisfied anyway, you got everything you asked for."

"I suppose so."

Bernstein mused for a moment. "It's a bad situation—a real crisis—but right now I feel optimistic. Something tells me we're going to lick it."

"It does?"

"Yes indeed. A few days ago I wouldn't have thought it possible. When your brother came into my office last week and told me the story—believe me, Chris, I'll never forget it. I thought to myself, 'There goes the company, there goes everything we've all lived and worked for all these years!'" He shook his head at the memory. "I just couldn't see a way out. Then I pulled myself to-

gether and I said to myself, 'We've got to fight this thing some-how.' "

Marshall looked at him with mild interest. It occurred to him that Bernstein was really quite a stupid man. To some extent it was concealed in the trappings of power. And there was always a tendency to assume, as Jeff had done, that because he held a position of such enormous authority he *must* have ability, even if it was not obvious on the surface, since if he had not, the implications were too appalling to contemplate. If a man without real capacity could reach the top by chance and then remain there by virtue of an amiable personality, a talent for minor personal intrigues, and the sheer inertia intrinsic to the structure of any large organization, then there was no use going on, the whole competitive system was a joke.

"So you fought it," he said.

Bernstein raised a hand. "With your help," he said handsomely. "It's due to you that we've managed to sit down together and find a solution to this problem. God knows what might have happened if one of our competitors had got onto this before you did. It was indeed fortunate for us that it was one of our own men, somebody with loyalty to the company." He was rather like a general making a speech before conferring a decoration. He said solemnly, "Your father would have been proud of you, Chris."

"You forget," said Marshall, "that the swindle was his idea in the first place."

Bernstein frowned. "I wouldn't call it a swindle exactly. Besides which," he continued, regaining confidence, "that was some time ago. Who can tell?—there may have been circumstances—— I don't think," he said, "that we have a right to set ourselves up in judgment. What I do know for sure is that if he'd been alive today he would have approved what you did a hundred per cent. I'm confident of that. And when all is said and done, I knew him better than most people."

"I guess so."

"He always thought very highly of you, Chris—better than you thought of him. It was a great grief to him that he couldn't build you up in the business as he wanted to."

The oysters were good, thought Marshall, if one refrained from dipping them in that revolting cocktail sauce. A little pepper and a squeeze of lemon . . . But he was growing a little impatient. He had not been invited to lunch purely as a social exercise. When was the old man going to get to the point?

"I'll be quite honest," said Bernstein, "and say that at one time I doubted his opinion of you. It didn't seem to me that you were cut out for the game at all. But it's always been my philosophy to admit when I make a mistake. I've made quite a few in my time," he admitted handsomely. "I know now that I made one with you."

With regret Marshall speared the last oyster and popped it into his mouth. He let it slide down his throat; an elusive tang of sea and surf lingered on the surface of his pharynx. So Jeff was right, he thought, Bernstein was going to offer him the International. Partly to silence him, but perhaps also to some extent because he had proved himself, shown that he could play the game with the best of them when necessity arose. For the first time they respected him. There was satisfaction in that—and even greater satisfaction in the thought that he did not need their respect, that he was prepared to throw their rewards back at them. That was something they would never succeed in understanding. "At one stage," he said, "you told me you didn't like my attitude."

"Well, that's true," admitted Bernstein without malice. "It did seem to me at the time that you were crowding me a little. But that's not so important. In business we fling around a few hard words now and then and it's all taken as part of the game. When the deal's over we shake hands and forget about it. Believe me," he said with some feeling, "I wouldn't be where I am today if I was a man who took offense too readily."

He paused while the waiter brought the next course and then went on.

"No, what *is* important is that in a difficult situation you showed drive and responsibility and a grasp of realities. You've realized that in administration it isn't possible to spend your life with your head in the air—you've got to grapple with facts—pleasant or unpleasant. That makes you just the kind of man we're looking for."

Marshall said nothing. It was coming now; this was the end of the build-up. Bernstein leaned toward him confidentially.

"But I didn't bring you here," he said, "to throw bouquets at you. I brought you here to offer you a job."

"Yes?" He gave a faint smile. He remembered that this was how it had begun, with his being offered a job. But he had moved a long way since April. He remembered his interview with Kingham ("How would you like to go to Europe, Chris? The job's made for you. What we need is someone with background—it could lead anywhere"). Well, that was true enough, it had led both himself and Kingham into positions which neither of them would have conceived possible a few months ago.

Bernstein looked at him benevolently, a dapper, custom-tailored fairy godmother. "How would you like to be general manager in India?" he said.

"India!"

Marshall was stunned. The contrast between expectation and reality had rendered him almost speechless. He was so taken aback that for the moment he felt no emotion except astonishment. Presently the first reaction would die down and give place to something more positive. He waited, wondering what it would be. At heart, was he angry—or simply amused?

Bernstein regarded him closely, searching for some clue to his state of mind. "It's a wonderful opportunity, Chris. Believe me, things are moving out there. In fact, if anybody were to ask me where I think the biggest possibilities for business expansion are right now, I'd answer without hesitation—the Far East. . . ."

He warmed to his theme. Professional pride was involved—this was a job of selling, and he had always flattered himself that he could sell a bill of goods as well as the next man. Gradually, as he spoke, Marshall's mood defined itself. He was not amused—far from it. He recognized that for some time now he had been deluding himself. Once again he had fallen a victim to flattery; he had allowed himself to think that they looked upon him differently, that they respected him, that everything was changed. But nothing was changed. Once they had wanted to get rid of him because they thought he was no use to them. Now the reason was different—

he was dangerous. But the methods, the cheap, contemptuous tricks were the same.

Bernstein continued, bland and optimistic as a travel poster, "You'll be right out there on your own. Have a chance to pick your own staff, work out some of your own ideas. I promise you," he assured, feeling around for the reason for Marshall's obvious lack of enthusiasm, "that there won't be any unnecessary interference from New York. Flack has definitely agreed——"

"Flack?"

"Yes." Bernstein smiled amiably. "He's going to take over the International."

There was a silence. Bernstein's smile became replaced by a look of concern; it was becoming apparent to him that he had lost his grip on his audience. From Marshall's mind all thought of the plans he had made before this meeting had completely disappeared. He could not even be bothered to decide whether Bernstein had offered him the Indian job seriously or merely as a way of trying to provoke him into resignation. Everything was obscured by the vision of Flack, the colorless, flat-voiced, frog-faced nonentity Flack, in charge of the International. Had he worked and suffered, cheated, threatened, betrayed—for this?

He shook his head. "No," he said.

Bernstein looked up at him sharply. "What do you mean—no?" His smile had disappeared, to be replaced by the expression of a man who has been tried almost to breaking point. His lips were tight, his eyes narrowed. He replaced the fork on his plate with a clatter. "Chris, I warn you, you can go too far. I've stood a lot from you because I understood how you felt——"

"You stood it because you had to. All you care about is your own safety and your own convenience." Why, he thought, why in God's name had Bernstein chosen Flack? Did he owe him something, for support once given at a critical time, a judicious silence when speech might have caused embarrassment? Did he like him? It hardly seemed possible. Was his very dullness attractive? There had been a note of fear in Bernstein's voice when he spoke of Kingham, a perceptible relief at the thought of getting rid of him. Kingham had grown strong in the last few years, strong enough to

threaten the men who sat above him. It might be by no means a disaster to have him removed and replaced by a safe, dull, aging man who owed his advancement to Bernstein himself. . . . "You know as well as I do," said Marshall, "that Flack isn't the man."

"I disagree. In my opinion he's an excellent man. But in any case, this isn't your affair. It's for me to make the appointment——"

"Why don't you stop pretending you don't have to listen to me?" said Marshall impatiently. "I tell you Flack isn't the man."

Bernstein breathed deeply. "I suppose now," he said with heavy sarcasm, "you're going to tell me who is?"

Marshall was silent for a moment. Then, as if he were being washed forward on a tide he had no power to stem, he said, "I am."

Bernstein gave a scornful, uncertain laugh. "You're crazy," he said.

"Why?"

"You haven't the experience, for one thing——"

"I have as much experience as some bull-witted lawyer you only pulled in because you needed somebody to talk you out of a spot." Marshall could hear his own voice rising in volume. He was tired of fighting. It was necessary to finish it for good and all. "I know you want to be rid of me and I know why. But you can forget it. You're stuck with me."

"Do you think I'm going to let you dictate to me what appointments I make——"

"You're going to do it," he said. "I tell you, you're going to do it." His father had had this same habit of repeating statements to emphasize his determination. "Otherwise I'll bring you down. I may not have meant it before, but I do now. Don't think I wouldn't."

He was almost shouting now. People at nearby tables had stopped their conversation to look at him. One of the waiters was whispering to the maître d'hôtel, who was looking anxiously at Bernstein. Was the young man drunk? his eyes asked. Was it necessary to interfere? But Bernstein was unaware of him. Tired, frightened, resentful, impotent, his face pale with anxiety, wrinkled with the memory of forty years of struggling toward the light, he looked helplessly at Marshall. Marshall stood up and dropped his napkin

onto his plateful of congealing, unregarded food. "Look around you," he said. With a wave of his hand he took in the smart restaurant, the scurrying waiters, the whole world of the prosperous and powerful and well fed. "Think of what you've got and what you had to do to get it. You could lose it all tomorrow—to please Flack——"

"It's nothing to do with pleasing Flack," he said weakly. "It's a matter of principle."

"You want to be a martyr to your principles?"

Bernstein squeezed his fingers together. "But I've actually spoken to Flack. I promised him——"

"Tell him you changed your mind. Tell him," said Marshall mercilessly, "that you made another mistake."

CHAPTER VI

HE PAID OFF his taxi at the hotel. The doorman helped him out of the cab; the girl at the cigarette counter smiled at him as she always did when he crossed the lobby to the elevator. Everything was as usual. Nobody looked at him with any special interest. It seemed strange to him that he should have passed through such an emotional upheaval and yet bear no signs of it on his face. He felt obscurely insulted by their lack of perception. His companions in the crowded elevator pushed against him listlessly; the operator intoned, with the flat indifference of a croupier at a gambling table, the numbers of the floors. In this city, he thought, everyone had his own worries—an ulcer, a drop in the stock market, a wife he couldn't trust . . . He passed by thousands of them every day and never noticed a thing. Why should they notice anything unusual about him?

He got out at the eighteenth floor and unlocked the door of his suite. Jane might be waiting for him—he had not been able to say when he would be returning. As soon as he opened the door he saw her. She was sitting on the sofa with her shoes off and her legs tucked beneath her, reading the paper. Discarded sections of the *Herald Tribune* lay strewn on the carpet beside her. In the middle of the room was a table with the remains of lunch.

Throwing his hat into a corner, he went to an armchair on the other side of the table and sat there for a moment in silence. Any elation he had felt following his victory over Bernstein had com-

pletely gone. All that remained was confusion and shame. It was as if in the course of some drunken escapade he had performed actions which he found impossible to explain. He had no confidence in his ability to handle this present situation. It was more, he felt, than could be reasonably expected. He needed time to think, to calm down; he needed a rest, a week at a sanatorium under sedatives. He said, "I'm glad you got something to eat."

She looked at him anxiously and walked over to him. "Darling, what's the trouble? You look terrible." At least, he thought, somebody was able to recognize it. She sat on the floor by his feet and took hold of his hand. "Darling—darling, what happened?"

"It's a mess," he said. "Everything's a mess."

"The meeting?"

He nodded.

"Did it go wrong?"

"No." He laughed shortly. "It went fine. I was terrific. I kicked them around. You should be proud of me. Everyone should be proud of me." He stopped for a moment and then said desperately, "But I don't know what I could have done. He *made* me do it. He practically forced it on me."

"Bernstein?"

"Yes." For the first time since he had entered the room he actually looked her in the face. "You saw me before I went, didn't you? I wasn't looking for trouble. I was prepared to be reasonable. I don't enjoy banging the table and threatening and pushing around old men who are scared for their skins. I never was like that, and I can't have changed so much. I'm not *such* a bastard, am I?" He demanded painfully, "Do you think I'm a bastard?"

"Of course not." She squeezed his hand. "Now please—tell me what it's all about."

"It's just that people won't leave you alone. You start off with the best of intentions, but for some reason they have to try to put something over on you, and that gets you mad and——" He stopped suddenly, trying to rearrange his thoughts. Then he said, "Bernstein's a fool—do you know that? The boss of the corporation, and he's a fool."

"What did he do?"

"He tried to play the same game as Kingham. After the meeting was over he took me out to lunch. He bought me a few drinks and told me what a wonderful guy I was and how he was so impressed by what I'd done that he'd saved a beautiful new important job for me"—he paused and then concluded with venom—"running a branch office in Calcutta."

There was a silence. She looked up at him in perplexity. Eventually she said, "Was that all?"

"All! Can't you see what he was trying to do?"

"Of course. But, in any case, you were going to resign——"

"You mean," he said, "that you can't see the difference? You mean that refusing the International and refusing the opportunity of being shunted into some garbage can in the Indian Ocean are the same thing to you?" He added hopelessly, "If that's how you see it, there's no point in going on."

"I can see the difference."

She was going to say something further, but she stopped herself. She wanted to say that the difference shouldn't matter, it was purely a matter of pride and prestige, that it had no essential importance. But this was something there was no use in explaining. To him, when the moment came, it *had* importance—and that was that. There was nothing more to be said about it. It occurred to her that this was the moment she had known must come eventually: the time when everything that mattered had been said, the point of no return.

"What did you do?" she asked.

He did not answer her directly. "What I want you to believe," he said earnestly, "is that when I told you the other night that I was going to quit, I meant it sincerely. And I meant it this morning too—right up to the point where he tried to sell me this job in India. I knew then that he'd never even considered me for the International. And so——" He hesitated.

"So you took it," she said. "Because he wouldn't offer it to you, you took it. Is that right?"

"Yes." He was relaxed now. The story was over. Whatever the result, there was nothing further he could do. "I suppose," he said vaguely, "it may be only temporary——"

"Don't fool yourself." Her voice was gentle. "You won't let it go. You wanted it all the time."

He shook his head violently. "No, you're wrong there. I never wanted it."

"You wanted to win."

"So did you."

"Yes, I won't deny it." She spoke with resignation. "It seems that once you start, you have to take it all the way."

As soon as she had said it, it surprised her that she had not realized this before. They were at the natural end-point of a process which she had herself initiated. She had said to him at the beginning that anything was better than to live out his life in futility and defeat. She had not expected or hoped for this result, but she knew now that it was the only result possible. Her reservations had been unreal, a childish desire to eat her cake and have it at the same time. She had driven him to action. She must accept what action had made of him. Love, if it meant anything, was a surrender without conditions.

She looked at him and saw on his face a bewilderment close to despair. It was as if he was not aware of what had happened to him. He said: "Are you going to leave me?"

It was important that he too should have no reservations. She said seriously: "You really want me to stay?"

"You know I do." Eagerly he went on: "We could be happy together. I'm sure of it. After all, we have so much——" Perhaps, she thought, we have too much—we should be so much safer with less. But safety was too much to ask for. He went on: "You might not like it over here as well as England just at first, but——"

"Places aren't important."

"You'd soon settle down, I'm sure. And I'll do everything I can." He paused and then said unhappily: "I know that what I did today must have been a shock to you. But now it's all over, I promise——"

"Please don't promise," she said. "Don't promise anything." When you took a man, you took him as he was, not as he hoped to be. It was not possible to guarantee the future. His sense of bewilderment would pass—and what then? Would he regard the events of today as a victory—or as a defeat? How much would he

understand, for how long would he remember? In the act of conquering, he had gone down before his enemies, Kingham, Bernstein, the Old Man—it was their world he had accepted. And now
that he had accepted it, he was bound by its rules. With Kingham
disposed of, the path was clear in front of him. Jeff was a nonentity,
Bernstein was growing old. She realized now that it had always
been inevitable. He had not wanted it consciously any more than
she had, but in the last instance what either of them wanted was
of little consequence. You could not get out while you were ahead
of the game, because the game never finished. Each move led to
another; there was no point at which you could relax without sac-
rificing what you had already gained. Men, like nations, acquired
power almost accidentally, to fill a vacuum, to establish order and
justice, to protect their interests. Afterward they felt a little ashamed
and tried to justify themselves. With their hands on their hearts
they protested that power was not of their seeking, it meant nothing to them personally but worry and overwork, that only a sense
of responsibility prevented them from handing over to others at the
earliest possible opportunity. . . . Nobody believed them. They
did not even know whether to believe themselves. Lonely, envied,
hated, they were fortunate to find a person here or there, a friend,
a wife, a mistress, to understand their isolation and comfort them
against the measureless hostility of the world.

She took him gently by the hand. She would not leave him now.

DATE DUE